THE CAMBRIDGE COMPANION TO
THE AGE OF CONSTANTINE

The Cambridge Companion to the Age of Constantine offers students a comprehensive one-volume introduction to this pivotal emperor and his times. Richly illustrated and designed as a readable survey accessible to all audiences, it also achieves a level of scholarly sophistication and a freshness of interpretation that will be welcomed by the experts. The volume is divided into five sections that examine political history, religion, social and economic history, art, and foreign relations during the reign of Constantine, a ruler who gains in importance because he steered the Roman Empire on a course parallel with his own personal development. Each chapter examines the intimate interplay between emperor and empire and between a powerful personality and his world. Collectively, the chapters show how both were mutually affected in ways that shaped the world of late antiquity and even affect our own world today.

Noel Lenski is Associate Professor of Classics at the University of Colorado, Boulder. A specialist in the history of late antiquity, he is the author of numerous articles on military, political, cultural, and social history and the monograph *Failure of Empire: Valens and the Roman State in the Fourth Century AD*.

The Cambridge Companion to

THE AGE OF CONSTANTINE

Edited by

Noel Lenski

University of Colorado

CAMBRIDGE UNIVERSITY PRESS
Cambridge, New York, Melbourne, Madrid, Cape Town, Singapore, São Paulo

Cambridge University Press
40 West 20th Street, New York, NY 10011-4211, USA

www.cambridge.org
Information on this title: www.cambridge.org/9780521818384

First published 2006

Printed in the United States of America

A catalog record for this publication is available from the British Library.

Library of Congress Cataloging in Publication Data

The Cambridge companion to the Age of Constantine / edited by Noel Lenski.
p.   cm.
Text in English; includes one essay translated from German.
Includes bibliographical references and index.
ISBN-13: 978-0-521-81838-4 (hardback)
ISBN-10: 0-521-81838-9 (hardback)
ISBN-13: 978-0-521-52157-4 (pbk.)
ISBN-10: 0-521-52157-2 (pbk.)
1. Rome – History – Constantine I, the Great, 306–337.   2. Constantine I,
Emperor of Rome, d. 337.   3. Church history – Primitive and early church,
ca. 30–600.   I. Lenski, Noel Emmanuel, 1965–   II. Title.
DG315.C36   2005
937'.08'092 – dc22   2005011724

ISBN-13   978-0-521-81838-4 hardback
ISBN-10   0-521-81838-9 hardback

ISBN-13   978-0-521-52157-4 paperback
ISBN-10   0-521-52157-2 paperback

piissimae et venerabili matri

Contents

ILLUSTRATIONS

FIGURES

PLANS

COINS

CONTRIBUTORS

BRUNO BLECKMANN is Professor of Ancient History at the University of Münster. His many publications on Constantine include the outstanding introduction *Konstantin der Große*.

SIMON CORCORAN is Senior Research Fellow in the Department of History, University College London. His *The Empire of the Tetrarchs: Imperial Pronouncements and Government AD 284–324* is now a standard work.

GEORGES DEPEYROT is a member of the Centre de recherche historique of the CNRS in Paris. His numerous publications on late Roman economic history include *Les monnaies d'or de Dioclétien à Constantin I (284–337)*.

H. A. DRAKE is Professor of History at the University of California at Santa Barbara. A long-time Constantinian scholar, he has recently published *Constantine and the Bishops: The Politics of Intolerance* to critical acclaim.

MARK EDWARDS is University Lecturer in Patristics and a Fellow of Christ Church Oxford. His masterful translations include *Constantine and Christendom* and *Optatus: Against the Donatists*, both excellent companions to this volume.

JAS ELSNER, a Fellow of Corpus Christi College Oxford, has published widely on Roman and Late Antique Art, including his sweeping *Art and the Roman Viewer: The Transformation of Art from the Pagan World to Christianity*.

HUGH ELTON is the Director of the British School of Archaeology at Ankara. His *Warfare in Roman Europe: AD 350–425* is the best study of its kind.

ELIZABETH KEY FOWDEN is an independent scholar who has published broadly on Late Antiquity, including her brilliant *The Barbarian Plain: Saint Sergius between Rome and Iran*.

ROBERT M. FRAKES is Professor of Roman History at Clarion University. His many publications include the important revisionist study *'Contra Potentium Iniurias': The 'Defensor Civitatis' and Late Roman Justice*.

CAROLINE HUMFRESS is Lecturer in Ancient History at Birkbeck College London. Her work on late Roman law and society has culminated in her monograph *Orthodoxy and the Courts in Late Antiquity*.

MARK J. JOHNSON is Professor of Art History at Brigham Young University. He has published a number of major articles on Late Antique and Byzantine architecture.

CHRISTOPHER KELLY is University Lecturer in Classics and Fellow of Corpus Christi College Cambridge. He has recently published the masterful *Ruling the Later Roman Empire*.

MICHAEL KULIKOWSKI is Associate Professor of History at the University of Tennessee. His important study, *Late Roman Spain and Its Cities*, will soon be joined by a book on the Goths.

A. D. LEE is Senior Lecturer in Classics at the University of Nottingham. His excellent source collection *Pagans and Christians in Late Antiquity* is a useful complement to this volume.

NOEL LENSKI is Associate Professor of Classics at the University of Colorado. He has published widely on late Roman history, including the monograph *Failure of Empire: Valens and the Roman State in the Fourth Century AD*.

SAMUEL N. C. LIEU is Professor of Ancient History at Macquarie University in Sydney. He has published extensively on Constantine, including two volumes co-edited with D. Montserrat, *From Constantine to Julian: Pagan and Byzantine Views* and *Constantine: History, Historiography and Legend*.

ACKNOWLEDGMENTS

This book represents a collective effort in the very best sense and thus leaves many people to thank. My greatest debt of gratitude is surely owed to the contributors, who were hardworking, prompt, and efficient. Second to these comes Beatrice Rehl, editrix extraordinaire, whose patient pressure makes things get done. The volume was also shaped in a profound way by the comments of six readers who reviewed two drafts of the original proposal and who helped change many of my wrongheaded ideas into better ones. Much of the editing for this volume was done while I held an Alexander von Humboldt Fellowship at the Institut für Alte Geschichte of the Ludwig-Maximilians-Universität in Munich in 2003. I am thankful to the the AvH Stiftung for providing me with time and to the Institut for providing me with facilities and assistance. Especially generous with their time and advice were Prof. Jens-Uwe Krause and Dr. Christian Witschel, both of them learned colleagues and true friends. While in Munich I also benefited from several conversations with Bob Frakes over many a Bierchen. Many of the photos for this book were taken during two brief stints in Italy funded by the University of Colorado's Graduate Committee on Arts and Humanities. During the first of these, Darius Arya kindly chauffeured me to many sites on his vespa. Several coins featured in the photographs come from Colorado University's (CU) newly acquired Wink Jaffee Collection, whose donor was of tremendous assistance to me on matters numismatic and historical. CU also funded undergraduate Jesse Vader who helped me assemble Constantinian laws. In the spring of 2004 Ray Van Dam hosted a seminar on "Constantine and His Age" at the annual meeting of the Association of Ancient Historians that brought together several of the contributors for a very helpful discussion of our work. Thanks are due to him and the audience, which included many luminaries of Constantinian studies, several of whom offered useful comments and suggestions that have shaped some of our ideas. I should also like to thank Ariel Lewin for inviting me to a conference at Matera in 2004 where I was able to air some of my work, and Vincenzo Aiello, Daniela Motta, Pietrina Pellegrini, and Umberto Roberto, whom I met there and who put me onto new bibliography and approaches. Most of the drawings and the stemmata were done by the magnificent Dave Underwood, and many of the graphics are the work of Tim Riggs, who also patiently taught me how "to photoshop." The prose of my chapter has been markedly improved by the careful editorial hand of Faith Orlebeke. Stepping back from this book, it is easy to see that I owe more to my family than anyone, to my parents and brothers, and my children Paul, Helen, and Chloe. Their love and encouragement are serious ingredients in this mix. My wife, Alison, who has weathered this book with many other storms over the past three years, is the true hero in my story. She deserves more credit than all the others combined.

ABBREVIATIONS

For abbreviations of primary source references not found here, see the bibliography of Primary Sources and Translations.

AE   *L'Année épigraphique: Revue des publications épigraphiques relatives a l'antiquite romaine* (Paris, 1888–)

BHG   *Bibliotheca Hagiographica Graeca*, ed. F. Halkin, 3d ed., 3 vols. (Brussels, 1957).

CCSL   *Corpus Christianorum, Series Latina* (Turnhout, 1967–)

CIL   *Corpus Inscriptionum Latinarum* (Berlin, 1862–)

CIS   *Corpus Inscriptionum Semiticarum* (Paris 1881–)

CPL   *Clavis Patrum Latinorum*, ed. E. Dekkers (Steenburgen, 1961)

CPR   *Corpus Papyrorum Raineri* (Vienna, 1895–)

CSCO   *Corpus Scriptorum Christianorum Orientalium* (Paris, 1903–)

CSEL   *Corpus Scriptorum Ecclesiasticorum Latinorum* (Vienna, 1866–)

CSHB   *Corpus Scriptorum Historiae Byzantinae*, 49 vols. (Bonn, 1828–78)

FGH   *Fragmente der griechischen Historiker*, ed. F. Jacoby et al. (Leiden, 1923–)

FHG   *Fragmenta Historicorum Graecorum*, ed. C. Müller, 5 vols. (Paris, 1841–70)

FIRA   *Fontes Iuris Romani Antejustiniani*, ed. S. Riccobono et al., 3 vols. (Florence, 1940)

GCS   *Die griechischen christlichen Schriftsteller der ersten Jahrhunderte* (1897–)

IGRR   *Inscriptiones Graecae ad Res Romanas Pertinentes*, ed. R. Cagnat et al., 4 vols. (Paris, 1906–27)

IK   *Inschriften griechischer Städte aus Kleinasien* (Bonn, 1972–)

ILAlg.	*Inscriptions Latines de l'Algérie*, ed. S. Gsell and H.-G. Pflaum, 2 vols. (Paris, 1976–7)
ILS	*Inscriptiones Latinae Selectae*, ed. H. Dessau, 5 vols. (Berlin, 1892–1916)
ILTun.	*Inscriptions Latines de la Tunisie*, ed. A. Merlin (Paris, 1944)
MAMA	*Monumenta Asiae Minoris Antiqua* (1928–)
MGH.AA	*Monumenta Germaniae Historica. Auctores Antiquissimi* (Berlin, 1877–1919)
NPNF	*The Writings of the Nicene and Post-Nicene Fathers*, ed. P. Schaff et al. (Peabody, MA [1887–92] 1995)
OGIS	*Orientis Graecae Inscriptiones Selectae*, ed. W. Dittenberger (Leipzig, 1905)
PG	*Patrologiae Cursus Completus, series Graeco-Latina*, ed. J. P. Migne et al. 162 vols. (Paris, 1857–66)
PL	*Patrologiae Cursus Completus, series Latina*, ed. J. P. Migne et al., 221 vols. (Paris, 1844–64).
P. Lond.	*Greek Papyri in the British Museum* (London, 1893–)
PLRE	*Prosopography of the Later Roman Empire*, vol. 1, AD *260–395*, ed. A. H. M. Jones, J. R. Martindale, and J. Morris (Cambridge, 1971)
P. Oxy.	*The Oxyrhynchus Papryi* (Oxford, 1898–)
P. Ryl.	*Catalogue of the Greek Papyri in the John Rylands Library, Manchester*, 4 vols. (Manchester, 1911–52)
PSI	*Papyri greci e latini della Società Italiana per la ricerca dei papiri greci e latini in Egitto* (Florence, 1912–)
RIC	*The Roman Imperial Coinage*, ed. H. Mattingly et al., 10 vols. (London 1923–94)
SCh	*Sources Chrétiennes* (Paris, 1940–)
SEG	*Supplementum Epigraphicum Graecum* (1923–)
TTH	*Translated Texts for Historians* (Liverpool, 1987–)

INTRODUCTION

Noel Lenski

The age of Constantine is one of the most fertile periods of historical change in all of antiquity. By itself, his elevation of the Christian faith from the depths of the persecution it suffered in his youth to the religion of his imperial household testifies to the growth of a new genus of government and a new sort of emperor. Cast by Constantine into the open light of toleration and imperial support, Christianity blossomed into a thriving offshoot of Mediterranean religious life. By the mid-fourth century, it had grown broad enough to cast its shadow over not just religious matters but art and architecture, philosophy and thought, literature and learning, politics and foreign relations, law and social practice. To be sure, Constantine was never so revolutionary that he turned up the roots of what had gone before and planted the field of history afresh. Rather, much of what he accomplished was to bring to fruition trends and tendencies that had sprung up long before his reign. Yet it was Constantine's genius to have distinguished between productive cultural strains and the infertile tares that were doomed by the climate of history to die out. The age of Constantine thus witnessed not so much a re-creation of the historical landscape as a new emphasis on the cultivation of those features that had previously been pruned back. The result was the growth of the period now referred to as late antiquity – roughly the fourth through sixth centuries AD – a period that has aroused tremendous interest among the present generation.

Historical change is, of course, inevitable and can hardly be traced to one man, but Constantine's position as *an* emperor and later *the* emperor of the Roman world for the first third of the fourth century gave him a greater role than any of his contemporaries in fostering productive change. Thus, while we can assume that, in the absence of

Constantine, the world of late antiquity would have shifted and developed into something different from what preceded it, it is impossible to conceive how it might have evolved. Without Constantine's patronage of holy men like Paphnutius and Anthony, we can hardly comprehend the rise of spiritual greats like the stylites Simeon and Daniel. His cultivation of theologians like Lactantius and Eusebius of Caesarea paved the way for powerful figures like Gregory of Nyssa and John Chrysostom. Without his support of powerful bishops like Ossius of Cordoba or Eusebius of Nicomedia, it is hard to believe that Augustine of Hippo and Cyril of Alexandria would have had the influence they did. His summoning and oversight of the Council of Nicaea established a precedent of imperial involvement in ecclesastical policymaking for centuries to come. His reclamation of the Holy Land for Christianity prepared the ground for Christians like Melania the Younger, Jerome, and even the empress Eudocia to refashion their lives in Palestine. Above all, his reworking of Christianity into a triumphalist religion allowed for the development of the Christian monarch in all its manifestations from late antiquity down to the Crusades. Indeed, Constantine's victorious Christian king, combined with his Christianization of the Holy Land, has had consequences throughout history, consequences with profound effects on Judaism, Islam, and Christianity, consequences that endure up to the present.

Nor was Constantine's vision for shaping history trained solely on the religious. Without his new emphasis on the gold currency, we can scarcely conceptualize the rebirth and growth of the late antique economy. His creation of new government offices and his reshaping of others set the stage for the development of the grand and powerful bureaucracy of the late Roman world. His deployment of barbarian military officers and auxiliary troops enabled the ongoing vitality of the late Roman army. And his creation of the new imperial capital in Constantinople permitted the Roman empire to transplant itself eastward so as to weather the barbarian invasions and survive down to the Renaissance. As the first in a series of Constantines to rule the Roman world, Constantine I has been awarded by history the epithet "the Great." The fact is, however, that regardless of his place at the head of an imperial tradition, Constantine well merits the epithet. He was a man whose impact on history was so profound that we continue to feel it today.

Strangely enough, even given the universal agreement on the importance of Constantine, few historical figures present us with as many puzzling questions. This is not because the events of his reign are obscured by a lack of relevant source material. Compared to the sources for other periods of antiquity, those for Constantine's life and times are strikingly rich in both quantity and quality. With these we can trace the broad outlines of Constantinian history quite boldly and distinctly: born of a powerful father and raised in the royal court, he was proclaimed emperor in 306, enjoyed considerable military success in his early years, defeated his rival Maxentius in 312, began openly advertising his conversion to Christianity, fought two wars that suppressed his coemperor Licinius by 324, presided over the ecclesiastical Council of Nicaea in 325, refounded the city of Byzantium in his own name, reclaimed the Holy Land for Christianity, died while preparing a campaign against the Persians, and left the empire to a cadre of dynastic successors. Despite this lucid larger picture, however, the finer features of this monolithic historical figure often remain obscured by enigmas and contradictions. And though many of these have been exhaustively debated, the problems still abide without any apparent hope of definitive resolution.

Precisely when, for example, was Constantine born? The range of possible dates spans a decade, and our choice of dates affects our interpretation of all the events of his career; nonetheless, there are no clear criteria by which to establish the truth beyond the shadow of a doubt. Other important dates are similarly disputed: the date of his first war with Licinius (314 or 316?), the date of his grandiloquent *Oration to the Assembly of the Saints* (a broad range between 315 and 328), the date of his refusal to perform public sacrifice in Rome (312? 315? 326?). Was Constantine originally intended by Diocletian to have succeeded to the throne? Was he born a bastard? Was his father Christian? Did he issue a law banning sacrifice? Did he attack his rivals Maxentius and Licinius because they were persecuting Christians? Where precisely did he fight his decisive battle against Maxentius? Why did he execute his son Crispus and wife Fausta? Why did he burden the empire with so many dynastic successors, and how precisely were these eliminated after his death? A series of questions also surrounds his foundation of Constantinople and his religious foundations in Palestine. How extensive were his building projects in Constantinople? Did he intend to create there a rival to Rome or merely another regional capital? Why did Constantine initiate his Holy Land reclamation project? How great a role did his mother Helena play? Did she or her contemporaries actually find what they believed to be the True Cross or did this happen later? Above all, there lingers the monumental question of Constantine's conversion, the "Constantinian question" par excellence. How many divine visions did he have leading up to his conversion: one, two, perhaps more? When precisely did he convert? Did he ever really convert? Scholars continue to argue these questions fiercely, yet opinion on all of them remains divided. Though general consensus has developed around some, none has been definitively solved and many remain wide open.

Constantine would surely have appreciated this situation. He was himself a lover of allusions, riddles, and secret messages in poetry and art, an interpreter and follower of ambiguous signs and puzzling portents, and a purveyor of legendary stories and frustratingly mixed messages. Examples abound. As to allusions and riddles, Constantine was convinced, as he states in his "Oration to the Saints," that the pagan poet Virgil, writing in the 30s BC, made vatic reference to the advent of Christ in his famous fourth *Eclogue* and that the mythic Sybil of Cumae tucked encrypted allusions to Christ into her oracles.[1] Indeed, the poet Optatianus Porfyrius was able to win his way back into Constantine's good graces and eventually secure plum political appointments by dedicating to Constantine a collection of poems larded with triply encoded messages layered throughout his verses in artfully shaped acrostics.[2] As to signs and portents, quite apart from his famous vision and dream of a crosslike symbol in the sky prior to the battle at the Milvian Bridge, Constantine is said to have witnessed a heavenly host coming to his aid on the day of that battle, October 28, 312.[3] He also had a vision of two youths – perhaps the Dioscuri – battering the enemy lines during a battle against Licinius at Adrianople (presumably the battle fought in 324); he believed he witnessed a light enclosing his camp during his siege of Byzantium in the summer of 324; he claimed God had appeared to him in a dream ordering him to found his new capital at Byzantium; and he had another vision during his wars with the Goths and Sarmatians.[4] As to legendary stories, Eusebius reports that Constantine himself regaled a group of bishops with tales of his vision(s) and military successes, and Constantine must also be the source for the boast that he had manhandled wild beasts and personally captured barbarian chiefs in combat during his stay at Galerius's court.[5] Finally, Constantine's mixed messages are too numerous to catalog. A brief list might include his establishment at Constantinople of Christian churches alongside pagan temples and statues, some of the latter gathered for him by the pagan priest of the Eleusinian Mysteries;[6] or his famous letter to the eastern provincials where he excoriates pagans for holding onto their "sanctuaries of falsehood" but simultaneously refuses to coerce them to convert;[7] or his rescript to the people of Hispellum (AD 337) where he allows them to establish a cult temple to his family but refuses to let it be "defiled by the conceits of any contagious superstition."[8] To be sure, all of these seeming contradictions, these paradoxes, can be explained, though not always to everyone's satisfaction. If anything, all might agree that they reflect a consistently inclusive religious model that refuses to accept the contradiction in simultaneously fostering monotheist and polytheist belief. Yet the contradiction cannot be hidden, no more to us moderns than it could to many ancients. Constantine seems deliberately to have projected ambiguity, deliberately to have kept people guessing.

The fragments left to us to construct the events of his reign were thus already shrouded in mystery before he died, and their layers of complexity were brought into high relief by the strong feelings he evoked in all who experienced him or wrote his story. Thus, our most fulsome source, Eusebius's *Life of Constantine*, written shortly after his death, already presents so tendentious a picture in favor of Constantine that it has often been dubbed a tissue of lies or an outright forgery.[9] Though more recent scholarship has backed away from this extreme interpretation, Eusebius certainly set a high benchmark for slathering adulation. Nor was he alone, for his fellow Christian Lactantius and the pagans Praxagoras and Bemarchius were also quite lavish in their praise, albeit more restrained in expressing it. Very quickly, however, a contrapuntal reaction developed, first, apparently, in the writings of Constantine's own nephew Julian. The pagan Julian lampooned his Christian uncle as a spendthrift, a revolutionary, a sop to barbarians, and a murderer of his own kin who turned to the church in search of forgiveness for his unspeakable crimes.[10] Here, too, this tradition found adherents, the most notable being Eunapius and his transcriber Zosimus, who blackened Constantine's memory with scandalous accounts of his prodigality and maladministration and scurrilous reports of his family intrigues and love of luxury.[11] Nor was Constantine's reputation unblemished by Christians, for even the orthodox Jerome was quick to point out that he had been baptized an Arian heretic on his deathbed.[12] Thus did Constantine enter history with a reputation for a sort of ethical schizophrenia, all good to his advocates, who daintily sidestepped his foibles, all bad to his opponents, who trained their focus on his glaring faults.

By the fifth century, the history of this controversial figure had begun to meld with legend, at least in part as a way to iron out persistent contradictions. The earliest and most noteworthy among the legends – that of Helena and the True Cross aside – centers around the figure of Pope Sylvester, a contemporary of Constantine's, but one with whom he seems to have had little real contact.[13] The Sylvester legend portrayed the young Constantine as a bloodthirsty pagan who converted after allowing himself to be baptized by Sylvester in order to cure leprosy and eventually used the pope as his spiritual guide. This legend eventually gave rise to the eighth-century pseudojuridical document known as the Donations of Constantine, a pious forgery claiming that the emperor had turned over earthly and heavenly authority in Italy to Pope Sylvester and his successors. These ties forged (in both senses) between pope and potentate were variously exploited in subsequent centuries, as for example when the young German emperor Otto III installed his friend and teacher Gerbert of Aurillac as Pope Sylvester II in 999, at the latter's request, or when tensions between Pope Innocent IV and Frederick II in the thirteenth century were played out in the creation of frescoes of the Church of SS Quattro Coronati portraying a humbly genuflecting Constantine handing a tiara to a severe-looking Pope Sylvester (Fig. 38).[14] Only as late as 1440 was the Donations document decisively proven to be a forgery by Lorenzo Valla. By then, however, Constantine had already been cemented by the legends into his historical niche like some icon of the Christian prince locked in a love-hate wrestling match with the church over world rule.

Constantine thus entered the Enlightenment with plenty of baggage, baggage he would not shed any time soon, for modern historiography has been no less multivalent in its interpretations of and ultimately its uses of Constantine. The modern literature is staggering and cannot be done justice here. A glance across its surface is, nevertheless, revealing. In his breathtaking *History of the Decline and Fall of the Roman Empire* (1776–81), E. Gibbon presented a characteristically insightful interpretation of Constantine that combined his good and bad qualities into a dynamic portrait. Convinced of his divine right to rule, Gibbon's Constantine exploited the advantages of Christianity – its monotheism, its revelatory theology, its teleological cosmology, and its preexisting organization – to secure his claim to exclusive power. Once he had obtained this, however, he became personally convinced of the mythic narrative he had invented for himself:

> His vanity was gratified by the flattering assurance that he
> had been chosen by heaven to reign over the earth; success
> had justified his divine title to the throne, and that title was
> founded on the truth of Christian revelation. As real virtue
> is sometimes excited by undeserved applause, the specious
> piety of Constantine, if at first it was only specious, might
> gradually, by the influence of praise, of habit, and of example,
> be matured into serious faith and fervent devotion.[15]

Gibbon's Constantine is thus a victim of his own success, trapped in a fantasy of divine grandeur that was fed by his undeniable achievements. More pointedly, because in Gibbon's eyes the rise of Christianity spelled the fall of the Roman empire, his Constantine also becomes a tragic standard-bearer for the empire's demise.

The Swiss polymath J. Burckhardt, whose monograph *The Age of Constantine the Great* (first published in 1853) represents the first attempt to describe an "Age of Constantine," was less convinced of the emperor's self-deception. For him, Constantine was a calculating politician who shrewdly employed all means necessary to secure and maintain power. As such, he never gave himself over to any party – Christians, pagans, soldiers, senators, bishops, bureaucrats – but always played all sides against each other:

> In a genius driven without surcease by ambition and lust for power there can be no question of religiosity; such a man is essentially unreligious, even if he pictures himself standing in the midst of a churchly community. Holiness he understands only as a reminiscence or as a superstitious vagary.... He thinks that he will be at peace when he has achieved this or the other goal, whatever it may be that is wanting to make his possessions complete. But in the meantime all of his energies, spiritual as well as physical, are devoted to the great goal of dominion, and if he ever pauses to think of his convictions, he finds they are pure fatalism.[16]

Burckhardt's Constantine was thus a political impresario who feigned conversion and studiously avoided sincerity in his relentless drive for *Macht*. Nor was he alone in this assessment. Burckhardt's realist *tendance* found its culmination in the approach taken by a Belgian scholar of Constantine, H. Grégoire. Writing in the 1930s, Grégoire became a harsh critic of the authenticity of Eusebius's *Life* and saw Constantine's vision and conversion as a postmortem rewriting of events by his postulated pseudo-Eusebius. For him, Constantine remained a soldier emperor and political player whose interest in Christianity grew only after he witnessed the political usefulness of Christian religion as employed by his rival Licinius.[17] Burckhardt's opportunistic Constantine thus became Grégoire's exploitative Constantine.

This picture of the calculating pragmatist naturally provoked a reaction of its own, a reaction that came primarily in two flavors. The milder of these is well represented by the simple, even naive Constantine presented by the German O. Seeck in his monumental *Geschichte des Untergangs der antiken Welt* (1920–3). For Seeck, Constantine was very much a product of his world, a world rife with superstition and religious mysticism. His Constantine stood out in only one respect:

> What distinguished the character of this remarkable man was, above all, his deeply rooted feeling of duty and his religious sentiment that naturally bore the colors of its time and of his lowly social position, but was no less honest and pious for all that. Like most great military heroes, Constantine believed blindly in his good fortune. But like most all people of his era, who were ruled in one form or another by their fear of the divine, his sense of fortune was clothed in religious garb. After groping his way along and wavering considerably, he developed the conviction that he was the chosen instrument of the highest God, called to eliminate his enemies and to spread his kingdom on earth.[18]

Seeck's Constantine was thus an uncultured but generally sincere war hero whose faith in his own good fortune came to be translated into faith in his role as God's divine agent on earth. This Constantine's enigmas and contradictions were thus less a product of ingenious calculation than humble inconsistency. A not dissimilar Constantine appears in the Frenchman A. Piganiol's *L'empereur Constantin* (1932). For Piganiol, Constantine was neither a religious mystic nor an exploitative egotist; instead he was a sincere and simple man who sought truth and justice in religion and government but ultimately failed to achieve it. Though he was wise enough to have seen the value of Christian monotheism to the project of empire, he polluted his innate sense of equity with uncontrolled rage and surrendered too much of his power to the bishops he so labored to please. The result was a failed experiment in caesaropapism that, for all its good intentions, proved detrimental to the empire.[19] Less condemnatory were the related portraits by A. H. M. Jones and R. MacMullen, both of whom see in Constantine a less visionary and dynamic figure but more of what MacMullen calls "an impulsive, not overly subtle man, inclined to make decisions on inadequate grounds."[20] Thus was the masterfully conniving Constantine deflated, losing first his acumen to religious fanaticism, then even his standing as a religious icon.

The more assertive response to Burckhardt's realism came, however, with the reintroduction of Constantine the committed Christian. This approach was already heralded by N. Baynes's influential lecture cum monograph *Constantine the Great and the Christian Church* (1929), which argued for a Constantine who converted with some reluctance but soon became a committed Christian whose guiding principle was the establishment of unity among the members of the Church. What seems, then, like contradiction or wavering is in fact evidence of an effort to attract new adherents and absorb schismatics under the banner of a single *ecclesia*.[21] An even stronger representative of this school was the Hungarian A. Alföldi. He argued in *The Conversion of Constantine and Pagan Rome* (1948) that the best evidence for the genuineness and robustness of Constantine's conversion is the concerted retrenchment of a "pagan reaction" to him and his policies.[22] In the past two decades, most of the case for the rise of a pagan reaction – under Constantine or any emperor – has been discredited, but the image of Constantine the *Christianissimus imperator* has remained, indeed grown stronger.

The most developed and convincing defense of the Christian Constantine is to be found in the comprehensive and authoritative *Constantine and Eusebius* (1981) by T. D. Barnes:

> Constantine . . . was neither a saint nor a tyrant. He was more humane than some of his immediate predecessors, but still capable of ruthlessness and prone to irrational anger. As an administrator, he was more concerned to preserve and modify the imperial system which he inherited than to change it radically – except in one sphere. From the days of his youth Constantine had probably been sympathetic to Christianity, and in 312 he experienced a religious conversion which profoundly affected his conception of himself. After 312 Constantine considered that his main duty as emperor was to inculcate virtue in his subjects and to persuade them to worship God. Constantine's character is not wholly enigmatic; with all his faults and despite an intense ambition for personal power, he nevertheless believed sincerely that God had given him a special mission to convert the Roman Empire to Christianity.[23]

Barnes's Constantine is not nearly so radical as that of his forebears. Very much human and with all the attendant limitations, this Constantine nevertheless experienced a radical conversion, which he then actualized into a personal crusade to convert his empire. For Barnes, Constantine was a Christian sympathizer from the beginning and an unwavering proponent of Christianity from his conversion in 312 onward. The argument has strong merits, though at times it has been put forth without giving full weight to potentially contradictory evidence.[24] The argument for a firmly Christian Constantine reaches its zenith in T. G. Elliott's *The Christianity of Constantine the Great* (1996). Elliott's Constantine has no need for conversion, for he was already a committed Christian – as were his parents – from the start. Evidence of less-than-Christian behavior does not then convict him of a wavering faith, only of a faith imperfectly exercised. In Elliott the argument has come full circle. Like Grégoire, he discounts the stories of conversion as later falsifications. Yet his goal is no longer to prove Constantine a cynical opportunist but to show that Constantine was always a committed believer who, over time, developed the persona of the Christian prince.[25]

It should not go unremarked that the colorful Constantine we began examining – the warrior and statesman, the reformer of bureaucracy and economy, the builder of edifices and cities, the rebuilder of army and dynasty – has quickly become monochromatic as we turn to the history of legend and scholarship. No matter how hard the student of Constantine struggles, it is nearly impossible to avoid getting caught in the snares of the "Constantinian question," the question of conversion and faith.[26] This is precisely the predicament that I hope this volume goes some way toward avoiding. Important, indeed central, though the Constantinian question may be, it tends to overshadow the many facets of Constantine and his world that were unrelated or only tangentially related to Christianity and conversion. I hope with this text to move the debate outside this trap, without of course sidestepping it. The division of chapters should make it clear that religion, omnipresent though it is, is only one of the topics that will be illuminated in this book. Apart from this introduction and an overview of the sources, it consists of five sections, each with three essays. The first section is on politics and personalities, the second on religion and society, the third on law and economy, the fourth on art and literature, and the fifth on foreign policy. Most of the chapters have been assigned to younger scholars, and while some of the contributors are more seasoned and have previously written widely on Constantine, all, I hope, have been given a chance to express new ideas.

The volume begins with a survey of the sources by Bruno Bleckmann and then moves on with a chapter on the political situation before Constantine. In particular, Simon Corcoran examines the way that the comprehensive reforms undertaken by Diocletian and his fellow Tetrarchs set the stage for much of what Constantine would accomplish. I have written the second chapter, which surveys the political and military history of Constantine's reign in an effort to chart his progress from junior Tetrarch through tyrant-slayer and champion of the faith to divine visionary. Robert M. Frakes carries the story further with a look at how the elaborate dynastic edifice constructed by Constantine fell prey to the intrigues of his sons but eventually outlived the Constantinians by being grafted onto the next dynasty. The section on religion begins with a discussion of the meaning of Constantine's conversion by H. A. Drake, who shows that the supposed contradictions discussed earlier are evidence of an emperor bent on creating consensus through his commitment to religious toleration. Mark Edwards then expounds upon the growth of Christian religion in the age of Constantine more generally and emphasizes especially the rise of the cross as a new and powerful symbol of a triumphant Christianity. A. D. Lee goes on to look at pagan religion and its fundamental vitality in the age of Constantine, a vitality that guaranteed Constantine's cautious alliance with Christianity's former enemies. Turning to law and economy, Christopher Kelly shows what a fundamental role Constantine played in the creation of governmental structures that would endure throughout late antiquity. Caroline Humfress looks at Constantine's civil laws and finds less evidence of Christian ideology than of a fundamentally conservative moralism. Georges Depeyrot provides an overview of a basically faltering economy that was nevertheless shored up to a considerable degree by Constantine's monetary policies. Turning to high culture, Jaś Elsner describes the vitality of representative art in imperial and private circles, a vitality based on the productive reuse and re-formation of earlier artistic materials and forms. Mark J. Johnson covers the vast array of Constantinian architecture and demonstrates that, for all his innovation, Constantine always constructed buildings with an eye to the past. Finally, in the section on foreign policy, Hugh Elton maps out the workings of the late Roman army, an army every bit as powerful and dynamic as its early imperial predecessor. Michael Kulikowski presents the peoples of the northern frontier, first in macroscopic and then in microscopic perspective, and shows the surprisingly important role they played in shaping politics within the empire. And Elizabeth Key Fowden offers a sweeping survey of the peoples of the eastern frontier, whose assimilation into the Christian empire Constantine so longed to achieve that his dying efforts to invade Persia can rightly be taken as an accurate indicator of the teleological direction of his reign.

This is of course a collective effort and as such represents not one but a variety of perspectives and approaches. Every effort has been made to organize the contributions into a unified whole that will hopefully be greater than the sum of its parts. The reader should find very little overlap and redundancy. There are also no glaring contradictions or inconsistencies among the various contributions that might lead to outright confusion. In some instances, however, differences of opinion and interpretation will necessarily lead to differing conclusions. It is assumed that these will be viewed not as a deficit but rather as an asset of this collective approach. Not only will they allow readers to view the complexities and quandaries of Constantinian history from many sides, they will also hopefully bring the readers into these debates by providing all the pieces of evidence and modes of interpretation at our disposal.

NOTES

1   OC 18–20. In so doing, Constantine is following Lact. *Div. Inst.* 7.16–22.
2   See T. D. Barnes 1975; Levitan 1985.
3   *Pan. Lat.* 4(10).14.1–6; cf. Zon. 13.1.27.
4   On the two youths, see Zon. 13.1.27–8, with Bleckmann 1991, 351–2; cf. Eus. *VC* 2.6.1. On the foundation of Constantinople, see Soz. 2.3.3; cf. Philost. 2.9, which speaks of a waking vision. For the vision during the Gothic and Sarmatian wars, see Soz. 1.8.9. See also Soz. 6.33.3 and MacMullen 1968. More on the penchant of emperors to exploit portents and prophecies in Potter 1994.
5   On the vision, see Eus. *VC* 1.28–30; 2.8.2, 9.3. On the heroics, see *Origo* 3; Zon. 12.33; Lact. *DMP* 24.4; Praxagoras fr. 1.2 (*FGH* 2B219:948); cf. *Pan. Lat.* 7(6).3.3.
6   *OGIS* 720–1 with Fowden 1987. On the mix of pagan and Christian, see Chapter 7.
7   Eus. *VC* 2.56.1–60.2.
8   *CIL* 11:5256 = *ILS* 705, translated at Lee 2000, 92–3. On the phrase, see Gascou 1967, 651–5.
9   Most forcefully Grégoire 1938, 1939. Cameron and Hall 1999, 4–9, offer a summary of the arguments with bibliography.
10 Jul. *Caes.* 318a; 335b; 336a-b; cf. AM 21.10.8. For more on the ancient historiographic tradition concerning Constantine, see Chapter 1 herein and Neri 1992; Lieu 1996, 1–38.
11 Zos. 2.20.2; 29.1–30.2; 38.1–2; cf. Paschoud 1971a. Other fourth-century critics of Constantine included the pagans Ammianus and Libanius, on whom see Warmington 1981, 1999; Wiemer 1994a.
12 Jer. *Chron.* s.a. 337; cf. Aiello 1992b for the historiographic tradition on this lemma.
13 On the historical personage of Sylvester, see Aiello 2000b. On the legend, see Aiello 1992a; Fowden 1994a, 1994b; Lieu 1998; and Chapter 13.
14 More at Aiello 2000b; Marcone 2003, 319–20.
15 Gibbon [1776–81] 1994, 743; cf. 643–6, 725–50. The most lucid summary of what follows – i.e., the debate on the Constantinian question – can be found in Drake 2000, 12–34.
16 Burckhardt [1880] 1949, 281.
17 Grégoire 1930–1, 1938, 1939. The theory still has its adherents, e.g., Bleicken 1992.

18 Seeck 1920–3, 1:56, my trans.

19 Piganiol 1932. The outlines of this picture were darkened in Piganiol's *L'Empire Chrétien*, first published shortly after World War II; cf. Piganiol 1972.

20 MacMullen 1969, 237; Jones 1949.

21 Baynes 1929, passim. Baynes is especially concerned with Constantine's famous claim to have been "established by God as bishop of those outside (the church)," Eus. *VC* 4.24; cf. 1.54. This *bon mot* also forms the starting point of the recent book by S. Calderone 2001, a work very much in the tradition of Baynes in its insistence on Constantine's deliberate efforts to unify church and state. See also Fowden 1993, 80–99, whose Constantine strives to unite the entire world under the banner of Rome and Christianity.

22 A. Alföldi 1948.

23 T. D. Barnes 1981, 275.

24 See Cameron 1983; Drake 1983.

25 Elliott 1987, 1996, 17–72, esp. 63 n. 8. Odahl 2004 also portrays a very Christian Constantine.

26 T. D. Barnes 1981 is surely the best antidote to this problem, though even it has little to say on art, architecture, economics, and social history. Odahl 2004 also covers considerable ground, including the architecture.

1: SOURCES FOR THE HISTORY
OF CONSTANTINE

Bruno Bleckmann

Translated by Noel Lenski

What we can know about the history of an emperor is entirely dependent on our source base. For our knowledge of Constantine, the situation is actually quite favorable considering the usual standards in ancient history. To be sure, there is no longer extant a full-scale ancient historical work for the rule of Constantine. The historian finds compensation, however, in a large number of other sources whose breadth and complexity have made the treatment of the historical problem of Constantine's reign into something of a proving ground for ancient historical method. This method consists primarily in using the sources available to document a state of affairs in the most comprehensive way possible and then setting those sources in relation to one another, as for example through hierarchization.

To offer one example, the ancient historian could not settle the question whether Constantine the Great suddenly became Christian in the fall of 312 after the battle of the Milvian Bridge by looking only at the ecclesiastical historians of the fifth century, who preserve the well-known legend, often repeated into modern times, that Constantine saw a cross in the heavens before his victory over Maxentius and converted to Christianity out of gratitude for his success. On the contrary, he must investigate the origin of the legend and explain why already the contemporary Eusebius included this report in his *Life of Constantine* (*Vita Constantini*). He must further combine a plethora of contemporary and later source reports in order to derive arguments about the religious attitude of Constantine in 312: in this case, the inscription on the Arch of Constantine (Fig. 1), the Ticinum medallion (Coin 1), the contemporary report of the Christian pamphleteer Lactantius, and the decrees that Constantine made already in late fall 312 and spring 313 in favor of the metropolitan church of Carthage, preserved in their original wording.[1]

Further complications are added by the ever-broadening lack of familiarity with the source languages in which the original documents were written, even among classicists. This does not render all endeavors with the sources fruitless. We still stand to gain much relevant information and insight through the many fine translations recently produced, but we must always remain conscious of the fact that we are dealing with translations in which the finer nuances are often irretrievably lost, as for example when we are attempting to understand what it could mean that Constantine, according to the inscription on his arch, is supposed to have defeated his rival Maxentius "through the greatness of his mind and the impulse of the divinity" (*mentis magnitudine . . . instinctu divinitatis*). Is this supposed to mean that Constantine prevailed both through his own intellect and through the support of an anonymous divinity, or is *instinctu divinitatis* a mere variant on *mentis magnitudine* and thus means only that the emperor was directed by his own divine inspiration, as has recently been asserted?[2] Such an interpretation would prevent us from acknowledging any concrete allusion to the vision of 312 (and the consequent experience of divine support) in the inscription on the arch. The question cannot be determined by glancing at translations but only through the precise investigation of Latin parallels, especially in the panegyrics.

For an overview of the source material we can distinguish the following groupings, in keeping with the recognized system of division for historical sources:

1. Artifacts and remains created in the time of Constantine and, through the accidents of fortune, preserved up to the present: inscriptions, coins, papyri, archaeological remains, like the Arch of Constantine in Rome
2. Contemporary texts that the copyists of the Middle Ages have preserved, including in particular:
   a. The personal testimonies of Constantine, such as legal texts and speeches like the *Oration to the Assembly of the Saints*[3]
   b. Other contemporary literary texts, such as the orations of Gallic rhetoricians (*Panegyrici Latini*)[4] and Eusebius's biography of Constantine, composed immediately after the emperor's death[5]

3. Texts that were first composed one or more generations after
Constantine and describe the age of Constantine, such as the
ecclesiastical historians of the fifth century or the pagan historian Zosimus[6]

These three groups cannot be separated into entirely neat categories. There are always peculiarities and ambiguities. One of the
most important archaeological monuments of this period is the great
porphyry column that Constantine erected in the forum of his newly
founded city (Fig. 2). This is preserved as a stump of its former self, the
so-called Burnt Column (Çemberlitaş) in Istanbul. It originally served as
the base for a statue of Constantine. Later sources report the opinion that
this statue portrayed the emperor in the form of the sun-god. A minia-
ture on a Roman road map of the fourth century – the so-called *Tabula
Peutingeriana* (Fig. 3), which is preserved only as a medieval copy –
shows that Constantine was portrayed nude, like a divinity, while
a Byzantine chronicle transmits that Constantine also bore a radiate
crown, like the sun god. The original monument of the Constantinian
period must thus be reconstructed through various types of sources.
This reconstruction is important precisely because it shows clearly how
Constantine assumed that his profession of Christianity and his self-
representation in the context of Sol-Helios worship were compatible
right up to the end of his reign. Further, it becomes clear that the
lofty person of the heroic-divine emperor stood in the center of his
new foundation and that Constantinople, at whose center point this
quite ambiguous statue was located, was not conceived as a Christian
counterpoint to the pagan Rome.

Similarly complex is the situation with regard to the laws of Constantine. Many laws and imperial rescripts with legal force are known
through later codifications, especially the *Codex Theodosianus* (AD 438)
and the *Codex Justinianus* (AD 534).[7] Other laws were collected en bloc
as documents in church histories, where they served as evidence for the
Constantine's Christian stance. Some are also preserved in the original
form in which they were reported to individual cities of the empire, that
is, as inscriptions. This is the case with the dossier of Orcistus, which,
because of its strictly local relevance, was published only in Orcistus
itself. This dossier includes an imperial response with the force of law, a
so-called *adnotatio*, which gave local autonomy to Orcistus in answer to
a petition. To this *adnotatio* were added further documents (conditions
of implementation, the original petition to the emperor, etc).[8] Laws
with general validity are also partially preserved in epigraphic form so

that the versions of the *Codices* can be cross-checked against the epigraphic version, as for example the numerous copies of Constantine's well-known Edict on Accusations.[9] Above all the inscriptions offer the opportunity to gain more comprehensive information about the legislative activity of Diocletian, whose political order Constantine opposed and succeeded in overturning. Knowledge of the important epigraphically preserved edicts in the area of economic legislation (Diocletian's Price Edict[10] and Coinage Reform[11]) is essential for the comprehension of the preconditions that determined Constantine's politico-economic activities.

INSCRIPTIONS, COINS, AND ARCHAEOLOGICAL MONUMENTS

Having mentioned the epigraphically preserved documents, we can now turn to the first source group, the remains stemming from Constantine's immediate time period. The tendency to publish texts in costly form and present them to the public as inscriptions had certainly diminished markedly in late antiquity as compared with the high empire; nevertheless, we have a multitude of inscriptions from the time of Constantine whose historical importance is unequivocal. This is especially true of the emperor's religious policies: the previously mentioned monumental inscription from the Arch of Constantine in Rome, which was formally dedicated on the occasion of the emperor's *decennalia* in 315 by the Senate – but surely checked and approved by the imperial court – illustrates well a religious phase in which precise prescriptions regarding the identity of the almighty god were to be avoided.[12] In the dossier of Orcistus, also just discussed, which belongs to Constantine's late reign, this reluctance has been abandoned. On the contrary, Constantine clearly takes sides here in favor of the Christian community of Orcistus against its larger pagan rival Nacoleia. In an inscription from Hispellum (Fig. 4) very late in Constantine's reign, the emperor tolerates the expansion of the imperial cult but in the process forbids the pagan sacrificial rites that were so repugnant to Christians.[13]

Inscriptions also shed light on aspects of the emperor's rule other than religious politics. This is true of milestones, stone pillars used by travelers to measure distances along imperial roads, for these published the valid titulature of an emperor at the precise time they were engraved. The late empire was, of course, a period when multiple emperors ruled together in consort. When all the emperors of a current *collegium* are mentioned on milestones, this permits us to determine the hierarchy that existed between its members. We also have important indications about what themes played a contemporary role in imperial politics, from the time when Constantine first had to assert himself in the circle of shared rule requisite to the Tetrarchy up to the point where he worked to suppress his corulers. Especially interesting is the fact that Constantine did not attempt to assert himself as *maximus augustus* (greatest Augustus) – and thus claim clear precedence over his rival Licinius – immediately after his victory over Maxentius in AD 312 but only assumed this title beginning at the time of his decennalia in 315.[14] After defeating Licinius, his title *invictus* (unconquerable) – common among emperors of the time but also clearly identifying the emperor with the protective god *Sol Invictus* – was replaced by the religiously neutral *victor* (the conqueror). We must of course remember that, after victory over his last and most dangerous rival, Constantine embodied as sole ruler an especially charged aura of permanent triumph and that *victor*, a word of active agency, represented this. But the break with the epithet of the old solar deity remains unmistakable. In order to give still clearer expression to these ideas, after further successes on the borders of the empire, Constantine assumed the title *victor et triumphator*, which remained obligatory for future emperors in late antiquity.

Much of an emperor's program of self-representation is also on evidence in his coins. Their ability to reflect ever-changing propaganda on an easily datable basis lends coins special weight as interpretive tools even despite their rather stereotyped and formulaic nature in late antiquity. To be sure, the legends on coins generally consist of brief formulae and abbreviated imperial titulature, but when combined with changing pictorial representations they offer considerable scope for interpretation. One can only get an overview of the subjects treated in the coins by leafing through the pages of the corresponding volumes of *Roman Imperial Coinage*, especially volumes 6 (Sutherland) and 7 (Bruun).[15] Apart from the subjects introduced pictorially and in the legends, much can be learned from other qualities, like weight, size of issue, and place of minting (in late antiquity minting was decentralized and was conducted not just in Rome but also in other Tetrarchic capitals and significant provincial cities). Here we can give only a few examples of how many elements must be attended to in the interpretation of a coin:

1. In 322, just before the second war between Constantine and Licinius, a coin was minted in large numbers that celebrated the successes of Constantine on the middle and lower Danube

with the legend SARMATIA DEVICTA (Sarmatia [the barbarian territory north of the Danube bend] has been conquered; Coin 2).[16] With this, Constantine introduced himself to the western parts of the empire as the only capable defender of the Danube border and provoked his rival Licinius, who had not been in a position to restore order to this section of the Danube, although it was technically under his control. In the imperial territories of Licinius, no coins were minted to celebrate the victory of Constantine, and from a later source we learn that Licinius even forbade circulaton of these very coins of his rival in his domains.[17] Of note in this case, therefore, is the place of minting, the subject represented in the legend and image, and a textual notice preserved by historical accident.

2. From the 320s we have a coin with the seemingly unremarkable obverse legend D(ominus) N(oster) CONSTANTINVS P(ius) F(elix) AVG(ustus) (our lord Constantine pious and fortunate Augustus) — the standard designation for an emperor at this time — and SENATVS on the reverse (Coin 3). The concord between Senate and emperor is thus emphasized. This too initially seems unremarkable but gains a significant profile before the background of difficult relations between Constantine and the capital in the 320s described in pagan sources. We know that in order to counter resentment in Rome, Constantine repeated the celebrations of his twentieth anniversary as emperor (vicennalia) in Rome in 326 after they had already taken place in Nicomedia the year previously. The heavy weight of these medallions — 4.5 times the weight of a normal coin — indicates that the emperor put great stock in this demonstration of concord with the Roman Senate.[18]

3. Especially complex is the case of the medallion of Ticinum, minted in 315 (Coin 1). Its legends are conventional: on the obverse, we read the abbreviated titulature of Constantine: IMP(erator) CONSTANTINVS P(ius) F(elix) AVG(ustus) (Emperor Constantine pious and fortunate Augustus). On the reverse, another conventional notion is expressed that touches on the welfare of the commonweal: SALVS REI PVBLICAE (the safety of the state). The peculiarity of this coin lies, however, in the fact that the presentation of the emperor's military capacities — on the reverse, Constantine delivers a harangue before the soldiers, and on the obverse, he is shown with armor, horse, and shield — is connected with Christian symbolism for

the first time in Roman numismatic history. On the front-most rosette of the emperor's helmet, we find unmistakably the Chrismon (Chi-Rho), the initials for "Christ." After its discovery, the coin was naturally interpreted as an early demonstration of Constantine's acknowledgement of Christianity, yet the pictorial image is not entirely unequivocal. Whether the images behind the shield are really supposed to represent a Christian cross-scepter remains a subject of debate, and Constantine's shield portrays the Capitoline wolf with Rome's legendary founder Romulus, the deified son of the deity Mars. It is paramount that we are dealing with a medallion here, a special issue distributed for a special occasion to a specific cadre. We thus have relatively few extant coins – only three exemplars – of this sparingly minted issue, which was perhaps aimed at the specific interests of Christian recipients with imperial favor. Moreover, apart from this single coin with Christian symbolism, we have countless unequivocally pagan coins that were issued contemporaneously, for example, the famous Roman coin in which Constantine is portrayed in double profile with his protective deity Sol (Coin 4), very clearly expressing the identification of the emperor with solar religion: both figures, deity and emperor, resemble one another like twins, for Sol has taken on the features of Constantine.

Among the pertinent archaeological sources, we could rank not just the familiar Arch of Constantine in Rome or the "burned column" (Çemberlitaş) in Constantinople but also some new discoveries of recent years. Noteworthy is the palace in Gamzigrad-Romuliana (Serbia; Fig. 5), which Galerius had built as a residence for his planned retirement and whose remains, discovered just two decades ago, represent a major source for the reconstruction of the political system of the Tetrarchy against which Constantine struggled in his early years. The construction of a high-speed railway in Cordoba revealed a magnificent complex that lay 600 meters in front of the walls of the ancient city and that – at least according to the interpretation of its excavators – represents a Tetrarchic palace for Maximianus Herculius associated with the campaigns against the Mauri that he conducted from southern Spain.[19] Others argue, by contrast, that this complex of "Cercadilla" may simply be a governor's residence.[20] It is of course uncertain whether we will ever be able to separate imperial palace from governor's residence. The praetorium preserved in Cologne, for example, served the governor on the one hand but also sometimes the emperor, as when Constantine used it during the frontier wars in the first years of his reign or on other occasions, like the ephemeral usurpation of Silvanus. Regardless, the complex proves that Cordoba had a transregional importance in the context of imperial administration, and this helps to explain why the bishop of Cordoba, Ossius, came to serve as one of the most important theological advisors of Constantine, even to the extent of heading the Council of Nicaea (AD 325). Through his couplike takeover of the imperial territory of his father, Constantine had assumed control of Spain from the beginning of his reign and resided occasionally in Cordoba. In similar instances, bishops from other regions where Constantine often resided in the first years of his reign arose as important counselors and contacts, to wit, Arles and Cologne, even if contact with the emperor did not always guarantee a bishop influence, as was apparently the case in Trier.

CONTEMPORARY LITERARY EVIDENCE

Constantine's Personal Testimony

Constantine ranks first among those emperors for whom we have the greatest number of extant personal documents attesting to imperial affairs, and not simply because of his extremely long reign. His personal testimonia are in many ways the product of late antique literary workshops. They have been carefully prepared in the imperial chancery by specialists in the rhetorical art, generally in the typical overwrought style of late antiquity, and must thus not be taken as transparent windows onto the psychological judgment of the emperor. All the same, as contemporaneous documents describing in propagandistic fashion imperial actions from the perspective of the imperial administration, they are of inestimable worth. Personal testimonia of this sort are offered first and foremost in the law codes, usually in the form of letters directed to a specific addressee and then preserved in the *Codex Theodosianus* and the *Codex Justinianus*. Of course, the late antique codices offer only a selection of laws, and they are also presented only in abbreviated form so that the ideological basis for their justification is often lost. For this reason, we are fortunate to have some much more complete laws embedded in historiographic works where the emperor's more circumstantial argumentation is often seasoned with flourishes of late antique rhetoric. In contrast with the customs of classical historiography, according to which the unaltered and unelaborated citation of archival material was considered unacceptable and stylistically offensive, Constantine's contemporary, the ecclesiastical historian Eusebius (c. 260–339), followed a practice that arose in Hellenistic times, which was to present extensive and unaltered documents, not so much for scholarly as for polemical reasons.

Eusebius's goal with this documentary strategy was to demonstrate to his readers the truly Christian disposition of the emperor. Among the sources he incorporates into his *Ecclesiastical History*, for example, we must include several letters that Constantine had his chancery draft in connection with the debates in the African church, for example, a letter to Bishop Miltiades of Rome with a call to convene a synod in Rome or one to Chrestus of Syracuse with an invitation to the Synod of Arles.[21] So too the famous Edict of Milan (neither an edict nor from Milan), in which Licinius permitted the return of possessions confiscated in the Christian persecutions to churches, is offered in a Greek translation that can be compared with the Latin original recorded in Lactantius.[22] Eusebius follows this same technique with respect to original documents in his *Life of Constantine* (*Vita Constantini*), published shortly after the death of Constantine. This work consists in large part of Constantine's original personal testimonia (letters and laws), which are explained and interpreted within a narrative frame.[23] The opinion expressed in older historical research that some of the programmatic letters of Constantine embedded in the text were pure inventions of Eusebius (e.g., the letter that Constantine addressed to the inhabitants of eastern provinces after his takeover of this imperial territory from Licinius) has been considered obsolete ever since the discovery of a contemporary papyrus containing a fragment of an original document cited by Eusebius but quite independent of him.[24]

The ecclesiastical historians of the fifth century, Socrates, Sozomen, and Theodoret, discovered further documents from the period in collections of ecclesiastical law that assembled imperial pronouncements in favor of the Church and Christians. So too, in an appendix to his description of the conflict between the Catholic Church establishment and the schismatic Donatists, Optatus of Milevus included numerous documents in which Constantine took the side of the establishment against the Donatists after taking over Maxentius's territory.[25]

Pride of place among Constantine's personal testimonia surely goes to his own *Oration to the Assembly of the Saints*, which has been transmitted to us as an appendix to Eusebius's *Life of Constantine*.[26] It was apparently added by Eusebius himself as an example of the speeches the emperor supposedly composed in his free time. Because we are dealing here not just with the emperor's clear confession of his Christianity but also with a case of vehement polemic against traditional religions in the vein of apologetic, the dating of this oration is of the greatest importance for our understanding of Constantine's political and religious development.

The remaining personal testimonia of Constantine in which he clearly professes Christianity and upbraids pagans come from the period after the victory over Licinius, by which he gained control of the entire empire. As sole ruler, Constantine was able to appear less diplomatic toward pagans than he had previously. Above all, with the victory over Licinius he had taken over regions in which Christians constituted a very high percentage of the population and in which they had been much more intensely and mercilessly persecuted than their coreligionists in the west. In this situation, the emperor could not help but favor Christians more clearly and openly than he once had. Nevertheless, some scholars assert that the *Oration to the Assembly of the Saints* traces to the time when Constantine ruled only the western part of the Roman empire. The question hangs specifically on the interpretation of several passages from the twenty-second and twenty-fifth chapters of the speech, in which concrete historical allusions are made, first in the description of the decimation of Diocletian's army through civil wars, then in the mention of a "great city" that was witnessing Constantine's present successes, though having opted previously for the wrong champion. The speech mentions two "great cities," apparently Rome and Nicomedia, but if one sees an allusion to Rome in the "great city" and thus dates the speech immediately after the victory over Maxentius, it is impossible to reconcile the mention of the decimation of Diocletian's former army, which only truly occurred in 324. Nicomedia fits better, for it capitulated in 324 and numbered among Constantine's favorite residences for some time prior to the dedication of Constantinople. If we date the speech after 324, it belongs among the many testimonia in which Constantine congratulates himself unreservedly for his success in the civil war with Licinius.[27]

Contemporary Literary Texts

The contemporary literary texts have one characteristic in common: they all sing the praises of this surprisingly successful emperor in various ways, and they all come from authors who were more or less close to either the emperor himself or at least his court. Anything different would have been surprising in the age of Constantine. From the Latin west there are primarily sources that stem from the time in which Constantine had to fight against his rivals. Lactantius's pamphlet *On the Death of Persecutors* (*De mortibus persecutorum*), which hymns the praise of Constantine and Licinius, was written shortly after Maxentius and Maximin Daia had been extinguished in the wars of the crumbling Tetrarchy (312 and 313).[28] In lavish detail, it attempts to interpret the events following the abdication of Diocletian in a Christian light by offering a vehement attack against the religious policies initiated by Diocletian and championed above all by Galerius, which attempted to shore up the pagan basis of the Tetrarchy with Christian persecutions. In the process, Lactantius reports misleading information about the ambiguous opposition of Constantius Chlorus and his son Constantine to the Tetrarchic system and its religious policies. *De mortibus persecutorum* also offers our first report (albeit reduced to a single dream vision) of the Christian God's support of Constantine at the battle of the Milvian Bridge. He even offers a pendant that explains the Christian God's support for Licinius as well, a fact that helps date the work to c. 315, before Constantine's break with Licinius.

The *Panegyrici Latini* are a collection of orations delivered in the late third and fourth century in Gaul, primarily for celebratory occasions (imperial jubilees, etc).[29] The long-cherished notion that the imperial court would have dictated the desired propagandistic subjects to the orators is now considered obsolete. Even so, the orators, civic professors of rhetoric, must have had close connections with the imperial chancery and must also have had a sense for what subjects were in vogue at the time when they spoke. For this reason, these orations remain among the most important and fruitful sources we have. From them we can trace the history of the Tetrarchy's collapse and the rise of Constantine (up to the 320s) and can observe the political constellations and how current events were interpreted and then reinterpreted in the span of a few years. Thus, for example, the old emperor Maximianus, who attempted several times after his abdication in 305 to return to active politics and whose daughter Constantine married in 307, was still celebrated in the panegyric of 307 but was scorned as a doting codger in the panegyric of 310, immediately after his end in an attempted coup against Constantine.

For the period of Constantine's sole rule (324–37), there were undoubtedly further panegyrics delivered for the emperor in the west, but they failed to be included in the collection of the Gallic panegyrics. The Latin verses of Optatianus Porfyrius, which celebrate the definitive triumph of the emperor over Licinius and his assumption of sole rule, are rather sparse in content and reveal more about the aesthetics of the age than contemporary events.[30] Of contemporary rhetorical productions celebrating the emperor as ruler, we have extant only a few Greek works. One reflection of the themes that were treated in many speeches in the Greek cities after Constantine's takeover of power is offered by Praxagoras, whose two books on the emperor Constantine are known through a short excerpt made by the Byzantine patriarch Photius.[31] He portrayed how territory after territory was freed from the rule of the "tyrant" through the emperor's westward progress and how finally the empire, formerly fractured by the Tetrarchic order, flourished again under the hopeful sole rule of its savior Constantine. Precisely the same interpretations of Constantine's path to sole rule can be found in the parts of Libanius's fifty-ninth Oration that are devoted to the father of its imperial dedicatees, Constantius II and Constans.[32]

Finally, similar interpretations are also found in the previously mentioned *Life of Constantine* of Eusebius, who was not immune to general propaganda celebrating the takeover of the eastern territories by Constantine, even in the last books of his *Ecclesiastical History*, composed immediately after 324. The *Life of Constantine* thus appears as a sort of pendant to contemporary history that is appointed with especially rich facets. On the one hand, it continues the tradition begun in the *Ecclesiastical History* of presenting documents embedded in a narrative framework. On the other, it makes use of contemporary panegyrical discourse as presented in orations throughout the east. Because it reinterprets many actions of the emperor in a specifically Christian sense and presents the recently dead emperor to his sons as the model Christian emperor, the *Life* also takes on the characteristics of a *Fürstenspiegel*, or even a saint's life.

Less clear was the Christian interpretation in an oration that Eusebius delivered in honor of the emperor in his final years as ruler. The so-called *Oration in Praise of Constantine (Laus Constantini)* consists in reality of two clearly separable pieces,[33] a *basilikos logos* (imperial panegyric) delivered in 335 on the occasion of the dedication of the Church of the Holy Sepulcher[34] and an oration held in Constantinople for the thirtieth jubilee of Constantine's reign, the tricennalia.[35] While the former oration is primarily a long-winded description of the splendor of the new church, the tricennalian oration interprets the emperor as intermediary between heavenly and earthly spheres in formulations whose vague neo-Platonic content would have been acceptable even for non-Christians.

LATER SOURCES

The history of ancient historiography could easily be represented as an extended lament over what is lost. Because of the inadequate source tradition, we do not even know, for example, whether there ever was a detailed historiographical account of the period in which Constantine's sons battled one another after his death.[36] We are thus fortunate to have a very thorough fragment of text that covers especially the wars between Constantine and Licinius and is commonly known by the name *Anonymous Valesianus* (part I) or *Origo Constantini* (*Origin of Constantine*). Though typically dated shortly after the death of Constantine, it could very easily have been written at the end of the fourth century.[37] The first securely datable, extant historiographical treatment in the Latin west comes from the pen of Aurelius Victor, who wrote at the very end of the reign of Constantius II (c. 360) and whose account offers a correspondingly positive impression of the dead emperor despite some rather dark, strained, even seemingly critical formulations.[38] A new assessment of Constantine was offered in the short and failed reign of Julian, who wished to rescind the results of his uncle's religious policies, and then too the dynastic shift to the family of Valentinian in 364 offered the chance to reevaluate the reign of Constantine more freely, even if some elements of continuity were also restored – Valentinian's son Gratian married the daughter of Constantius II.[39] This can be seen in the short paragraph that Eutropius devotes to the reign of Constantine in his outline of Roman history dedicated to the emperor Valens (364–78).[40] To be sure his source base was probably the same as that of Aurelius Victor, the so-called Enmann's Kaisergeschichte, a lost historical work whose existence can be securely demonstrated based on commonalities between Eutropius, Aurelius Victor, and others. Yet his overall impression is considerably more negative. In his account, Constantine was so desirous of sole rule that he not only initiated a war of aggression against Licinius but also broke his oath by having his defeated rival killed; incapable of enduring his success, he killed his son, his nephew, his wife, and countless friends; only in the early years of his reign was he comparable to the best emperors, afterward only with the mediocre; and he was known for having issued not only good but also many superfluous laws. The relativization of Constantine's achievements by Eutropius is best explained as stemming from dynastic rivalry with the Valentinians rather than debates about the religious shift introduced by Constantine. The ideological differences with this shift expressed in Julian's oeuvre were first fully revitalized in Theodosian times (379–450), and then only in new circumstances, including the beginning of serious attacks on paganism after a period of relative tolerance in the 360s and 370s and a church reinvigorated by the universal dominance of "Orthodox" Christianity achieved in the 380s.

Forced onto the defensive by this Christian zeitgeist, pagan intellectuals attacked Constantine from their side as the originator of all evil. This polemical interest in his reign led ironically to the fortunate preservation of valuable historical details that, even if tendentious in their overall presentation, might otherwise have been totally lost. This is true, for example, of facts that one finds in the so-called *Epitome de Caesaribus*, a short work in the style of the *breviaria* of Aurelius Victor and Eutropius that was composed in the immediate aftermath of Theodosius's death.[41] The author of the *Epitome de Caesaribus* was himself only a marginally talented compiler who, like Aurelius Victor and Eutropius, used the work of a rather important pagan intellectual whose interpretive viewpoint still glimmers through this atrophied biography of Constantine. All in all, the pagan source seems to have painted an unfavorable picture of Constantine, who is portrayed as ruling satisfactorily only in the first ten years of his reign but then ever more perversely.[42] Even Constantine's positive beginnings are colored with a certain ambiguity when the author of the *Epitome* makes clear that Constantine owed his elevation primarily to the support of the Alamannic king Crocus, who belonged to the immediate military entourage of the emperor. This datum about Crocus is found only in this source. Despite its tendentious context, it is clear that we are dealing with an authentic detail, for the prominence of Germanic princes in the immediate military entourage of late-antique emperors is well attested elsewhere.[43]

Ammianus Marcellinus, the greatest late Roman historian, also wrote in the Theodosian period. His work is, however, only preserved from the fourteenth book onward (that is, the period beginning in AD 353), thus the books dedicated to Constantine are unfortunately lost. Nevertheless, because Ammianus had the habit of regularly referring to the content of lost books, there remain some few references to the history of Constantine.[44] Thus we learn for example that the Frankish commander Bonitus was among the most important members of Constantine's following (*comitatus*), which agrees well with the tenor of the *Epitome*'s presentation connecting Constantine with barbarian generals.[45] At the outbreak of the Romano-Persian wars of the fourth century, which only ended with a shameful treaty by emperor Jovian (363–4), we learn that Constantine was actually the one responsible because he had only too eagerly believed the "lies of Metrodorus," that is, false reports concerning the Sassanian empire.[46] A few other passages show that Ammianus must have offered a rather jaundiced sketch of Constantine's reign and thus took a clear position in the ideological controversies of the Theodosian era.[47]

Finally, the extended accounts of late Greek historians also return to the ideological debates in which pagans and Christians became embroiled during Theodosian times. Zosimus, the author of a *New History* whose second book treated the reign of Constantine and included important details about his murder of his son Crispus and his foundation of Constantinople, wrote his history only in the sixth century.[48] The chronicle of the Byzantine monk Zonaras, which also offers important details about the reign of Constantine, dates to the twelfth century.[49] Because, however, ancient and Byzantine historical writers shared the peculiarity of recycling material from previous narratives without great changes, the gap that separates historical events from historiographic accounts can often be much narrower than first appears. Zosimus and Zonaras report from and thus transmit narratives that existed in the last years of the fourth century. Zosimus, for example, essentially preserves the report – rewritten in simpler Greek – of the strongly tendentious author Eunapius of Sardis,[50] who lamented the neglect of pagan cults by the emperor in his history and saw in this the reason for the catastrophes of the barbarian invasions. The situation is somewhat more complicated in the case of Zonaras, who used legendary narratives from the Byzantine epoch, in which Constantine was revered as a saint, alongside a secular author of the fourth century (through intermediate sources, especially Petrus Patricius), who was also used by other Byzantine chroniclers. The use of this fourth-century secular author explains why there is so much overlap of content between, on the one hand, the Byzantine tradition in Zonaras, Cedrenos, and Leo Grammaticus, and, on the other, Ammianus and the *Epitome*.[51] Thus, for example, the story of how Metrodorus fabricated stories that provoked Constantine to attack Persia, a story that we have just seen received passing mention in Ammianus, is thoroughly laid out in this tradition and can thus be more thoroughly unpacked based on the Byzantine sources.[52]

The polemic of pagan intellectuals, with its differentiated and richly illustrated portrait of Constantine's reign, did not fail to exercise influence over Christian ecclesiastical history. Eusebius's presentations in the *Ecclesiastical History* and *Life of Constantine* came to be considered insufficient in the Theodosian era, especially because their author was suspected of Arianism. How many continuations of and improvements on Eusebius there were up to the Theodosian period remains an open question; we can reconstruct in outline the works of Gelasius of Caesarea and of the anonymous homoian historian.[53] At any rate, a true boom in ecclesiastical history writing was first experienced in the reign of Theodosius II (408–50). From this period we have three completely preserved *opera magna*: the ecclesiastical histories of Socrates, Sozomen, and Theodoret.[54] They generally continue the ecclesiastical history of Eusebius, which concluded in 324, and in the process take sides against Arianizing tendencies and against pagan historical interpretation, which still had its proponents in fifth-century Constantinople. Different tendencies are evident in each. Bishop Theodoret appears particularly intolerant and also quite careless with his factual data.[55] By contrast, the layman Socrates stands out for his respectful and nuanced portrait of Julian,[56] while Sozomen argues extensively and forcefully in long digressions with the pagan version of Constantine's conversion.[57] Nevertheless, all three orthodox ecclesiastical historians preserve in equal measure extremely interesting and authentic material that illustrates especially well Constantine's ecclesiastical politics after his takeover of the Greek east. A unique perspective is offered by the historical work of the radical Arian Philostorgius, which appeared somewhat before the just mentioned orthodox ecclesiastical historians. It is not preserved in its entirety but must be reconstructed out of summaries and citations from other works.[58] The peculiar worth of this source lies in the fact that Philostorgius transmits important and interesting details about secular history in order to lend his work greater authority. Without doubt, for example, Philostorgius is the source for the saying of a Byzantine author of a life of Constantine (*BHG* 365) that the emperor had donned his diadem as a sign "of his sole rule and victory over opponents." Philostorgius is thereby the only writer who offers explicit and correct information about the symbolic content of the ruler insignia assumed in the immediate aftermath of Constantine's victory over Licinius in 324. This confirms well how even distant sources, sometimes hidden from immediate view, deserve ongoing attention.

FURTHER READING

Further information and a bibliography can be found in S. N. C. Lieu and D. Montserrat's *From Constantine to Julian: Pagan and Byzantine Views* (1996, 1–38). Most of the epigraphical material is collected in T. Grünewald's *Constantinus Maximus Augustus* (1990).

NOTES

1 See Chapter 3 in this volume.
2 Grünewald 1990, 78–86.
3 See the translation of Edwards 2003.
4 See the translation of Nixon and Rodgers 1994.
5 See the translation of Cameron and Hall 1999.
6 See the translation of Ridley 1984.
7 For the *Codex Theodosianus*, see the translation of Pharr 1952. There is, as yet, no comprehensive English translation of the *Codex Justinianus*.
8 *MAMA* 7:305 with Feissel 1999. See the translation at Lee 2000, 90–2.
9 *CIL* 5:2781,1–30; *CIL* 3:12034, 12133; *AE* 1957, 158; and Habicht and Kussmaul 1986. See also Corcoran 2002 for the possibility that the edict may be Licinian.
10 Giacchero 1974. See the partial translation of Lewis and Reinhold 1990, 422–6.
11 See the edition of J. Reynolds in Rouéché 1989, 252–318.
12 *CIL* 6:1139 = *ILS* 694. See the English translation below at Chapter 3 n. 61 from Lee 2000, 83.
13 Gascou 1967 supercedes *CIL* 11:5265 = *ILS* 705. See the translation at Lee 2000, 92–3.
14 Grünewald 1990, 89.
15 Sutherland 1967; Bruun 1966.
16 *RIC* 7 London 289–90; Lyons 209, 212, 214, 219–22; Trier 429, 435–8; Arles 257–8; cf. Simium 48.
17 *Anon. Cont. Dio* fr. 14.1 = *FHG* 4:199.
18 *RIC* 7 Rome 272. Cf. Grünewald 1990, 141.
19 Hidalgo 1996.
20 Arce 1997.
21 Eus. *HE* 10.5.18–20; 21–4. For Eusebius *Ecclesiastical History* (*HE*), see the translations of Lake and Oulton 1926–32 or Williamson and Louth 1989.
22 Eus. *HE* 10.5.1–14 and Lact. *DMP* 48.2–12.
23 For Euesbius's *Life of Constantine* (*VC*), see the translation and commentary of Cameron and Hall 1999.
24 Compare Eus. *VC* 2.24–42 with *P. Lond.* 3:878; cf. Jones and Skeat 1954.
25 See the translation of Edwards 1997 for Optatus's text and the accompanying documents. Cf. the French translation and notes of Maier 1987–9 for the documents.
26 See the translation of Edwards 2003.
27 On the date, see Bleckmann 1997 and T. D. Barnes 2001, with arguments for 328 and 325, respectively, not 315, as Edwards 2003, xxiii–xxix, assumes.
28 See the Latin translation and commentary of Creed 1984; cf. Moreau 1954.
29 See the translation of Nixon and Rodgers 1994.
30 See the Latin text and commentary of Polara 1973. There is no English translation.
31 See the Greek text at *FGH* 2B:219:948-9 and the English translation at Lieu and Montserrat 1996, 7–8; cf. Bleckmann 1999.
32 See the translation at Lieu and Montserrat 1996, 164–205.
33 Drake 1976.
34 Eus. *LC* 11–18.
35 Eus. *LC* 1–10. For both, see the translation of Drake 1976.

36 The existence of a source common to Theophanes, the *Chronicon Paschale*, Jerome, and an anonymous homoian historian who, at any rate, treated the "persecution" of the Christians under Julian (361–3) has long been acknowledged; cf. Bidez and Winkelmann 1981, cli–clxiii.

37 See the translation at Lieu and Montserrat 1996, 43–8.

38 See the translation of Bird 1994. Neri 1992, 1–64, arrives at a different assessment on the basis of a subtle interpretation of certain passages.

39 Lenski 2002b, 97–104.

40 See the translation of Bird 1993.

41 See the translation at Lieu and Montserrat 1996, 4–5.

42 *Epit.* 41.16.

43 Frank 1969.

44 Warmington 1999. See the translations of Rolfe 1935–9 and Hamilton 1986.

45 AM 15.5.33.

46 AM 25.5.23.

47 T. D. Barnes 1998, 178–80.

48 See the translation of Ridley 1982; cf. Paschoud 1971b.

49 See the translation of Constantinian material in Di Maio 1977.

50 The preserved fragments directly from Eunapius are found at Blockley 1983, 2–127.

51 Bleckmann 1992.

52 These source relations were not fully recognized by Warmington 1981 and 1999.

53 Neither source has been translated.

54 Leppin 1996; Urbaincyk 1997 and 2002; Wallraff 1997.

55 The translation of Walford 1854 is to be preferred to that of Jackson 1892.

56 See the translation of Zenos 1890.

57 See the translation of Hartranft 1890.

58 There is no English translation.

SECTION I

POLITICS AND PERSONALITIES

2: BEFORE CONSTANTINE

Simon Corcoran

When Apharban, envoy from the Persian king Narseh, came before the Caesar Galerius Maximianus to beg favourable terms for his defeated sovereign, his rhetoric met an angry rejoinder from the Caesar:

> You observed the rule of victory towards Valerian in a fine way, you who deceived him through stratagems and took him, and did not release him until his extreme old age and dishonourable death. Then after his death, by some loathesome art you preserved his skin and brought an immortal outrage to the mortal body.[1]

Thus, at his moment of triumph, the Caesar referred back to one of the darkest episodes of recent imperial history. In AD 260, between Carrhae and Edessa, Narseh's father, Shapur I, had decisively defeated a Roman army and captured the emperor Valerian (see Map 2). He recorded these deeds for posterity in both words and images at Naqsh-i Rustam and on the Kaᶜba-i Zardušt near the ancient Achaemenid capital of Persepolis, preserving for us a vivid image of two Roman emperors, one kneeling (probably Philip the Arab, also defeated by Shapur) and the second (Valerian), uncrowned and held captive at the wrist by a gloriously mounted Persian king (Fig. 6).[2] The equally decisive victory of Galerius over Narseh in 297 marked a dramatic reversal of fortune and can indeed stand as symbolic of how the rulers of the first Tetrarchy and their immediate predecessors had managed to regain firm military and political control over the empire.

A little over ten years before Valerian's catastrophe, the emperor Philip had in 248 celebrated Rome's first millennium in grand style, little knowing that Rome's second millennium was to open with a series of disasters. Plague struck Italy. Philip himself was killed the next year in battle against his successor, Decius. With Goths and Carpi (see Map 1) threatening the Danube frontier, Decius, still mindful of the millennial celebrations (during which he may have been urban prefect at Rome), seems to have felt that divine protection for the empire needed to be assured. And so in 250 he commanded universal sacrifice from the population, the first time the Roman state had made such an ambitious demand, requiring of its subjects proof of obedience in the form of certificates of sacrifice.[3] Many Christians did not comply and so were punished, making this the first general persecution. Despite his efforts, however, Decius fell in battle with the Goths in the following year. The pressure on the northern frontiers did not lessen, indeed they were repeatedly breached, a powerful force of "Black Sea" Goths became a naval threat in that region, while the king of Persia started operations on the eastern frontier. Becoming emperor in 253, Valerian also sought divine favour in unity around traditional religion, as had Decius. This time, however, he directly attacked the clergy and Christians of high rank in 257 and 258. Then followed his humiliating capture.[4] His son Gallienus granted a peace to the Christians that would last for forty years. This did not preserve his authority as emperor intact, as the empire effectively split into three, with Gallienus retaining control of only the central core. Gaul, Britain and Spain were ruled by the so-called Gallic emperors,[5] while in the east, the dynasts of the caravan city of Palmyra, who had turned the tide against the Persians, took control of Syria, gradually extending their rule to other eastern provinces.[6] Both regimes, however, can be characterized as essentially loyalist rather than separatist. Further, peoples from beyond the Rhine and Danube repeatedly breached the imperial frontiers, reaching as far as northern Italy and even Spain, sacking Athens[7] and engaging in pirate raids around the Aegean. The empire, for the first time, found itself more or less continuously on the defensive, responding not initiating. The mountain region of Isauria fell into ongoing revolt,[8] and some imperial territory even had to be abandoned permanently, such as the *Agri Decumates* (the reentrant angle between Rhine and Danube) and most importantly Dacia, whose population was evacuated by Aurelian and resettled in a renamed Dacia south of the Danube.[9]

This essentially military emergency has often been seen as part of an overall crisis in which economic and social factors combined to weaken the empire internally and threaten its disintegration in the face of strong external enemies, a crisis which the empire only surmounted by transformation into the grimmer and grittier *dirigiste* state of late antiquity. Thus plague and depopulation, abandonment of agricultural land by peasants fleeing as taxes weighed ever heavier on the reducing tax base, the decline of slavery, coinage debasement, inflation, demonetization of the economy, the demoralization of the educated curial elites who had maintained classical culture, the expansion of new religions: all these and more were woven into a "theory of everything" to explain both crisis and transformation. Current views tend to greater caution. Part of the problem is that, in assessing the crisis, the ancient evidence is essentially thin and uneven, as well as ambiguous. For instance, can we tell whether the plague, which spread across the empire in the 160s and recurred periodically thereafter, had a debilitating effect on the population, thus causing or exacerbating agricultural decline, tax deficits, and military manpower shortage? Was apparent depopulation in Egyptian villages the result of plague mortality, flight, or migration, and might these be temporary or permanent? And if the empire did indeed suffer population decline in the mid-second century, had it in fact largely recovered by the opening of the third century, long before the "crisis"? It is true of course that two mid-third century emperors died of plague at critical moments (Hostilian in 251, Claudius Gothicus in 270), while direct experience of plague was perceived by writers such as Dionysius of Alexandria as a sign of moral decay or divine judgement. But in this, as in other areas, the sense of crisis or doom expressed by contemporary authors is too impressionistic for us to take them as a reliable confirmation of demographic realities.[10]

The crisis that can be seen most clearly, therefore, is essentially a crisis of emperor and army, brought on by military emergencies. The fault lines of the Roman Principate had been exposed. The empire of the Severan dynasty (193–235) was still in most essentials that of Augustus and the Principate. The Roman republic had foundered on the bloody military rivalry of its leading men. Augustus, the ultimate victor of those civil wars, sought to provide future stability by monopolizing military power and glory to prevent conflict on the battlefield. To be sure, he also co-opted the Senate and existing institutions of the "restored" republic to run the empire and even to command the armies themselves, but the old aristocracy always operated under the emperor's aegis. Thus there was just sufficient honour all round. This sleight of hand worked well for long periods, with politics revolving around the emperor and Senate in Rome and with the army distantly loyal upon the frontiers.

Unfortunately, the question of the imperial succession and dynastic security was never settled, and times of crisis, such as the fall of Nero and the "Year of the Four Emperors" in AD 68–9 and the aftermath of the murder of Commodus in 193–7, showed what could happen when emperors lost their the grip on the ears of the wolf that was the Roman state.[11] After Septimius Severus emerged triumphant from the civil wars of 193–7 and gained glory from emulating Trajan's capture of the Parthian capital, Ctesiphon, in 198, the military underpinnings of his regime were less cloaked than in earlier periods. Yet the formal pattern of government continued, with the emperor still spending extended periods of time in Rome and central Italy, conducting business through the Senate (to pass legislation) and employing senators (to command provinces and armies). The political story of the third century represents how all this vanished, being refashioned over several decades before being consolidated and given firm shape by the organizational ability of Diocletian (Coin 5).

Given the poor sources for the mid-third century, the details of this process are somewhat obscure, but the broad pattern is clear. In the east, the Parthian Arsacid dynasty, which had always constituted more of a notional than a real threat, was replaced by the Persian Sassanids, ambitious, capable and energised, who saw no reason why they should not covet Syria, just as the Romans had long coveted Mesopotamia. The former shadow-boxing with Parthia was replaced by war in deadly earnest between two adversaries too evenly matched for either to vanquish the other permanently. In the west, German tribes merged to create arguably more formidable new coalitions east across the Rhine (the Franks and Alamanni), while other peoples such as the Goths and Heruli pressed upon the long Danube frontier. The empire was not prepared for war on two fronts. Despite its great territorial size, its army and administration, as also its taxation, were relatively modest. There was little in the way of reserve, in terms of troops or money.

With this military situation obtaining on the edges of the empire, the relationship of emperor and army was thrown into sharp relief. Antoninus Pius (138–61) had governed for over twenty years in the mid-second century without leaving Italy (and thus without seeing his armies). This was now a forgotten luxury. Emperors had to fight, and fight effectively. The first emperor to suffer from this new reality was Alexander Severus (222–35). Having failed to win decisively over the Persians, he was eliminated at Mainz by his own troops, who had found on their return west that their homes had been ravaged by tribes from across the Rhine. Emperors who failed were swiftly punished, those who were absent and seen as neglectful saw usurpers raised to meet regional needs, until eventually military proclamations of emperors became almost casual, as soldiers sought not just effective commanders but personal enrichment from overfrequent donatives.

Yet the empire weathered the military crisis. After the assassination of Gallienus (268), a series of emperors, largely from the Danube provinces and not from the traditional senatorial or even equestrian elites, regained the upper hand. Claudius Gothicus (268–70) well earned his name defeating the Goths, while Aurelian (270–5) traversed much of the empire as he brought the Gallic and Palmyrene territories back under central control. Yet even at the height of the crisis, we should not imagine war overwhelming all parts repeatedly. Many areas were largely unaffected by distant fighting or suffered only occasionally.[12] In general, Roman forces could and still did win their engagements, only now they could not count on perpetual victory. The most crucial issue, however, was the vulnerability of the emperor, whom compulsory sacrifice, tutelary deities, and titles such as *dominus et deus* (lord and god), did little to protect from arbitrary liquidation. As the empire became more secure, what of the security of the emperors?

It was against this background, with the imperial administration and army restructuring even as they weathered and finally surmounted the crisis, that Diocletian became emperor. The young emperor Numerian (283–4), travelling with his troops westwards from Mesopotamia (where his father had mysteriously died), had reached Nicomedia in Bithynia and then also died (mysteriously as well), his death apparently concealed by his father-in-law, the praetorian prefect Aper. On November 20, 284, the troops acclaimed Diocles, commander of the bodyguard, as emperor, and he promptly and by his own hand "executed" Aper as a regicide. Changing his name to the more Latinate and grand "Diocletianus" shortly after his accession, the new emperor then advanced into the Balkans to confront the already existing emperor Carinus, Numerian's brother (spring 285). In the ensuing battle, which does not seem to have been going Diocletian's way, the unpopular Carinus was assassinated by his own side, and Diocletian was left as sole emperor. The truth about the messy disposal of the two sons of Carus and Diocletian's role in it will never be known. Yet regardless of how he had risen to the top, the new emperor proved to have both the energy and ingenuity to stay in power for two decades and carry out a wide array of reforms, building, it is true, on already existing trends and the efforts of his predecessors, but giving a new coherence and shape, durability and effectiveness to the imperial administration. This earns him a place as one of the "great" rulers of the empire, a moulder of a new imperial matrix, even as was Augustus. As the latter stood at the beginning of the Principate, so, conventionally, Diocletian is seen standing at the threshold to the Dominate, a period characterised by a more authoritarian, militaristic, ceremonial, and bureaucratic style of imperial rulership.

One of the first acts of Diocletian was probably also his most important decision.[13] He appointed a comrade-in-arms, Maximian, to be his coruler (Coin 7). The exact chronology is uncertain, but Maximian was made Caesar in 285 and then a full Augustus in 286. The appointment of a coruler was nothing new. Augustus had shared key imperial powers with colleagues, and formal coemperors had from time to time existed from the reign of Marcus Aurelius. Many third-century emperors shared office with others (usually their sons) bearing either the lesser title of "Caesar" or the full title of "Augustus." The appointment of Maximian, however, was to prove crucial. Maximian was not always militarily effective and certainly seems to have had many moral deficiencies, but in one area he did not lack: as both contemporary panegyric and invective agreed, he was unswervingly loyal to Diocletian, and so the axis between them provided the necessary stability that allowed their rule to survive and their reforms to be enacted. The assumption of the titles *Iovius* and *Herculius* by Diocletian and Maximian c. 287 symbolised their relationship, with Diocletian, Jupiter-like, devising and commanding, and Maximian as Hercules heroically performing his allotted tasks (Coins 6 and 7).[14]

Maximian's first task was to pacify the revolt in Gaul of the Bagaudae – often seen as rural insurgents although their leaders claimed imperial titles – which he successfully completed. Meanwhile, raiding by Saxon pirates in northern Gaul was suppressed by Carausius, a commander subsequently suspected of inappropriately siphoning off booty – if not collaborating with the enemy. Usurpation still seemed the answer to any local difficulty, so Carausius declared himself emperor, seizing control of northern Gaul and Britain, yet claiming to rule as a legitimate colleague. This usurpation Maximian was unable to suppress, especially given barbarian crossings of the Rhine frontier, most memorably during Maximian's inauguration ceremony as consul on January 1, 287. Campaigning against the German tribes was a priority, which Maximian carried out with success both on his own and later in a joint operation with Diocletian in 288. Diocletian himself was also busy both in the east and on the Danube. When they met again in northern Italy to confer early in 291, it was becoming clear that even two joint-emperors were overstretched.[15]

Thus on March 1, 293, two more rulers were appointed, endowed with the lesser rank of Caesar, one in effect to serve under each Augustus: thus the first Tetrarchy was born. The men chosen were Constantius (Coin 8) and a second Maximian, usually referred to as Galerius from his *nomen* (Fig. 7). Diocletian had no son, and Maximian no grown son, and these two men were obvious choices. Each originated from the Balkans, had an army background, and, it seems likely, had already been married to an imperial daughter (Galerius to Diocletian's daughter Valeria, Constantius to Maximian's daughter Theodora).[16] The new Tetrarchy soon proved itself militarily effective. In 293 Carausius, losing his Gallic territory when Constantius took Boulogne, was murdered by one of his own officials, Allectus. In 296 Constantius then invaded Britain, brought the rebel regime to an end, and proudly proclaimed that he had "restored eternal light."[17] Maximian, after a sojourn in Spain, campaigned across North Africa against rebel tribes called in the sources *Quinquegentiani*, ending up triumphantly in Carthage in 298. Meanwhile Diocletian campaigned successfully on the Danube, and Galerius, having suppressed one Egyptian revolt in 293 or 294, was directed towards the eastern frontier. A second serious rebellion in Egypt in 297 was suppressed by Diocletian, who forced the bloody surrender of Alexandria in 298. In 296, Galerius suffered an initial reverse at the hands of the Persians – being in consequence humiliated by Diocletian – but in 297 he regrouped and went on to win a spectacular victory over the Persian king Narseh, capturing the king's harem and eventually taking the capital at Ctesiphon. The subsequent peace treaty secured Roman territory in Mesopotamia and even a protectorate over regions beyond the Tigris, as well as the tenure of the Armenian throne by the Roman client Tiridates (Trdat) III.[18] The last years of the reign were largely – though not entirely – peaceful, so that when Diocletian and Maximian visited Rome in November 303 for their twentieth anniversary (*vicennalia*), they could celebrate a well-deserved triumph. Their Prices Edict of 301 describes "the peaceful state of the world seated in the lap of a most profound calm," a picture of a world at peace that was not optimistic propaganda but a fair description of reality.[19]

Military needs may have driven Diocletian's decision to create his imperial college but did not limit his sphere of activity. His reign saw a whole series of reforms enacted that largely set the pattern for the later Roman empire. This does not mean that these all happened at once. Few, indeed, can be exactly dated, although the mid-290s following the creation of the Tetrarchy seems to have been a key period. The four rulers must also have built on what had already been done by earlier emperors less well served by the surviving evidence.[20] Certainly, however, many things crystallized and took firm shape, because Diocletian, unlike his immediate predecessors, managed to stay in power for two decades and in control of most of the empire for most of the time. Planning, experimentation, development and implementation became more practicable.

The first point to note is that the imperial office itself had mutated. The origin of emperors had dramatically changed. The first emperors were aristocrats of ancient Roman lineage, but as local elites were incorporated into the imperial system, emperors came from all round the empire: Gaul, Spain, North Africa and Syria. Yet no-one became emperor who had not first become a senator until the praetorian prefect Macrinus, of equestrian rank, gained the throne in 217. As military proclamations subsequently became the norm, many men became emperors who had risen through the ranks of the army and had little or no connection to existing elites, especially after 268. It was the Danubian provinces, by no means the richest or most cultivated in the empire, which provided most of these third-century "soldier emperors," men often characterized as rude and unlettered. Following this pattern, Diocletian and his three colleagues in the first Tetrarchy were all from the Balkans and seem to have risen through the ranks. Diocletian himself, from Salona in Dalmatia, is said to have been of servile origin, although more likely the son of a freedman (like the emperor Pertinax) than a freedman himself. Whatever his personal education, however, he was happy to encourage the traditional liberal arts, at least in their Latin guise – he summoned the eminent rhetor Lactantius from Africa to be professor of Latin rhetoric at his new capital of Nicomedia.

Another obvious change in the imperial office was its multiplication. As already noted, there had been joint emperors at various times since the reign of Marcus Aurelius and Lucius Verus (161–9), and third-century emperors had routinely made their sons Caesars or even coequal Augusti. The constant usurpations and proclamations, especially the fragmentation of the empire under Gallienus, showed clearly how difficult it was for a single emperor to meet all challenges and be in all necessary places at once. It is true that Aurelian as sole ruler managed in a crowded five years to reunite the empire, but Diocletian does not seem to have considered that reigning alone was a realistic option. The appointment of Maximian as Caesar, then Augustus, was his initial approach, and it took him several years to decide what further manner of imperial collegiality was needed. The pattern of the first Tetrarchy, with two Augusti and two Caesars, seems too crafted to be simply an unplanned response to crisis. It not only created more princes to deal with multiple emergencies but implied an order of succession fixed in advance within a new dynastic framework – marked also by the appellations *Iovius* and *Herculius* in, respectively, east and west. Whether Diocletian had already mapped out all aspects of this system, however, can hardly be known. His eventual abdication was certainly not something that ordinary provincials were led to expect in advance.[21]

A major change of style took place in the imperial office. In place of the quasi-republican "first among equals" façade adopted by Augustus (defined as *civilitas*), the emperor was set apart, purple-robed, diademed, even his shoes studded with gems: subjects now had to prostrate themselves before him, and the most fortunate were permitted to kiss the hem of the imperial robe (*adoratio, proskynesis*). Eunuchs attained new prominence as palace servants.[22] The relatively informal council (*consilium*) of advisers chosen by the emperor and before whom he conducted much business was still in existence under Diocletian, and indeed under Constantine,[23] but the greater formality of court ceremonial must already have been transforming it into the consistory (*consistorium*) of later emperors, so called because all except the emperor had to stand. We do not know the exact chronology of this development, but it is almost universally attributed in the ancient sources to Diocletian himself. Yet the emperors still seem approachable, given the number of responses to petitions (rescripts) they issued, even to those of low status.[24] They spent much time on the dusty road, in motion, on campaign, not permanently immured in tightly controlled palace spaces. People would flock from miles around to see the imperial train pass by, as happened when Diocletian and Maximian came to Milan to confer in the winter of 290/1, and the formal entry of an emperor into a city was a much repeated ceremony.[25] Emperors remained highly visible.

The position of Rome had also changed, despite the focus that the millennial celebrations of 248 had brought upon the city. The emperors of the mid-third century spent time there when they could, and taking possession of Rome was still a primary aim for any emperor who wanted to be seen as legitimate. Even an emperor as militarily busy as Aurelian found time to intervene in the affairs of the city, and of course he provided the city with its first new circuit of walls in more than five hundred years. However, the succession of invasions and usurpations made spending time in Rome increasingly difficult, and with the accession of Diocletian, the imperial presence there largely ceased. Despite his entering northern Italy in 285, it is far from certain that he came down to Rome at this time, so that his only visit would be for the *vicennalia* celebrations in 303.[26] Even Maximian, based in Italy, seems seldom to have been in Rome. Only his son Maxentius, already resident before usurping the purple in 306, made Rome his principal base.

For more than a hundred years after Diocletian, Rome was not an imperial seat, only the venue for occasional ceremonial visits. Diocletian's Rome was still of course the proper capital, privileged, untaxed, fed with free wheat and pork (to maintain its swollen population), kept amused by games and races, and provided with other amenities. It was the seat of the wealthy but largely decorative and impotent Senate and the principal home of the Praetorian Guard, both of which bodies had long since lost their influence in choosing emperors. A large area of the Forum Romanum had been destroyed by fire under Carinus and was extensively rebuilt – so that the Senate House (*Curia Julia*) we see today, after thirteen centuries of existence as the Church of S. Adriano, is the building restored to its Tetrarchic form.[27] When he returned in triumph from Carthage in 298 or 299, Maximian matched the baths he had had built there in his own name by providing Rome its largest ever bath complex, the Baths of Diocletian (see Map 3.1).[28] Yet when Galerius approached Rome to besiege Maxentius in 307, he was, according to Lactantius, surprised at the city's size, having never seen it before. Perhaps this inadvertence explains also his disastrous decision to try and tax the population of Rome in 306.[29] Galerius's situation was Gallienus's in reverse, with "legitimate" rulers everywhere but Rome. Rome was still powerfully symbolic, but for an emperor it was more a luxury than a strategic necessity.

Since emperors could no longer govern from Rome, they needed other bases, and although emperors had travelled and rested in many places over the years, it was only during the Tetrarchic period that a number of strategic cities around the empire came to serve sufficiently often and for sufficiently long to be considered as virtually alternative imperial seats, and indeed were adorned with suitable buildings. There were, however, dozens of cities overall which enjoyed occasional or frequent imperial visits, and emperors are better seen as men constantly on the move, not men at rest.[30] Further, not every monumental building of the period betokens an emperor's presence.[31] Nevertheless, the typically favoured Tetrarchic residence could boast an imperial palace, often attached to a circus, as well as other newly built amenities such as grandiose baths. Imperial mausolea, the permanent resting places for rulers and their dynasties, were also built in such cities or at other sites distant from Rome. Among the most prominent of the new "imperial" cities were now, in Italy, Milan (main capital of Maximian); in Gaul, Trier (capital of Constantius) as well as Arles; in the Balkans, Sirmium (the best launching place for campaigns on the Danube), Serdica and Thessalonica;[32] and in the east, Nicomedia[33] (Diocletian's favourite) and Antioch (the main base for overseeing the frontier with Persia). Even in Rome, home of the original palace-circus complex (Palatine-Circus Maximus), Maxentius built himself a Tetrarchic imitation a short way beyond the walls along the Via Appia, comprising a palace, circus and mausoleum.[34]

With the emperor, wherever he travelled or resided, went his *comitatus*, the core of the imperial court, administration, and army, and just as there were multiple emperors, so there were multiple *comitatus*, staffed in a largely identical manner. The chief officials at court were now almost exclusively of equestrian rank, holding offices that were not new, although sometimes restyled. At the top were the praetorian prefects, one at the side of each Augustus, holding the rank of *vir eminentissimus* (the highest equestrian rank, reserved for them alone) and acting as a college like the emperors they served, although none was ever again elevated to become emperor, as Macrinus, Philip and Carus had been. Although not yet entirely devoid of a military role in the Tetrarchic period (thus Asclepiodotus played a key part in the reconquest of Britain), they were now principally civilian officials, with wide powers, even inappellable jurisdiction, and concerned most of all with provisioning of the armies.[35] The remaining officials were ranked *viri perfectissimi*. Among these were the chief financial officers (*rationalis summae rei* and *magister privatae*, for respectively public finances and the imperial estates), below whom was an expanded hierarchy of officials at the diocesan and provincial level. There were also the "palatine secretaries," concerned with the emperor's correspondence and judicial functions (including the *magistri epistularum*, one each concerned with correspondence in Latin and in Greek, the *magister libellorum*, concerned with rescripts issued in reply to petitions, and the *magister memoriae*, exact duties unspecified).[36] The officials in this imperial civil service in fact had a very military appearance. Their service was called "*militia*," and their insignia and dress were largely military as well. Coupled with this grew a tendency, discernible though not yet universal under Diocletian, for officials to mark their status in the imperial service by adapting their names. Thus, in the Tetrarchic period many governement officials assumed the nomen "Valerius" (as carried by Diocletian, Galerius and Maximian). This trend became much more marked from Constantine onwards with the widespread adoption of "Flavius" (as carried by Constantius and Constantine).[37]

As regards the army, Lactantius accused Diocletian of "multiplying the armies, since each of the four [Tetrarchs] strove to have a far larger number of troops than previous emperors had had when they were governing the state alone." On the other hand, Zosimus praises Diocletian for keeping troops strung out along the borders and strengthening frontier defences, in contrast to Constantine's withdrawal of troops to distant inland cities.[38] Both these views are at least in part true – despite the bias of each writer, and in Zosimus's case two centuries' worth of hindsight. There was certainly a marked increase in the overall size of the army, as fighting units were smaller but vastly more numerous. These units generally fell under the control of *duces* (equestrian generals) rather than provincial governors as previously, although many were also unified to form the growing mobile field armies which followed each emperor's *comitatus*. Several emperors, each with an army, meant that multiple military operations could be carried out, but emperors sometimes came together to co-operate (as did Diocletian and Maximian in 288), and some campaigns required the gathering and relocation of troops on an extensive scale, as for the campaign against Narseh.[39]

As regards provincial administration, the provinces were now "sliced and diced" (*in frusta concisae*).[40] Subdivision of provinces was not new, but Diocletian seems to have undertaken much more extensive reorganization than his predecessors (even if not necessarily as part of a single act). Almost all provinces now had an equestrian *praeses*, who came to be shorn of any remaining military duties and so was primarily concerned with matters of law and tax. But the provinces were also grouped together into twelve larger administrative units called dioceses, each in the charge of a *vicarius* or vicar (literally "a deputy") of the praetorian prefects, representing an intermediate level of jurisdiction between governor and prefect or emperor. In theory, by concentrating the efforts of governors on purely civil matters in smaller provinces and providing an extra-regional layer of government, greater efficiency and control should have been achieved. Given the largely parallel provincial/diocesan organization of the financial departments, the *summa res* and the *res privata*, the size of the civil service was certainly much increased and, with the often minute regulation of seniority and remunerations, gives a strong impression of a "bureaucratic" state apparatus. It is difficult to audit the true effectiveness of this expanded administration, but there is no dispute that there was more government than previously.[41]

This provincial reorganization for the most part excluded senators, who in Diocletian's reign reached their nadir in terms of participation in administration and government. Gallienus is credited in the sources with banning senators from the army, but this probably stands as symbolic not of a single legislative act but of a longer process during the third century, as more army officers rose from within the ranks and aristocrats increasingly avoided an unduly dangerous calling. Thus, by the time of the Tetrarchs, a typical senatorial career was at once civil in nature and largely Italian in setting. Senators might hold the traditional magistracies and other administrative posts in Rome and Italy, including the governorships (often with the title *corrector*) of the newly created Italian provinces and curatorships of individual cities. The highest magistracy, the consulship, was still held, although 60 percent of consulships in the period 285–305 were held by members of the imperial college and still others by their praetorian prefects promoted into the Senate. The more successful senators would go on to enjoy the traditional proconsulships of Africa and Asia, both much reduced in size by the calving of new provinces.[42] The most powerful senatorial post, however, was probably that of urban prefect, in charge of the city of Rome and its environs, a post which was enhanced in importance by the more or less permanent absence of the emperor and which, like the praetorian prefecture, came to entail an inappellable jurisdiction, as if of a surrogate for the emperor.[43]

In many ways the true administrative unit in the empire had not been the province but the city. In the early empire, the local aristocracies of each city focussed much attention on local politics, with traditional political rivalries limited to competitive extravagance, adorning towns with public buildings, and setting up endowments for games and free distributions ("civic euergetism"). Indeed, much of our sense of what antique cities were like physically – especially the well-preserved cities in Anatolia, Syria, or North Africa – derives from the outburst of building in the first two centuries AD. This confident local activity stalls in the third century. For instance, the imperial letters confirming its traditional privileges sent to Aphrodisias in Caria and proudly inscribed in public come to an end after Valerian and Gallienus. The next imperial texts carved are proactive imperial edicts, set up on the orders of the provincial governor.[44] Surplus wealth was now scarcer, or at least more carefully guarded, as the most successful of the local elites joined the imperial aristocracy and redirected their interests. And they were certainly glad to gain immunities from various impositions upon their persons and property (*munera*, or liturgies) required by their city and the central government. There was still sometimes competition to join the city council. After all, decurions (members of the local city councils, or *curiae*) counted as the lowest level among the *honestiores* (those citizens entitled to more lenient treatment at the hands of the law, being exempt, for instance, from torture). And Diocletian and Galerius both granted the privilege of city status in response to petitions, with the express wish to foster the increase of the number of cities in the empire.[45] At the same time, the burdens on decurions had increased, especially as they often seemed little more than unpaid tax collectors or providers of services for the central government. Cities fell under tighter control by provincial governors, they ceased to mint their own coinages by the 270s, and increasingly they lost any financial independence.[46] The reign of Diocletian saw the introduction of the new offices (although with old titles) of *curator, defensor,* and *exactor,* tied closely to the imperial administration.[47] The long tradition of the self-governing city was severely dented. Indeed, local initiative could be viewed with suspicion. The city council of Antioch was executed by Diocletian for having raised forces to defeat an attempted usurpation in 303.[48] In response to these pressures, decurions attempted to find some means to gain immunity or exemption from their curial duties (a common theme in petitions to emperors), usually through the acquisition of a higher rank, especially those consequent to holding particular offices; such promotions were all the better if they could be achieved by notional office-holding without the need actually to have performed any duties.[49] Indeed, the equestrian order itself, never a truly uniform body, seems to have been changing into an aristocracy of office. It was no longer the case that men already possessed of the rank were eligible for the office; rather, men who acquired the office became appointed to the correct rank. Yet the more who escaped into the higher ranks (usually the wealthier), the greater the burden on those left behind. In extreme cases, decurions might simply flee, in the manner of an oppressed peasant or slave.

One particularly severe problem for the emperors was imperial finance. The principal drain upon resources was paying the soldiers their regular salary, but additional burdens included distributing frequent donatives, now expected rather than being a rare bonus, as well as keeping them supplied and fed. The state had always had fairly shallow reserves, easily squandered by a profligate emperor or eaten up by a prolonged military campaign, and liquidity had been maintained by a gradual adulteration of the main silver coinage. By the mid-third century, this had become a base metal coinage coated in a silver wash and thus bore little relationship to its old face value. Coinage never ceased to be generally used, but for the government, direct requisition became more significant, making the raising and spending of money taxes of reduced importance. Some such levies had long existed (such as the *annona*, the grain supply for Rome), but they became more widespread, although extraordinary rather than systematic. This Diocletian sought to regularize.

As already noted, the financial administration mirrored the provincial, with the central officials of the *comitatus* at the top and subordinates at both the diocesan and provincial levels. There is clear evidence now for state factories established in many provinces, producing arms, clothing, purple dyed cloth, and linen for both types of *militia*. There now existed a mint in almost every diocese. The five-year census cycle was revitalized so that the whole empire could be assessed on a more systematic basis, with the previous patchwork of exempt city territories and other anomalies (principally Italy) overwritten. When the various taxes, whether in kind or money, were to be levied, it would be on a census assessment designed to give a theoretically fair estimate of wealth in land and the size of the (rural) population. *Urban* areas and populations were generally exempt under Diocletian (although certain types of impost did fall upon the urban populations). This new Diocletianic system is generally referred to as *iugatio vel capitatio*.[50] Land of different types was reduced to notional units called *iuga*, similarly individuals to notional units called *capita*, and then these were added up to a total for a city or village. How such units were measured or counted, as also the terminology, varied between provinces or dioceses, so the system was not entirely uniform. But it was broadly speaking consistent. It also brought officials of the central government into contact with the minutiae of local conditions: *censitores* in Syria fixed village boundaries, while in the diocese of Asiana (in western Anatolia and the Aegean islands) inscriptions were erected to record the assessed value for various estates in regard to their differing types of agricultural land, their livestock, and their tenants and slaves.[51] Lactantius describes the system in typically unforgiving fashion, as characterized by waves of officials resorting to torture of the taxable population in order to maximize the value of census returns. This was no distant farming out of taxes (although some indirect taxes were still put out to farm) but the state's projecting its will directly down to the lowest level.[52]

In a related area, Diocletian sought to stabilize the currency through a sweeping coinage reform in the mid-290s, which also saw the ending of the last separate coinage in the empire (that of the Alexandrian tetradrachm). In addition to a more plentiful gold coin (the aureus, struck at sixty to the pound, valued at 1,000 denarii), a new true silver coin (the argenteus) was introduced, with the low-value copper coins still freely minted, representing vestiges of the old denarius.[53] The government tried where possible to pay out in base metal, as with donatives to soldiers mentioned in the Panopolis Papyri of AD 300, or to make compulsory purchases of precious metal.[54] But Diocletian's manipulation was not successful. The coinage had to be retariffed in 301 in a series of decrees, while the most famous of Diocletian's enactments, the monumental Prices Edict, also of 301, sought to put a ceiling on prices for several hundred categories of goods and services.[55] The ambition of this measure is quite staggering, as is the fact that some governors were sufficiently behind it to cause at least forty copies to be inscribed on stone across their provinces. The emperor's perception of the problem was probably distorted, unduly influenced as it was by temporary price fluctuations wherever his massive and disruptive *comitatus* appeared. But the aim of price control was certainly valid and operated in the immediate interest of army and administration. The market, by contrast, did not prove amenable to such attempts at fixing. Goods disappeared. Inflation continued. The measure was a bold failure.

The mass of the free population had been enfranchised and made Roman citizens (carrying the *nomen* "Aurelius") by an edict of Caracalla in AD 212 (the *Constitutio Antoniniana*). Following this, the citizenship, once prized, was no longer so valuable, as the real distinction had come to be that between the upper echelons of society (*honestiores*: the more honorable) and all the rest (*humiliores*: the more lowly), who came to suffer the judicial treatment and punishments reserved for subjects and slaves. In theory, however, Roman law was now applicable to entire provincial populations. Even if in practice most people would continue their lives as before, following local custom and remaining distant from legal institutions, the law was there for those who chose to use it. The emperors themselves, aside from the direct hearing of cases and appeals, issued many rescripts on points of law in response to petitions from all manner of their subjects. Diocletian himself seems to have been chauvinistically Roman in approach, with a stress on traditional Roman values and institutions. He set his face against bigamy, incest, and certain other non-Roman practices. Just as he tried to foster Latin in his newly chosen capital Nicomedia by appointing Lactantius as professor of rhetoric, so it is no surprise to find that the first two Roman law codes, the Gregorian and Hermogenian Codes, consisting largely of rescripts in Latin, were issued in the 290s. The extent of Diocletian's direct involvement is unknown, although the lack of imperial nomenclature for the codes suggests that these were not, strictly speaking, official projects. But both codes comprised principally rescripts of Diocletian, his colleagues and his imperial predecessors, and one of the compilers, Hermogenian, went on to become Diocletian's praetorian prefect. These new resources would have been tremendously useful for his expanded roster of governors as they attempted to apply Roman law to the mass of theoretical Roman citizens in their provinces, citizens whose legal status and cultural identity interacted in varied and complex ways.[56]

As regards religion, Diocletian was conservative. However diverse the religions of the empire, and in contrast with a ruler such as Aurelian, who had favoured the cult of the Sun (Sol) with a fine new temple in Rome, Diocletian seems to have sought security in the traditional. To symbolize his rule, as noted above, he chose two tutelary deities, the ruler-god Jupiter and his son Hercules, and adopted the sobriquets for himself and his appointee Maximian, *Iovius* and *Herculius* respectively. The imperial colleagues thus assumed the divinized roles of commander and subordinate. Seemingly, this was a matter not simply of seeking divine favour from traditional gods but also of the reverse, of Diocletian publicly asserting his confidence in them. Although not generally used as part of the emperor's otherwise extensive titulature, these titles recur regularly as a matching pair to designate imperial entities – military units, provinces, buildings. They were also intended to mark out the line of succession in east and west – with *Iovius* passing to Galerius and Maximin and *Herculius* to Constantius and Severus. Jupiter and Hercules (also Mars) are, not surprisingly, prominent on the coinage (Coins 6 and 7). So too are images of all four emperors embracing or performing a traditional sacrifice in unison (Fig. 8, Coin 9). This emphasis on the Roman manner found in some of Diocletian's legal rulings includes an emphasis on the consonance of old Roman virtue with divine favour and the importance of both being maintained. This is clearly expressed in an edict issued by Diocletian from Damascus in 295 against incest, which is characterized as both impious and un-Roman. But unwarranted religious novelty was also seen as the mark of a subversive fifth column. In a famous rescript sent to the proconsul of Africa from Alexandria in 302, Diocletian decreed strong action against the Manichees – a dualist religious sect that combined elements of Jewish, Christian, and Persian religion – as surrogates of the Persians.[57]

Given this attitude, it is perhaps not surprising that, despite the long years of peace for Christians which seem to have brought them deep within both army and court, Diocletian and some around him saw them as endangering the conformity necessary to ensure divine favour. Diocletian is depicted as highly superstitious, constantly seeking divine indications for the future, and thus easily roused against Christians at court blamed for hindering the success of his sacrifices. Others at court, such as Sossianus Hierocles and Porphyry, seem to have been engaged for much longer in intellectual battle with Christians, which they were prepared to continue in a more deadly manner.[58] And so, with the army already purged of Christians as early as 299,[59] an edict was promulgated from Nicomedia in February 303 under which churches were to be pulled down, Christian scriptures surrendered for destruction, Christians of rank stripped of their status, and even those who were imperial freedmen reenslaved. The edict was being enforced in Palestine by March and in Africa by May. There followed later in 303 the arrest of clergy, to be freed if they apostasized by offering sacrifice – although many were freed after coerced or even only notional compliance under an amnesty for the *vicennalia* in November 303. In 304 a further measure requiring universal sacrifice was implemented. After Diocletian's and Maximian's abdication in 305, the impetus of the persecution seems to have abated, and in the western provinces it was formally terminated by Constantine and then Maxentius in 306.[60] The strongest continuation was in the eastern territory of the new Caesar Maximin whose fervour continually renewed the persecution. He used the census registration as a tool to enforce sacrifice, ordered the sprinkling of polluting libations in public places, thus effectively denying to Christians participation in civic life, and also attempted to set up a pagan hierarchy in imitation of church organization. He then neutered Galerius's eventual edict of toleration of April 311, orchestrating a series of petitions as a pretext for expelling Christians entirely from various cities during 312. Even he, however, when defeated and near death, was forced to concede toleration in 313, thus marking the end of the "Great Persecution."[61] The whole enterprise had sought to eviscerate the church by assaulting its fabric, its hierarchy, its holy books, and by making Christianity simply too costly for those of any rank or aspiration. Success in persecution was best assessed not by the numbers tortured to death but by the numbers who apostasized. Nevertheless, enforcement was uneven, depending largely on the enthusiasm of governors or local magistrates, or even on the propensity of eager would-be martyrs seeking confrontation. Not all measures were promulgated equally everywhere, and even within the imperial college Constantius seems to have complied only reluctantly and minimally,[62] in contrast to Maximin's later zeal. The persecution had been launched at a time when the empire was more stable and peaceful than for many years, with Christians having enjoyed toleration since the capture of Valerian over forty years before. Indeed, in contrast to spontaneous local outbursts of persecution in the early imperial period, this empire-wide official persecution – as earlier those of Decius and Valerian – does not seem to have rested upon significant popular support.[63] The most long-lasting effect of the persecution was unintended, the enduring divisions it created between Christians over treatment of the lapsed, most particularly the Donatist schism in Africa. Thus a style of government that was immensely ambitious – not just in rhetoric but in attempts at enforcement, although apparently successful in implementing detailed census arrangements – could not impose its will in other areas, whether the control of prices or the suppression of Christianity.

So not all the projects that Diocletian undertook were successful. But our judgement upon him and the Tetrarchy should not rest upon certain failures but take account of their considerable achievements. By surviving for twenty years, Diocletian was able to enact directly or otherwise enable or complete an extensive reorganization of provincial government, taxation and finance, law and the administration of justice, as well as restyle the very office of emperor and enjoy significant military success, both controlling internal revolt and external aggression and even extending the empire in Mesopotamia. Diocletian's last act is one of his most innovative but least successful. There was no close parallel for the voluntary abdication of an emperor – the closest is perhaps Sulla's surrender of his dictatorship in 80 BC, an act later viewed by some as folly.[64] The symmetry of the Tetrarchy, with two Augusti and two Caesars, suggests that Diocletian envisaged not simply a military partnership to deal with multiple emergencies but in due course the promotion of the Caesars to Augusti, with new Caesars appointed to fill their place, thus solving the perennial problem of the succession. There is, however, no way of knowing whether a planned abdication, as opposed to the chances of mortality, was in truth part of Diocletian's original plan. For instance, we cannot tell when the monumental palace at Split on the Dalmatian coast, to which Diocletian retired, was begun (or finished), or if it was originally intended for a retired emperor at all.[65] It does seem, however, that, during the *vicennalia* celebrations in Rome in November 303, Diocletian extracted on oath a promise from Maximian to join him in abdication.[66] The exact timing, however, appears in the end to have resulted from a combination of Diocletian's failing health and Galerius's impatient ambition. In May 305, Diocletian surrendered power in his beloved Nicomedia, with Galerius now Augustus and Galerius's nephew Maximin as Caesar, and Maximian resigned at Milan, with Constantius now Augustus and the otherwise unknown Severus as Caesar.[67] In many ways, Galerius is the proper heir of Diocletian, striving to imitate Diocletian's policy as Tiberius did that of Augustus. Ignoring Constantius the theoretical senior and anticipating his death, Galerius strove to maintain the Tetrarchic structure on his own terms, parodying the pivotal role that Diocletian had played previously, envisaging for himself also an abdication and retirement to a vast palace after twenty years of rule – planned for 312 (see Fig. 5, which shows the model of Galerius's recently excavated palace Romuliana at Gamzigrad).[68]

But the simultaneous management of four rulers and four potential lines of succession was too much. Diocletian had been forced to choose colleagues not related by blood, simply because of a lack of alternatives – just as the "adoptive" second-century emperors only adopted so long as they had no sons of their own. But by the time the first Tetrarchy was ready to give way to the second, there were two adult sons of existing rulers – Constantine, son of Constantius I, and Maxentius, son of Maximian. While hereditary succession had never safeguarded an emperor against rebellion or assassination, leaving imperial heirs alive but excluded proved an extremely dangerous policy, which may help to explain the brutal extermination of imperial relatives by Licinius in 313 and the sons of Constantine in 337. Within eighteen months of Diocletian's abdication in May 305, the attempt to replicate Tetrarchic symmetry broke down as the ailing Constantius died in July 306, and first Constantine and then Maxentius seized power. Even Maximian undid his abdication. Diocletian, by contrast, famously refused to resume the purple. At a conference held at Carnuntum in 308, he resisted calls for his resumption of power, having limited himself to the assumption of the consulship for that year and lending what prestige he had left to shore up Galerius's attempt to preserve the Tetrarchic structure. Although the Tetrarchic idea succeeded as a solution to the problems of imperial government as long as Diocletian ruled, it failed to provide a definitive blueprint for collegiality. Even so, given the undoubted need for multiple emperors, as shown by the non-consensual division of the empire into three parts under Gallienus, Diocletian had demonstrated that harmonious collegiality of some sort was not only necessary but both possible and effective.

FURTHER READINGS

Although there is now less optimism about the possibility of definitive histories for any period, the first recourse for the third century and the Tetrarchy is now likely to be the second edition of *The Cambridge Ancient History*, vol. 12, *The Crisis of Empire, AD 193–337*, ed. A. Bowman, A. Cameron, and P. Garnsey (2005; replacing the previous 1939 volume). There is also the recent volume of the *Routledge History of the Ancient World* entitled *The Roman Empire at Bay AD 180–395* (2004), by D.S. Potter. Many invaluable articles (often in English) are contained in *Aufstieg und Niedergang der römischen Welt*, vol. 2.2, ed. H. Temporini (1975). For regional views, see J. Drinkwater, *The Gallic Empire* (1987); R. Stoneman, *Palmyra and Its Empire* (1992); F. Millar, *The Roman Near East, 31 BC–AD 337* (1993); and D. Rathbone, *Economic Rationalism and Rural Society in Third Century AD Egypt* (1991). The emperor's legal role from Severus to Diocletian is examined by T. Honoré in *Emperors and Lawyers* (1994). On Diocletian and the Tetrarchy, S. Williams's *Diocletian and the Roman Recovery* (1985) is very serviceable, although Chapter 1 of T. D. Barnes's *Constantine and Eusebius* (1981) is the most powerful and succinct account. T. D. Barnes's *The New Empire of Diocletian and Constantine* (1982), with updates in Barnes, "Emperors, Panegyrics, Prefects, Provinces and Palaces (284–317)," *Journal of Roman Archaeology* 9 (1996a): 532–52, remains an invaluable reference tool. Volumes 2 and 3 of the journal *Antiquité Tardive*, ed. J.-M. Carrié (1994, 1995), are devoted to the Tetrarchy and provide a range of up-to-date evidence, views and discussions. Aspects of law and government are covered by S. Corcoran in *The Empire of the Tetrarchs* (2000). P. J. Casey's *Carausius and Allectus* (1994) deals with the 'British' usurpers. The paucity of ancient sources makes good editions of important surviving texts crucial for approaching the period. For the mid-third century, D. S. Potter's *Prophecy and History in the Crisis of the Roman Empire* (1990) provides an exhaustive commentary on the *Thirteenth Sibylline Oracle*. For Diocletian, C. E. V. Nixon and B. S. Rodgers's *In Praise of Later Roman Emperors* (1994) gives a similarly detailed treatment of the Latin Panegyrics, also well covered by R. Rees in *Layers of Loyalty in Latin Panegyric* (2002). Briefer is J. L. Creed's *Lactantius: De Mortibus Persecutorum* (1984). The more plausible Diocletianic martyr acts are included in H. Musurillo *Acts of the Christian Martyrs* (1972), nos. 17–27. Of documentary material, the Panopolis papyri brightly illuminate Diocletian's Egypt; these are edited as in T. C. Skeat, *Papyri from Panopolis in the Chester Beatty Library* (1964).

NOTES

1   Petr. Patr. fr. 13 (*FHG* 4:186). English translation at Dodgeon and Lieu 1991, 132.

2   Shapur's account, *ŠKZ* 18–39, can be found at Huyse 1999, 1:34–52. See the English translation at Dodgeon and Lieu 1991, 57. For a survey of the evidence for Valerian's defeat, see Potter 1990, 331–41.

3   Potter 1990, 261–8; McKechnie 2002.

4   Christian writers, of course, see divine judgement in the fates of Decius and Valerian, Lact. *DMP* 4.1–6.7.

5   Drinkwater 1987 . Cf. the important recently discovered inscription of Postumus; Bakker 1993a, 1993b.

6   Stoneman 1992; Millar 1993, 159–73.

7   For the dramatic archaeological evidence for the sack of Athens, see Frantz 1988, Chapter 1; cf. Millar 1969.

8   Lenski 1999; cf. Mitchell 1995, Chapter 6.

9   More details at Bowman, Cameron, and Garnsey 2005, Chapter 2, and Christol 1997.

10 The most recent reassessments of the 'crisis' in Bowman, Cameron, and Garnsey 2005; Potter 2004; Carrié and Rousselle 1999, esp. Chapters 2, 8, and 9. Witschel 1999 reexamines much archaeological information for the western provinces. For the issue of plague, see Carrié and Rousselle 1999, 521–4, and Bagnall 2002. Letters of Dionysius of Alexandria on the plague are preserved at Eus. *HE* 7.21–2. Alföldy 1974 surveys third-century authors, perhaps with a little more credence than warranted.

11 The wolf metaphor, first attested in Latin at Terence *Phormio* 506, was used for ruling Rome by Tiberius (Suet. *Tib.* 25.1): *saepe lupum se auribus tenere diceret.*

12 For instance, Africa (see Carrié and Rousselle 1999, 526–8), and Egypt (see Rathbone 1991).

13 General accounts of Diocletian's reign at Jones 1964, Chapter 2; T. D. Barnes 1981, Chapter 1; Williams 1985; Demandt 1989; Christol 1997, 4.2–3; Carrié and Rousselle 1999, Chapter 3; Potter 2004, Chapters 7 and 9; Rees 2004; Bowman, Cameron, and Garnsey 2005, Chapter 3. The chronology is best presented by T. D. Barnes 1982, with some revision at T. D. Barnes 1996a. These various accounts provide the background for the following discussion; detailed references are not provided for all individual statements.

14 For the elevation of Maximian, the 'dyarchy', and *Iovius* and *Herculius*, see Kolb 1987, Chapters 3 and 5; Kuhoff 2001, Chapter 1.2; Bowman, Cameron, and Garnsey 2005, 69–74, 171, 556. For the ideology of the early relationship of Diocletian and Maximian, see especially Rees 2002, Chapters 1–2, on *Pan. Lat.* 10(2) (289) and 11(3) (291).

15 For a detailed account of the 'British' usurpers, see Casey 1994.

16 Kolb 1987, Chapter 4; Kuhoff 2001, Chapter 1.4–5; Potter 2004, 280–90; Bowman, Cameron, and Garnsey 2005, 74–8. See Stemma 1 in the Appendix.

17 A famous medallion from the Arras horde depicts Constantius at London, with the legend '*redditor lucis aeternae,*' *RIC* 6 Treveri 34.

18 The sources for the Persian campaign are collected in English translation by Dodgeon and Lieu 1991, 124–35. The chronology as currently accepted is given by Zuckerman 1994b, followed by T. D. Barnes 1996a, 543–4.

19 For the Prices Edict's claim (*tranquillo orbis statu et in gremio altissimae quietis locato*), see Corcoran 2000, 208.

20 Note Philip's reforms in Egypt; Bowman, Cameron, and Garnsey 2005, 316–7. There is also new information about the administration of the east, where his brother Priscus held an overall regional command, following the publication of papyri from Syria; Feissel and Gascou 1989, 1995; Carrié and Rousselle 1999, 143; Potter 2004, 239; Bowman, Cameron, and Garnsey 2005, 161, 277.

21 To judge by Eus. *HE* 8.13.10–11; cf. Eus. *MP* 9.5–6.

22 Carrié and Rousselle 1999, 151–3.

23 Corcoran 2000, 255–6, 260–3.

24 Corcoran 2000, Chapter 5.

25 On Milan, see *Pan. Lat.* 11(3).10–12. On the imperial *adventus* (formal arrival), see MacCormack 1981, 17–33. As to controlled spaces, note that during his residence in the palace at Nicomedia (November 304–March 305), Diocletian's state of health became mired in mystery; Lact. *DMP* 17.5–9.

26 T. D. Barnes 1981, 5; 1996a, 537.

27 Bartoli 1963.

28 For Maximian in Rome, see Nixon and Rodgers 1994, 201. For the Baths of Diocletian, *CIL* 6:1130, 31242; cf. *ILS* 646.

29 Lact. *DMP* 26.2–3, 27.2.

30 On imperial journeys, see T. D. Barnes 1982, Chapter 5; Bowman, Cameron, and Garnsey 2005, app. 2. On Tetrarchic 'residences', see Carrié and Rousselle 1999, 157–60; Kuhoff 2001, Chapter 2.1.3.

31 E.g., Piazza Armerina (Wilson 1983) or Cordoba (Arce 1997); cf. Lavan 1999.

32 Srejović 1993.

33 Foss 1996, 1–4; cf. Lact. *DMP* 7.8–10.

34 For late Roman circuses, see Humphrey 1986, Chapter 11 (Nicomedia, Trier, Sirmium, Milan, Aquileia, Thessalonica, Rome).

35 T. D. Barnes 1982, Chapter 8; 1996a, 546–8; cf. Chapter 8 in this volume.

36 Corcoran 2000, Chapter 4.

37 Salway 1994, 137–9.

38 Lact. *DMP* 7.2; Zos. 2.34.

39 See in general Chapter 14 in this volume; cf. Nicasie 1998, Chapter 1; Carrié and Rousselle 1999, Chapters 3 and 9; Bowman, Cameron, and Garnsey 2005, Chapter 5. For Tetrarchic defences, see Millar 1993, 174–89, on Syria, and Zahariade 1997, on the Danube frontier.

40 Lact. *DMP* 7.4.

41 On provincial reorganization and dioceses, see Kuhoff 2001, 327–81; Bowman, Cameron, and Garnsey 2005, Chapter 6d, Chapter 8, app. 1. On governors and vicars, see T. D. Barnes 1982, Chapters 9 and 12; 1996a, 548–51; Carrié, Feissel, and Duval 1998.

42 On senatorial careers in the period, see T. D. Barnes 1982, Chapter 6; Jacques 1986; Christol 1986; Chastagnol 1992, Chapters 13 and 14; Bowman, Cameron, and Garnsey 2005, Chapter 7.

43 Chastagnol 1962, Chapter 1; T. D. Barnes 1982, Chapter 7.

44 Roueché 1989.

45 See the examples of Tymandus, where civic status was possibly granted by Diocletian (Feissel 1995, 37 no. 14; *MAMA* 4:236), and Heraclea Sintica, where it was certainly granted by Galerius (Mitrev 2003).

46 Harl 1987, Chapters 8 and 9. Note that there was a brief revival under Maximin c. 312; Corcoran 2000, 149 n. 122.

47 Bowman, Cameron, and Garnsey 2005, Chapters 9 and 10; Frakes 2001, Chapter 2.

48 Lib. *Or.* 19.45, 20.17–20.

49 Millar 1983; Corcoran 2000, 101–5.

50 Carrié and Rousselle, 1999, 593–615; Bowman, Cameron, and Garnsey 2005, 374–9; cf. below Chapter 10.

51 For Syria, see Millar 1993, 535–44; for Asiana, see Corcoran 2000, 346–7. See also census edicts in Egypt, *P. Cair. Isid.* 1; *CPR* 23.20.

52 Lact. *DMP* 7.3–5, 23.

53 Carrié and Rousselle 1999, 195–208; Bowman, Cameron, and Garnsey 2005, Chapter 11.1. See also Chapter 16 in this volume.

54 On the Panopolis Papyri, see Skeat 1964. On compulsory gold purchase, see *P. Oxy.* 17:2106.

55 On retariffing, see Roueché 1989, 254–65 no. 230. On the Prices Edict, see Giacchero 1974, with Corcoran 2000, Chapter 8.

56 On the Diocletianic jurists and the law codes, see Honoré 1994, Chapter 4; Corcoran 2000, Chapters 2 and 4; Bowman, Cameron, and Garnsey 2005 Chapter 7b. For the major cultural divide between Greek and Latin reflected in the language chosen to promulgate imperial pronouncements, see Feissel 1995; Corcoran 2002. For issues of cultural identity in the third century, see Clark 1999.

57 For Diocletian's *romanitas*, see Corcoran 2000, 173. For the laws on incest and Manichees, see *Coll. Mos. et Rom. Leg.* 6.4, 15.3, with translation at Lee 2000, 66–7. For the Persians as touchstones of un-Romanness but also as models of both persecutors and proselytizers, see McKechnie 2002.

58 See T. D. Barnes 1976a.

59 See, e.g., T. D. Barnes 1996a, 542–3.

60 On the Great Persecution, see T. D. Barnes 1981, Chapter 2; Bowman, Cameron, and Garnsey 2005, 645–63; below Chapters 5 and 6.

61 Mitchell 1988.

62 Lact. *DMP* 15.7; contrast Eus. *HE* 8.13.13, *VC* 1.13.2.

63 Digeser 1998.

64 Sulla is criticized at Suet. *Iul.* 77.1 but praised at App. *B. Civ.* 1.12.103–4. Lact. *DMP* 18.2 has Galerius refer inaccurately to the example of Nerva and Trajan.

65 On Diocletian's palace, see Wilkes 1993.

66 *Pan. Lat.* 6(7).15.6; Kolb 1987, 143–50; Nixon and Rodgers 1994, 241; cf. Nixon 1981.

67 Kolb 1987, Chapter 7; Kuhoff 2001, Chapter 1.5.4; Potter 2004, 340–2; Bowman, Cameron, and Garnsey 2005, 86–8.

68 For Gamzigrad, see Srejović and Vasić 1994, with further articles in Carrié 1994.

3: THE REIGN OF CONSTANTINE

Noel Lenski

BIRTH AND EARLY CAREER

The details of Constantine's birth are enigmatic. We know that he was born in or near the Moesian city of Naissus (Niš: see Map 1) and that he was the eldest son of Flavius Valerius Constantius, soon to become Caesar. The year of his birth, however, is hardly certain. Most historians agree that he was born on February 27, 272, though one good contemporary source indicates 276, and some scholars have argued for a date as late as 288.[1] Behind much of the confusion stands Constantine himself, who regularly had himself portrayed in art and panegyrics as much younger than he actually was.[2] The question of Constantine's legitimacy has also long plagued historians. The Christian chronographer Jerome, writing in the 380s, claimed that Constantine's mother, Helena, was a mere concubine of Constantius I; the anonymous author of the *Origo Constantini*, a source quite favorable to Constantine, calls Helena "extremely lowly"; and bishop Ambrose, Jerome's contemporary, reports that she had been a mere stable maid when she met Constantius.[3] Whatever the exact status of their relationship, then, Constantine's mother was hardly of noble stock, a fact that eventually provoked his father to leave her c. 289 in order to marry the princess Theodora, stepdaughter of the emperor Maximian.[4]

When Constantine was born, his father, a native of Illyricum (the Balkans), was serving as an imperial bodyguard (*protector*) to the emperor Aurelian (r. 270–5).[5] This position would prove quite favorable after two other Illyrian officers of Aurelian, Diocletian and in turn Maximian, took over corulership of the empire in 284 and 285, respectively (Coins 5 and 7). From 288, Maximian, the western emperor, selected Constantius to serve as his praetorian prefect and shortly thereafter arranged for Constantius's marriage to his stepdaughter. When Diocletian and Maximian decided to promote two junior emperors (Caesars) to help them in the conduct of warfare, Diocletian promoted his confidant Galerius (Fig. 7), also an Illyrian and former soldier of Aurelian's, and Maximian promoted Constantius (Coin 8). Thus was formed, on March 1, 293, the first Tetrarchy, a quadripartite rule governed by two senior Augusti and two junior Caesars and cemented by the bonds of marriage: not only was Constantius married to Theodora, but Galerius was married to Diocletian's daughter Valeria.[6]

Constantine benefited markedly from his father's promotion. He received a formidable education, sufficient to render him an aficionado of literature in his native Latin, a capable if not fluent speaker of Greek, and an adept in philosophy.[7] As the son of a military emperor, however, Constantine's most important obligations were on the battlefield, and it was with this in mind that he was co-opted for employment by the Tetrarchy. In the 290s, his father, operating in the western empire, farmed Constantine out to the eastern rulers Diocletian and Galerius. This was intended in part to initiate his son's military training, in part also as a security for his own loyalty to the eastern Tetrarchs. The *Origo* reports that Constantine fought under Diocletian and Galerius in Asia, and other sources indicate he held a series of military tribunates. Eusebius claims to have seen the young Constantine traveling with Diocletian's court through Palestine. And Constantine himself claims in his *Oration to the Assembly of the Saints* that he had witnessed in person the ruins of Babylon in Mesopotamia and Memphis (see Map 2) in Egypt. This has been taken to indicate that he accompanied Galerius on his expedition into Persia in 298 and that he also participated in one of Diocletian's Egyptian journeys, probably in 301/2.[8] Constantine had thus seen more than ample service in his early career, experience that would be put to good use in the years to come.

On May 1, 305, when Constantine was probably thirty-three, Diocletian formally retired from the throne in Nicomedia (Kocaeli) and forced his western colleague Maximian to do the same in Milan, thus putting his Tetrarchic machine to its greatest test yet. Diocletian had established a system based on merit rather than dynasty and intended for successive instantiations of the Tetrarchy to operate in the same way. Thus, the two Caesars, Constantius and Galerius, duly ascended to the rank of Augusti, and both received Caesars to fill their former posts: Constantius took Severus, and Galerius chose Maximin Daia. Both were from Illyricum and both had been soldiers, Maximin another former *protector*.[9] Naturally, this had entailed passing over the children of emperors. Constantius had not only Constantine but also three sons by

Theodora, albeit too young to rule, and Maximian also had a son, Maxentius, a slightly younger contemporary of Constantine.[10] This dynastic slight naturally created discontent, discontent compounded by the fact that family had played a role in Galerius's choice of Maximin Daia, his nephew.[11] Galerius, who remained Constantine's overseer and thus the master of his fate, must have been aware of this tension and is reputed to have sent Constantine into harm's way more than once in hopes of eliminating him. Constantine's propagandists report that he was made to lead an advance unit against the Sarmatians along the middle Danube and even that he was forced into single combat with a lion for Galerius's amusement.[12] How much of this can be trusted is unclear, but Constantine had at least acquitted himself admirably enough to attain the rank of tribune of the first order by late 305.[13]

It was around this time that Constantius petitioned for his son to be sent to the western frontier to help in military operations against the Picts in Britain. Galerius is reported to have resisted but eventually to have granted reluctant permission. The next morning, when he awoke late after one of his notorious drinking revels and attempted to revoke his order, it was already too late; Constantine had fled the night before. The story has it that Constantine rode posthaste using the *cursus publicus*, a sort of ancient Pony Express with stables of fresh horses every fifteen to twenty miles on the imperial highways. To evade pursuit by Galerius's agents, which inevitably followed, Constantine supposedly selected for himself the best horse at each stop and maimed the rest. He also apparently took the longer route north of the Alps so as to avoid contact with the western Caesar, Severus, then resident in northern Italy.[14] Again it is legend, albeit the contemporary legend of Lactantius, that reports that he reached Constantius only as his father lay on his deathbed. Since Constantius died at York (Eburacum), one might assume Constantine first met his father in Britain. In fact, the more reliable *Origo* and Constantine's own panegyrist of 310 confirm that he found Constantius in Bononia (Boulogne) in northwestern Gaul shortly before Constantius returned to Britain to fight.[15] Only many months later did Constantius then expire in Britain, with his son at his deathbed.

ELEVATION TO THE THRONE AND DEFEAT OF MAXENTIUS

The date was July 25, 306. What happened that same day was entirely predictable: the dying Augustus, the imperial army, and even a Germanic king, who was fighting with the Roman auxiliaries, joined together in supporting the elevation of Constantine to emperor, indeed to the rank of full Augustus.[16] It had been standard practice through much of Roman history for the imperial army to elect a successor on the death of the emperor, and it was only natural for them to favor the emperor's son, himself a tested commander. But this was by no means the manner in which the Tetrarchy was meant to function. From the perspective of the other Tetrarchs, and indeed of many contemporaries, Constantine was a usurper. His promotion set off a firestorm of resentment. Galerius, the ranking Augustus, is reported to have reacted first with rage, which he then tempered with a realistic acceptance of the inevitable fact of Constantine's acclamation, though he insisted on his demotion to the rank of Caesar and the consequent promotion of Severus to Augustus.[17] Maxentius, the slighted son of the former Augustus Maximian, was less restrained. When Constantine's imperial portrait was exhibited in his home city of Rome, as was customary, Maxentius mocked Constantine as the son of a harlot and lamented that he, the legitimate son of an emperor and the son-in-law of Galerius to boot, remained a private citizen.[18] No longer content to remain on the sidelines, Maxentius persuaded a coterie of imperial guardsmen to gather on October 28, 306, six miles north of the city on the Via Labicana, and acclaim him emperor (Coin 10), albeit with the archaizing title "*princeps*" (prince). At the same time, Maxentius also convinced his father, the ex-Augustus Maximian, then living in retirement in Lucania (southern Italy), to resume the purple robe of empire and join his cause.[19]

Maxentius had capitalized on a collective wave of discontent in Rome and Italy and hoped that his skill in harnessing it would make up for the fact that he was generally lacking in the key ingredient to successful rule in this period, an army. His father had chafed under the retirement forced on him by Diocletian and was more than happy to join his son.[20] The praetorians and their counterparts the urban cohorts, Rome's military police force, were also restive after Diocletian and Galerius had reduced them to a rump of their formerly glorious selves, and they saw in Maxentius a champion of their cause. The Roman people also happily abetted the usurper, for they had watched their power and privileges steadily erode in the Tetrarchic period and were irate that Galerius had instituted measures to removed their tax-exempt status.[21] Maxentius fostered the support of these allies by promoting a program of Roman revivalism: he increased the size and prestige of the guards, maintained the privileges of the *populus Romanus*, and pumped hoards of money into a building program that saw the restoration and construction of temples, the expansion of the Circus Maximus, and the construction of Rome's largest public basilica (see Map 3.1). All the while he promoted his own image as Rome's paladin on his coins and even named his son Romulus after Rome's legendary founder.[22]

Though his charades played well on the Italian stage, Maxentius had much greater trouble winning approval from the remaining Tetrarchs, particularly Galerius, the senior Augustus. Within months of Maxentius's elevation, Galerius sent the emperor Severus from Milan to Rome to put a stop to what both regarded as a shameless usurpation. As Severus approached the walls of the city, however, he was surprised to witness his soldiers desert to Maxentius, who enticed them with bribes and probably appealed to their loyalty to his father, under whom many of them had served until less than two years previously. In the face of this setback, Severus fled north to Ravenna, a city rendered virtually impregnable by the marshlands that surrounded it. Maximian was sent to negotiate with Severus and eventually coaxed him out of the city with false promises of amnesty, only to arrest him and have him imprisoned in the town of Tres Tabernae, south of Rome.[23]

With Severus as his hostage, Maxentius now braced himself for the inevitable onslaught from Galerius himself. This arrived in mid to late 307, when Galerius reached the walls of Rome swearing he would obliterate its Senate and slaughter its people. When Maxentius declined Galerius's overtures to begin negotiations and even murdered Severus, Galerius realized he was in for a lengthy siege. And when Galerius, like Severus, began witnessing the support of his men erode in the face of Maxentius's money and propaganda, he found himself pleading with his own troops, whom he convinced to accompany him out of Italy on the condition that they be allowed to plunder its countryside in exchange for their loyalty.[24] More than anything, Galerius, who had never been to Rome, had underestimated the risks involved in besieging so well fortified a city. Here again Maxentius had calculated shrewdly in falling back on the resources of Rome as the bulwark of his power.

Constantine, meanwhile, remained in Gaul and operated in the mode of the junior Tetrarch by asserting Roman rule along the frontier. In early 307 he had campaigned against the Frankish tribes along the lower Rhine, captured their chieftains Ascaric and Merogaisus, paraded them in a triumphal procession, and had them fed to the beasts in the arena of Augusta Treverorum (Trier).[25] Again in 308 he campaigned on the lower Rhine against the Frankish Bructeri and even constructed a bridge near Colonia Agrippinensium (Cologne) to expedite future attacks.[26] Also like a good junior Tetrarch, Constantine was working to secure his own position by strengthening his alliance with a senior Augustus, in this instance the superannuated Maximian. Maximian had begun courting Constantine in the aftermath of his return to power in 306 and even came north of the Alps in 307 to strengthen the alliance by marrying his young daughter Fausta to Constantine (Coin 11). Like his father, Constantine put aside his erstwhile companion Minervina and happily assumed the role of son-in-law to the senior Augustus.[27] The accompanying festivities are well described by the panegyrist of 307, who reports two important things about the bargain Constantine and Maximian had struck. First, Constantine won permission from Maximian to claim for himself the title Augustus, formerly denied him by Galerius.[28] Second, despite this promotion, Constantine was still willing to advertise himself as Maximian's subordinate:

> It becomes you, father [i.e., Maximian], to survey from your pinnacle of command the world you share, and with celestial nod decide the fate of human affairs, to announce the auspices for wars which have to be waged, and to impose the terms when peace is to be concluded. You, young man, it behooves to traverse frontiers tirelessly where the Roman Empire presses upon barbarian peoples, to send frequent laurels of victory to your father-in-law, to seek instructions, and to report what you have accomplished. So it will come about that both of you will have the counsel of one mind, and each the strength of two.[29]

Another striking feature of the panegyric of 307 is its studied refusal to make any direct mention of Maximian's son Maxentius back in Rome. This omission was probably not accidental, for despite his skill at exploiting political advantage, Maxentius was not so adept at keeping his constituents satisfied. In the aftermath of Severus's murder and Galerius's discomfiture before the walls of Rome, Maxentius seems to have begun drifting apart from his father, who was thus actually protecting his own interests by turning to Constantine as an ally. In 308, after his return to from Trier to Rome, Maximian's discontent even led him to hold an assembly at which he attempted publicly to strip Maxentius of his imperial vestments. Maxentius once again threw his lot in with the soldiers and succeeded in chasing his father out of Italy and back to Constantine in Gaul.[30] Despite this success, however, the event was a sign that Maxentius's lockhold on power was beginning to weaken. The break with Maximian, who had been extremely popular in North Africa, also alienated the provincials there, and these eventually acclaimed the vicar of Africa, L. Domitius Alexander, emperor.[31] The usurper turned to Constantine for support, which Constantine seems to have offered, albeit very cautiously, in a bid to keep pressure on Maxentius.[32] More importantly, the volatile populace of Rome was heavily dependent on African grain for its daily bread, a fact that rendered Domitius Alexander's control of Africa and even Sardinia extremely dangerous. Not surprisingly, a famine ensued in Rome and eroded Maxentius's support in his home base for at least a year before Domitius Alexander could be suppressed. By 309 a fire was set to the temple of Fortuna near the Colline Gate, a member of Maxentius' praetorian guard was murdered, and riots broke out, leading Maxentius to unleash his praetorians on the populace and slaughter as many as six thousand civilians.[33] Other charges reported in the sources, including the imprisonment and murder of senators, attempted rape of aristocratic women, and dissection of babies, are either exaggerations or outright fabrications, but they confirm an atmosphere of brooding discontent among the inhabitants of Rome.[34]

Even before things reached these straits, Galerius, the senior legitimate Augustus, was appalled at the chaotic state of affairs in the west. By November 11, 308, he had convinced Diocletian to emerge from retirement and attend an emergency conference along the Danube border at Carnuntum (Petronell). Present at the conference was also Maximian, who was hoping to win approval for his own resumption of power. In typically magisterial fashion, Diocletian laid down the law without, however, resuming the throne. Indeed, he resisted calls for his return to power by insisting that he much preferred the cultivation of vegetables at his retirement complex at Split.[35] Instead, he ordered that Maximian abdicate a second time and that Galerius take a new colleague to replace Severus in the west. Galerius chose his confidant and former military commander Licinius, another Illyrian, and − to the consternation of both Constantine and Maximin Daia − he promoted him forthwith to Augustus (Coin 12).[36]

Despite being formally demoted to Caesar at Carnuntum, Constantine maintained his own assertion of the title Augustus. Naturally he also continued to show deference to the man who had granted it, even despite Maximian's second forced abdication. Nevertheless, after having subdued the Franks on the lower Rhine in the summer of 310, Constantine was informed that Maximian had once again resumed the purple and convinced a group of soldiers in Augustodunum (Autun) to revolt. He hastened "with admirable speed" from Cologne overland to the Sâone River, down it to the Rhone, past Autun – which Maximian had abandoned – and on to Massalia (Marseilles) on the coast of the Mediterranean. In this nearly impregnable city Maximian had barricaded himself, but Constantine easily convinced his reluctant troops to turn over the two-time usurper.[37] Remarkably, Constantine spared his father-in-law, keeping him under house arrest, until the incorrigible Maximian hatched a final plot to assassinate Constantine (if we can believe Lactantius), in consequence of which he was arrested and forced to commit suicide.[38]

Maximian's revolt and forced suicide were naturally delicate matters and were thus only discussed in guarded terms by a panegyrist who addressed Constantine in July of 310. Eager as he was to change the subject, the same panegyrist turned to two new themes that heralded a volte-face in Constantinian imperial propaganda. The first was the revelation – in reality the invention – of a new imperial ancestor:

> I shall begin with the divinity who is the origin of your family, of whom most people, perhaps, are still unaware, but whom those who love you know full well. For an ancestral relationship links you with the deified Claudius, who was the first to restore the discipline of the Roman Empire when it was disordered and in ruins, and destroyed on land and sea by huge numbers of Goths who had burst forth from the straits of the Black Sea and the mouth of the Danube.[39]

The ancestor was Claudius Gothicus, the beloved emperor who had rescued the empire from a Gothic invasion before his premature death in 270. Scholars agree that his purported connection with the lineage of Constantine is a fabrication, but it recurs in the lore and propaganda of the Constantinian family through the rest of the fourth century.[40] Here we must remember that Constantine's three-year-old dynastic link to the house of Maximian had just lost all publicity value, and the suspicion of bastardy, which always besmirched Constantine's claim to noble ancestry, was continuously raised by Maxentius in Rome. In a world where four emperors were competing simultaneously for a claim to precedence, the discovery of a long-lost imperial ancestor was meant to bolster Constantine's bid for supremacy.

So, too, was a second bold new revelation. While Constantine was returning to Trier after having defeated Maximian, he had turned off the main road to visit a temple of Apollo, probably at Grand, Vosges.

There he claimed to have seen, to his amazement, not just the god's temple but the god himself:

> For you saw, I believe, O Constantine, your Apollo, accompanied by Victory, offering you laurel wreaths, each one of which carries a portent of thirty years. For this is the number of human ages which are owed to you without fail – beyond the old age of a Nestor. And – now why do I say "I believe"? – you saw, and recognized yourself in the likeness of him to whom the divine songs of the bards had prophesied that rule over the whole world was due.[41]

The panegyrist's description has long been taken to relate to an image commonly portrayed on imperial *vota* coins that display a series of Xs inside a circular laurel wreath, with each X representing a decade (X years) of imperial rule (Coin 13). Constantine must, then, have seen something that looked like this ✕✕✕ or perhaps this ✳ in the heavens (see the striking image on Coin 14). The fact that the vision occurred near the temple of Apollo and apparently in broad daylight was interpreted to mean that it had been sent by the god of the sun. Not surprisingly, then, from 310 onwards Constantine began trumpeting the idea that he had special connections to Apollo or to an even more popular sun god among previous emperors, Sol (Greek Helios). From this period, Sol, often referred to as "Sol Invictus" (Unconquerable Sun), shows up with especial regularity on Constantine's coins as his official "comrade" (*comes*), and Constantine began portraying himself on coins with the attributes of or in association with Sol Invictus (Coins 4 and 15).[42] What precisely Constantine saw that day in 310 remains a matter of dispute, but the German researcher P. Weiss elaborated a theory in 1993 that has won growing acceptance. Weiss contends that Constantine witnessed a documented atmospheric phenomenon called a "solar halo," a credible and convincing hypothesis that will be more fully explained in what follows.[43] Here it suffices to say that Constantine believed he had seen a divine vision that, at the time, he believed to have come from the god of the sun.

Constantine's interest in divine support was hardly unique. Imperial efforts to court the favor of the gods stretched back to Augustus and had reached new heights under the Tetrarchs. Diocletian, the self-proclaimed son of Jove, and Maximian, who claimed Hercules as his father (Coins 6 and 7), had even launched Rome's longest and most systematic persecution against the Christians in an effort to rebalance the delicate equilibrium between empire and gods. This so-called Great Persecution, begun in February of 303, had reputedly been master-minded by none other than Galerius, and even after it had ceased in the west following Maximian's abdication in 305, Galerius had stubbornly prolonged persecutions in the east down to 311.[44] In that year he fell ill with a repugnant degenerative bowel disease and ultimately repented of his project. While defending the soundness of his original intent – to bring Christians in line with traditional worship – he admitted that his violent methods had failed to achieve their end. Shortly before his death, in spring 311, he issued an edict of toleration allowing freedom of worship to pagans and Christians alike.[45] This did not, however, put a definitive stop to the persecutions, at least not in the easternmost empire. There, within six months of the Edict of Toleration, Maximin Daia renewed them with increased vigor. While pretending to favor religious tolerance, he gladly entertained pleas from local city coun-cils to expel Christians from their towns, he ordered published and taught in schools forged "Acts of Pilate" slandering Christianity, and he put credence in oracles that called for renewed attacks on high-profile Christians.[46] Such was the religious atmosphere of the early 310s in the eastern empire. Constantine, meanwhile, had little stomach for reli-gious persecution. As a young soldier in the company of Diocletian and Galerius, he had witnessed the beginnings of the Great Persecution in person. His father, Caesar in the west at the time, had given only halt-ing support to the violence and apparently never murdered Christians.[47] Thus when Constantine was acclaimed emperor, one of his first mea-sures was to proclaim religious freedom for Christians.[48] Persecution, he had seen, could only sow discord and could never compel con-sent. Despite his paganism, despite his Apolline visions, Constantine self-identified early as a friend of Christians.

By 312 Constantine's elimination of Maximian had fanned the flames of Maxentius's resentment to a new pitch. Despite the total rup-ture of their relations in 308, Maxentius rediscovered his filial piety after Maximian's death in 310 and began advertising portraits of his deified father on his coins and proclaiming his resolve to avenge his murder.[49] Constantine responded by systematically eliminating Maximian's images from public places and his name from public inscriptions – a politi-cal practice called *damnatio memoriae*.[50] All the while, Maxentius faced an ever-deteriorating situation in Rome, where his early support had eroded into open protest.[51] In these circumstances, Maxentius would have been hard pressed to steal a move on Constantine. This does not mean, however, that either he or Constantine avoided preparations for a conflict. Knowing that he would require the support of Licinius, whose Balkan realm abutted Italy, Constantine forged an alliance with him by betrothing to Licinius his half-sister Constantia. Maxentius, in turn, accepted an alliance with Maximin Daia, who though farther afield was eager to join forces with any enemy of Licinius.[52] Maximin had always resented Licinius's direct promotion to Augustus, and by the summer of 310 he had himself proclaimed Augustus by his troops.[53] Ultimately his goal was the elimination of Licinius, who in his turn was well aware of Maximin's hatred and thus gladly accepted Constantine's overtures.

Chief among Constantine's many virtues as a military leader was his willingness to act boldly and swiftly. Rather than bide his time as relations deteriorated or wait for Maxentius to attack him, Constantine assembled a compact crack force and vaulted over the Alps in the spring of 312.[54] When he encountered resistance in the Alpine town of Segusio (Susa), he burned it. By the time he reached Augusta Taurinorum (Turin) he met a sizable force of Maxentius's troops outside the city's walls but outmaneuvered and defeated them. With this setback, Maxentius's support in northern Italy began to erode, and Milan soon welcomed Constantine without resistance. Continuing eastward, he faced another serious battle at Verona, where Maxentius's praetorian prefect, Ruricius Pompeianus, and his army were stationed. In a scene still commemorated on his triumphal arch in Rome, Constantine faced a battle on two fronts as he was attacked by Pompeianus's reinforcements outside the walls while laying siege to resisters inside (Fig. 17). Yet again he prevailed and captured massive numbers of Maxentius's troops. Upon news of this victory, Aquileia, at the easternmost foot of the Alps, surrendered, and Constantine became master of northern Italy.[55]

Without hesitating, Constantine descended through central Italy for a final face-off with Maxentius, who remained walled off in Rome, no doubt hoping to repeat his successes resisting the sieges of Severus and Galerius. He had already laid up stores of supplies in the city and had cut bridges, especially the Milvian Bridge just north of Rome over the Tiber along the Via Flaminia.[56] Constantine had camped along this road, probably at a place now called Malborghetto, a site where he later erected a four-bayed triumphal arch (Fig. 10).[57] He seemed, then, to be heading into the same trap as his predecessors. At the last minute, however, Maxentius had a boat bridge constructed alongside the broken Milvian Bridge (Fig. 9 and Map 3.2) and prepared a force to face his rival in battle. On October 28, 312, the sixth anniversary of his reign, he exited the city and headed north on the Flaminia, in part prodded by a riotous Roman populace, in part by an oracle predicting "the enemy of Rome would be killed that day."[58] At the ninth milestone, at a place called Saxa Rubra, his forces met Constantine's but were routed.[59] Maxentius fled back to the Tiber, where the battle continued as his men attempted to cross the boat bridge alongside the broken Milvian Bridge back into the city. Many were forced into the Tiber, and many others, including apparently Maxentius, fell off the wobbly pontoons in the crush of fugitives. Weighted down as they were with heavy armor, soldiers and emperor alike drowned.

MAXIMUS AUGUSTUS: MILITARY TRIUMPH AND CHRISTIAN TRIUMPHALISM

Maxentius's body washed ashore nearby and was fished out of the Tiber. His head was lopped off, placed atop a pike, and paraded into Rome the next day with Constantine's victorious army.[60] Constantine himself appears to have celebrated a triumph, a slightly unusual maneuver in the aftermath of a civil war. Yet his propaganda only barely admitted this grim truth, for the panegyrics, histories, and inscriptions of the day portrayed Maxentius not as a rival emperor but rather as a cruel tyrant from whom the city and people of Rome were glad to be freed. Nowhere is this clearer than on the dedicatory inscription above his victory arch near the Colosseum (Fig. 1):

> To the emperor Caesar Flavius Constantinus the greatest, dutiful and blessed, Augustus, the Senate and people of Rome dedicated this arch, distinguished by [representations of] his victories, because, by the inspiration of divinity and by greatness of his mind [*instinctu divinitatis mentis magnitudine*], with his army he avenged the state with righteous arms against both the tyrant and all of his faction at one and the same time. To the liberator of the city, and the establisher of peace.[61]

The panegyrist who addressed Constantine in 313 spoke of Maxentius as a veritable monster whom the Romans were glad to see removed.[62] Little wonder then that, like his father's, Maxentius's images and inscriptions were systematically obliterated in a *damnatio memoriae*. Most of his unfinished building projects were taken over in Constantine's name, and Constantine even built another tetraconchic arch in the Forum Boarium, the epicenter of Roman provisioning, as if to symbolize the end of famines (Fig. 11).[63] Finally, Constantine cultivated goodwill by showing clemency to most of Maxentius's supporters; he even appointed his confidant and former praetorian prefect C. Ceionius Rufius Volusianus to the post of urban prefect and elected him consul for 314.[64]

Perhaps the most striking thing about the inscription on Constantine's triumphal arch is the expression "by the inspiration of divinity," an allusion left deliberately vague by the arch's dedicators in 315.[65] Allusive though the wording may be, its referent is seems clear enough thanks to details provided by other sources. At some point not long before the battle of the Milvian Bridge, Constantine was visited by a dream in which

> he was advised to mark the heavenly sign of God on the shields of his soldiers and then engage in battle. He did as he was commanded and by means of a slanted letter X with the top of its head bent round, he marked Christ on their shields.[66]

Thus Lactantius, writing from good sources not long after the event. Once again we encounter Constantine the visionary claiming divine epiphany and the revelation of some holy sign.[67] The symbol (☧ or ⳨) has changed only slightly from what he saw in 310, but Constantine's interpretation of it had metamorphosed considerably. Here again P. Weiss's interpretation remains the most convincing: in 312 Constantine had no new waking vision, nor is one reported in contemporary sources. Rather he had a dream ordering him to emblazon the shields of his soldiers with a sign remarkably like the one he had seen in 310, the primary difference being that it had changed into a monogram of the letters chi and rho, the first two letters of Christ's name in Greek. Such monograms, like the *vota* symbols of his earlier interpretation, were common in the period, but Constantine's decision or perhaps revelation that the sign stood for Christ was up to that point unique.[68] He had converted to Christianity.

Oddly enough, we have very little evidence that the Chi-Rho (☧: also called the "Christogram" or "Chrismon") became a common symbol of Constantine's Christianity in his iconography or propaganda before the 320s. Prior to that we have only one obvious instance of its use as a Christian symbol, on a very rare but clearly important medallion of Ticinum dated to 315 (Coin 1).[69] This does not mean, however, that Constantine simply hid his conversion. On the contrary, in numerous ways he made it abundantly clear that he was now a Christian. Most obvious to the Romans, in the three months he spent in the city following his victory, was his initiation of the construction of a number of massive Christian churches, the most important of which – the Lateran Basilica – he erected over the razed camp of Maxentius's trusted guard unit, the Equites Singulares (Fig. 12, Plan 1).[70] Also while in Rome, he issued a letter to the Proconsul of Africa, Anullinus, ordering him to restore to Christians any property that they had lost in the persecutions. The following spring he wrote to the bishop of Carthage, Caecilianus, conferring emoluments on Christian clergymen in North Africa, and again to Anullinus exempting clergy from public service.[71] Very quickly his favoritism toward the established Catholic clergy in North Africa drew him into a debate over the Donatist controversy, which will be discussed in later chapters.[72] Here it suffices to say that, within a year of his victory at the Milvian Bridge, Constantine had ordered a conference in Rome to examine the issue, and by August of 314 he called and attended a much larger council at Arelate (Arles). Finally, Constantine also chose to meet with Licinius in early 313 at Milan, and there he both consecrated the promised marriage between Licinius and his half-sister Constantia[73] and also convinced Licinius to extend some pro-Christian measures into his realm. The result is the so-called Edict of Milan, actually preserved as a letter by Licinius to a governor ordering not only that Christians be granted freedom of worship but also that any property confiscated from them be restored.[74] Within half a year of converting, then, Constantine was promoting his new religion empirewide.

THE FINAL COLLAPSE OF JOINT RULE

Licinius had a number of reasons to temper antagonisms against the Christians in the east. Chief among these was the threat posed by his own rival, Maximin Daia, an avowed persecutor. Although the two had ironed out their differences at a meeting on the Bosporus in the summer of 311, the very fact that negotiations had to be conducted on the watery no-man's land between their two realms confirms that relations were hardly cordial.[75] Thus while Constantine went back to Gaul in the spring of 313 to enjoy his new exclusive control of the western empire, Licinius traveled to Thrace to square off against Maximin. Maximin had taken advantage of Licinius's absence in Milan to march his army from Syria across Anatolia, over the Bosporus, and deep into Licinius's territory of Thrace. He had, however, miscalculated the effects of this winter slog on his troops. As the two approached battle in May of 313,

Licinius put to use publicity tactics similar to those employed recently by Constantine. He claimed to have seen a vision of the Supreme God (*summus deus*) in a dream and commanded his troops to memorize and recite a prayer conveyed in the dream before engaging battle.[76] When his forces prevailed in the ensuing conflict near the key city of Adrianople, Maximin abandoned his shattered army and fled in disgrace back to Anatolia. After collecting a makeshift force in Cappadocia, he retreated to the Cilician Gates, a formidable pass over the Taurus mountains, and, again repulsed, to the city of Tarsus. There, hemmed in and powerless, he seems to have gone insane, whether by having taken a poison or through some wasting disease, before he finally died in August. Licinius obliterated all remnants of his family and condemned Maximin with a *damnatio memoriae*.[77]

This brought to a definitive close the Tetrarchy as established by Diocletian. There were now just two rulers, both still allies, but not so firmly enmeshed in the intricate webs of power binding the earlier system.[78] Even so, peace prevailed inside the empire as Licinius engaged the Persians and Goths and Constantine the Germans in 314.[79] The mood is well reflected in an inscription of the following year from Tropaeum Traiani (Adamklissi) along the Danube recording the construction of a fort dedicated "to the avengers of Roman security and liberty, our lords Flavius Valerius Constantinus and V[alerius Licinianus Licinius]."[80] The very ordering of names confirms that the eastern emperor was willing to concede precedence to Constantine (compare Coin 16 of 320). But Constantine began pushing the situation ever more in his favor. In an incident only vaguely understood, he seems to have sent another brother-in-law of his, named Bassianus (married to his half-sister Anastasia), to Licinius for approval as a candidate for Caesar in 315. Far from representing an attempt to revive the Tetrarchy, however, the proposal must have been designed to help Constantine secure control over his succession with a dynastic ally. Licinius, who took the proposal amiss, had Bassianus's own brother Senecio arm Bassianus against Constantine instead. Constantine was thus forced to defeat and kill Bassianus, after which he ordered Licinius to turn over Senecio as well. Licinius refused and began having statues of Constantine desecrated in the city of Emona (Ljubljana), on the border between their realms.[81]

This constituted grounds for war. Constantine had spent the summer of 315, the year of his *decennalia*, or tenth regnal anniversary, in Rome. After returning to his base in Gaul for the winter, he was back in northern Italy by autumn 316, and by October he had moved into Licinius's realm and captured the Pannonian capital of Siscia (Sisak).

Licinius, meanwhile, took up a position to halt his eastward progress at the crossroads city of Cibalae (Vinkovci). On October 8, Constantine once again took the initiative, attacked, and, after a momentous battle, prevailed. Licinius, who had lost nearly two-thirds of his army, fled to Sirmium (Sremska Mitrovica), where he had left his wife, son, and treasury.[82] With these in tow he continued his flight eastward and, after having broken down the bridge over the River Savus (at Singidunum), he made his way into Thrace. The need to rebuild the bridge delayed Constantine, of course, and this bought Licinius enough time to regroup his army at Adrianople, where he had defeated Maximin in 313. During this period he appointed his own co-Augustus, a general named Valens, in a move that angered Constantine. Thus, after Constantine had reached the Thracian city of Philippopolis (Plovdiv) and Licinius refused his demands to remove Valens as a condition of peace, battle was resumed. Once again Licinius was worsted, at a site called Campus Ardiensis (probably Harmanli, between Philippopolis and Adrianople). Even after this second blow, however, Licinius did not lose his wits: rather than flee eastward, as Constantine might have expected, he took advantage of the cover of darkness to escape northwest to Boroea. Constantine, who did in fact continue east all the way to Byzantium in blind pursuit, only learned the truth of Licinius's whereabouts after his rival effectively controlled the highway to his west and thus his supply line back to the west.[83] Outfoxed, Constantine was forced to negotiate. As the clear victor, Constantine received favorable terms, but these fell short of Licinius's removal from power: Valens was dethroned; Constantine gained control of the central Balkans all the way up to Thrace; and his sons Crispus and Constantine II (Coin 17), along with Licinius's homonymous son, were to be appointed Caesars.[84]

The negotiations probably dragged on into early 317, and it was not until March 1 of that year that the new Caesars were formally acclaimed.[85] This date was far from accidental. Constantine had chosen it because it was the anniversary of his father's elevation to Caesar; as such it highlighted the fact that the elevation of Crispus and Constantine II carried the dynasty into a third generation – fourth if one includes Claudius Gothicus. Constantine and Licinius were thus pushing things ever further from the Tetrarchic model and back toward dynasty. Indeed, Crispus was at most seventeen years old at the time, Licinius II only twenty months, and Constantine II only seven months.[86] Constantine, however, was well aware that dynasty provided stability, and it was this that he sought more than adherence to Diocletian's system. He also stabilized his new holdings in the Balkans by shifting his primary residence from Trier, where he had been headquartered since 306, to Serdica (Sofia), which he took to calling "my Rome."[87] By the time Crispus reached full manhood the following year, however, Constantine sent him back to Trier to continue the job of defending the Rhine frontier against the barbarians.[88] And in the summer of 322, Constantine himself undertook a major war against the Sarmatians, who had ravaged the cities along the Danube bend, especially Campona. His successes were advertised in the poetry of Optatianus Porfyrius and in coins proclaiming SARMATIA DEVICTA (Sarmatia has been subdued; Coin 2).[89]

Relations with Licinius of course remained tense, and things only grew worse when Licinius began, c. 320, taking measures against Christians that could be construed as persecution: expelling Christians from imperial service, forbidding synods, and perhaps even condoning executions.[90] By now Constantine had begun to portray his civil war against Maxentius as motivated by the need to protect Christians against persecutions and had become increasingly bold in his self-advertisement as a champion of the faith.[91] By 321 he and Licinius began refusing to recognize one another's annually appointed consuls, and in 322 Licinius refused to distribute coinage advertising Constantine's Sarmatian victory.[92] Things came to a head in 323 when Constantine encroached on Licinius's territory in order to suppress yet another barbarian invasion, this time by the Goths.[93] Licinius could legitimately argue that Constantine had broken their treaty, and preparations were made for war.[94]

THE FINAL CONFLICT WITH LICINIUS

Constantine established a base on the Aegean at the port city of Thessalonica, where he began constructing a massive fleet. Crispus, his son and Caesar, now an experienced commander after six years of campaigning on the Rhine, was summoned and given command of these ships. In the summer of 324, Constantine moved out from Thessalonica with his army and met Licinius once again near Adrianople. Here too he seized the initiative by crossing the river Hebrus and taking the battle to Licinius on July 3. After an extended engagement in which Constantine himself was wounded, he defeated his rival and forced his flight to Byzantium.[95] There a mighty siege was undertaken against a city now packed with Licinius's tattered army.[96] Sitting as it does on a horn of land projecting into the Propontis, Byzantium offers excellent protection against a siege. It is approachable by land armies only from the west and then only by a narrow peninsula, while the sea surrounding the rest permits easy provisioning. It was with this in mind that Constantine had sent Crispus with his new fleet to wrest control of the Propontis from Licinius; Licinius, however, had anticipated this, assembled his own fleet under the commander Amandus, and sent him to guard the sea-lane.[97] Crispus, still in his early twenties, followed his father's example and took the battle to Licinius's admiral at the mouth of the Hellespont near Elaius (Seddülbahir). Knowing that this strait is narrow and its current swift, Crispus wisely deployed only eighty ships for the first engagement. These easily outmaneuvered and defeated the bloated 300-ship fleet deployed by Amandus. The next day, when Amandus's remaining ships squared off against Crispus's full fleet – near Callipolis (Gallipoli) at the inlet of the Propontis – they were crushed against the shore by strong winds. With just four ships remaining, Amandus retreated to Byzantium to meet Licinius, who realized that his hopes of retaining the city had been lost with his fleet and fled across the Bosporus to Chalcedon (Kadiköy).[98]

There Licinius repeated his earlier tactic of naming a co-Augustus, this time Martinianus, his former master of the offices.[99] Licinius was acutely aware of the advantage enjoyed by Constantine in having a loyal son of the age and experience to be useful as a coruler and deputy commander.[100] Martinianus, although not a relative, was appointed to play a similar role and was promptly dispatched with an army to Lampsacus (Lapseki) to prevent Constantine from crossing the Hellespont. Constantine, however, once again outmaneuvered his opponent by building a separate fleet of transport skiffs – quite apart from the fleet he had occupying the Propontis – and ferrying his army across to Asia near the northern end of the Bosporus at the Sacred Promontory, 35 kilometers from Licinius in Chalcedon.[101] Again caught by surprise, Licinius desperately recalled Martinianus – 400 kilometers away by land route – and marched north to meet Constantine. It is not clear whether Martinianus reached him before September 18, when Licinius engaged battle one final time at Chrysopolis (Skutari). The remains of his army were crushed by Constantine's, and he narrowly escaped to Nicomedia 100 kilometers away.[102] With no troops to support him, Licinius initiated negotiations through his wife, Constantia, who managed to convince her half-brother to spare the life of Licinius and his son, provided the two abdicate. Martinianus was also removed from power and shortly thereafter eliminated. The two Licinii were sent to Thessalonica, where they were kept under house arrest. Their acts and images were nullified through *damnatio memoriae*, and by 325 and 326, respectively, father and son were executed on suspicion of treason.[103]

CHRISTIANISSIMUS IMPERATOR

Constantine and his empire had entered a new era. It had been nearly four decades since Rome had fallen under the control of a single ruler. With his victory over Licinius, Constantine had captured sole power for himself and his dynasty for the next four decades.[104] Almost immediately he began ushering in the profound changes that would leave a Constantinian stamp on Roman history for centuries to come. Chief among these was his choice to refound Byzantium as his eponymous capital of Constantinople. In both of his wars against Licinius, and indeed in wars stretching back through Roman history, Byzantium had played a significant role. Its strategic location within the empire, its comfortable proximity to the Danube frontier, its defensibility, and its crucial role as a gateway between west and east rendered it ideal to serve as capital of an empire whose center of gravity had long been moving northward and eastward. Though much about Constantinople's foundation remains shrouded in legend, Themistius gives us good reason to believe that its new status had already been proclaimed by November of 324.[105] By May 11, 330, Constantine believed that the new capital was ready for dedication in a ceremony at which he himself presided.[106] To be sure, most of the Tetrarchs had founded new capitals of their own beginning already in the 290s,[107] but Constantinople represented something new both in scale and claims to status (see Map 4). It was furnished by its founder with a new fortification wall on its western end, a rationalized street grid, a new imperial palace with direct access to a newly extended hippodrome, a bath complex, a capitolium, a grand circular forum, a senate house, two martyria, and two further churches – Holy Peace and the emperor's new mausoleum church Holy Apostles (Plan 2). Its people were endowed with food rations like Rome's, a new senate like the Roman Senate, and a new mint.[108] In gestures typical of his polyvalent religious politics, the Christian emperor even built or rebuilt several temples, and in the middle of his forum he erected a column of porphyry featuring at its pinnacle a statue of himself holding a globe and scepter and bedizened with sunrays projecting from its head (Figs. 2 and 3).[109] No observer could escape the visual parallel with the standard image of Sol Invictus, Constantine's favored pagan god from 310 onward, who appears regularly on Constantinian coins down to

325 (Coins 4, 14, and 15).[110] Constantinople was thus hardly a water-tight Christian levee against the receding tides of paganism.

Pagans did, however, find room to grumble that many of the statues that adorned the new capital were pilfered from their shrines, and much of the wealth used in its construction was confiscated from pagan temple treasuries.[111] Indeed, it would be hard to deny that there was something of an air of Christian triumphalism behind the new foundation, which Constantine claimed to have renamed at God's command, even if this message was always dampened with the usual ambiguity.[112] More than anything, Constantinople began challenging Rome, a city long favored by Constantine, with claims to the status of being the "New Rome," an eastern rival to its Italian forebear. This claim had already been asserted by 326 and became widely accepted by the last quarter of the fourth century.[113] By the fifth century, public awareness had grown that Constantinople was to inherit Rome's role as the imperial capital, a legacy that guaranteed its lofty status down to its surrender to the Ottomans in 1453, nearly a millennium after the fall of the western capital.

These were heady times for Constantine and his family. With no rival to challenge his authority, he could bolster his dynastic arrangements with members of his sizable clan – by 324 he had four sons, Crispus, Constantine II, Constantius II, and Constans; two daughters; and a host of extended relatives. On November 8, 324, he elevated Constantius II to Caesar (Coin 18),[114] thus joining him to Crispus and Constantine II. Around the same time, he also elevated his wife Fausta and mother Helena to Augusta and began striking coins featuring their images and titles (Coins 11 and 19).[115] Similarly, his half-sister Constantia, though recently tarnished by her association with Licinius, was soon restored to favor, exercised tremendous influence over her brother's religious policies, and eventually won the honor of having a Palestinian city named after her (Constantia, formerly Maiuma).[116] Not since the age of the Severans had the royal women played such an important role in imperial politics, and none was more powerful than the queen mother. By her death in 328/9 Constantine had refounded the coastal city of Drepanum, home of the shrine of her favorite martyr Lucian, as Helenopolis (Hersek).[117] She was not buried there, however, but in Rome, in a mausoleum and indeed a sarcophagus that Constantine may have originally intended for himself while still resident in the west (Figs. 21 and 22, Plan 3).[118] After his relocation eastward, Constantine had established his mother in the revamped Sessorian palace on the city's southeastern edge.[119] There he probably met her in July of 326 when he returned to Rome to repeat the celebrations for his *vicennalia* (twentieth regnal anniversary), having already celebrated the same event the previous summer in Nicomedia.[120]

In the course of these celebrations, however, things turned sour. Probably during this, his third visit to Rome, Constantine refused for the first time to mount the steps of the Capitoline hill for the celebration of a sacrifice to Jupiter, Rome's state god. This religious slight, coupled with the obvious rivalry introduced by the refoundation of Constantinople as a rival to Rome, created tensions that erupted in vehement protests and eventually led to a permanent cooling of relations with the Senate and people of Rome.[121] In addition, in the late summer or early autumn of the same year, Constantine had his son Crispus, by now a military hero, executed. Shortly thereafter he ordered his wife Fausta killed in gruesome fashion – cooked to death in a superheated bath chamber. The reason for these brutal family murders remains a mystery. Sources favorable to Constantine, especially Eusebius, gloss over the events without mention. Those that report details are generally hostile and thus biased. The most complete version traces back to a pagan account used by Zosimus and Zonaras. According to this version, Fausta fell in love with Crispus but was rebuffed. After she went to Constantine to accuse Crispus of attempted rape, he had his son murdered, only to learn the truth, then ordered Fausta's extermination as well.[122] The story is so redolent of Greek tragedy that many modern critics have dismissed it out of hand. But Constantine was, at this very time, obsessed with punishing adultery,[123] and Fausta would have had good grounds to wish her stepson dead in order to remove an older and more impressive rival from her sons' path to rule. There may then be a kernel of truth in this pagan version.[124]

It was with these executions weighing on her that Helena journeyed to the Holy Land in 327 with the intention of rediscovering the sacred topography of Christ's life. Her journey cannot have been without the support of her son, but her driving role in revivifying the Holy Land as a center of sacred geography has often been unjustly underplayed by moderns.[125] While there, Helena claimed to have found the cave in which Jesus was born in Bethlehem and the point from which he ascended to heaven on the Mount of Olives. At the same time, Macarius, bishop of Jerusalem, helped disencumber what he believed to be the tomb in which Jesus's body was laid, the Holy Sepulcher, and legend has it that Helena also believed she had found the very cross on which Christ died.[126] At each of these sites, and especially at the site of the Holy Sepulcher, major building operations were undertaken that culminated in a dedication ceremony for the church at that site (Plan 4) during which Eusebius delivered a still extant panegyric in 335.[127] As with the refoundation of Byzantium as the new imperial capital of Constantinople, the reinvention of the Holy Land as a site of Christian pilgrimage and a locus of Christian spiritual power would have profound effects that lasted through the middle ages and down to the present.

The church too, however, seemed to slip from Constantine's grasp just as he gained control of world empire. Even before his acquisition of the eastern empire, a bitter controversy had begun to roil in the church of Egypt. The already contentious Alexandrian diocese witnessed the rise of a heated dispute between its bishop Alexander and his priest Arius over the nature of Christ's person: Was Christ created or had he always been? Was Christ of the same nature as the Father or in some way different and thus inferior? After securing Licinius's surrender in the summer of 324, Constantine appears to have proceeded eastward as far as Antioch and from there to have addressed a letter of rebuke to the instigators of the controversy; shortly thereafter he called a council to be held the following spring.[128] When it met at Nicaea in May 325, he presided over the roughly three hundred bishops summoned from across the empire and succeeded in imposing his decision on all but a few recalcitrants: Christ was unequivocally uncreated and of the same nature as the Father! With this, Constantine probably assumed that he had stamped out the fires of controversy. Instead, he had merely scattered its sparks across the empire, where they would flare up for the rest of the century. Even so, Constantine's efforts to impose concord on a contentious church were genuine and reflected part of a larger program of spirituality that characterized the last decade of his reign. By now in his late fifties, he transformed himself from an energetic soldier and tyrant slayer into a spiritual monarch.[129]

THE FINAL YEARS

This transformation rendered Constantine content to leave most of the business of warfare to his Caesars. Four years after gaining control of Thrace (328), Constantine had constructed a massive stone bridge across the Danube at Oescus (Gigen) and a fortified bridgehead on the opposite shore of the river from Transmarisca (Tutrakan), which he named Constantiana Daphne (Spantov; Coin 20).[130] These greatly facilitated access into Gothic territory when a group of Goths crossed into the Hungarian Banat and attacked the neighboring Sarmatians. Constantine was able to send his eldest living son, Constantine II, north of the Danube to corner the Goths, defeat them in battle, and starve them into making a treaty favorable to the Romans in 332.[131] In keeping with his policy of gradually transferring power to his successors, Constantine added to his roster of coemperors by elevating his youngest son, Constans, to Caesar on December 25, 333 (Coin 21).[132] The following year, the same Sarmatians, who had armed their slaves as a defense against the Goths, found themselves expelled from their territory by those same slaves and required resettlement in Roman territory. Again Constantine II seems to have been heavily involved.[133] Also in 334 Calocaerus, whose unenviable title of "Master of the Flock and Camels" says much about his status, broke into revolt on Cyprus but was easily suppressed, not by Constantine but by his half-brother Dalmatius.[134] Constantine was thus ceding the duties of the soldier emperor to his dynastic successors.

Only one barbarian people remained as yet unconquered, the Persians. From early in his reign, Constantine seemed to have a sense of a natural west to east progress of his dominion. In speeches and documents, he often repeats the mantra that he had raised up the whole world beginning at the western ocean and the shores of Britain and moving to the east.[135] In some sense, he had laid the groundwork for a Persian campaign shortly after gaining control of the east when he answered embassies from the Persian Shah Shapur II with a long letter reporting his Christian faith, his successes over its persecutors, and his desire to see Shapur protect the Christians in his own realm.[136] In many ways, then, Shapur played into Constantine's hands c. 334 when he removed from power the Christian king of Armenia and replaced him with a Persian appointee.[137] Shapur had long been awaiting an opportunity to regain control over a series of territories on the Perso-Armenian border that his grandfather had lost to emperor Galerius in 298.[138] His theft of suzerainty over Armenia thus represented the opening gambit in a foreign relations match that would last down to the 380s. Constantine countered Shapur's seizure of Armenia by appointing a fourth Caesar, the homonymous son of the aforementioned Dalmatius, to manage Thrace, Macedonia, and Achaea; by naming another of Dalmatius's sons, Hannibalianus, "King of Kings and of the Pontic Peoples," to assert control over the sub-Caucasus region (both in 335); and by dispatching his own son Constantius II to Antioch to confront Shapur directly.[139] Subsequent negotiations soon broke down, and Constantine pushed ahead with plans to lead an army personally against Shapur. Well aware of the infirmity of his age, however, he probably intended less to battle down the Persians than to scare them into submission with some close-in saber rattling.[140] Perhaps with this in mind, he plotted a route to the

Persian frontier replete with nonessential stops, including a layover in the Holy Land, where he hoped to be baptized in the Jordan River.[141] Instead, only 80 kilometers into his journey the infirm emperor fell deathly ill at Nicomedia, where he received baptism at the hands of the Arianizing bishop Eusebius.[142] He died shortly thereafter at a suburban villa named Achyron on May 22, 337.[143]

His son Constantius II hastened from the eastern frontier to Nicomedia and transported his father's body in a golden casket to Constantinople. It lay in state for a considerable time, enough for the citizens of Rome to petition for its interment in their city. Constantius, however, chose to entomb it in Constantinople in Constantine's new Mausoleum of Holy Apostles after an elaborate Christian funeral.[144] There it received its place amidst the remains of Andrew and Luke and among cenotaphs for the remaining apostles, thus making Constantine into something of a thirteenth apostle.[145] Coins were struck for the deified Constantine, described by Eusebius as "portraying the Blessed One on the obverse in the form of one with head veiled, on the reverse like a charioteer on a quadriga, being taken up by a right hand stretched out to him from above"[146] (Coin 22). Much of this ceremonial was new and distinctly Christian. Much, however, only slightly modified the pagan traditions of imperial consecration from previous centuries. Even on the coins, the emperor's symbolism was polyvalent, for strikingly similar consecration issues had been common for deified emperors since the first century AD.[147] In death as in life, Constantine remained an enigma, a man whose ongoing self-refashioning rendered him at once a brilliant politician and an incredibly complex study.

FURTHER READING

To number the books and articles that narrate the reign of Constantine would be like counting the sands of the sea or the stars of the sky. I point here to only a sample of the resources available in the western languages most likely to be useful to the readers of this book. The most comprehensive and reliable treatment in English remains T. D. Barnes, *Constantine and Eusebius* (1981), though it is superceded in some details. For a shorter but generally accurate account, see H. A. Pohlsander, *The Emperor Constantine* (1996). Odahl 2004 is rich in dramatic detail, not all of it traceable to the sources. An excellent new survey of the broader period can be found in D. Potter, *The Roman Empire at Bay AD 180–395* (2004). In German, several introductions to the reign of Constantine have appeared in the last decade, the best being B. Bleckmann, *Konstantin der Große* (1996), though H. Brandt, *Geschichte der römischen Kaiserzeit von Diokletian und Konstantin bis zum Ende der konstantinischen Dynastie (284–363)* (1998), is also quite useful for the sources it provides. In Italian, A. Marcone, *Costantino il Grande* (2000), is short but accurate and insightful. There have been no recent monographs in French. One awaits with anticipation the appearance of the second edition of *The Cambridge Ancient History* vol. 12, which will no doubt add immensely to the discussion.

NOTES

1   See T. D. Barnes 1982, 39–42; Kienast 1996, 298; Potter 2004, 663 n. 46; contrast Nixon 1993, 240. The place is taken from *Origo* 2; Firm. Mat. *Math.* 1.10.13. The day is from *Chron. 354* and Polemius Silvius, both at *CIL* 1^2:255, 258, 259. The year derives from Jer. *Chron.* s.a. 337; Eutr. 10.8; Soc. 1.39.1. For the year 276, see Aur. Vict. *Caes.* 41.16; cf. Eus. *VC* 1.8.1, 4.53.1.

2   E.g., Eus. *VC* 2.51.1, 4.53.1; *Pan. Lat.* 7(6).5.2–3, 6(7).17.1, 4(10).16.4; cf. Lact. *DMP* 18.10, 24.4, 29.5. On art, see Chapter 11 in this volume.

3   Jer. *Chron.* s.a. 306; *Origo* 2; Ambrose *De Obit. Theod.* 42; cf. Zos. 2.8.2; Eutr. 10.2; Zon. 13.1.4. Her lowly status and tenuous conjugal ties were whitewashed in Constantinian propaganda; cf. *CIL* 10:517 = *ILS* 708. See also *PLRE* 1 Fl Iulia Helena 3; Drijvers 1992, 9–19; Leadbetter 1998.

4   Sources at *PLRE* 1 Theodora 1.

5   See *PLRE* 1 Fl. Val. Constantius 12; Kienast 1996, 280–2.

6   More on the formation of the Tetrarchy in Chapter 2 of this volume.

7   See T. D. Barnes 1981, 73–5; Millar 1992, 205–6; Corcoran 2000, 259–65, 253–4.

8   *Origo* 2–3; *OC* 16; Eus. *VC* 1.12.1–2, 1.19.1; cf. *Pan. Lat.* 7(6).5.3, 6(7).3.3; Lact. *DMP* 18.10; Theophan. a.m. 5788. On Constantine's early career, see T. D. Barnes 1976a, 250–1; 1982, 41–2; and below n. 12.

9   See *PLRE* 1 Galerius Valerius Maximinus Daia 12; Fl. Val. Severus 30; Kienast 1996, 288–90.

10 See *PLRE* 1 Flavius Dalmatius 6; Iulius Constantius 7; Fl. Hannibalianus 1; M. Aur. Val. Maxentius 5. See also Kienast 1996, 291; T. D. Barnes 1981, 39–43; 1996b, 544–6; cf. Mackay 1999, on the possibility that Constantine and Maxentius were originally intended as successors but later passed over.

11 Lact. *DMP* 18.13–14; *Epit.* 40.1, 18; Zos. 2.8.1, with Mackay 1999, 202–5, and T. D. Barnes 1999, on whether Maximin was also related to Galerius by marriage.

12 *Origo* 3; Praxagoras fr. 1.2 (*FGH* 2B219:948); Zon. 12.33; cf. *Pan. Lat.* 6(7).3.3; Lact. *DMP* 24.4; Eus. *VC* 1.20.1–2.

13 Lact. *DMP* 18.10.

14 *Origo* 4; Lact. *DMP* 24.3–9; Praxagoras fr. 1.2 (*FGH* 2B219:948); Aur. Vict. *Caes.* 40.2–3; *Epit.* 41.2; Zos. 2.8.3; Eus. *VC* 1.21.

15 *Origo* 4; *Pan. Lat.* 6(7).7.5; cf. Lib. *Or.* 59.17–18; *AE* 1961, 240, with König 1987, 71–4. For the deathbed legend, see Lact. *DMP* 24.8; Eus. *VC* 18.2, 21.1–2; cf. Aur. Vict. *Caes.* 40.3; *Epit.* 41.2.

16 On the date, see *CIL* 1²:268–9; *Cons. Const.* s.a. 306; Soc. 1.2.1. For a full list of sources, see *PLRE* 1 Fl. Val. Constantinus 4, esp. Lact. *DMP* 24.8. See *Pan. Lat.* 7(6).7.3–4 for Constantius's approval and *Epit.* 41.3 for the role of the Alamannic *rex* Crocus. T. D. Barnes 1996a, 539–41, offers discussion and bibliography on the vexed question of a possible alternate *dies imperii* for Constantine.

17 Lact. *DMP* 25.1–5; cf. *Pan. Lat.* 6(7).8.2; *ILS* 657, 682. Grünewald 1990, 14–16, shows that Constantine initially accepted this demotion.

18 Zos. 2.9.2.

19 Lact. *DMP* 26.1–3, 6–7; Zos. 2.9.3; *Origo* 6; Eutr. 10.2.3; Aur. Vict. *Caes.* 40.5; *Epit.* 40.2, 10–12; Jer. *Chron.* s.a. 307; Soc. 1.2.1. For the title *princeps*, see *RIC* 6:338–9, 367–70. For commentary, see especially Paschoud 1971b, 194.

20 Lact. *DMP* 26.6–7; Eutr. 10.2.3; cf. *Pan. Lat.* 7(6).8.7–12.8 for the sanitized "official" version.

21 Lact. *DMP* 26.2–3; cf. Aur. Vict. *Caes.* 39.47.

22 See Curran 2000, 50–63; cf. Cullhed 1994, with caution.

23 *Pan. Lat.* 12(9).3.4; Zos. 2.10.1–2; *Origo* 9–10; Lact. *DMP* 26.4–11; Eutr. 10.3.4; Aur. Vict. *Caes.* 40.6–7; *Epit.* 40.3; Jer. *Chron.* s.a. 307; *Cons. Const.* s.a. 307. The sources are contradictory about precisely when Maximian joined Maxentius's revolt. I follow Lact. *DMP* 26.6–9 in assuming he was already with Maxentius when Severus reached Rome with his army; cf. Paschoud 1971b, 195–6.

24 *Pan. Lat.* 12(9).3.4; Lact. *DMP* 27.1–6; *Origo* 6–8; Aur. Vict. *Caes.* 40.8–9; Zos. 2.10.3; Zon. 12.34. On the timing of Severus's death, see *Origo* 10, with Creed 1984, 107–8.

25 *Pan. Lat.* 7(6).4.2, 6(7).10.2–11.6, 4(10).16.5–6; Eutr. 10.3.2.

26 *Pan. Lat.* 6(7).12.1–13.5, 4(10).18.1–19.2. On the bridge, see Nixon and Rodgers 1994, 235–6 n. 56.

27 *Pan. Lat.* 7(6) passim, esp. 6.1–7.4; Lact. *DMP* 27.1; Zos. 2.10.5–7; Zon. 13.1; *RIC* 6 Trier 639–4, 744–6. Fausta was probably about 17 at the time; cf. T. D. Barnes 1982, 34; contra Potter 2004, 347. There is no proving whether Minervina was Constantine's wife or concubine; contrast Nixon and Rodgers 1994, 195 n. 10, with Pohlsander 1984, 80.

28 *Pan. Lat.* 7(6).1.1, 2.1, 5.3, 8.1; cf. Nixon and Rodgers 1994, 179–81. Grünewald 1990, 16–41, which shows that Constantine began distancing himself from his Tetrarchic colleagues already in 307.

29 *Pan. Lat.* 7(6).14.1–2 (trans. Nixon and Rodgers). On this speech, see Nixon and Rodgers 1994, 178–90. Grünewald 1990, 25–41, demonstrates that the marriage took place in Arles.

30 *Pan. Lat.* 12(9).3.4; Lact. *DMP* 28.1–4; Eutr. 10.3.1–2; *Origo* 8; Zos. 2.11.1.

31 Zos. 2.12.1–3, with Paschoud 1971b, 199; Aur. Vict. *Caes.* 40.17–19; *Epit.* 40.2, 20; *CIL* 8:7004 = *ILS* 674; *CIL* 8:22183 = *ILS* 8936; *AE* 1966, 169; *RIC* 6:434 n. 66; Polemius Silvius 1.62 (*MGH.AA* 9:522). On dates, see T. D. Barnes 1982, 14–15.

32 Alexander recognized Constantine on his inscriptions (*CIL* 8:22183 = *ILS* 8936). Constantine did not reciprocate in kind but probably offered some limited support; cf. Aiello 1988; Kuhoff 1991, 136 n. 24. Though earlier scholarship had argued that Constantine took advantage of Domitius Alexander's revolt to wrest Spain from Maxentius's control, it is probable that Constantine controlled it from the beginning of his reign; see Christol and Sillières 1980.

33 *Pan. Lat.* 12(9).4.4; Zos. 2.13.1; Aur. Vict. *Caes.* 40.24; *Chron. 354* (*MGH.AA* 9:148); Eus. *HE* 8.14.3; *VC* 1.35.1.

34 Eus. *HE* 8.14.1–6; *VC* 1.33.1–36.2; *Pan. Lat.* 4(10).8.3, 12(9).3.1–4.4; cf. *Liber Pont.* 31. See also T. D. Barnes 1981, 38–9, 303–4; Curran 2000, 63–5.

35 *Epit.* 39.6.

36 Full details and sources at T. D. Barnes 1981, 32–3. Cf. *PLRE* 1 Val. Licinianus Licinius 3; Kienast 1996, 294–7.

37 *Pan. Lat.* 6(7).14.1–20.4; Lact. *DMP* 29.3–8; Aur. Vict. *Caes.* 40.21–2; *Epit.* 40.5; Jer. *Chron.* s.a. 308; *Cons. Const.* s.a. 310; Eutr. 10.3.2; Zos. 2.11.1; Eus. *HE* 8.13.15; *VC* 1.47.1; Zon. 12.33.

38 Lact. *DMP* 30.1–6; cf. *Pan. Lat.* 6(7).14.5, but see T. D. Barnes 1973, 41–3.

39 *Pan. Lat.* 6(7).2.1–2 (trans. Nixon and Rodgers). On this oration, see Nixon and Rodgers 1994, 211–7.

40 See, e.g., *Pan. Lat.* 5(8).2.5, 4.2; *ILS* 699, 702, 723, 725, 730, 732; *AE* 1952, 107; Optat. Porf. *Carm.* 8.11–12, 27–8, 10.28–32; Jul. *Or.* 1.6d, 3.51c; *Caes.* 336b; *Origo* 1; Eutr. 9.22; Jer. *Chron.* s.a. 289–91. For the mendacity of this legend, see Syme 1974; cf. Grünewald 1990, 46–50.

41 *Pan. Lat.* 6.21.4–5 (trans. Nixon and Rodgers). Nixon and Rodgers 1994, 248–51, offer commentary and bibliography; see also Rodgers 1980 and Grünewald 1990, 50–61.

42 Bruun 1958; M. Alföldi 1964; Christodoulou 1998, 56–65.

43 Weiss 1993, translated with addenda in Weiss 2003. The same hypothesis, mentioned, e.g., at Jones 1949, 96–7, goes back centuries but had not been adequately elaborated. It is by no means universally accepted.

44 On the Great Persecution, see above Chapter 2 and below Chapter 5 in this volume.

45 Lact. *DMP* 33.1–35.4; Eus. *HE* 8.16.1–17.11; *VC* 1.57.1–3; cf. *Origo* 8; Aur. Vict. *Caes.* 40.9–13; *Epit.* 40.4; Jer. *Chron.* s.a. 309; Eutr. 10.4.2; *Chron. Pasch.* pp. 522–3. On the date of Galerius's death, see T. D. Barnes 1982, 31–2.

46 Lact. *DMP* 36.3–37.2, 48.4; Eus. *HE* 8.14.7–10, 9.2.1–7.16, 9.9.13–10.12; *Chron. Pasch.* pp. 519–20. More on the chronology of Maximin Daia's persecution at T. D. Barnes 1982, 67–8. Important epigraphic finds confirm the written sources; cf. *CIL* 3:12132 = *IK* 48 nr. 12 (Arycanda); Mitchell 1988 (Colbasa); Merkelbach and Stauber 1999. See also Nicholson 1994.

47 Eus. *VC* 1.13.1–3, 16.1–17.3, 20.3, 2.49.1; Optat. 1.22; cf. Lact. *DMP* 8.7, 15.7; Eus. *HE* 8.13.12–13; Soz. 1.6.1–4. Some have argued that Constantius was even Christian, e.g., Elliott 1996, 17–27. Most of the evidence, however, indicates he was pagan, e.g., M. D. Smith 1997, who also shows that he was not particularly devoted to the sun god Sol, as often assumed.

48 Lact. *DMP* 24.9; *Div. Inst.* 1.1.13. Maxentius had also proclaimed tolerance for Christians at the beginning of his reign; Eus. *HE* 8.14.2; Optat. 1.18.

49 Lact. *DMP* 43.4–6; Zos. 2.14.1; *RIC* 6 Roma 243–4, 250–1; Ostia 24–6; cf. *CIL* 9:4516 = *ILS* 647; *CIL* 10:5805.

50 Lact. *DMP* 42.1; Eus. *HE* 8.13.15; *VC* 1.47.1. On the timing, see T. D. Barnes 1973, 34–5; 1982, 34–5.

51 Lact. *DMP* 44.2; Aur. Vict. *Caes.* 40.18–19, 28; Zos. 2.14.2–4.

52 Lact. *DMP* 43.1–4; *Pan. Lat.* 4(10).9.1–12.3; Zos. 2.14.1. *ILAlg.* 3949, an inscription of Maxentius and Constantine, shows evidence that Constantine's name was hammered out after the rupture with Maxentius.

53 Lact. *DMP* 32.1–5; Eus. *HE* 8.13.15. Cf. Lact. *DMP* 44.11–12; Eus. *HE* 9.10.1 on Maximin's yearning for preeminence.

54 Constantine had fewer than 40,000 men; *Pan. Lat.* 12(9).5.1–2; contrast Zos. 2.15.1–2. Burckhardt [1880] 1949, 259, compares Constantine's blitzkrieg to Napoleon's youthful Italian campaign; cf. Potter 2004, 357.

55 On the battles in northern Italy, see *Pan. Lat.* 12(9).5.1–11.4 and 4(10).17.3, 21.1–27.2, with commentary at Nixon and Rodgers 1994, 303–13, 367–72; cf. *Origo* 12; Aur. Vict. *Caes.* 40.20–22; Eus. *HE* 9.9.2–3; *VC* 37.2.

56 The details in the sources on the battle of the Milvian Bridge are often contradictory. I assemble them from various sources in a way that seems fitting. See *Pan. Lat.* 12(9).15.1–17.3, 4(10).28.1–29.6; *Origo* 12; Lact. *DMP* 44.1–9; Eus. *HE* 9.9.2–8; *VC* 1.38.1–5; Praxagoras fr. 1.4 (*FGH* 2B219:948); Zos. 2.15.3–16.4; *Epit.* 40.7; Lib. *Or.* 59.19–21; Jer. *Chron.* s.a. 312; Eutr. 10.4.3; Aur. Vict. *Caes.* 40.23; *Chron. 354* (*MGH.AA* 9:148).

57 On the monument, see Messineo and Calci 1989; Holloway 2004, 53–4.

58 On the date, see *CIL* I²:274; cf. Lact. *DMP* 44.4. On the oracle, Lact. *DMP* 44.8; Zos. 2.16.1; cf. *Pan. Lat.* 4(10).27.5–6.

59 I accept the report of Aur. Vict. *Caes.* 40.23 that the first major engagement took place at Saxa Rubra, although this contradicts the contemporary testimony at *Pan. Lat.* 12(9).16.3–4 and 4(10).28.1–5 that Maxentius chose to line up with the Tiber at his rear. Tactically this makes no sense, nor does the notion that Maxentius would cross the Tiber to meet Constantine if his men were already pressing down on the city. Fuller arguments at Kuhoff 1991, 147–62.

60 *CIL* I²:274; *Pan. Lat.* 12(9).16.2, 18.3–19.4, 4(10).30.4–32.5; Lact. *DMP* 44.10–12; Eus. *HE* 9.9.8–11; *VC* 1.39.2–3; Praxagoras fr. 1.4 (*FGH* 2B219:948); *Origo* 12; Zos. 2.17.1–2; Aur. Vict. *Caes.* 40.24–5; *Chron. Pasch.* p. 521.

61 *CIL* 6:1139 = *ILS* 694 (trans. Lee 2000, 83); cf. Grünewald 1990, 63–86. On the arch, see Holloway 2004, 19–53, and Elsner 2000a.

62 *Pan. Lat.* 12(9).3.6–4.5, 14.2–15.2; cf. *Pan. Lat.* 4(10).6.2–13.5, 33.1–34.1; and above n. 34.

63 See Holloway 2004, 55–6, and below Chapter 12 in this volume.

64 On clemency, see *Pan. Lat.* 12(9).20.1–21.3; *PLRE* 1 C. Ceionius Rufius Volusianus 4; and esp. *CIL* 6:1140 = *ILS* 692.

65 See the similar allusiveness at *Pan. Lat.* 12(9).2.4–6. On the phrase, see Jones Hall 1998.

66 Lact. *DMP* 44.5–6 (trans. Creed).

67 See above notes 41–3.

68 This explains the conflation of vision and dream by Eus. *VC* 1.28.1–32.3; cf. Soc. 1.2.4–7; Soz. 1.3.1–3; Philost. 1.6. For a different interpretation, see the important article by Van Dam 2003.

69 Bruun 1962; cf. Eus. *VC* 1.31.1; M. Alföldi 1964; and Bruun 1965.

70 See Curran 2000, 93, and below Chapter 12. Taking over another structure from Maxentius, his massive basilica, Constantine completed it and graced it with a colossal statue of himself bearing a cross and a triumphal Christian inscription; Eus. *HE* 9.9.10; *LC* 9.8–11; *VC* 1.40.1–2. Unfortunately, we cannot know the statue's date, but from iconography it would appear to fall later in his reign.

71 Eus. *HE* 10.5.15–17, 6.1–5, 7.1–2, with Maier 1987–9, 1:139–44. Cf. Eus. *VC* 1.41.3–42.1; Optat. *App.* 10; *CTh* 16.2.2.

72 See Chapters 5 and 6 in this volume.

73 Lact. *DMP* 45.1; Eus. *HE* 10.8.3–4; *VC* 1.49.2–50.1; *Epit.* 41.4; *Origo* 13; Aur. Vict. *Caes.* 41.2; Zos. 2.17.2.

74 Lact. *DMP* 48.2–12; Eus. *HE* 9.9.12, 10.5.1–14; cited below at Chapter 5 n. 25 in this volume. On this vexatious decree, see recently Calderone 2001, 135–204.

75 Lact. *DMP* 36.1–2; cf. *CIL* 3:7174 = *ILS* 663.

76 Lact. *DMP* 46.3–7. The prayer was very similar to that used by Constantine with his troops; see Eus. *VC* 4.19–20.

77 Lact. *DMP* 45.1–47.6, 49.1–50.7; Zos. 2.17.2–3; Aur. Vict. *Caes.* 41.1; *Epit.* 40.8; Jer. *Chron.* s.a. 311; *Chron. 354* (*MGH.AA* 9:148); *Chron. Pasch.* p. 521; Eutr. 10.4.4; Eus. *HE* 9.9.1, 10.13–15; *VC* 58.1–59.1.

78 Diocletian, meanwhile, had died in retirement, probably on December 3, 312; cf. Nakamura 2003.

79 Sources at T. D. Barnes 1982, 72, 81.

80 *CIL* 3:13734 = *ILS* 8938.

81 *Origo* 14–15, with König 1987, 113–7. Cf. Eus. *HE* 10.8.5–7; *VC* 1.47.2. Zos. 2.18.1 attributes the falling-out to Constantine's efforts to gain control of some of Licinius's provinces. If this is not simply a confusion with the events leading up to the civil war of 324, it may imply that Constantine wished his subordinate Bassianus to take over rule in the western Balkans.

82 Zos. 2.18.1–5; *Origo* 16–17; Eutr. 10.5; Aur. Vict. *Caes.* 41.2, 6; *Epit.* 41.5. *Cons. Const.* dates the battle of Cibalae to 314 (cf. Jer. *Chron.* s.a. 313), which had been the traditional dating until Bruun 1953, 15–21, showed that the coins point to a date of 316; cf. Bruun 1961, 10–22. Habicht 1958 demonstrated that other sources confirm this; cf. Barnes 1973, 36–8. Subsequent arguments for both dates are summarized in Pohlsander 1995, who argues rightly for 316.

83 Zos. 2.18.5–19.3; *Origo* 17–18; *Epit.* 40.2. Though the sources call Valens merely Caesar, his coins prove he was full Augustus; *RIC* 7 Cyzicus 7; Alexandria 19. On the location of the battle, see König 1987, 128–9.

84 Petr. Patr. fr. 15 (*FHG* 4:189–90); Zos. 2.20.1–2; *Origo* 18–19; Aur. Vict. *Caes.* 41.6; Eutr. 10.5; *Epit.* 41.4; Jer. *Chron.* s.a. 317; Zon. 13.1. For details, see Paschoud 1971b, 210–13; T. D. Barnes 1981, 198; Pohlsander 1984, 86; König 1987, 131–4.

85 On the date, see *Cons. Const.* s.a. 317; *Chron. Pasch.* p. 523.

86 On these ages, see T. D. Barnes 1982, 44. Pohlsander 1984, 81–4, and König 1987, 137, argue Crispus was only twelve.

87 *Anon. Cont. Dio* fr. 15.1 (*FHG* 4:199); cf. Zon. 13.3.

88 On Crispus's military exploits, see Optat. Porf. *Carm.* 5.30–2; 8.33, 10.24–31; *Pan. Lat.* 4(10).17.1–2; Pohlsander 1984, 87–8.

89 Zos. 2.21.1–2; Optat. Porf. *Carm.* 6.14–28, 7.31–32, 18.5–12; *RIC* 7 London 289; Lyon 209, 212, 214, 219, 222; Trier 429, 435; Arles 257; Sirmium 48.

90 Jer. *Chron.* s.a. 320; Oros. 7.28.18; Eus. *HE* 10.8.1–9.3; *VC* 1.49.2–54.1; 2.1.1–2.3; 66.1; Soc. 1.3.1–4; Soz. 1.7.1–4; Theophan. a.m. 5811; cf. *CTh* 16.2.5; Aur. Vict. *Caes.* 41.3–5. Eus. *VC* 2.20.2–21.1, 30.1–39.1 discusses Constantine's efforts to rectify the effects of persecution in the east in 324, though not all of the punishments mentioned were initiated by Licinius.

91 This despite the fact that Maxentius actually granted indulgence to Christians; Optat. 1.18; Eus. *HE* 8.14.1; cf. T. D. Barnes 1981, 37–9; Curran 2000, 63–5. Maxentius's religious policy is treated extensively in De Decker 1968.

92 On the consuls, see Bagnall et al. 1987, 176–7. On the coins, see *Anon. Cont. Dio* fr. 14.1 (*FHG* 4:199).

93 The only confirmed testimony to this campaign is *Origo* 21, but this generally reliable source is quite circumstantial here and should not be dismissed. *CTh* 7.1.1 and 7.12.1, both from April 323, seem to hint at related problems, and Paschoud 1971b, 213 n. 31, has argued that Zos. 2.21.3 represents a confused reference to the same event. Even so, many regard the *Origo*'s testimony as a confusion for Constantine's Sarmatian campaign, which they would date to 323. It is certainly true that there is no numismatic or epigraphic testimony for a Gothic victory. The situation is thus open to dispute; contrast below Chapter 15 n. 67 in this volume.

94 *Origo* 21–2.

95 *Origo* 24–5; Zos. 2.22.3–23.1; cf. *Chron. Pasch.* p. 524; Aur. Vict. *Caes.* 41.8; Eus. *HE* 10.9.4–6; *VC* 2.5; Zon. 13.1.28. On the date, see sources at T. D. Barnes 1982, 75.

96 *Origo* 25–7; Zos. 2.23.1, 24.2–25.1

97 *Origo* 23; Zos. 2.22.1–3. On whether the name of Licinius's admiral was "Amandus" or "Abantus," see *PLRE* 1 Amandus 2; contrast Seeck 1920–3, 1:512. On naval warfare in this period, see Aiello 2000a.

98 Zos. 2.23.2–25.1; *Origo* 25–7; Optat. Porf. *Carm.* 19.35–6; Aur. Vict. *Caes.* 41.8. Though Eus. *HE* 10.9.4–6 and *VC* 2.6.1–18.1 contain information relevant to Constantine's wars against Licinius, their utter disregard for chronology renders them all but useless.

99 *Origo* 25; Aur. Vict. *Caes.* 41.8–9; *Epit.* 41.5–6; Zos. 2.25.2; cf. Joh. Lyd. *De mag.* 2.25. On the place and date, see Paschoud 1971b, 217, contra König 1987, 156–7. Once again, written sources refer to Martinianus as Caesar but the coins prove that he was full Augustus; *RIC* 7 Nicomedia 45–7; Cyzicus 16.

100 Cf. *Anon. Cont. Dio.* fr. 14.2 (*FHG* 4:199).

101 Zos. 2.25.1, with Paschoud 1971b, 217.

102 *Origo* 27; Zos. 2.26.2–3; Praxagoras 1.6 (*FGH* 2B219:949); Leo Gramm. p. 85; cf. Aur. Vict. *Caes.* 41.8; Eus. *VC* 2.15; Soc. 1.4.2. On the date, see sources at T. D. Barnes 1982, 75.

103 Praxagoras fr. 1.6 (*FGH* 2B219:949); Optat. Porf. *Carm.* 9.5–8; *Origo* 28–9; Zos. 2.18.1–2, 28.2; *Cons. Const.* s.a. 325; Jer. *Chron.* s.a. 323, 325; *Epit.* 41.7–10; Eutr. 10.6.1–3; Zon. 13.1.22–6; Leo Gramm. p. 85; Soc. *HE* 1.4.3–4; Soz. 1.7.5. For the *damnatio memoriae*, see *CTh* 15.14.1, with Gothofredus's emendation; cf. Corcoran 1993. Licinius may actually have had two sons: the younger, Constantine's nephew, was made Caesar in 317 and killed in 326; the elder may have been the bastard mentioned at *CTh* 4.6.2–3 who was made a slave in an imperial clothworks. See König 1987, 124–6, 140, 167; contrast Corcoran 2000, 291.

104 As if to signal a change, Constantine altered his official epithet from "Invictus" (unconquerable) to "Victor"; cf. Chastagnol 1966a.

105 Them. *Or.* 4.58b. At *RIC* 7:562–4 Bruun shows that the mint was operating by 326; cf. Preger 1901; A. Alföldi 1947, 10.

106 On the dedication, see *Cons. Const.* s.a. 330; Malalas 13.7; *Chron. Pasch.* p. 529; Philost. 2.9; Hesychius *Patria Constantinopoleos* 42 (Preger p. 18); cf. Jer. *Chron.* s.a. 330. More on the foundation of Constantinople at Zos. 2.30.1–32.1, 35.1; Malalas 13.7–10; *Chron. Pasch.* pp. 527–9; Hesychius *Patria Constantinopoleos* 39–41

(Preger pp. 16–18); *Origo* 30; Eutr. 10.8.1; Praxagoras 1.7 (*FGH* 2B219:949); Zon. 13.3.5; Soc. 1.16.1–4; Soz. 2.3.1–8.

107 E.g., Trier, Milan, Aquileia, Sirmium, Antioch, Nicomedia, Thessalonica. Constantine himself had added much imperial luster to Trier (Chapter 12 in this volume) and Aquileia (Rieß 2001). He is even reputed to have toyed with the idea of a new capital at Troy; cf. Zos. 2.30.1; Soz. 2.3.1–3; Zon. 13.3.1–2, with Paschoud 1971b, 224–5.

108 On the buildings, about which there is much dispute and little evidence, see Mango 1990c, 23–36; cf. Dagron 1974, 388–409 and Chapter 12 in this volume. On privileges and administration, see Dagron 1974, 29–47.

109 On the temples, see Zos. 2.31.2–3; Malalas 13.7 (p. 320); cf. Malalas 13.13; Bassett 2004, 22–36; Chapter 11 nn. 56–7 in this volume. On the column, see Mango 1965, 306–13; 1993a, Fowden 1991.

110 Bruun 1958; M. Alföldi 1964; Christodoulou 1998, 62–3; cf. Wallraff 2001. Philostorgius 2.17 even reports that Constantine's statue was worshipped like a pagan deity. See also Eus. *LC* 3.4 and Tantillo 2003.

111 Zos. 2.31.1–3; Lib. *Or.* 30.6, 37, 62.8; Eun. *VS* 6.1.5; Jul. *Or.* 7.228b; cf. Eus. *LC* 8.1–4; *VC* 3.54.1–7; Jer. *Chron.* s.a. 330; *DRB* 2.1–4; Bassett 2004, 50–78. More on Constantine's measures against pagans at Chapter 7 in this volume.

112 *CTh* 13.5.7: *urbis, quam aeterno nomine iubente deo donavimus.* Cf. Raimondi 2003, 188–94, on the new city as a "temple."

113 The earliest reference is Optat. Porf. *Carm.* 4.6: *altera Roma*, properly translated "second Rome," not, as Potter 2004, 383, "another Rome." See also Optat. Porf. *Carm.* 18.33–34; *Origo* 30; Jul. *Or.* 1.8b; Them. *Or.* 3.41c–42b. Socrates. 1.16.1 even claims that Constantine ordered this title inscribed on a publicly posted decree. See A. Alföldi 1947, 1948, 110–23; Calderone 1993.

114 *PLRE* 1 Fl. Iulius Constantius 8; cf. Kienast 1996, 314–37.

115 See Drijvers 1992, 39–54.

116 See sources at *PLRE* 1 Constantia I; cf. Pohlsander 1993.

117 On Helena's death, see Drijvers 1992, 73–5. On Helenopolis, see Mango 1994.

118 Eus. *VC* 3.46.1–47.3; *Liber pont.* 34.26; Deichmann and Tschira 1957.

119 Drijvers 1992, 45–8; Blaauw 1997, 60.

120 See esp. Jer. *Chron.* s.a. 326; cf. *Cons. Const.* s.a. 326; Eus. *VC* 3.15.1–2.

121 Zos. 2.29.5; cf. Lib. *Or.* 19.18–19, 20.24. The dating is vexed. I follow Wiemer 1994b; cf. A. Alföldi 1947, 12–15, against Paschoud 1971b, who dates to 315, and Straub 1955, who dates to 312.

122 Zos. 2.29.2; Zon. 13.2.37–41; Philost. 2.4; Soz. 1.5.1–2; *Epit.* 41.11–12; cf. Jul. *Caes.* 336a–b; Aur. Vict. *Caes.* 41.11; Jer. *Chron.* s.a. 325, 328; *Cons. Const.* s.a. 326; Eutr. 10.6.3; *Chron. Pasch.* p. 525; AM 14.11.20.

123 *CTh* 9.7.1–2, 8.1, 24.1 (early 326); Optat. Porf. *Carm.* 3.29–30; *Pan. Lat.* 4(10).38.4; cf. Evans Grubbs 1995, 203–25.

124 For other scenarios, see Guthrie 1966; Pohlsander 1984, 99–106; Woods 1998; Potter 2004, 380–2; and Chapter 4 in this volume.

125 See Lenski 2004; contrast Hunt 1997; Drijvers 1992, 55–72; Cameron and Hall 1999, 291–5.

126 On the legend of the True Cross, see Chapter 6 in this volume. I hold with those – in the minority – who would date the finding of the True Cross to Constantine's reign; see Rubin 1982; Drake 1985; Borgehammar 1991.

127 Eus. *VC* 3.25.1–42.4; *LC* 9.16–19; cf. *VC* 3.51.1–53.4. See also Cameron and Hall 1999, 274–94, and Chapter 12 in this volume.

128 Eus. *VC* 2.64.1–72.3. On Constantine's journey to Antioch, see Eus. *VC* 2.72.2 with T. D. Barnes 1982, 76; Lane Fox 1986, 638–43; contrast Burgess 1999b, 191. Cf. Chapter 5 in this volume.

129 Eus. *VC* 4.14.1–25.3, 4.29.1–33.2; *LC* 2.5, 5.1–8, 9.9–12.

130 Aur. Vict. *Caes.* 41.18; *Epit.* 41.14; *Chron. Pasch.* p. 527; Theophan. a.m. 5820; *RIC* 7 Constantinople 29–38; cf. Eus. *VC* 1.8.2. See more below in Chapter 15.

131 *Origo* 31; Eus. *VC* 4.5.1–2; Aur. Vict. *Caes.* 41.13; Jul. *Or.* 1.9d; *Cons. Const.* s.a. 332; Jer. *Chron.* s.a. 332; cf. Zos. 3.31.3; Eutr. 10.7.1; *AE* 1934, 158. For the time of year, see *CIL* 1²:258.

132 *PLRE* 1 Fl. Iul. Constans 3; cf. Kienast 1996, 312–3.

133 *Origo* 32; Eus. *VC* 4.6.1–2; Aur. Vict. *Caes.* 41.13; *Cons. Const.* s.a. 334; Jer. *Chron.* s.a. 334; *RIC* 7 Trier 532–3.

134 Aur. Vict. *Caes.* 41.11–12; *Origo* 35; Jer. *Chron.* s.a. 334; Polemius Silvius 1.63 (*MGH.AA* 9:522); Theophan. a.m. 5825. Dalmatius had also been awarded the consulship in 333 and was sent to preside over the church council held in Antioch in 334. See *PLRE* 1 Fl. Dalmatius 6.

135 Eus. *VC* 1.8.2–4, 2.28.2–29.1, 4.9.1, 4.50.1; cf. *P. Lond.* 3:878 with Jones and Skeat 1954 and Soz. 1.8.2. The mantra stretches back to at least 316; cf. Petr. Patr. fr. 15 (*FHG* 4:190). For expressions of a desire for dominance over Persia see *Pan. Lat.* 4(10).38.3; Optat. Porf. *Carm.* 5.1–5, 14.9–27, 18.4.

136 Eus. *VC* 4.9.1–13.1.

137 *BP* 3.21. For what follows, above all see Barnes 1985b; Fowden 1994b, 146–53.

138 Sources at Dodgeon and Lieu 1991, 125–31.

139 On Dalmatius, see *PLRE* 1 Fl. Iulius Dalmatius, 7; cf. Kienast 1996, 307, and esp. Eus. *LC* 3.2–4. On Hannibalianus, see *PLRE* 1 Hannibalianus 2; cf. Kienast 1996, 308, and Wirth 1990. On Constantius in the east, see Jul. *Or.* 1.13b–d, 18b–19a; Lib. *Or.* 59.60, 72–79; Soz. 3.5.1.

140 *Origo* 35; Eus. *VC* 4.56.1–57.1; Lib. *Or.* 59.60–73; Festus 26–7; Theophan. a.m. 5815; cf. Gel. Cyz. *HE* 3.10.26–7; Ruf. *HE* 10.12; Philost. 2.16; Soc. 1.39; Soz. 2.34.21. More sources on this conflict at Dodgeon and Lieu 1991, 143–79, esp. AM 25.4.23 with Warmington 1981.

141 Eus. *VC* 4.61.1, 62.2; Soc. 1.39.1; Soz. 2.34.1; Cedrenus p. 519; Zon. 13.4.

142 Jer. *Chron.* s.a. 337; Soc. 1.39.2–4; cf. Eus. *VC* 4.61.1–62.5.

143 On the date and place, see *Cons. Const.* s.a. 337; Aur. Vict. *Caes.* 41.16; Soc. 1.40.3; *Festal Index* 10; *Chron. Pasch.* p. 532; Jer. *Chron.* s.a. 337; cf. Jer. *Chron.* 306; Eutr. 10.8.2–3; Malalas 13.14. Further sources and discussion at Burgess 1999a. The rumor that he was poisoned by his brothers (Philost. 2.4, 16; Cedrenus p. 520; Zon. 13.4) is surely false.

144 See Eus. *VC* 4.65.1–71.2; Lib. *Or.* 59.74; Aur. Vict. *Caes.* 41.17.

145 On Andrew and Luke, see Burgess 2003. On the thirteenth apostle, see Rebenich 2000; cf. Amici 2000 on the conferment of the standard title *divus* (deified).

146 Eus. *VC* 4.73.1 (trans. Cameron and Hall).

147 See Koep 1958; cf. Wallraff 2001, 263–4.

4: THE DYNASTY OF CONSTANTINE DOWN TO 363

Robert M. Frakes

From the elevation of Constantius I as Caesar in 293 to the death of the emperor Julian in 363, the family of Constantine would play a direct and major role in the later Roman empire for seventy years. The actions of Constantius I's first son, Constantine, would forever change the nature of the Roman empire and of Western civilization. In an effort to elucidate this impact, this chapter will begin by examining the ways in which Constantine adopted and adapted the Tetrarchic system established by Diocletian into a family dynasty.[1] It will then investigate how this plan was followed – and sometimes not – in the period after Constantine's death up to the death of his nephew Julian, the last male dynast to rule as emperor. As we shall see, however, the next dynasty, the house of Valentinian, established connections to the Constantinians through marriages to a granddaughter and, probably, a grandniece of Constantine, with the result that the bloodline of the family continued to run through the veins of Roman emperors well into the fifth century. The chapter ends with a quick look at the afterlife of the image of Constantine in the later Roman empire and in world history.

FAMILIAL AND TETRARCHIC *CONCORDIA*

The prudence of Diocletian discovered that the empire, assailed on every side by the barbarians, required on every side the presence of a great army and of an emperor. . . . The suspicious jealousy of power found not any place among them; and the singular happiness of their union has been compared to a chorus of music, whose harmony was regulated and maintained by the skilful hand of the first artist.[2]

Thus Edward Gibbon described the plan and *concordia* of the Tetrarchy. While the fifty years before the accession of Diocletian (Coin 5) had seen immense internal and external problems – including secessions of breakaway empires, inroads of folk migrations, and attacks from a revived Persian empire – Diocletian had reformed the army and administration to deal more effectively with threats on the frontiers and with internal problems. The most important part of his reforms was the creation of a college of first two and then four emperors with no relation by blood, the Tetrarchs. In 285 Diocletian raised Maximian (Coin 7) as his colleague, first with the title of Caesar (assistant emperor), then in 286 with the title of Augustus (full emperor), and placed him in charge of the western half of the empire, while he himself kept dominion over the eastern (Greek-speaking) half. Apparently, however, Diocletian felt that even two emperors did not provide enough executive authority for the demands of the empire, for six years later he added as Caesars Galerius (Fig. 7) in the east and Constantius (Coin 8) in the west.

Diocletian was not the first emperor to have appointed an imperial colleague or coruler; indeed the practice became common by the mid-third century, though most of those chosen were blood relations of the reigning emperor. With Diocletian, however, the practice of sharing the executive power became more systematized and above all moved away from dynastic models. Thus, Diocletian set up the system so that the most able younger generals were chosen as Caesars, not just those most closely related to the Augusti. In this regard Diocletian followed a system based on merit rather than dynasty and thus broke with traditions generally followed since the Julio-Claudian emperors. Even so, dynastic models were not entirely shunned, in part because of the weight of tradition, in part because there was no getting around the collegiality fostered by family relations. Marriages were thus arranged between the different members of the Tetrarchy: Constantius I set aside his concubine Helena and married Theodora, the stepdaughter of Maximian, and Galerius took as his wife Diocletian's daughter Valeria.

After a reign of twenty years, Diocletian retired from public life on May 1, 305, and used his powers of persuasion to compel Maximian to do the same. Both Caesars, Galerius and Constantius, then assumed the position of Augusti and chose two new Caesars, Maximin in the east and Severus in the west. This was clearly part of Diocletian's plan to have an orderly and peaceful succession. In avoiding dynastic appointments, however, the plan passed over several potential royal successors, including Constantine, the son of Constantius by Helena, who was being kept at the court of Galerius in the east, presumably as a further security on the concord of the next stage of the Tetrarchy. The power of dynasty, however, proved too strong to be repressed, and the concord of the Tetrarchs began to break down within a year.

In late 305, Constantine managed to be released from Galerius's court and promptly traveled to be with his father, who was campaigning in Britain. When Constantius I died at Eburacum (York) on July 25, 306. Constantine was conveniently on hand to be hailed as Augustus by his father's troops. Though the eastern Augustus, Galerius, recognized him as a Caesar shortly afterward, Constantine's accession quickly provoked resentment from another dynastic claimant who had been passed over in 305, Maxentius (Coin 10), the son of Maximian. He, like Constantine, had himself proclaimed emperor in October 306.

Maximian, meanwhile, took advantage of his son's acclamation to resume the purple but fairly quickly fell out with Maxentius. Already in 307 he began establishing new political connections when he sealed an alliance with Constantine that was consummated by Constantine's setting aside his former concubine Minervina – who had already given birth to his first son, Crispus – and marrying Fausta (Coin 11), the daughter of Maximian (see Appendix I). Yet tensions between the various rulers continued to run high, a fact that led Diocletian and Galerius to call their famous Conference of Carnuntum in 308, where they formulated a series of compromises. Galerius would take a new Augustus, the distinguished soldier Licinius (Coin 12), to replace the now dead Severus in the west. Maximin, the eastern Caesar, would remain, while Constantine would be the western Caesar. Maximian was, once again, to abdicate, and Maxentius was given no official standing. This arrangement was also short-lived. Constantine and Maximin began to assert claims to the status of Augustus, and Maximian once more tried to reassert a bid for the purple before being forced to commit suicide. Galerius died in 311, and Maximin and Licinius split his territory, although not without tension. Licinius and Constantine soon thereafter tightened their alliance, and Licinius sealed it by marrying Constantine's half-sister, Constantia.[3]

These links helped Constantine and Licinius to rule as co-Augusti after each had defeated his respective rival – Maxentius in 312 and Maximin in 313 – once again following Diocletian's pattern of shared empire. Nevertheless, they also cleaved to the older, dynastic model when each chose his son or sons as Caesars: Constantine promoted Crispus, his son by Minervina, and Constantine II, his son by Fausta, and Licinius elevated Licinius II, his son by Constantia. Despite marriage alliances and careful planning, however, the two Augusti still squared off against one another in a series of wars down to 324, when Constantine became the ultimate victor and Licinius was forced into retirement (within a year Licinus was executed). Licinius's homonymous son also had to give up his title of Caesar and was himself executed a year later.[4]

The *concordia* of the Tetrarchy lasted only as long as it was supported by the power and prestige of Diocletian. Personal ambition and, above all, family links led the sons of Tetrarchs to tear the orderly, if somewhat idealistic, system of Diocletian apart. Constantine would replace it with an adapted model – one where a single Augustus would share the purple with his sons as Caesars. Though Diocletian's model seems rational to modern students of history and politics, it failed to take account of the power of dynasty among members of the imperial family, the army, and the people. Constantine's hybrid system, which shared rule among family members, while far from problem-free, proved more attractive and more durable.

DYNASTIC ARRANGEMENTS DOWN TO 337

With the defeat and deposition of Licinius in 324, Constantine arranged for his sons and a nephew to be the Caesars and thus eventual successors to his reinvention of the model of shared rule. Of his own sons, Crispus was initially the obvious leading figure in that he was much older, was more experienced, and had played a decisive role in the defeat of Licinius. Nevertheless, in one of the most puzzling events of the reign of Constantine, he ordered his eldest son executed in mid to late 326.[5] Our sources are spotty and late for this event. Because Crispus's death is followed shortly afterward by the execution of Constantine's wife Fausta, later sources attribute both to a scenario like that of Hippolytus and Phaedra in Greek mythology or Potiphar's wife and Joseph in the Hebrew Bible: an older woman avenged herself on a younger male by claiming rape when her advances were declined. Although delightfully juicy, this scenario is unlikely because the future emperor Julian (Coin 23) praised the moral character of Fausta in a panegyric to her son Constantius II (Coin 18).[6] Julian need not have raised the topic if it would have embarrassed Constantius; thus it seems logical to assume that Fausta did not attempt to seduce her stepson or have an illicit relationship with him.[7] Another explanation advanced by some scholars is that Fausta wanted to eliminate Crispus so that only her own sons would inherit the throne.[8]

The real motivation may have been rather more complicated. Licinius's son, a former Caesar, was also executed in 326. Gibbon long ago hypothesized that the wife of Crispus, another Helena, might have been a daughter of Licinius.[9] Our sources for this Helena are even murkier than for Crispus, but we do know from a law of the Theodosian Code that she and Crispus had already had a child in 322.[10] It was only natural that Constantine and Licinius attempted to tighten their alliance in 312–13 by various means, and it would have been quite logical and in keeping with standard practice for Crispus to marry an early daughter of Licinius. But even if this hypothetical connection is accepted, marriage alliances were no guarantee of safety, as Fausta herself confirms. Since Licinius I was killed early in 325, followed by Crispus and Licinius II in 326, it could be that Fausta fanned fears of a conspiracy of state by the remnants of a Licinian faction to advance the future power of her own sons, only to have her plan backfire. The fact that Constantine then had Fausta killed suggests that she urged her husband to suspect his eldest son too quickly and that Constantine intensely regretted his rashness.

Whatever the cause of the purge, and we will probably never know it exactly, Constantine was now left with three surviving sons. The eldest, Constantine II, had already been made Caesar in 317. The second surviving son by Fausta, the wily Constantius II, was made Caesar in 324. The youngest, Constans, became Caesar in 333. Constantine also entrusted two of his great-nephews with imperial positions as well. He proclaimed Flavius Julius Dalmatius, son of Flavius Dalmatius – a half-brother of Constantine by Constantius I and his second wife, Theodora – Caesar in 335 with special dominion over Thrace. He also appointed Dalmatius's brother Hannibalianus *rex regum et ponticarum gentium* ("King of Kings and of the Pontic Peoples") in an attempt to control more tightly Armenia and its neighbors as a buffer zone against Persia.[11] Constantine strengthened Hannibalianus's status further by arranging for his marriage to his own daughter Constantina in 335.

By 335 Constantine had thus set up an elaborate and top-heavy system of dynastic succession in which his sons and nephews held power over various zones of the empire, while he remained the sole Augustus. He apparently sought to circumvent any succession problems by preparing the various Caesars to move up to the status of Augustus upon his death. This was certainly the case with his three sons, though his nephews may have been intended to continue managing regional hot spots as Caesars even after Constantine's decease. Here we can see how Constantine was adopting and adapting the imperial model of Diocletian. While retaining the concept of multiple emperors and of peaceful succession, Constantine was using bloodlines instead of merit as the basis for sharing the purple.

THE ROLE OF THE EMPRESS IN CONSTANTINIAN POLITICS

Constantine's transition to blood instead of merit may have been the inevitable result of the use of female relatives to seal alliances in strategic marriages even in the original Tetrarchy. Descendants of these privileged marriages would naturally feel that they had a right to positions as rulers. These strategic marriages already began with the establishment of the Tetrarchy. As we have just seen, such marriage ties were used in the next generation as well. Constantine set aside Minervina to marry Maximian's daughter Fausta, and Maxentius, the son of Maximian, married Valeria Maximilla, the daughter of Galerius. Lastly, Licinius married Constantine's half-sister Constantia (see stemmata in Appendix I).

The third generation of Constantius I's family used familial marriages to intertwine the dynasty even further, creating a family tree that begins to approach Oedipean levels of consanguinity. Constantine's daughter Helena married Julian, the son of Julius Constantius, Constantine's half-brother, and Basilina. Constantine's other daughter, Constantina, first married his nephew Hannibalianus (a grandson of Constantius I by Theodora and thus a son of Constantine's half-brother and confidant, Fl. Dalmatius). After Hannibalianus's murder in 337, she married Gallus, Julian's older half-brother (son of Constantine's half-brother Julius Constantius and Galla) and thus also a nephew of Constantine, to whom she would bear a daughter. Constantine's son Constantius II would marry three times: first to a daughter of Julius Constantius whose name is unknown;[12] second to a certain Eusebia, another marriage with no issue; and finally to Faustina, who bore him a posthumous daughter named Constantia. This Constantia would go on to marry the emperor Gratian (reigned 367–83), which would tie the Valentinianic dynasty directly to the house of Constantine.

Another probable princess of the family is Justina. As a mere girl, she had been drafted to marry the usurper Magnentius in 351/2; she would later marry the emperor Valentinian I in 369.[13] Since she went on to have four children by Valentinian, she was probably still relatively young in 369. Magnentius appears to have sought her hand for dynastic reasons, for he married her only after attempts to marry Constantina, daughter of Constantine and former wife of Hannibalianus, had been rebuffed.[14] A long-held suspicion of scholars has been that Justina was somehow another female member of the Constantinian dynasty and that she offered Magnentius a second chance to bolster his claims to legitimacy.[15] She was the daughter of Justus, a Roman senator, and an unknown woman. While it is possible that Justus was somehow related to the Constantinian family himself, it seems more probable that his anonymous wife carried the connection, perhaps as a daughter of Julius Constantius and Galla. The latter was half-sister to Constantius II's senatorial confidant Vulcacius Rufinus and full sister of another of Constantius II's favorites, Neratius Cerealis. Julius Constantius and Galla's children included the future Caesar Gallus (born in 325), an elder son, and at least one daughter (the first wife of Constantius II). As the emperor Julian was born to Julius Constantius and his second wife, Basilina, in 331, an additional daughter of Julius Constantius would have to have been born sometime between 324 and 331 for the hypothesis to work.[16] It is possible that this hypothetical daughter could have married Justus while quite young and born Justina c. 340, thus allowing Justina to have been twenty-nine years old at the time of her marriage to Valentinian.

The evidence for this identification lies in the names of Justina's children by Valentinian. Aside from their son Valentinian II (obviously named after his father) and daughter Grata (named for Valentinian's father Gratian), her other girls were Justa and Galla. Justa clearly hearkens back to Justina's father, Justus, while Galla suggests her probable grandmother, Galla.[17] Indeed, Justina's daughter Galla would marry Theodosius I, and their daughter also would be named Galla (Placidia). Valentinian's marriage to Justina may thus have tied him to the great Constantinian dynasty, and Theodosius's marriage to Galla Placidia would do the same.[18] Further confirmation of Justina's connection to this wing of the family can be seen in the names of her siblings. One of her brothers was named Cerealis, the name of the first Galla's brother. Another, who was killed while serving in Valentinian's army in 369, was called Constantinianus, a name whose obvious resonance further indicates a connection to the Constantinians. The names "Cerealis," "Constantinianus," and "Galla/us" are thus strong evidence of a family connection – one that Magnentius already hoped would give his usurpation an air of legitimacy.

Constantinian empresses thus provided important links to further legitimize the emperors' authority. As these women had been born, raised, and lived among imperial politics and intrigue, they would naturally have intimate knowledge of imperial affairs. Many of them would thus influence their male relatives in various aspects of policy. Helena played a decisive role in fostering the construction of churches in the Holy Land and achieved eminence in her symbolic role as queen mother. Constantia, Constantine's half-sister, helped settle the final peace that brought about the surrender of her husband Licinius to Constantine and later played a crucial role in Constantine's ecclesiastical politics. Constantine's daughter Constantina served as a dynastic wife to the princes Hannibalianus and Gallus, was herself a great ecclesiastical-builder in Rome, and even interceded to encourage a general named Vetranio to revolt as a way to protect her brother Constantius II from the much more dangerous usurper Magnentius. Helena the younger, another daughter of Constantine, was also used to strengthen the dynasty when she was married to Julian, over whom she exercised considerable influence in his years as Caesar. Indeed, had she lived longer, she might have been able to broker a peace between her brother Constantius II and her husband. The youngest princess of the house, Justina, not only carried the Constantinian dynasty into the next century through her descendants, she played a major role in ecclesiastical politics during the reign of her son Valentinian II – to the point that the irate bishop Ambrose labeled her "Jezebel."

THE COLLAPSE OF *CONCORDIA*

> And close kinsmen as we were, how this most humane Emperor treated us! Six of my cousins and his, and my father who was his own uncle, and also another uncle of both of us on the father's side, and my eldest brother, he put to death without a trial... they kept telling us, and tried to convince us that Constantius acted thus, partly because he was deceived, and partly because he yielded to the violence and tumult of an undisciplined and mutinous army.[19]

Julian's satirical invective summarizes how Constantine's elaborate plans for the succession after his death lasted only briefly after he died on May 22, 337. There followed what has been called "the massacre of the princes" – a purge of male relatives of Constantine, especially those descended from Theodora, including the Caesar Dalmatius and the *rex regum* Hannibalianus.[20] All together, Julian describes how nine males were killed. Only the young Julian and Gallus, Constantine's nephews, still mere boys, survived.

Julian indicts Constantius II as the culpable party, as do some other sources.[21] He was the first emperor on the scene in Constantinople after Constantine's death and was commander of the troops who carried out the executions. He seized much of the territory of the murdered Dalmatius and, presumably, also had designs on the territory of Hannibalianus. Even so, our sources are not entirely clear on how this purge came about. Even Julian, attempting to downplay any extenuating factors, mentions a mutinous army and "lies" to which Constantius II fell victim.[22] A later source, Philostorgius, clarifies that a rumor circulated that Constantine had been poisoned by his half-brothers and their followers – those descended from Constantius I by Theodora.[23] It could be that the rumor spread through military and government circles immediately following Constantine's death, and owing to misplaced loyalty and fear of losing privileges, leaders of factions in the army purged those suspected of playing a role in the alleged poisoning. Nevertheless, Constantius was certainly on the spot and stood to benefit from the purge. Most likely is the compromise view that he saw what was happening and did not intervene to stop it out of self-interest.[24] He may even ultimately have stepped in to save Julian and Gallus in order to preserve some semblance of clemency, ensure that there were successors to keep the image of a strong family dynasty alive, and preserve the boys as brothers of his wife – although this did not protect their eldest brother.

In this regard, we should perhaps keep in mind that Constantius had the model of Constantine to follow. Constantine had killed his own son Crispus, as well as his brother-in-law Licinius and his nephew Licinius II, in a possible purge. Constantius followed up the massacre of the princes with the assassination of the experienced praetorian prefect Flavius Ablabius and several other notables in late 337.[25] This must be somehow connected to the dynastic purge, but the connection is obscured by our scanty source record. By early September 337, we have only the three sons of Constantine on the imperial playing field, and at this point they begin to use the title Augustus: Constantine II in Gaul, Spain, and Britain; Constans in Italy, North Africa, and Illyricum; and Constantius II in Thrace and the east. The last was perhaps the strongest of the three but was occupied at the start of his reign with an invading Persian army.

In its turn, this triad also did not last long. Later sources describe how Constantine II was jealous of Constans, the youngest of the three brothers – just seventeen in 337 – because he had gained so much territory in the Balkans after the assassination of Dalmatius. Constantine II thus attempted to bully his youngest brother into giving up some lands.[26] Another source claims the argument arose over North African territory, though it could be that Constantine II desired this as compensation for the Balkan territory that his two younger brothers had gained with Dalmatius's execution.[27] This seems likely, if unprovable. Regardless, Constantine invaded Italy in 340 but was soon killed in a skirmish near Aquileia. At the time, Constantius II was occupied in resisting a Persian invasion, leaving Constans to become master over almost two-thirds of the Roman world by age twenty. He would maintain power for ten years, during which time (the sources indicate) he had to deal with problems along the Rhine and in Britain and North Africa. There are also indications in our meager sources that Constans's relationship with his brother was often tense, as both sparred over matters ecclesiastical and territorial.[28] The sources also criticize him scathingly for his lascivious homosexual conduct.[29]

THE PROBLEM OF USURPATION

The problem of usurpation, so familiar in the third century but largely brought to heel under Diocletian's and Constantine's reigns, reemerged after Constantine's death. It appears that structural arrangements of succession, whether dynastic or Tetrarchic, proved successful only when a strong emperor was in power. Of course, Constantine's own usurpation, the massacre of the princes, and Constantine II's civil war with Constans all provided recent models for those interested in using war or conspiracy to establish and consolidate power.

A new spate of usurpations began in 350, when Constans was overthrown by a conspiracy that replaced him with the general Magnentius, a usurper of Frankish origin, as Augustus. In the midst of the coup, Constans fled into a church and was assassinated in February of that year. This usurpation in turn unleashed a wave of reaction by those connected to the Constantinian dynasty. Another young prince of the imperial dynasty, Julius Nepotian (the son of Eutropia, a daughter of Constantius I and Theodora), seized Rome with a troop of gladiators but was quickly executed by Magnentius's operatives.[30] At the same time, a general, Vetranio, also claimed the purple in Sirmium. Vetranio had been the *magister militum* under Constans and was in that emperor's Illyrian territories during the assassination in early 350. When he heard of his emperor's death, he was allegedly persuaded by Constantius II's sister Constantina to claim the title of Caesar and seize Illyricum so that Magnentius would not have it.[31] Constantina then may have communicated to Constantius II the motives behind the usurpation, for he temporarily recognized Vetranio's authority, even if only as an expedient while he faced the Persian threat.[32] Vetranio sought military aid from Constantius for a campaign against Magnentius, but Constantius was fully occupied with the Persian frontier.[33] Meanwhile, Magnentius attempted to negotiate a peace treaty with Vetranio. Finally, both sent a joint delegation to Constantius, by means of which Magnentius seems to have sought a marriage alliance with Constantius's sister Constantina herself, the widow of Hannibalianus.[34]

At this point Constantius, feeling the eastern frontier had been pacified, finally rejected any possibility of shared rule with either Vetranio or Magnentius. In December 350 he persuaded Vetranio to give up his claim to the throne and live out his natural life as a private citizen with a handsome state pension.[35] Around the same time, Constantius claimed to have had a dream in which his younger brother's corpse had appeared begging for revenge and inspiring him to declare war on Magnentius.[36] In early 351 he marched west with a massive force to face the usurper, but to guard his rear flank against the Persian threat, Constantius appointed his cousin Gallus (one of the two survivors of the massacre of the princes) as Caesar in the east and married him to the same Constantina who had brokered relations with Vetranio. Constantius won a decisive, though costly, victory against Magnentius at the Battle of Mursa later that year and then spent two more years engaged in mop-up operations before he finally hunted down Magnentius and executed him and his relative Decentius, to whom Magnentius had awarded the title of Caesar.[37]

Within a year of defeating Magnentius, Constantius reverted to his earlier conduct and ordered the arrest and execution of Gallus. Again the cause of this is rather obscure. It appears that Constantius had surrounded Gallus with a cadre of officials who had also been given the additional duty of spying on their Caesar. More importantly, some sources indicate that Gallus was beginning to careen out of control, perhaps even toward usurpation, and that his wife, the princess Constantina, was urging him on to savage violence.[38] It could simply be, however, that Constantius's spies whipped up exaggerated charges and preyed upon Constantius's suspicious nature for their own ends. Regardless, Gallus was executed in 354, leaving his younger half-brother Julian as Constantius's sole surviving male relative.

After stabilizing the west, and executing his cousin Gallus Caesar, Constantius faced another crisis in the usurpation of Silvanus. This general had defected from Magnentius's forces to the side of Constantius at the Battle of Mursa and was then appointed to an important command in Gaul by the victorious emperor. However, a cabal of Constantius's administrators, perhaps jealous of Silvanus's successes in Gaul, altered some of Silvanus's correspondence to make it appear that he was plotting a usurpation in 355. Once again they appealed to Constantius's suspicious nature, and he recalled Silvanus. Nevertheless, the falsely accused general heard of what was transpiring and, figuring there was nothing to lose, claimed the purple in August. Constantius sent his reliable general Ursicinus to Gaul to settle the problem, and Ursicinus succeeded in having Silvanus assassinated in September.[39]

Following the successive deaths of Gallus and Silvanus, Constantius was persuaded by his second wife, Eusebia, that he should elevate his last remotely close male relative, Julian, to the position of Caesar. Constantius proclaimed Julian in November 355 and gave him authority over Gaul and the northwestern frontier. His position was solidified further by a marriage between Julian and Helena, another of Constantius's sisters. Although Julian had had no prior military or administrative experience and had spent his youth under virtual house arrest and in studies, he proved to be quite successful in campaigns against the Germanic Alamanni and Franks and in administering Gaul. Indeed, his success was so great, especially after his victory at Argentoratum in 357 (Strasbourg), that Constantius grew suspicious of Julian's abilities and possible ambitions. To weaken the threat posed by Julian's army and to bolster his own troop strength, Constantius ordered the transfer of several of Julian's military units from Gaul to the east in early 360.[40]

Julian's troops, who opposed this transfer from Gaul, chose instead to hail him as a full Augustus in early 360, a promotion that would inevitably provoke Constantius. Julian made a show of reluctantly accepting and immediately sent a letter to Constantius explaining, and justifying, what had happened. Both emperors eyed each other with suspicion for over a year while dealing with threats on their respective frontiers. Meanwhile, their one hope of reconciliation, Helena, died of natural causes in the early 360. Finally, in late summer of 361, Julian marched east to confront his cousin – and, he insisted, the murderer of his family – but Constantius died of natural causes before they met on the battlefield. He left behind a pregnant young third wife and allegedly bequeathed the empire to Julian.[41]

Julian's flamboyant short reign would be marked by his attempt to turn back the tide of Christianity and restore paganism to its former glory. Though his religious convictions certainly appear to have been very personal and genuine, the murder of many of his relatives in 337 by the Christian Constantius traumatized the young Julian and contributed at some subconscious level to his desire to reject the religion championed by his family. What might have become of his religious volte-face had he reigned longer we will never know. This is because Julian also launched a major invasion of Persia that ended disastrously in his untimely death in June 363. After this, the Christian Jovian was elected emperor by a group of generals. Although he died only nine months later, another Christian, Valentinian I, was elected in his place and proved successful in establishing a new dynasty that would reinstall some stability for the empire and for Christianity. This he did at least in part by building connections to the Constantinian dynasty with the marriage of his son to the princess Constantia (the posthumous daughter of Constantius II) and of himself to Justina, both discussed earlier.

The period from 337 to 363 is thus marked by a series of civil conflicts and violent usurpations. An underlying cause for this situation may have been the need for a strong imperial presence in frontier areas threatened by foreign enemies, such as the Germanic tribes in the north and Persians in the east. When these same threats grew critical in the mid to late third century, they also led to frequent usurpations, but Diocletian's strong leadership and his establishment of the Tetrarchy had reestablished stability. Constantine was able to continue this stability by means of his own forceful personality and was able to take advantage of a window of peace, with few major foreign threats, in the second half of his reign. Under his sons, however, the Persian threat grew strong again and preoccupied Constantius II – the strongest and most capable of the three – while various groups continued to pressure the west. It was only after Constantius II had stabilized the east that he was able to restore order throughout the empire and continue his father's adapted model of a dynastic shared rule, with Julian as his Caesar. Though Julian's reign is full of "what if's" for the modern student of history, one cannot help but wonder what the empire and imperial dynasties might eventually have looked like if he had not rushed into invading Persia. As it was, the ruling house changed, but the Valentinianic dynasty did retain the Constantinian model of dynastic coemperors – Valentinian ruled with his brother Valens and his son Gratian – and this model continued to be followed into the fifth century and beyond.

THE USE OF CONSTANTINIAN IMAGES
FOR LEGITIMACY

Constantine was very careful in appealing to religion while always focusing squarely on the loyalty of his armies for legitimacy. Descriptions of his victory at the Milvian Bridge indicate how he publicly acknowledged the help of Christ as his divine comrade, as do his policies toward the Church. However, Constantine was careful not to alienate traditional pagans. So, in a variety of public images he would create a middle, tolerant stance that would appeal to both Christians and pagans by using images with which both could identify. His successors, who, as we have seen, had to deal with a variety of internal and external threats, would follow in his footsteps. The most famous of Constantinian images is of course the Chi-Rho (☧). This was emblazoned on the labarum, a battle standard, by Constantine. Such a symbol was abstract enough that it could be perceived differently by different audiences. It is strikingly similar to a symbol for a sun god from the Danubian region from which Constantine's ancestors came.[42] Indeed, it has been argued that it is also similar to the Egyptian ankh, a pagan symbol of life.[43] At the same time, it would be hard for an educated Christian not to notice that this symbol could also be seen as composed of the first two Greek letters of Christ's name. In this instance and others, Constantine's genius was to use vague symbols and language that could resonate well with multiple audiences. His sons, by contrast, pushed the Christian interpretation much further.

Another example of the use of Constantinian images can be seen in the coins struck during his reign. Coins in the Roman world are among the best indicators of how the emperor wished to have his public image portrayed in that they were minted – and thus "printed" – by imperial order.[44] Under the legend *Gloria Exercitus* (the Glory of the Army),[45] for example, a series of coins was introduced in 330 that displayed a variety of images honoring the success of the army in establishing peace following the war against Licinius and various successes against the barbarians (Coin 24).[46] After Constantine's death, his sons continued to use the same coin legend and types, thereby linking the legitimacy of their rule with that of their father.[47] Some mints even used the Chi-Rho on the banner on these coins, further enhancing the appeal to religious authority and to their father's victory and power. In an even bolder ploy to build on the symbols of their father's rule, the Constantinian dynasts minted a series of coins under the legend *Hoc Signo Victor Eris* (by this sign you will conquer), a direct allusion to Constantine's victory at the Milvian Bridge, which also reinforced their claim to legitimacy through

Christianity.[48] Constantine had not used the phrase on his own coins and indeed had continued to mint coins with images of solar deities and other pagan gods for some time (Coins 4 and 15).[49]

One new coin type created by Constantine's successors was the famous *Fel(icium) Temp(orum) Reparatio* series (Coin 25). The Latin is translatable as something like "the restoration of happy times," and this widely minted series of bronze coins was probably instituted in 348, which was the eleventh centenary of the founding of Rome in 753 BC as well as the tenth Etruscan *saeculum* (a "century" of 110 years), a festal event redolent with traditional pagan symbolism.[50] This double reminder of the antiquity and glory of Rome, issued in a period when Constans and Constantius had temporarily achieved peace in the empire, linked Rome's glorious and remote pagan past with an equally glorified Christian present. In fact, this new series made great use of the Chi-Rho on the labarum[51] while intermingling typical images of Roman military victory with more pagan allusions to rebirth, like the Phoenix. With this series, then, Constantius and Constans, like their father, succeeded in striking something of a balance between pagan and Christian symbolism. Not surprisingly, when the later usurper Procopius – a remote relation of the dynasty – challenged Valens's authority as eastern emperor in 365–6, he courted both pagan supporters of Julian and Christian adherents of Constantius with propaganda emphasizing his own connection to the house of Constantine. To drive home the point, he issued a series of gold solidi under the legend *Reparatio Fel(icium) Temp(orum)*.[52]

Constantine's use of Christian symbols on his coinage, although nonexclusive, would set a precedent for his sons. As they reigned in an increasingly Christian empire, they began to use them more and use pagan symbols and imagery less. Ultimately, by the succession of Christian emperors after Julian, the Romans came to view the legitimization of power through the Christian deity as normal, thus laying the groundwork for medieval concepts of kingship in the west.

FURTHER READING

There is no single work focused on the dynasty of Constantine and the period from 325 to 361. T. D. Barnes's *The New Empire of Diocletian and Constantine* (1982) provides a sound outline of the major people and events in the early fourth century. His *Constantine and Eusebius* (1981) and *Athanasius and Constantius: Theology and Politics in the Constantinian Empire* (1993) provide in-depth treatments of these two emperors' activities, especially as they related to the church. R. Klein's *Constantius II. und die christliche Kirche* (1977) remains of interest, especially for its review of earlier scholarship. A. H. M. Jones's magisterial survey *The Later Roman Empire, 284–602: A Social, Economic, and Administrative Survey* (1964) still provides a useful starting point, as do E. D. Hunt's recent chapters "The Successors of Constantine" and "Julian" in *The Cambridge Ancient History*, vol. 13, *The Late Empire*, ed. A. Cameron and P. Garnsey (2nd edition, 1998). Lastly, the articles on pertinent emperors in *De Imperatoribus Romanis* (at http://www.roman-emperors.org) offer sound overviews and a regularly updated bibliography.

NOTES

An Alexander von Humboldt Stiftung Research Fellowship at the Leopold Wenger Institute at the University of Munich in the summer of 2003 made revisions of this chapter possible. I would also like to thank Raymond Van Dam and members of the seminar on Constantine and his Age at the 2004 meeting of the Association of Ancient Historians for their comments on a truncated version of this chapter.

1 Such a task is not easy because our sources are scarce, late, and sometimes problematic for this period up until 353, when the extant books of the history of Ammianus Marcellinus begin. See also Frakes 1995. For the use of the twelfth-century chronographer Zonaras as a source for the fourth century, see Di Maio 1977 and 1988 and Bleckmann 1992.

2 Gibbon [1776–81] 1994, 361–2 (Chapter 13).

3 See Chapter 3 in this volume.

4 The only indications of date fall at Jer. *Chron.* s.a. 325 and Eutr. 10.6.3, both of which indicate that Licinius II was executed at the same time as Crispus, i.e., in 326.

5 See, in general, Pohlsander 1984.

6 Jul. *Or.* 1.9b–d.

7 See the recent radical attempt by Woods 1998 to blame Fausta's death on an attempted abortion of Crispus's love child.

8 Guthrie 1966.

9 Gibbon [1776–81] 1994, 650 n. 18. See also Potter 2004, 380–2, for a somewhat different analysis.

10 *CTh* 9.38.1 (October 30, 322).

11 See Baynes 1910, 627–9; Jones 1964, 85; Hewsen 1978–9, 109–11; and Wirth 1990.

12 Possibilities are Galla, after her mother, or Julia or Constantia, after her father.

13 See *PLRE* 1 Iustina and Lenski 2002b, 103–4.

14 Petr. Patr. fr. 16 (*FHG* 4:190).

15 T. D. Barnes 1982, 44, hypothesizes that she was perhaps a granddaughter of Crispus.

16 Like her sister, her name was likely Galla, Julia, or Constantia.

17 Rougé 1958, 8–9.

18 Rougé 1958, 10–11, esp. 11 n. 33.

19 Jul. *Ep. ad Ath.* 270c–271b (trans. Wright).

20 Lucien-Brun 1973; cf. Di Maio and Arnold 1992.

21 Cf. Zos. 2.40.

22 Cf. Eutr. 10.9.1.

23 Philost. 2.4, 16. Cedrenus 520 and Zonaras 13.4 accept the rumor as fact.

24 Lucien-Brun 1973, 600–2.

25 Eun. *VS* 6.3.9–13; Zos. 2.40.3; Jer. *Chron.* s.a. 338.

26 Zon. 13.5.5–15.

27 Zos 2.41.

28 Portmann 1999.

29 Aur. Vict. *Caes.* 41.23–4; Zos. 2.42.1; cf. Eutr. 10.9.3; AM 16.7.5.

30 Aur. Vict. *Caes.* 42.6–8; Eutr. 10.11.2; *Epit.* 42.3; Oros. 7.29.11; Jul. *Or.* 2.58c; Zos. 2.43.2–4.

31 Philost. 3.22; *Chron. Pasch.* p. 539.

32 *Artem. Pass.* 11; Zon. 13.7.16–18. See also Di Maio 1977, 291.

33 Jul. *Or.* 1.26c; 2.76c.

34 Zon. 13.7.18–20; Petr. Patr. fr. 16 (*FHG* 4:190).

35 Zos. 2.44.3–4; Eutr. 10.11.2; Zon. 13.7.21–22.

36 Zon. 13.7.20–22.

37 Eutr. 10.12.1–2; Aur. Vict. *Caes.* 42.9–10; *Epit.* 42.4–6; Jul. *Or.* 1.39b–40b; Zos. 2.49.2–53.3.

38 AM 14.1.1–3.

39 AM 15.5.1–34; Aur. Vict. *Caes.* 42.15–16; *Epit.* 42.10–11; Eutr. 10.13; Jul. *Or.* 2.97–98.

40 More on Julian in Bowersock 1978 and at Matthews 1989, 81–179.

41 AM 21.15.3–6.

42 Drake 1976, 73–4.

43 Bruun 1966, 61.

44 See Charlesworth 1937 and, more recently, Noreña 2001. More generally, see Howgego 1995.

45 Bruun 1966, 20.

46 *RIC* 7 pp. 137–41, 214–8, 270–9, 336, 339, 341–6, 407–10, 453–60, 524–6, 529–30, 557–61, 579–82, 589–90, 633–5, 653–60, 693, 697, 711–12.

47 *RIC* 8 pp. 143–4, 178, 205–6, 249–51, 316, 354–5, 407, 431, 449–50, 471–2, 490–1, 515–6, 539–40.

48 *RIC* 8 pp. 369, 386.

49 For solar deities, see Bruun 1966, 243, 246, 248, 286, 415, 488, 713. For a recent article attesting to the continuation of pagan symbols, see Vanderspoel and Mann 2002.

50 Mattingly 1933.

51 Mattingly 1933, 190–1.

52 Lenski 2002b, 97–104.

Section II

RELIGION AND SPIRITUAL LIFE

5: THE IMPACT OF CONSTANTINE ON CHRISTIANITY

H. A. Drake

The impact of Constantine on Christianity can be summarized fairly quickly: during the thirty years of his reign, more change took place in the status, structure, and beliefs of the Christian Church than during any previous period of its history. In 306, when Constantine was first elevated by his father's troops, the imperial government was in the middle of a concerted effort to remove all traces of Christian presence from the empire. When he died in 337, Christian leaders had assumed the rank, dress, and, increasingly, the duties of the old civic elite. Before the century ended, the tables were turned completely, with traditional sacrifices outlawed and the old state cults forbidden. But Constantine's role in bringing about this reversal is more problematic. At one time, the only question that needed to be asked about that role was how "sincere" Constantine's conversion had been. Was he in truth a pious son of the church, or was he rather a political mastermind who seized on the power he could gain by subordinating this well-organized and doctrinaire group to his will? Admirers pointed to the enormous powers and benefactions he bestowed upon the church, the Christian character of his laws, and his suppression of pagan cults. Those who argued the opposite pointed disdainfully at the continued presence of pagan images on his coins for some time after 312, his unwillingness to use any but the most general terms for deity in his public utterances, and, most damningly of all, evidence that he not only permitted the old cults to survive but even actively patronized them, at least on occasion.

Newer scholarship and thinking has made most of this old argument obsolete. For one thing, it depended too heavily on the notion of a monolithic Christian Church; that is, the idea that there was only one kind of Christian that Constantine could become. In the scholarly world, this normative Christian was invariably unyielding and intolerant, which is why Constantine's "sincerity" was measured by the extent to which he himself tolerated other beliefs. But scholars now recognize that the Christianity of Constantine's day, while more organized than any ancient religion had ever been, was still by later standards simply a loose assemblage of local congregations, held together by regular meetings of their bishops, but still differing significantly in character and even in the fine points of belief.[1] Constantine thus had a variety of Christians with whom he could choose to work – some certainly determined to war to the death against the old gods, but others prepared to live in harmony with their pagan neighbors. This choice in turn means that the question about Constantine's conversion needs to shift from "Did he become a Christian?" (about which there can be very little doubt) to "What *kind* of Christian did he become?" This question can be answered by paying closer attention to the types of Christians with whom he associated and the types he sought to avoid. To anticipate, this chapter will argue that it is a mistake to think Constantine's aim was to make the empire Christian, at least in any doctrinaire meaning of that word. He conceived of a Christian *public* religion that set a fairly low threshold for membership, and he threw in his lot with Christians who he thought would help him achieve this goal.

But if it is a mistake to think of Constantine as a doctrinaire Christian, it is an even greater mistake to think of him as a politician interested only in the power the church could help him achieve. There was no separation between church and state in antiquity; indeed, except among Christians, there was no idea of a "church" that was anything other than the "state." For this reason, the task of sorting out "political" from "religious" motives in a ruler like Constantine is bound to fail. It is possible, however, to consider the political *implications* of his actions without having to conclude that these actions were politically *motivated*. In fact, it could be said that the mistake of earlier scholarship was to ignore such political considerations and depend too heavily on the theological implications of Constantine's behavior, forgetting that theology is a very weak tool for analyzing developments in the public sphere. To understand Constantine's impact on Christianity, a different set of questions needs to be asked: What problems did he have to address, and why? What solutions did he devise? Were these solutions viable?

For good reason, the changes that took place during Constantine's reign have been connected with his conversion; but the motives and procedures for this dramatic realignment can properly be understood only in the broader context of traditional imperial practice. More important even than his conversion is the way that, in response to a sequence of events, Constantine worked out a role for himself in the governance of Christian affairs that allowed him to build a viable coalition around a policy of broad inclusion. Only after studying these events can Constantine's impact on Christianity be adequately assessed.

CONSTANTINE'S CONVERSION

Two separate accounts of Constantine's conversion survive in works written by Christian contemporaries. The earliest was written, probably in 315, by Lactantius, a Christian rhetorician who became tutor to Constantine's oldest son. After describing events leading up to the decisive battle for Rome on October 28, 312, Lactantius writes that

> Constantine was advised in a dream to mark the heavenly sign of God on the shields of his soldiers and then engage in battle. He did as he was commanded and by means of a slanted letter X with the top of its head bent round, he marked Christ on their shields.[2]

Without further elaboration, Lactantius moves swiftly to the defeat and death of Maxentius. The classic account of Constantine's conversion, however, is contained in the *Life of Constantine*, written shortly after the emperor's death in 337 by his older contemporary, Bishop Eusebius of Caesarea, who reports that he heard the story "a long while after" from the emperor's own lips:

> About the time of the midday sun, when day was just turning, he said he saw with his own eyes, up in the sky and resting over the sun, a cross-shaped trophy formed from light, and a text attached to it which said, "By this conquer." Amazement at the spectacle seized both him and the whole company of soldiers which was then accompanying him on a campaign he was conducting somewhere, and witnessed the miracle.[3]

Eusebius is vague about the time and place of this miracle, but he places it squarely in the context of Constantine's preparations for war against the "tyrant" Maxentius. Constantine, he writes, "became aware that the head of the whole, the imperial city of the Roman Empire, lay oppressed by bondage to a tyrant" and sought the aid of some god himself because he knew

> that he would need more powerful aid than an army can supply.... He regarded the resources of soldiers and military numbers as secondary, for he thought that without the aid of a god these could achieve nothing; and he said that what comes from a god's assistance is irresistible and invincible.[4]

Like Lactantius, Eusebius also reports a dream in which Christ himself explains the meaning of the vision to Constantine and bids him to use the sign he has seen "as protection against the attacks of the enemy."[5] But in his version, the dream is completely overshadowed by a far more spectacular celestial miracle – a miracle that is completely absent from Lactantius's comparatively spare report. What accounts for this difference? Some scholars have traced it to an even earlier story, told by a pagan source, of a vision involving the god Apollo that occurred in Gaul some two years earlier, in 310, and they have concluded that Eusebius merely added an acceptable Christian gloss to this event. Those who need natural explanations for spiritual phenomena take comfort in the occurrence of a "solar halo phenomenon," which can produce effects similar to what Constantine said he saw – although, as the best of these studies points out, cultural conditions determine what viewers make of such signs.[6]

In all of the arguing over these accounts – which typically has focused on what they reveal about Constantine's "political" motives and whether these taint the sincerity of his belief – an obvious central point has been ignored, which is that neither Lactantius nor Eusebius seem to find the combination of religious and political events in their story detrimental in any way to the image they wish to convey of a pious prince. Lactantius was a rhetorician and might be excused from such sensitivities. But Eusebius was both a bishop and author of a path-breaking *History of the Church*; he is widely regarded as the most learned Christian of his day. Yet in his account of this event Eusebius betrays not the slightest embarrassment over an emperor who connected earthly power with divine support. Why is that?

Properly read, Eusebius's text is a primer on late Roman imperial ideology. From the start, Roman emperors had always performed religious duties as *pontifex maximus* (head of the Roman state religion); symbolically, the title of Augustus – a word with vague connotations of prosperity ensured by the gods – was even more significant, for it added an aura of sacrosanctity to their person. Although Christians liked to portray emperors as believing they were gods, none but a deranged few ever thought of themselves as such. But they did believe they played a role in the divine order – "last among gods, and first among men," as an ancient tract put it.[7] By the mid-third century, this role in the divine order had expanded to the point that a successful emperor had to demonstrate, above all else, ties to divine power.[8] As Eusebius's text shows, Christians shared this worldview. Hence, even though Eusebius himself describes how Constantine had been proclaimed emperor by the army, within a few paragraphs he also asserts,

> In such a way then did God, the President of the whole world, of his own will elect Constantine, sprung from such a father, as universal ruler and governor, that no man could claim the precedence which he alone possessed, since the rest owed the rank they held to election by others.[9]

To say this is not to say that Constantine's conversion, whenever it happened, was "insincere" even by modern standards that struggle to divorce piety and politics. Rather, the point is that, to understand the religious environment of the late Roman world, modern students must always be aware that that world had no room for a deity like the "Master Clockmaker" envisioned by European thinkers in the eighteenth century – a deity who, having once established physical and natural laws for the universe, now keeps apart from their regular operation. Christians and pagans alike in that world believed in a deity who did intervene, and did so with disturbing regularity. This deity took sides, as did the malevolent deities who intervened just as frequently on behalf of Rome's enemies. In such an environment, ensuring divine support was prudence, not politics.

An important clue for understanding Constantine's conversion lies embedded in Eusebius's narrative at the point where he says that the emperor told the story "a long while after" the event. It is a point easily overshadowed by the dramatic story that follows, but modern studies of conversion experiences suggest that a dramatic 180-degree turn – even if not replete with angels and anthems – is the way converts typically remember the event long after it has happened. The questioning and searching that lead up to the moment become forgotten, as does the long period of socialization in the new religious community that follows.[10] Constantine fits this model. Little is known of his religious views before

312, but what little there is all points in the same direction: Constantine, probably like his father before him, began as a solar monotheist, belonging to the popular cult of the Unconquerable Sun God, Sol Invictus.[11] Indeed, his first recorded vision experience, described by a panegyrist in 310, involved a meeting with Apollo, a god tied to solar religion, and on a commemorative medallion issued only months after the battle of the Milvian Bridge, Constantine appears in twin profile with this deity (Coin 4).

There is no longer any need to choose between these two accounts. Both tell of an emperor seeking a divine champion and protector. If a change occurred in this protector's identity, it happened as Constantine himself remembered a critical time in his early career through the lens of his Christian understanding.

The point Constantine wanted to be sure all his hearers understood was that he had been called by God to rule. This need to demonstrate his qualifications for Christian rule is what is missing from most studies of the impact of Constantine. Instead, the conversion story leads to the conclusion either that the church became immediately submissive to his will or that he himself was so awed by the experience that he slavishly delivered the empire to the church. Both alternatives ignore the great diversity in the number and condition of Christian communities that prevailed in the early fourth century, some of which did not define themselves in a way that precluded being both "Christians" and "Romans." In such conditions, it is better not to proceed with preconceived outcomes in mind but to study how both Christians and Constantine reacted and adapted to conditions that were, in many ways, utterly novel. By looking at some well-known conflicts as a series of choices Constantine had to make between competing parties, it will be possible to answer the question, "What kind of Christian did he become?"

DONATISM

While Constantine – at least in Eusebius's version – was mulling his options for divine sponsorship, a controversy was brewing in the large and influential North African Christian community that soon would force him to make many more choices more quickly than he may initially have intended. The subject was clergy who had become tainted during the persecution by surrendering sacred books and objects to imperial officials. This made them, literally, "traitors" (*traditores* in Latin, people who hand things over). All sides agreed that such individuals had to be dismissed from office. The problem concerned acts that they had performed while in office. The position of the hierarchy in Carthage was that sacraments remained valid, even if administered by tainted clergy. But a rigorist group that came to be called the Donatists after their most tenacious leader, the priest Donatus of Casae Nigrae, insisted that the sacraments themselves – and particularly baptism – were tainted and had to be administered anew. To preserve the purity of their community, they chose to separate themselves from their laxer brethren.

Thus began the Donatist schism, which would embroil the North African Church for more than a century. Conceivably, Constantine might never have gotten involved in it, and the issue would then be absent from these pages. But as Eusebius's discussion showed, both Roman emperors and their subjects assumed it to be both a right and a duty of emperors to ensure proper worship of divinity. Accordingly, when they were rebuffed in Carthage, the Donatists appealed their case to the emperor. Being a Christian might have made Constantine even more inclined to intervene, but there was precedent for Christians to appeal to the emperor for help in settling internal disputes, whether he was Christian or not. Some forty years earlier, eastern bishops had asked the emperor Aurelian to oust Bishop Paul of Samosata from the church in Antioch, which he had defiantly refused to leave even after being deposed by a church council. Aurelian was no Christian; indeed, later tradition branded him a would-be persecutor. But he turned the case over to the bishop of Rome and undertook to enforce whatever judgment was issued.[12]

With a similar goal in mind, the Donatists appealed to Constantine in the spring of 313 for help in settling their dispute. Instead of Rome, however, they asked the emperor to assign their case to bishops from Gaul, whom they believed to be free of any taint thanks to the mild rule there of Constantine's father, the Tetrarch Constantius I.[13] At this early stage of the conflict, however, Constantine evidently saw no reason to deviate from precedent. In a letter that made its way into the final book of Eusebius's *Church History*, Constantine turns the case over to the bishop of Rome, Miltiades, informing the pontiff that he has arranged for Caecilian, the accused bishop of Carthage, to be brought to Rome along with ten of the bishops accusing him and ten others chosen by himself for his defense.[14] Significantly, Constantine adds that he has also arranged for three bishops from Gaul, whom he identifies by name, to coadjudicate with Miltiades. Constantine had been ruling in Gaul for the previous six years and had also inherited all the contacts his father had developed during his own dozen years there. The three Gallic bishops – Reticius of Autun, Maternus of Cologne, and Marinus of Arles – were all certainly known to him. Their inclusion was a concession to the Donatists; it indicates that Constantine had given some thought to their petition.

Although he explicitly left procedural details to Miltiades, Constantine probably had in mind the relatively relaxed arbitration procedures that bishops used to mediate disputes between members of their flock – procedures that many years later he would compare favorably to the "captious bonds of legal objection" (*captiosa praescriptionis vincula*) that could keep the truth out of formal legal proceedings.[15] Miltiades, however, had other plans. Exploiting a loophole, he packed the court with an additional fifteen Italian bishops and, when the session began in October, informed the parties that they would be held to the strict rules of Roman civil procedure. When the Donatists could not present a case, he declared Caecilian innocent by default.

What might have happened had Miltiades followed Constantine's original instructions? The emperor's role to this point had been largely passive and administrative.[16] His selection of Gallic judges was prudent, however much it might have infringed on the primacy and independence that Roman bishops, as the successors of Peter and Paul, always claimed was uniquely theirs. Had the Donatists been given a full and fair airing of their grievances and a decision, even an unfavorable one, rendered by Miltiades and the Gallic judges alone, Constantine might well have concluded that any reasonable demands made by the schismatics had been satisfied. As it was, when the stunned Donatists howled with outrage, Constantine proved once more receptive to their complaints.

This time Constantine took matters into his own hands and summoned a council of bishops from all the western provinces to assemble the next summer (314) in Arles. This was a major departure from precedent, one that would have far-reaching consequences. For the first time, a Roman emperor had taken the initiative in convening a council of bishops, on any scale. His action instantly elevated the status of such a meeting and changed its nature. A surviving letter shows that he put the public post at the disposal of the bishops he summoned, a move that instantly guaranteed them not only swifter and more comfortable travel but also higher status and visibility.[17] Further, his summons gave at least a quasi-official character to whatever decision this council might reach, meaning that their internal disputes were now matters of public concern, and meaning further that the emperor was now committed in one way or another to resolving them. Constantine's decision to convene bishops from all the provinces he controlled thus dramatically underlined the novelty of their relationship, for the church as well as the empire.

The Council of Arles ruled decisively against the Donatists.[18] Once again they appealed to the emperor, and once again – despite eloquently complaining to the bishops, whose decision he was about to snub, that "they demand my judgment, when I myself await the judgment of Christ" – Constantine agreed to hear the Donatists himself. But another part of this same letter indicates that now the emperor was far less disposed to entertain their complaints. Appeals from decisions fairly rendered were, in Constantine's eyes, devices used by "heathens" (*gentes*) to circumvent justice: "It is true that the heathen, fleeing from a lesser tribunal, where justice can be soon obtained, are wont to betake themselves to an appeal, since authority intervenes more for greater tribunals." In resorting to this tactic, the Donatists ceased to look like injured parties to Constantine; instead, they were looking more and more like obstructionists. His aim this time evidently was to hold the leaders of both sides in Italy while he dealt with other matters, perhaps hoping that this cooling-off period would bring them to their senses.[19] Instead, first one side and then the other slipped away and returned to North Africa.

The Donatist case dragged on, and there is no need here to pursue the many ironies and reversals that lay in store. Only two points need to be kept in mind. The first, a simple one, is that the Donatists represent a certain type of Christian: rigid, unyielding, puritanical, and in the event more than willing to use violent means to achieve their ends. The bishops who met at Arles represent a different kind of Christian. Not only did they respond favorably to the emperor's summons, but while in session they adopted canons that paved the way for Christians to hold imperial office and serve in the army.[20] The scholarly argument over the "sincerity" of Constantine's Christianity implicitly depends on the assumption that Christians like the Donatists were the normative Christians. But the bishops at Arles show that Donatists were not the only Christians. It should be noticed, therefore, that Constantine ultimately, and decisively, declined the opportunity to espouse their cause. Rigorists clearly were not the type of Christian he favored.

The second point is a little more difficult to establish but ultimately of far greater significance. It is that during these years Constantine eventually renounced force as a means to achieve religious conformity, though he came close to using it. Frustrated by the intransigence of the Donatists, Constantine threatened late in 315 to come to North Africa and personally take charge of the situation. "Those same people who incite and do things of this nature," he wrote Celsus, the vicar of Africa, "so that the supreme God is not worshipped with the requisite devotion, I shall destroy and scatter."[21] This was precisely the type of imperial thinking that had eventually led Constantine's predecessors into the Great Persecution. But Constantine had personally witnessed the failure of that policy, and he soon drew back from a commitment that would have repeated the blunder. Instead, by 321 we find him counseling the bishops of North Africa that the situation called for patience, not force:

> Our faith ought to be confident that whatever suffering result from the madness of people of this kind will have value in God's eyes by the grace of martyrdom. For what is it in this age to conquer in the name of God, if not to bear with unmoved breast the lawless attacks of those who harry the people of the law of peace?[22]

Prestige was an emperor's most precious commodity, and cynics might argue that Constantine merely resorted to face-saving rhetoric once he realized his bluster would not work. Even if so, his choice of this particular line of rhetoric, deeply embedded as it was in Christian teaching, would remain significant. So, too, would be his decision not to follow the path that led to the use of force to compel belief. But there is reason to believe Constantine's decision to eschew coercion was more firmly grounded in principle. Within months of seizing the eastern empire from Licinius in 324, Constantine issued a letter to his new subjects urging toleration:

> However let no one use what he has received by inner conviction as a means to harm his neighbor. What each had seen and understood, he must use, if possible, to help the other; but if that is impossible, the matter should be dropped. It is one thing to take on willingly the contest for immortality, quite another to enforce it with sanctions.[23]

At this point in his career, when he had defeated his last rival and was the uncontested sole ruler of the empire, Constantine was under no pressure to exercise such restraint; indeed, according to the assumptions of modern scholars, he should at this period have been advocating just such coercive treatment. Yet even five years later he wrote in the same

vein to bishops in Numidia, urging them to show Christian patience in
their dealings with Donatists:

> Indeed it is by this that the judgment of God appears
> manifestly more great and righteous, that he bears them
> [Donatists] with equanimity and condemns by his patience,
> enduring all the things that come from them. God indeed
> promises to be the avenger of all; and thus when vengeance
> is left to God a harsher penalty is exacted from one's
> enemies.[24]

There is no reason to believe Constantine followed such a policy for
any other reason than conviction. The reason for imperial intervention
grows out of a different set of imperatives that are reflected in another
document from this period.

The Edict of Milan

Within months of his victory over Maxentius, Constantine met in Milan
with his eastern ally, Licinius. The purpose of the meeting was to
cement their new alliance in the traditional Roman fashion by a marriage between Licinius and Constantine's half-sister, Constantia. While
there, they also agreed on a common policy with regard to the religious
turmoil to which the empire had been subjected for the previous decade.
Commonly known as the "Edict of Milan" – even though in the form
we have it, it was not an edict and was not issued in Milan – the document legalizes Christianity and promises restoration of property seized
during Diocletian's persecution.[25] These are the passages that Christian
authors rightly emphasize, but only in retrospect did the protections
extended to Christianity seem paramount. Reading the document in
light of the previous policy of persecution, its center of gravity amounts
to a repudiation of coercion as a means to achieve religious unity. The
emperors proclaim that

> in accordance with salutary and most correct reasoning we
> ought to follow the policy of regarding this opportunity
> [given the Christians] as one not to be denied to anyone at
> all, whether he wished to give his mind to the observances
> of the Christians or to that religion which he felt was most
> fitting to himself.

The disavowal of their predecessors' policy of coercing belief in a limited set of approved deities could not have been clearer – making allowances, of course, for the circuitous and overblown nature of late imperial rhetoric. Instead, diversity of belief was now to be accepted as a matter of imperial policy.

The new policy took an even more radical departure, whose full import can only be gauged by keeping in mind the efforts made by the previous regime to identify itself specifically with the gods Jupiter and Hercules. In this document, Constantine and Licinius use only general terms for deity – "Divinity" and "Supreme Divinity" (*summa divinitas*) – thereby making clear that their policy required no such specificity. Instead, the emperors show a refreshing uncertainty about the nature of that divinity, saying that their aim was to appease "whatever divinity there is in the seat of heaven" (*quicquid <est> divinitatis in sede caelesti*).[26] Tetrarchic certainty has been replaced by a novel modesty. The Edict of Milan defines Constantine's religious policy. Though he was himself a Christian and made no effort to hide his allegiance to that faith, he would not return to the policy of coercion, whose disastrous consequences were apparent to all. This policy underlay his decision to forgo force in dealing with the Donatists and to enjoin Christians in the east from physical attacks on nonbelievers. By the time he wrote the Numidian bishops in 330, he had found a firm grounding for this policy in the Christian admonition to "turn the other cheek."

At the same time, other parts of this document explain why Constantine intervened in the Donatist affair, and why intervention at some point was probably inevitable. In the same breath with which they grant religious rights to all, the emperors repeatedly explain that they were taking this step to ensure the security of the Roman state, "in order that whatever divinity there is in the seat of heaven may be appeased and made propitious towards us and towards all who have been set under our power," as they state at the outset.[27]

Such thinking reflects the universal belief of this age that divine support was essential to success and prosperity in this world and that the emperor was responsible for gaining and maintaining that support. Precisely this thinking underlay the earlier decision to persecute Christians. In his edict calling off the persecution in 311, Galerius explained that it was undertaken "for the advantage and benefit of the state," in order to "set everything right in accordance with the ancient laws and public discipline of the Romans."[28] Constantine and Licinius had made Christianity one of the state's licit religions. But their express belief that doing so would contribute to "the public well-being" (*beatitudine publica*) shows that they continued to believe in this tie between divine favor and material benefit. Thus it was now their duty to ensure that the Christian god's cult would be conducted properly. It is probably significant that when Constantine wrote his fiery letter to the vicar of Africa in 315, the focus of his anger was those who were not giving the Supreme God his proper veneration.[29]

How seriously did Licinius take his own commitment to the Edict of Milan? After Constantine seized control of the eastern empire in 324, Licinius came to be ranked among the Christian persecutors. But when the rhetoric is stripped from the account of Eusebius of Caesarea, what we learn is that Licinius deposed some bishops, some of whom were even executed by his governors, and that in the city of Amaseia in Pontus churches were closed and Christians barred from assembly.[30] These actions provided sufficient pretext for Constantine to act. Some of them, however, might have been the result of a new controversy that was raging through the eastern Church and that immediately engulfed Constantine himself.

HERESY AND UNITY

The issue this time was not moral rectitude but the even more central problem of correct belief (orthodoxy). Since correct belief was essential to believers' hopes for an afterlife, and since the utter novelty of the Christian understanding of deity produced a stream of teaching that tried to explain this novelty despite a theological vocabulary that later ages would consider grossly deficient, incorrect belief, or heresy, was a problem that always threatened to destroy the unity of the Christian body. At this moment, the controversy focused on the Alexandrian priest Arius, whose teaching addressed the central question of the relationship of the Son to the Father in the Christian trinity. Put simply, Arius reasoned that because fathers precede sons, there must have been some point at which the Son did not exist. Arius stressed that this point would have occurred before there was any such thing as time or created existence, but his enemies seized on this part of his teaching to claim that he had reduced the divine nature of Christ to that of a mere creature and thereby effectively denied his ability to provide eternal life for those who believed in him. The issue, of course, was not that clearcut; indeed, then and now there have been thinkers deeply immersed in Christian belief who have concluded that his accusers, not Arius, were the ones in error.[31] Our concern here, however, is not to determine which side was right or wrong but to understand Constantine's role in a situation that proved to be pivotal for the future of both church and state. For the church, the Arian controversy produced a credal statement that ultimately became the touchstone of Christian orthodoxy; for the state, it committed the emperor to the use of his coercive powers to enforce conformity to that creed. Taking into account universal belief in the direct role divinity played in human affairs and the direct role the emperor played in ensuring the goodwill of that divinity, it is not difficult to understand how, in short order, enforcing correct belief became the prime mission of the Christian emperor.

Constantine's intervention began with an effort to resolve the dispute amicably by reconciling Arius with his bishop, Alexander. A letter that the emperor dispatched to the two antagonists survives in the second book of Eusebius's *Life of Constantine*. Here Constantine demonstrates that theology was not his primary concern. The issue dividing them, he says repeatedly, was a "trivial" matter, a "very silly question." It should never have been broached in the first place, but now that it had been, both should realize that this "slight difference" should not be the cause of either heresy or schism.[32] Instead, what mattered to Constantine was that division had been created: "the most holy people were divided in two and forsook the concord of the common body." He then spelled out his own standards for achieving a restoration of unity:

> On the subject of divine Providence therefore let there be one faith among you, one understanding, one agreement about the Supreme; the precise details about these minimal disputes among yourselves, even if you cannot bring yourselves to a single point of view, ought to remain in the mind, guarded in the hidden recesses of thought.[33]

Theologians rightly scoff at the naivete of this letter, but as a political statement it is of paramount importance. As with the Donatists, Constantine hoped to achieve unity and to avoid public disorder. More than that, the letter shows that at least a dozen years after his personal commitment to Christianity, Constantine still envisioned it as a faith that could produce "one united judgment in reference to God" without stumbling over such trivial matters as the nature of Christ and the Trinity. His own priorities are clearly marked out: publicly, all that was needed was belief in a monotheistic Divine Providence that guides human affairs; any further stipulations, conditions or definitions were private matters that should not be brought into the public sphere. Along with a recognition of the close personal ties between Divine Providence and the emperor, and of divine support for the emperor and his dynasty, this belief was both necessary and sufficient to ensure the well-being of the empire.

Given his previous experience dealing with the Donatist issue, Constantine might not have been completely surprised when his effort to reconcile Arius with his bishop failed. Because of that previous experience, however, he also knew in advance what his next move must be. By the end of 324, plans evidently were already underway to summon a general council along the lines of the one he had summoned to Arles a decade earlier. Just as that council was attended by bishops from all the provinces under his rule, so too would this one be. But in 314 his rule had been limited to the western provinces; now it encompassed the entire empire. Accordingly, this council again would be precedent setting: the first ecumenical, or "worldwide," council of the entire church. If everything had gone according to plan, this council would have been held in Ancyra, the modern Ankara in central Asia Minor, and Christians today would be reciting the Ancyrene Creed instead of the Nicene Creed. But at the last minute Constantine shifted the locale to Nicaea on the Aegean coast of the province of Bithynia. Ostensibly, he intervened because the site was more accessible, especially for bishops from the west, and the climate nicer.[34] But a far more interesting, and revealing, story lurks beneath the bland surface of this decision. For Ancyra was the see of Bishop Marcellus, a virulent opponent of Arianism, and Constantine had learned from Miltiades's actions at Rome in 313 just how much sway the presiding bishop could have over a council. This time, Constantine did not wait on the outcome before intervening. In changing the site to Nicaea, he signaled his intention to follow the model of the Council of Arles without the preceding disaster of the rigged Council of Rome.

The switch indicates that Constantine had been listening to another Eusebius, this one bishop of Nicomedia, capital city of the province of Bithynia. Eusebius was Arius's most important and most skilled patron. When he heard Ancyra was to be the site of the great council, Eusebius evidently complained to Constantine. Mindful of his mistake with the Donatists, the emperor swiftly intervened.[35]

A SAINTLY EMPEROR

Constantine summoned the council, but why did the bishops come? This is a question that never would occur to a reader of Eusebius of Caesarea's *Life of Constantine*. Once they received Constantine's summons, he writes, the bishops "all dashed like sprinters from the starting line, full of enthusiasm. They were drawn by the hope of good things, the opportunity to share in peace, and the spectacle of that strange marvel, to see such a great Emperor."[36] There is no reason to doubt the picture Eusebius draws. But the success of Constantine's effort should not blind us to certain political realities. Constantine's defeat of Licinius had won him, if Eusebius is to be believed, enormous popularity among Christians throughout the east, and Constantine had moved rapidly to consolidate that position with a program of restitution and patronage.[37] But accepting imperial largesse was one thing; allowing the Roman emperor to control the definition of Christian belief was quite another. Constantine, moreover, carried a number of liabilities that the miracle legend has obscured for later ages but that would have been all too easy for a hostile Christian contemporary to recall. He had held a favored position at Diocletian's court, for instance, and despite eloquent condemnations of the persecution after the fact, nothing indicates that Constantine opposed it especially strenuously at the time. Early in his reign, he had formed a dynastic alliance with the persecutor Maximian, and in the ten years that he had been in sole control of the west, he had taken no active steps to suppress traditional religion.

That no such challenge to his authority survives is mute testimony to the skill with which Constantine worked to establish his legitimacy in Christian eyes. Evidence for this effort survives in an intriguing speech he delivered to a Christian assembly, in all likelihood within a few months of seizing the east from Licinius.[38] Labeled the *Oration to the Assembly of the Saints*, it is on the surface a lengthy refutation of critics of Christianity in which he sets out to demonstrate, to an audience that scarcely needed it, the truth of the Christian faith. Scholars have predictably worried this part of the speech to pieces for what it says about the purity of the emperor's belief. But they have paid far less attention to what was certainly the speech's most important goal: to convince its audience of the constancy of their new emperor's faith and thereby make them willing to accept his leadership. Constantine's argument is that there is a Divine Providence governing the universe and that it has pleased this Providence to restore order to the political and natural universe by appointing this emperor to protect the righteous and proclaim the truth to all parties.[39]

Eusebius of Caesarea, who preserved this quirky document for us by attaching it to his *Life of Constantine*, describes it as typical of the kind of speech the emperor was always giving.[40] That is the reason for thinking about it here. The speech is an opportunity to observe how Constantine went about staking his claim to a leadership position in an organization that had developed completely independent of imperial control and to observe as well the direction in which he meant to lead it. In its present form, the oration is divided into twenty-six chapters that, according to one estimate, would have taken about two hours to deliver.[41] The general plan of the oration is fairly simple – it can be divided into three parts either by content (a section on the Father, another on the Son, a third on the working of God in the present age) or method (theological, philosophical, historical). But such abstract division fails to capture the very personal nature of the emperor's argument and leads scholars to classify it too readily into the genre of apologetic. Although the emperor puts forth his arguments in apologetic fashion, his goal clearly differed significantly from that of the Christian apologists. For one thing, apologists generally directed their defenses *to* the emperor, whereas this one was coming *from* an emperor. Moreover, apologists aimed their works at nonbelievers – even if, in fact, believers were their true consumers – while Constantine delivered his remarks to an audience that was clearly Christian.

Read as mere apologetic, the speech comes across, at best, as a marginally competent rehash of well-worn themes.[42] Taken instead as an effort by Constantine to demonstrate his *bona fides* as a Christian ruler, the speech magically blossoms into an orchard of imperial thought on the role religion would play in the new government. Constantine rejects polytheism, for instance, because it is an organizational nightmare. "To whom should I pray?" he asks. "To whom could I pay especial worship without impiety to others?" Worse, even if he did choose, the god in question might not have jurisdiction if the case is not within the scope of its authority.[43] Worse still, polytheism fosters belief in more than one ruler. If all things, "both things in heaven and those on earth," were not "subjected to his sole rulership," then "there would be share-outs and divisions of the elements . . . envy and avarice, dominating according to their power, would mar the harmonious concord of the whole."[44] In a world that thought of itself as a mirror of the heavenly realm, polyarchy was a concept with immediate, and dangerous, consequences.

In a central chapter, Constantine makes several references that sound autobiographical. He reports, for instance, that he himself has put aside "all that the inferior condition of fortune haphazardly imposed upon me in a state of ignorance, for I consider the greatest salvation to be repentance." His next words are striking:

> I wish this revelation had been given to me long ago, for blessed is he who from childhood has both been grounded in knowledge of divine matters and greatly delighted by the beauty of virtue. This I can say in all modesty; for even if the best of men do not become wise at the earliest age or, as they say, while still in swaddling clothes, it is equally welcome if they attain wisdom in the prime of life.[45]

However obliquely, these statements together seem to address the very issues that a Christian critic might have seized upon to challenge Constantine's authority: for years he lived at Diocletian's side and thereby shared responsibility for the persecution. The modesty of these sentences, cast in tones of confession and repentance, was designed to evoke understanding and forgiveness, thereby neutralizing any negative effects that might result from failure to disclose and confess. As with the miracle story, Constantine's confession seems designed as well to evoke the image of St. Paul, another persecutor converted by a divine vision into a great evangelist – an association that would be made even closer by Constantine's posthumous designation as "equal to the Apostles" (*isapostolos*).[46]

Given that ancient speeches were not policy addresses, Constantine is remarkably direct about his intentions. In the same passage where he makes those apparently revealing autobiographical remarks, Constantine speaks quite specifically about what he intends to do:

> We, indeed, strive as much as possible to fill the uninitiated with such words of good hope, calling on God to be our help in the enterprise. For it is no easy task to turn the minds of our subjects to the service of God if they happen to be good, and more difficult still to reverse the course of those whose minds are bad and senseless, and make useful those who are useless.[47]

He will work to convert the empire, in other words. But how? As this chapter progresses, Constantine makes equally clear what his terms are, in a way that is uniquely late Roman: he talks about God and what God wants. For example, at one point he speaks of "certain witless and impious men" who do not realize that the way to deal with opponents is "with the confidence of reason and magnanimity."[48] We may take this characterization of God's policy as code for Constantine's own. In his plan, people were to be led to Christianity through acts of moderation and reason; they were not to be coerced. "This is the noble victory," he exclaims; "this the true power and the greatest act: the moderate governance of the entire population."[49] Constantine's "defense" of Christ takes on a new meaning in this light, for it means that he was arguing not simply against pagans but also against certain Christians. By casting his message in terms of God's will rather than his own, Constantine at one and the same time was able to isolate these Christians by lumping them together with those who "hate Christ" and to protect himself against a charge of improperly asserting imperial influence.

The sentiments in the *Oration to the Assembly of the Saints* lead the mind back to his judgments on the Donatists and to injunctions in the Edict to the Provincials and forward to the Council of Nicaea. Writing of Constantine's behavior in such venues, Eusebius of Caesarea observed that "such as he saw able to be prevailed upon by argument and adopting a calm and conciliatory attitude, he commended most warmly, showing how he favored general unanimity, but the obstinate he rejected."[50] In his opening speech at the Nicene Council, summarized by Eusebius in the *Life*, Constantine thanks God for the blessing of being allowed to behold such an assembly "united in a common harmony of sentiment." Reminding the attendees of the evils of his persecuting predecessors, he commits himself to the struggle against dissent within the church, which he describes as "graver than any war or fierce battle." The greatest favor they can do him, he concludes, would be to "loosen all shackles of dispute by the laws of peace."[51] The political importance of this speech is immense. In a relatively few sentences, Constantine has made unity, not purity, the goal of the session. To bishops completely unused to such flattering attention, the prospect of a Roman emperor saying that he wanted nothing more than that which would most please them and the God they serve was irresistible. Small wonder that no one objected when Constantine took part in the sessions and even contributed to the debate. "He addressed each person gently," Eusebius wrote in the *Life*, "and by speaking Greek – for he was not ignorant of that language either – he made himself pleasant and agreeable, persuading some and shaming others with his words, praising those who were speaking well, urging all towards agreement, until he had brought them to be of one mind and one belief on all the matters in dispute."[52]

Eventually, Constantine oversaw and sanctioned the creation of a creed that equated the Father and Son by using the extremely controversial term *homoousios* (of the same substance). Though the term, never found in scripture, soon provoked a vigorous and protracted new debate, it was accepted at Nicaea by all of the bishops except two, who were deposed and sent into exile, along with Arius himself, who, since he was not a bishop, had no say in the decision. This as well as anything testifies to Constantine's power as an arbitrator.

As with the Donatists at Arles, the Council of Nicaea did not fully resolve the Arian controversy. Within a few years, Constantine would reverse himself about Arius's orthodoxy and send Athanasius into exile for refusing to admit him into communion with the church in Alexandria. In the final irony, the emperor's deathbed baptism would be performed by an Arian, the same Eusebius of Nicomedia whose interests Constantine had protected in 325. The letter Arius used to regain Constantine's favor is preserved in the fifth-century *Church History* of Socrates Scholasticus. After reciting a generic creed that sidestepped the word *homoousios*, Arius wrote,

> God is our judge both now, and in the coming judgment. Wherefore we beseech your piety, most devout emperor, that we who are persons consecrated to the ministry, and holding the faith and sentiments of the Church and of the holy Scriptures, may by your pacific and devoted piety be reunited to our mother, the Church, all superfluous questions and disputations being avoided: so that both we and the whole Church being at peace, may in common offer our accustomed prayers for your tranquil reign, and on behalf of your whole family.[53]

It is obvious why Athanasius found this confession wanting. But bearing in mind the agenda Constantine laid out in his original letter to the two disputants, it is just as easy to see why the emperor thought the problem resolved. Arius expressed a commitment to concentrate on his ministry and put aside "all superfluous questions" so that appropriate prayers for the empire and the dynasty will reach God's ear. Embedded in the letter is a program that explains why, for the remainder of Constantine's reign, bishops identified with Arius's cause actually gained the upper hand at Constantine's court. They did so not with theological arguments but by painting the opposition, now led by Athanasius, as intransigent and unwilling to compromise.

CONCLUSION: A NEW WORLD?

When, after Constantine's death, his son Constans attempted to resolve the Donatist schism – this time with cash instead of troops – an angry Donatus responded with a frosty question: "What has the Church to do with the emperor?"[54] This was a question Constantine had worked tirelessly, and successfully, to avoid. The vision story helps explain his success while also explaining the failure of his son. The whole force of the vision story was its uniqueness; it endowed Constantine with a charismatic authority that he could not pass on to his successors. But that is only part of the explanation, for it seems certain that Donatus would have been no more receptive to an overture from Constantine himself. So political skill is another reason why Constantine succeeded in keeping this question at bay: he knew the limits of his power and never gave hotheads like Donatus the opportunity to contest it.

But the hotheads were there. We can see them peeping around the edges of Constantine's criticisms in the *Oration to the Assembly of the Saints*, and clearly they are the ones in control by the end of the century, when famous temples were falling to the blows of Christian axes. As this story is usually told, such destruction was an inevitable consequence of Christianity's inherent intolerance.[55] Do Constantine's efforts to build a more broadly based and inclusive church around the general principle of monotheism confirm or deny this premise? At the very least, by showing that a viable alternative was possible, Constantine shows that intolerance by itself cannot explain the coercive turn Christianity took. Such success as Constantine had came from his ability to use Christianity's central message – to return hatred with love – to neutralize extremists like Donatus.

As much as intolerance, the dynamics of the new arrangement between emperor and bishops worked out under Constantine explain this change. As we have seen, divine support was *the* imperative for successful rule in the late empire. The one thing the Christian God had that no other deity in the ancient world could match was, not the advantages of either monotheism or intolerance, but an organizational core in the person of its bishops – local leaders who held their local communities together and who also had a tradition of periodic meetings to work out solutions to common problems. This tradition gave the bishops an institutional base that allowed them to function in a way roughly analogous to the way the Senate had in earlier days – as a sounding board for emperors and a formal means for them to receive periodic affirmations of their legitimacy. Just as the Senate's ceremonial importance made emperors of the Principate sensitive to the standards and values of that class, so Christian emperors now were obliged to demonstrate their commitment to Christian principles and values. As one scholar put it, "By the end of the fourth century Christian orthodoxy had been added to the traditional list of virtues required in a legitimate emperor."[56]

Orthodoxy did not necessarily require the suppression of paganism, but it did require the suppression of heresy, the wrongful teaching that jeopardized every Christian's prospects for immortal life. Prior to Constantine, bishops could meet and agree on articles of faith, but – as the bishops who tried to eject Paul of Samosata from the church of Antioch discovered – they were powerless to enforce their decisions. By legalizing Christianity, the Edict of Milan had created the necessary preconditions for imperial intervention, and Constantine's summons of Church councils to deal with Donatism and Arianism established the precedent for a regular mechanism whereby that intervention could be effected. The prospect of using the coercive powers of the state to suppress heresy greatly enhanced the attraction of the empire in the eyes of the bishops and provided the incentive for them to cooperate. From the use of coercion against internal enemies to its use against external enemies was a small, but fateful, step.

Was this Constantine's impact? Indirectly, yes. He legalized their god and created a mechanism for imperial involvement in the regulation of their cult. In so doing, Constantine made Christian bishops politically relevant, and by endowing them with churches and patronage resources, he greatly enhanced their power as well as their status. But impact and intent are not identical. Constantine had learned from Christians the principle that true belief cannot be coerced. Ironically, what he taught them in return was the important role deity played in the late Roman version of national security and the many benefits that accrued from participation in that relationship.[57] A cynic might say that everything had changed and nothing had changed.

FURTHER READINGS

In his 1918 Raleigh Lecture on *Constantine the Great and the Christian Church* (published in 1929), N. Baynes referred to Constantine as "an erratic block which has diverted the stream of human history." Few would dispute that judgment, but in every other way scholars continue to differ over the extent and purpose of Constantine's impact. T. D. Barnes, in *Constantine and Eusebius* (1981), sees Constantine attaching himself to a faith that by his day had become virtually unstoppable, while R. Lane Fox concluded in *Pagans and Christians: Religion and the Religious Life from the Second to the Fourth Century A.D.* (1986) that Christianity was moribund prior to Constantine's conversion. T. G. Elliott argues for a very Catholic Constantine in *The Christianity of Constantine the Great* (1996), whereas I have attempted to shift the argument from theology to social process in *Constantine and the Bishops: The Politics of Intolerance* (2000).

Even though they were written more than two centuries ago, E. Gibbon's chapters (15–20) on Constantine and Christianity in *The History of the Decline and Fall of the Roman Empire* [1776–81] 1994 are still worth reading. His admonition that "Eusebius and Zosimus [a hostile pagan author] form indeed the two extremes of flattery and invective" is judicious, but overall Gibbon's view is informed by Enlightenment attitudes toward religion. Similarly, J. Burckhardt's powerful 1853 image of a Constantine driven solely by power reflects nineteenth-century fascination with "The Great Man." The second edition of 1880 is available in an English translation by M. Hadas as *The Age of Constantine the Great* (1949).

H. Dörries undertook a thorough, albeit theologically oriented, study of all of Constantine's writings in *Das Selbstzeugnis Kaiser Konstantins* (1954, trans. 1972). T. Grünewald's *Constantinus Maximus Augustus: Herrschaftspropaganda in der zeitgenössischen Überlieferung* (1990) is a similarly exhaustive review, this time with an eye on propaganda. The new role of the Christian bishop is brought into focus by H. Chadwick in *The Role of the Christian Bishop in Ancient Society* (1980) and by G. Bowersock in "From Emperor to Bishop: The Self-Conscious Transformation of Political Power in the Fourth Century A.D.," *Classical Philology* 81 (1986a): 298–307. See also G. Fowden, "Bishops and Temples in the Eastern Roman Empire, A.D. 320–435," *Journal of Theological Studies* n.s. 29 (1978): 53–78, and the new book by C. Rapp, *Holy Bishops in Late Antiquity: The Nature of Christian Leadership in an Age of Transition* (2005). For the religious controversies of the age, W. H. C. Frend's venerable *The Donatist Church: A Movement of Protest in Roman North Africa* (2nd ed. 1971) remains important, and R. P. C. Hanson's *The Search for the Christian Doctrine of God: The Arian Controversy, 318–381* (1988) is a good guide to the problems encountered at Nicaea.

NOTES

1 The pioneering work is W. Bauer 1971. For a critique, see Harrington 1980.

2 Lact. *DMP* 44.5. Unless otherwise noted, translations are from Creed 1984. See his n. 7, pp. 118–19, on chronological inaccuracies in the passage. On its date, see T. D. Barnes 1973.

3 Eus. *VC* 1.28.2. Unless otherwise noted, translations are from Cameron and Hall 1999.

4 Eus. *VC* 1.26–7.

5 Eus. *VC* 1.29.

6 Weiss 1993, translated at Weiss 2003, is judicious on the halo phenomenon. For the pagan account, see *Pan. Lat.* 6(7).21.3–5; Seston 1936; Grégoire 1939; Hatt 1952.

7 Spoken by Isis to her son, Horus, in *Kore kosmou*; Stob. 1.49.45.

8 Nock 1930, 1947.

9 Eus. *VC* 1.24; cf. 1.22.

10 Stark 1993, 172.

11 The panegyrist at Constantine's wedding in 307 depicts his father looking down on the proceedings from the chariot of the sun; *Pan. Lat.* 7(6).14.3. Preger 1901 drew attention to Constantine's use of a statue of Apollo-Sol for himself in Constantinople, on which see also Fowden 1991. For the use of Sol on Constantine's coins, see Bruun 1958; M. Alföldi 1964; see also Wallraff 2001; Tantillo 2003.

12 Eus. *HE* 7.30.19. Eusebius goes on to say (*HE* 7.30.20–1) that Aurelian was planning a persecution when he was killed, a charge repeated by Lactantius (*DMP* 6.1–3). On Paul of Samosata, see Millar 1971.

13 Optat. 1.22; cf. Maier 1987–9, 1:146–8 no. 15. Translations are from Edwards 1997.

14 Eus. *HE* 10.5.18.

15 *Const. Sirm.* 1 (AD 333).

16 Cf. Millar 1992, 588.

17 Eusebius includes Constantine's letter summoning Bishop Chrestus of Syracuse to the council at *HE* 10.5.22. On the speed and prestige of the public post, see Matthews 1989, 264; cf. Kolb 2000.

18 For the council's report to Bishop Sylvester of Rome, see Optat. *App.* 4; cf. Maier 1987–9, 1:160–7 no. 20.

19 Constantine's letter to the bishops at Arles is at Optat. *App.* 5; cf. Maier 1987–9, 1:167–71 no. 21.

20 See canons 3 and 7 in Hefele 1907–52, 1.1:186–7.

21 *easdem personas quae res istius modi concitant faciuntque, ut non cum ea qua oportet ueneratione summus deus colatur, perdam atque discutiam,* cited at Optat. *App.* 7; cf. Maier 1987–9, 1:194–6, esp. n. 2 on the date.

22 Letter to African Bishops, c. 321, cited at Optat. *App.* 9; cf. Maier 1987–9, 1:239–42 no. 30.

23 Eus. *VC* 2.60.1. For a very different interpretation, see T. D. Barnes 1986, 49, where it is characterized as "a long and fiery letter."

24 Optat. *App.* 10; cf. Maier 1987–9, 1:194–6 no. 26.

25 The "edict" as we have it is actually a letter (*epistula*) sent to provincial governors in the east by Licinius, reporting on agreements reached by the two emperors

when they met in Milan. Lactantius reproduces a Latin version at *DMP* 48.2–12; Eusebius provides a slightly different Greek version at *HE* 10.5.2–14. See also Chapter 10 n. 67 in this volume.

26 Lact. *DMP* 48.2.

27 *DMP* 48.2. Cf. 48.3: "so that the supreme Divinity, whose religion we obey with free minds, may be able to show in all matters His accustomed favor and benevolence towards us," and 48.11: "[so] that the divine favor towards us, which we have experienced in such important matters, will continue for all time to prosper our achievements along with the public well being."

28 Lact. *DMP* 34.1.

29 See n. 21.

30 Eus. *VC* 2.1–2.

31 Wiles 1962; Gregg and Groh 1981 redefine the issues; see also R. Williams 1987 and Beatrice 2002.

32 Eus. *VC* 2.64–72.

33 Eus. *VC* 2.71.7.

34 The surviving Syriac version of the letter, along with a Greek translation by E. Schwartz, is printed at Opitz 1934a, 41–2 no. 20. See also Opitz 1934a, 36–41 no. 18, where Constantine gives his reasons for the change of venue.

35 Constantine writes of Eusebius's fears in a letter that he sent to the congregation of Nicomedia subsequent to the Council of Nicaea. See Opitz 1934a, 58–62 no. 27.

36 Eus. *VC* 3.6.2.

37 Eus. *VC* 2.19–22. Constantine's edict recalling exiles and restoring property is at *VC* 2.24–42. On his churches, see *VC* 2.45–6 and 3.25–6, 48–52. For a very different view of events leading to the Council of Nicaea, see Elliott 1992–3.

38 Doubt was cast on the authenticity of the oration by Rossignol 1845, 112, supported by Heikel 1902, lxxix–cii. Most of the issues raised have been adequately addressed, and scholars are now inclined to accept it as genuine; see Pfättisch 1913; Kurfess 1948; T. D. Barnes 1976b; Fischer 1982; Ison 1985; Lane Fox 1986, 627–53. An exception is Cataudella 2001. On the date, see Bleckmann 1997; this date was argued for earlier by Ison 1985. The argument is accepted, with modification, by T. D. Barnes 2001. Edwards 1999; 2003, xiii–xxix, prefers an earlier date.

39 *OC* 26.2. Translations, unless otherwise indicated, are from Edwards 2003.

40 Eus. *VC* 4.32.

41 Lane Fox 1986, 628.

42 So Ison 1985, 115–16.

43 *OC* 3.3–4.

44 *OC* 3.2.

45 *OC* 11.1, my translation.

46 Compare *OC* 11.2, "My education never at any time partook of human concerns, for all habits and traits that are valued by those who have understanding are entirely gifts of God" (my translation), with Gal. 1:1, "From Paul, an apostle, not by human appointment or human commission, but by commission from Jesus Christ and from God the Father who raised him from the dead," and Gal. 1:12, "I must make it clear to you, my friends, that the gospel you heard me preach is no human invention. I did not take it over from any man; no man taught it me; I received it through

a revelation of Jesus Christ." For "bishop of those outside," see Eus. *VC* 4.24. Constantine arranged to be buried among memorials to the twelve apostles; Eus. *VC* 4.60.

47 *OC* 11.1, my translation.

48 *OC* 11.4 my translation. The passage is corrupt in the final part, but this is the clear sense.

49 *OC* 11.6.

50 Eus. *VC* 1.44.3.

51 Eus. *VC* 3.12.2, 5.

52 Eus. *VC* 3.13.2.

53 Soc. 1.26.6.

54 Optat. 3.3. On the significance of this complaint, see the comment by P. Brown at Chadwick 1980, 20.

55 The classic statement is by Gibbon, who listed "[t]he inflexible, and, if we may use the expression, the intolerant zeal of the Christians," as the first of five reasons for the success of Christianity at the start of Chapter 16 of his *History of the Decline and Fall of the Roman Empire*; cf. Gibbon [1776–81] 1994, 515. See also Drake 1996.

56 T. D. Barnes 1993, 174.

57 Garnsey 1984 is important.

6: THE BEGINNINGS OF CHRISTIANIZATION

Mark Edwards

D uring the reign of Constantine, Christianity was the religion
of the emperor but not yet the religion of the empire. His
policies and enactments on behalf of the church established
the conditions in which Christianity could flourish and thus prepared
his subjects for the Christianizing measures of his successors. If it were
true, as some contend, that Christianity was but one of many converg-
ing "monotheisms," the present chapter would not need to be carried
beyond the first section. In the second, however, I shall argue that –
considered as a cult, if not as an intellectual system – Christianity took
on features under Constantine that precluded assimilation to its rivals.
In the third, I shall follow the advance of synodal government and the
rise of the episcopal grandees, who, as I argue in the fourth and final
section, repaid the patronage of Constantine by hallowing his ambitions and endorsing a tacit parallel between earthly despotism and the
monarchy of God.

CONVERSION: FROM WHAT TO WHAT?

It is probable that by the mid-fourth century Christians made up more
than half the entire population of the empire. The sociologist R. Stark
has tentatively proposed that if the church had grown at a constant
rate of 40 per cent each decade since the time of the apostles, it
would have arrived at this preponderance without incurring any debt
to Constantine.[1] Yet even if every generation had spread the word with
the same zeal as the first, and even if Christian families were regularly
larger than those of pagans who were free to practice abortion and
infanticide, such increments could hardly have been sustained for three

hundred years. In fact, it seems that the epoch of evangelism ended with the first century;[2] Tertullian, near the close of the second century, could boast of the sudden proliferation of Christians in North Africa,[3] but if we ignore a tendentious epigram in his *Apology*, no ancient testimony lends support to the claim that pagans were converted by the fortitude of martyrs.[4] War, forensic torture, the arena and imperial caprice had together inured all ranks of society to the suffering of the innocent – and where the Christians suffered most, they were not deemed innocent by the applauding mob. Even where the spectacle was observed with admiration rather than ridicule, there would always be an equal number of apostates to justify cowardice or excite disgust. Our witnesses in the third century confirm what common sense would have predicted – that the strength of the church was lessened periodically by deaths and defections during persecution and that, when peace came, a number of the lapsed did not live long enough to complete the lengthy penances imposed as a condition of their return.

Of course, we must suppose that the church was large enough at all times to survive repeated massacres and lynchings; the Christians who inspired the abuse of Celsus and the ridicule of Lucian must already have been more conspicuous in the second century than the errant devotees of other gods.[5] Frequent correspondence was maintained between distant churches from the first century – hardly possible, one might argue, if the Christian population of the empire never rose above a few hundreds in this period, as K. Hopkins has surmised. Hopkins draws analogies with the growth of religious movements in the modern age, where every innovation must compete with at least one well-established form of Christianity; in the ancient world, however, there was nothing that resembled Christianity – no cult with such a compendious philosophy, and, even in the Indian summer of Neoplatonism, no philosophy that was so much of a cult. As Stark perceives, the most credible statistics are supplied by papyrology, and R. Bagnall calculates that, once the church was freed from persecution in 311, it recruited heavily until it came to account for 18 per cent of the Egyptian population.[6] Nevertheless, by 321 a tapering-off is visible, and if we attribute this to the repressive laws enacted by Licinius, we admit that the church was not immune to the vacillations of the civil power.

Egypt was in any case the cockpit of theological controversy and hence a region where educated men might seek advancement among the clergy while the ignorant may have been drawn into the church by the fascination of their quarrels. In Asia Minor and proconsular Africa, Christians may have been more numerous; on the other hand, no mission could bear fruit in northern Gaul, in Britain, or in any hinterland remote from an urban centre until the law began to work in favour of the evangelists. It is simply undeniable that Constantine's conversion and his repeal of persecution were propitious to a growth in Christian numbers. Few consciences perhaps were forced or bribed, but it is impossible to guess how many neophytes were created by the mere removal of obstacles and dangers. W. Cobbett thought that from the dimensions of a church one could deduce the size of its parish; yet even in Rome, where Constantine endowed more sacred buildings than in any other part of his realm, there was evidently not sufficient room within walls to accommodate the whole Christian community. In that case, one might ask what marks would identify a Christian. Baptism might be regarded as a measure of sincerity, but the number of those who underwent aspersion in the new baptisteries will never have been coterminous with the number of the faithful, for in certain regions infants received the sacrament whereas in others it was frequently deferred until the postulant was deemed incapable of further sins.[7]

From a paucity of monuments, we may safely infer a low incidence of Christians, as at Gaza, where eight temples overshadowed the single church at the beginning of the fifth century.[8] Among the Goths there were Christians already, the neophytes and children of prisoners carried home from raids in the late third century. It was only after Constantine's death, however, that the Gothic Christian Ulfila, a descendant of Gothic prisoners from Roman Asia Minor, was able to put a Gothic rendering of the Gospels into the hands of the evangelist.[9] Another missionary is said to have won Iberia,[10] while it may have been at the end of Constantine's reign that the trader Musonius began to enlarge the numbers and influence of the small Christian Church in India.[11] It is, however, unlikely that the Gospel was heard, let alone believed, by the mass of people in either of these regions. Exhortation through the megaphone of flattery should not be mistaken for bare reporting, even when the medium is an inscription like the one which commends the unanimous Christianity of the inhabitants in the Phrygian town of Orcistus.[12] Orcistus was petitioning Constantine for civic status and thus independence from its pagan neighbour Nacoleia. Though it obtained its request, it remained an obscure see. Emulation may have inspired the conversion of the magistrates in Maiuma close to Gaza, but Eusebius surely exaggerates when he tells us that the whole population took leave of its gods.[13] Constantine renamed the town Constantia – after his sister – and granted to it the status of a *civitas*, but according to Sozomen, Maiuma soon lost its status under the emperor Julian.[14] Constantine himself, although most members of his family took the colour of his religion, retained among his allies up to 331 the Neoplatonist Sopater, who made no pretence of Christianity.[15]

Why did Romans turn to Christianity? The poor, no doubt, had always had good reason to join the "Christian republic" (as Gibbon styled it), which preserved their lives in time of want and promised them a dignified interment with the hope of resurrection to better things. The conversion of the rich amazed contemporaries, and modern scholars have not been wholly incredulous of the stories which attribute it to miracle. At the same time, it may be that what Weber called the "intellectualism" of the privileged class[16] disposed them to admire the frank philosophers who not only participated in the ridicule of the ancient gods but refused them the formality of worship. Once Constantine's accession had removed the worldly barriers to conversion, it was natural that educated men should become more numerous in the church and that their works should be better known to those without. If we may believe the ecclesiastical historians, public debates were staged before the Nicene Council, and in its wake the orthodox were obliged to vanquish pagan defenders of the Arian heresy.[17]

Two monotheists are no more bound to be allies than two monarchists who favour different monarchs. The One of the Neoplatonists, for example, is incommensurable with the God of the Christian fathers, though the two have been compared from ancient times. For one thing, *theos* (Greek for "god") is not a proper name but a conventional appellative, and one that could be expunged from Plotinus's *Enneads* without damage to his intellectual system. In his work, it solicits admiration rather than worship, and while the One is at times *ho theos* (God) in a peculiar sense, the term *theos* is rejected at other times for this very reason, while the plural form is applied to lower entities with no fear of solecism, let alone blasphemy. Will and love are not ascribed to the One in Plotinus's work, except to intimate that, as the highest principle, it is sole cause of itself and free of all prior determination by an essence. Plotinus exercised the philosopher's privilege of "atheism" – abstinence from common religious festivals – declaring that "the gods should come to me, not I to them."[18] Eusebius of Caesarea likened the persons of the Trinity to a triad of higher principles in a pseudo-Platonic letter.[19] But the triad of Plotinus is "One, Mind, Soul," not Father, Son and Spirit, and the title was supplied by Porphyry, one of his disciples and a keen foe of Christianity, for all that he admired the monotheism of the Hebrews. Porphyry was a theist for whom all images, myths, and sacramental rituals were inferior representations of the "God above all";

nevertheless, because his full divinity would blind us, we must be content with shadows, and it is arrogance in the Christians to suppose that they possess the only avenue of salvation.[20] Porphyry's young contemporary Iamblichus was even prepared to justify magical practices, the interrogation of stars, and the propitiation of demons – at least for the simple pietist who had not discovered the greater efficacy of mathematics. It was on Iamblichus's teachings that the "apostate" emperor Julian was later to erect his pagan rival to the church.

In these times, strict monotheism – the choice of a single god to the exclusion of all others – was a rarity, but it was common style in magic, prayer, and literature to adopt a single patron who subsumed the deities of many lands. A simple faith, unencumbered by expensive rites, a hereditary priesthood, and fixed monuments, was especially congenial to the army, the source of a number of converts in the New Testament and the object of a purge by Diocletian on the eve of his Great Persecution. Constantine owed his coronation in 306 to his father's troops; it was also, we are told, from the example of Constantius I that he imbibed his disposition to monotheism.[21] Of course, a political autocrat will always find it expedient to suppose that heaven also is a monarchy; of course, his soldiers will be inclined to adopt the sun, the ubiquitous companion of their travels, as the ensign of that monarchy. Constantine's *Oration to the Saints* reveals that he, like all good Christians, saw the solar disc as nothing more than an icon of the Sun of Righteousness, but demotic piety may have been less austere.

The learned spoke equivocally, with an eye to future changes on Olympus. The panegyrists of Constantine, for example, avoid the names of pagan gods and any hint of emperor worship after the capture of Rome in 312, but they do not give a name to the sovereign power who ordained this victory. In the work of Firmicus Maternus, two species of enlightened monotheism are juxtaposed, if indeed they do not coalesce. In the *Mathesis*, he commends astrology as the science which discerns in the constellations the inexorable design of the God who moves them. This deity he flatters with an ardour not unworthy of a Christian, referring with esteem to Constantine,[22] while he ridicules Plotinus as a mortal who had thought himself superior to his fate. In the tract *On the Error of Profane Religions*, he vents his wit on the mysteries of Attis, Mithras, Isis, and Cybele, challenging the two young emperors Constans and Constantius to suppress them in the name of Christianity. Since churchmen of his day opposed all theories of malign predestination, it is generally assumed that he composed one work as a pagan and the other as a Christian. Yet he never defends the mysteries in his *Mathesis*, and there is no religious opinion in this book that he repudiates in his Christian petition. In the latter work, he allots each of the four pernicious cults to a different element and its associated clime and thus appears to endorse the geographic determinism of astrological writings such as Ptolemy's *Tetrabiblos*. Both books were published under Christian rulers, and if they represent incompatible convictions, we cannot say which he wrote as his most mature.

It was easy to be a Christian and something else, so long as one was not a severe philosopher or a bishop. The notion that Christianity is one, perhaps the best, of many roads to God was entertained by Zosimus the alchemist of Panopolis, who promised in his *Treatise on the Omega* to show the "Son of God becoming all things" to his novice Theosebeia.[23] It may be that he meant to exhibit a physical metamorphosis resembling the ostensible transmutation of wine to blood in the eucharists of the second-century heretic Mark the Mage.[24] Theosebeia's name suggests a Christian and may be intentionally reminiscent of the term *theosebes*, which was applied to believing Gentiles who frequented the synagogue. Pagans, Jews, and Christians used to congregate at Mamre, the site of Abraham's vision, in a festival that Constantine attempted to purify but did not turn into a Christian monopoly.[25] The relation between these three groups and the devotees of the "Most High Zeus" (*Hypsistos*) continues to exercise scholars. Evidently they worshipped the God of Abraham under a title more congenial to the Gentile settlers in Palestine; the frequency of this title in inscriptions throughout the empire may suggest that syncretism had become fashionable, or that Jews or Christians sometimes found it politic to employ an ambiguous sobriquet in worship.[26] Yet one of Constantine's aims, as we shall see in the following section, was to remind the world that Christians were not simply monotheists but the sect of Christ – the Christ of Calvary, which, as Paul said, was a scandal to Jews no less than it was foolishness to Greeks (1 Cor. 1:21–4).

THE DEMARCATION OF CHRISTIANITY UNDER CONSTANTINE

From early times the church's feasts and usages were discriminated carefully from those of Judaism. Such legislation was all the more necessary after persecution had driven some weak spirits into the synagogue: in 305 the Council of Elvira was obliged to forbid the sharing of meals with Jews, though the sufferings of the churches had been lighter in Spain than elsewhere.[27] Perhaps it was through fear of assimilation that the Latin-speaking apologists Lactantius and Arnobius waived the customary appeal to the antiquity of Moses. Palestine had been the seat of the fiercest persecution under Maximin Daia, and the separation between the two indigenous faiths was jealously maintained by the church, which now rose to prominence under Macarius of Jerusalem and Eusebius of Caesarea. The latter was in no doubt that God had revoked his pact with Israel when he gave Jerusalem over first to riot and then to Rome in AD 70. He magnified the event with lurid excerpts from Josephus in his *Ecclesiastical History*, where he also urged, improving on a hint in the ancient letter ascribed to Barnabas, that only the patriarchs, not the Jews of the Exodus, were the true precursors of Christianity.[28] Constantine's legislation is more temperate, designed at once to contain and to protect the people of the first covenant. Elders of the synagogue and those who were still called priests were now exempted from the burden of civic office; on the other hand, the circumcision of Christian slaves was rendered unprofitable by a law which required the involuntary convert to be freed without delay.[29] The mild tone of this ruling makes us doubt the authenticity of an edict in the *Theodosian Code* which forbids the Jews to punish apostates and promises harsh penalties to anyone who joins the "nefarious sect."[30] This might have been the language of a bishop but not of Constantine, at least not in his laws.

Nevertheless, one cannot mistake the tone of his letter endorsing the Nicene canon which required that the date of Easter should be calculated everywhere by the Roman and Alexandrian reckoning rather than by the "Quartodeciman" rule, which made Good Friday coincide with the Fourteenth Nisan of the Jewish Passover. Constantine does not appeal, as the Synod of Whitby did in 664, to the authority of St. Peter; he does not adduce the practical necessity of observing a uniform date for the greatest festival in the calendar. Instead, he insists that "nothing be held in common with the murderers of the Lord."[31] This is hardly fair to the Asiatics, who were accustomed to defend their own Quartodeciman computation by appealing to the chronology of the Fourth Gospel; on the other hand, the decision must have brought relief to those churchmen who had hitherto felt obliged to await the signs of a Jewish holiday before they could keep their own.

Constantine's own testament of his devotion to Passiontide is the *Oration to the Assembly of the Saints*, which salutes Good Friday as a day whose "splendour shines further than the sun's."[32] The published text contains a Sibylline oracle in which the initial letters of consecutive lines spell *Iesous Christos Theou Huios Soter* (Jesus Christ, Son of God,

Saviour). The acrostic was known already to Lactantius, but it is in the royal version that a stanza is appended spelling out the word *Stauros* (cross).[33] The vision that converted Constantine induced him not only to have a cross engraved on the shields of his troops but to build it into a colossal statue which he erected on entering Rome.[34] Only in the fourth century did the crucifixion become a subject for painters, while apologetics took for its theme not merely the necessity of Christ's death but the manner of it. Whereas Eusebius stresses the penal function of the cross, Athanasius writes that the elevation sealed Christ's victory over the demons of the air and that he spread his arms in token of his desire to embrace the world.[35]

In the cross the church had found a symbol that was simple, pathetic and eminently portable. It flung the "crucified sophist" in the teeth of pagan satirists[36] and separated Christian from Jew without transgressing the second commandment. It could not, however, satisfy the desire for cultic images which must have increased as pagans entered the church in greater numbers. The representation of Christ or God continued to be forbidden by the guardians of orthodoxy – whose intervention shows, of course, that some congregations were of a different mind. Popular devotion found a substitute in the relics of the martyrs, which pagans believed to be part of the furniture of Christian worship as early as 177, when they drowned the corpses of martyrs at Lyons.[37] The clergy of Lyons were quick to gainsay them,[38] but the Montanists' cult of martyrs was denounced in Asia only because the martyrs were unworthy, and churches of the third century permitted intercessions to the departed.[39] The honouring of martyrs was a spur to fortitude under persecution, and such obsequies are assumed to be both familiar and acceptable to the audience of Constantine's *Oration to the Assembly of the Saints*.[40] In Egypt, Athanasius deplored the lavish ceremonies which had no doubt been devised in emulation of the rites for the dead Osiris.[41] Nevertheless the custom of preserving relics spread, with its attendant prodigalities: neither could be restrained with any force by the episcopate when they were fostered with such enterprise by Helena, the mother of Constantine.

Helena did not profess Christianity before Constantine adopted it as his own religion; nor was she a personage of note before his accession, as Constantius had put her away for a wife of nobler birth (Coin 19). Eusebius makes Constantine the author of her conversion,[42] which, for all his praise of her mental powers, was evidently sentimental rather than intellectual and bore fruit both for herself and for the church in 327, when she set out for Palestine in search of relics. The Church of the Nativity in Bethlehem (Plan 5) and the Church of the Ascension on the Mount of Olives were her greatest projects. Legend wrongly credits her with the foundation of the Church of the Holy Sepulchre, the foundations of which had already been laid on the putative site of Jesus's tomb before her expedition (Plan 4).[43] The first witness to her most famous deed, the invention or discovery of the True Cross, is Ambrose, writing in 395.[44] Some detect an allusion to the trophy in Eusebius,[45] but he has nothing to say of Helena's part in finding it; no display of the cross in Jerusalem is recorded before 350 (Fig. 13).[46] Even if the story is apocryphal, it attests this low-born woman's reputation as the tribune of a lay piety which outran the deliberations of the clergy. At the same time, we observe that Bishop Macarius of Jerusalem – most probably the true founder of the Church of the Holy Sepulchre – is introduced in the narrative to orchestrate a miracle which picks out the Cross of Christ from the other two.[47] Constantine did not expect that the church, any more than the empire, would be governed by the consensus of the faithful: the function of a bishop in his see, like that of a general in the army, was to lead.

ALTAR AND THRONE

Almost simultaneous with the first preaching of the Gospel was the appearance of the *ecclesia*, or church, which sought to anticipate the kingdom by submission to an exigent rule of conduct and an ostentatious cult of Christ as Lord. Initially those teachers who were recognised as apostles (that is, emissaries of Christ) were the authorities in everything, and obedience was enforced by the consensus of the laity. By the end of the second century, however, the majority of congregations relied on a body of presbyters, or elders, to ward off heresy, while the power to exclude or reprimand the wicked was entrusted to the monarchical *episkopos*, or bishop. Dissent was now repressed by appeal to a rule of faith, the common patrimony of those churches which had been planted by the apostles or their deputies. The guardians of this rule were ancient bishoprics in the centres of population, and most venerable of all (says Irenaeus) was the see of Rome, which Peter and Paul had watered with their blood.[48] Differences between prelates might require the arbitration of a synod, where the dissident was first interrogated by a presbyter and then chastised by the suffrage of the bishops. If he remained both obstinate and powerful, the juridical pronouncement could be rendered effective only by the interposition of the secular magistrate. When in

271 the pagan emperor Aurelian deposed Paul of Samosata, bishop of Antioch, he decreed that the "bishops of Italy" should determine the succession to this see.[49] By the time of Constantine, then, the Christian might be subject to half a dozen modes of governance – presbyteral, episcopal, patriarchal, synodical, pontifical, imperial – and it was often left to character or historical circumstances to decide which would prevail.

Constantine's conversion and accession armed the church with a chief executive of unprecedented power. It was, however, his custom to form his judgements with the assistance of the bishops, and the teaching office came to be regarded as their prerogative. "How," asked the Council of Antioch in 341, "can we, being bishops, follow a presbyter?"[50] In Carthage, where the legitimacy of the bishop was disputed, Constantine himself, after some disclaimers, took a hand in the controversy. Although he declared in favour of Rome's candidate Caecilian, the Catholic Church in Africa was irreparably weakened by the schism, with the consequence that the bishop of Rome became the undisputed primate even of western synods which he did not attend in person. In the east, on the other hand, the bishoprics of Antioch, Nicomedia, Caeasarea, Alexandria and, in time, Constantinople claimed a parity of honour which was calculated to heighten any dissonance in practice or opinion. The same divisions and rivalries that necessitated the summoning of councils also robbed their deliberations of integrity in the eyes of the vanquished parties; usually the minority was intractable, and the emperor did not escape the task of adjudication, since he might be obliged to temper a decree that he was unwilling to enforce. Since not only the punishment of malcontents but the composition, locality and presidency of the council were at the discretion of the sovereign, the session itself was merely one event in a protracted contest for the royal favour. Hence arose a generation of bishops who combined theological acumen with eloquence and ambitious statecraft in the classic vein.

The most important example of this heightened interaction of altar and throne surely came in the Council of Nicaea in 325. Its chief aim was to arrest the controversy which ensued when Arius, an Alexandrian presbyter excommunicated by Bishop Alexander, sought asylum with Eusebius of Nicomedia, a former protégé of the pagan emperor Licinius.[51] Eusebius found no scandal in his suppliant's view that Christ, the Word and Son of God, was created out of nothing; Alexander, on the other hand, maintained that he was eternally of one nature (*homoousios*) with the Father, and therefore God. It is said that Alexander was accompanied to the council by his deacon Athanasius, who succeeded to his chair. Two other eminent clerics who brought their quarrel to the meeting were Marcellus of Ancyra, the modern Ankara, and Eusebius the great historian, who regarded his bishopric in Caesarea as the metropolis of Christian Palestine. All five left writings to show that, even before the accession of Constantine to the eastern throne, the bishop of a major see was a man of parts and learning, was not unacquainted with philosophy, and was capable of labouring Christian thoughts into classic periods with an artifice that could only have been acquired at some pecuniary expense.

Marcellus held that the Caesarean Eusebius had compromised the unity of God in his exposition of the Trinity, and Eusebius charged him with the converse error. Although neither of the Eusebii was an Arian, both suspected that the Alexandrian watchword *homoousios* would compromise the primacy of the Father. When a creed was issued which contained the word, both subscribed it, but Eusebius of Nicomedia was deposed because he refused to sign the anathemas which were appended to the document. Yet the Alexandrian victory was soon annulled, for within five years the newly-founded see of Constantinople had received Eusebius as its first incumbent, while Arius was restored to communion with his reluctant countrymen by order of Constantine. Socrates's conclusion that the emperor cared for nothing so much as concord would be unavoidable even if Constantine himself had not said as much in his letter to Aelafius at the height of the Donatist schism.[52] Even before the council he had reprimanded Arius for his contumacy and Alexander for testing the conscience of his subordinate.[53] Knowing, like any autocrat, that one choir can accommodate many voices, he was readier to embrace a penitent Arius or Eusebius than to countenance those whose strong convictions still untuned the harmony of the church.

What is pragmatism in Constantine becomes intellectual principle in Eusebius, the forgotten theologian of this epoch, though perhaps, as M. R. Barnes contends, the most representative.[54] He is not to be considered an Arian merely because he endorsed his master's strictures on the controversy and branded Athanasius as a meddler when he stood in the way of reconciliation. That unity mattered more to him than purity of doctrine or antiquity of discipline is obvious from those portions of his *Ecclesiastical History*, undoubtedly completed before the reign of Constantine, in which he enumerates the presidents of the major sees, pours obloquy on the antipope Novatian, discovers an almost uniform canon of scripture in every period, and expunges from his chapters on Paul of Samosata all rumour of the doctrinal controversies which were still reverberating in his own time.[55] At Nicaea he was irenic to a fault, for he accepted the *homoousion*, explaining to his bewildered congregation in Caesarea that the word meant nothing new and that the emperor had demanded its inclusion in the creed.[56] To him, therefore, an ordinance from the throne – which pagan usage had already described as sacred – outweighed the murmurs of a whole diocese; but was the emperor then a theologian? Certainly Eusebius credits him with sermons of great insight in the *Life of Constantine*, while he praises the emperor in the *Tricennalian Oration* of 336 as an omniscient vigilante, forcing demons from their altars with the zeal of a second Christ.

The doctrine that the civil power is also the chief authority in ecclesiastical matters may be embraced for worldly ends or from a conviction that the godly king is the voice of the whole congregation. The Caesarean Eusebius may be acquitted of ambition, since he refused the see of Antioch when Constantine offered it to him,[57] and as T. D. Barnes points out, he was no court bishop, since his duties in Caesarea kept him far from the seat of power.[58] The politician among his fellow clergy was his namesake, "the great Eusebius," who, before his promotion to Constantinople, had migrated to Nicomedia from the flourishing city of Berytus. Throughout his life it appears that he owed his eminence to royal favour rather than to his own talents or the suffrage of the people to whom he ministered. Nevertheless, we can call him neither heretic nor toady, for he never espoused the "Arian" position that the Son had been created "out of nothing," and he could not have been such a powerful figure at the Council of Antioch in 341 had his views not coincided with the second thoughts of the Greek Church outside Egypt.[59] To judge by ecclesiastical declarations, the arch-heretic of this period was Marcellus, who after his deposition in the 330s was repeatedly condemned by eastern councils, although during the reign of Constantine he found a temporary berth in Rome.

The most buffeted man of these years was Athanasius, in his own estimation bishop of Alexandria from 328 to his death in 373. Like his predecessor, Alexander, he was challenged by the party of Melitius, a rival for the see of Alexandria who had assumed the office of bishop during the time of persecution. The Council of Nicaea allowed the Melitians to retain their ordinations under Alexander's authority, but it seems that Athanasius felt obliged to overawe them by strong measures. He remained the favourite of the populace, and a phalanx of Egyptian bishops demurred to his condemnation before his peers at Jerusalem in 335. The grounds of deposition included the charge that Athanasius had obstructed the grain supply from Alexandria – a tribute to the power that an ecclesiastical luminary could now wield under a sympathetic ruler. Relying, however, less on his popularity than on his own enterprise, Athanasius fled to Constantinople, where he seized the bridle of the emperor's horse before an astonished crowd and persuaded Constantine to commute the deposition to a suspension.[60] The deposition was ratified in 339 by Constantine's heir Constantius II, but neither the Christian nor the pagan mob in Alexandria would tolerate the successors who were imposed by royal decree.[61] Athanasius himself fled to Rome, and during the twenty years that followed he was by turns restored and banished, a rebel in Italy and a fugitive in Egypt, the champion of the undivided Trinity and the mascot of the Roman claim to primacy – though in his own diocese it was he, and not his western sponsors, who was known by the title of pope.

The one ecclesiastic who retained the unbroken confidence of the emperor was Ossius of Cordoba, who accompanied him to the east as his confessor in 324. His counsel was indispensable, as he knew more Greek than the easterners knew Latin and could be trusted to speak the mind of the Roman Church in all debates. It is plausibly surmised from Syriac records that he presided in 324 at a synod in Antioch, where Eusebius of Caesarea was subjected to a hostile inquisition.[62] He may have presided at the Nicene Council in 325,[63] and it is said he became the keeper of the sovereign's conscience after 326, when Constantine learned that his execution of Crispus, the heir apparent, had been a judicial murder. What advice the Spaniard gave on the Arian controversy we do not know, but at the western Council of Serdica in 343 it was he who affirmed that the see of Rome was entitled to reverse decisions taken by bishops in another province.[64] He was generally regarded as a defender of the Nicene *homoousion*, and his subscription in 357 to the "Blasphemy of Sirmium," a council which prohibited all cognates of the noun *ousia*, was explained as the aberration of an old man under intolerable tortures.[65] After all, it had never been his custom to be at war with God's vicegerent; in 343 he had set his face against churchmen of a different breed, who had set themselves not only above the throne but above the concord of the churches, east and west.[66]

RESTRAINING DISSENT

To borrow a trite antithesis, the authority of the clergy under Constantine was institutional rather than charismatic, in that it rested on their ordination rather than on any display of superhuman merits. Now that persecution had ceased, there was little opportunity in civil life to imitate the fortitude, the vigour, or the spectacular defiance of the martyrs. It was remembered against some bishops, including the great Eusebius of Nicomedia, that they had failed in the hour of trial; on the other hand, to enjoy a reputation as a confessor was to win a vote without speaking, as the old Paphnutius proved in his defence of clerical marriage at Nicaea.[67] The rise of asceticism in the fourth century has sometimes been explained as an attempt to re-enact the heroic sufferings of the church under pagan tyranny; yet this will not hold for Antony, who acted on Christ's command to "sell thy goods to feed the poor" and then departed to the Egyptian wilderness still in the heat of the eastern persecution in 306.[68] It might be true of the next generation of eremites, who gathered in the same desert around Pachomius after 320. But unlike Antony, many of these were men with an aspiration to learning, and the self-imposed austerities of philosophers may have seemed to them more instructive than the transient affliction of the saints. Pythagoras and his like had been commended as a pattern to the confessor by Tertullian and by Origen, the latter himself a martyr; even under Diocletian's flail, however, the Christian often met with no privation but captivity, and the plaudits that were readily bestowed upon the Greek might not be extended to the Christian who had voluntarily run upon his death.[69]

P. Brown has shown that in late antiquity the holy man was the bearer of great though unofficial power, receiving suppliants and deciding village lawsuits where the magistrate was absent or untrusted.[70] In theological controversy, bishops sometimes found monastic disputants intractable, except to the assaults of other monks. But this was to come: the patriarchs Alexander and Athanasius lived on good terms with these athletes of the desert. Athanasius relates that Antony and a party of troops descended on Alexandria in support of the Nicene formula, and the accusations levelled against Athanasius by the Melitians confirm that he had such forces at his beck.[71] Even such interventions as the Council of Gangra's interdict on the use of male attire by women need not betoken a general state of war between monks and bishops:[72] the latter could not have hoped to impose their canons from without if they could not reckon on a majority within. The ascetics did not contradict the view of the episcopate that a man without an office had no authority, even if God had loaded him with spiritual honours. The hierarchy was itself divided by the opposite case, when the conduct of the man had shamed his office. Some thought it impossible to restore a fallen bishop or to keep fellowship with one who had connived at the fall of others by restoring apostates. Hence arose the great schisms, behind which some historians now glimpse forces as invisible to the actors as Homer's gods were to the combatants at Troy.

Perhaps the tamest schism to trouble the fourth-century church was Novatianism. Novatian, the earliest Roman theologian to write in Latin, was the rival of Cornelius for the vacant bishopric of Rome in 251. Neither before nor after his defeat is there any evidence to associate him with the Greek-speaking populace of the capital, but fifty years before the Nicene Council, the Novatianists of the east made common cause with the Asiatics by adopting the Quartodeciman date for Easter.[73] Constantinople, the New Rome, appears to have been the headquarters of the movement after Constantine, though it persevered for another hundred years in Italy; in neither area were they much molested in the fourth century, except by legislation. Constantine forbade them to assemble and promiscuously joined them in his edict with other "heretics" who had compromised the unity of Christendom; yet he summoned their leader Acesius to the Nicene Council, if only to tell him mockingly to "get himself a ladder and climb to heaven on his own."[74] Eusebius thought it profitable to transcribe Cornelius's sallies against Novatian in his *Ecclesiastical History*;[75] other Greeks, including the Nicene Fathers, dubbed them *katharoi*, or puritans, extending the name to a small brigade of Donatists who had seized a hill near Rome.[76] By superimposing one schism on another, they could safely gratify the western patriarch without seeming to have passed a conscious judgement on the unextinguished feud in Africa.

Seeds of wrath in the African church were sown by Diocletian's persecution. Mensurius, the undisputed bishop of Carthage during the troubles, died in 311, and Caecilian, one of his deacons, was installed as his successor. A party of Numidian bishops, led by Secundus of Tigisita and Purpurius of Limata, challenged his ordination and elected one Majorinus in his stead.[77] The causes of secession were variously reported. One story ran that, during the persecution, Caecilian had caused the deaths of a number of Christian prisoners by obstructing supplies of food. Another laid a charge of *traditio* (handing over scriptures to be burned) against Mensurius, another against Bishop Felix of Abthugni, who took part in the consecration of Caecilian.[78] A third maintained that Secundus and his acolytes had been suborned some years earlier by a rich woman named Lucilla, whom Caecilian had rebuked for her devotion to an undeserving martyr.[79] If we accept this third account but assume that the objection was to any cult of martyrs and not merely to a false one, the Donatists will appear to us as champions of an austere demotic piety against the mitred sycophants who had neither withstood the season of adversity nor honoured those who did. We must, however, remember that the anecdote was told in the Catholic interest, that it echoes second-century invectives against the new prophecy of Montanus,[80] and that the heroes of the Donatist martyrologies were not volunteers but casualties of imperial repression. The unwordliness which is frequently imputed to the malcontents would have sorted ill with the typical cult of martyrs, in which lachrymose penitents helped themselves to indulgences from a treasury of merits.[81] In fact, we cannot be certain that the discipline of the people in the Donatist church was stricter than elsewhere: it is one thing to ask that the clergy be untainted by apostasy, another to force an impossible perfection on the laity. The Donatist Tyconius, acknowledged by Augustine as his mentor in the exegesis of scripture, also anticipates his argument that in this world the wheat is inseparable from the tares.[82]

If the Donatists were sectarian – refusing, for example, to reciprocate the Catholic acknowledgement of their baptisms – it was not because they cherished either a loftier or a more popular understanding of the Gospel. With lawyerlike and self-protective logic, they taught that anyone who took part in a eucharist administered by a successor of Caecilian, or even a bishop of the same communion, was breaking bread with apostates and shared the guilt of those who had bought immunity by sacrificing to pagan gods in the age of persecution.[83] It followed that any magistrate who lent troops to the cause of unity was a persecutor; Donatus himself addressed a contumelious letter to Gregory, Prefect of Africa, and flung back Daniel's saying "Thy gifts remain with thee, O King" at Constans, son of Constantine.[84] Catholics in reply professed a patriotism unusual in the literature of African Christianity: for Optatus, all outside the Roman empire are barbarians, and obedience to the Roman see is the test of ecclesiastical fellowship.[85] Under his guidance, some modern commentators have discerned behind this schism a revolt of the native Berbers against the economic tyranny of Carthage, once their Punic and now their Roman overlord.[86] As evidence, one can cite the humiliation of the Catholics in Cirta, principal city of Numidia;[87] the jejune and ungrammatical Latin employed in correspondence by the enemies of Caecilian; and the readiness of the fifth-century Donatists to ally themselves with roving marauders known as Circumcellions.[88] Yet as to the first point, Cirta, too, was a colony; as to the second, Paul wrote barbarous Greek and yet was proud to be a citizen of both Tarsus and Rome; and as to the third, it is usual for disaffected parties to become confederates, even when the roots of disaffection are not the same. Donatus enjoyed enough support in

Carthage to be recognised at the eastern Council of Serdica in 343 as the bishop of that city;[89] no distinction of ancestry, no social inequality, is needed to engender strife between a flourishing colony and its mistress overseas.

What the pagans made of these divisions we do not hear, except for a sarcastic animadversion to the belligerence of prelates in Ammianus Marcellinus.[90] They must have perceived at least that, with the rise of the episcopate, city was set against city in a manner unknown under any pagan ruler and that for the first time the religion which the emperor chose to patronise was defined as much by doctrine as by cult. The presence of pagan onlookers was no restraint but an irritant to those who believed, with Constantine, that a unified church was the necessary instrument by which the "Catholic faith" was to take possession of the world. Athanasius's lucid classic *Against the Nations*, for example, borrows an argument from Constantine – that a single world requires single ruler.[91] At the same time, as though the ecclesiastical corollary was not clear enough already, he dwells – as the older apologists seldom did – on the divinity of Christ the Word, thus hinting that the merely superhuman Christ of Arius could not have restored to a fallen race the image that God himself vouchsafed to Adam. Eusebius, on the other hand, believed that the church should be governed by consensus, not by faction, and that God had now appointed as its head the same legislator whom he had given to the nations; no wonder that in his panegyric on Constantine he maintains that a certain knowledge of God has been dispensed to all peoples through their common participation in the Word.

No more to Eusebius than to Constantine did it seem that a belief in the universality of reason ought to entail a universal toleration. On the contrary, it is reason that exposes the absurdity of the ancient myths and tears away the specious veils of allegory that philosophers cast upon them.[92] Constantine acts not merely as the image of Christ the logos but as the plenipotentiary of the common logos, which has dispensed to the wise in every nation, when he suppresses pagan obscenities at the holy site of Mamre, the "school of vice" at Aphrodite's shrine in Phoenician Aphaca, and the impostures practised under the name of Asclepius in Cilicia.[93] Reason should dissuade us, in Eusebius's view, from idolatry, the bloodying of altars and the supplication of any local deities, and hence he ascribes to Constantine an edict against all sacrifice which is not transmitted in the Theodosian Code.[94] The mistake betrays the ambitions of the newly-ennobled clergy; the even-handed statesmanship of Constantine was better understood by his fellow-Latins. Lactantius and

Arnobius find a charter for theological scepticism in the great moralists of Rome's heyday; from the same source, however, they imbibe republican principles which the Seleucids and Ptolemies had extinguished in the Greeks. Moreover, they were laymen to whom the accession of a Christian monarch promised freedom but not a benefice. Lactantius therefore commends in his *Divine Institutes* a provisional indulgence of the false cults,[95] and they are granted a sort of parity in Constantine's *Oration to the Saints*: "Go then, impious ones . . . to your slaughter of victims, your immolations, surfeits and carousings, as you pursue unbridled pleasure under cover of sacrifice."[96] Eusebius is sometimes thought to have tampered with the *Oration* (which survives as the fifth book of his *Life of Constantine*), but he could not have forged this passage, any more than he could have coined the emperor's saying that he wished to be the "bishop (*episkopos*) of those outside."[97]

In origin, the Greek noun *episkopos* means "overseer," and the symbol of the emperor's benign but inescapable surveillance was the Unconquered Sun, which continues to be depicted on coins long after his first profession of Christianity (Coins 4 and 15). In Constantinople, a famous statue represented Constantine in the guise of Apollo Helios (Fig. 3).[98] Yet he banished his likeness from pagan shrines, and a similar prohibition may have been implied when he asked that a temple erected in his honour should be kept free of all "pestilent superstition" (Fig. 4).[99] Chrysostom relates that when he learned that one of his statues had been overthrown and shattered, he showed no anger but passed his hand across his face and professed surprise that he could detect no injury.[100] No wonder that Eusebius, when he illustrates the distinction between the persons in the Godhead by analogy with the ruler and his statue, insists that the original and the image, though entitled to equal honour, are not identical.[101] By contrast, Athanasius employs the same analogy to demonstrate the unity of worship and assumes that this implies unity of nature.[102] He was writing under Constantius II, and it may seem paradoxical that the latter should have been hostile to a theology that enhanced the sanctity of his own insignia. No doubt he perceived that Athanasius flattered the image to divide the monarchy: since the filial image is coeval with the Father, power should never be a monopoly, in heaven or on earth. Eusebius, on the other hand, having hinted in an early work that Father and Son were related more by fiat than by nature, could proceed without hypocrisy to suggest in his later writings that this God had now inaugurated a human regency in Constantine.

Notes

1 Stark 1996, 10–14. Hopkins 1998 finds that a similar projection yields corollaries which shed light on the facts of history. It teaches us, for example, not to anticipate a general persecution before the middle of the third century, when there would at last have been a million Christians in a world of a hundred million; and it shows us why it was only at the beginning of the fourth century, as the figure approached ten million, that an aspirant to the throne could forge a profitable alliance with the church.

2 If the church grew little in the second century, numbers must have been higher in the first than many scholars have surmised. The paltry figures entailed by the rising graphs of Stark and Hopkins seem hard to reconcile with other data. If, for instance, there were only ten thousand Christians in the empire at the time of Pliny's governorship in Bithynia (*Ep.* 96), how could he pretend that they were so numerous in that province that they threatened to drain the commerce of the temples? And if its population at the end of the second century did not exceed that of Iceland today, how could the oppressed and largely illiterate church have nourished such a generation of writers as Tertullian, Clement, Origen, Hippolytus, and Julius Africanus?

3 Tert. *Apology* 37.

4 Tert. *Apology* 50: "the blood of the martyrs is seed." Lactantius states that the sufferings of the church under Diocletian provoked both sympathy and reflection (*Div. Inst.* 5.23), but even if his evidence can be trusted, the circumstances were extreme.

5 Cornelius's (d. 253) enumeration of his clerical staff in Rome (Eus. *HE* 6.43.11) bespeaks at most a Christian population of fifty thousand in a city whose population is generally reckoned at a million; Lane Fox 1986, 47, 268–9. This implies that even in the metropolis of the Christian world, no more than 5 per cent of the inhabitants were Christian in the middle of the third century, and it therefore tends to verify Hopkins' estimate that 1 per cent of the empire had adopted this religion. Yet the figures of Cornelius may not be typical, since he wrote at a time when the Roman church had suffered more than others and the clergy more than the laity in that city.

6 Bagnall 1982.

7 Such delays were especially prudent in a time of persecution, since baptism was regarded as a plenary absolution for the lapsed. See Jonkers 1954, 32 (canon 12 of the Council of Ancyra, AD 314).

8 Marc. Diac. *V. Porph.* 17.

9 Ruf. *HE* 10.9; Soc. 1.19; Philost. 2.5. Heather and Matthews 1991, 142–3 date the beginnings of Ulfila's mission to 340. T. D. Barnes 1990, by contrast, dates Ulfilas's consecration to the last year of Constantine's reign.

10 Soc. 1.19.

11 Philost. 3.4–6.

12 *MAMA* 7:305 = *ILS* 6091, translation at Lee 2000, 90–2. See also the more recent text and commentary of Feissel 1999.

13 Eus. *VC* 4.37.

14 Soz. 5.3.6–9.

15 On his death, cf. Eun. *VS* 6.2.10–12 with Zos. 2.40. Compare also Constantine's close relations with the pagan priest Nicagoras of Athens (*OGIS* 720–1, translated at Lee 2000, 88; cf. Fowden 1987) and the praise he received from the pagan historians Praxagoras (Phot. *Bibl.* 62 = *FGH* 2B219:948–9) and Bemarchius (Lib. *Or.* 1.39 = *FGH* 2B220:950), on whom see now Bleckmann 1999 and Raimondi 2003.

16 M. Weber 1963, 118–36.

17 Soc. 1.8; Gel. Cyz. *HE* 2.14.1–24.30. This debate is no doubt fictitious, though it is hard to see why an author who was engaged in free invention should have weakened the orthodox case with an apocryphal quotation that is detected by the "Arian" interlocutor. Occasions of this kind are described, for example, in Augustine's recantations, and it was common before the Council of Nicaea for the defendant at a synod to be interrogated by a presbyter; see Lim 1995.

18 Porph. *V. Plot.* 10.35.

19 Eus. *PE* 11.20, citing [Plato] *Ep.* 2.

20 Fragments of Porphyry's treatise *On the Return of the Soul* are appended to Bidez 1913.

21 Eus. *VC* 1.27.2.

22 And to his "deified" father Constantius at 1.10.13–14.

23 See W. B. Scott 1936, 104–53.

24 Irenaeus *Adv. Haer.* 1.13.2.

25 Though their own altar was demolished and they were debarred from the Christian sanctuary, the pagans continued to offer sacrifice to Abraham's angels, according to Sozomen (2.4.2); cf. Eus. *VC* 3.52–3.

26 Zeus Hypistos predominates in inscriptions of Caria, Syria, and mainland Greece, Theos Hypsistos elsewhere; see Mitchell 1999, 128–47. Assuming that the appellations are nonetheless synonymous, Mitchell posits a cult which grew from "local roots" in Greece and neighbouring areas but spread by "cross-fertilisation" with Judaism and was fitted to survive though not to prevail because it was not allied to civic or imperial institutions (pp. 126–7). I cannot, however, follow him when he implies that the Novatianists espoused the cult in Phrygia in accordance with a general design of accommodation to Judaism (p. 123): the ancient accusation of Judaizing is calumnious; the Hypistarian doctrines find no home in Novatian's classic exposition of the Trinity; and had his followers not upheld the divinity of Christ, the wider church would have deemed their baptisms invalid.

27 Canon 50 in Jonkers 1954, 16.

28 Eus. *HE* 3.6; cf. Eus. *PE* 7.3–8.

29 *CTh* 16.8.2, 16.9.1.

30 *CTh* 16.8.1.

31 Eus. *VC* 3.19.1.

32 For translation and review of scholarship, see my *Constantine and Christendom* (2003). The date of the *Oration* is still unknown, though its authenticity is now admitted by almost every commentator.

33 *OC* 18; *Sibylline Oracles* 8.217 ff.; Lact. *Div. Inst.* 7.19.9.

34 Eus. *VC* 1.39–41, esp. 1.40.1–2; cf. Eus. *HE* 9.9.10; *LC* 9.8–11.

35 Athan. *De Incarn.* 25 (*SCh* 199:356–8).

36 E.g., Lucian *Peregrinus* 13.

37 Eus. *HE* 5.1.62.

38 They are not refuted by the *Acts of Polycarp*, where it is said that the admirers of this martyr requested his body from the prefect after his death, which occurred sometime between 142 and 165. The object was to honour the body, not to venerate it.

39 Origen *De oratione* 14.6.

40 *OC* 12.

41 Athan. *V. Anton.* 90.

42 Eus. *VC* 3.42.1.

43 Stemberger 2000, 57.

44 Ambrose *De obit. Theod.* 73.

45 Drake 1985.

46 Cyr. Hier. *Cat.* 10.19.

47 On the growth of the legend, see J. W. Drijvers 1992.

48 Irenaeus *Adv. Haer.* 3.2.

49 Eus. *HE* 7.30.19.

50 Jonkers 1954, 57.

51 Theod. *HE* 1.20.1.

52 Eus. *HE* 1.27.5; Optat. *App.* 3.

53 Eus. *VC* 2.69.1.

54 M. R. Barnes 1998, 52.

55 Eus. *HE* 6.43, 7.27–30.

56 Soc. 1.8 passim.

57 Eus. *VC* 3.61.2.

58 T. D. Barnes 1981, 266.

59 See J. N. D. Kelly 1972, 263–74.

60 On this incident see Chapter 8 n. 53 in this volume. All panegyrics or satires on Athanasius rely primarily on his writings from exile – *Apology to Constantius, History of the Arians, On the Decrees.*

61 See AM 22.11.3–10 on the violent end of George of Laodicea.

62 Chadwick 1958.

63 T. D. Barnes 1981, 215.

64 Jonkers 1954, 67.

65 Athan. *Hist. Arian.* 2.

66 Jonkers 1954, 65.

67 Soc. *HE* 1.11.4.

68 Athan. *V. Anton.* 2.

69 See Elvira canon 60 (305?) at Jonkers 1954, 18.

70 Brown 1971.

71 See esp. Brakke 1995.

72 Jonkers 1954, 83–4.

73 Soc. 4.28 passim. See above n. 31.

74 Eus. *VC* 3.64.1; Soc. 1.10.4.

75 Eus. *HE* 6.43.3–22.

76 Epiph. *Anc.* 13; *Pan.* 59.13.

77 Optat. 1.19.

78 Aug. *Brev.* 3.25; *Pass. Mart. Abit.* 15; Optat. 1.27. The authority of scripture became more absolute, but the codices less precious, under a sovereign who was able to commission fifty leather-bound copies in a single draft; Eus. *VC* 4.36.

79 Optat. 1.16–19; Aug. *Cresc.* 3.29; *Brev.* 3.31–2.

80 Eus. *HE* 5.16–17 passim.

81 E.g., Cyprian *Ep.* 22.

82 Aug. *De doct. Christ.* 3.45.

83 E.g., Optat. 3.14.

84 Optat. 3.3.

85 Optat. 2.4–5, 3.3.

86 Frend 1971.

87 Constantine's donation of a new basilica to the Catholic bishops of Cirta (Optat. *App.* 10) implies that the Donatists were in possession of the old basilica.

88 See Optat. 3.4.

89 Aug. *Cresc.* 3.38.

90 AM 21.16.18.

91 Athan. *Con. gen.* 36-8; cf. Eus. *LC* 6.

92 Eus. *PE* 3.7–14.

93 Eus. *VC* 3.51–8; cf. Robert 1973, 188–92.

94 Eus. *VC* 2.45.1.

95 See Digeser 2000.

96 *OC* 11.

97 Eus. *VC* 4.24.

98 Fowden 1991. Pictures of the saints could be owned (Eus. *HE* 7.18.4) but not displayed in churches (Elvira 30, at Jonkers 1954, 13).

99 Eus. *VC* 4.16; *CIL* 11.5265 = *ILS* 705; cf. Gascou 1967.

100 Joh. Chrys. *De statuis* 1.

101 Eus. *DE* 5.1.4.

102 Athan. *Apol. con. Arian.* 3.5.

7: TRADITIONAL RELIGIONS

A. D. Lee

T he world in which Constantine grew up during the late third century was a world "full of gods."[1] It was full of gods in the sense that "religion pervaded every aspect of political and social life"[2] and that religious life in the Roman empire encompassed an extraordinary diversity of deities and of expressions of devotion to those deities. This diversity was observable in any part of the Roman empire, but even in the late third century, when it was increasingly marginalised as a locus of political power, it was the city of Rome which continued to offer the most conspicuous and concentrated exemplar of this phenomenon.

TRADITIONAL RELIGIONS OF ROME: AN INTRODUCTORY TOUR

Had the young Constantine visited the city of Rome in the 280s, he would have been confronted by a vast array of temples and shrines, their history reflecting the evolution of Roman power over the course of a millennium, and he would no doubt have marvelled at them in the same way that his son was to do during a famous visit three-quarters of a century later (see Map 3.1).[3] Entering the traditional heart of public life in the city, the forum, his gaze might well have been drawn first to the temple of Jupiter, which occupied a commanding position on the Capitoline hill overlooking the forum and was still regarded by one fourth-century writer as "the most magnificent building in the whole world."[4] A temple dedicated to the chief deity of the original Roman pantheon – which he shared with his consort Juno and daughter Minerva – had been sited here since the late sixth century BC, and it had provided an important focus for Roman civic life across the centuries.

Among other major ceremonial occasions, it was here, at the start of the new year, that the consuls offered vows for the well-being of the state during the republic and for the health of the emperor and his family during the empire, and it was here, too, that successful generals made sacrifices as the culmination of triumphal processions through Rome – something the adult Constantine himself was to have the opportunity to do, though not without controversy, as will be seen later in this chapter.

At the opposite end of the forum, the young Constantine would have been able to observe the circular shrine of Vesta, another cult of great antiquity and importance dedicated to the goddess of the hearth-fire.[5] The maintenance of the perpetual flame within the shrine had long been viewed as vital to the welfare of the Roman state, and so it was tended by a special band of priestesses, the Vestal Virgins, priestesses who came under the authority of the chief priest (*pontifex maximus*) – an office always held by the reigning emperor and therefore another issue of potential significance for Constantine in later life.

Facing the forum and immediately adjacent were the temples of Vespasian and of Antoninus and Faustina respectively, which reflected a relatively more recent development in the religious life of Rome – the emergence of the imperial cult.[6] The initiative for this seems to have come from the provinces, particularly in the eastern Mediterranean, where the ruler cult was a well-established feature of Hellenistic monarchies. Augustus and most of his more immediate successors exercised considerable caution in accepting offers of divine honours in their lifetime, but by the late first century AD the monarchical system of government established by Augustus had become sufficiently accepted for temples to deceased emperors to be constructed in the heart of the capital. During Constantine's youth, a further variation on this theme came about with the close identification of the emperors Diocletian and Maximian with Jupiter and Hercules, respectively (Coins 6 and 7),[7] and in this area also Constantine himself was to confront issues in due course.

Ascending the adjacent Palatine hill, Constantine would have come upon temples dedicated to Apollo and Cybele. In contrast to the indigenous Roman deities encountered so far, these were originally official "imports" from the eastern Mediterranean. Although the Palatine temple of Apollo was the work of the emperor Augustus, another temple to this deity, associated in the Greek world with healing, prophecy, and the sun, had apparently been constructed on the Campus Martius in the late fifth century BC in response to an outbreak of plague. A time of crisis had also been the occasion for the introduction to Rome of the even more exotic deity Cybele, the "Great Mother" from Phrygia in Anatolia. The strong ecstatic dimension of this cult and the fact that her priesthood comprised castrati made this a somewhat surprising choice for importation in the late third century BC, to be explained in part by the exigencies of the Hannibalic War; however, the fact that both cults had been admitted on the initiative of the Senate no doubt meant that there was a strong degree of state control and, in the case of Cybele, "domestication."[8]

Turning to the south-west, Constantine could then have descended from the Palatine, crossed the Circus Maximus, and proceeded up the nearby Aventine hill, where, with help from local inhabitants, he might have been able to find the entrance to one of a number of underground shrines set up by devotees of Mithras in Rome – in this case, the "Mithraeum" now located under the church of S. Prisca.[9] This was yet another cult of eastern origin, but one which never achieved official recognition in the way that the others encountered so far had – and indeed the very different character of the sacred space in which Mithraic ritual was performed, compared with the standard temple, emphasised this cult's divergence from more traditional ones. Had he been able to gain admission to the cave, he would have observed frescos depicting the seven grades of initiates, a cult statue of Mithras slaying a bull and an inscription including the words "who saved us with the shed blood."[10] This exclusively male cult, whose hierarchical structure appealed particularly to soldiers and bureaucrats, appears to have given greater emphasis to the individual and to soteriological ideas than other cults in ancient Rome.

Returning northwards from the Aventine and following the course of the Tiber as it curved away to the west, Constantine would have reached the Campus Martius. Once a large open area for the assembly of citizens in Republican times, it had become increasingly monopolised during the empire by an array of imperially sponsored public amenities such as baths and theatres. Scattered among these structures were various temples, including one dedicated to the goddess Isis, yet another eastern import, initially without official sanction.[11] The Egyptian deity Isis had become an enormously popular object of devotion in the eastern Mediterranean during the Hellenistic period, due particularly to her association with fertility and the protection of women – especially in the context of marriage and motherhood – and it was natural that, as Rome's importance grew during the late republic and the Principate, the city should attract immigrants from all over the Mediterranean world, who naturally brought with them their gods.[12]

A short distance away, the young Constantine would have encountered the most recently completed of the structures on his tour, a temple in honour of Sol, the sun, erected in the mid-270s by the emperor Aurelian on his return from his eastern campaign.[13] Aurelian no doubt saw himself as simply adding yet one more element to the Roman pantheon, but the popularity of the cult of Sol in this period may have reflected an apparently widespread view that Sol was in some sense the supreme deity who subsumed all others – a form of quasi-monotheism whose adherents may have included Constantine's own father, Constantius.[14]

The young Constantine's tour of the religious landmarks of Rome could have continued for many more hours and taken in many more buildings, but it is perhaps more interesting to imagine him wearying of his sightseeing after the temple of Sol and beginning his northward journey home by proceeding along the nearby Via Flaminia – a route which would have taken him out of the city over the Milvian Bridge.

TRADITIONAL RELIGIONS: THE WIDER PICTURE

The approach so far has been to provide an entrée into the traditional religions of the Roman world through their most visible and potentially permanent manifestations – temples and shrines – concentrated in a relatively small area which had, until recently, been the focal point of the empire. As a description of religious life in the Roman world, however, it is obviously only very partial, for at least three reasons: first, it only hints at the diversity of religious cults in the provinces of the empire; second, it risks overlooking the more transient, impermanent expressions of religious sentiment, such as sacrifice and festivals; and third, it tends to privilege public religion over private. Each of these aspects needs to be investigated if a more rounded sense of traditional religions in this period is to be gained.

The fact that a number of the cults noted in the previous section had their origin in the eastern Mediterranean is a reminder that the empire encompassed a large number of regions, each with its own religious traditions. Some of these gained wider currency, while others remained more restricted in terms of their appeal. In the east, Egypt, Syria, Anatolia, and Greece each had indigenous pantheons and religious practices of great antiquity, as also did North Africa and the Celts of Spain, Gaul, and Britain in the west (see Maps 1 and 2). Moreover, many of these regions had already been subject to other significant cultural influences prior to conquest by the Romans, notably the diffusion of Hellenism in the east, especially in the centuries after Alexander, and the impact of the Phoenicians on North Africa, influences which left their mark on religious life. In Anatolia, for example, cults of Greek deities were prominent alongside those of indigenous mother goddesses and of the widely-revered Anatolian moon-god Men.[15]

Two further broad features of provincial religion warrant particular comment – syncretism and localisation. Many provincial cults involved deities with a double name, where one name is that of an indigenous deity assimilated to a non-indigenous but analogous deity. So in Anatolia, dedications have been found to Zeus Abozanos, Zeus Alsenos, Zeus Thallos and a host of other Zeus combinations, just as in Gaul there is evidence for Mars Camulus, Mars Caturix, Mars Lenus, and many others, as well as a range of Hercules and Mercury hybrids.[16] This syncretic phenomenon also highlights the way in which many deities were specific to a particular locality, whether it be an individual community or a natural feature such as a spring or a grove. From the perspective of inhabitants of rural villages, these localised cults are likely to have been of greater significance than the widely diffused cults which inevitably tend to be featured more prominently in the surviving evidence.

Whether one is considering religious life in the metropolis or the provinces, in urban or rural contexts, another important dimension is that of praxis. In contrast to the Christian emphasis on doctrine and creed, religious allegiance in traditional cults was expressed above all through ritual, and the pre-eminent ritual was sacrifice. The most dramatic form of this was the public slaughter of an animal, parts of which would then be burnt on an altar in honour of the deity while the remainder was cooked for consumption by participants.[17] The centrality of sacrifice is particularly evident from the fact that when in 249 the emperor Decius decided that all inhabitants of the empire should participate in an empire-wide expression of devotion to the gods, it was the offering of sacrifice which his edict stipulated.[18] At the same time, the offering of sacrifice was typically one part of more general festivities, which might include a procession through the town or countryside, perhaps to the accompaniment of music, and was sometimes associated with cultural or sporting events extending over a number of days.[19]

On such occasions, the emphasis was on public, communal celebration of the gods, but religious devotion could also take forms which were more private and/or individual. Such features are apparent to some extent in the cult of Mithras, as also, in different ways, in the common east Mediterranean phenomenon of pilgrimage, particularly to consult oracles or seek healing,[20] and in domestic religious observance, reflected, for example, in the wall shrines (*lararia*) which have survived in houses at Ostia and Pompeii and in the terracotta figurines from Roman Egypt.[21] They are also apparent in the areas of astrology and magic – the latter typically employed with a view to achieving practical success in love, sport, or the law court. Although these can hardly be described as forms of religious *devotion*, and although their relationship to "religion" has long been the subject of debate, it is legitimate to treat them as a form of religious engagement in at least a broad sense, since magic was essentially an attempt to manipulate spiritual forces, while Roman astrology had close links with magic and divination, and the stars whose movements were the focus of astrology were identified with immanent powers.[22] The popularity of magic is attested by the large numbers of so-called magical papyri which have survived from Roman Egypt and the substantial quantities of curse tablets and amulets from around the Roman world,[23] and the popularity of astrology is reflected in astrological treatises and surviving horoscopes.[24]

TRADITIONAL RELIGIONS: TERMINOLOGY AND TOLERATION

The religious profile of the Roman world, as briefly sketched in the preceding sections, presents a terminological challenge which highlights some important issues. This vast array of cults and practices has traditionally been referred to as "paganism," but this is a term that has been increasingly subjected to critical scrutiny in recent years. One problem is that "paganism" implies a degree of coherence belied by the sheer diversity of the phenomena the term is supposed to encompass. A second is that it was a term not used by pagans to define themselves but rather by their critics, the Christians.[25] Not surprisingly, adherents of traditional cults did not have an agreed common designation for themselves or their cults: even as late as the end of the third century, the emperor Diocletian is found using the rather vague phraseology of *vetus religio* and *veteriores religiones*, both perhaps best translated simply as "traditional practices."[26] This reflects the fact that

> they had no tradition of discourse about ritual or religious matters (apart from philosophical debate or antiquarian treatise), no organised system of beliefs to which they were

asked to commit themselves, no authority-structure peculiar to the religious area, above all no commitment to a particular group of people or set of ideas other than their family and political context.[27]

It was only the process of confrontation with Christianity in the third and fourth centuries which began to create a growing sense of identity, reflected for example, in the apostate emperor Julian's use of the designation "Hellenes" for his co-religionists.[28]

"Polytheism" has seemed to some scholars preferable to "paganism," because, although another "–ism," it explicitly acknowledges the plurality of cults.[29] Others, however, have deemed it unsatisfactory, above all because the term is unable to accommodate an important feature of religious life in the Roman world which has so far only been hinted at − namely, the fact that the Roman religious scene included monotheists who were neither Jews nor Christians. To start with, there was a long tradition in Greek philosophy which acknowledged the existence of one god; indeed, "the vast majority of philosophers in antiquity believed in one God who providentially governs the universe."[30] More specifically, the dominant philosophy during the third and subsequent centuries was Neoplatonism, which, as developed by Plotinus (205–69/70), laid great emphasis on "the One" and on achieving unity with it.[31]

It might be tempting to minimise the significance of "pagan monotheism" as the preserve of an intellectual elite were it not for the fact that there is a large body of evidence attesting the existence of another, much less rarefied form of the phenomenon. This was the cult of Theos Hypsistos (the Highest God), whose "worship from the Hellenistic period until the fifth century was found in town and country across the entire eastern Mediterranean and the Near East . . . [and whose] worshippers came mostly from the humbler levels of society."[32] Its significance has perhaps been masked by the fact that the inscriptions which constitute the primary evidence for the cult are scattered across a wide geographical area and a vast number of specialist publications.[33] One of the most informative as to the character of the cult is the following third-century text from Oenoanda in south-western Anatolia:

> Born of itself, untaught, without a mother, unshakeable, not contained in a name, known by many names, dwelling in fire, this is god. We, his angels, are a small part of god. To you

who ask this question about god, what his essential nature is, he has pronounced that Aether is god who sees all, on whom you should gaze and pray at dawn, looking towards the sunrise.[34]

A further feature of the cult which is of interest is that worship of this deity seems to have focused on the medium of light, whether in the form of the natural rays of the rising and setting sun or the artificial illumination of lamps and torches, while animal sacrifice apparently had no role in cult ritual – a view which can be paralleled in ancient philosophical thought.[35] Generalising about "the uncontrollably complex heritage"[36] of traditional religions in the Roman world is therefore difficult in the extreme.

The diversity of traditional religions raises another issue of broader significance, that of toleration. The apparent willingness of the Roman state to accommodate new cults in Rome and allow the continued practice of local religions in the provinces prompted Gibbon to write of "the universal spirit of toleration" which characterised the empire in the second century AD, in contrast to "the intolerant zeal of the Christians."[37] Nevertheless, Roman incorporation of novel cults should not be seen as reflecting a fundamental attitude of openness to all new religious ideas, as the strength of the rhetoric in Diocletian's edict against the Manichaeans (297/302) makes clear:

> A new cult ought not to find fault with traditional practices. For it is a most serious offence to re-examine matters decided and fixed once and for all by our ancestors, which retain their standing and contain the path to be followed. For this reason we are very keen to punish the obstinate and perverse thinking of these utterly worthless people. For they introduce strange new creeds in opposition to the traditional cults, excluding by their own perverse judgement the practices which divinity granted to us in former times.[38]

Some cults, such as those of Apollo and Cybele, were initially accepted only under the pressure of circumstances, while others were added as an extension of military conquest. The Roman approach can therefore only be described as toleration in a very loose, weak sense – at best, "toleration by default" as opposed to "toleration born of principle."[39] "The Romans tolerated what seemed to them harmless, and drew the line whenever there seemed to be a threat of possible harm"[40] – hence the persecution of the Bacchanals in the 180s BC, the periodic expulsion of other religious groups from Rome (Chaldaeans, adherents of Isis, Jews), the repression of Druidism in the north-western provinces, and ultimately the persecution of Christians. The fact that such action was not taken more often shows rather "an appreciation of the limits of [government] power or a passive acquiescence in the presence of cults which they could not control."[41]

TRADITIONAL RELIGIONS: VITALITY OR DECLINE?

An important but difficult question is the vitality or otherwise of traditional religions in the late third century, since the answer to this question obviously has implications for the significance attached to Constantine's religious policies. The "vitality" of a religion, however, is a very slippery concept in any context, and the problem is compounded in this period by the plethora of cults, some of which may have been thriving, while others may have been static or in decline, whatever those terms may mean. In the early twentieth century, the German scholar Johannes Geffcken thought he had identified conclusive proof of the decline of many traditional cults in the form of the dramatic falling off of inscriptions commemorating dedications to gods from the mid-third century onwards. Since this falling off coincided neatly with the years of severe military and economic crisis experienced by the empire, it was tempting to posit a causal link between these two broad developments and deduce that the cumulative hardships and insecurity of the 260s and 270s prompted a "loss of faith" in traditional deities.[42]

This argument, however, is open to criticism and qualification on a number of fronts. In the first place, "if times were hard, pagans had their own explanation: the gods were showing their anger or quarrelling among themselves. The remedy was not to abandon belief in them, but to try to identify and appease the aggrieved party."[43] Second, although the economic travails of the empire must have reduced the ability of communities and individuals to fund the setting up of inscriptions, this says "nothing about people's faith. It is not the priest who is stilled but the stonecutter."[44] Third, evidence from Egypt ("the only province where we can look beyond the inscriptions" because of the survival of papyri) shows "traces of continuing pagan festivals and cult, even in the most obscure and difficult decades . . . suggest[ing] that inflation did not destroy the traditional patterns of public cult in the towns."[45] Finally, it underplays the significance of forms of religious devotion whose vitality was not dependent on major economic resources. The cult of Theos Hypsistos, for example,

> was not linked, like the worship of emperors or the main civic deities, to sporting or musical competitions, grand festivals, lavish euergetism, or even to animal sacrifice. It was therefore ideally equipped to weather the storms of economic recession, social change, and the militarization of the Roman world in the third and fourth centuries.[46]

If, however, reports of the death of traditional religions in the mid-third century have been greatly exaggerated, it nevertheless remains the case that certain forms of traditional public cult increasingly struggled to maintain their popularity during the first half of the fourth century; under the pressure of imperial disapproval, but also because of the impact of Neoplatonic philosophy, a decline in the frequency of rituals involving blood sacrifice has been identified as a trend of particular significance.[47] At the same time, less public forms of traditional devotion clearly continued throughout the fourth century and beyond, even as imperial sanctions progressively reduced the formal room for manoeuvre.[48] Those sanctions were directed particularly at sacrifice, but

> polytheists had been accustomed to offering prayers to the gods in innumerable ways – at the healing springs of Britain, Spain and Gaul, in caves cluttered with late Roman lamps, as in Attica, and with lights and with heavy clouds of incense all over Syria. Though essential to the Christian representation of the end of polytheism, and deeply resented, laws against sacrifice may have been less disruptive to traditional piety than we might suppose.[49]

CONSTANTINE AND TRADITIONAL RELIGIONS: TO 312

This, then, was the general religious context in which Constantine grew up. Of course, he was born in a particular geographical location within the empire – Naissus in the northern Balkans – so presumably his experience of localised indigenous cults will initially have been of those specific to that region, probably various Thracian deities and rider-god cults.[50] However, his close involvement in army life from an early age will also have resulted in steady exposure to many of the deities worshipped more widely in the Roman empire. The famous early third century calendar of religious festivals preserved among the papyri recovered from the Roman military outpost on the Euphrates at Dura-Europos testifies to the regular performance, in military camps around the empire, of rituals associated with the traditional state deities of Rome such as Jupiter, Juno, and Mars, as well as the imperial cult,[51] and the popularity of the cult of Mithras among soldiers has already been noted.

All this can be no more than plausible surmise, however, because so little is known about Constantine's early years. Attempts to gain a clearer perspective on his stance vis-à-vis traditional religions before 312 have focused on two issues: the religious views of his father, Constantius, and Constantine's religious policies and attitudes during the years following his proclamation as emperor in 306. The limited nature of the evidence for Constantius's religious position has made it possible for scholars to adopt a spectrum of positions, ranging from "traditional pagan" to "solar monotheist" to "Christian or Christian sympathiser," of which "solar monotheist" has proved the most popular. The numismatic evidence, however, tends to tell against that view, although the alternatives are no more strongly supported.[52] The best evidence for the idea of Constantius as a Christian or a Christian sympathiser is his limited enforcement of the Diocletianic persecution in the territory under his control and the fact that one of his daughters was named Anastasia (from the Greek word for resurrection), but neither of these items is compelling. Constantius may not have martyred any Christians, but he did destroy church property, and even Eusebius acknowledged that persecution in Gaul and neighbouring regions lasted for nearly two years;[53] moreover, Maxentius ended persecution of Christians after he came to power in 306, yet he has not been labelled a Christian. As for the name "Anastasia," the most that can be claimed is that it implies the presence of someone with Jewish or Christian sympathies in Constantius's household;[54] alternatively, "she may have taken the name herself after 312 at baptism when other members of the family became Christians."[55]

As for Constantine's own religious policies and attitudes in the period 306–12, the most widely accepted view is that he was a tolerant pagan with monotheistic tendencies, though this is based in part on assumptions about his father's religious sympathies. Some, however, have seen him as more definitely committed to the Christian cause from at least 306.[56] The most important evidence in support of this position is Lactantius's statement that "the first act of Constantine Augustus on assuming imperial power was to restore the Christians to their worship and their God."[57] Yet as the case of Maxentius again shows, toleration of Christianity need not presuppose personal commitment. There is also the well-known story of his apparent encounter with the god Apollo at a shrine in Gaul in 310, as recorded by an anonymous panegyrist:

> You had turned aside toward the most beautiful temple in the whole world, or rather, deity made manifest, as you saw. For you saw, I believe, O Constantine, your Apollo, accompanied by Victory, offering you laurel wreaths, each one of which carries a portent of thirty years. For this is the number of human ages which are owed to you without fail – beyond the old age of a Nestor. And – now why do I say "I believe"? – you saw, and recognized yourself in the likeness of him to whom the divine songs of the bards had prophesied that rule over the whole world was due.

The allusive style of this particular genre and the difficulty in determining the extent to which the content of panegyrics received prior "official" approval pose problems in unravelling precisely what happened here, but the emphatic identification of "your Apollo" and the fact that Constantine's coinage began in the same year to bear representations of the sun (Coins 4, 14, and 15) – with which Apollo was of course closely associated – strongly imply that Constantine's primary loyalty still lay with traditional cults.[58]

CONSTANTINE AND TRADITIONAL RELIGIONS: 312–324

Constantine's defeat of Maxentius at the Milvian Bridge in October 312 effectively gave him control of the western half of the empire. It is also from this point onwards that there is incontrovertible evidence of Constantine giving positive support to the Christian Church in a way which leaves no doubt about his personal religious allegiance. How, then, did this affect his attitudes to and treatment of traditional religions during the twelve-year period until the next critical juncture in his political career, his defeat of Licinius and acquisition of the eastern half of the empire in 324?

The first test may have come immediately with his triumphal entry to Rome, since the traditional climax of such occasions was the victorious general offering a sacrifice in the temple of Jupiter on the Capitoline. However, the sources for Constantine's entry leave it unclear whether he staged a formal triumph or not, and if he did, whether he offered sacrifice or refrained from doing so. The picture is further complicated by the fact that Constantine subsequently made visits to Rome in 315 and 326 to celebrate the tenth and twentieth anniversaries of his accession to the imperial throne and apparently on one of these occasions pointedly refused to participate in sacred rites on the Captoline, alienating the Senate and the urban populace. It is, however, unclear whether this episode, reported by the unsympathetic historian Zosimus in a confused and tendentious manner, should be assigned to 315 or 326, or indeed to 312. It would be understandable if Constantine had offered sacrifice in October 312, both in terms of political calculation and his then limited understanding of the demands of Christianity, but the state of the evidence means that the issue must remain unresolved.[59] At any rate, Zosimus himself admits that Constantine continued to hold the title of chief priest of the Roman cults (*pontifex maximus*) down to the end of his reign.[60]

In February 313 Constantine and Licinius held a summit meeting in Milan, one of the outcomes of which was a declaration of religious toleration traditionally, though somewhat misleadingly, known as the "Edict of Milan." The primary interest of this document has usually been its explicit statement of toleration for Christians and restoration of their property throughout the empire, but from the perspective of this chapter, the crucial point is that this measure also explicitly guaranteed the freedom of worship of non-Christians:

> We have likewise granted to others the open and free right
> to observe their own religion in accordance with the peace
> of our time, so that everyone may have the free opportunity
> to worship whatever they choose. We have done this so that
> we do not appear to have acted to the detriment of any cult
> or religion.[61]

In other words, the fact that Constantine now favoured the Christian Church in no way meant that non-Christians under his rule would be the object of discrimination.

Nevertheless, this did not prevent him from issuing a number of laws which placed restrictions on certain forms of traditional religion.

An imperial letter of 318 prohibited the practice of certain forms of magic, but the fact that it distinguished between "bad" magic used to plot against men's lives and "good" magic intended to heal or protect crops places Constantine's concerns in a long tradition in Roman law. Similarly, measures issued in 319 and 320 limiting the legitimate activities of diviners to public contexts are consistent with long-standing imperial worries about the potential political threat that divination in private might pose.[62] These measures, then, cannot be regarded as violating the principles enshrined in the Edict of Milan.

In this period, therefore, Constantine did not initiate any policies that actively discriminated against adherents of traditional cults except in ways for which there were well-established precedents. One possible explanation of this is in terms of political pragmatism: during this phase, Constantine ruled only half of the empire, and that half had been exposed to Christianity less intensively than the east and included a powerful bastion of traditional religious sentiment in the form of the senatorial aristocracy; it would therefore have been unwise politically for Constantine to take any steps in the religious field which might alienate the substantial non-Christian population of the west. If political pragmatism was the primary determinant of policy, however, then one would expect to see more stringent policies implemented once Constantine was sole ruler of the empire. A critical question, then, is whether 324 marks a watershed in Constantine's behaviour and whether tougher policies are evident during the years that follow.

Constantine and Traditional Religions: 324–37

There can be no doubt that Constantine's pronouncements from 324 onwards sometimes indicated a more critical attitude against traditional religions. Consider the following excerpt from his *Letter to the Eastern Provincials* in 324, reproduced by Eusebius in his *Life of Constantine* – where Constantine's remarks are, at this point, directed to God himself:

> Right-thinking people should be confident that only those whom you call to rest their hopes on your sacred laws will live holy and upright lives. As for those who draw back, let them have the temples of falsehood they desire – we have the most radiant dwelling place of your truth which you have given in accordance with your nature.[63]

Elsewhere he talks about non-Christians as having "the violent rebel-liousness of injurious error . . . obstinately fixed in their minds" and as being in need of healing.[64] Expressions of contempt, however, are one thing; the crucial question is whether this sort of attitude was trans-lated into action. The first hint that this was unlikely to be the norm comes in the same document, where it is evident that Constantine is at least partly concerned to prevent a backlash against the adherents of traditional religions by Christians resentful at the persecution they had endured in recent decades, and where he explicitly eschews the use of compulsion in the promotion of Christianity: "it is one thing to take on willingly the contest for immortality, quite another to enforce it with sanctions."[65]

In view of these features, the *Letter to the Eastern Provincials* has usually been seen as in effect another edict of toleration, even if some of its language is dismissive or critical of traditional cults.[66] However, the matter is complicated by the fact that, a couple of chapters before reproducing the letter, Eusebius states that Constantine issued a law that "restricted the pollutions of idolatry which had for a long time been practised in every city and country district, so that no one should presume to set up cult-objects, or practise divination or other occult arts, or even to sacrifice at all."[67] Prohibition of divination and occult arts is consistent with the laws of 318–20 noted in the previous section; it is particularly the claim about a ban on sacrifice which has generated scholarly controversy.

The controversy has arisen in part from the fact that the relevant section of the Theodosian Code preserves no law of Constantine. It does, however, include the following excerpt from a law of his sons, issued in 341:

> Let there be an end to superstition, let the madness of sacri-fices be done away with. For anyone who dares to perform sacrifices in contravention of the law of the holy emperor our father and this decree of Our Clemency shall experi-ence the appropriate penalty and an immediate sentence of judgement.[68]

Many scholars, however, remain unconvinced that Constantine imple-mented a ban on sacrifice: it goes against the general tenor of the *Letter to the Eastern Provincials*. The panegyrical character of the *Life* and the fact that Eusebius does not quote the law directly has aroused the suspicion that his primary concern – writing as he was soon after Constantine's death – was to bolster his image as an emperor resolutely opposed to traditional cults, and the 341 reference to "the law of the holy emperor our father" could be a looser phrase referring to Constantine's views rather than specific legislation.[69] Moreover, the staunch pagan Libanius is emphatic that, whatever else he may have done to weaken pagan cults, Constantine allowed traditional temple rituals to continue unchanged.[70]

This is not to deny that Constantine took active steps against temples in the east after 324. Eusebius records five specific cases of temples being destroyed – those of Aphrodite in Jerusalem, Heliopolis, and Aphaca, a temple of Asclepius at Aegae in south-eastern Anatolia, and an unspecified shrine at Mamre in Palestine.[71] As has been noted by various scholars, however, special circumstances can be seen to account for the targeting of these particular sites: the temples of Aphrodite were associated with ritual prostitution, and the one in Jerusalem was thought to have been built over the location of the Holy Sepulchre; Mamre was likewise a place of special significance to Christians, while the temple of Asclepius had associations with Apollonius of Tyana, who had featured prominently in anti-Christian polemic during the Diocletianic persecution.[72] There is no reason to generalise from these cases to an empire-wide policy of temple destruction, particularly since it is clear that there remained numerous long-established temples throughout the empire which became a focus for attacks later in the fourth century. On the other hand, it has generally been accepted that Constantine sanctioned the transfer to government coffers of significant quantities of gold and silver from temple treasuries.[73]

The fourth-century Antiochene rhetor Libanius claimed that Constantine needed this gold and silver to help with the costs of establishing his new capital Constantinople.[74] Whether this was the case, the establishment of Constantinople has provoked debate of relevance for other reasons: according to different sources, Constantine adorned the city with statues of deities taken from temples, prominent adherents of traditional cults are said to have played a role in the dedication ceremony, a representation of the Tyche (guardian spirit) of the city also featured at the dedication, and Constantine erected a porphyry column surmounted by a radiate figure identified by some as Helios, the sun-god (Figs. 2 and 3; cf. Coin 15).[75] Most of the relevant sources are from the sixth century or later, but even if they preserve reliable information, it is possible to read too much significance into them. Eusebius goes to great lengths to try to excuse the presence of the cult statues in the city, suggesting that Constantine displayed them in order for them to be the object of derision, but it is surely more plausible that Constantine saw them as works of art intended to enhance the beauty of the city; one of the prominent pagans said to have been involved in the dedication ceremony was Sopater, a leading Neoplatonic philosopher who is known from other sources to have enjoyed Constantine's favour during the second half of the 320s;[76] the city's Tyche was a very ill defined entity; and the radiate figure could just as well have been a calculated exploitation of the scope for overlap between solar monotheism and Christian ideas of light.[77]

A final episode which has prompted debate of relevance is Constantine's response to the Italian community of Hispellum (Spello) in the mid 330s when it requested permission to build a temple in honour of Constantine and his family (Fig. 4). Contrary to what one might have expected, Constantine acceded to this request. Had this occurred in the years soon after 312, one might have explained it in terms of his not yet understanding the full implications of his adoption of Christianity, but that argument can hold no force by this late stage of his reign, particularly when Constantine had been having temples destroyed in other parts of the empire. There are, however, two points of fundamental importance here: first, it is the imperial cult which is at issue in this case, and that cult was as much about expressing political loyalty as about religious allegiance; second, Constantine grants the request "on the express condition that this temple dedicated to our name should not be defiled by the deceits of any contagious superstition" – almost certainly a reference to sacrifice. Constantine, then, can be seen making a modest concession while maintaining his integrity on what he regarded as the crucial religious issue in the situation.[78]

How, in the end, should Constantine's attitudes and policies towards traditional religions be characterised and explained? This will depend in part on the view one takes of the central issue of whether he banned sacrifice. For some of those who accept that he did, Constantine becomes an individual stridently opposed to traditional cults – precisely the image, in fact, which Eusebius projects in his *Life of Constantine*. But there remain features of his behaviour which are not easy to reconcile with such an image – his willingness to associate with prominent adherents of traditional cults such as Sopater, his allowing the community of Hispellum to build a temple, his retention of the office of *pontifex maximus*, apparently without demur. These features suggest that a more subtle and nuanced approach is required. Political calculation may well have been a factor in the period from 312 to 324 and perhaps continued to be so subsequently; a majority of his subjects must still have been non-Christians, even after the acquisition of the more heavily Christianised east. However, another possibility has also been proposed – namely, that Constantine, although firmly committed to Christianity himself, pursued a considered policy of seeking religious consensus and toleration; after all, "it is not necessary to have weak beliefs to be tolerant of religious diversity."[79] From this perspective, which takes for granted that there was no outright ban on sacrifice, it was sometimes necessary for Constantine to adopt strongly worded rhetoric which denounced traditional cults in order to maintain his credibility with more militant Christians, even while his actions communicated a different, more balanced message.[80] The Constantine who emerges from such an analysis is certainly a more complex and convincing character than Eusebius's rather one-dimensional portrait.

FURTHER READING

For good surveys and discussions of traditional religions in the Roman world, see J. North, *Roman Religion* (2000) (succinct); R. MacMullen, *Paganism in the Roman World* (1981) (fuller); M. Beard, J. North, and S. Price, *Religions of Rome*, 2 vols. (1998) (detailed and well illustrated, with the second volume a valuable sourcebook); and H.-J. Klauck, *The Religious Context of Early Christianity: A Guide to Graeco-Roman Religions* (2000) (a clearly organised reference work which focuses on *Realien* rather than broader interpretation). For particularly well-documented regions, see Part I of R. Lane Fox, *Pagans and Christians* (1986) (on Anatolia), and D. Frankfurter, *Religion in Roman Egypt* (1998). P. Athanassiadi and M. Frede's *Pagan Monotheism in Late Antiquity* (1999) is an invaluable collection of essays on an important but neglected dimension of Roman religious life.

One of the most important ancient sources for Constantine's religious policies is Eusebius's *Life of Constantine*: Averil Cameron and S. G. Hall offer a good translation and judicious commentary on this difficult and tendentious work (1999). Modern biographies of Constantine obviously include much of relevance to the themes of this chapter; the most recent comprehensive biography in English is that of T. D. Barnes, *Constantine and Eusebius* (1981), which is firmly grounded in the sources, though also sometimes a little too ready to take Eusebius's testimony at face value, with the result that the Constantine who emerges is thoroughly pro-Christian and anti-pagan from the outset; see the important reviews by H. A. Drake in *The American Journal of Philology* 103 (1983): 462–6, and Averil Cameron in *JRS* 73 (1983): 184–90.

S. Bradbury "Constantine and the Problem of Anti-Pagan Legislation in the Fourth Century," *Classical Philology* 89 (1994): 120–39, H. A. Drake "Constantine and Consensus," *Church History* 64 (1995): 1–15, and the relevant sections of W. Liebeschuetz, *Continuity and Change in Roman Religion* (1979) and J. Curran, *Pagan City and Christian Capital: Rome in the Fourth Century* (2000) provide valuable discussions of aspects of Constantine's religious evolution and policies towards traditional cults.

NOTES

1 To use the felicitous phrase from the title of Keith Hopkins's (1999) entertaining and provocative study.

2 Hopkins 1999, 43.

3 For Constantius II's visit to Rome in 357, see AM 16.10 and Symm. *Rel.* 3.6–7. It is not known whether Constantine's upbringing included a trip to Rome – his triumphal entry after his victory over Maxentius in 312 may well have been his first visit to the city – but an imaginative exercise in virtual history, such as follows in this section, can still serve a serious didactic purpose.

4 AM 22.16.12. For the archaeology and history of the temple site, see Platner and Ashby 1929, 297–302; L. Richardson 1992, 221–4; Steinby 1993–2000, 6:144–53.

5 For the archaeology and history of the shrine, see Platner and Ashby 1929, 557–9; Richardson 1992, 412–13; Steinby 1993–2000, 5:125–8.

6 For the archaeology and history of the sites, see Platner and Ashby 1929, 13–14, 556; Richardson 1992, 11–12, 412; Steinby 1993–2000, 1:46–7, 5:124–5. For the imperial cult more generally, see Hopkins 1978, 197–242; Liebeschuetz 1979, 64–78; Price 1984; Gradel 2002.

7 For this development, see Liebeschuetz 1979, 235–44.

8 For the temples of Apollo and Cybele, see Platner and Ashby 1929, 15–19, 324–5; Richardson 1992, 12–13, 14, 242–3; Steinby 1993–2000, 1:49–57, 3:206–8. For the cult of Cybele (Magna Mater) in Rome, see Beard, North and Price 1998, 1:96–8, 164–6, 2:43–9.

9 For the specific shrine, see Richardson 1992, 257–8; Steinby 1993–2000, 3:268–9; Vermaseren and Van Essen 1965. For the cult, see Gordon 1996; Beard, North and Price 1998, 1:278–91.

10 Vermaseren 1956–60, no. 485.

11 For the site and its history, see Platner and Ashby (1929) 283–5; Richardson (1992) 211–12; Steinby (1993–2000), 3:107–9; for the cult, see Beard, North and Price (1998) 1:278–91.

12 Cf. Noy 2000.

13 For the site and its history, see Platner and Ashby 1929, 491–3; Richardson 1992, 363–4; Steinby 1993–2000, 4:331–3. For the cult, see Halsberghe 1972; Liebeschuetz 1979, 277–91; 1999a, 187–92.

14 See M. D. Smith 1997 for references and a revisionist critique.

15 Mitchell 1993, 2:11–31.

16 Mitchell 1993, 2:22–4; Derks 1998, 95–9.

17 Lane Fox 1986, 69–72; Beard, North, and Price 1998, 2:148–52.

18 Rives 1999.

19 MacMullen 1981, 18–28; Lane Fox 1986, 66–8, 90–2; Beard, North and Price 1998, 2:116–47.

20 MacMullen 1981, 28–9; Lane Fox 1986, 41–2, 168–261; Frankfurter 1998, 145–97.

21 Orr 1978; Frankfurter 1998, 131–42.

22 Lane Fox 1986, 36–8; Betz 1991; Barton 1994, 27–71.

23 Betz 1986; Gager 1992; Kotansky 1994; Michel 2001.

24 MacMullen 1971; Barton 1994, 27–94.

25 For the history of the term, see O'Donnell 1977.

26 In his notorious edict against the Manichaeans of 297/302, see *Coll. Mos. et Rom. Leg.* 15.3.2–3 with the translation at Lee 2000, 66–7.

27 North 1992, 187.

28 North 1992, 188–9; cf. Rives 1999.

29 For discussion and further references, see Drake 1996, 3 n. 1; Athanassiadi and Frede 1999, 4–7; Lee 2000, 10.

30 Frede 1999, 56.

31 Rist 1967; Edwards 2000, vii–xxix.

32 Mitchell 1999, 125–6.

33 Mitchell 1999, 128–47 assembles a catalogue of nearly 300 epigraphic texts.

34 *SEG* 27 (1977) no. 933 (trans. Mitchell), with discussion and further references in Mitchell 1999, 81–92.

35 Cf. Lee 2000, 32–3.

36 Fowden 1993, 38.

37 Gibbon [1776–81] 1994, 56, 447; cf. Drake 1996, 7–11.

38 *Coll. Mos. et Rom. Leg.* 15.3.2–3 – a text which, interestingly, Gibbon does not appear to discuss.

39 Garnsey 1984, 9.

40 North 2000, 63.

41 Garnsey 1984, 9; cf. Beard, North, and Price 1998, 211–44.

42 Geffcken [1920] 1978, 25–30; cf. Liebeschuetz 1979, 231–4.

43 Lane Fox 1986, 575.

44 MacMullen 1981, 127. Indeed, as MacMullen has shown elsewhere, not just religious dedications but all forms of public inscriptions dropped off markedly from the mid-third century.

45 Lane Fox 1986, 578–81. Though Bagnall 1993a, 260–73, argues that pagan temples, dedications, and practices seem to have been in serious decline from the mid-third century.

46 Mitchell 1999, 127.

47 Bradbury 1995.

48 Bowersock 1990; MacMullen 1997; Fowden 1998.

49 Brown 1998, 645.

50 Mócsy 1974, 253–4.

51 *P. Dura* 54 (= Beard, North and Price [1998] 2:71–4; Lee [2000] 16–19).

52 M. D. Smith 1997, with full references to those who favour Constantius as a solar monotheist. See Elliott 1987, 421–3, 1996, 17–27, for Constantius as a Christian.

53 Lact. *DMP* 15.7, Eus. *MP* 13.12.

54 M. D. Smith 1997, 200–1.

55 Lane Fox 1986, 611.

56 T. D. Barnes 1985c; Elliott 1987, 1996.

57 Lact., *DMP* 24.9 (trans. Creed).

58 *Pan. Lat.* 6 (7).21.3–6 (trans. Nixon and Rodgers). See the discussion and further references in Nixon and Rodgers 1994, 248–51 nn. 91–3 and in this volume at Chapter 3 n. 41.

59 Curran 2000, 71–5, for good discussion of the ancient sources (esp. Zos. 2.29.5) and modern debate, esp. Paschoud 1971a and Wiemer 1994b.

60 Zos. 4.36.4.

61 Lact. *DMP* 48.6.

62 *CTh* 9.16.3 (318); 9.16.2 (319); 9.16.1 (320), with discussion in Curran 2000, 172–4.

63 Eus. *VC* 2.56.2. Cf. also Constantine's *Oration to the Assembly of the Saints* 11 with discussion in Drake 1995.

64 Eus. *VC* 2.59–60.

65 Eus. *VC* 2.60.1 (trans. Cameron and Hall). For commentary on the whole letter, see Cameron and Hall 1999, 244–8.

66 See Bradbury 1994, 124–6, for discussion; T. D. Barnes 1981, 210–12, takes a different view.

67 Eus. *VC* 2.45.1 (trans. Cameron and Hall).

68 *CTh* 16.10.2.

69 Lane Fox 1986, 667; Cameron and Hall 1999, 243–4, 247–8, 319–20; Curran 2000, 175–85. For arguments in favour of a Constantinian ban, see T. D. Barnes 1984; Bradbury 1994, though the latter acknowledges that the impact of such a ban during Constantine's reign will have been minimal.

70 Lib. *Or.* 30.6. The fact that this assertion was made half a century later and occurs in a context where it suits Libanius's argument need not compromise its significance, since making a false claim on this point would not have helped Libanius's case. See Wiemer 1994a, 520–3, building on Errington 1988.

71 Eus. *VC* 3.26–7, 51–3, 55–6, 58. See Robert 1973 on the history of Aegae, including its destruction under Constantine, which clearly did not obliterate its cult of Asclepius.

72 Lane Fox 1986, 671–2; Cameron and Hall 1999, 301–4.

73 References in Jones 1964, 1083 n. 33.

74 Lib. *Or.* 30.6. See more at Chapter 10 in this volume.

75 Eus. *VC* 3.54; *Chron. Pasch.* pp. 527–31; Joh. Lyd. *De mens.* 4.2.

76 Eun. *VS* 6.1.1–12. See also the case of Nicagoras of Athens, a leading initiate in the Eleusinian Mysteries; Fowden 1987. See also Chapter 6 n. 15 in this volume.

77 For discussion of different aspects, see Cameron and Hall 1999, 303–4; Dagron 1974, 37–45; Fowden 1991; Mango 1993a. See also Chapter 11 n. 48 in this volume.

78 *CIL* 11:5265 = *ILS* 705; cf. Gascou 1967. See the translation at Lee 2000, 92–3, with further references, and Curran 2000, 181–2.

79 Chadwick 1978, 12.

80 Drake 1995, 2000.

SECTION III

LAW AND SOCIETY

8: BUREAUCRACY AND GOVERNMENT

Christopher Kelly

On September 18, 324, at Chrysopolis, just across the water from Byzantium, Constantine's army won a decisive battle. This victory over the emperor Licinius (who had ruled most of the eastern half of the empire since 313) established Constantine's control over a reunified Roman world. It effectively doubled his domains. But like all military successes – no matter how glorious or divinely inspired – the reconquest of the eastern Mediterranean posed a series of difficulties: practical, political, administrative, economic, and ideological. This chapter looks at one particular problem which might confront any government attempting to assimilate a large and recently subdued territory. The challenge Constantine and his advisers faced was, of course, not how to "Romanise" or "civilise" the eastern provinces – the very idea would have seemed farcical – but rather how to control and exploit its resources. One tactic was to strengthen the apparatus of central government control. The evidence is patchy and unsatisfactory, but it does seem that both after the victory at the battle of the Milvian Bridge in 312 (which confirmed Constantine's rule in the west) and especially following the defeat of Licinius, a series of reforms significantly altered the duties of the empire's most important civil and military officials. These innovations saw the consolidation and systematisation of distinct areas of responsibility under the supervision of high-ranking office-holders closely associated with the emperor himself.

The development of a more highly centralised administration was undoubtedly important in securing the eastern provinces, but it also risked the exclusion and alienation of local élites whose complicity was essential to the effective operation of government. The second part of this chapter surveys some of the tactics which were deployed under Constantine to link imperial centre and provincial periphery. Its focus is on social and political measures rather than on the more obviously ideological or religious. It explores the impact of imperial benefactions and the blurring of traditional expressions of rank and status with the newer expressions of a powerful and increasingly centralised officialdom. In the cities of the eastern Mediterranean, it was important that the wealthy and well educated – many once enthusiastic supporters of Licinius – were made aware of the immediate and tangible advantages of a willing participation in the administration of a reunified empire. It was important too that they should be prepared – in the elegant phrase of a late fourth-century law – "to associate themselves with immortality"[1] by joining their own concerns and ambitions with those of a victorious emperor and his new régime.

A CENTRALISED ADMINISTRATION

There is – regrettably – no comprehensive or coherent record of the organisation of the imperial administration under Constantine. Much depends on chance references to individual office-holders; even then, the allocation of specific responsibilities to particular high-ranking officials is often and unavoidably subject to speculative retrojection from later information. Nor, of course, should it be simply assumed that the first attestation of a particular post is always or necessarily closely coincident with its establishment. That said, it is possible to reconstruct a reasonably certain sketch of the empire's principal administrative structures under Constantine, even if the result is inevitably more static and less sophisticated than it might have seemed to contemporaries.

The most orderly blueprint of the administration of the later Roman empire is contained in the one surviving copy of a document known as the *Notitia omnium dignitatum et administrationum tam civilium quam militarium*. The *Notitia Dignitatum* is, as its full title grandly proclaims, "a list of all ranks and administrative positions both civil and military." The surviving version of what, in fact, is little more than a simple checklist of offices offers a fairly comprehensive overview of the empire's military and administrative establishments in the eastern half of the empire at the end of the fourth century, and somewhat later, and more haphazardly, for the west.[2] In all, the *Notitia Dignitatum* listed over one hundred provinces. These were grouped into fourteen dioceses, the majority under a *Vicarius*, who exercised a general supervisory role over provincial governors and in some cases heard appeals from their courts.

Dioceses, in turn, were grouped into four praetorian prefectures: Gaul (which included Britain and Spain), Italy (which included Africa and the western Balkans), Illyricum (roughly Crete, modern Greece, and the Balkan states to the north of Macedonia) and the east (see Maps 1 and 2).[3] Praetorian prefects were the most powerful civil officials in later Roman government. They had overall responsibility for the administration of the empire and in many judicial matters presided over the final court of appeal. They also headed important financial departments, levying taxation to finance "the major and essential needs of the state," including the administration, the army, and imperial public works.[4]

Such a system was slow to emerge. In the early 290s, the emperor Diocletian reorganised the empire's provincial administration, roughly doubling the number of provinces. Many were split in two, and Africa was divided into three provinces, Asia into seven. A snapshot of these important changes is offered by the so-called Verona List (*Laterculus Veronensis*), a simple catalogue of the provinces of the empire as they stood probably sometime around 314.[5] Diocletian also grouped the provinces into dioceses. The diocese was an innovation, as was the official responsible for this new administrative unit, the *vicarius*, or *vices agens praefectorum praetorio* (deputy to the praetorian prefects). The Verona List – like the empire itself – was divided into twelve dioceses: Oriens, Pontica, Asiana, Thracia, Moesia, Pannonia, Britannia, Gallia, Viennensis, Italia, Hispania, and Africa. This basic scheme was retained by Constantine following his reunification of the empire in 324.[6] In addition to a *vicarius*, Constantine in some dioceses also made use of an official known as a *comes provinciarum*. The precise relationship between these two posts is unclear: both *comites* and *vicarii* are attested in several dioceses (Oriens, Hispania, Africa).[7] The degree of subordination of these officials to the Praetorian Prefects, at least in some judicial matters, is also uncertain. In a law of 331 issued "to all in the provinces," Constantine confirmed that appeals lay to the imperial court from decisions of both *comites* and *vicarii* but not from praetorian prefects, "who alone may truly be said to judge in place of the emperor (*vice sacra*)."[8]

The territorial logic which led to the creation of dioceses was not systematically extended by either Diocletian or Constantine to embrace (as in the *Notitia Dignitatum*) the praetorian prefectures. The evidence is fragmentary and any reconstruction correspondingly tentative.[9] Under Diocletian and the Tetrarchy (perhaps until as late as 306), there seem to have been only two praetorian prefects at any one time. The division of responsibilities – if any – is unclear. It may be that one Prefect was attached to the staff of Diocletian in the eastern half of the empire and one to Maximian in the west.[10] The Tetrarchic prefect was a powerful figure. He acted as "a kind of grand vizier, the emperor's second in command, wielding a wide authority in almost every sphere of government, military and judicial, financial and general administration. He was the emperor's chief of staff, adjutant-general, and quartermaster-general rolled into one."[11]

In the civil wars following Diocletian's abdication in May 305, the main contenders (Constantine, Maxentius, Severus, Maximin, Galerius, and Licinius) are each attested as having appointed their own praetorian prefect.[12] From 313 to 324, with Constantine in control of the western half of the empire and Licinius in control of the east, it seems likely that there were again only two praetorian prefects in the whole empire.[13] This pattern of the close association of praetorian prefects with particular emperors seems to have been significantly broken after 324. A dedicatory inscription on an arch erected probably sometime around 332 at Ain Rchine in modern Tunisia honoured the imperial family – Constantine I, Constantine II, Constantius II, and Constans – and listed five prefects (not all the names are preserved in full). A second inscription honouring Constantine II known from both Tubernuc (near Carthage) and a statue base from Antioch, and probably dating to around 335/6, also listed five prefects.[14]

The division of responsibility between these prefects is not specified; indeed only a bare list of names was recorded. Importantly, unlike later fourth century inscriptions, the prefects' names were not followed by an explicit reference to the region for which they were primarily responsible (Gaul, Italy, Illyricum, or the east). This lack of formal specification makes it clear – contrary to the claim of the late fifth century historian Zosimus[15] – that "regional prefectures" in the manner set out in the *Notitia Dignitatum* were not officially established under Constantine. That said, it is equally clear that after 324 individual prefects in the exercise of their duties were often understood to have a particular expertise in the governance of certain dioceses. Two laws issued to the praetorian prefect Valerius Felix in 334 and 335 assume his oversight of Africa, a specialist responsibility for a particular geographical area which may have resulted from the continuing unrest associated with the Donatist controversy.[16]

Valerius Felix is also included amongst the prefects on the inscriptions honouring Constantius from Tubernuc and Antioch, and it may be that his name should also be restored on the earlier dedication to the imperial family from Ain Rchine.[17] T. D. Barnes has argued that the five prefects who are listed on the Tubernuc and Antioch inscriptions should be associated with Constantine's envisaged division of the empire amongst his sons after his death: L. Papius Pacatinus, prefect of Constans; Flavius Ablabius, Prefect of Constantine I; Valerius Felix, prefect of Africa; C. Annius Tiberianus, prefect of Constantine II; Nestorius Timonianus, prefect of Constantius II.[18] At first sight, such an arrangement might seem to represent a return to Tetrarchic practice (with four of the five prefects closely associated with emperors), but as Constantine – in addition to maintaining Africa as a distinct area of responsibility – also allocated specific areas of the empire to his sons, it might equally be a further indication of a growing regional specialism amongst praetorian prefects. From that point of view, Constantine's scheme, in its careful elaboration of the territorial logic of Diocletian's provincial reorganisation, might fairly be regarded as a close foreshadowing of the later formal division of the empire into regional prefectures.

The greater geographical definition of responsibilities in the latter half of Constantine's reign should also be closely associated with other changes clearly intended to modify the role of the praetorian prefects. Most probably immediately following his victory over Maxentius at the battle of the Milvian Bridge in 312, Constantine instituted a series of major military reforms encompassing both the disposition of troops and the balance of strength between an enhanced mobile field army and those units stationed on the frontiers. Towards the end of his reign, the field army was placed under two newly created senior-ranking officers, the *magister peditum* (in command of the infantry) and the *magister equitum* (in command of the cavalry).[19] Praetorian prefects no longer commanded any troops. This was an important shift. Amongst those appointed by Constantine to the empire's most senior posts, there was now a sharp division between those with civil and those with military responsibilities and expertise. In part, this firm separation recognised – as A. H. M. Jones noted – the practical difficulty of finding suitable candidates for praetorian prefect who combined military, judicial, financial, and administrative abilities and experience.[20] It also undoubtedly had the advantage – at least from an emperor's point of view – of reducing the possibility of any senior figure at court being able to accumulate a threateningly powerful range of resources and responsibilities.

The influence of the praetorian prefects was also circumscribed by the development and consolidation of a set of officials (and their staffs) principally associated with the emperor himself. The *Notitia Dignitatum* lists two high-ranking officials responsible for the administration of significant aspects of central government: the imperial *quaestor* and the *magister officiorum.* The quaestor was responsible for drafting legislation and the responses to petitions and letters addressed to the emperor.[21] According to the late-fifth-century pagan historian Zosimus, the office was established under Constantine.[22] In its origin, the imperial *quaestor* was probably connected to the *quaestores caesaris*, who since the first century AD had been responsible for reading out imperial communications to the Senate. At some point, Constantine detached the most senior *quaestor* from his colleagues, giving him a senior position in the palatine administration and putting him in charge of a consolidated set of legal tasks.[23]

Overall control of the palatine administration was the responsibility of the *magister officiorum.* He supervised the *sacra scrinia* (the three principal imperial secretariats, from which the *quaestor* also drew his staff), which dealt with a wide range of matters, including petitions, reports, judicial records, the issuing of letters of appointment to various senior civil and military posts, the requests of embassies, and the day-to-day running of the palace.[24] The institution of the *magister officiorum* represented a significant aggregation and systematisation under one senior official of a series of disparate functions. Many of these – particularly the core tasks concerned with petitions, correspondence, and embassies – connect this post with a range of departments responsible since the first century AD for the conduct of these key aspects of imperial administration.[25] The *magister officiorum* may perhaps have been created by Diocletian, but on balance it seems more likely that the position was established – in the separate administrations of both Constantine and Licinius – sometime soon after 312.[26] The main palatine secretariats, which had varied in number, title, and duties, are first recorded in 314 in the tripartite division which became standard for the late empire: *scrinium memoriae, scrinium epistularum,* and *scrinium libellorum.*[27]

It is also possible to date the establishment of the *agentes in rebus* to roughly the same period. The *agentes* were the successors of the *frumentarii:* a *corps* under the direct control of the praetorian prefect formed from legionaries on secondment who acted as confidential imperial messengers between provincial governors and Rome.[28] The *frumentarii* – at least in the form they had operated in the first three centuries AD – were disbanded by Diocletian. It may be that their functions – clearly important to the effective operation of government – were transferred to some more tightly regimented and centralised group with less obviously divided loyalties.[29] Certainly under Constantine – and arguably attested as early as 319 – the *agentes in rebus* were responsible for the delivery of imperial dispatches, for the oversight of some operational aspects of the imperial post, and more generally for monitoring and reporting on the administration of the provinces. Most importantly, although *agentes* were still ranked according to military grades, they were now serving palatine bureaucrats and responsible not to the praetorian prefect but to the *magister officiorum*.[30]

The inception of the *magister officiorum* under both Constantine and Licinius reflected the consolidation in one office of a number of civilian administrative duties. Indeed, it may be possible to see something of this transformation in the organisation of central government – under both Constantine and Licinius – just before the decisive civil war of 324. The earliest attested *magistri officiorum*, Heraclianus in 320 and Proculeianus in 323, are both mentioned in laws which refer to them as *tribunus et magister officiorum*.[31] The rank of *tribunus* may indicate that the *magister officiorum* was, at least in some of his duties, regarded as subordinate to the much higher ranking prefect. At some point in the first half of the fourth century, the *magister officiorum* was raised from the rank of *tribunus* to the newly formalised rank of *comes* (imperial companion).[32] It is not possible securely to date the *magister's* promotion – the new title is not firmly attested until 346[33] – but it may be that it should be placed just before 324. Perhaps reflecting this change, Peter the Patrician (*magister officiorum* for nearly three decades in the middle of the sixth century), in his history of the post, listed no office-holders before Palladius (known to have served under Constantine in 323/4) and Martinianus (known to have served under Licinius in 324).[34]

It is certainly attractive to regard the elevation of the *magister officiorum* as coherent in its intent with Constantine's transfer near the end of his reign of the praetorian prefects' military functions to the *magister peditum* and *magister equitum* – with supervision of the palace guard assumed by the *magister officiorum*.[35] As with the establishment of these two posts – which also carried the rank of *comes* – the promotion of the *magister officiorum* might be understood as marking out (or perhaps reinforcing) a new pattern of responsibilities.[36] A set of tasks most closely concerned with the effective operation of imperial government was no longer under the undisputed control of the praetorian prefecture. Importantly too, the distribution of duties allowed for significant overlaps, reflecting both the process of reallocation and an imperial concern that no one official should have an easy monopoly of control over strategically sensitive resources. Supervision of the *cursus publicus* (the imperial post) and the *fabricae* (the imperial arms manufactories) was the concurrent responsibility of both the *magister officiorum* and the *praetorian prefects*.[37]

Nor in the conduct of imperial business was the emperor restricted to using only the administrative staff headed by the *magister officiorum*. He could also draw on the *notarii*, who formed a parallel and to some extent an independent secretariat headed by the *primicerius notariorum*. The *primicerius* was also in charge of issuing documents of appointment for high-ranking officials and for drawing up the *Notitia Dignitatum*.[38] The origins of the *notarii* are not clear; but there are good reasons for suggesting that they were established – by both Constantine and Licinius – around the same time as the *magister officiorum*.[39]

A similar pattern of specialisation and the careful allocation of strategically sensitive tasks amongst senior officials can also be traced in the development of the empire's financial administration. Here the most important official remained the praetorian prefect, who since Diocletian had been in charge of the calculation, collection, and redistribution of most direct taxes, either in kind or gold.[40] Alongside the fiscal duties of the prefects, the *Notitia Dignitatum* lists two other high-ranking officials directly concerned with the administration of the imperial treasury: the *comes sacrarum largitionum* and the *comes rei privatae*. The *comes sacrarum largitionum* was responsible for the collection of indirect taxes, such as customs dues, and direct levies of precious metals. He also supervised the administration of state mints, mines, quarries, and textile factories. The *comes rei privatae* controlled imperial properties, their acquisition, leasing, rents, sale, and revenues. The money so raised was in large part used for the maintenance of the imperial household and for paying out disbursements or pensions granted at the emperor's discretion.[41] As with the *magister officiorum*, the responsibilities of these posts represent the consolidation of a series of duties previously carried out by more junior officials.[42] R. Delmaire has also suggested that an imperial law specifically mentioning the *comes sacrarum largitionum* should be dated to 326, making the establishment of the post roughly coincident with the raising of the *magister officiorum* from *tribunus* to *comes*. The creation of a *rationalis rei privatae* may also be dated to the same period; by 339 this official had been promoted to the higher rank of *comes*.[43]

In the end, given the difficulties in dating the establishment of these offices, any overall reconstruction of the chronology of these administrative changes must be knowingly fragile. Even so, and despite these difficulties, it may be possible to see Constantine's innovations falling roughly into three phases. The first, after the victory over Maxentius in 312, might include the reform of the palatine administration with the establishment of the *magister officiorum*, the *notarii*, and the imperial *quaestor*. The second, after the defeat of Licinius in 324 and the reunification of the empire, would then encompass the reorganisation of imperial finances and the elevation of at least some key palatine posts to the superior rank of *comes*.[44] The third and most important phase, near the end of Constantine's reign, saw the splitting of the praetorian prefects' remaining military and civil functions and the creation of the *magister equitum* and *magister peditum*, changes perhaps carried out as preparation for the succession of his sons.

Whatever the precise order of these reforms or their details, the twenty-five years from 312 to 337 saw the emergence of a range of high-ranking officials whose areas of responsibility were systematically consolidated and more clearly defined. The restructuring of these posts helped to secure Constantine's own position, both by impeding the possibility of any rival gaining control of both army and administration and by creating – as a fundamental part of central government – a set of powerful officials directly answerable to the emperor. Overlapping responsibilities in sensitive areas also helped to ensure that senior office-holders might police the actions of their colleagues. Most importantly, it was now more likely that an emperor would be surrounded by a series of advisers – each of whom might jockey for influence – rather than remain crucially dependent on one or two alone.

From one point of view, these changes, particularly in their allocation of the various responsibilities of high-ranking officials, can be seen as extending and refining existing Tetrarchic arrangements – neatly illustrated before 324 by parallel changes under Licinius. Indeed, in some cases, the division of tasks has a close affinity with the distribution of duties in the comparatively underdeveloped central government of the first two centuries AD. Yet such relationships should not be allowed to obscure either the importance of Constantine's innovations or their internal logic. The fragmentation of the praetorian prefects' vast area of responsibility, the foreshadowing of regional prefectures, and the institution and promotion of a series of high-ranking military and civil offices represented both a definite break with the structures of Tetrarchic government and a coherent attempt to deal with the new demands of ruling a reunified empire. Most importantly, the reorganisation of the palatine administration strengthened the institution of central government. A range of specialist tasks and strategic responsibilities was distributed across a number of departments headed by senior officials closely associated with the emperor. In its delineation of the basic scope, functions, and status of these powerful posts, Constantine's reform established a lasting and effective framework for one of the basic aspects of Roman imperial government. It marked a clear and decisive step towards that highly centralised administrative world so splendidly idealised in the *Notitia Dignitatum*.[45]

RÉGIME BUILDING

Looking back – even from the late fourth century – it is easy to exaggerate the importance of Constantinople: to see its foundation as celebrating the establishment of an explicitly Christian capital and a self-conscious rival to Rome.[46] But to contemporaries, the contrast may not have been so pronounced. Constantine's decision to found a new capital, or at least not to modify an existing Tetrarchic capital such as Nicomedia, Thessalonica, or Sirmium, could also be seen as a straightforward and sensible defensive measure. The military and economic advantages of the new site were undoubted and universally recognised. Significantly, too, the failure to remodel an existing capital was part of a consistent policy of marking out a discontinuity with both the Tetrarchy and Licinius. Such a disjunctive strategy demanded that Constantine trace his own descent from the third-century emperor Claudius Gothicus.[47] It was also expressed in his refusal to base his own court and administration within a city and palace complex closely associated with a defunct régime which he claimed to have surpassed.

It was perhaps that distance with the recent past which mattered most, a distance emphasised in one contemporary description of Constantinople as a "second Rome."[48] This was a connection nicely elaborated in the tradition that the porphyry column erected in the Forum of Constantine to celebrate the foundation of the city (Figs. 2 and 3) contained in its base the *palladium*, the ancient image of Pallas Athena taken by the fleeing Aeneas from the ruins of Troy and previously preserved in the innermost sanctum of the temple to Vesta in Rome. Constantine is said to have had this ancient talisman removed, perhaps secretly, and to have consecrated it at the centre of his new city. Constantinople might thereby lay claim to a direct link not only with Rome but also with Troy.[49] Indeed, the early fifth century ecclesiastical historian Sozomen suggested that Constantine had originally intended to establish his new city in northern Asia Minor on the ancient site of Troy.[50] With such a foundation, Virgil's *Aeneid* would have come full circle as the new hero of Mediterranean reunification returned to rebuild a city once sacked by the cunning of Odysseus and the treachery of the wooden horse. But for all its literary attractions, such a project – if it were ever conceived by Constantine – would perhaps have been too symbolically unambiguous, too stark a contrast to the new city's Christian imagery, too antagonistic a commentary on the defeated Greek supporters of Licinius.

Constantinople was more subtle. It was at once – and not always consistently – a Christian city, an imperial capital in the Tetrarchic manner, and the centre of Constantine's administration and court. Within these contexts, explicit parallels with Rome should not be seen as a crass attempt at disadvantageous comparison or outright displacement. Rather, like Constantine's fictive imperial lineage, they fashioned an imaginary history for a new foundation. That Constantinople was in some way connected to Rome helped mark it out from other important urban centres. It was a city whose mythical origins linked it to the most important heroic story of classical literature and – again eliding the achievements of both the Tetrarchy and Licinius – to the imperial capital of the Mediterranean world for the last half millennium.

But in the eastern empire, it was perhaps less the contrasts with Rome which mattered and more those with cities such as Antioch and Nicomedia. Of course, these cities, like many others, received huge imperial benefactions that allowed them to add impressive buildings – many of them explicitly Christian – to their already monumental centres.[51] Indeed, Antioch, with its extensive palace complex on an island in the middle of the Orontes, could fairly claim to be an imperial city. It was the frequent residence of emperors and a vital base for military operations along the Persian frontier. Even so, it was Constantinople which had been designed to function as the political, administrative, and ceremonial hub of the eastern Mediterranean world. It was at Constantinople – in his newly constructed Great Palace – that Constantine spent most of his time from 330 until his death in 337.[52] It was to Constantinople and to its court that those who wished to influence imperial policy had to travel. Not that obtaining an audience was always easy. In 336, Constantine summoned the bishops involved in the synod of Tyre (in modern Lebanon), which had been convened to hear various – and in some cases clearly fabricated – charges against Athanasius, bishop of Alexandria. The emperor had been persuaded to act following the intervention of Athanasius, who had himself fled the synod fearing condemnation, sailing in an open boat to Constantinople. In the capital he had adopted equally desperate measures to bring his case to the emperor's attention. The dramatic account of his success is preserved in a letter of Constantine to the bishops in Tyre explaining why he had ordered them to court:

> As I was entering the ever all-blessed city of Constantinople, a city which bears our name, and on this occasion I happened to be riding on horseback, suddenly in the middle of the road Athanasius the bishop and several others who were with him approached so unexpectedly as to cause alarm. The all-ruling God is my witness that at first sight I would not have known who he was had not some of my retinue inquired, as was only reasonable, who he was and what wrong he had suffered and so reported the matter to me.[53]

Not all who journeyed to Constantinople to seek royal favour had to risk being trampled underfoot by the emperor's entourage or pushed aside by his guards. In his *Life of Constantine*, Eusebius of Caesarea was keen to emphasise the emperor's seemingly boundless beneficence:

> Just as the sun rises and spreads the beams of its light over all, so also Constantine shone forth with the rising sun from the imperial palace, as though descending with the heavenly luminary, and shed upon all who came before his face the sunbeams of his own generous goodness. It was not possible to come near him without receiving some benefit, nor would the good hopes of those who looked to him for support ever be disappointed.[54]

Such well-worn themes of imperial praise must, of course, be treated with considerable caution. But in this case it may be significant that in more hostile traditions Constantine's open-handedness is also emphasised: in this case as one of his chief defects.[55] For Zosimus, Constantine "continued to exhaust his revenues by making unnecessary gifts to undeserving and useless people."[56] For Julian in his *Caesares* – an apparently witty satire on his own imperial predecessors written in 361 – it was again the emperor's liberality which was to be held up to ridicule. In a contest held by the gods on Olympus to award the prize to the best ruler – Marcus Aurelius was the outright winner – the heavenly question-masters Hermes and Silenus also interviewed Constantine:

> Hermes asked, "What do you consider honourable?" Constantine answered, "To amass a great fortune and to spend it

freely fulfilling my own desires and those of my friends." At this Silenus laughed loudly and said, "But if it was a banker that you wanted to be, how did you so forget yourself as to lead the life of a chef and a hairdresser?"[57]

Aside from the Constantine's often lavish funding of individuals and cities – however this should be judged or joked about – the many concessions granted government officials also offered clear proof of the signal benefits of close association with the imperial centre. Palatine officials were, in the words of one of Constantine's own laws, "deluged with privileges."[58] Most valuably, they were released, as were their sons and grandsons, from any obligation to serve on the municipal council in their home-towns and from the considerable financial liabilities such office-holding entailed. Their property was to be exempt from the various charges collectively known as *munera sordida*, these included grinding corn and baking bread for troops, billeting travelling officials and supplying them with animals for transport, and providing materials and labour for public works and for the upkeep of roads and bridges.[59] The laws conferring these immunities clearly emphasised that they were a fitting reward for "those who have blamelessly held office in our service" and "who on account of their work of proven quality have been granted a peaceful retirement."[60]

The award of such privileges – like memorable tales of Constantine's justice or generosity – openly advertised the advantages of a close connection with the new régime. Indeed, the foundation of Constantinople itself, with its imposing concentration of splendid palaces and grand official buildings, unmistakably expressed the powerful position of central government. Importantly, too, the decision not to remodel any existing major urban centre gave the new capital a certain independence. It allowed the emplacement of imperial court and palatine administration without its entanglement in ancient intercity rivalries or the more recent preferences of a defeated emperor. But its disadvantages were also clear. Any significant sense of detachment or separation could impede progress towards effective reconciliation with local élites. P. Heather has neatly summed up these pressing political difficulties:

> Having defeated Licinius, Constantine faced a huge governmental problem. He had already ruled for the best part of twenty years, but only in the west; now he had taken over the east by force, where he knew nobody, and where all the senior appointees were Licinius' men, and where all local

men of importance were used to operating through channels set up by Licinius. In essence, Constantine had to begin
from scratch to establish the chain of relationships which
would make the east governable.[61]

In confronting this problem, Constantine and his advisers pursued two distinct tactics, ideally complementary but at times inescapably
antithetical. The benefits of contact with the imperial centre were continually proclaimed and extravagantly demonstrated. The influential
inhabitants of the eastern Mediterranean were encouraged to accept –
gratefully – the self-evident rewards of cooperation with an emperor
in his own city. Yet matchless acts of imperial generosity could also be
seen as marking out the distance between the provinces and the capital,
between individuals regarded as wealthy in their own communities and
a ruler who commanded the vast resources of empire. Spanning this
dangerous divide was important to the success of Constantine's new
régime. The coalition of traditional and more recently established ranks
and titles offered one means of "bringing together and to some extent
fusing the old senatorial and new imperial aristocracies."[62] It allowed a
greater facility of movement between centre and periphery. It held out
the possibility that status achieved at court could be of advantage in the
prosecution of smaller scale home-town rivalries. For some amongst
the provincial élites, the disruption of traditional patterns of power and
influence was itself emblematic of the empire's steady decline. For others, the intrusive presence of imperial government might be tolerated –
if not welcomed – as long as it could be seen as a means of reinforcing,
rather than eroding, their own dominant local position.

Imperial grants of ranks or titles gave formal and permanent
expression to connections with the ruling régime. Following victory at
the Milvian Bridge, Constantine established the order of *comites* (imperial companions). Sometime in the 330s they were classified into three
grades.[63] Neither the reason nor the basis for this division is known, but
it may reflect something of the success and expanding membership of
an order created to embrace a wide range of the emperor's supporters.
Indeed, the use of the traditional term *comites* itself stressed the particular
link between these companions and Constantine himself. Any doubt as
to how the title should be understood was dispelled by its full form: *comes
domini nostri Constantini invicti et perpetui Augusti.*[64] It was this association
with the emperor, rather than any other social or political advantage,
which was central to an order which included high-ranking palatine
officials, those entrusted (in addition to *vicarii*) with the governance of

dioceses (*comes provinciarum*), those who undertook important missions on behalf of the emperor, and prominent provincials.[65] Constantine, here again hinting at some deep connection with an ancient Roman past, also revived the traditional title of "patrician" (*patricius*), transforming what had once been a hereditary title borne by the noblest families into a distinction to be granted by the emperor only to his most loyal associates.[66]

Alongside the promotion of these new distinctions, traditional expressions of high status were also remodelled. Perhaps in the late 320s, a senate was established in Constantinople.[67] Like so much else in the city, the foundation – or duplication – of an ancient institution in "another Rome" carefully situated the past within a novel imperial context. The senate was firmly embedded within both the physical and political structures of the capital. It met in one of two buildings: one adjacent to the porphyry column in the Forum of Constantine, the other sited between the Grand Palace and the great church of Hagia Sophia.[68] More significantly, its membership – modest at only three hundred – epitomised a much more extensive restructuring of the order as a whole. Senatorial status – marked by the formally designated rank of *clarissimus* – was regularly extended to include those who had held high administrative office.[69] This was a two-way process. The opportunities for existing senators to hold government positions were broadened by the upgrading of a number of provincial governorships, including Syria, Bithynia, Campania, Sicily, and Byzacena, now open only to *clarissimi*.[70] At the same time, the number of senators was greatly expanded through direct imperial grants of status or through grants associated with the holding of a particular post. By the mid-330s, for example, the title of *clarissimus* might comfortably encompass a member of an established Roman aristocratic family, a former praetorian prefect of comparatively obscure background who had spent the first fifteen years of his career in a range of junior palatine offices, and perhaps a former *magister officiorum* or imperial *quaestor*. All of these might also have been granted the title of *comes*.[71]

Such associations with the imperial centre resonated powerfully in the provinces. Of course, not everyone always applauded the possibilities for advancement which Constantine's new titles afforded. Writing towards the end of the fourth century, the famous Antiochene orator Libanius frequently presented himself in his speeches as an avowed traditionalist and – despite himself holding the honorary rank of praetorian prefect – unremittingly hostile to any novel form of status. He affected to regard the advancement of Flavius Optatus (the only known *patricius* under Constantine) with extreme distaste. In Libanius's sketch – almost cartoon – biography, Optatus was a poorly paid "teacher of letters" who had tutored the son of the emperor Licinius. After Licinius's defeat in 324, Optatus allegedly owed his continued success to his wife, the daughter of an innkeeper, who – as Libanius coyly suggests – was ever willing to bestow her favours in order to secure her husband's advancement.

The history of Optatus's career is almost entirely obscured by Libanius's seductive rhetoric. If anything certain can be made out, it is more likely – as R. Kaster has suggested – that, like most known imperial tutors, Flavius Optatus was an established and well-respected rhetor: perhaps rather like Libanius at the start of his own career.[72] Even so, Optatus's elevation to the new rank of *patricius* is still a significant formal register of the change in social status which the association with an emperor might confer. And no doubt many well-educated provincials clearly saw the benefits of such a connection, both at court and in their own home-towns. In the mid 350s, the then seventy-year-old Joseph of Tiberias recounted his life story to Epiphanius, later bishop of Salamis (in northern Cyprus) and a famous cataloguer of Christian heresies. Joseph told of how, having abandoned Judaism for Christianity, he had travelled to the imperial capital. Constantine had warmly welcomed a convert from such a prominent family. He granted him permission to build churches in several mainly Jewish towns in Palestine and admitted him to the order of imperial *comites*. Much later, Joseph who had remained staunchly orthodox but was now living in Scythopolis, a city well-known for its strong Arian community, was persecuted by the city's bishop. In these difficult times, Joseph insisted, the chief thing which had protected him was his rank of *comes*.[73]

Such stories help to calibrate something of the effect of these shifts in status now formalised in the range of new ranks and titles. Despite the comparative lack of evidence about individual careers – only one *patricius* and fewer than twenty-five *comites* are known between 312 and 337 – the possibility that such information might illustrate a wider pattern is again strengthened by ancient critiques, both laudatory and antagonistic, of Constantine's reign. For the ever-hostile late-fifth–century pagan historian Zosimus, the emperor's reforms to ancient traditions were clear portents of the empire's fall, his benefactions a waste of valuable revenue:

> He utterly confused long-established magistracies . . . he bur-
> dened those who paid taxes, enriching those who were

unable to contribute anything; for he regarded prodigality as munificence . . . . After damaging the state in all these ways, Constantine died from a disease.[74]

In his imperial biography, Eusebius, before moving on to describe the emperor's peaceful death and magnificent funeral, offered his readers a different perspective in a brief review of Constantine's political programme:

> Some received money in abundance, others goods; some acquired posts as prefects, others senatorial rank . . . some were appointed *comites* of the first order, others of the second, others of the third. Similarly many thousands more shared honours as *clarissimi* or with a wide range of other titles; for in order to promote more persons the Emperor contrived different distinctions.[75]

However praised or condemned, the pursuit of these policies was important to the institution of Constantine's rule in a reunified Roman empire. The elaboration and reorganisation of major palatine offices, now splendidly accommodated in a new purpose-built capital, consolidated the effective apparatus of central government control. It also helped to ensure that an emperor would not need to rely either for advice or information on any one senior official. The basic division of responsibilities worked out across the 320s and early 330s – in particular, the splitting of civil and military authority and the move towards regional praetorian prefectures – was maintained in its essentials by Constantine's imperial successors for the next two hundred years.

Alongside these reforms, Constantine's new administration also sought to establish permanent links with wealthy and influential provincials. Key tactics included well-directed imperial generosity and the fusing of traditional and more recently created ranks and titles. In terms of status, privilege, and position, involvement with central government was made increasingly and deliberately attractive. The pressing long-term need to secure this relationship continued to shape imperial policy. It remained one of the principal fault lines in the social landscape of late antiquity. Of course, Constantine cannot have foreseen subsequent developments, nor should his own particular innovations be taken as in some way "setting the agenda" for later fourth-century emperors. Rather, the measures pursued in the latter half of his reign, especially after the victory at Chrysopolis, should be understood as a clear and perceptive recognition of an immediate need to bridge the gap between the periphery of the empire and its centre. They represent an attempt to reconcile both imperial advantage, so forcibly expressed in the foundation of Constantinople, and deep-seated provincial particularities. This gradual conjunction of interests – in part competing, in part complementary – was a fragile and delicate process but a vital one. It was on the continued willingness of local élites to cooperate with a conquering power that the lasting success of Constantine's régime significantly depended.

FURTHER READING

Useful general introductions to late antique bureaucracy and government are offered in A. H. M. Jones, *The Later Roman Empire* (1964), esp. Chapters 11–13 and 16 (which still remains fundamental), and C. M. Kelly, "Emperors, Government and Bureaucracy," in *The Cambridge Ancient History*, vol. 13, *The Late Empire A.D. 337–425* (1998), 138–83, and above all in C. M. Kelly, *Ruling the Later Roman Empire* (2004). R. Delmaire offers the best up-to-date institutional study in his *Les institutions du Bas-Empire romain de Constantin à Justinien* (1995). There are a number of highly technical studies on individual offices. Three are outstanding: J. Harries, "The Roman Imperial Quaestor from Constantine to Theodosius II," *Journal of Roman Studies* 78 (1988): 148–72; M. Clauss, *Der Magister Officiorum in der Spätantike (4.–6. Jahrhundert)* (1980); and R. Delmaire, *Largesses sacrées et res privata: L'aerarium impérial et son administration du IV*ᵉ *au VI*ᵉ *siècle* (1989). On the complex issue of "regional prefectures" and the details of Constantine's administration, see the lucid account in T. D. Barnes, *The New Empire of Constantine and Diocletian* (1982), with most recent revisions in his "Emperors, Panegyrics, Prefects, Provinces and Palaces (284–317)," *Journal of Roman Archaeology* 9 (1996a): 532–52 and the detailed discussion in P. Porena, *Le origini della prefettura del pretorio tardoantico* (2003).

The foundation and development of Constantinople is magisterially discussed in G. Dagron, *Naissance d'une capitale: Constantinople et ses institutions de 330 à 451* (1974). Both C. Mango, *Le développement urbain de Constantinople (IV*ᵉ*–VII*ᵉ *siècles)* (1990c), and R. Krautheimer, *Three Christian Capitals: Topography and Politics* (1983), offer good, accessible introductions. S. Bassett, *The Urban Image of Constantinople* (2004), catalogues the classical sculpture on display in the city.

For Constantine's reform of the senatorial order, see the important contribution by P. Heather, "Senators and Senates," in *The Cambridge Ancient History*, vol. 13, *The Late Empire A.D. 337–425* (1998b): 184–210, and the discussions in Jones, *The Later Roman Empire*, Chapter 15, and A. Chastagnol, *L'évolution politique, sociale et économique du monde romain de Dioclétien à Julien* 3rd ed. (1994). A thoughtful exploration of the implications of these changes is offered in P. Brown, *Power and Persuasion: Towards a Christian Empire* (1992), Chapter 1.

NOTES

1   *CTh* 6.22.6 (381).
2   Jones 1964, 1147–50, and articles in Goodburn and Bartholomew 1976 provide helpful introductions to the complexities of the text. Brennan 1995 offers an important and perceptive understanding of the document as a whole. His translation and commentary, soon to appear in the *Translated Texts for Historians* series will make the *Notitia* more accessible to students. For the dating, a vexed question, see the opposing views of Zuckerman 1998a and Kulikowski 2000.
3   Jones 1964, Map II.
4   Jones 1964, 448–62, quoting 449; Stein 1928, 179–81; Karayannopulos 1958, 80–84, 94–112.
5   T. D. Barnes 1996a, 548–50; Jones 1954, 1964, Map I. The text is most easily available in T. D. Barnes 1982, 201–3.
6   T. D. Barnes 1982, 141–7; 1996a, 550; Chastagnol 1994, 245–9.
7   Seeck 1900, 631–2; Jones 1964, 105; T. D. Barnes 1982, 141–7; Piganiol 1972, 353–5; Migl 1994, 54–69, esp. 66–9.
8   *CTh* 11.30.16; Jones 1964, 374–5, 481–2.
9   Migl 1994, 33–94, offers a detailed overview, and Porena 2003 now treats the problem in exhaustive detail. See also the important discussions in T. D. Barnes 1987, 13–15; 1992, 249–51; 1996a, 546–8, modifying some of the suggestions in T. D. Barnes 1982, 123–39, and Chastagnol 1994, 249–51. For an alternative reconstruction, see *PLRE* I, neatly summarised in Table A at p. 1048.
10   T. D. Barnes 1996a, 546–8; Chastagnol 1989.
11   Jones 1964, 371.
12   Porena 2003, 187–291; T. D. Barnes 1982, 124–8; 1996a, 547–8.
13   Porena 2003, 291–302, 409; see also Jones 1964, 101; T. D. Barnes 1982, 128–31.
14   On the inscription from Ain Rchine (*AE* 1981, 878), see Chastagnol 1986, 263–70; T. D. Barnes 1992, 249 n. 2; Migl 1994, 33–8; Porena 2003, 398–466. On Tubernuc (*AE* 1925, 72 = *ILTun.* 814) and Antioch (*AE* 1985, 823), see Feissel 1985; Chastagnol 1986, 270–3; T. D. Barnes 1992, 249–51; Migl 1994, 84–94; Porena 2003, 466–96.
15   Zos. 2.33.1–2 with Paschoud 2000, 247–50. For a different view, defending Zosimus and arguing that fully-fledged regional prefectures were established by Constantine between 324 and 330, see Porena 2003, 496–562.
16   *CTh* 12.1.21 and *Const. Sirm.* 4 = *CTh* 16.8.5 + 16.9.1, with T. D. Barnes 1982, 133; Migl 1994, 69–84; Porena 2003, 431–42.

17 Grünewald 1990, 202 no. 133; Migl 1994, 34.

18 T. D. Barnes 1992, 249–51, and, more generally, Piganiol 1972, 355–6; Migl 1994, 39–49.

19 Boak 1924, 29–30; Jones 1964, 97; Demandt 1970, 560–2; T. D. Barnes 1981, 256–7; Chastagnol 1994, 260–2; Austin and Rankov 1995, 228–9; Porena 2003, 555–6.

20 Jones 1964, 101.

21 *Not. Dign. or.* 12, *oc.* 10; see Harries 1988, 159–69; Delmaire 1995, 57–63. The fuller form of the title – *quaestor sacri palatii* – is not common until well into the fifth century; see Harries 1988, 154–5.

22 Zos. 5.32.6 with Bonfils 1981, 57–9; for the one possibly attested office-holder under Constantine, see Millar 1992, 100–1; *PLRE* 1 Fl. Hermogenes 9.

23 Jones 1964, 104; Bonfils 1981, 46–57; Harries 1988, 153–6; Millar 1992, 304; Delmaire 1995, 58–9.

24 *Not. Dign. or.* 11, *oc.* 9. See Boak 1924, 63–8, 82–6, 91–100; Jones 1964, 368–9, 575–8, 582–4; Piganiol 1972, 347–8; Clauss 1980, 15–21; T. D. Barnes 1981, 256; Delmaire 1995, 69–73, 78–85, 91–4.

25 Clauss 1980, 8–9; Millar 1992, 224–5. On the early empire, see Millar 1992, 83–110, 213–52; cf. Purcell 1983.

26 Stein 1928, 172–3; Clauss 1980, 9–14. Contrast Boak 1924, 24–8.

27 *CTh* 6.35.1 = *CJ* 12.28.1 with Clauss 1980, 12–13.

28 Jones 1964, 103–4; Clauss 1973, 82–109; Austin and Rankov 1995, 136–7.

29 Clauss 1980, 28.

30 *CTh* 6.35.2 (319) with Clauss 1980, 13, 24, who, nevertheless, accepts an earlier date of 315. The date of *CTh* 6.35.3.3 = *CJ* 12.28.2.3, which unequivocally mentions *agentes in rebus*, is also disputed; see Clauss 1980, 23–4; Delmaire 1989, 32–4; 1995, 98; Porena 2003, 256–71. On the duties of the *agentes*, see conveniently Jones 1964, 578–82; Clauss 1980, 27–40; Delmaire 1995, 102–18; Austin and Rankov 1995, 219–21. On ranks and grades, see Clauss 1980, 24.

31 *CTh* 16.10.1 (Heraclianus), 11.9.1 (Proculeianus).

32 See below n. 63.

33 *CTh* 12.1.38; see Clauss 1980, 13–14.

34 *PLRE* 1 Palladius 2 and Martinianus 2. Peter's work survives only in fragments; the reference to the list of *magistri officiorum* is made by Peter's contemporary John Lydus (*De mag.* 2.27), a high-ranking official on the judicial side of the eastern praetorian prefecture and, like Peter, the author of a detailed history of his own administrative department.

35 Jones 1964, 613–14; Frank 1969, 50; Demandt 1970, 565; Clauss 1980, 13, 40–1; Porena 2003, 500–1.

36 Boak 1924, 31–2; Stein 1928, 172–3. Note also Delmaire 1989, 30–84; 1995, 75–7, 88, with a different but complementary argument linking changes in the remit of the praetorian prefecture and the *magister officiorum* soon after 324. See too Sinnigen 1962; Giardina 1977, 13–18; below n. 43.

37 On the *cursus publicus*, see Boak 1924, 74–80; Clauss 1980, 45–51; A. Kolb 2000. On *fabricae*, see Giardina 1977, 66–9; Clauss 1980, 51–4; S. James 1988, 273–4, 291–4; Delmaire 1995, 85–90. More generally on the overlapping of administrative functions, see C. M. Kelly 1998, 169–71.

38 *Not. Dign. or.* 18, *oc.* 16. Jones 1964, 572–5; Clauss 1980, 22–3; Teitler 1985, 19–26; Delmaire 1995, 52–3.

39 Jones 1964, 103; Teitler 1985, 54–6; Delmaire 1995, 48–9. See too – although with a different view on their origin – Stein 1928, 171–2; Sinnigen 1959, 1962, 379–81; Chastagnol 1994, 204–5.

40 See above n. 4.

41 *Not. Dig. or.* 13–14, *oc.* 11–12. Delmaire 1989 offers a detailed and comprehensive treatment of both officials, usefully summarised in 1995, 119–47. See too Karayannopulos 1958, 54–72; Jones 1964, 411–37; King 1980.

42 Jones 1964, 411–12; Delmaire 1989, 703–4. On the early empire, see Millar 1992, 144–201.

43 Delmaire 1989, 30–8; 1995, 120. On the dating of *CTh* 6.35.3 = *CJ* 12.1.3 + 12.28.2 to 326, see Delmaire 1989, 32–4, and the counter arguments in Porena 2003, 256–71.

44 The exception may be the imperial *quaestor*. The first securely attested office-holder with the rank of *comes* was in post in the mid-350s (*PLRE* 1 Flavius Taurus 3). The argument for the *quaestor* holding the rank of *comes* under Constantine rests on a claim of likely coincidence with the *magister officiorum* and *comes sacrarum largitionum*. See Harries 1988, 156–7; Delmaire 1995, 58–9.

45 For an alternative reconstruction to that offered here, dating the establishment of the *notarii*, the *comes sacrarum largitionum*, and *comes rei privatae* to the reign of Constantius II, and similarly the promotion to the rank of *comes* of the *magister officiorum* and the imperial quaestor, see, in particular, Weiss 1975, 42–55; Vogler 1979, 183–210, 220–30; Bonfils 1981, 59–68.

46 On Constantinople and its foundation, see usefully Janin 1964, 21–60; Dagron 1974, 13–76; T. D. Barnes 1981, 222–3; Krautheimer 1983, 41–67; Mango 1990c, 23–36; Millar 1992, 53–7.

47 Syme 1974.

48 Optat. Porf. *Carm.* 4.6; Dagron 1974, 43–7; Calderone 1993, esp. 733–44.

49 *Chron. Pasch.* p. 528; Malalas 13.7; Procop. *BG* 1.15.9–14; cf. Dagron 1974, 39; C. M. Kelly 1999, 170–1.

50 Soz. 2.3.2.; cf. Zos. 2.30.1.

51 Eus. *VC* 3.33–43, 50, and, generally, Krautheimer 1993; on Constantinian building in Antioch, see Downey 1961, 342–50; in Rome, Curran 2000, 70–115.

52 Dagron 1974, 78–9; T. D. Barnes 1982, 78–80.

53 Athan. *Ap. con. Arian.* 86.6; Millar 1992, 603–5; T. D. Barnes 1981, 235–40.

54 *VC* 1.43.3 (trans. Cameron and Hall); cf. 4.1, 28.

55 Heather 1994, 15–16; 1998b, 186; Cameron and Hall 1999, 309–11.

56 Zos. 2.38.1 with T. D. Barnes 1981, 255–6; Chastagnol 1966b, 45–6.

57 Jul. *Caes.* 335b; cf. *Or.* 1.8b. On this theme, see also Chapter 10 n. 64 in this volume.

58 *CTh* 6.36.1 = *CJ* 12.30.1 (326); cf. C. M. Kelly 2004, 186–8.

59 *CTh* 6.35.1 = *CJ* 12.28.1 (314); *CTh* 6.35.2 (319); *CTh* 6.35.3 = *CJ* 12.1.3 + 12.28.2 (for the date, see n. 43); *CTh* 6.35.4 (321); *CTh.* 6.35.5 (328); *CTh* 6.36.1 = *CJ* 12.30.1 (326). See Jones 1964, 104, 452.

60 *CTh* 6.35.1 = *CJ* 12.28.1 (314); *CTh* 6.35.4 (321).

61 Heather 1998b, 185–6; cf. 1994, 14–16, and generally Grünewald 1990, 134–44.

62 Jones 1964, 106.

63 Eus. *VC* 4.1.2 (quoted below at n. 75). See Jones 1964, 104–5, 333–4; Millar 1992, 117–19; Seeck 1900, 629–36, 644–6; Weiss 1975, 18–28.

64 *CIL* 6:1707 = *ILS* 1213 honouring *PLRE* 1 C. Ceionius Rufius Volusianus 4.

65 On individuals, see Jones 1964, 105–6 and nn. 61–2; Bonfils 1981, 2–25.

66 Ensslin 1934; Jones 1964, 106, 534 n. 28; Piganiol 1972, 346–7.

67 Chastagnol 1976a, 1976b, 343–48; 1994, 227–31; Heather 1994, 12; 1998b, 184–6. For doubts and discussion, see Jones 1964, 132–3; Dagron 1974, 120–4.

68 Mango 1959, 56–8; Janin 1964, 154–6; Dagron 1974, 138–9.

69 Jones 1964, 106–7, 525–30, 545–52; Chastagnol 1970, 1976a; Piganiol 1972, 71–2, 389–91; Dagron 1974, 154–90; Heather 1998b, 195–7.

70 T. D. Barnes 1982, 153, 155, 163, 165, 168.

71 *PLRE* 1 Fabius Titianus 6 with Bonfils 1981, 14–15; *PLRE* 1 C. Caelius Saturninus signo Dogmatius 9 with Bonfils 1981, 6–7. It seems reasonable to assume that the clarissimate was open to holders of the four chief palatine offices following the promotion of their posts to the rank of *comes*. The evidence is patchy, but such an imperial grant probably remained discretionary until at least the 360s, when the clarissimate was conferred. For discussion, see Delmaire 1989, 38–9, with Weiss 1975, 50 n. 130; cf. Jones 1964, 528; Clauss 1980, 100.

72 Lib. *Or.* 42.26; cf. Kaster 1988, 419–21, no. 241; *PLRE* 1 Flavius Optatus 3.

73 Epiph. *Pan.* 30.4.1, 5.1–6, 11.7–9; Millar 1992, 118.

74 Zos. 2.32.1, 38.1, 39.1.

75 Eus. *VC* 4.1.2 (trans. Cameron and Hall).

9: CIVIL LAW AND SOCIAL LIFE

Caroline Humfress

> That noble man [Constantine], who dearly loved the honorable
> and who was a most conscientious judge of morals.
>
> Marcian *Novels* 4.2

I n AD 454 a constitution of the emperor Constantine, originally
issued 118 years previously, was still creating doubt and confusion
in the law courts of the Roman empire. Constantine's ruling, issued
on July 21, 336, had targeted senators, *perfectissimi* and those "adorned"
with various high-ranking provincial and municipal dignities who were
treating children whom the civil law classed as *de facto* illegitimate as
if they were legitimate.[1] According to Constantine's law, this newly-
defined group of elite men were "to become foreigners in the eyes
of Roman law" – to lose the protection that their Roman citizenship
guaranteed to their (elite) civil status, their (considerable) property, and
their (high-class) households – if they attempted to transfer any gifts or
inheritances to children not born of a union befitting their rank and dignity. With characteristic precision, Constantine's enactment catalogued
certain "types" of women who by simple virtue of their own civil status
(or lack thereof) were to be classed as producing illegitimate offspring
with these elite men:

> a slave woman, the daughter of a slave woman, a freed-
> woman, a daughter of a freedwoman, whether made a
> Roman or a [Junian] Latin, a woman of the stage, a daughter
> of a woman of the stage, a mistress of a tavern, a daughter of a
> tavern keeper, a low and degraded woman [*humilis abiectaque
> persona*], the daughter of a procurer or of a gladiator or a
> woman who has charge of wares for sale to the public.[2]

This list may seem peculiar to us, but none of the various types of "infamous" women (i.e., women who by birth or occupation were deemed "alien" or outside the Roman civil law) would have sent shock waves through the ranks of the early fourth-century élite. The classifications and categorizations of those who counted as "the élite," the vanguard of Roman mores and respectable social values, had certainly shifted over time. The ideal of the respectable stay-at-home girl, on the other hand, seems to have remained fairly constant. Likewise, the integrity and status of the top-ranking social groups – their (oftentimes fictional) cohesiveness, what they did with their property, those to whom they donated their wealth, how they transmitted their patrimonies – had been a driving force within Roman civil law since its inception.

What was at stake in Constantine's 336 law was not so much the prohibition of unions with the types of women listed as the fact that key high-ranking men were simply acting as if these unions and their offspring *were* legitimate, either by their own conduct – such as designating their children by such women as legitimate heirs in their wills or donating gifts to them *as if* they were legitimate – or by petitioning the emperor for personal *beneficia* (privileges or exemptions) which would legalize the relevant property transactions and by implication the children themselves.[3] The drafter of Constantine's 336 constitution was equally well aware that powerful, high-ranking men, their friends, and indeed their relations might attempt to circumvent the spirit of the emperor's legislation by using mechanisms readily available within Roman civil law itself: for example, by naming a third party as a "legitimate" heir who was then to pass the property on to its originally intended beneficiary or by having other "legitimate" family members swear oaths or pacts that they would not challenge a will which instituted the "illegitimate" children as heirs.[4] The fact that the 336 law explicitly prohibited these dodges and rackets is an important reminder that the relationship between civil law and social life in late antiquity involved rather more than an emperor simply laying down the law and expecting it to be followed in practice. Constantine, like his predecessors, worked within a system of private law that, at base, was founded on "remedies," on finding legal solutions to tricky social situations, disputes, and case-specific problems. The élite, those with the most to lose, also had the most to gain from attempting to maneuver the civil law to their own (particular) advantages. The drafters of Constantine's laws were certainly concerned with the abuses of *potentiores* (powerful men) against the *mediocres* or *tenuiores* (the weak and defenceless).[5] But, as we shall see, the emperor and his officials were frequently willing to aid the propertied classes in their attempts to exploit the flexibility of Roman private law to their own advantage.

By 454 the Constantinian text at *Codex Theodosianus* 4.6.3 had assumed a virtual life of its own. The interpretative emphasis being given to Constantine's enactment in the mid-fifth century was that it *prohibited* certain types of immoral and illicit marriages, with a strong overtone of Christian rectitude. The trouble arose specifically in connection with the Constantinian phrase *humilis abiectaque persona*. To what type of "low and degraded" persons did this phrase actually refer? Had Constantine intended to forbid the unions of senators and high-ranking dignitaries with freeborn, poverty-stricken women?[6] Marcian looked back to the golden age of Constantine, the (Christian) spirit of his reign, and decided that an emperor who so dearly loved the honourable and judged so conscientiously concerning morality could never have intended a meaning so manifestly unfair: "For who could suppose that Constantine of renowned memory, when he prohibited the nuptial couches of Senators to be contaminated with the vileness of polluted women, preferred the gifts of fortune to natural virtues ?"[7] Having thus interpreted the spirit of the law, Marcian provided his own definition for the phrase *humilis abiectaque persona*; henceforth it should not be interpreted as applying to freeborn, poor women but should be treated simply as identifying the "class" under which all the other types of women mentioned in Constantine's 336 law should now be seen to fall. Given the overwhelming concern with property and wealth transference in the original law, it is certainly a moot point whether a judge deciding a case in 336 or 337 would have arrived at the same conclusion.

The emperor Marcian's interpretation of Constantine's 336 constitution highlights two major pitfalls of which the modern historian should be aware when attempting to explore the relationship between civil law and social life in the early fourth century. First, the modern historian may be tempted, as Marcian was, to attribute a particular spirit or policy to Constantine's extant legislation and then use that attribution to reason out the imperial intention behind any given legislative text. In this context, Constantine's status as the first Christian emperor looms large. Constantine's contemporary Eusebius certainly saw the laws of Constantine through a (particularly coloured) Christian lens, as did the later, fifth-century church historians Socrates and Sozomen. Historical scholarship written within the last decade has begun to turn the tide back, undermining the idea of a general Christian influence on the extant corpus of Constantinian legislation in favour of cautiously identifying a spirit which looks back to the statutes of the first emperor, Augustus (and even further into remote antiquity).[8] What is striking, however, about the three hundred and thirty or so extant (or rather partially extant) laws issued by Constantine between 312 and 337 is not their attempt to implement any legislative programmes of either innovation or conservatism but rather their "reactive" quality.[9] The drafters of Constantine's laws respond to concrete situations: they clarify, tinker with, elaborate, and occasionally repeal various substantive principles of Roman law already in existence. As far as Constantine was concerned, litigation in private civil matters (at least) should end to the satisfaction of the litigants.[10]

The second pitfall highlighted by Marcian's interpretation of Constantine's 336 law is the tendency to treat the reign of Constantine as a watershed in the history of late Roman law itself. Marcian, like the mid-fourth-century apostate emperor Julian and in turn most emperors after Theodosius II and his Codex of 438, looked back to Constantine as the beginning of a new era in imperial law-making.[11] There are certainly arguments in favour of this view, but it is worth noting from the outset that the specific provisions within Constantine's legal texts invariably demand a knowledge of relevant strands of existing Roman law and treat these strands as part of an operative legal system. On occasion the legal decisions of previous second- and third-century emperors – preserved today in the form of the sixth-century Justinianic Codex and Digest – are cited in Constantine's laws as a springboard to new Constantinian "adjustments," especially with respect to litigation involving civil status and family/inheritance law.

SOCIAL STATUS IN CONSTANTINE'S LAWS

New laws have been established for regulating morals and quashing vices; the cunning evasions of earlier times have been cut short and have lost their snares for entrapping honesty. Modesty is safe, marriage protected. Properties, free from worry, take pleasure in being sought and there is no fear of having as much as possible, but in so large a profusion of blessings there is a great dread of not having any.[12]

Nazarius *Panegyric of Constantine*

In the minds of conservative upper-class Romans, and within the civil law which had been primarily elaborated to protect their interests, wealth, civil status and moral excellence went hand in hand. Nazarius, in the quotation given above, expected the emperor whom he praised to share this ideology. The "haves" of late Roman society were those who had both Roman citizenship and enough wealth to access the various "blessings" of the legal system (and if necessary the emperor himself) and to make it worth their while to do so. An individual's place in an empire-wide sociolegal order determined the justice they could expect as well as the social and financial obligations (the personal and/or patrimonial *munera*) which civil life demanded from them. In practice, Constantine's own legislation developed a piece-by-piece mosaic of ordinary and extraordinary obligations and exemptions which covered all classes, from *clarissimi* down to *coloni*, via *perfectissimi, palatini*, professors, architects, military veterans, decurions, *navicularii* (shipmasters), plebeians, urban bakers, and even "pigmen." Constantine's legislation also records the extraordinary (il)legal dodges to which some members of the aforesaid groups would resort in order to escape the personal and patrimonial burdens that they were deemed to owe.[13]

Traditionally, the senatorial class, those of the *clarissima dignitas*, stood at the apex of the sociolegal order. In 317 Constantine seems to have revoked an important senatorial privilege in ruling that *clarissimi* accused of certain specified (capital) crimes had to be tried in the province where the crime had been committed rather than at Rome itself. Here, however, Constantine was extending an already established juristic principle that "an accusation excludes all prerogatives of rank when a criminal case, not a civil or pecuniary suit, is brought." Constantine states that senators should not petition him for any particular exemptions from this ruling – the implication being that said *clarissimi* can continue to petition him for particular exemptions and privileges in civil and pecuniary cases.[14] In theory, this relationship between emperor and citizen also held good at the lowest gradations of the "haves." An early law of Constantine dated June 2, 315, and addressed *ad universos provinciales* grants relief to certain litigants (lacking alternative financial resources) who are having their slave-plowmen and plow-oxen dragged away by judicial order as pledges for debts demanded in civil proceedings. Constantine threatens a capital sentence against any member of the judge's office staff, or any creditor, who follows this practice. What was the emperor's specific concern? That the payment of imperial taxes was being delayed by the removal of essential items for working the land.[15]

The "have-nots" of the early fourth century included groups outside the Roman empire (barbarians and those taken in captivity beyond the frontiers) as well as subgroups of "aliens" within. The legal categorizations of these internal subgroups could include slaves and *de facto* particular gradations within the slave "class," the *coloni* (free rural serfs), the urban and rural poor, and a whole host of ever-shifting sociolegally defined types of marginalised individuals (including those tainted with the stain of *infamia* by reason of judicial sentence, birth, or occupation). Each of the aforementioned subgroups came under the gaze of Constantine's legislation with specific reference to judicial sentencing in both private and criminal disputes. Differential penalties for those of high and low rank appear in a number of Constantine's laws, as well as instructions to judges that sentencing in specific cases should be adjusted "according to distinctions of sex and differences in legal status."[16] Once again Constantine is building upon a legal framework already in existence, developed in particular by classical jurists who recognized that inflicting a pecuniary fine or confiscating someone's property would not function as a punishment for those who possessed nothing to begin with. *Codex Theodosianus* 16.2.5 – to be dated to December 25, 323 – fits well within this classical juristic context. The constitution states that if any person should force a cleric, or any other servant of the Catholic *secta*, to perform lustral (i.e., "pagan") sacrifices, he should be

> beaten publicly with clubs, provided his legal status so permits. If, however, the consideration of his honorable rank protects him from such an outrage, he shall sustain the penalty of a very heavy fine, which shall be vindicated to the cities.

The penalty for any given offence could depend not only on the act that was committed but also on who was committing it and against whom.[17] Although high-ranking magistrates had a certain leeway in deciding upon an appropriate penalty, the emperor also provided them with rules for particular cases. The judicial sentences to be issued against the "have-nots" are marked by an increasing severity, if not savagery, from Constantine's reign onwards.[18]

In the case of a criminal accusation for adultery, the social status of the accused could even determine whether the prosecution was to be undertaken or not. Two Constantinian constitutions issued in 326 concern the statutory crime of adultery. Under the Augustan *Lex Iulia de adulteriis* (c. 18 BC), adultery was classified as a public criminal offence, but one committed specifically against a wronged husband and the agnatic relations of the woman accused (i.e., to those related through the male line).[19] Constantine limited the right of accusation for adultery to close kin and the husband especially.[20] In *Codex Theodosianus* 9.7.1 (= *CJ* 9.9.28, dated February 3, 326), the emperor tackled a specific situation concerning the application of the *lex Iulia de adulteriis* to one of the very lowest rungs of the sociolegal hierarchy. The extant text – an excerpt of a longer original – is so specific that it should be read as a response to a particular query, a clarification of the law in force issued for the benefit of either a private petitioner or a legal official. The question is whether the female owner of the tavern and the servant woman should be hauled equally before a judge on the basis of a criminal accusation for adultery. The text begins, "It will have to be inquired whether the woman who committed adultery was the owner of a tavern or a servant." If the latter, then the drafter of the text assumes that as part of her job the servant woman also serves "the wines of intemperance," that is, she sleeps around or even "prostitutes herself." Constantine's answer is that the owner can be legally accused, but "in consideration of the baseness of the woman who is brought to trial," the servant cannot,

> since a condition of modesty [*pudicitia*] shall be required from those women, who are held by the bonds of the law, but those shall be proven immune from judicial severity whom the baseness of their life [*vilitas vitae*] has not considered worthy of the observation of the laws. (trans. Grubbs)

It had previously been assumed that the servant in question was a slave, but more recent investigation has determined that she was most likely free and thus at least theoretically subject to the law on adultery. The phrases *viles vitae* and *viles personae* had been used in earlier juristic discussion to signify a composite though loosely defined category of freeborn persons who, from the jurists' perspective, existed either on the fringes of society or beyond the purview of the law altogether.[21] In Constantine's legislation, marginal freeborn individuals, such as the tavern servant woman, continued to fall between the legal cracks. A (moral) crime committed by a "respectable" freeborn person reflected on society as a whole, but it seems that the *vilitas* of the tavern servant in *Codex Theodosianus* 9.7.1 reflected on no-one but herself. It was not worth pursuing a person for a public crime which epitomised her lack of civil standing and respectable *mores* when the individual in question was already deemed to have none.

THE 'FAMILY' IN CONSTANTINIAN LAW
AND LEGAL PRACTICE

This law is better than the ancient one.

Codex Justinianus 5.37.22, AD 329

"To most Romans property and rank, or lack of them, came through inheritance within the family."[22] In Roman civil law the term *familia* covered a juridically ordered set of social relationships. Those relationships stretched upwards to one's ancestors and *parentes* (close lineal ascendants), downwards to one's descendants, and outwards according to the rules of agnatic kinship. The head of any given *familia* was the *paterfamilias*, in most instances the oldest living free male in the extended family. Within this juridical unit, this was the individual who was *sui iuris* (in his own legal power) and consequently held other members of the *familia* within that power (*potestas*). As far as the civil law was concerned, the *paterfamilias* also held the purse-strings: hence the term '*familia*' also covered *res*, or property (i.e., the family patrimony). Individuals within the *potestas* of the *paterfamilias* could include his children and their descendants (unless emancipated or adopted into another *familia*), as well as slaves. A slave could not form his own *familia* – he had no legal power independent of his owner or possessor – but even in the late republic, jurists had begun to argue that some of their elaborate classificatory terminology could be loosely applied to *de facto* relationships based on affection or kinship between slaves.[23] The *materfamilias* (the wife of the *paterfamilias*, the "respectable" female head of the household) was either within the *potestas* of her *paterfamilias* or else *sui iuris* herself. The legal power of a woman who was juridically independent was not the same, however, as that of an independent man.[24] Any married woman, whether *sui iuris* or *in potestate*, could also be classed as belonging to her husband's *domus*, a broad term encompassing the idea of the (physical) house and cognatic relationships. A "freed person," a slave who had been manumitted and had received either full or limited citizenship, was *sui iuris* but owed certain duties and obligations to the patron(s) who had freed him or her. The obligations and entitlements of this "belonging," the sociolegal duties owed by a freed person to his or her patron and vice versa, had different effects according to the particular terms under which the slave had been legally freed.[25] An individual's age, sex and place within a *familia* affected his or her legal capacity: the ability to make a dowry or a will; to be a party to a contract, pledge, or donation that would stand up in court; to bring a legal action; or to act as a defendant in a case. It is to Constantine's legislation concerning the family that we shall now turn.

Within the extant corpus of Constantine's legislation, there are nineteen constitutions which specifically and self-consciously state that the legislator is altering, amending, or even repealing law that was currently in force. Out of these nineteen constitutions, fourteen fall within the subject area of the family. Even allowing for the fact that – almost without exception – we do not have the full texts of most Constantinian laws, this number is striking. It is in the area of family and inheritance law that the drafters of Constantinian constitutions seem most self-consciously aware of the past legal sources they are working with as well as the changes and developments they are introducing. This legislative preoccupation makes perfect sense: when it came to the transference of patrimonial property, citizens were expected to be secure in their knowledge of what legal actions and defences were available to them given their age, sex, and juridical capacity – or lack thereof. Of course, those with the most to lose had the most to gain from understanding how to negotiate the complex system of civil law within which they operated and from keeping up with the pace of new imperial rulings.

Constantine's legislation, like that of emperors before him, was concerned with the practicalities and consequences arising from a number of different kinds of male-female unions.[26] *Codex Theodosianus* 12.1.6 (318) begins by stating a traditional legal definition concerning "mixed" unions between slaves and the freeborn: "a *conubium* [lawful marriage] cannot exist with servile persons, and from a *contubernium* [cohabitation] of this kind, slaves are born." *Contubernium* could exist freely between Roman citizens not otherwise within a *conubium*,[27] although any children born from the former kind of union would count as illegitimate in the eyes of the law. *Contubernium* between a freeborn man and a female slave was not prohibited by law. In this respect, the Constantinian drafters of *Codex Theodosianus* 12.1.6, however, had their eye on a particular problem. Despite the apparent social stigma, men from the decurial class were not only cohabiting with female slaves but alienating their patrimony to the (high-ranking) masters of those female slaves. The practice of decurions alienating their property to the heads of powerful houses threatened the finances, manpower, and resources of the empire's cities. Constantine thus laid down differential penalties for the decurion and the slave woman as well as for her master and any overseers/procurators of the rural or urban property where the said *contubernium* was taking place. The municipalities were also authorized to seek the restoration of the decurion's alienated property. A freeborn woman of honourable status living – of her own volition – in *contubernium* with a male slave, on the other hand, automatically forfeited her own freedom and gave birth to slaves.[28] In fact, any mother of servile status could only give birth to slaves, even if they were the natural children of her master. A law issued in 331, however, testifies to an ingenious legal loophole being pleaded in court by parties attempting to claim citizenship for children born to master-slave unions. It had been granted previously that any person who lived in good faith as freeborn for sixteen years could not have that personal status challenged in court – some individuals pleaded that master-slave children aged sixteen years and above should also have this benefit. Having been brought to the attention of the emperor, this dodge was henceforth to be understood as an "empty usurpation of freedom."[29]

In the early fourth century, the path to *matrimonium iustum* was marked increasingly by the exchange of betrothal gifts. The drafter of a 319 law declared the emperor to be "displeased with the *sententia veterum* that gifts to a betrothed woman were valid even if marriage did not follow."[30] The law then lays out a number of different scenarios in which gifts given in contemplation of marriage should be returned and circumstances in which they should not. One of the legislator's main concerns was to ensure a "no-fault" situation if either party should pull out from the anticipated matrimony. Allegations against the morals or social status of a repudiated fiancé or fiancée were not to be taken into account by a judge when deciding whether betrothal gifts ought to be returned to the giver. In 335 Constantine supplemented his 319 ruling in order to differentiate between gifts made before and after "a kiss has been exchanged as a pledge."[31] Other Constantinian texts speak of a two-year limit for betrothals[32] as well as criminal penalties against *raptus* (the forcible marriage/rape of young daughters *in potestate*). *Raptus* was only classified as a crime affecting all women (slave women included) by the emperor Justinian in the early sixth century.[33] Strictly speaking, *matrimonium iustum* was founded on a husband's and wife's intention, but the giving of a dowry from the woman's *familia* could act as a crucial means of differentiating a respectable marriage from a *contubernium* if the status of the union was ever brought into question. The dowry was owned by the husband (or his *paterfamilias*) for the duration of the marriage as a means of underwriting the expenses of the household – any property owned by the bride and not classified as dowry remained hers after marriage.[34]

The marriage bond itself could be broken by either death or divorce, the latter of which came in two sorts: *divortium* and *repudium* (respectively, bilateral and unilateral divorce). Under Constantine, as before, both parties were free to divorce each other mutually without legal penalty. In 331, however, Constantine issued a law that attempted to restrict unilateral *repudium*.[35] A woman who henceforth sent a notice of divorce "on trumped-up grounds" (like alcoholism, gambling, or philandering!) was to forfeit all of her property down to the last hairpin to her husband and be deported to an island. Only if a wife could prove that her husband was guilty of a serious public crime (murder, sorcery, or the violation of tombs) could she repudiate him, earn commendation for the accusation, and at length recover her dowry. If a man wished to repudiate his wife, Constantine laid down much less stringent legal grounds for doing so (that she was an adulteress, a sorceress, or a "procuress"). The penalties in the husband's case were also lighter: a man who effected an "illegal" repudiation had to restore the entire dowry to his cast-off wife, and if he married again, his ex-wife was granted the legal right to storm into the new matrimonial home by force and appropriate the second wife's dowry for herself. This law is certainly fraught with a heavy moralizing tone. The marriage bond is prioritized over the (private) wishes of the wife or husband seeking divorce, except where one of the partners threatened the moral fabric of society as a whole through the worst kinds of criminal activity traditionally associated with their sex. The fact that Constantine did not legislate against divorce by mutual agreement, however, suggests that this law was not primarily motivated by Christian ethics, which strictly prohibited divorce.

Viewed from a legal perspective, the main reason for contracting a bond of legitimate marriage was the production of legitimate offspring. In 320 Constantine famously repealed "old law" (*ius vetus*) by rescinding the penalties put in place by the emperor Augustus in the first century BC against the childless – penalties which had long been circumvented in practice.[36] The drafter of the same constitution was also careful to specify that the strict traditional limits on gifts between husbands and wives remained in force. Thus even this pathbreaking law upheld the old standard that any property held by a wife's independent right should be protected from encroachment by her husband. On the other hand, in 315 Constantine had restated a principle from earlier imperial rescripts that, in the event of courtroom litigation, "a husband has a perfect right to undertake the management of the affairs of his wife without any mandate." In this way, respectable married women were to be protected from incurring "contempt for the modesty of their sex" by being forced to appear in the assemblies of men.[37] An oppressively protective attitude to women is characteristic of Constantine's legislation, although we should not assume that all women found themselves equally subdued.[38]

Since the age of Augustus, a woman with three legitimate (surviving) children could petition for the so-called *ius liberorum*, thereby freeing her from some of the legal restrictions normally imposed on the female sex. In 318 Constantine reinforced a woman's (cognatic) rights within her husband's *familia* by stating that even without the *ius liberorum* a woman could inherit a third of the property of an intestate child who predeceased her. This Constantinian development in favour of the mother was in line with earlier statutes – the *senatus consultum Tertullianum* and the *senatus consultum Orphitianum* – which granted a woman previously forbidden claims to inherit from her children if they died intestate. From at least the mid-third century onwards, men had also taken advantage of a rather different type of *ius liberorum*. Five legitimate children could earn a man exemption from the performance of compulsory extraordinary burdens (*munera*). This last privilege was apparently open to abuse, forcing Constantine to prohibit men pleading the *ius liberorum* from exhibiting "the children of others as their own" in order to qualify.[39]

Legitimate children owed legally defined duties of respect and obligation to their *paterfamilias*. In one constitution Constantine refers to a particular advantage to be gained by dutiful sons and daughters: they could expect to be emancipated from paternal power. *Codex Theodosianus* 8.18.2 (318) even implies that this emancipation could be taken for granted as part of the normal course of things; a father would be "led to emancipate his children by the fact that they have arrived at legal age and he wishes to see his own children heads of households [*patresfamilias*]."[40] A Constantinian rescript, however, responds to a situation where an emancipated son has had his emancipation revoked because he treated his own son "arrogantly" and "cruelly."[41] On occasion, Constantine was also concerned to emphasise that the legal relationship between child and *paterfamilias* was a two-way street. *Codex Theodosianus* 9.43.1.2 (321) states that a father who had lost his civil status but then had it reinstated

> must perform his paternal duty, uncorrupted by any baseness, so that he may protect and increase his children's property. For if he should misuse the *patria potestas* as a license for injuring and squandering their patrimony, as in the case of

an insane and demented person, and likewise of a prodigal,
enslaved to all lusts and vices, the children's property must
not be entrusted to him.

The drafter of the law attributes the particular legal principle he is working with to an opinion of the classical jurist Papinian.[42] The idea that
a dutiful father must protect and increase the family property, however,
underpinned the very institution of *patria potestas* itself.

If children below the age of puberty – twelve years for girls, fourteen for boys and, according to Diocletian, eighteen for eunuchs (!) –
found themselves free from paternal power (*sui iuris*), then Roman public law demanded that they be provided with a *tutor*, "in imitation of
the guardianship of the father."[43] Under classical Roman law, women
were expected to have tutors for life, but by the early fourth century this
requirement and the general rule that women could not act for themselves in law and business had become redundant.[44] Male and female
children below the age of puberty (*impuberes*) had a very limited legal
capacity, "their age does not understand what it sees,"[45] and certain
restrictions could remain with a "minor" up to the age of twenty-five
years. Constantine's legislation considerably strengthened the rights of
independent *impuberes* and minors vis-à-vis their guardian's obligation
to administer capably and expand their patrimony.[46] Money was not
everything. A law of 329 forbids tutors from the almost total liquidation of their wards' inheritance, presumably in the context of turning
property into cash that could then be invested or loaned at a higher
rate of return. The children affected by this 329 ruling were expected
to be of a very high social class; the drafter envisages a patrimony that
could include gold, silver, pearls, gems, vases, clothing, urban estates
and slaves, buildings and baths, warehouses and animals, as well as rustic
estates and the slaves tied to them. A particularly striking phrase in the
text specifies that "it is not permitted to sell the house in which the
father died or the minor was brought up, for it would be sad enough
not to see the statues of the family ancestors fastened therein, or to have
them torn away."[47]

The death of a *paterfamilias* necessitated the transmission of the
patrimony to his heirs. In the late republic and early empire, a complex
set of (frequently conflicting) rules concerning inheritance had been
elaborated, particularly with respect to intestate succession. Constantine responded to these circumstances with a law of 324 that addressed
the problem of a *paterfamilias* making an "imperfect" will (a testament

begun but not completed, lacking legally binding words or the requisite formality). If the *paterfamilias* had instituted as heirs those persons who were under his power at the time of his death (*heredes sui*), Constantine rules that the intention of the deceased should stand "among the aforesaid class of heirs only," even despite the document's lack of legal formality.[48] The constitution goes on to state that the *ius civile* and the praetor (i.e., the existing law on intestacy) already granted to children and grandchildren the right to inherit anyway, if perhaps in proportions different to those expressed in the will.[49] Constantine's legislation in this field thus attempted not to subvert but to clarify or supplement the rules already in force.

A law dated 321 shows the drafter of the text developing existing principles by reasoning from analogy: just as a legitimate child omitted as heir from a parent's testament could challenge that testament as "undutiful" (*inofficiosus*), so, too, a mother should be granted the right to proceed against her son's testament on the same grounds.[50] Mothers could expect to inherit from sons. Conversely, three constitutions spanning the beginning and end of Constantine's reign guarantee the rights of underage minors *in potestate* to inherit goods from their mother (termed *bona materna*).[51] Rather than the children's *paterfamilias* formally entering upon the estate of their mother as heir (thus "owning" the *bona materna* for them), the three laws outline a scheme whereby the father becomes a quasi-owner with the right of use (*usufructus*) but not the right of alienation over said maternal goods. The maternal inheritance is to be restored to the children in the event of emancipation, but they should offer a third back to the father by way of gratitude for his solicitude in conserving the *bona materna* for them – though the legislator suggests that "good" fathers may not wish to accept it. The final constitution of 334 irons out complications arising when a father decides to contract a second marriage. In attempting to provide a particular legal defence for the rights of dependent children with respect to their maternal inheritances, the drafters of these Constantinian texts are self-consciously aware of doing something new while at the same time working within a general trend dating back to the early empire.

It is perhaps in this vein that we might interpret Constantine's confirmation of the validity of all testamentary dispositions "to the most holy and venerable council of the Catholic church."[52] The practice of bequeathing gifts to pagan temples had long been common, and Constantine was simply extending this to the recently legitimized Christian religion. Moreover, Christians had manifestly made many gifts to the church long before Constantine's reign.

SLAVES AND MASTERS

A number of different owners of slaves appear in Constantine's extant legislation: alongside those attached to the urban and rural estates of *potentiores* there are references to slaves belonging to decurions and wealthy independent minors, as well as to the children and grandchildren of *palatini* (imperial officials), the sons of military veterans, and the households of Christian clerics.[53] Slaves were also held by the emperor as part of his own patrimony. When gifts of land were made from the imperial fisc, the ownership of any slaves attached to that land was transmitted as part of the property.[54] Slaves were also owned publicly by municipalities, and Constantine was (characteristically) concerned to protect the rights of cities as slave-owners against any encroachment from private would-be masters. Thus at *Codex Theodosianus* 6.1.5 (319) he orders that municipal slaves and freedmen "skilled in certain trades" had to remain in their respective towns; if they fled to another master and were not recovered, the cities' *defensores* were held legally and financially responsible.[55] Whether in private, imperial or corporate ownership, the price value of an individual slave was determined by his or her sex, age and skill (*ars*).[56] Judicial fines for harboring any given slave without the master's knowledge were based on an average slave's estimated value, 20 solidi.[57] A master's legitimate power over any slave included "disciplinary beatings." *Codex Theodosianus* 9.12.1 (319) allows for the disciplinary killing of slaves. If, however, the death resulted from a whole catalogue of "cruel and unusual punishments" designed to inflict death, then a charge of homicide could be brought against the master. A constitution from seven years later revises this principle: if a master beats a *household* slave to death in the exercise of his "domestic power," no criminal investigation for homicide should ensue.[58] In a similar vein, the torture of slaves to the point of death remained a standard procedure for gaining evidentiary testimony in court.

Establishing whether a person was in fact a slave or not could be complicated. Classical Roman law had established exact procedural regulations for a legal case concerning freedom (*causa liberalis*).[59] The fifth-century compilers of the Theodosian Code included a separate section entitled *de liberali causa*, title eight of book four. All but one of the constitutions excerpted under this title are Constantinian. Constantine's laws deal with a series of complexities arising from cases where either a slave claims free status on the basis of mistaken enslavement or else a master appears as plaintiff claiming a freeborn person as his or her slave. *Codex Theodosianus* 4.8.4 (322) gives a ruling on the personal status of a child born while the mother's claim for freedom is pending in the courts. When "free" persons appeared as defendants in a *causa liberalis* – or indeed when "slaves" appeared as plaintiffs – they could not act for themselves; they had to find a Roman citizen who would assert free status on their behalf, an *assertor libertatis*. *Codex Theodosianus* 4.8.5 (322) orders that anyone who has trouble finding an *assertor libertatis* must be led through the people of the province bearing a written notice that he or she is seeking such a person. One of the intended effects of this practice was "show and tell" – provoking testimonies from the defendant's local community concerning his or her "true" personal status. This "show and tell" must have been a relatively effective practice in a society with limited instruments of registration. Other means of attempting to prove legally an individual's personal status included birth registrations, documents of sale, contracts, and the torture of any slaves who were liable to have information. *Codex Justinianus* 7.16.41 (possibly a constitution of Licinius) rules out letters from a lover as valid documentary evidence.

At the opposite end of the spectrum, masters could manumit (free) slaves within their ownership through a simple legal procedure before the emperor or a competent imperial bureaucrat.[60] A manumitted slave thereby became a freedman and the master a patron. From shortly after his conversion, Constantine seems to have extended the list of those allowed to oversee formal manumissions to include bishops. Our first evidence of this is a constitution of 316 in which Constantine gave legal validity to the "pious intent" of freeing a slave within the walls of a church.[61] Constantine also issued two much discussed laws which seem to authorize the transferral of civil cases to an *episcopalis audientia* (a "hearing" by the bishop).[62] Constantine thus opened the church to much greater involvement in civil law, but we must not carry the argument too far, for Constantine himself did not intend to replace civil with ecclesiastical judges, only to supplement the judicial pool with these trusted local leaders. Bishops were not, for example, competent to adjudicate the "cases concerning freedom" outlined above.

Slaves had no independent power to perform a legal act under the civil law. They could, however, be appointed to act on their master's behalf in a number of legal situations. Constantine's laws refer to slaves acting as business agents, managing a house or landed estate for an absentee master, and even guarding young masters against fraudulent activities by unscrupulous *tutores*. A constitution issued in 313 (addressed to the city council of Byzacium) very carefully outlines how a slave can be used legally to dodge the penalties and stigma associated with bankruptcy.[63] None of the aforementioned was new. In general, the picture painted in Constantine's legislation concerning slaves and masters is a traditional one, with the particular exception of manumission in Christian churches.

The drafters of Constantine's legislation exhibit a mixture of idealized traditional sentiments concerning social and familial relationships and a stereotypical distrust that these sentiments were being effected in practice. "Dissolute" women who abandon their children for new husbands; the "terrible" crime of parricide committed by children against parents and also vice versa; the exposure of newborn infants, who can then be taken up as either freeborn or slave according to the desire of the person who rears them – all these situations and more are covered by Constantinian laws.[64] By the same token, certain of Constantine's laws exhibit a particular distrust of the cohesiveness of Roman family units, such as those that concern secret trusts being transferred between close kin (illegal and to the detriment of the imperial fisc), family members pledging to stand false witness for each other in court, and the houses of powerful men absorbing free persons as slaves and quasi-slaves. *Codex Theodosianus* 8.12.5 (333) sums up the problem nicely: "since indeed in the case of clandestine and domestic frauds anything you please can be easily devised in accordance with the opportunity of the situation, or that which has been actually done can be nullified." The forces that governed social life and influenced law in the age of Constantine were bigger than the emperor and his legal texts.

In practice, "clandestine" or "illegal" agreements between family members could, and did, go unnoticed by the law. And the same must be true for the vast majority of individuals of questionable or uncertain legal status. The civil law would be invoked only when a given interested party had the inclination and resources to prosecute a case: "In the ordinary life of families in Roman society, what mattered was not so much the legal status of the people involved, as whether there was anyone in whose interest it was to insist upon the legalities being observed."[65] Constantine and his legislators tackled the problems which did come to their notice with only a modest degree of innovation. Radical change was out of the question, and even when legislative changes were made, they were always rooted in the principles of the past and sometimes watered down in subsequent laws. In so far as there was any idealism, religious or moral, it was so heavily tempered with an innate Roman conservatism and a characteristically Constantinian pragmatism that it can scarcely be discerned by the modern eye.

Further Reading

The relevant laws of Constantine are collected in the *Theodosian Code* (trans. Pharr, 1952), the *Code of Justinian* (ed. Krueger, 1895) and the *Vatican Fragments* (ed. Riccobono, 1940). P. Silli, *Testi Costantiniani nelle fonti letterarie* (1987), collects laws preserved in non-legal literary sources. J. Matthews, *Laying Down the Law: A Study of the Theodosian Code* (2000), gives a full introduction to the complex compilation and transmission of this crucial source as well as elucidates the problems confronted by historians in its use.

Detailed studies of the Constantinian legislative corpus are provided by C. Dupont in *Le droit criminel dans les constitutions de Constantin* (1953) and *Les constitutions de Constantin et le droit privé au début du IVe siècle: les personnes* (1968). S. Corcoran, *The Empire of the Tetrarchs: Imperial Pronouncements and Government AD 284–324* (2000), provides a full and methodologically aware study of the extant legislation up to the year 324. The secondary literature, in general, is preoccupied with assessing the impact of Christianity on the laws. See especially F. Amarelli, *Vetustas Innovatio: Un'antitesi apparente nella legislazione di Costantino* (1978), and J. E. Grubbs, *Law and Family in Late Antiquity: The Emperor Constantine's Marriage Legislation* (1995). The influence of Christian and/or traditional morality on the late Roman family is dealt with more briefly in A. Giardina, "The Family in the Late Roman World," in *The Cambridge Ancient History*, vol. 14, *Late Antiquity: Empire and Successors AD 425–600* (2000): 392–415, and Y. Rivière, "Constantin, le crime et la christianisme: contribution à l'étude des lois et des moeurs de l'antiquité tardive," *Antiquité Tardive* 10 (2002): 327–61, the latter of which discusses the special problem of the brutality of Constantine's criminal law. For specific studies on the legal position of women in the late empire, see J. Beaucamp, *Le statut de la femme à Byzance (4e–7e siècle)* (1990), and J. E. Grubbs, *Women and the Law in the Roman Empire: A Sourcebook on Marriage, Divorce and Widowhood* (2002), a sourcebook of relevant translated texts. A. Arjava, *Women and Law in Late Antiquity* (1996), also discusses explicitly the legal relationship between fathers and children (Arjava has updated his bibliography to 2005 and posted it at: http://www.nipissingu.ca/department/history/muhlberger/orb/arjava3.htm). On social status, in the absence of a specific study relating to Constantine's laws, see in general P. Brown, *Poverty and Leadership in the Later Roman Empire* (2002). J. A. Schlumberger, "*Potentes* and *Potentia* in the Social Thought of Late Antiquity," in *Tradition and Innovation in Late Antiquity*, ed. F. M. Clover and R. S.

FIGURES

FIGURE 1. Arch of Constantine, Rome, north face. Photo by Koppermann, DAI Inst. Neg. 61.2297. Copyright Deutsches Archäologisches Institut.

FIGURE 2. Remains of the porphyry column of Constantine (Çemberlitaş), Istanbul. Photo by G. Fowden, reproduced with permission.

FIGURE 3. Personified Constantinople seated next to the column of Constantine, *Tabula Peutingeriana*, detail of segment VIII, Österreichische Nationalbibliothek, Vienna. Copyright Bildarchiv der Österreichischen Nationalbibliothek.

E.   S.   R.
IMP CAES FL CONSTANTINVS
MAX GERM SARM GOT VICTOR
TRIVMP AVG ET FL CONSTANTINVS
ET FL IVL CONSTANTIVS ET EI-
CONSTANS.

OMNIA QVIDEM QVAE HVMANI GENE-
RIS SOCIETATE TVENTVR PERVIGILI VM CV-
RAE COGITATIONE COMPLECTIMVR SED PRO-
VISIONVM NOSTRARVM OPVS MAXIMVS
EST VT VNIVERSAE VRBES QVAS IN LVMINIBVS PROVIN-
CIARVM HAC REGIONVM OMNIVM SPECIES ET FORMA DIS-
TINGVITVR NON MODO DIGNITATE PRISTINAM TENEANT
SED ETIAM AD MELIOREM STATVM BENEFICENTIAE NOS-
TRAE MVNERE PROBEANTVR CVM IGITVR ITA VOS TVS SCI-
AE AD SE RERE TISSE SE CONIVNCTOS VT INISTITVTO
CONSVETVDINIS PRISCAE PERSING VLAS ANNORVM VI-
CES A VOBIS AD QVE PRAEDICTISSACERDOTES CREENTVR,
QVI APV TVVLSINIOSTVS CIAE CIVITATE LVDOS
SCHENI COSET GLADIATORVM MVNVS EXIIIBEAN T,
SED PROPTER ARDVAM ONTIVM ET DIFFICVLTATE SITI-
NERVM SALT VOSA INPENDIO POSCERE TIS VT INDVLTO
REMEDIO SACERDOTI VESTRO OBEINTIONES CELE-
BRANDAS VVLSINIOS PERGERE NE CESSEN ONESSET
SCILICET VT CIVITATIC VI NVNCHIS PELLVM NOMEN
EST QVAM QVE FLAMINIAE VIAE CONFINE MADQVE CON-
TINVAM ESSE MEMORAT ISDE NOSTRO COGNOMINE
NOMEN DAREMVS IN O VAT EMPLVM FLAVIAE AE GENT IS
OPERE MAGNIFICONI MIRV M PROAMPLIT VDINEM
NVNCVPATIONIS EXSVRGERE IBIDEM QVEI IIS
SACERDOS QVEM ANNIVERSARIA VICE VMBRIA DE-
DIS SET SPECTACVLVM TAM SCENICORVM LVDORVM
QVAM GLADIATORII MVNERIS EXHIRE REMANENTE
PERTV SCIAE A CONSVETVDINE VT INDIDEM CRE-
ATVS SACERDOS A PVTVVLSINIOS VT SOLEBAT
ED TIONVM ANTE DICTARVM SPECTACVLA FRE-
QVENTARE PRAECATION I HAC DESIDERIO VESTRO
FACILI SACCESSITNOSTER ADSENSVSNAM CIVI-
TAT IHISPELLO AETERNVM VOCABVLVM NOMEN Q
VENERANDVM DE NOSTRAN VNCVPATIONE CONCES-
SIMVS SCILICET VT IN POSTERVM PRAEDICTA VRBS
FLAVIA CONSTANS VOCETVRINC VIVS CREMIO
AEDEM QVOQVE FLAVIAE HOC EST NOSTRAE GEN-
TIS VT DESIDERATIS MAGNIFICO OPERE PERFICI
VOLVMVS EA OBSERVATIONE PER SCRIPTAN EAE-
DIS NOSTRO NOMINI DEDICATA CVIVS QVAM CON-
TAGIOSE SVPERSTITIONIS FRAVDIBVS POLLVATVR
CONSEQVENTER ETIAM EDITIONVM IN PRAE-
DICTA CIVITATE EXHIBENDORVM VOBIS
LICENTIAM DEDIMVS SCILICET VT SICVTI
DICTVM EST PER VICES TEMPORIS SOLLEM-
NITAS EDITIONVM VVLSINIOS QVOQVE NON DE-
SERAT VBI CREATI ET VSCI A SACERDOTIBVS MEMO-
RATA CELEBRITAS EXHIBENDA EST ITA QVIPPE NEC
VETERIBVS IN STITV TIS PLVRIMVM VIDEBITVR
DEROGAT VM ET VOS QVI OB PRAEDICTAS CAVSAS
NOBIS SVPPLICES EXTITISTIS EA QVAE IN PEN-
DIO POSTVLAS TIS IMPETRATA ESSE GAVDE-
BITIS.

FIGURE 4. Hispellum Decree (*CIL* 11:5265 = *ILS* 705 of AD 333/7), Spello, Italy.
Photo from *Spello: Guida storico-artistica* (Spello, 1995), p. 42. Reproduced with
permission of the Associazione Pro Spello.

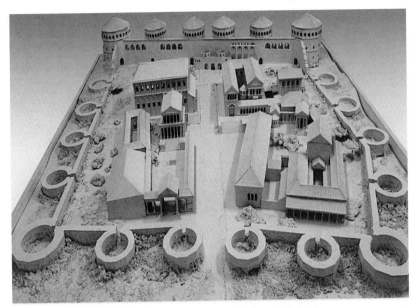

FIGURE 5. Model of the imperial villa Romuliana (Gamzigrad), Narodni Muzej, Zaječar, Serbia. Photo B. Dimitrijević, reproduced with permission.

FIGURE 6. Monumental rock-cut relief of Shapur I, mounted before Philip the Arab (kneeling in obeisance), and grasping the wrist of the captured Valerian (standing), Naqsh-i-Rustam, Iran. Photo Orinst. P 58746/N 38603. Copyright The Oriental Institute, Chicago.

FIGURE 7. Porphyry bust of emperor Galerius from the imperial villa Romuliana (Gamzigrad), Narodni Muzej, Zaječar, Serbia. Photo by B. Dimitrijevic, reproduced with permission.

FIGURE 8. Porphyry Tetrarchs, Piazza San Marco, Venice. Photo by Singer, DAI
Inst. Neg. 68.5152. Copyright Deutsches Archäologisches Institut.

FIGURE 9. The Milvian Bridge, Rome, Via Flaminia. The superstructure of the bridge was rebuilt after its destruction in 1849, but its original piers remain. Photo by N. Lenski.

FIGURE 10. Constantinian Quadrifrons reconstructed into a medieval *palatium* (Malborghetto), Via Flaminia. The arch may mark the site of Constantine's encampment before the battle of the Milvian Bridge. Photo by N. Lenski.

FIGURE 11. Constantinian Quadrifrons (Janus Quadrifrons), Forum Boarium, Rome. This arch, now shorn of its attic, is probably the *Arcus Divi Constantini* mentioned in the *Notitia Urbis Romae* Regio XI. Photo by N. Lenski.

FIGURE 12. Basilica of St. John Lateran, Rome, aerial view. The nave of the Constantinian basilica, now surrounded by later additions, remains visible in the center, and the octagonal baptistery on the lower right. Photo by G. A. Rossi. Copyright TIPS images/G. A. Rossi.

FIGURE 13. Thirteenth-century icon of Constantine and Helena, Benaki Museum, Athens. Copyright Scala/Art Resource, NY.

FIGURE 14. Colossal marble bust of Constantine, Musei Capitolini, Rome, originally part of an enthroned colossus in the Basilica of Constantine. Photo by N. Lenski.

FIGURE 15. Colossal bronze bust of Constantine, Musei Capitolini, Rome. Copyright Archivio Fotografico dei Musei Capitolini.

FIGURE 16. Recut portrait head of Constantine from the Arch of Constantine, Rome, north face, boar hunt tondo. Photo by Faraglia, DAI Inst. Neg. 32.36. Copyright Deutsches Archäologisches Institut.

FIGURE 17. Relief showing the siege of Verona from the Arch of Constantine, Rome, south face. Detail of Alinari 17328. Copyright Fratelli Alinari.

FIGURE 18. Relief of Constantine's address in the Forum from the Arch of Constantine, Rome, north face. Detail of Alinari 17326. Copyright Fratelli Alinari.

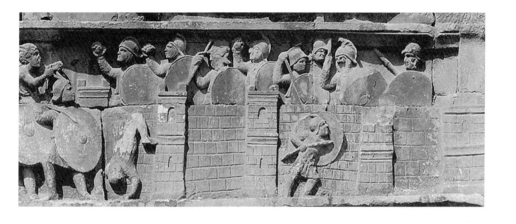

FIGURE 19. Intaglio-cut amethyst with Constantine's portrait, Antikensammlung,
Staatliche Museen, Berlin. Photo I. Geske-Heiden, Object inv. 30931. Copyright
Bildarchiv Preussischer Kulturbesitz/Art Resource, NY.

FIGURE 20. Over-life-sized statue of Constantine, porch of the Basilica of St. John in Lateran, Rome. Photo by Brenci, DAI Inst. Neg. 78.2242. Copyright Deutsches Archäologisches Institut.

FIGURE 21. Mausoleum of Helena (Tor Pignatara), Via Labicana, Rome. Photo by
N. Lenski.

FIGURE 22. Porphyry sarcophagus of Helena, Vatican Museum, Rome. Photo by Como, DAI Inst. Neg. 63.2339. Copyright Deutsches Archäologisches Institut.

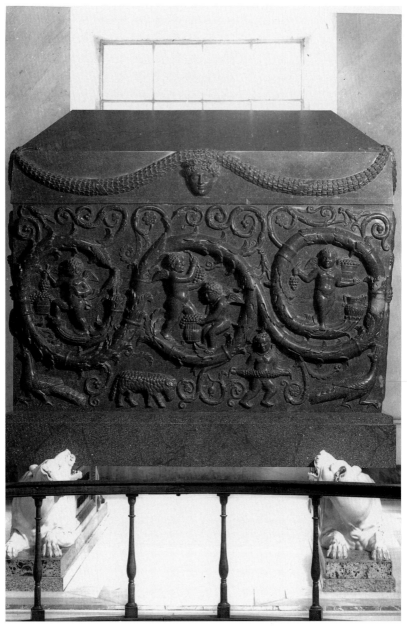

FIGURE 23. Porphyry sarcophagus of Constantina, Vatican Museum, Rome. Photo by Como, DAI Inst. Neg. 63.2342. Copyright Deutsches Archäologisches Institut.

FIGURE 24. Ceiling mosaic showing vintaging scenes from the church of S. Costanza, Via Nomentana, Rome. Photo by N. Lenski.

FIGURE 25. Ceiling fresco of a nimbate woman with jewel box from the imperial palace at Trier, Bischöfliches Dom- und Diözesanmuseum. Copyright Bischöfliches Dom- und Diözesanmuseum Trier.

FIGURE 26. *Opus sectile* panel of a consular driving a chariot from the Basilica of Junius Bassus, Museo Nazionale, Rome. Copyright Scala/Art Resource, NY.

FIGURE 27. Artemis of Saint Georges de Montagne, Museum of Bordeaux. Photo by M. Bergmann, reproduced with permission.

FIGURE 28. Cameo of Constantine (second from left) and his family from the cover of the Ada-Evangeliar, Statdtbibliothek, Trier. Copyright Stadtbibliothek Trier.

FIGURE 29. Sardonyx cameo of Constantine(?) mounted, trampling conquered barbarians, Narodni Muzej, Belgrade. Photo by T. Čvjetićanin, reproduced with permission.

FIGURE 30. Seasons sarcophagus in the Dumbarton Oaks Byzantine Collection, Washington, DC. Copyright Dumbarton Oaks Byzantine Collection.

FIGURE 31. Fresco showing the ascension of Elijah from the Via Latina Catacomb, cubiculum B, Rome. Copyright Pontificia Commissione di Archeologia Sacra.

FIGURE 32. Interior of the Aula Palatina, Trier. Fototeca Unione FU 14. Copyright Fototeca Unione/American Academy in Rome.

FIGURE 33. Baths of Constantine on the Quirinal, Rome. Engraving by E. Du Pérac 1575. Fototeca Unione no. FU 4769. Copyright Fototeca Unione/American Academy in Rome.

FIGURE 34. Licinian Garden Pavilion (Minerva Medica), Rome. Drawing by F. J. B. Kobell 1780. Fototeca Unione FU 9079. Copyright Fototeca Unione/American Academy in Rome.

FIGURE 35. View of the interior of the Constantinian Basilica of St. Peter, Rome. Fresco by G.-B. Ricci da Novara from the Cappella della Madonna della Bocciata. Copyright Grotte Vaticane/Fabbrica di San Pietro.

FIGURE 36. Model of the Basilica Apostolorum (S. Sebastiano), Rome. Copyright Pontificia Commissione di Archeologia Sacra.

FIGURE 37. Remains of the apse of the church of S. Agnese, now the backdrop of a tennis club, Via Nomentana, Rome. Photo by N. Lenski.

FIGURE 38. Romanesque fresco showing the Donations of Constantine, Church of the Santi Quattro Coronati, Rome. Copyright Scala/Art Resource, NY.

FIGURE 39. Silver dish with Constantius II mounted, accompanied by a guardsman (*candidatus*) bearing a shield emblazoned with the Chi-Rho monogram and a laurel bearing Victory, Hermitage Museum, Leningrad. From J. P. C. Kent and K. S. Painter, *Wealth of the Roman World AD 300–700* (London, 1977), fig. 11. Reproduced with permission of the Trustees of the British Museum.

FIGURE 40. Relief showing armored cavalry in close company with the emperor, on the right (now headless), from the Arch of Galerius, Thessalonica. DAI Inst. Neg. Athen Sal. 225. Copyright Deutsches Archäologisches Institut.

FIGURE 41. Tetrarchic fort of Mobene (Qasr Bshir), Al-Kerak, Jordan. Photo by D. Kennedy, reproduced with permission.

PLAN

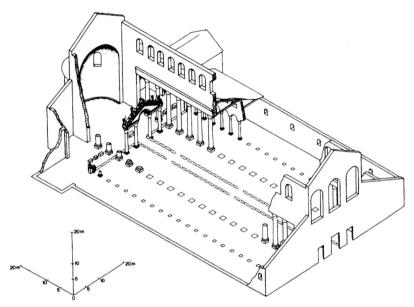

PLAN I. Basilica Constantiniana of the Lateran in Rome, isometric reconstruction with *fastigium* and *solea*. Plan by S. L. de Blaauw, reproduced with permission. First published in *Acta ad Archaeologiam et Artium Historiam Pertinentia* 15 (2001), fig. 2.

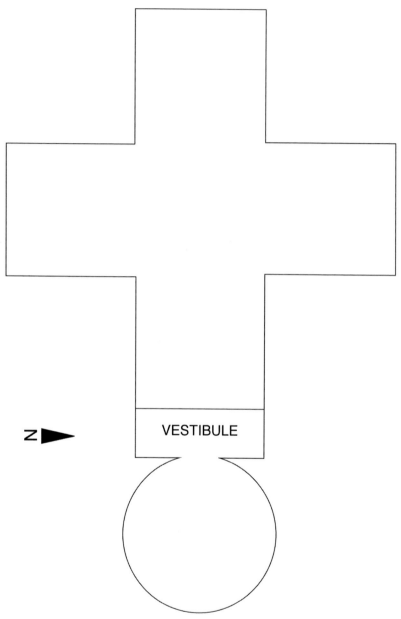

PLAN 2. Church of the Holy Apostles in Constantinople, hypothetical plan. Drawing by D. Underwood, based on a drawing by M. Johnson.

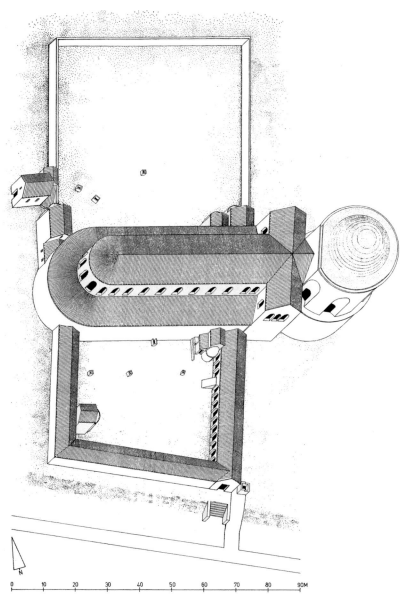

0 10 20 30 40 50 60 70 80 90M

PLAN 3. Church and cemetery complex *ad duas lauros* (Tor Pignatara/SS. Marcellino
e Pietro) on the Via Labicana in Rome. Hypothetical reconstruction by J. Rasch
Das Mausoleum der Kaiserin Helena in Rom und der "Tempio della Tosse" in Tivoli
(Mainz, 1998), fig. 98, based on a drawing by U. Colalelli in J. Guyon *Le cimitière
"Aux deux lauriers"* (Rome, 1997), fig. 142, with permission of J. Rasch.

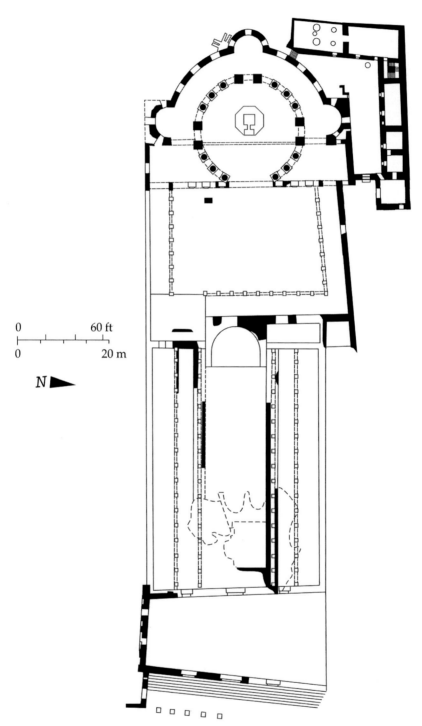

0   60 ft

0   20 m

N ▶

PLAN 4. Church of the Holy Sepulcher in Jerusalem. Drawing by D. Underwood, based on the hypothetical plan at R. Krautheimer *Early Christian and Byzantine Architecture*, 4th ed. (New Haven, 1986), fig. 27(B).

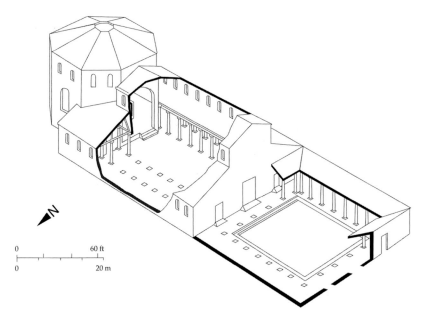

PLAN 5. Church of the Nativity in Bethlehem. Drawing by D. Underwood, based on the isometric reconstruction in R. Krautheimer *Early Christian and Byzantine Architecture*, 4th ed. (New Haven, 1986), fig. 26.

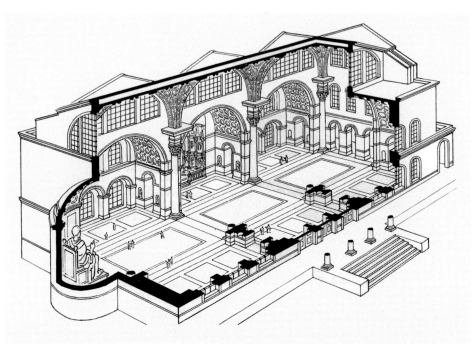

PLAN 6. Basilica of Maxentius and Constantine in Rome, reconstruction in cutaway view. From H. Leacroft and R. Leacroft, *The Buildings of Ancient Rome* (Hodder and Stoughton/Addison-Wesley Publishing, 1969), p. 20. Copyright lapsed.

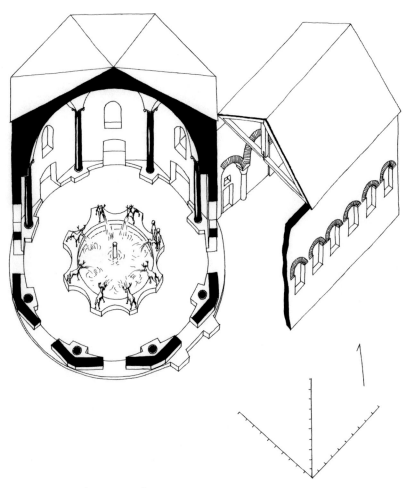

PLAN 7. Lateran baptistery of Constantine in Rome. Reconstruction by O. Brandt, "Il battistero laternanense da Costantino a Ilaro," *Opuscula Romana* 22–3 (1997–8), fig. 67, reproduced with permission.

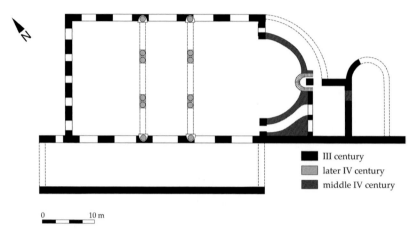

III century
later IV century
middle IV century

0   10 m

PLAN 8. Church of S. Croce in Gerusalemme in Rome. Drawing by D. Underwood, based on the hypothetical plan at S. de Blaauw, "Jerusalem in Rome and the Cult of the Holy Cross," in *Pratum Romanum* (Wiesbaden, 1997), p. 57, fig. 1.

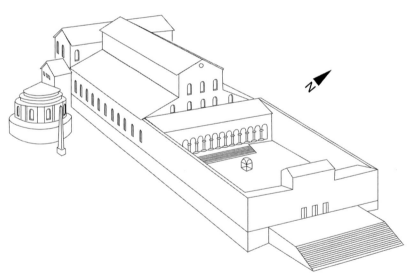

PLAN 9. Constantinian Basilica of St. Peter in Rome. Drawing by D. Underwood, based on the isometric reconstruction at R. Krautheimer, *Early Christian and Byzantine Architecture*, 4th ed. (New Haven, 1986), fig. 21.

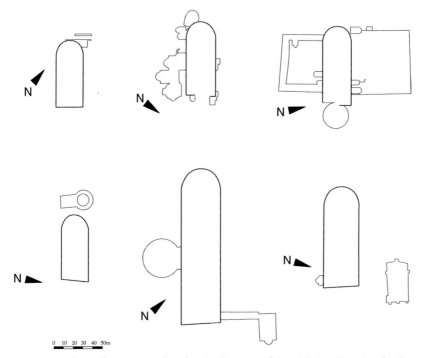

0 10 20 30 40 50m

PLAN 10. Plans of cemetery churches in Rome and its vicinity. Drawing by D. Underwood, based on the plan at V. Fiocchi Nicolai, *Strutture funerarie ed edifici di culto paleocristiana di Roma dal IV al VI secolo* (Vatican City, 2001), fig. 39.

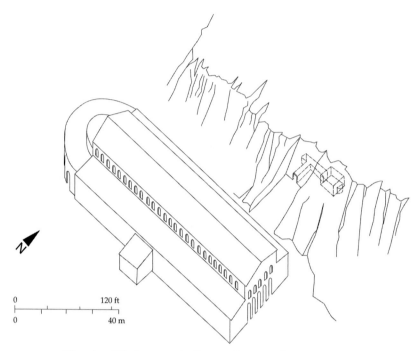

PLAN II. Church of S. Lorenzo in Rome. Drawing by D. Underwood, based on the isometric reconstruction at R. Krautheimer, *Early Christian and Byzantine Architecture*, 4th ed. (New Haven, 1986), fig. 18.

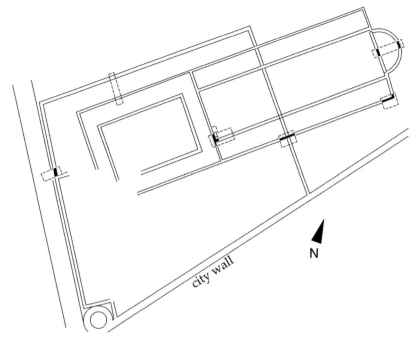

PLAN 12. Constantinian bishop's church at Ostia. Drawing by D. Underwood, based on the archaeological plan at F. A. Bauer, "The Constantinian Bishop's Church at Ostia," *Journal of Roman Archaeology* 12 (1999), fig. 3.

COIN 1. Ob. IMP CONSTANTINVS PF AVG: Constantine three-quarters facing, with a helmet bearing a Chi-Rho emblem, holding a horse by the bridle and a shield emblazoned with the Roman wolf suckling Romulus and Remus, silver medallion (*RIC* 7 Ticinum 36). Copyright Hirmer Verlag, Munich.

COIN 2. Rev. SARMATIA DEVICTA: Victory holding palm branch and trophy, spurning captive on the ground, bronze follis (*RIC* 7 London 289). Copyright The British Museum.

COIN 3. Rev. SENATVS: Togate figure standing, holding globe and scepter, 4.5 solidus gold medallion (*RIC* 7 Rome 272). Copyright Narodni Muzej, Belgrade.

COIN 4. Rev. INVICTVS CONSTANTINVS MAX AVG: Constantine and Sol Comes jugate, 9 solidus gold medallion of Ticinum. Copyright Bibliothèque Nationale de France, Paris.

COIN 5. Ob. DIOCLETIANVS AVGVSTVS: Diocletian laureate, gold aureus (*RIC* 6 Antioch 1). W. Jaffee Collection, University of Colorado, Boulder.

COIN 6. Rev. IOVI CONS CAES: Jupiter standing nude holding staff and thunderbolt, gold aureus (*RIC* 6 Antioch 10). W. Jaffee Collection, University of Colorado, Boulder.

COIN 7. Ob. MAXIMIANVS PF AVG: Maximian laureate, and Rev. HERCVLI VICTORI: Hercules holding lion skin, leaning on club, gold aureus (*RIC* 6 Nicomedia 3). W. Jaffee Collection, University of Colorado, Boulder.

COIN 8. Ob. CONSTANTIVS NOB CAES: Constantius I laureate, gold aureus (*RIC* 6 Antioch 8). W. Jaffee Collection, University of Colorado, Boulder.

COIN 9. Rev. VIRTVS MILITVM: Four emperors sacrificing over a tripod before a fortification (*RIC* 6 Trier 102a). W. Jaffee Collection, University of Colorado, Boulder.

COIN 10. Ob. MAXENTIVS PF AVG: Maxentius facing, bare headed, gold aureus (*RIC* 7 Ostia 3). Copyright The British Museum.

COIN 11. Rev. SALVS REI PVBLICAE: The empress Fausta standing, holding two babes in her arms, gold solidus (*RIC* 7 Ticinum 182). Copyright Hirmer Verlag, Munich.

COIN 12. Ob. LICINIVS AVG OB D V FILII SVI: Licinius facing, bare headed, gold aureus (*RIC* 7 Nicomedia 41). Copyright The British Museum.

COIN 13. Rev. VOTIS XXX MVLTIS XXXX: Inscribed within wreath, silver siliqua (*RIC* 8 Sirmium 66). W. Jaffee Collection, University of Colorado, Boulder.

COIN 14. Rev. VIRT EXERC: X-shaped pattern with Sol standing above, holding globe, bronze follis (*RIC* 7 Thessalonica 71). Copyright The British Museum.

COIN 15. Rev. SOLI INVICT COM DN: Sol radiate, standing, holding globe with victoriola in left hand, bronze follis (*RIC* 7 Rome 48). Copyright The British Museum.

COIN 16. Ob. DD NN CONSTANTINVS ET LICINIVS AVGG: Confronted busts of Licinius and Constantine holding a statuette of Fortuna, bronze follis (*RIC* 7 Nicomedia 39). Copyright The Ashmolean Museum, Oxford.

COIN 17. Ob. FL CL CONSTANTINVS PF AVG: Constantine II rosette diademed, gold solidus (*RIC* 8 Siscia 26). W. Jaffee Collection, University of Colorado, Boulder.

COIN 18. Ob. DN CONSTANTIVS PF AVG: Constantius II pearl diademed, silver siliqua. W. Jaffee Collection, University of Colorado, Boulder.

COIN 19. Ob. FLAVIA HELENA AVGVSTA: Empress Helena with elaborate headdress, bronze medallion (*RIC* 7 Rome 250). Copyright The British Museum.

COIN 20. Rev. CONSTANTIANA DAPHNE: Victory standing on *cippus* beside trophy, spurning captive on the ground, bronze follis (*RIC* 7 Constantinople 32). Copyright The British Museum.

COIN 21. Ob. CONSTANS AVGVSTVS: Constans pearl diademed, gold solidus (*RIC* 8 Trier 129). W. Jaffee Collection, University of Colorado, Boulder.

COIN 22. Rev. No legend: Constantine veiled, rides a chariot heavenward with the hand of God reaching down to him, bronze follis (*RIC* 8 Alexandria 4). Copyright The British Museum.

23

24

25

26

27

28

29

30

31

32

33

34

COIN 23. Ob. DN IVLIANVS NOB CAES: Julian bare headed, gold solidus (*RIC* 8 Antioch 163). W. Jaffee Collection, University of Colorado, Boulder.

COIN 24. Rev. GLORIA EXERCITVS: Two soldiers standing, holding spear and shield, between them two standards, bronze follis (*RIC* 7 Antioch 86). University of Colorado, Boulder.

COIN 25. Rev. FEL TEMP REPARATIO: Helmeted soldier bearing shield spears a horseman, bronze (*RIC* 8 Constantinople 109). University of Colorado, Boulder.

COIN 26. Ob. CONSTANTINVS NOB C: Constantine square jawed, brow furrowed, with close cropped beard and hair, gold aureus (*RIC* 6 Rome 141). Copyright Hirmer Verlag, Munich.

COIN 27. Ob. CONSTANTINVS PF AVG: Constantine facing right, diademed, gold solidus (*RIC* 7 Trier 21). Copyright The British Museum.

COIN 28. Ob. CONSTANTINVS PF AVG: Constantine nimbate, facing, gold solidus (*RIC* 7 Ticinum 41). Copyright The Ashmolean Museum, Oxford.

COIN 29. Ob. No legend: Constantine with plain diadem, looking upwards, 1.5 solidus gold medallion (*RIC* 7 Siscia 206). Copyright The British Museum.

COIN 30. Ob. CONSTANTINVS MAX AVG: Constantine rosette diademed, gold solidus (*RIC* 7 Thessalonica 174). W. Jaffee Collection, University of Colorado, Boulder.

COIN 31. Rev. SPES PVBLIC: Labarum crowned by Chi-Rho piercing a serpent, bronze follis (*RIC* 7 Constantinople 19). Copyright The British Museum.

COIN 32. Rev. ALAMANNIA DEVICTA: Victory holding trophy and palm branch, spurning captive on the ground, bronze follis (*RIC* 7 Sirmium 49). Copyright The British Museum.

COIN 33. Rev. GLORIA SAECVLI VIRTVS CAESS: Constantine seated holding scepter, offering globe with phoenix to Caesar, a panther at his feet, bronze medallion (*RIC* 7 Rome 279). W. Jaffee Collection, University of Colorado, Boulder.

COIN 34. Rev. FELICITAS PVBLICA: Euphrates personified reclining, silver siliqua (*RIC* 7 Constantinople 100). Copyright Bibliothèque Nationale de France, Paris.

Humpheys (1989), 89–104, and P. Rosafio, *Studi sul Colonato* (2002), provide introductions to *potentiores* and *coloni,* respectively. On social status during the age of Constantine viewed from a number of different angles, see A. Cameron and P. Garnsey, eds., *The Cambridge Ancient History*, vol. 13, *The Late Empire AD 337–425* (1998), especially the articles by P. Heather (Senate), C. Kelly (bureaucracy), E. D. Hunt (church) and C. Whittaker and P. Garnsey (rural relations).

NOTES

1   *CTh* 4.6.3.
2   *CTh* 4.6.3. Translations from the Theodosian Code follow those of Pharr 1952, with some revisions.
3   *CTh* 4.6.3 ends with a specific reference to "the son of Licinianus who . . . shall be bound in fetters and consigned to service in the imperial weaving establishment in Carthage." The same individual is the subject of *CTh* 4.6.2 (read at Carthage April 29, 336). Corcoran 2000, 291, discusses whether this "son of Licinianus" should be identified as an illegitimate son of the (executed) emperor Licinius but concludes, "The easiest solution is to suppose that the son of Licinianus is no relation of Licinius at all." In any event, we should note that the issuing of *CTh* 4.6.2–3 was prompted by a particular case.
4   *CTh* 4.6.3.2–3.
5   *CTh* 11.16.3 (325, possibly Licinius) and *CTh* 1.16.4 = *CJ* 1.40.2 (328). See in general Schlumberger 1989.
6   Marcian *Novels* 4.2.
7   Marcian *Novels* 4.1.
8   Cautious assessments in Grubbs 1995; McGinn 1999; and Rivière 2002. For arguments in favour of the influence of Christianity as a pervading spirit within Constantine's laws, see Dupont 1968; Amarelli 1978; T. D. Barnes 1981, esp. 50–2 and 220–1; Nathan 2000.
9   For extensive background and discussion, see Millar 1992. In some areas Constantine and his administration were proactive: *CTh* 11.3.1 (313) refers to the emperor himself checking the tax accounts province by province. The Constantinian legislation on legal procedure and the appeals system overhauls previous practice. It is within these "procedural" areas that Constantine reveals himself most clearly as a legal innovator.
10   *CTh* 2.18.1.
11   Marcian *Novels* 4.4. On Julian, see AM 21.10.8. The earliest laws in the *Codex Theodosianus* date to 312/13.
12   *Pan. Lat.* 4(10).38.4–5 (321) (trans. Nixon and Rodgers).
13   *CTh* 14.3.1 (319) is a good example: breadmakers are transferring their property to third parties (in trust) and then claiming exemption from their patrimonial *munera* of breadmaking on the grounds of financial insolvency!
14   *CTh* 9.1.1. Cf. *CTh* 9.19.1 (316): the same principle applies to decurions charged with criminal forgery.
15   *CTh* 2.30.1.
16   *CTh* 9.21.1 (319).

17 Bagnall 1993, 236, discusses this point with reference to classical jurisprudence and fourth-century papyri.

18 Beaucamp 1990 argues for an increase in the brutality of the law due to a Constantinian crystallization of moral attitudes. On Constantine's criminal law, see Dupont 1953, and on judicial savagery in general, see MacMullen 1986.

19 This Augustan *lex* was originally part of a broader package targeted at regulating marriages, morals, and testamentary dispositions. See Grubbs 1995, 94–5. On Constantine's two laws, see ibid. 205–16. It should be noted that *CJ* 9.9 includes twenty-seven pre-Constantinian imperial rescripts on adultery and its prosecution.

20 *CTh* 9.7.2 (326).

21 *Dig.* 50.2.12 (Callistratus) gives an exception: where there is a shortage of suitable candidates, "base persons" can be considered for the office of decurion. Similar avenues for social mobility also existed in the early fourth century.

22 Saller 2000, 855. See also Giardina 2000.

23 For example, *Dig.* 2.4.4.3 (Ulpian): Labeo argued that the term *parentes* could be used of slave mothers and fathers. On the same terms being applied to slave and free family relations in epigraphical data, see Martin 1996, 42.

24 Women's legal capacity: *CTh* 9.1.3 (322), 3.5.3 (330), 8.15.1 (334), the last of which concerns a woman litigating before Constantine himself. On the general status of women in late antiquity, see Beaucamp 1990, esp. 35–45; Arjava 1996.

25 Freedmen not fulfilling their duties to patrons could be sent back into slavery: *CTh* 4.10.1 (313); *CJ* 6.7.2 (320). Cf. *CTh* 2.22.1 (320).

26 For background and discussion, see Grubbs 1993; 2002, 136–186.

27 *CJ* 5.26.1 (326).

28 *CTh* 4.12.1 (314), 4.12.4 (331). *CTh* 4.12.3 (320?) amends the *ius vetus* and rules that free women can live with fiscal slaves (i.e., those belonging to the emperor's patrimony) without loss of civil status: any resulting children receive an intermediate civil status and are held bound by legal obligations to the emperor as their "patron."

29 *CTh* 4.8.7.

30 *CTh* 3.5.2.

31 *CTh* 3.5.6.

32 *CTh* 3.5.4, 5 (332): a girl cannot be kept waiting for two years and then sued for fraud if she marries someone else! Previous imperial rescripts, dating from the mid-second century onwards, refer to four or five years.

33 *CTh* 9.24.1 (320/6), and see Beaucamp 1990, 342. Compare *CTh* 9.18.1 (315) on kidnapping children in general.

34 Saller 2000, 859–61. Limiting gifts between husband and wife also conserved the patrimony for agnatic kin.

35 *CTh* 3.16.1.

36 *CTh* 8.16.1 (addressed to the Praetorian Prefect Ablabius). The Christian inspiration (or lack thereof) behind the repeal of the "celibacy" penalties and the future effects of that repeal are discussed by Arjava 1996, 78–9, and Grubbs 1995, 103–9; 2002, 103–4. *CTh* 8.16.1 was originally issued as part of a much broader law concerning succession and property transfer. Matthews 2000, 232–40, carefully discusses its original context and rejects any Christian influence.

37 *CJ* 2.12.21.

38 See Clark 1993, 7–8; Arjava 1996, 111–56.

39 *CTh* 12.17.1 (324).

40 Cf. *CTh* 8.18.1.2 (315).

41 *Frag. Vat.* 248 (330).

42 The celebrated "law" on the classical jurists Papinian, Paul, and Ulpian (*CTh* 1.4.1) was originally part of *CTh* 9.43.1. The Constantinian text was chopped up and placed under different titles by the compilers of the Theodosian Code.

43 *CTh* 9.43.1.2.

44 As argued by Dixon 2001, 73–88.

45 *CTh* 9.21.4 (324).

46 Age and legal capacity: *CTh* 3.17.1 (318), 2.16.2 (319), 2.17.1 (324). Tutors' or curators' personal liability for the property of their wards: *CTh.* 3.30.1 (314), 2.16.1 (326); *CJ* 5.37.22 (329).

47 *CJ* 5.37.22; cf. *CTh* 3.30.3.

48 *CTh* 2.24.1.

49 *CJ* 3.36.16 (293); *CJ* 3.36.21 (294); and *CJ* 3.36.26 (318/21) had all previously elaborated similar principles.

50 *CTh* 2.19.2.

51 *CTh* 8.18.1–3.

52 *CTh* 16.2.4 (321).

53 *CTh* 4.7.1.1, 6.35.1, 3, 7.22.2.

54 *CTh* 10.1.2. For *coloni* on imperial estates in Constantine's constitutions, see *CJ* 11.68.1–2. On *coloni* in general, see *CTh* 11.7.2 (319); 11.63.1 (319); 11.50.1 (Constantinian, undated); and *CTh* 5.17.1 (332). For the background and complex development of the colonate in the early and late empire, see Rosafio 2002.

55 See Frakes 2001, 39–40.

56 *CTh* 4.9.1 (319) and *Frag. Vat.* 34 (313). *Dig.* 50.15.4.5 (Ulpian) states that a slave's race, age, duties, and skills should be declared separately in an individual's census return.

57 *CJ* 6.1.4 (317).

58 *CTh* 9.12.2.

59 See *Dig.* 40.12 and *CJ* 7.16, with forty imperial rulings that predate Constantine.

60 *CJ* 7.1.4 (Constantinian, undated). Cf. *CTh* 4.9.1 on "mistaken" manumissions and their annulment.

61 *CJ* 1.13.1, addressed to Bishop Protogenes. See also *CTh* 4.7.1 (321), to Bishop Ossius.

62 *CTh* 1.27.1; *Const. Sirm.* 1. See Harries 1999, 191–211, and Lenski 2002a for discussion of the complex problems associated with these two Constantinian constitutions.

63 *CTh* 2.19.3: the institution of a "necessary heir."

64 On abandonment, see *CJ* 5.37.22. On parricide, see *CTh* 9.15.1, 11.27.1. On exposure, see *CTh* 5.9.1; 5.10.1 = *CJ* 4.43.2.

65 Gardner 1997, 53.

10: ECONOMY AND SOCIETY

Georges Depeyrot

Translated by Noel Lenski

A DIFFICULT PERIOD?

From an economic perspective, it is difficult to speak of a "Constantinian period." The economy, in contrast with legislation or politics, evolved slowly. Thus, regardless of whether we think of the Constaninian period as the short duration of Constantine's sole rule, the period of his entire reign, or even more broadly the period of his family dynasty, we still fail to arrive at the long and slow process whereby economies change. If, however, we understand Constantine's reign as part of a larger period of late antiquity, it must first be stated that, from an economic perspective, it was a period many have characterized as troubled. Some attribute this to natural disasters: seismic activity in Greece, for example, seems to have increased in the period of the fourth to sixth centuries relative to the previous nine hundred years.[1] Others have argued that climatic change around the Mediterranean and in western Europe – particularly a third-century shift to a much cooler and drier climate and a net rise in sea level – led to reforestations, swampification, and the decline of settled agriculture.[2] The consequences could obviously have been profound, including increased mortality rates, a decline in agricultural production, and even increased pressure from barbarian peoples hoping to migrate to more temperate regions. Unfortunately, no cause-to-effect links between these geographical phenomena and the contemporary economy can be measured directly in the sources available to us.

Indeed, it is far from obvious that the economy of the fourth century was in an irredeemable state of decline. Any diminution in agricultural production across the empire was in some ways offset by

226

an increase in productivity on better lands. The increase in the output of large centers of production required, of course, a corresponding increase in commerce to supply markets. The consequences could be beneficial for both agriculture and manufacturing. For example, the growth in specialized olive plantations in North Africa presupposed the distribution of oil with commercially produced amphorae.[3] So too in the southeast of England, it has been possible to gauge soil productivity based on the size of archaeologically attested granaries. The proportion of yield grain to sown has been estimated at 12:1, 8:1, and 5:1, the last probably the most normal.[4] In the course of the fourth century, the surface area of grain storehouses also increased in areas situated near armies or larger cities, which archaeologists again interpret as a sign of agricultural specialization.[5] Such specialization is also confirmed by the discovery of specialized milling installations, as for example the water mill installation of Barbegal (Bouches-du-Rhône). Undoubtedly constructed in Constantine's reign, it had sixteen conduits each with its own mill.[6] Rather than universal decline, one can thus speak of contrasts, above all regional contrasts, with some areas in economic decline while others prospered, and with commerce and trade often compensating for regional disparities.

If large production centers could not exist without large-scale commerce, the economy of large estates could not help but tend toward self-reliance. Here state policies were surely at play, for commercial activities within the confines of a single estate were not subject to the business tax, the *chrysargyron*. This concession led large holders to develop their estates into coherent ensembles which could meet their own commercial needs independently. At the same time, fiscal and juridical limitations worked to limit commerce outside these estates. All this meant that several levels of commerce coexisted with more or less difficulty. High-level commerce in either bulk products or particularly expensive commodities continued. But smaller-scale commerce and artisanal activity tended to flourish only in the context of larger estates.[7]

AGRI DESERTI

As noted earlier, large tracts of land seem to have become marginal in late antiquity, and others were simply abandoned. Several explanations can be advanced. The climate certainly played a role, as noted even by contemporaries, who lamented the trend toward increasing drought.[8]

Then, too, barbarian raids, which had been on the rise since the third century, particularly in the west, contributed to the agricultural crisis. Some indication of the problem can be seen in the census and cadastre of Diocletian, which served as a basis for fiscal calculations when it was assembled but was already out of date by 312.[9] Thus Constantine was forced to grant the city of Autun a tax reduction to accommodate its reduced number of producers:

> That city [Autun] lay prostrate, not so much because of the collapse of its walls as because of the exhaustion of its strength, from the time when the harshness of the new census drained it of life.... One saw everything devastated, uncultivated, neglected, silent and gloomy.... As a result, it often happens that our obligations are discharged late.... Having made up your mind to reduce the load of the census, you [Constantine] fixed its number; intending to remit our outstanding debts, you asked us how much we owed.... Through your remission of 7,000 *capita* [tax units] you have given strength to the 25,000 remaining.... Five years' arrears you have waived for us![10]

Many Egyptian papyri mention the flight of farmers from the land and workers from the cities. To take just one example, a papyrus of 332 reports this complaint:

> We, these three aforesaid, are the persons in the village, lord prefect, who contribute for the whole village, for 500 arouras [c. 335 acres]...though the individual list...[contains] twenty-five names, so that from this cause the village has got into greatly straightened circumstances. In the search for our fellow villagers we visited the Oxyrhynchite nome, and we found...a total of six men.... We also found three other men..."[11]

The later empire was thus a period of shrinkage in the structures of agricultural production.

There has been some recent debate over whether the *agri deserti* mentioned in our sources really represented a major problem. C. R. Whittaker has argued that *agri deserti* were nothing more than lands that had traditionally remained uncultivated and holds that the complaints about the issue actually trace to literary topoi without necessarily conveying real contemporary concerns.[12] This is not a view I share. *Agri deserti* were in fact a real and contemporary issue, even if the problems they caused were in part ameliorated by an increase in productivity on the lands that remained in cultivation. Indeed, in as far as contemporaries recognized a real problem, they often discovered creative solutions that went some way toward solving it. We have already seen how Constantine's relaxation of tax levies in Autun led his panegyrist to claim that the remaining tax units would be worked much more productively. With similar foresight, Constantine devised another scheme that simultaneously filled abandoned land and helped reintegrate military veterans back into civil society by offering them gifts of *agri deserti*, matched with money or grain subventions and accompanied by exemption from taxes. Thus in 326 Constantine issued a law ordering that "veterans shall receive vacant lands, and they shall hold them tax exempt in perpetuity,"[13] thereby bringing fields into production while serving the needs of the powerful constituency represented by veterans. Yet another solution to the problem of *agri deserti* was to install captured barbarians, sometimes individually, sometimes in groups, on deserted lands or understaffed estates. This technique was employed, for example, by Constantine's father in an incident that drew great praise from the panegyrist of 297:

> And so it is for me now that the Chamavian and Frisian plows and that vagabond, that pillager toils at the cultivation of the neglected countryside and frequents my markets with beasts for sale, and the barbarian farmer lowers the price of food.[14]

Here too the problem was solved while relieving pressure on the frontiers and diffusing a real and present threat from barbarians, who now worked on behalf of the empire.

THE CITIES

The dominant urban phenomenon in this period was certainly the reduction in the overall surface area of towns and their reinforcement with walls. Much of this was already initiated at the end of the third century, when invasions in the west had led to large-scale urban destruction and in turn the desire to enclose cities within walled circuits as part of

Table 10.1. *North African Storage Inscriptions*
(293–350)

Time span (AD)	Number of Inscriptions
293/305	20.5
305/312	0
312/324	7
324/337	10.5
337/350	6.5

the painful process of rebuilding.[15] A. Grenier first surveyed the surface areas of cities in Gaul during the high and later empire and established that the average surface area for seven cities in the high empire (Autun, Nimes, Cologne, Avenches, Lyon, Vienne, and Saintes) was 168 hectares and that this figure diminished by almost 90 percent in the later empire. Thus Avenches went from 150 to 9 hectares, Amiens from 100 to 10. Setting aside the two capitals in the north (Trier and Mainz at 285 and 120 hectares, respectively), the average city size was just 18 hectares. In addition, while the largest cities of the high empire were concentrated in the south of Gaul, those of the late empire were nearer the frontier, Trier, Mainz, and Metz.[16] Many cities also built walls to protect themselves from invasions, yet another phenomenon that – to limit the costs of construction – forced contractions in the surface area of cities.[17] Similar fortifications were built across the empire throughout the fourth century, but the phenomenon of urban contraction was particularly marked in the early part of the century. Perhaps this led the historian Zosimus to state this criticism:

> By such exactions the cities were exhausted; for these demands persisted long after Constantine, they were soon drained of wealth and most became deserted.[18]

Yet here, too, the situation was far from uniform across the empire, leading us to question the general validity of Zosimus's complaints. The North African inscriptions studied by C. Lepelley show the ongoing construction or restoration of urban buildings. Especially striking is his study of inscriptions from 332 grain storage facilities, of which 326 are datable and 236 attest to construction activity, many precisely during the period in question (Table 10.1).

Thus in the Tetrarchic and Constantinian periods the relative constancy of inscriptions attesting to construction indicates a certain stability in building activity.[19] So, too, the outstanding archaeological excavations in North Africa and recent work in northern Italy, especially at Aquileia, have allowed us to demonstrate the maintenance of building activities.[20] Even the Italian city of Bologna, which had been hard hit in the third century, enjoyed a period of rebuilding, as did Sirmium and other cities in Pannonia, and Emona in Istria.[21] In fact, this phase of reconstruction was widespread in the early fourth century and was generally heavily supported with sponsorship from the emperor:

> In addition Diocletian had a limitless passion for building, which led to an equally limitless scouring of the provinces to raise workers, craftsmen, wagons, and whatever is necessary for building operations. Here he built basilicas, there a circus, a mint, an arms-factory.[22]

Lactantius's exaggeration reveals an underlying truth, for Dioceltian – like his successors – was an extremely active builder, as archaeolgical remains have amply revealed. Constantine's building projects in Trier, Rome, Constantinople, and Jerusalem continued the trend and thus lend credence to the assumption that building activity under imperial sponsorship had hardly ceased in the age of Constantine.[23]

RURAL LABOR

The later empire has been considered a pivotal period in the history of slavery. Many factors contributed to the changes that occurred: a probable reduction in the supply of slaves, the influence – albeit limited – of the church, and social changes. To be sure, slavery remained a structural element in the Roman economy throughout late antiquity, but it seems to have lost the role it had played in early imperial Italy as a dominant mode of production.

Some shrinkage in the slave supply can be traced in our records for slave prices. Already at the turn of the fourth century, the relative rarity of slaves is attested by the high prices listed for them in Diocletian's Price Edict: a male slave of sixteen to forty years is valued at the equivalent of 0.4 pounds of gold.[24] This price seems to have climbed throughout the fourth century, for a letter of the Roman Senator Symmachus written in 394 judges prices twice that high to be acceptable: he offers 1,000 solidi for twenty slaves, which is the equivalent of 0.7 pounds of gold per slave.[25] The source of these slaves appears to have been primarily the barbarian territories beyond the northern frontier. This was true even in Egypt, from which we have numerous papyri that speak of Gallic, Pontic, Gothic, and Sarmatian slaves. The historian Ammianus tells much the same story when he claims that Julian turned down the chance to campaign against the Goths: "for the Goths, said Julian, the Galatian slave traders were enough, by whom they were offered for sale everywhere without distinction of rank."[26]

The position of the Christian Church toward slavery naturally became important as the church gained in power in the wake of Constantine's conversion. As an increasingly important political player and a growing landholding institution, the church had to face questions like the morality of using slave labor on its property (which it continued to do), appointing other people's slaves as clergy, and accepting their runaways as fugitives (which it generally refused to allow).[27] Scripture nowhere explicitly condemns slavery as an institution, and thus the church refused to condemn it as well: Cyprian and Basil called on slaves to be obedient to their masters as part of their duty to God.[28] Even so, the writings of the Church Fathers reveal a decided effort to ameliorate the situation of slaves: Augustine and Ambrose asked masters to show respect for their slaves and avoid cruelty.[29] Caught in a sort of contradiction between a fundamental acceptance of slavery but discomfort with its consequences, the church and in turn the emperor favored a gradual improvement in the slave's juridical condition. Thus Constantine forbade the tatooing of slaves on the face – which, he reminded, reflected the image of God – and created a new mode of freeing one's slaves whereby the master could manumit them in churches. In 321 Constantine also granted clerics greater ease in freeing their own slaves.[30]

Any attempt to draw broader conclusions from these laws or even from our sources showing a decline in the use of slaves, however, should not blind us to the more basic question of dependent labor. In the forefront of an emperor's mind were always the interests of landholders in securing a stable labor pool. Thus even while emperors were improving the conditions of slaves, they were simultaneously expanding the juridical possibilities for constraining labor from peasants by creating a new category of bound laborer, the *colonus*. It is eminently possible to argue that the colonate arose out of the agricultural reforms of Diocletian and particularly his creation of tax registers. This system's insistence on maintaining small farmers and seasonal laborers in place led to the development of *origo* (the juridical connection to the land whence laborers "originated") and in turn to the devolution of tax collection responsibilities onto large landholders.[31] Naturally landholders also favored the new system as a way to maintain their labor force in place. And as the colonate developed, it soon spawned other forms of dependency for related groups of laborers, as for example members of the bakers guild in Rome and Constantinople (*pistores*) or weavers in imperial cloth factories (*gynaeceia*).[32]

The first mentions of *coloni* occur at the beginning of the fourth century and are restricted to imperial estates. Beginning in 319, *coloni* of the *res privata* (imperial estates) in the east were bound to their land: it was forbidden for them to work for other proprietors or to change their line of work.[33] And from 332 all *coloni* were threatened with enslavement if they attempted to flee their place of origin.[34] This new social stratum was, as mentioned, subdivided into several groups (imperial and ecclesiastical *coloni*, private and public *coloni*), and initially several juridical terms were used to distinguish the most common categories of laborers (*servus, ancilla, colonus*).[35] Over time, however, the differences between the categories and between *coloni* and *servi* grew ever hazier in the law codes, so that by the sixth century the distinctions had become difficult to draw. This new system of bound labor offered at least one advantage over slavery, even if a very small one: the *colonus* was attached to the land but had the right to utilize it as a free man. Because of this attachment, *coloni* were sold with the land where they originated and attached to that land for purposes of tribute.[36] Although an owner could transfer slaves from one property to another, this was forbidden for *coloni*, a measure that helped emperors calculate tax levels for a given landholding but also limited the geographic mobility of laborers.[37]

Though the *colonus* was attached to the soil, he still had to pay taxes and tribute on his produce. In earlier periods, sharecroppers (also called *coloni*) on imperial domains paid one-third of their own revenues under the *Lex Manciana*, though at times this could climb as high as one-half. This older law was repeated and confirmed in 319 in a law that forbade the *colonus* to pay in money. This return was due to the landowner, and it was forbidden for him to increase it, on pain of prosecution.[38] Conceived of as a simple element in the process of agricultural production, the *colonus* had a miserable status; like the slave, for example, he was forbidden to take refuge in the church in order to change his status. And even if the *colonus* was initially granted some advantages over other free laborers – for example, the right to sell his produce at market without paying the business tax on the sale – his status became ever closer to that of a slave.

Elements of Political Economy

The third and fourth centuries were indelibly marked by the great inflationary crisis that destabilized the once solid monetary system of the high empire. The rise in prices beginning in the third decade of the third century caused the disappearance of gold and silver coinage from the market so that only the Antoninianus, a coin tariffed at two denarii but containing only a few miligrams of silver, remained. The resolution of this monetary crisis was possible only in a climate of political stability, which was attainable only beginning in the 270s, when Aurelian initiated the process of putting the monetary system back on a more sound footing.[39]

Economic problems were not, however, at an end. Diocletian of course wanted to believe that inflation had been strangled. In fact, however, it continued, above all in the areas around military camps, where a massive growth in demand effected a flare-up in prices. In September 301, through an edict now preserved in a copy inscribed at Aphrodisias, he doubled the face value of the coins, a move that naturally ruined creditors. This the emperor had been able to foresee, even if he did nothing to forestall it:

> As to debtors who prior to the first of September either are found to have debts to the imperial fisc or are locked into private arrangements, it is by all accounts just and concordant with the strictest equity that the following rule should be applied: they are obliged to pay the same number of coins they had already paid according to the recognized face value that the money had before the augmentation took place in accordance with our provision.[40]

Worse still, in as far as this decision followed a diminution in the money supply, the revaluation of the current silver coin (argenteus) was attributed to the avarice of Diocletian by the likes of Lactantius:

> This same Diocletian with his insatiable greed was never willing that his treasuries should be depleted; he was always amassing surplus wealth and funds for largess so that he could keep what he was storing complete and inviolate. Since too by his various misdeeds he was causing an immense rise in prices, he tried to fix by law the prices of goods put up for sale.[41]

Though Lactantius does not understand the economic causes behind the process, Diocletian's regrettable decision to revalue the currency certainly caused a new rise in prices, which Diocletian then attempted to combat with his famous Prices Edict from the end of 301. This ambitious order listed maximum prices to be applied throughout the entire empire for literally all goods and services. It was inscribed and posted in numerous cities and has thus survived to the present in numerous, generally fragmentary copies. The preamble of the Prices Edict offers a wonderful analysis of the mechanism of price elevation as it was understood in the late empire:

> Who indeed is so obtuse in spirit or deprived of all sense of humanity that he could ignore, or rather not even perceive that money transactions occurring in markets or conducted in daily commerce in the cities have fallen into such an uncontrolled state of pricing that it could not be mitigated either by the unbridled desire of thievery nor the abundance of goods or fertility of harvests? So that there is obviously no doubt that businessmen forever contemplate and watch for enriching rains through the motions of the stars, nor are they able to tolerate in their iniquity that fertile fields be watered with heavenly showers in hope of future harvests, as if they considered it a personal misfortune that an abundance of goods should be produced from the storms of heaven itself... And though each of them is overflowing with the greatest riches, which could supply entire populations, yet they chase after tiny amounts of money and pursue exacting percentages. Oh my provincials, the reason of common decency persuades us to put a limit on their avarice![42]

For Diocletian, the only engine driving the increase in prices was the speculation of greedy traders. In his eyes, the problem was thus a moral one, and the appropriate administrative response had to be nothing less than repression and the limitation of prices backed up by penalties against speculators. Given the failure of its assumptions, the failure of the edict was assured. By the end of 301, Diocletian had exhausted all the resources of monetary politics he could muster: floating rates, doubling the value of the coins, legal price limitations. For him, these were the only conceivable means of intervention available to an emperor.

Table 10.2. *Percentage Price Increases for Commodities*
(c. 300–c. 367)

Product	Time span	Increase/year
Gold	300/367	16.90%
Silver	301/359	17.46%
Wheat	301/359	16.25%
Meat (pork?)	301/360	17.25%
Fish (low quality)	301/338	17.69%
Common oil	301/c. 340	17.36%
Donkeys	307/314–16	18.90/23%
Horses	313/367	18.53%

THE REALITY OF PRICES

The information available to us on the question of prices is both abundant and lacunary: abundant because, for certain products like wheat, we have several dozen attestations; lacunary because it is essentially impossible to understand price development for the broader range of products used by modern economists to calculate inflation. We can thus only offer possible reconstructions of price fluctuation. For these purposes, it is perhaps best to use as our benchmark the price of a pound of gold. Our sources for datable prices make it apparent that there was a long period of strong price increase from the end of the third century up to the 360s. In this period the value in units of account of a pound of gold increased from 40 to almost 1,000,000 talents. After the 360s, this increase continued but at a slower pace.

Our first figures (from around 300 to 310) come from official price lists and are consistently in the same order of magnitude (40, 48, 66.6, 73, and 80 talents).[43] By the 350s, however, we have a document recording a price of 648,000 talents.[44] Inflation in the price of gold was thus massive in the period beginning around 300 and apparently lasted until Valentinian's coinage reform in 367. Using the data available to us in papyri, we might propose an estimate of 17 percent for the annual average increase in the price of gold during this period. Similar results obtain when we compare the nominal increase in the gold price with the increase in a certain number of products for the period from around 300 to around 367 (Table 10.2). Constantine's entire reign was thus subsumed within a period of strong price inflation.

THE CREATION OF THE SOLIDUS AND THE PREDOMINANCE OF GOLD

The creation of the solidus in 309 remains the most important economic reform of the fourth century. In reality, this new coin represented no particularly great departure from earlier monetary policy: Constantine simply reduced the weight of Diocletian's gold aureus from about 6 grams to about 4.5 grams (contrast Coins 5 and 27). Nevertheless, this change initiated a long period of stability in the gold coinage, which, despite crises, invasions, and the division of the empire, did not witness a weight reduction before the Byzantine empire began to experience difficulties in the tenth century. The perfect stability of the solidus makes it one of the rare examples of a monetary reform that succeeded.

As noted, the reform was characterized by a small reduction in the weight of the previous gold coin. This was, however, coupled with the maintenance of its purity and especially the introduction of a rather plain engraving that simplified the process of production. The role of the solidus became all the more important in 324, when Constantine took over the empire of Licinius and thereby acquired control of the mines in the central regions of the empire and access to new metal sources from regions beyond the eastern frontier. Above all, however, the conquest of the east gave Constantine access to the enormous metal reserves of the pagan temples there, which he promptly and brutally converted into coin. This sudden influx of gold allowed Constantine to convert the solidus into a viable, empire-wide, standard currency. This new predominance of gold coin corresponded with a shrinkage in the issue of silver coin. The monetary system that resulted consisted, on the one hand, of a mass of coins minted in bronze whose supply continuously increased with each monetary reform or weight reduction (310, 313, 318, 324, 330, 336) and, on the other hand, of an ever-growing and ever more powerful gold coinage.

Calculations I have made allow us to follow the evolution of the production of gold in the empire (Table 10.3). The production of gold shows a period of regular growth from 294 to 313, probably because of civil wars; a phase of regular decline until Constantine's acquisition of the eastern reserves (from 313 to c. 330); and finally a period of increase in issues from 330 until the emperor's death.[45]

Through another set of calculations, I have demonstrated the increased role of eastern imperial mints in the overall stock of solidi empire-wide (Table 10.4). In the space of a few years, the disappearance

Table 10.3. *Production of Gold per Year*

Time span	Index
294/305	100
305/309	128
309/313	155
313/318	102
318/324	90
324/330	81
330/335	98
336/337	179

of silver money and the considerable production of gold coinage transformed the money supply. This transformation was all the more important because the bronze coinage became ever lighter and more poorly struck, resulting in a net decrease in its value over against the gold. All of our literary sources – patristic, legal, and historical – testify to the growing importance of gold coin in all forms of economic and fiscal exchange. Indeed, this widespread diffusion of gold met with serious criticism from several authors. Written in the middle of the fourth century, probably in 368, the famous text *On Military Matters* (*De rebus bellicis*) described the situation in scathing terms:

> It was in the reign of Constantine that extravagant grants assigned gold instead of bronze (which earlier was considered of great value) to petty commercial transactions; but the greed I speak of is thought to have arisen from the following causes. When the gold and silver and the huge quantity of precious stones which had been stored away in the temples long ago reached the public, they enkindled all men's possessive and spendthrift instincts. And while the

Table 10.4. *Evolution of the Effective Coin Stock of the Empire*

Date	Total strikes	Percentage of eastern strikes
310	924	52
320	1,046	51
330	1,011	65
340	1,257	79

expenditure of bronze itself... had seemed already vast and burdensome enough, yet from some kind of blind folly there ensued an even more extravagant passion for spending gold, which is considered more precious. This store of gold meant that the houses of the powerful were crammed full and their splendor enhanced to the destruction of the poor, the poorer classes of course being held down by force. But the poor were driven by their afflictions into various criminal enterprises, and losing sight of all respect for law, all feelings of loyalty, they entrusted their revenge to crime.[46]

Although it was impossible for historians of the period to comprehend the reality of monetary phenomena, it remains true that they agree in attributing to Constantine a decisive role in the evolution of the monetary system and in the augmentation of the role of gold in the diverse spheres of economic life in the empire.

A STABLE NEW GOLD CURRENCY

Thus Constantine's creation of the solidus and his massive increase in its output in the second half of his reign significantly transformed the economy of the Roman empire. From the moment of its creation, the solidus constituted a standard currency and unit of value while other coins were relegated to secondary functions. Thus the mints could suspend their output of silver money and manipulate the weight of their bronze issues without destabilizing the system. The solidus quickly gained strength as an empire-wide unit of value and then retained that strength because of the choice of Constantine and his successors never to alter its characteristics. This made the solidus an excellent monetary instrument for estimating debts, so much so that it quickly became standard to reckon loans only in gold solidi.

The role conferred on the gold currency from the 310s onward made it the center not only of the monetary system but also of the economy. Gold coin gained a supramonetary value. By overtaking fixed relations of exchange with the silver coin, it became a true floating currency. The fact that taxes were demanded in gold contributed, for example, to a growth in the demand for the solidus as a commodity. Thus, the value of the solidus regularly increased at times when taxes were collected. This valorization of gold devalued the other means of exchange and, in a sort of feedback loop, reinforced the dominant role of gold.

Thus the solidus was at one and the same time an element of stability and instability. Imperial soldiers and officeholders, for example, began demanding a growing part of their pay, much of which was formerly received in kind (grain, clothing, and supply rations), to be commuted to gold coin. As it became more and more the possession of the economic, military, and bureaucratic elite, gold gradually modified the relations between those who possessed solidi and those who did not, and it helped to broaden the gap between mass and elite. By and large, however, the advantages of the solidus greatly outweighed the troubles it created. The monetary unity and stability it afforded reinforced the political unity established by Constantine and helped to stabilize long-distance exchange and loans, thereby facilitating commerce.

STATE FINANCES IN THE AGE OF CONSTANTINE

The Constantinian epoch was characterized by an effort to maintain and even increase the importance of gold in the system of taxation. The crisis of the third century had caused the fiscal system to contract considerably. The restoration work undertaken by Aurelian and continued by Diocletian and Constantine attempted to shelter the revenues of the state from any new inflationary crisis. For this purpose, it was important to have a perfectly stable coinage on which to base the fiscal system. The primary objective of that system was of course to effect a steady return of gold coin into state coffers. This was then recirculated in the payment of bureaucratic and military allowances and donatives.

The relation between the collection of gold and its distribution to the troops played a crucial role in the development of the late antique economy. Many texts draw the link between the increase in fiscal pressure, the development of gold currency, and the growth of the armies. Lactantius, for example, offers a scathing condemnation of the growing weight of taxation and its roots in the growth of the army and bureaucracy:

> [Diocletian multiplied] the armies since each of the four [Tetrarchs] strove to have a far larger number of troops than previous emperors had had when they were governing the state alone. The number of recipients began to exceed the

number of contributors by so much that, with farmers' resources exhausted by the enormous size of the requisitions, fields became deserted and cultivated land was turned into forest. To ensure that terror was universal, provinces too were cut into fragments; many governors and even more officials were imposed on individual regions: accountants, controllers and prefects' deputies.[47]

As a Christian, Lactantius was extremely biased against the persecutor Diocletian and was thus inclined to criticize the Tetrarch for his fiscal policy as well. Yet much the same assessment is offered by the more objective Aurelius Victor some forty years later, even though Victor was anything but a Christian propagandist.[48]

As part of the legacy of the collapse of the fiscal system in the third century, there were many taxes that were in theory paid in kind rather than money. Chief among these was the *annona*, or grain levy, designed to meet the provisioning needs of the army. Because it was a system of requisitioning and thus best adapted to meet the needs of armies stationed in permanent camps, it quickly became outmoded with the growing development of a mobile army under Constantine. This new army was better paid in gold coin – an extremely mobile bearer of value – rather than bulky grain rations. Similar were two other taxes in kind, the *equorum collatio*, or horse levy, designed to equip cavalry riders with horses, and the *vestis militaris*, designed to outfit soldiers with clothing. Fairly early in the fourth century, these latter taxes began to be collected in gold and then paid entirely or partially to the soldiers as money. Indeed, the fourth century is generally characterized by a tendency to commute taxes formerly collected in kind into their money value in gold. Even the *annona* could be commuted to its equivalency in gold from at least 299, and this occurred with increasing frequency after 313.[49]

This process of commutation (*adaeratio*), a process that only increased in the reign of Constantine and his successors, went hand in hand with the growing importance of gold all across the economy.[50] The increase in taxes evaluated using the gold solidus and its fractions – which go as low as 1/72 of a coin in some papyri – forced some taxpayers to have recourse to an intermediary who could pay their debts, which were usually lumped together with the debts of a larger group of small taxpayers of more modest means. Fiscal debt thus became an element of social domination as small landholders or moderate urban taxpayers found themselves bound by debt to more powerful individuals who could cover their tax burdens in gold and thus win patronage claims over them in a broader social sense. The *annona* and related military supply taxes were, however, hardly the only sources of revenue for the late Roman state. Though we cannot detail all the remaining taxes assessed in the period, it is worthwhile to review the most important. *Aurum coronarium*, or crown gold, was theoretically a voluntary levy that was assessed primarily on the towns and their decurions at the accession of an emperor to the throne and every major anniversary thereafter. Along similar lines, senators, who were exempt from the *aurum coronarium*, were allowed and indeed expected to offer their own separate voluntary gift (*aurum oblaticium*) to the emperor – the senator Symmachus reports, for example, that the Roman Senate decided to offer 1,600 pounds of gold for Valentinian II's *decennalia* in 384.[51] In addition, the senators were required to pay a separate obligatory tax in gold based on an assessment of their landed wealth.

Ultimately, however, the fiscal system rested most heavily on two further taxes that are relatively well documented. The first was a tax on merchants, often called the *chrysargyron*,[52] and the second was the *capitatio*, or head tax. The merchant tax was created by Constantine around 314, not without protest:

> It was he [Constantine] who also imposed the payment of gold and silver on those who sold any sort of wares in the cities, even down to the most humble, without even allowing unfortunate prostitutes to escape the tax, so that, when the end of the period of four years approached and it was necessary to pay up, one could witness tears and lamentations throughout the city and, once the term was past, beatings and tortures were inflicted on the bodies of those who could not bear the weight of the fee because of their extreme poverty.[53]

The Theodosian Code reflects the fact that a growing number of groups were offered permanent exemptions from the *chrysargyron*, including shippers and veterans (from 326), then ecclesiastics (from 346), and later peasants selling their produce (from 361).[54] These exemptions surely reflect pressure to relieve what was commonly regarded as a heavy burden and a burden that, to judge by the laws in the Theodosian Code, became particularly acute in the later fourth century. The passage just quoted from Zosimus, for example, was written over a century and a half after Constantine's death, leading one to assume that the burden of the *chrysargyron* really only became unbearable after heavy inflation in the gold price and the growth in the number of exemptions. It is no surprise, then, that Zosimus's contemporary, the emperor Anastasius, finally abolished this tax in 498.

Last but by no means least, the *capitatio* was a tax on individual taxpayers, in theory the simplest assessment conceivable. In fact, however, the term *capitatio* actually covered several sorts of taxes that varied in nature and scope from region to region. In cities it was a head tax, though women, children, and slaves were often evaluated at less than a full head (*caput*). In the country, by contrast, it was a tax based on landholdings and their surface area and quality. Here too exemptions were numerous. Soldiers and former bureaucrats, for example, were exempt. The tax was also gradually transformed during the course of the fourth century. Diocletian's formulation of the tax reckoned assessments according to persons, animals, and lands, a structure typical of the Tetrarchy in its obsession with complicated systems of recording. This required public administrative offices to maintain registers of all possessions, which then formed the basis for all fiscal assessments. Yet from the 310s, the papyri show that this system was abandoned in Egypt in favor of a classification of land types, which was in turn abandoned for a unique system of taxation linked to the development of the Egyptian system of *iuga*, which is attested from 349. Fundamental changes were also made to the system in the west. Constantine's reduction of 7,000 *capita* for Autun cited above shows explicitly alterations to Diocletian's work while still emphasizing the ongoing importance of land registers. Even at the end of the fourth century the capitation system remained tied to land, not persons. Thus a law of the western emperor Honorius from 398 affirms, "The glebal tax is attached to landholdings and not to persons ... When the declaration of the tax payable in gold is filed on the tax lists, this declaration cannot be lost, even when the ownership is transferred."[55]

Finally, surprising though it is to moderns, confiscations were a significant element of the Roman state budget. Thus Diocletian, Maximian, and Galerius have left a lasting impression as emperors who relied on this source of wealth too heavily:

> I pass over the numerous people who perished because of their property or their wealth; for as people became used to trouble, this became normal, almost legitimate; but the outstanding feature of Diocletian's behavior here was that, whenever he saw a field rather better cultivated than most or a house rather more finely adorned, a false accusation and

capital punishment were immediately at hand for use against the owner, as if he could not seize other people's property without shedding their blood.[56]

Under the Tetrarchs, of course, Christians in particular suffered from the confiscations that went along with the Great Persecution. Yet Constantine himself after his conversion organized a similar transfer of wealth from pagan temples and Donatist schismatics to the state and the church. And Constantine's sons continued the politics of their father by despoiling temples, a policy with which Christian authors, in a paradoxical twist, fully agreed:

> Take away, yes, calmly take away, Most Holy Emperors, the adornments of the temples. Let the fire of the mint or the blaze of the smelters melt them down, and confiscate all the votive offerings to your own use and ownership.[57]

This vast transfer of wealth, as noted earlier, helped spur the abundant production of gold that allowed for the success of the solidus and the conversion of the fourth-century economy into a gold-based system.

THE COST OF THE ARMY

The single biggest expense faced by any Roman emperor was financing the army. The single biggest problem faced by modern historians trying to calculate this cost is estimating the total number of soldiers. Much of the problem stems from the lack of information on this question in ancient sources. The Latin panegyrist of 313, for example, reports the size of Constantine's and Maxentius's forces before the battle of the Milvian Bridge as forty thousand and and one hundred thousand respectively. These figures are probably accurate, but the number for Constantine's men reflects only the size of the expeditionary force he led into Italy; according to the same panegyrist, Constantine left three-fourths of his troops (thus 120,000 additional men) back in Gaul.[58] Moreover, these figures represent only the size of the western armies, not those held by Licinius and Maximin Daia at the same time. In the end, then, we can only estimate the total size of the army at somewhere around four hundred thousand under Diocletian, five hundred thousand under Constantine, and two hundred thousand by the fifth century.[59]

The costs for an army this size would have involved between 16 million aurei under Diocletian and 30 million aurei under Constantine, for not only did the army grow in size under the latter, but its costs per soldier increased. To cope with these costs, Diocletian worked hard to regularize payments to the troops. Apart from supply rations, much of a soldiers pay came in donatives (formal cash gifts), which had formerly been irregular and thus difficult to estimate and control. Diocletian regularized donatives with fixed dates, generally linked to the accession and birth dates of the reigning emperors. As P. Bastien recognized, the resumption of regularly minted gold issues from 286 corresponded with the need to ensure distributions of a uniform coin throughout the empire for precisely these occasions.[60]

Several donatives are known for the reign of Diocletian and the Tetrarchs. The discovery of two important papyri from Panopolis, both dating to the winter of 299/300, has permitted us to comprehend better the question of how these worked. Both report orders of transfer for sums designated for donatives. One, for example, reads as follows:

> See that you pay out to the mounted archers under the command of the *praepositus* Valerius, stationed in the fort of Potecoptus, on account of donative for the accession of our ruler Diocletian, the senior Augustus, on November 20th in the most happy 7th and 6th consulate of our rulers Diocletian and Maximian the Augusti, 30 myriads of denarii and 2,500 *atticae* [drachmas]; and on account of donative for the birthday of the same our ruler Diocletian, the senior Augustus, on December 22nd in the same consulate, 30 myriads of denarii and 2,500 *atticae*, making a total altogether of 60 myriads of denarii and 5,000 *atticae*.[61]

P. Bastien has attempted to transform these units of account into sums of coin.[62] According to his figures, the commander of the Equites Promoti in the Legio II Traiana received a donative in the amount of 2,500 denarii of account = 20 small folles = 2 aurei. Lesser soldiers (the *lancearii*, those in the *vexillatio*, the *equites sagitarii*, and those in the *vexillatio legionum orientalium*) got 1,250 denarii each = 10 folles = 1 aureus. Finally, the donative of the Ala II Herculia Dromedariorum amounted to only 250 denarii of account = 2 folles = 1/5 aureus. Reading the figures slightly differently, R. P. Duncan-Jones argues that the Panopolis papyri show that the payments of soldiers could be established according to the following schema:[63]

stipendium	1,800 denarii/year
annona	600 denarii/year
birthday and accession donatives, Augusti	2,500 denarii/year
birthday and accession donatives, Caesars	1,200 denarii/year
oil	1/11 sextarius/day

Such a calculation would entail a minimum of 6,100 denarii, or 4.88 aurei, per soldier per year. Assuming a Diocletianic army of 400,000, this would translate into a mininum of 1,952,000 aurei, or about 33,000 pounds of gold, per annum in state expenses for military pay alone.

With the end of the civil war years, the rhythm of donatives diminished considerably. Only twelve distributions took place between 313 and 325, and only eight between 325 and 337, figures that confirm a deceleration in the rhythm of *donativa*. The decline in frequency did not, however, help Constantine avoid the reputation of being a spendthrift or even prodigal emperor. While still Caesar, Julian thought it proper to praise the action of his uncle Constantine to his cousin and superior Constantius II. Once he had become emperor, however, Julian attacked Constantine for his prodigality when he posed him in a comic scene in his dialogue *Caesares*:

> Hermes asked Constantine, "And what was the height of your ambition?" "To amass great wealth," he answered, "and then to spend it liberally so as to gratify my own desires and the desires of my friends."[64]

The historian Zosimus looked on Constantine even more harshly:

> Constantine continued wasting revenue by unnecessary gifts to unworthy and useless people, and oppressed those who paid taxes while enriching those who were useless to the state; for he thought that prodigality was liberality.[65]

To be sure, Constantine was not alone among emperors in drawing fire for his reputed prodigality. In fact, such criticisms are generally based more on moralism than reality, and they almost always reflect the complaints of those opposed to other imperial policies – in the instance of Julian and Zosimus, religious policies.[66] As we shall see, Constantine's gifts, particularly those to the Christian Church, were elaborate, but his maintenance of responsible fiscal practices seems beyond doubt. By the time of his death, both empire and emperor were on sound financial footing, which could not have been said forty years earlier.

GIFTS TO CHURCHES

The intrusion of the Christian Church into political and then economic life was certainly one of the major revolutions of the later empire. In the space of a few years, the church assembled landed estates and riches that allowed it to play an ever-growing role in politics. These endowments could not have come into being before Constantine's legislation. We have already seen that Constantine's conversion marked the beginning of a period of massive transfers of funds between pagan temples, the church, and the state. In a related move, Constantine quickly repaired most of the economic damage done to the church during the period of the persecutions. Thus the Edict of Milan in 313 already provided for the restitution of goods confiscated from the church and individual Christians:

> [Constantine] commanded that all those who, on account of their confession of Christ, had been sent to banishment... should be restored to liberty and he returned to them their confiscated goods... In the case of those who had been slain, and whose property had been confiscated, he enacted that the inheritance should be transferred to the next of kin, or, in default of heirs, to the church belonging to the locality where the estate was situated; and when the inheritance had passed into other hands and had become either private or national property, he commanded it to be restored. He likewise promised to resort to the fittest and best possible arrangements when the property had been purchased by the exchequer, or had been received therefrom by gift.[67]

Constantine also funded the church in more active ways. Shortly after his conversion, he introduced a tradition of endowments to the church, first in Rome and then in the provinces: "Under the government of Constantine the churches flourished and increased in numbers daily, since they were honored by the good deeds of a benevolent and well-disposed emperor."[68] And he invited governors to follow his example:

> He then wrote to the governors of the provinces, directing that provision-money should be given in every city to virgins and widows, and to those who were consecrated to the divine service; and he measured the amount of their annual allowance more by the impulse of his own generosity than by their need. The third part of the sum is distributed to this day. Julian impiously withheld the whole. His successor [i.e., Jovian] conferred the sum which is now dispensed, the famine which then prevailed having lessened the resources of the state.[69]

The various members of his imperial family also signed onto this same politics of ecclesiastical endowment.[70] Our most detailed evidence for the scale and range of Constantine's endowments to churches is the *Liber pontificalis*, which records the nature of those endowments as they affected the church in Rome. These consisted of precious vessels made of gold or silver transferred directly to the church's treasury, of gifts of land and buildings whose revenues were transferred to the church, and even of spices and other rare commodities. Though this text presents a number of problems with authenticity and interpretation, we can derive from it tentative figures for Constantine's total endowments to the Roman church in the years from 314 to 336 at 963 kilograms of gold and 5,300 kilograms of silver – consisting mostly of sacred vessels – and revenues from landed properties of 32,469 solidi (148 kilograms of gold) per year.

CONSTANTINE AND THE TRANSITION FROM ANTIQUITY TO THE MIDDLE AGES

Constantine's image in the tradition is above all that of a great reformer in monetary matters. The creation of the solidus remains, from a numismatic perspective, one of the most important reforms ever. This coin continued to be minted for almost seven centuries, and even when monetary crisis ultimately modified the characteristics of the gold coinage, it was the ancient solidus that eventually determined the new money that emerged. Ultimately the term "solidus" remained in the vulgar languages a general name for money or units of account (thus the Italian "soldi" and the French "sous"). The great reform represented by the solidus and the possibility it offered of mass minting and the creation of a viable empirewide gold currency thus made Constantine the creator of a major new monetary system.

Although the creation of a new gold coin constituted a major and beneficial reform, Constantine could also be charged with reducing the bronze coinage to a secondary role. His reductions in the weight of the bronze coinage between 320 and 330 coincided with massive increases in the money supply as millions of coins per year were minted. Constantine thus also set the preconditions for a period of major inflation in the bronze currency used by the empire's less privileged social groups. Here, too, the impact was long lasting, if only because this abundance of bronze was so great that his coins continued to circulate for centuries. Even in the Merovingian period, three hundred years later, certain gold coins copied the types on Constantinian bronzes. Constantinian era bronzes also turn up in droves in archaeological sites or in certain hoards of medieval or even modern times.

From an economic perspective, the age of Constantine is characterized by a series of major developments, especially the development of a fiscal system based on gold. This system of valuation and regulation of taxes favored the development of networks in which one person paid for a collective of people who were then indebted to him. The age of Constantine is also the period of the first legislative texts that tended to limit the freedom of peasants and certain professional groups – for example, bakers – to alter their status or homeland. For some time historians have seen in these evolutions the beginnings of the feudal system. This is far from certain. What is certain is that the Constantinian period represented one (or perhaps the last) of the great periods of peace in the Roman empire. The development of rich villas that sprang up across the countryside, the renewal of banking, the security of the frontier zones, and the stability of the fiscal system and of the functioning of the state explain why one speaks of a "Constantinian renaissance."

FURTHER READING

There has been considerable recent work on the ancient economy more broadly and the late Roman economy more particularly. In general terms, M. I. Finley's *The Ancient Economy* (1985) remains fundamental, though it has come under considerable recent criticism. A good example of a new approach to economic history in the Mediterranean is the provocative study of P. Horden and N. Purcell, *The Corrupting Sea* (2000). Fiscal concerns are solidly researched in R. P. Duncan Jones's *Money and Government in the Roman Empire* (1994), though not all will agree with the conclusions. The late Roman economy is covered in Chapters 9 and 10 of A. Cameron and P. Garnsey's *The Cambridge Ancient History*, vol. 13, *The Late Empire A.D. 337–425* (1998), and fiscal matters are covered in M. F. Hendy's *Studies in the Byzantine Monetary Economy, c. 300–1450* (1985). Again, a recent revisionist treatment, J. Banaji's *Agrarian Change in Late Antiquity: Gold, Labour, and Aristocratic Dominance* (2001), goes some way toward rewriting the story. It is continued in two more recent studies, M. McCormick's *Origins of the European Economy: Communications and Commerce, AD 300–900* (2001) and the three-volume collection edited by A. E. Laiou, *The Economic History of Byzantium: From the Seventh through the Fifteenth Centuries* (2002).

Notes

1 Plassard 1968; Bousquet and Péchoux 1977.
2 Fritts 1976. On new methods of historical climate research, see the special editions of *The Journal of Interdisciplinary History*, Rabb and Rotberg 1980. See also Brooks 1950, 364; Lamb 1977, 374, 424–7; Noel 1972, 72–3. On swampification, see Richard 1988. On rises in the sea level, see Somme 1977, 545–55.
3 Panella 1981; Keay 1984.
4 Jardé 1925; Black 1987; Demarez 1987. Though these numbers seem high, they are derived from careful calculation.
5 Black 1987, 58–60; Demarez 1987.
6 Grenier 1960, 79–82.
7 Banaji 2001 explains how these larger estates came to dominate in the east in very productive ways.
8 Leclercq 1907, 371. Contrast, however, Witschel 1999, 42–6, and passim for a broader critique of the "third-century crisis."
9 Jones 1959; Lallemand 1964, 16.
10 A pastiche of *Pan. Lat.* 5(8).5.4, 7.2–3, 10.5, 11.3, 13.1 (trans. Nixon and Rodgers). The city had originally been responsible for 32,000 *capita* (tax units), an indication that 22 percent of the land had been abandoned. Cf. Cérati 1975, 322.
11 *P. Thead.* 17 = *P. Turner* 44 (trans. J. Rea); cf. *P. Cair. Isid.* 68 (314).
12 Whittaker 1976. See also Bravo 1979.
13 *CTh* 7.20.3 (326; trans. Pharr). The law was repeated and extended several times in the fourth century; *CTh* 7.20.4 (325), 8 (370), 11 (373).
14 *Pan. Lat.* 8(5).9.3 (trans. Nixon and Rodgers).
15 Drinkwater 1987.
16 Grenier and Déchelette 1931, 282–484.

17 On the towns in Gaul, in general, Grenier 1931, 362–592. See also the collection *Topographie chrétienne des cités de la Gaule*, edited by Gauthier, Picard, and Duval since 1986. Their surveys tell a somewhat different story: an ecclesiastical building boom occurred precisely when other traditional civic structures were being neglected – a shift in priorities rather than prosperity.

18 Zos. 2.38.2–4 (trans. Ridley). More on the late Roman city in Ward-Perkins 1984 and Liebeschuetz 2001, esp. Chapter 2. Liebeschuetz emphasizes a distinction between the west, where the classical Roman city did not survive the third century, and the east, where in many aspects it survived, albeit transformed, until the seventh, and also a distinction between the late Roman city of the fourth century and the later Roman city of the fifth and sixth centuries.

19 Lepelley 1979, 60–108.

20 Février 1964; Tavano 1970; Depeyrot 1999.

21 Scagliarini 1970; Popović 1971; Bosković et al. 1973; Plesnicar-Gec 1970–1, 1972; Poulter 1992, 1995.

22 Lact. *DMP* 7.8 (trans. Creed).

23 See chapter 12 in this volume.

24 *Ed. de pretiis* 29.1. The same amount could purchase roughly 300 modii of grain, enough to feed twelve people for one year.

25 Symm. *Ep.* 2.78, though the text at the crucial point remains problematic.

26 AM 22.7.7–8; cf. 29.4.4 for slave traders along the Rhine and 31.4.11 with Zos. 4.20.6 for slave trading along the Danube.

27 On runaways, see already Paul's letter to Philemon 8–17; cf. *Regula Pachomii* 49 (*PL* 23.73). On clergy, see, e.g., *CTh* 9.45.5; cf. Klein 1993.

28 Cyprian *Ad Demetrium* 8 (*CSEL* 467:86); Basil *De Sp. Sanct.* 20 (*SChr* 17bis:204–6); *Mor.* 75.1 (*PG* 31:856); cf. Klein 2000.

29 Aug. *CD* 14.14–15; Amb. *Ep.* 2.31; cf. Klein 1988.

30 *CTh* 9.40.2 = *CJ* 9.47.17; *CTh* 4.7.1 = *CJ* 1.13.2.

31 See Rosafio 2002.

32 E.g., *CTh* 14.3.2 (355).

33 *CJ* 11.63.1, 68.1–2.

34 *CTh* 5.17.1.

35 *CJ* 6.4.2, 11.68.4; *CTh* 5.17.3.

36 *CTh* 11.1.4 (366), 13.10.3 (357).

37 *CTh* 11.1.26 (399).

38 *CTh* 11.16.1; cf. *CJ* 11.50.1 (325).

39 On this period, see Depeyrot 1991, 1995a.

40 Edict of Aphrodisias fr. E ll. 5–10, at Roueché 1989, 259.

41 Lact. *DMP* 7.5–6 (trans. Creed).

42 *Ed. de pretiis* praef. 65–85.

43 P. *Panop. Beatty*, 2.219 (300), *Ed. de pretiis* 28.1; P. *Oxy.* 2:106; P. *Ryl.* 616; *PSI* 310.

44 P. *Oxy.* 3:401. More on prices in Bagnall 1985.

45 Depeyrot 1995b, 1996; cf. Hendy 1985, esp. 378–80, 462–7, on the development of the monetary economy.

46 *DRB* 2.1–2.

47 Lact. *DMP* 7.2–4 (trans. Creed).

48 Aur. Vict. *Caes.* 39.31–2.

49   On taxation, Jones 1964, 411–69, remains fundamental; cf. Depeyrot 1991; Bagnall 1993a, 153–60. Eus. *VC* 4.2–3 asserts that Constantine cut tribute by one-fourth, though the assertion is otherwise hard to document. See T. D. Barnes 1981, 255–8.

50   On *adaeratio*, see Mickwitz 1932; Mazzarino 1951, 193–8; see Carrié 1993 for a different assessment.

51   Symm. *Rel.* 13.1–3.

52   The tax actually bore various names, including *collatio lustralis* and *aurum commerciorum*. More at Karayannopulos 1958, 129–37.

53   Zos. 2.38.2–4.

54   *CTh* 7.20.2, 13.1.3, 16.2.10.

55   *CTh* 6.2.21 (trans. Pharr).

56   Lact. *DMP* 7.4, 11–12 (trans. Creed).

57   Firm. Mat. *Err.* 28.6 (trans. Forbes).

58   *Pan. Lat.* 9(12).3.3, 5.1–2. Zos. 2.15.1–2 pegs the numbers at 98,000 for Constantine and 185,000 for Maxentius, surely too high.

59   These are the figures established by Segré 1942–3. Similar numbers at Elton 1996b, 210–13; Lee 1998, 219–20.

60   Bastien 1988; cf. Burgess 1988.

61   *P. Panop. Beatty* 2.161–3 (Skeat 1964, 82–3, with this translation).

62   Bastien 1988, 32–4; cf. Jones 1964, 187–8.

63   Duncan Jones 1978.

64   Jul. *Caes.* 335b (trans. Wright).

65   Zos. 2.38.1 (trans. Ridley). On this theme, see also *Epit.* 41.6, AM 16.8.12, and Chapter 8 n. 57 in this volume.

66   Compare the complaints at *Epit.* 41 against Licinius.

67   Soz. 1.8.3–4 (trans. Hartranft), which summarizes Eus. *VC* 2.20–21; cf. Lact. *DMP* 48.2–12; Eus. *HE* 9.9.12, 10.5.1–14.

68   Soz. 1.6.1 (trans. Hartranft).

69   Theod. *HE* 1.11 (trans. Jackson); cf. 3.6. See also Elliott 1978.

70   See, e.g., the Arab Jacobite Synaxarion 13 Sept. at *Patrologia Orientalis* 1.

SECTION IV

ART AND CULTURE

11: PERSPECTIVES IN ART

Jaś Elsner

INTRODUCTION: PERSPECTIVES AND PROBLEMS

onstantine ruled longer than any other Roman emperor after Augustus. The changes inaugurated in his Principate were arguably still greater and longer lasting for European history even than those instigated by his illustrious predecessor. In the visual arts, my subject here, developments under Constantine can be seen from more than one perspective. In one sense they represent a moment of major transformation in the history of art: the state began actively to sponsor the architecture and imagery of Christianity and thus to put the force of the establishment behind changes in image-making that would culminate in the move from pagan to Christian art and the (not wholly unrelated) move from the practices and aesthetics of Graeco-Roman art to those of the early Middle Ages. This latter is a long process, beginning well before Constantine's reign (scholars have sought its inception as early as the Flavian period and at numerous occasions thereafter)[1] and ending perhaps as late as the sixth century. It is a process which some have attributed to the internal dynamics within Roman image-making and others to the influence of external traditions of art, especially from the Near East.[2] From a narrower perspective, the images produced in Constantine's reign allowed for significant innovations within the dynamics of imperial propagation of Roman state art. Whether these innovations constituted a "revolution" of the kind associated with Augustan image-making is perhaps a moot point – very difficult to assess because of the relatively poor state of the empirical evidence. But there can be no doubt that the visual messages of Constantine's reign were as significant as those of Augustus for helping to construct a new monarchical system and for conveying its affiliations (above all its support for Christianity) to the populace. Both these perspectives – large scale and relatively narrower – will be discussed here, but first some problems.

One difficulty in assessing Constantinian art is precisely the double perspective from which it must inevitably be studied. When we look at such canonical images as the great marble head from the basilica of Constantine in the Roman Forum (now in the Museo Conservatori; Fig. 14), are we to regard it within the dynamic of its specific relations to earlier imperial imagery and especially by contrast with the Tetrarchic images that preceded the visual patterns of Constantine's own reign? Or are we to see its place in the much bigger picture that led from the conception of Roman to Christian emperorship, from antiquity to Byzantium? A version of this problem of perspective is the fraught and unresolved question of the extent and exclusivity of Constantine's specifically Christian affiliations. Many arguments have been advanced on this issue; suffice it to say that in the visual arts as in other fields of expression the régime seems to have given a variety of contradictory signals on this matter. Certainly there was a significant and parallel Constantinian cult of the Sun, whose roots lay deep in the imperial past and which had flourished during the third century.[3] A further problem is the relative paucity of evidence: by contrast with hundreds of surviving portraits of Augustus,[4] for example, we have only about fifty that survive of Constantine,[5] and many of these are disputed. This comparatively weak evidentiary base may reflect a more restricted level of production in a relatively poorer empire. But it may also be related to the vulnerability of late antique works of art to the various depredations of war and invasion that beset the empire both east and west throughout the early medieval period. These difficulties mean that we cannot trace the range of Constantinian art, its penetration into the private and non-official sphere, or its empire-wide impact beyond certain urban capitals on anything like the same level we can for imperial art in, say, the period of Augustus.[6]

To compound the paucity of evidence and our uncertainties about the material we do have, problems of dating bedevil our desire for precision about works created or used in the reign of Constantine. Even the Arch of Constantine, for instance, which can at least in its final form be securely attributed to the emperor's reign, has raised controversy when precise dates are suggested (Fig. 1).[7] With the imperial portraits, insofar as we are secure about their identification, there is a good likelihood that most belong to Constantine's reign, though the chances of posthumous images being made for the founder of a dynasty are not unlikely – as in the case of several portraits of Augustus and possibly with the bronze colossus from Rome now thought to represent Constantine rather than his son Constantius (Fig. 15). But what about other portraits? The usual means for dating these is by comparison with the styles of the imperial images – and the examination of especially "fashion-dependent" items like hairstyles and earrings which can be compared with independently dated examples.[8] But this assumes that cosmopolitan styles were immediately adopted, without a significant time lag, and that old fashions were dropped rather than continued in distant provinces. The absence of a collected corpus of Constantinian (and indeed fourth-century) private portraiture hardly helps the process.[9]

In the case of most images broadly attributable to the first third of the fourth century – as opposed to fifty years before or after – on stylistic grounds, we have no objective or external verification. Even when we have such evidence, what does it mean? The so-called Constantinian villa in Antioch, many of whose finest mosaics are now in Paris, is dated by a coin of Constantine found in the mortar where the mosaics were laid.[10] But when I was a boy in the 1970s, before the arrival of decimalisation of the coinage in England, we regularly used pennies from the later part of Queen Victoria's reign, eighty years before. If I had dropped such a penny in newly laid concrete, what would it have told us about chronology? So much for the security of precise dating by coin finds. The worst problem lies in relation to what was clearly Constantine's greatest single act of artistic patronage – namely, the foundation of Constantinople. It is partly a sign of his success in establishing a capital which would be the centre of a Christian empire for over a thousand years that most of Constantine's own works were embellished and built over in subsequent centuries. Our evidence for the period of the city's foundation comes from fragments of (usually poor) archaeology and from late, often legendary and unreliable, literary traditions in which a medieval dream of the first Christian emperor is much more significant than an interest in anything that we might regard as valuable empirical or factual evidence. If we followed these kinds of traditions too closely, then the great gilded bronze equestrian statue of Marcus Aurelius from Rome would have a rightful pride of place in this account – for it survives because it was believed to be Constantine throughout most of the Middle Ages.

Let us begin by looking at arguably the most famous monument that survives from Constantine's own lifetime to illustrate the problems of perspective and evidence I have just raised. The emperor's arch in Rome, probably voted him by the Senate after his conquest of 312 and probably dedicated in 315, is in remarkably good condition – especially by contrast with the loss or radical rebuilding of so many of Constantine's other prestige dedications, like the churches or his mausoleum in Constantinople.[11] Yet even here there are numerous losses which make the Constantinian appearance of the monument uncertain – especially the loss of the (bronze?) statue group at the top, a small frieze of coloured marbles beneath the cornice on which the attic storey stands, most of the porphyry background to the eight tondi dating from Hadrianic times, and a number of imperial heads in the reliefs.[12] Added to this is the intense debate about whether the basic structure of the arch goes back to Domitian or Hadrian or whether it is a Constantinian – or a Constantinian adaptation of a Maxentian – copy of the Arch of Septimius Severus, a debate which has recently been rejoined with much passion in the 1990s, after the 1980s cleaning and excavations.[13] These archaeological uncertainties make it difficult to assess, within the relatively narrow perspective of the arch's impact in its own time, the extent to which it was an innovative or conservative monument. Clearly its architectural form and its placement within a specific complex of buildings – many new in the fourth century and rededicated by Constantine – are traditional.[14] The use of relief sculpture showing the emperor in his main roles of state belongs to a practice of celebrating leading Romans in public reliefs that reaches back to the republic. But the arch borrows many of its sculptures from earlier monuments – possibly dismantled for the purpose but more likely the victims of damage by fires or other disasters in the later third century. These include panels from major decorative programmes celebrating Hadrian, Trajan, and Marcus Aurelius, which are juxtaposed against the Constantinian sculpture,[15] as well as eight statues of defeated Dacians probably from Trajan's forum.[16] Interestingly the heads of the emperor on these reused panels were rather brilliantly recarved with excellent new heads mainly of Constantine and, in four of the Hadrianic medallions, of another figure, perhaps his father Constantius Chlorus (Fig. 16).[17] This kind of recarving was normal in Roman culture – and it is thought that many of Constantine's surviving portrait heads in marble were in fact recut in this way.[18] But normally in Roman culture, when a relief had its portrait changed, this was a sign of the condemnation of the figure recarved,[19] whereas the makers of the arch either passed no judgement on the reused materials, taking them entirely for pragmatic reasons,[20] or, as I think more likely, engaged in the singularly innovative practice of using such recutting to bolster Constantine by presenting him in the bodies, as it were, of some of his most illustrious deified predecessors.[21]

Again, the general subject matter of the arch's sculpture is traditional – the imagery of imperial triumph, sacrifice, hunting, addressing the troops, entering cities. But its context, in celebration of a victory in civil war in which Rome itself had fallen to what might be regarded as a conquering usurper rather than in relation to a triumph over foreign enemies, was unprecedented. The motifs employed for the fourth-century frieze, which winds its way around the monument just above the two smaller bays to the east and west sides of the arch, are highly familiar in Roman imperial art: the setting out of the army; sieges and wars (Fig. 17); a victorious entry; the emperor addressing the populace in the Roman Forum, whose buildings are depicted with a certain documentary accuracy (Fig. 18); the giving of largesse.[22] But the subject is a narrative of Constantine's campaign against Maxentius, his victory and his taking of Rome. Even if one might interpret the theme as the return of the rightful ruler to his city and the overthrow of what the arch's inscriptions calls "tyranny," the opportunity for taking this imagery as the boasting of an upstart usurper must have been hard to resist for anyone invested at any stage in the Maxentian cause. This was especially so given Maxentius's singular concentration on Rome as a centrepiece for imperial patronage and Constantine's usurpation not just of power but also of Maxentius's entire building programme in Rome. Again, rather startling innovation is wrapped up together with a striking traditionalism. We might add that the arch's inscriptions made it clear that the monument was a dedication to or for the emperor by the Senate. But in the absence of secure fourth-century evidence about Constantine's own dedications and about other civic benefactions in his honour, it is very difficult to know how to interpret the issues of patronage and intentions, beyond the obvious point that the Senate would not have built the new conqueror an arch that he positively disapproved of or detested.

With regard to the broader perspective of the arch's place in the changes in visual production characteristic of late antiquity, the monument's lack of reference to Christianity is striking. Nonetheless, a number of its visual strategies are highly novel in ways that point towards medieval rather than traditional visual practices. First, the recycling of earlier materials, often referred to in the scholarly literature as *spolia* (by no means just relief sculpture but also carved architectural elements like capitals and columns and even blocks of marble), is the most notable and characteristic feature of this monument.[23] This became a fundamental feature of Constantinian building and decoration of all sorts[24] and was to have a long-term future in medieval art. The arch of Constantine is the first surviving public monument to boast that eclecticism of styles and that juxtapositional bricolage of objects from different periods which was to become common during the early and High Middle Ages in such diverse contexts as church buildings, jewelled display crosses and gilded gospel covers containing fragments from antiquity, from Byzantium, and from Islam displayed in contemporary settings. Moreover, in juxtaposing fourth-century friezes depicting Constantine's recent victories over Maxentius with the near canonical victories of Trajan and Marcus over the Dacians and the northern barbarians and with the hunting feats of Hadrian, the makers of the arch appear to have seized on the kinds of typology developed in the same period to brilliant effect in Christian art. Just as the images of Jonah vomited by the whale or Daniel in the lion's den are used in Christian sarcophagi or catacomb painting to prefigure the resurrection of Christ, so the military feats of Trajan and Marcus prefigure those of Constantine. Just as Christ fulfils the promise and prophecy of the Old Testament, so Constantine – literally embodied in the earlier emperors once his face has come to replace theirs – fulfils the eternal promise of Rome's former imperial glories in his reunification of the empire and his charismatic arrival in Rome as sole emperor of the west.[25] Again, the message being proclaimed is rather traditional here, even if the circumstances of victory in civil war make it somewhat delicate, but the means used are radically new. This is not Christian typology – with its correspondences of Old and New Testament themes – of the sort that would come to dominate Christian art in the Middle Ages and indeed even in the Constantinian period, but it is the same method applied to the relations of past and present in Roman imperial history and ideology.

THE IMPERIAL IMAGE

Huge claims have been made for the portraiture of Constantine – the radical, even unprecedented, ways in which it changed over the period of his reign and its innovative qualities in relation to earlier Tetrarchic imagery.[26] Several points need to be emphasised before an assessment is possible. First, there is an outstanding coin record giving high-quality dated examples of the emperor's portrait, not only in profile, as was usual, but also in a three-quarters turn and full frontal. One can certainly examine these coins alongside a couple of carved gems and the sculpture in marble and bronze. But it is worth worrying about whether these different media reflect a single policy and image or different ones – mutually influenced, no doubt, but not a concerted campaign. Likewise it is worth asking whether the intended viewers of coins and statues responded in the same or similar ways to these very different kinds of media: the coins, intrinsically valuable, exchangeable and handleable; the statues, grand recipients of ritual honours and a backdrop for public life. Second, in relation to both media, the image of the emperor always participated in a complex dynamic whereby any portrait both reflected continuity with the great tradition and at the same time attempted to mark the special and individual difference of the currently portrayed imperial subject from that tradition.

In the Tetrarchic visual culture within which Constantine had grown up, the imperial portrait both on coins and in stone sculpture had taken on an iconic quality. The emperor was figured in a geometric, even an abstract form, whose schematism might be said to emphasise the office over the individuality of its holder. The extreme examples of this kind of image are the porphyry groups of Tetrarchs, now in Venice and in Rome (Fig. 8), where the group of four emperors are represented without individualization or identification, their images frozen into an identikit ideal of collegiate emperorship. This kind of portraiture, in which the identity of an individual is entirely subsumed into his role as ruler, went side by side with much more individualized portraits – in late antique style and usually in stone – although in the absence of inscriptions on the surviving corpus, it is hard to know which emperor is represented by which portrait type.[27]

Constantine's earliest portrait type, as seen on coins of 306–7 struck in Rome after he had just been hailed Augustus by his troops in York in succession to his father, follows the model of Tetrarchic portraiture. With square head, cropped hair, moustache and beard he looks every bit the mid-thirties commander he was when he assumed the throne (Coin 26).[28] But rapidly – especially in the coins struck at Trier, his own imperial capital – a new portrait type emerged which might be defined as mature but youthful, on the model of Augustus, clean-shaven and with a fine Trajanic coiffure (Coin 27).[29] This new type, common to coins, gems, and the three-dimensional portraiture of Constantine, was both a visual break with Tetrarchic patterns of portraiture and at the same time a strong affirmation of age-old Roman visual traditions going back to the ideal emperorship implicit in the images of Augustus – who also remained perpetually youthful in his portraiture – and Trajan. In the sense that the imperial ideal was now to be vested in the single charismatic person of Constantine, this looks back to a period well before the collegiate idealism visually promulgated by the Tetrarchs and projects what may be taken as a bid for unique sole emperorship, which the reign was subsequently to enact. The characteristic nose and large eyes that appear in both coins and portrait heads imply a personal individuality in which that charisma resided (in contrast with the Tetrarchs); they also allowed a familial type to be taken up and exploited by Constantine's heirs as the visual signature of their succession – much as Augustus's portrait type formed a model for the Julio-Claudian princes of his family.

Within the established image, numerous options for nuance were possible. In the years of the dyarchy with Licinius, there are various coin versions of Constantine the military hero, in purposeful profile beside Sol as divine protector (Coin 4)[30] or wearing a high-crested helmet with the Christogram above his brow in a three-quarter turned image alongside a shield emblazoned with the wolf of Rome and what appears to be an orbed cross-sceptre in the background (Coin 1).[31] These kinds of images indicate the complex balancing act of pagan and mythological reference beside Christian affiliation – indeed, Constantine's marked absence of discomfort with the simultaneous use of Christian and pagan imagery may stem from a conception of Christ as something closer to an additional personal protector deity beside the rest of the Roman religious pantheon rather than in place of it. Likewise, Constantine appears fully frontal – like the other late Tetrarchs Maxentius and Licinius – in military dress but with a nimbus (Coin 28).[32] In later years, after the defeat of Licinius and Constantine's assumption of sole emperorship, there is a move to an upturned profile bust with jewelled diadem and enlarged eyes, modelled on the ideal imagery of the Hellenistic kings – a type that has been variously interpreted as flooded with Christian religious enthusiasm or ancient royal charisma (Coin 29).[33] Here the military emphasis is replaced by an inspired regal grandeur. Finally, in the 330s, a last profile type emerged that retains the royal diadem and the staring eyes but has the emperor robed in the vestments of state. This more naturalistically fleshy and finely-modelled image was to establish the type of the imposing majesty of the late Roman emperor (Coin 30).[34] It was to be the model for the portraiture of his dynastic successors (Coin 17). The portrait gems, with Constantine's image incised in amethyst, echo the diadem-wearing profile of charismatic majesty (Fig. 19).[35]

We find the same range of nuance in the imperial role in stone sculpture. The recut second-century reliefs of the Arch of Constantine, as well as the arch's fourth-century sculpture – some of which, it has been suggested, may be reused from Maxentian originals[36] – depict the emperor in a variety of roles of state: as soldier, triumphator, general addressing the troops, priest conducting sacrifice, orator speaking to the populace of Rome, benefactor distributing largesse. A series of statues in Rome (now on the porch of the Lateran and on the balustrade of the Palazzo dei Conservatori) show Constantine, and in one case his son Constantine II, standing in military garb (Fig. 20). These may have been recut from Tetrarchic originals and then possibly displayed in Constantine's baths on the Quirinal.[37] By contrast with this militaristic emphasis, the great colossal statue from the Basilica of Constantine in Rome – perhaps recut from a statue of Maxentius itself recut from a statue of Hadrian – was seated and bare-chested, perhaps in the pose of Jupiter (Fig. 14).[38] The head, breast, arms and legs were fashioned in white marble, while the mantle, which no longer survives, even in fragments, may well have been bronze. It is not impossible that this image carried a sceptre with Christian insignia or with a Victory. The intimations – military, civilian, or divine – of the great bronze head now in the Palazzo dei Conservatori, part of a five-times-life-size colossus from Rome, are not clear (Fig. 15).[39] This image, once earlier considered a portrait of Constantius II but now generally thought to represent Constantine in old age – even posthumously – and to reflect the late type of his coinage, is an outstanding piece of bronze-casting in the late antique style. It falls into a great Roman tradition that looks back most notably to the colossus of Nero and offers a major objection to those who have argued that a decline in technical skill or artistic competence underlies the stylistic changes of the Constantinian period.

The potential ritual significance of these kinds of images is perhaps best examined by turning from the surviving portraits to some lost but well-attested examples. According to the eighth-century *Parastaseis Syntomoi Chronikai*, a Byzantine collection of legends about the foundation of Constantinople, one of the principal acts of the city's consecration on May 11, 330, was the bringing of a gilded statue of Constantine in a chariot to the great porphyry column which had been set up at the centre of the emperor's forum (Fig. 2) and the placing of the statue atop the column.[40] The appearance of the statue is controversial – was it nude or clothed, and if clothed, how? Was it new-cast (like the Rome colossus) or reused (perhaps from a statue of Sol or Apollo)? Was it brought from elsewhere (for instance, from Troy, Heliopolis, or Athens)? What is certain is that it held a lance in the left hand and a globe – perhaps surmounted by a Victory – in the right and wore a radiate crown in emulation of Sol-Helios-Apollo, who not only was a protector of Constantine but was specifically associated with imperial colossi, like that of Nero in Rome (Fig. 3, Coin 15).[41] Every year on May 11 – perhaps starting after Constantine's death in 337 – a festival commemorating the city's birthday was celebrated in which a second gilded wooden statue of Constantine bearing the Tyche of the city in its right hand was escorted in a triumphal chariot from the forum to the Hippodrome. After taking a turn around the course, the image of Constantine met the reigning emperor in his imperial kathisma, provided he was in Constantinople; received his homage; and thence returned to its depository in the forum of Constantine. How long this festival survived is unclear, but it certainly was held through most of the fourth century.[42]

These specific cases from Constantinople, reported by admittedly late and unreliable sources, are a useful reminder that the imperial image in the Constantinian period – and indeed in Roman culture much more generally – played a deeper role than simply establishing a more or less life-like portrait type. The link of Constantine to Sol-Helios, with its echoes of Aurelian's cult of the Sun and of Augustus's affiliation to Apollo, may have had as much significance for the emperor's largely pagan subjects as his affirmation of Christ had for Christians. Indeed, a (biasedly) Christian source, Eusebius's *Life of Constantine*, reports that a wax-encaustic painting showing Constantine and his sons trampling a dragon with "the Saviour's sign placed above" the emperor's head was displayed over the entrance to the imperial palace in Constantinople.[43] One might see this as a visual affirmation of Christianity to go side by side with the visual link to Sol. Moreover, the cultivation of images in ceremonial contexts and on festival days – a usage with deep roots in the polytheistic past – points to an animation of the portrait beyond simply visual likeness into a kind of embodiment of the portrayed. This is apparent in such practices as *damnatio memoriae*, where the images and inscriptions of a condemned person were destroyed,[44] and in the use of the imperial image for purposes of sanctuary or asylum. Little wonder then that the Church Fathers of the fourth century, in the years after Constantine, theorised the relationship of image and prototype as one in which the honour done to an image was transmitted to the emperor himself.[45]

THE IMPERIAL PROGRAMME: PUBLIC ART AND COURT CULTURE

The most striking aspect of Constantine's public monumental programme today is his building of churches in Rome, Palestine, Antioch, and Constantinople.[46] In his own time, however, arguably the most impressive gesture was the founding of a new capital at Constantinople. Both these undertakings had major effects in marking the novelty of the reign's affiliations – a new religion, or perhaps an idiosyncratic cult specially favoured within the mass of polytheistic religions, and a new conceptual centre for the empire in situating its capital so far to the east. Both reorchestrated established space. The churches in Rome and Jerusalem redesigned traditional civic topography through the placement of major imperial benefactions according to an entirely novel pattern (of largely scriptural or martyrological significance) which was to have fundamental effects for the patterns of urban ritual – in the case of Rome, by establishing a new focus of patronage and liturgy on the periphery rather than in the centre of the city. The foundation of Constantinople took the imperial centre to the east of the Mediterranean and demanded a redrawing of the political map quite as radical as that of the religious map – according to which Jerusalem was now the privileged spiritual centre of the Roman world.[47] What might be stressed on the visual side of both these projects is the extensive use of spolia – not only in the architectural fabric of the churches but also in the decoration of Constantinople, which was literally crammed with statuary gathered, in Jerome's words, "by the virtual denuding" of every city in the east.[48]

The vogue for ancient spolia (such as the serpent column still in the Hippodrome in Constantinople, which had originally been part of a tripod from Delphi, or the porphyry statue group of the Tetrarchs that is now on the south-west corner of San Marco in Venice but had been in the Philadelphion in Constantinople) not only lavished an antique dignity on the new capital but also signalled the desacralisation of many of the objects moved to their new locations. In their collection, these kinds of images – including ancient cult statues – became not works of pagan sanctity but aesthetically, as opposed to religiously, valued museum pieces for decorating a city. This interest in collectables from the past appears to be paralleled in private collections of the period, for instance, in the great range of works – from as early as the republic through to the fourth century – found at the late antique villa at Chiragan in southern Gaul.[49] Like the sculptures on the Arch of Constantine, these collections boast a stylistic eclecticism coupled with a rich variety of subjects. By and large these assemblages are not Christian in theme or context, but the very reappropriation and redeployment into private collections of these objects, many with pagan themes, helped to neutralize their religious value to a sort of antiquarian chic which was hardly in opposition to the new Christianising tendency.

Almost nothing survives of the original decoration of any Constantinian church. But the – admittedly problematic – sixth-century *Liber Pontificalis*, which lists Constantine's donations to the Lateran basilica, implies that he adorned Rome's main Christian cathedral with statuary in precious metals that was equivalent to the grandest cult image in any pagan temple:

> A hammered silver *fastigium* [probably a colonnaded canopy] – on the front it has the Saviour seated on a chair, 5 ft in size, weighing 120 lb, and 12 apostles each 5 ft and weighing 90 lb with crowns of the finest silver; for someone in the apse looking at it from behind, it has the Saviour sitting on a throne, 5 ft in size, of finest silver weighing 140 lb, and 4 spear-carrying silver angels, each 5 ft and weighing 105 lb, with jewels of Alabanda in their eyes.[50]

As so often when ancient texts are adduced to reconstruct lost images, this is highly obscure, its details are controversial, and its reliability is at best uncertain.[51] But if we believe any of this, then somewhere between apse and altar, in the most sacred part of the church and precisely where the cult statue would have stood in a pagan temple, was an elaborate statue group in precious metal centred on two figures of Christ enthroned back to back (see the attempted reconstruction at Plan 1 in this volume).[52] The impressive visual impact of pagan cult statuary appears to have been marshalled here to the cause of Constantine's new cult. Similar effects were also achieved in the Lateran baptistery, if we are to believe the *Liber Pontificalis* in its account of Constantine's gift of a golden lamb between five-foot-high silver statues of the Saviour and John the Baptist (see the partial reconstruction at Plan 7 in this volume).[53]

We should not exaggerate the Christianity of these gestures. Although Constantine certainly built one church in his new capital at Constantinople, St Irene,[54] as well as his mausoleum, which may also have been a church,[55] he also consecrated three pagan temples and endowed them with cult images. These were the Capitol, with its triad of Jupiter, Juno, and Minerva (the traditional state deities of the city of Rome),[56] and two temples in the area known as the Basilica, one dedicated to Cybele (a mystery goddess of great significance in both Rome and Asia Minor) and the other to Tyche (or Fortune, a goddess traditionally associated with the protection of eastern cities).[57] We are told relatively little about the images, but the fifth-century historian Zosimus reports that the Cybele, brought to Constantinople from Cyzicus, was a venerable statue, said to have been dedicated originally by Jason and the Argonauts, and if the Tyche was that of Constantinople, who later appears regularly on coins minted there, then the statue was probably newly made in the fourth century (cf. Fig. 3).[58] In effect, in the visual and highly public venue of his religious buildings, Constantine maintained a traditional stance of pious temple dedication while attaching a new significance to Christianity. Architecturally, however, Constantine's Christian churches added a new focus – almost inestimably influential in future patterns of church building – on edifices large enough to contain a sizeable congregation and on sites with a scriptural history, as in the Holy Land, or a reliquary significance, like St. Peter's in Rome. One might argue that the pattern of moving relics to churches, which may have been inaugurated by Constantine himself in his mausoleum at Constantinople,[59] was the brilliant fusion of the aesthetics and pragmatics of the taste for spolia with the rising Christian religious need for holy objects.[60] Effectively, relics – fragments borrowed from the bodies of the saints, just as spolia were fragments borrowed from the fabric of earlier buildings – enabled a genuinely Christian antiquarianism in which the Christian, as opposed to pagan, past could be treasured as a series of collectable material remains with huge sacred potency.

In the matter of burial – one of the most significant forms of imperial self-promotion since Augustus had inaugurated his Principate with the building of a mausoleum in Rome – Constantine seems to have broadly followed the pattern of his Tetrarchic colleagues and predecessors. Like Diocletian, Galerius and Maxentius,[61] Constantine and his family built domed mausolea on a round, octagonal or square plan, large enough to be monumental but small enough to be individual rather than dynastic tombs. The ruins of the mausoleum of the empress Helena, Constantine's mother, survive as the Tor Pignatara adjoining the Constantinian funerary and basilica complex of SS. Marcellino e Pietro on the Via Labicana in Rome (Fig. 21, Plan 3).[62] We do not know its decoration, but – to judge by the extant slightly later mausolea of other family members, namely, S. Costanza in Rome (probably the mausoleum of Constantine's daughter Constantina) and Centcelles near Tarragona in Spain (possibly the burial site of his son Constans) – it was very likely adorned with mosaics in the vault. While the porphyry sarcophagi of Helena (Fig. 22) and Constantina (Fig. 23) were not specifically Christian in theme (and that of Helena rather unsuitably militaristic in subject matter), the mosaics of the vaults of both

Centcelles and S. Costanza mixed generic antique imagery (hunting, vintaging, animals, seasons, and so forth) with at least some explicitly Christian iconography, now largely lost (Fig. 24).[63] These two imperial sarcophagi inaugurate a tradition of the use of porphyry – the purple and hence imperial stone, which had been heavily used by the Tetrarchs – for the coffins of the reigning family. In both cases, the sarcophagi appear to have been visual and virtually reliquary centrepieces within the tombs built around them. Indeed, Tor Pignatara and the sarcophagus of Helena may have been intended for Constantine himself before the move of the capital to Constantinople. Constantine's own mausoleum, established in Constantinople at the end of his reign, is highly controversial – many have argued that it was actually a church, built on the Greek cross plan, although recent arguments for a traditional circular mausoleum may well be correct (Plan 2).[64] What is uncontroversial is the explicitly and unambiguously Christian nature of the building, with monuments (possibly tombs, possibly statues) for the twelve apostles surrounding the tomb of Constantine, which – like those of Helena and Constantina – stood as the building's ostentatious centrepiece.[65]

Very little survives of what might be called the court art of the imperial dynasty. The impressive coffered ceiling of a room from the imperial palace at Trier of the 310s or 320s remains, with painted pairs of putti, philosophers, and busts of female figures jewelled and in one case carrying a jewell box (Fig. 25).[66] But whether this was from a principal chamber or a relatively unimportant room, and therefore whether this decoration was considered grand or commonplace in Trier, is impossible to determine. Certainly the lack of gilding and precious stones and the mere use of paint and trompe l'oeil argue for relative insignificance. But the imposing scale of these figures, their relative frontality, and the lack of interest in background – which they share with the surviving "Roma Barberini" fresco from Rome (perhaps representing Minerva) – as well as a focus on adornment, jewellery, and conspicuous display on the part of the female figures nonetheless illustrate at least some aspects of elite taste in the period. Something more of the grand style of high aristocratic decoration may be gleaned from the surviving remains of the basilica of Junius Bassus, consul in 331, on the Esquiline in Rome. Here the walls were covered with spectacular figurative subjects executed in *opus sectile* technique from sawn marble, hard stones, and glass paste (Fig. 26).[67] The lavish extent and sophisticated panache of the floor mosaics of the period, from the Constantinian villa at Antioch to the elite country villa at Piazza Armerina in rural Sicily, again point to the magnificent decorative possibilities available to those at the peak of the social spectrum in the first third of the fourth century.[68] Like-wise the characteristic fourth-century mythological sculpture associated with Aphrodisian workshops – found not only in Constantinople and Rome but also in villas scatterd across the empire, from St. Georges de Montagne and Chiragan in France, to Valdetorres de Jarama in Spain, to Carthage in North Africa and Amman in the east – indicates something of the wealth of contemporary collectables available to the aristocracy (Fig. 27).[69] These sculptures, all probably from the later rather than the early fourth century,[70] give a suggestion – alongside the other luxury arts – of what sorts and styles of objects were likely to have been in use amongst the elite.

Only one group of objects can be certainly said to have been made for the Constantinian court, and these are the gems. Unfortu-nately, much is controversial – especially the date – about each individual cameo associated with Constantine. They may have been executed in an impressive revival of Claudian style, may have been recut from Julio-Claudian originals, or may in fact be much earlier works mistakenly attributed by modern scholarship to the fourth century.[71] The cameos offer imperial dynastic iconography in the case of the Ada cameo now in Trier (Fig. 28); military imagery, parallel to, say, the sarcophagus of Helena, in the large fragment from an enormous oval plaque now in Belgrade (Fig. 29); and pagan mythological imagery in the case of a gem once drawn by Rubens and now in the Hague.[72] As in the elite imagery from the private sphere in mosaics and prestige sculpture, the gems show a general antiquarianism in both style and subject matter with a taste for traditional themes and little interest in Christianity. In the absence of other evidence, one might conclude that this mix of sophisticated traditionalism and classical antiquarianism represents a likely profile of artistic taste among the elite, at least in the private sphere, during the Constantinian period generally.

ART AND RELIGION

The Constantinian policy on religious toleration clearly took the brake off artistic development in a Christian religious context. Not only in the churches – sponsored by the imperial family and increasingly by local elites and the clergy – but also in more humble commissions like the painted rooms of catacombs or marble sarcophagi, Christian themes were developed with an invention and panache impossible before.[73] It is likely that the workshops responsible for the fourth-century sculptures on the Arch of Constantine also produced a number of surviving sarcophagi.[74] These were both traditional in theme, with mythological subjects like the narrative of Adonis, for instance,[75] and Christian, such as the impressive double-register "Dogmatic Sarcophagus" from the Lateran collection, now in the Vatican.[76] This mix of clientele for workshops meant a constant demand for artists to adapt themes to satisfy the needs of different religious cults or funerary tastes. The popular theme in seasons sarcophagi, for instance, of a tondo with a couple or an individual above vintaging erotes, appears in various third-century sarcophagi and in the great Constantinian Barberini sarcophagus now in Dumbarton Oaks (Fig. 30).[77] It reappears, this time in a Christian iconographic context, in a probably post-Constantinian sarcophagus from San Sebastiano,[78] while the vintaging motif – its significance now presumably Eucharistic rather than Dionysiac – emerges on the lid of the early fourth-century Claudiano sarcophagus[79] and appears repeatedly in such major later monuments as the Junius Bassus and Three Good Shepherds sarcophagi,[80] as well as the mosaics of S. Costanza and the porphyry sarcophagus of Constantina which stood beneath those mosaics (cf. Figs. 23 and 24).[81] The emergence of Christian art as something more than simply a specialised mythological iconography within Roman art more generally owed much to this period of experimentation inaugurated in the early fourth century.

In the case of the catacombs, where dating is largely based on the stylistic comparison of paintings, there appears to have been a clear expansion of both construction and decoration in the aftermath of the Edict of Toleration (Fig. 31).[82] Interestingly, the major attempts to mix pagan subjects with Christian ones – or to replace Christian images with pagan mythological subjects – in both the Via Latina and Marcellino and Pietro Catacombs probably belong to later phases of decoration, when patrons or artists who wanted to assert traditional religion – either against or alongside Christianity – felt the need to do so in the face of what had become, or was increasingly becoming, Christian predominance.[83] The great difficulty in assessing Constantinian art is neither overly to expect earlier Roman patterns of religious patronage, when Christianity was restricted, nor – and this is the major problem – to retroject patterns of patronage and religious affiliation from later in the fourth century, when Christianity took on an increasingly militant ascendancy and pagan polytheism responded with resistance and even some aggression. Under Constantine, there appears to have been a broad tolerance in which – just about for the last time in the Roman world – the numerous cults which together made up Roman religious "pluralism" could indulge in a kind of visual competition in both providing decorated ambiences for their adherents and in potentially using images to attract converts from among the other religions.

Alongside Christianity, the various cults of the Roman empire continued to produce sacred iconography throughout the fourth century and of course continued using ritual artefacts made earlier. A number of securely dated early fourth-century objects and inscriptions have survived from the cult of Cybele and Attis – especially in the area around Rome – and likewise from the religion of Mithras, which is best attested in its archaeological and artistic remains.[84] In Egypt a number of significant examples of traditional cult survive (probably) from the fourth century, including cult images and reliefs of Isis and Horus.[85] Both in Palestine and elsewhere, the fourth century proved a rich era for the production of Jewish iconography and especially synagogues.[86] In the later fourth century, legislation of various kinds would attempt to speed the suppression of these religions and of the great established civic cults of antiquity. Constantine's own subjects, however, would have seen few indications in their visual world that pointed to the radical change of attitudes toward traditional religion which was just around the corner. This was, after all, an emperor who may have legalised Christianity but who also built pagan temples in his new capital city.

CONCLUSION: THE CHIMAERA OF DECLINE?

The literature on the Arch of Constantine, from Raphael's letter to Pope Leo X in the early sixteenth century to Bernard Berenson's monograph of the 1950s, was systematically obsessed with stylistic and qualitative decline.[87] The one valiant exception was the work of Alois Riegl in 1901, which posited a fundamental – and positive – change in artistic attitudes and perceptions in late antiquity, of which the arch served as a paradigmatic case.[88] In the latter part of the twentieth century, as scholars have become increasingly wary of passing qualitative judgements – especially using the criteria of naturalistic style as the benchmark for quality – we have become careful not to be too explicit about "decline." On the other hand, the paradigms for writing the art history of antiquity – which usually end the history of Greek and Roman art with Constantine and start the history of early Christian and Byzantine art at the same moment – might be said to have institutionalised the value judgement of radical change combined with a qualitative dip. How else to explain the break in the seamless flow of history?

The question of decline – which is a long-term issue – returns us directly to the problem of perspectives with which this chapter began. For good or ill, Constantinian art has always been caught in the long view, encapsulated by the arch's juxtaposition of second- and fourth-century relief sculpture, in which its particular manifestations are more frequently judged against past and future productions than most arts of most periods. There are, as I have attempted to suggest, good reasons for this in the problems of evidence and the lack of accuracy with which we can date the objects we do have. But it also means that in studying the arts under Constantine we must inevitably bring to bear a series of more or less explicit assumptions and presuppositions about the "long view." These include, first, the fundamental question of whether one prefers the classical naturalism of the bulk of Graeco-Roman art to the more abstract schematism of medieval art, of which the arts under Constantine were a harbinger – or vice versa. Second, there is the deep and in a post-Christian culture still unavoidable issue of one's Christian investments, or their opposite, and of whether the Christianisation inaugurated by Constantine was more or less of a good thing. Not wholly separate from this is the complex issue of the extent to which Constantine had a Christian programme. In principle, these are questions historians should decide on the basis of the evidence, but here the evidence is so bitty, diffuse, and complicated that its very interpretation usually depends on an implicit position. More than usual, then, the range of the visual arts under Constantine challenges their student to take a position founded on principle or prejudice and to live with the consequences. So, dear reader, over to you!

FURTHER READING

The bibliography on Constantinian art is large and mostly in German. This paragraph is a brief guide to some of the more accessible items (mainly) in English. For late antique art generally – and extending well beyond Constantine – see H. P. L'Orange, *Art Forms and Civic Life* (1965); R. Bianchi Bandinelli, *Rome: The Late Empire* (1971); and J. Elsner, *Imperial Rome and Christian Triumph* (1998a). There is no synoptic view covering all aspects of the art under Constantine – hence I suppose the need for this chapter – but much is discussed (in German) in R. Leeb, *Konstantin und Christus* (1992). There is a useful sketch of much sculptural material in the Constantine chapter of D. Kleiner, *Roman*

Sculpture (1992), with bibliography. For portraiture, see N. Hannestad, "The Ruler Image of the Fourth Century: Innovation or Tradition," in *Imperial Art as Christian Art – Christian Art as Imperial Art*, Acta ad archaeologiam et artium historiam pertinenda XV, ed. J. R. Brandt, and O. Steen (2001): 93–107; D. Wright, "The True Face of Constantine the Great," *Dumbarton Oaks Papers* 41 (1987): 493–507; and R. R. R. Smith, "The Public Image of Licinius I: Portrait Sculpture and Imperial Ideology in the Early Fourth Century," *Journal of Roman Studies* 87 (1997): 170–202. For the Arch of Constantine, see P. Peirce, "The Arch of Constantine: Propaganda and Ideology in Late Roman Art," *Art History* 12 (1989): 387–418; and J. Elsner, "From the Culture of Spolia to the Cult of Relics: The Arch of Constantine and the Genesis of Late Antique Forms," *Papers of the British School at Rome* 68 (2000a): 149–84, with bibliography. On the catacombs, see V. Fiocchi Nicolai, F. Bisconti, and D. Mazzoleni, *The Christian Catacombs of Rome* (1999), and L. Rutgers, *Subterranean Rome* (2000).

NOTES

1   For a brief synopsis, see Elsner 2000b, 261, with nn. 44 and 45.
2   The argument has raged since Riegl 1901 and Strzygowski 1901, on which see Brendel 1979, 25–68, and Elsner 2002.
3   See Bergmann 1998a, esp. 267–81 on the third and fourth centuries and 282–90 on Constantine.
4   Boschung 1993 catalogues 217 items, excluding uncertain and later examples as well as fakes.
5   L'Orange 1984 catalogues fifty examples.
6   I am thinking especially of Zanker 1988 for Augustus.
7   For AD 325–6, see Richardson 1975; for AD 312–15 (the majority view), see Buttrey 1983, 375–80.
8   See, e.g., S. Walker and Bierbrier 1997 for the application of these principles to the (re)dating of the Fayum portraits.
9   For some reflections, see M. Bergmann in Ensoli and La Rocca 2000, 237–43.
10 See Levi 1948, 226.
11 The literature on the arch is vast. Fundamental is L'Orange and von Gerkan 1939. For photographs, see esp. Giuliano 1956. In English, see Berenson 1954; Brilliant 1984, 119–23; Peirce 1989; Elsner 2000a; Holloway 2004, 19–53; Marlowe 2004, 158–204.
12 On some of these losses, see Gradara 1918; Magi 1956–7; Pensabene and Panella 1993–4, 184, 191–2.
13 The recent polemic about when the arch was first constructed and how it was adapted is intense. See Melucco Vaccaro and Ferroni 1993–4 against Pensabene and Panella 1993–4 and 1999, with further references. For what it is worth, I agree with the majority view that the arch is a fourth-century creation.

14 On the complex, see, e.g., Bergmann 1998b, 11–125.

15 The specific literature is again large; see Kleiner 1992 for discussions and bibliography on the Hadrianic (pp. 220–3, 264), Trajanic (pp. 251–3, 265) and Aurelian (pp. 288–95, 314) materials.

16 See Waelkens 1985, 645; Packer 1997, 1:437–8.

17 On this recutting, see Elsner 2000b, 163 with n. 22, for the still very active argument about which other Tetrarch was portrayed.

18 See Evers 1991 on recuttings of Hadrian and Giuliano 1991 on recuttings of Augustus.

19 This activity is described by the modern term *damnatio memoriae*. See, e.g., Vittinghoff 1936; Kinney 1997; Stewart 1999; Varner 2000.

20 See Ward-Perkins 1999, 227–33, on pragmatism, and see Kinney 1997, 146, for the argument that the recarving of an earlier emperor meant his eradication.

21 See Elsner 2000b, 173–4.

22 See L'Orange and von Gerkan 1939, 34–102; Koeppel 1990, 38–64, with previous bibliography; Kuhoff 1991; Giuliani 2000.

23 On spolia in general, see, e.g., Deichmann 1975; Pensabene 1995; Poeschke 1996; Kinney 1997, 2001b.

24 On Constantinian spolia, see Pensabene 1993, 1999; Pensabene and Panella 1993–4, 125–37; Kinney 1995; Elsner 2000a, 153–62; Meier 2001, 63–8; Wohl 2001.

25 See Elsner 2000a, 163–75.

26 E.g., Wright 1987, 507: "No other emperor changed his public image as drastically or so often, and none was more resourceful in manipulating his portrait for propagandistic effect"; Kleiner 1992, 434: "The most extraordinary transformation of an emperor in the history of Roman portraiture." The literature is large and mostly German. See Delbrueck 1933, 110–32; L'Orange 1933, 47–65; 1984, 38–80, 118–28; Harrison 1967; Sydow 1969, 22–43; Calza 1972, 209–47; Leeb 1992, 53–70; M. Alföldi 1999, 172–89. Specifically on coinage, see M. Alföldi 1963 and Kent and Hirmer 1978, 48–52, for an overview with excellent photographs.

27 On Tetrarchic portraiture, the literature again is large and mainly in German. Fundamental are L'Orange 1933, 15–46; 1984, 3–36; Sydow 1969, 5–16; Calza 1972, 14–208; Bergmann 1977, 163–79, very incisive on stylistic matters; Baratte 1995. Recent accounts in English include Kleiner 1992, 400–8; Rees 1993; R. R. R. Smith 1997, 179–83.

28 E.g., *RIC* 6 Rome 141 (pl. 6).

29 *RIC* 7 Trier 21 (pl. 3). Cf. Zanker in Fittschen and Zanker 1985, 147–52, no. 122, Wright 1987; R. R. R. Smith 1997, 185–7; Hannestad 2001, 95–8.

30 Kent and Hirmer 1978, no. 648. Also at R. R. R. Smith 1997, pl. 11.3.

31 *RIC* 7 Ticinum 36 (pl. 9). Also at Kleiner 1992, 435, no. 395.

32 *RIC* 7 Ticinum 41 (pl. 9) = Kent and Hirmer 1978, no. 629. Also at M. Alföldi 1963, pl. 4.61; R. R. R. Smith 1997, pl. 11.2. On the nimbus, see Hannestad 2001, 99–100; Ahlquist 2001.

33 *RIC* 7 Siscia 206 (pl. 13). Also at R. R. R. Smith 1997, pl. 11.5. See analysis at Wright 1987, 505–6; R. R. R. Smith 1997, 187 and n. 100.

34 *RIC* 7 Thessalonica 174 (pl. 16). See analysis at Wright 1987, 506; R. R. R. Smith 1997, 187.

35 See M. Alföldi 1963, 129. For the gems in general, see Zazoff 1983, 328 and n. 149;
    cf. Ensoli and La Rocca 2000, 77 and nn. 55 and 56, with up-to-date bibliography.
    They are conveniently illustrated and collected in Delbrueck 1933, pl. 74.

36 E.g., Knudsen 1989 and 1990.

37 See Heintze 1979; Zanker in Fittschen and Zanker 1985, 144–7, 151, nos. 120 and
    121, and C13, for no. 122.

38 See Zanker in Fittschen and Zanker 1985, 147–52, no. 122; Nicholson 2001b,
    178–84.

39 See Zanker in Fittschen and Zanker 1985, 152–5, no. 123; Ensoli 2000; Lahusen
    and Formiglioli 2001, 315–7.

40 See Bauer 2001, 31–4, with bibliography.

41 For recent discussion of the statue, see Fowden 1991, 125–31; Leeb 1992, 12–17;
    Mango 1993a, 1–6; La Rocca 1993, 557–61; Bergmann 1998a, 284–7.

42 See Bauer 2001, 34–6. It is worth noting that the seventh-century *Chronicon Paschale*
    dates the erection of the statue on the porphyry column to 328 but records this
    ceremony with the gilded wooden statue in May 330; *Chron. Pasch.* pp. 529–30.

43 Eus. *VC* 3.3.1; cf. Cameron and Hall 1999, 255–6, with bibliography.

44 Briefly, Elsner 1998a, 54–8.

45 See Setton 1941, 196–211.

46 Generally see Alexander 1971 and Krautheimer 1993, though these are more
    optimistic in attributing foundations to Constantine than is perhaps warranted. Cf.
    Leeb 1992, 71–92, and Chapter 12 of this volume. On Rome, see Curran 2000,
    90–114, with bibliography, and Holloway 2004, 57–155. On Jerusalem, Mamre, and
    Bethlehem, see, e.g., Hunt 1997 with bibliography. On Antioch, see Krautheimer
    1993, 539–40, 547, with bibliography. Constantinople is particularly difficult, as
    the foundations of many of the city's churches were later attributed to Constantine.
    Largely following Dagron 1974, 388–409, I would prefer to be cautious and accept
    only St. Irene and the mausoleum – itself not certainly a church – as Constantinian.

47 For some reflections on this issue, see Elsner 2000c, 189, 194–5.

48 Jer. *Chron* s.a. 314. On this spolia, see, e.g., Mango 1990c, 55–9; Bassett 1991,
    1996, 2004, and Chapter 7 in this volume.

49 See Hannestad 1994, 127–41; Bergmann 1999, 26–43, 55, 68–70; Stirling 2005,
    49–62.

50 *Liber pont.* 34.9–10 (trans. Davis); cf. Duchesne 1955, 1:172. On altars in Constan-
    tine's Roman churches, see Blaauw 2001b, 969–73.

51 The *Liber pontificalis* admits that the fastigium was plundered by the Goths and
    replaced by the emperor Valentinian III at the request of Pope Xystus in the 430s,
    a strong indication that the details of the Constantinian fastigium, unless the result
    of an accurate archival record, may well be embroidered with later fantasy. See
    Liber pont. 46.4; Duchesne 1955, 1:233.

52 See Teasdale Smith 1970; Krautheimer, Corbett, and Frazer 1937–77, 5:88; Blaauw
    2001a with recent bibliography.

53 *Liber pont.* 34.13; cf. Duchesne 1955, 1:174. On Constantine and the Lateran bap-
    tistery, see O. Brandt 2001 with bibliography.

54 E.g., Alexander 1971, 318–9. Unless we add the two martyr churches on the out-
    skirts (St. Mokios and St. Akakios) on the model of Rome's extramural churches,
    with Mango 1990c, 35–6; but need these be Constantinian (Dagron 1974, 383–5),
    and need the model of Rome apply in Constantinople?

55 The literature is vast and filled with much uncertainty. See the discussions and bibliography in Mango 1990a; Leeb 1992, 93–120.

56 See Mango 1990c, 30; Bassett 2004, 31–2, 35, 124.

57 See Mango 1959, 44; Bassett 2004, 24, 34, 72, 155–6.

58 On Cybele, see Zos. 2.31.2, referred to as Rhea; cf. Amelung 1899. On Tyche, see Zos. 2.31.3; Soc. 3.11.4; cf. Toynbee 1947, 136–7, but beware the Christian bias here. Mango 1959, 44, suggests that Cybele/Rhea was dedicated as the Fortune of Constantinople and Tyche as the Fortune of Rome.

59 Again this is controversial. See Mango 1990b; Woods 1991; Burgess 2003.

60 See Elsner 2000a, 157–62.

61 For a brief discussion and bibliography, see Curcic 1996; Elsner 1998a, 158–65; and Chapter 12 in this volume.

62 See Deichmann and Tschira 1957.

63 On Centcelles, see Schlunk 1988. On S. Costanza, see Stern 1958.

64 Mango 1990a with Curcic 1996, 55–6. Also Leeb 1992, 93–120, for the traditional view.

65 See Elsner 2000a, 157–8, with bibliography.

66 Discussions in W. Weber 1984; Brandenburg 1985; Simon 1986.

67 Becatti 1969, 181–215; Sapelli in Ensoli and La Rocca 2000, 137–9, 534–6, with bibliography.

68 On the Constantinian villa at Antioch, see Levi 1948, 236–44. On Piazza Armerina, see Carandini, Ricci, and de Vos 1982.

69 See Bergmann 1999.

70 See Bergmann 1999, 15–17. So too the extensive survivals of mid to late fourth-century silver plate, on which see, e.g., Kent and Painter 1977.

71 For an inclusivist view, see Bruns 1948 and Zadoks-Josephus Jitta 1966. More circumspect are Spier 1993, 43–5, and Sande 2001, 150–2, who argues for fourth-century recutting of first-century products in all cases.

72 Brief accounts with bibliography in Spier 1993, 44–5.

73 For Constantinian sarcophagi, see Koch 2000, 249–80 (Rome), 476–9 (Gaul). For the catacombs in the Constantinian period and its immediate aftermath, see Fiocchi Nicolai, Bisconti, and Mazzoleni 1999, 37–48; Rutgers 2000, 108–17.

74 See L'Orange and von Gerkan 1939, 219–29.

75 E.g., for the fragment from the Museo Pio Clementino, see Brandenburg 1979b, 453–4.

76 See Bovini and Brandenburg 1967, no. 43.

77 See Hanfmann 1951; Kranz 1984, no. 34. Cf. Kranz 1984, nos. 52, 54, 66, for other examples.

78 See Bovini and Brandenburg 1967, no. 188.

79 See Bovini and Brandenburg 1967, no. 771.

80 Respectively Bovini and Brandenburg 1967, nos. 680 and 29.

81 See Stern 1958, 198–200; Bovini and Brandenburg 1967, no. 174.

82 To this period may be dated various sections of the Catacombs of Priscilla, the Via Anapo, and Marcellino e Pietro (including most of the famous painted decoration there in sections X and Y), as well as the "Eusebius" region of the Callistus Catacomb, and cubicula A–C in the the Via Latina Catacomb. See, e.g., Fiocchi Nicolai, Bisconti, and Mazzoleni 1999, 37; Tronzo 1986, 11–15.

83 So room 79 of the Marcellino e Pietro Catacomb (where Orpheus appears) is dated to the era of Valentinian (AD 364–75) by Deckers, Seeliger, and Mietke 1987, 348–50; cubicula E and N of the Via Latina Catacomb respectively to the 340s and 370s by Tronzo 1986, 15–17. However, room 66 (the "athletes room") of Marcellino e Pietro is thought to be Constantinian by Deckers, Seeliger, and Mietke 1987, 319–20. This mixing of pagan and Christian subjects is true not only of catacomb painting but also of other later fourth-century examples of "syncretism" on silverware, for instance, or in the texts of the Codex Calendar of 354. On aspects of the syncretism question, see Elsner 1998b, 744–8; 2003, 76–89.

84 For the certainly dated items on Cybele and Attis, see Vermaseren 1977–89, vol. 3, nos. 8, 226, 234, 315; vol. 4, no. 84; vol. 5, nos. 50, 94, 97, 182, 209, 210; vol. 6, nos. 8 and 188. On Mithras, see Vermaseren 1956–60, 1:362, 2:439.

85 For Isis Lactans, see, e.g., Tran Tam Tinh 1973, 54–5; Mathews and Muller 2005. For Horus, see, e.g., Effenberger et al. 1996, 84.

86 See Hachlili 1988, 396–400, on the Holy Land, and Hachlili 1998, 454–8, on the Diaspora.

87 For a brief review of this literature, see Elsner 2000a, 149–52.

88 See Elsner 2002, 361–70.

Addendum: In the summer of 2005 a 60 centimeter marble head of Constantine was discovered in the Forum of Trajan in Rome that will add important insights into ongoing discussions of his portraiture.

12: ARCHITECTURE OF EMPIRE

Mark J. Johnson

A mong the emperor's vast responsibilities was the duty to build. Every emperor who ruled for more than a short time became responsible for founding or refounding cities, renovating or rebuilding old public buildings, and constructing new ones. Temples, public basilicas, baths, palaces, and mausolea were all objects of imperial patronage with a variety of functions. Constantine followed his predecessors in this regard; indeed, he would surpass most of them. A variety of conditions determined who among the emperors would be great builders. First, the emperor needed the disposition and desire to commit resources to the construction of public and private structures. Some felt this impetus more strongly than others. In addition, an emperor who wanted to build needed the resources of land and money and the willingness to commit these to construction endeavors. The builder also needed a motive, whether to make a political statement, to engage in a heartfelt or public display of piety or largesse, or simply to fulfill the genuine needs of a city or province. Finally, the great builder needed time. Large construction projects often took years to complete, and thus the longer one ruled, the greater the opportunities to build. In Constantine's case, all of these factors obtained.

Like other great builders, Constantine possessed a desire to leave his mark in various cities of the empire and especially in his two capital cities, Rome and Constantinople. The defeat of his rivals gave him the resources needed to launch numerous construction projects, and his reign of three decades the time to see most of those to completion. He was also motivated by necessity and desire and was involved with projects that had traditionally been a part of imperial patronage, such as public baths. Beyond these usual motivations, an important aspect of Constantine's building program was the fact that, for the first time in

Roman history, an emperor was actively involved in the promotion of the Christian religion. Previously the growing Christian communities in the cities of the empire had never enjoyed the privilege of meeting in public buildings and had instead been relegated to house-churches, the residences of wealthy congregants that were often left as legacies to the local Christian community. The growth of Christianity and the emperor's involvement with it demanded a massive new building campaign that would both accommodate the day-to-day needs of the various Christian congregations throughout the empire and also honor the sites most significant to the faith.[1] A need and an opportunity had arisen, and Constantine responded with the resources of an emperor to take advantage of that opportunity and meet that need.

The earliest building project attributable to Constantine is the audience hall known as the Aula Palatina or Basilica, a part of the palace complex at Trier (Fig. 32).[2] Located in the northeastern quarter of the city, most of the palace is now in ruins and remains largely unexcavated. The audience hall, its only standing remnant, was nevertheless preserved because of its conversion into a church, and thus it remains unquestionably the best preserved Constantinian architectural monument in the world. The basilica can be dated by a coin found embedded in the mortar of one wall that dates to 305 and by the panegyric delivered to Constantine at Trier in 310, which seems to mention the newly completed structure when it refers to the *sedes iustitiae* (seat of justice) of the city.[3]

The audience hall is unique not just as the largest fully standing Constantinian building but also as the only fully standing example of Roman palace architecture to survive to the present day. The type, a rectangular structure with an entrance at one short end and an apse at the other, had been used in palace architecture going back at least to Domitian and the Flavian Palace on the Palatine hill in Rome. The exterior, typical of late Roman architecture, is austere, with red brick – faced concrete articulated by large arches on piers extending up through two tiers of windows. Gone are the two courtyards that once flanked the building as well as any other exterior decoration. Inside is a single large hall covered by a wood truss roof whose beams are exposed to view. Now as austere as the exterior, the interior walls originally were covered with slabs of marble revetment that added color and variegated patterns to the interior. Where now stands the altar once stood the imperial throne, at the far end of the building's axis as one entered the door. As significant as the building is for its place in palace architecture, it also holds one of the keys for understanding the development of monumental early Christian church architecture. The plan – its arrangement of door and apse as well as the simplicity of its construction – and the symbolism of the audience hall would be repeated in the large Christian churches that Constantine would begin building within a few years.

By the end of 312 Constantine had taken possession of Rome, where he would spend relatively little time, choosing to rule from other cities and eventually founding a new capital at Constantinople. Rome, however, was rich in tradition as the historical seat of the empire, and it also contained numerous sites important to the growing Christian faith. These factors kept Constantine's interest in the city alive despite his unconcern for living there and would create the motives leading to Constantine's significant architectural patronage in the city (see Map 3.1).[4]

Though his more revolutionary projects would be in the realm of Christian church architecture, the emperor did not neglect his responsibilities to all Romans, nor did he ignore the imperial tradition of bestowing largess upon the capital city in the form of monumental architecture. Maxentius had initiated work on numerous buildings, some of which Constantine himself completed, and Constantine also added others as the ongoing work of beautifying the city continued.

Perhaps the most striking and certainly the most grandiose of Maxentius's Roman projects was the Basilica Nova, a massive public hall in the heart of the city on the Via Sacra. The Basilica Nova was apparently nearing completion in October 312, so Constantine's role was in overseeing its end phase and adding some modifications (Plan 6).[5] The building, a huge structure designed along the lines of a cross-vaulted rectangular *frigidarium* (cold bathing room) like that in the recently completed Baths of Diocletian, had its entrance and vestibule facing the temple of Venus and Rome to the east and had an apse on the west. A new entrance with a monumental staircase facing the Palatine to the south was built and a new apse, aligned to this entrance, was built on the north side of the building. In the original apse was placed the famous colossal enthroned statue of Constantine, parts of which are now in the Capitoline Museum (Fig. 14). The building, like other late Roman structures, was plain on the exterior, with its brick covered in stucco drafted to look like ashlar masonry, but its interior was lavishly appointed with marble revetment and stucco decoration, bits of which remain in situ. Its tall central space was directly illuminated by light entering through enormous thermal windows placed under the cross vaults; its side aisles were darker but impressively covered with a series of coffered barrel vaults set at right angles to the main axis of the building.

Not far away to the east stood the Flavian Amphitheater, and near it – at the point where the Via Sacra began its climb up the Velia hill and down into the Forum – a triumphal arch was erected to honor Constantine and his victory over Maxentius (Fig. 1).[6] The form of the arch was derived from that of Septimius Severus in the Forum, with a large central archway flanked by two smaller ones that pierce the wide piers of the structure. Freestanding columns are placed in front of the piers, and a large attic bearing the dedicatory inscription completes the structure. Relief sculpture – some made expressly for this arch, most borrowed from other commemorative structures originally built to honor Trajan, Hadrian, and Marcus Aurelius – decorate the monument. Another, typically Tetrarchic victory monument, a four-piered archway known as the Janus Quadrifrons, was built on the other side of the Palatine in the Forum Boarium (Fig. 11). A very similar quadrifrons archway – called Malborghetto since its transformation into a medieval palace – was also built along the Via Flaminia just north of Rome near where Constantine defeated Maxentius's forces on October 28, 312 (Fig. 10).[7]

Like many of his predecessors, Constantine also erected a large public bath complex, the last of the imperial baths to be constructed in Rome. Located on the Quirinal hill and partially constructed on an artificial terrace, the Baths of Constantine survive in only a few tracts of walls, though Renaissance plans and drawings offer a reasonable impression of their original appearance (Fig. 33). Smaller than other imperial bath complexes, Constantine's shared the same basic design, employing axial symmetry, with the principal rooms of the *frigidarium, tepidarium* (warm room), and *caldarium* (hot room) aligned on the short axis of the building, and other rooms arranged symmetrically to either side of this axis. As at the Baths of Caracalla, the *caldarium* was a domed rotunda and was placed on the southern side of the building. Most of the brickstamps found on the site are Maxentian, leading to the supposition that here too Constantine may have finished a building that had been begun by Maxentius.[8] On the other hand, the stamps could simply mean that the bricks were produced during his predecessor's reign but used here in a project initiated by Constantine, to whom the baths are, after all, attributed by Aurelius Victor.[9]

In the southeast corner of the city, the Sessorian Palace complex, consisting of a residence, circus, small amphitheater, gardens, and public baths of Severan date, received the emperor's attention when it became the residence of his mother Helena, perhaps around 317.[10] The baths were remodeled and became known as the Thermae Helenianae. Little survives of the palace itself, though part of an audience hall stands, as does another structure, converted by Helena into a church. The nearby Licinian pavilion was probably built as a place for entertaining guests within its private garden (Fig. 34).[11] Its date is given variously, from c. 300 to 320, and whether it was built by Constantine or one of his predecessors, he at least had a role in its remodeling. An unusual decagonal plan is defined by ten piers that rise to support a drum and dome, representing an important example of a point support system. Between the piers are niches, except on the sides in which the spaces were left open, allowing a view of the surrounding gardens, a design that clearly demonstrates the continuing high level of innovation found in Roman architecture even at this late date.

In completing these projects, Constantine was simply fulfilling one of the expectations of an emperor, that of funding and constructing buildings that would benefit the population of the city or his imperial family. In the projects connected with the remodeling of the Sessorian palace on behalf of Helena, Constantine was also demonstrating an interest in this particular part of the city, the Caelian hill. This quarter had evolved into one of the nicer residential districts of the city, a place where several of the most important families had their homes. Constantine's patronage in this area would not be limited to the residence, for it was here, just a short walk from the palace, that he choose to build a much more revolutionary structure, the first great Christian church building, the Lateran Basilica (Fig. 12).[12]

Prior to the time of Constantine, Christians had apparently been meeting for the most part in simple structures, often houses converted into meeting halls, a number of which are known through excavations in Rome and elsewhere. Sources talk of Christian churches before the time of Constantine, often in the context of their destruction during the persecutions, especially the Great Persecution, but nothing is really known of their form and appointments, so it is hard to say just how innovative the design of Constantine's new building really was. It is a safe assumption, however, that none of the earlier churches would have been built on the scale that he envisioned. This was to be a grand building, one that befitted both its importance as an imperial foundation and the importance of the bishop and city of Rome (see Map 3.2).

There is reason to believe that idea of constructing a major Christian building to service the needs of the bishop and faithful of Rome arose almost immediately after the victory at the Milvian Bridge. A later medieval source indicates that it may have been founded as early as November 312, meaning that the construction of the first major church building in the Roman world was one of the first actions taken by Constantine following his victory.[13] Although the sources are silent on the process that led to the initiation of this project, it can be imagined that Constantine would have met with the bishop of Rome soon after his entry into the city and discussed it. There was a need for a building large enough to accommodate a sizable congregation and a place suitable for the bishop of the capital, but there was also the likelihood that Constantine wished to signal his support for the Christian faith in a highly visible manner.

Much has been written about the choice of the site for this large, new Christian edifice. Located just inside of the Aurelian Walls at the Porta Tuscolana, the church rose on ground recently cleared by the destruction of the barracks of the Equites Singulares, Maxentius's elite imperial horseguard, which Constantine had just disbanded. It has been argued that Constantine choose this site on the edge of the city as a way of avoiding upsetting the still pagan aristocracy of the capital.[14] While in some sense the choice of location represented a shrewd political move on the part of Constantine, it was also very much a practical and logical decision. Land under direct imperial control for building a large structure was available here, whereas in all likelihood it would have been much more difficult to obtain suitable land near the city center. All the same, it must have been striking to the Roman public that a massive monument to the emperor's newfound Christian religion stood over the former headquarters of his pagan rival's first line of defense.

Known as the Basilica Salvatoris and the Basilica Constantiniana, it eventually came to be called St. John in Lateran and remains the pope's official *cathedra* in Rome. The new church was completed no later than the early 320s and was richly endowed by Constantine with precious gifts for liturgical use and lands to provide income for its continued maintenance.[15] None of these dependent tracts was located in the east, that is, none was acquired by Constantine following his defeat of Licinius in 324, an indication that the building was completed and functioning by that date.

The church was clearly designed to serve as more than a neighborhood meeting place. It is a large structure, over three hundred feet long from its entrance to the end of its original apse (Plan 1). The design of the building was another permutation of the common Roman type, the basilica. The building faces east, towards the rising sun, in the manner of a pagan temple. A large central nave, illuminated with clerestory windows and covered by an open-beam roof, is flanked on each side by double side-aisles. Columns in the nave were of red granite, those separating the side aisles were of green granite. Two lateral spaces occupied the location of the present transept, while the apse was semicircular, inside and out. Although the building was heavily remodeled by the architect Borromini in the seventeenth century, it was not destroyed but largely encased within new walls and piers, a remodeling that hides the details of the structure but maintains its original sense of space and spatial divisions.

Much has been written about the origins of the Christian basilica as seen here and in the churches to follow soon after. The completed Basilica Constantiniana would not have struck contemporary Romans as an unusual building. Although it might have seemed strange that such a large edifice was dedicated to Christian use, the architectural type would have been familiar enough. The rectangular plan, the rows of columns, the clerestory windows, and the open-beam roof would all have been familiar as components of the Roman public basilica and also of an imperial audience hall like the one in Trier. While many public basilicas had entrances on their long sides and apses on both short ends, there were also some that had the major entrance on one short end, on axis with the apse at the opposite end.

Much has also been written concerning the symbolism of the building and whether or not people would have found imperial associations with the type and with the particular axial design used here and in other Christian basilicas.[16] Here, too, the sources are not as explicit as could be hoped, but it is hard to believe that most Romans would not have been aware of some connections with the imperial court and its ceremony. It is probably more in how the building was decorated and used, rather than its design, that those connections would have been clearest to the Roman viewer. The axial design lent itself well to accommodating liturgical processions, which were in part based on the ceremony of the court. The decoration – especially the gift of an enormous silver *fastigium* that Constantine commissioned for the church – would also have been recognized as an imperial symbol.[17] In short, the typical Roman would probably not have confused a Christian basilica with either a public basilica or an audience hall but would have recognized elements common to both. The emperor's new religion was thus to be endowed with the trappings of empire, a move that probably seemed more natural to contemporaries than we moderns might suspect.

Further speculation centers around Constantine's role in the choice of this particular architectural type for Christian use.[18] Here, too, the sources are silent on what his exact role may have been. In the one example of a building where his role is documented, that of the Holy Sepulcher in Jerusalem, Constantine seems not so much to have chosen exactly what to build as to have approved the project and helped facilitate its completion.[19] It could be surmised that, as the project for the Basilica Constantiniana was being discussed, the need for a large structure that could accommodate processions was expressed. A variation of the basilica must have been put forth as a logical solution, yet it can be imagined that, while Constantine approved the plan, the site, and the budget, he might not have taken an active role in delineating the particulars of the design.

Constantine also provided a place for the bishop to live, perhaps centered around the Domus Faustae located nearby and mentioned in sources as having hosted a church council. This palace would evolve and grow over time before being destroyed and replaced in the 1580s. And a baptistery was constructed on the site, located behind the apse of the church (Plan 7).[20] A bathhouse was destroyed to make way for the new building, and its plumbing reused to service the font. The walls of the new structure were laid out in an octagonal plan, and a rectangular vestibule with apses at each end was added later. The baptistery, with its plain brick-faced concrete walls, still stands, surrounded by structures added by later popes. Inside, eight porphyry columns originally stood in the corners of the octagon while a circular font stood in the center, the whole covered by a dome. Here, too, Constantine provided sumptuous gifts of silver and gold, including silver statues of stags seemingly drinking from the fountain of life represented by the font.[21]

As for the previously mentioned Sessorian Palace, a largely private imperial structure, Constantine also decided to convert a part of the complex into a church called Hierusalem (Jerusalem);[22] greatly expanded, this became the church now called S. Croce in Gerusalemme. At some point this church came to house a relic of the True Cross, purportedly discovered by Helena during her pilgrimage to the Holy Land, probably in 327. In this case, a rectangular hall, in essence a basilica-like form, was remodeled with the addition of an apse on the east end and transversal arcades set into the hall (Plan 8). Created from a room in the palace, it may have served as a palace chapel for Helena and her court, though it eventually was opened for the entire Christian community. Apart from this and the Lateran basilica, Constantine built only one other church within the walls of the city, a basilica constructed at the behest of Pope Mark and dedicated to St. Mark.[23] Largely replaced in the ninth century by the present church of S. Marco set within the later

Palazzo Venezia, very little is known of the original church, though it seems to have been modest.

To judge by sheer numbers and the level of resources allocated, Constantine's building interests in Rome were focused heavily, not so much on these intramural churches, but rather on the growth of the cult of the saints and the elevation of the tombs of martyrs that were found along the major roads leading out from the city.[24] The most important of these was surely his church to St. Peter, which stood on the site now still occupied by the Renaissance structure that replaced it.[25] According to a very early tradition, Peter was buried in a tomb in the Vatican region west of the Tiber River, in a cemetery located next to the Circus of Caligula and Nero, in or near the imperial Gardens of Domitilla. The tomb, which was rediscovered through excavations in the mid-twentieth century, had been the object of veneration from an early period and had received modest architectural embellishment in the form of a simple aedicula in around AD 200. At an uncertain date, but probably close to 320, Constantine made the decision to honor it on a grand scale with a large basilica, placed so that the chord of its apse would be aligned with the aedicula marking the burial place of Peter. The location, on the slope of the Vatican hill, necessitated the leveling of the site and the covering of the cemetery – with its mostly pagan tombs – under the floor of the new building.

The tomb of Peter dictated the layout of the building, whose apse, set at the west end of a long basilica, marked its location (Plan 9). As at St. John in Lateran, the church of Old St. Peter's was orientated to the east. It was preceded by a propylea (monumental gateway) that led into an atrium (a courtyard surrounded by columned porticoes). The portico on the west acted as a vestibule to the basilica proper and gave entry to the nave and its flanking double side-aisles. The nave, taller than the side aisles, was illuminated by clerestory windows (Fig. 35). Large columns and capitals, reused from earlier structures, supported the nave wall and, in turn, an open-beam roof. Between the end of the nave and the apse was a transept, or transversal hall, as tall as the nave itself. This created a large space in front of the top of the aedicula of Peter's tomb, which rose out of the floor in front of the apse.

The transept would eventually become a very common element in church design, but in early Christian architecture, especially in Italy, it was rare. Its appearance here is a sign of the unique function of this particular church. The transept here served as the setting for the veneration of Peter in his tomb. Connected with this idea is the fact that the nave and side aisles functioned not only as a setting for processions and the gathering of a congregation but also as a covered cemetery for literally hundreds of faithful who chose to be buried near Peter in his tomb. Those seeking this afterlife connection with the saint would eventually include the western Roman emperors, many of whom were buried in the rotunda of S. Petronilla, attached to the south transept arm probably by Honorius in the early fifth century. Other changes, including the creation of a crypt and the raising of the floor of the apse as well as decoration in fresco and mosaic, would be added over the years. After almost twelve hundred years of existence, Pope Julius II decided that the crumbling structure needed to be replaced, and the project to build a new church in place of the old was begun. Over the next century as work progressed on the new church, the remnants of the old were torn down until nothing remained save for a few tracts of the foundation walls, a few pieces of the decoration, and some salvaged architectural elements.

The date of the construction of Old St. Peter's is not specified in any of the literary sources, and, while several inscriptions from the church are known, their interpretation has varied.[26] Regardless, the dating can be narrowed to the period of the 320s. First, a coin found in a closed urn in one of the tombs under the basilica provides a lower terminus of 317–20. Second, the lands that Constantine donated to the church for its upkeep were all located in the east, in territory acquired following Constantine's victory over Licinius in September 324, suggesting the church was completed – or was nearing completion – after that date. Finally, the inscription of a gold cross donated to the church by Constantine and his mother Helena refers to her as Augusta, a title first accorded her in 324.[27] The date of Helena's death, though uncertain, probably falls between 328 and 329, thus the cross bearing her name as donor had to have been given by the end of the decade. There is no valid reason to suppose that construction would have dragged on for decades, as some have suggested. Other buildings as large or larger, some with complicated vaulting systems such as the Baths of Diocletian, had been constructed by the Romans in five to seven years.

At the same time, Constantine also embarked on a campaign of building memorial churches that would both honor the location of martyrs' burials and, like Old St. Peter's, provide a covered cemetery for those seeking burial near the martyrs and a setting for the funerary feasts held in honor of dead relatives. These churches were also linked by a particular architectural form, yet another variation on the basilica (Plan 10). The cemetery church type is characterized by an entrance wall on the east that is angled slightly so that the long walls of the church behind it are slightly off perpendicular. On the opposite end, the aisles curve around the end of the nave and join together in an ambulatory, providing a path for processions, presumably for the *circumambulatio* performed to honor the dead in their graves, which would be under the floor of the nave and aisles. The rectangular structure with one oblique end angled like the *carceres* (starting gates) of a circus and the opposite end curving like the *sphendone* (curved end) of a circus has led to the designation "circiform." It has also invited iconographic interpretation on the part of scholars who have noted how circus imagery is found in a funerary context in Roman art and how this seems to have been adopted by the Christians.[28]

These churches outside of Rome have been, for the most part, directly linked to Constantine. They include the churches of SS. Marcellino e Pietro on the Via Labicana (modern Via Casilina), S. Lorenzo at the base of the Verano hill, S. Agnese on the Via Nomentana, a newly discovered church on the Via Ardeatina, S. Sebastiano, earlier known as the Basilica Apostolorum, on the Via Appia, and one of unknown dedication in the area of the Villa Gordiani on the Via Prenestina. Most of these were built near but not directly over the tombs of the saints whom they honored, and all acted as covered cemeteries for individuals desiring a close connection with the particular saint. Tombs also surrounded the churches, many of them connected directly with the side aisles and ambulatory. When the practice of the funerary banquet was banned in the fifth century, these churches fell out of use and were abandoned. Only the Basilica Apostolorum survived largely intact.

This same Basilica Apostolorum (Fig. 36) may have been the earliest of the type, located as it was near the complex of buildings – palace, mausoleum, and circus – built by Maxentius after 307 on the Via Appia.[29] This proximity, along with some similar architectural details in the two buildings, Maxentius's known religious tolerance, and the lack of any attribution to a patron in surviving sources has led to speculation that it was perhaps built during his reign.[30] The church is located above a catacomb in which the Apostles Peter and Paul were venerated during the mid-third century, indeed where some even believe their remains may have been sequestered for safekeeping during the persecutions of Decius and Valerian. Whether or not the remains of the apostles were ever there, the site itself had become associated with them and became a desirable place of burial for the faithful. Although remodeled at a later date, the church retains its original walls and interior space. The curving end is clearly visible, with its early-fourth-century masonry composed of alternating bands of brick and white stone. While the building is not mentioned in the list of churches constructed by Constantine in and near Rome contained in the *Liber pontificalis*, this does not necessarily mean that Constantine played no role in its construction or completion.

The cemetery church of SS. Marcellino e Pietro was unequivocally the work of Constantine (Plan 3).[31] Constructed on land that had held a cemetery of Maxentius's horseguard, the Equites Singulares, as well as a subterranean Christian catacomb and abutting an area of suburban land owned by Helena, the church was also the site of her burial. Between the Via Labicana and the basilica was a porticoed courtyard that gave access to the basilica. The church ran parallel to the road, and its entrance was on its south side (one of its long sides). A narthex separated it from the circular domed mausoleum that abutted the east end of the basilica. The basilica, with wide aisles separated from the nave by rectangular piers, had the characteristic rounded west end with ambulatory. On the north side was another walled enclosure, though without porticoes for additional burials.

The large mausoleum is one of several late Roman imperial mausolea to be built in the form of a domed rotunda, though it was the first to be attached to a church (Fig. 21).[32] Some 28 meters in diameter on its exterior, with niches placed on its interior walls, it has a tall drum with large windows that supported a dome. The dome is mostly gone now, but it and the walls of the interior may have been decorated with mosaics and colored marbles. The niche opposite the door probably housed the large porphyry sarcophagus holding the remains of Helena (Fig. 22). The *Liber pontificalis* states that Constantine built the church and mausoleum and provided gifts of liturgical items for both as well as an endowment of lands to furnish income for the maintenance of the complex.[33] These domains were all found in territory controlled by Constantine prior to 324, which again is likely evidence that the buildings were nearing completion before his defeat of Licinius. In addition, a coin found in the mortar used to hold the interior decoration of the mausoleum dates from 324–6 and indicates that finishing work was being done on the building at that time, perhaps as late as 328 when Helena probably died.

It has been suggested that Constantine originally built the mausoleum for himself, but there is no good reason to believe this.[34] The strongest support for this hypothesis rests on the sarcophagus, with its distinctly martial themes. To be sure, its high relief with cavalry formations seems somewhat militaristic for an empress, but it need not have been intended for Constantine. Moreover, the church and mausoleum were built on land belonging to Helena, near her suburban villa. Even if at some point Constantine considered using the mausoleum as his own, by 326, as it was nearing completion, he had already made the decision to move his capital to Constantinople and was probably changing his funeral plans accordingly.

Just outside of the city on the Via Tiburtina, Constantine built another cemetery church on the Verano hill near the tomb of the martyr Lawrence on land that had belonged to the imperial fisc for more than a century.[35] Like the other cemetery basilicas, it was occidented with the east end straight and the west end curved (Plan 11). In this case, the curved west end actually faced the road and so was opened with seven arched doorways to provide direct access. Remnants of the basilica are known from excavations, though the church itself was replaced by a sixth-century structure built directly over the tomb of the saint. The *Liber pontificalis* attributes the construction of the church to Constantine and notes that he also provided a direct access with steps to the tomb of the saint and embellished the tomb with silver decoration, including candelabra, lamps, and medallions depicting Lawrence's *passio*.[36]

The *Liber pontificalis* also claims that Constantine was responsible for the construction of the cemetery church of S. Agnese on the Via Nomentana, built at the request of his daughter, Constantina, on property she owned near the tomb of the saint (Fig. 37).[37] An acrostic inscription placed in the church after its completion attributes the work to Constantina, but the sources are not mutually exclusive: both father and daughter could be seen as patrons, with Constantine providing the initial funding and Constantina overseeing the work. Though in ruins, large tracts of the exterior walls and their supporting foundations, raised high to compensate for the slopping terrain, remain visible. Excavations inside the curved end of the nave have revealed a small rectangular apsidal structure whose function is unclear. Near the entrance on the south side of the building the circular and domed mausoleum that housed the porphyry sarcophagus of Constantina was constructed. Both the mausoleum, with its fine fourth-century mosaics, and the sarcophagus, now in the Vatican, are well preserved (Figs. 23 and 24).

Constantine's involvement with the construction of the recently discovered and partially excavated cemetery church on the Via Ardeatina is also attested by the *Liber pontificalis*.[38] Though it was built by Pope Mark in 336, Constantine, at the pope's request, donated income-producing property to help sustain it. It was here, not far from the catacomb of Callixtus, that Mark would be buried. The excavations undertaken to this point provide a crystal clear archaeological understanding of the function of these cemetery churches: every available space under the floor of the building was filled with tombs.

The emperor's patronage of churches extended outside of Rome, with contributions made towards the construction of churches in Italy at Ostia, Albano, Capua (modern S. Maria Capua Vetere), and Naples; in North Africa at Orleansville; and on the northern frontier at Trier. At Capua, a large basilica – with its entrance facing east and a separate octagonal baptistery – was built to the east of the amphitheater.[39] Remains of the church at Ostia, also attested in the *Liber pontificalis*, have recently been discovered and partially excavated (Plan 12).[40] Located just inside the town walls on the south flank of the city, the church fronted a street on the west with an atrium that gave access to a basilica with nave and side aisles and an apse on the east end – contrary to the usual orientation of Constantinian churches. Though not as grand as the major churches in Rome, it nevertheless was a fairly large structure, measuring some 51 meters in length. Constantine's former capital of Trier also received a new cathedral after a part of the palace was demolished to make way for the new structure around 326.[41] This was a double cathedral, two parallel basilicas built side by side, each with an atrium preceding its facade, and connected by a large square baptistery.

Constantine's victory over Licinius in 324 and his mother's pilgrimage to the Holy Land soon afterward provided a new focus for imperial building activities. His decision to enlarge the ancient city of Byzantium, rename it Constantinople after himself, and make it his capital led to numerous projects there and elsewhere. Located on a peninsula jutting into the Bosporus that separates Europe from Asia, the site was obviously chosen for its location nearer the eastern border, its ease of access to major roads and the sea, and its own natural defensive qualities (see Map 4).

Constantine founded the new city soon after his victory and reputedly dedicated it already on May 11, 330. His intention from the beginning was to restructure Constantinople on a grandiose scale. He thus removed the old city walls and had a new wall on the landward side of the peninsula constructed in a place that allowed room for future growth. Just outside of what had been the old city wall, Constantine built a new forum, circular or oval in plan and surrounded by porticoes, in the middle of which he ordered the placement of a large column of porphyry that remains standing – if truncated (Fig. 2). This forum was to act as the new centerpoint for the enlarged city. On the top of the column, in keeping with the tradition of Roman honorific columns, was placed a large statue of the emperor (Fig. 3), and its base was apparently decorated with relief carvings of victories, both now gone.[42] From the forum a porticoed street later called the Mese extended westward to the edge of the city.

Little remains of Constantine's other buildings in the city, though literary sources provide an idea of the scope of his projects for the new capital.[43] Taking advantage of the existing hippodrome (or circus), Constantine had a palace constructed on its eastern side, on a site overlooking the Bosporus. The hippodrome was remodeled to include a kathisma (imperial box) that had a direct connection with the palace in an arrangement that echoed that of the Circus Maximus and Palatine in Rome. The palace apparently consisted of several structures and would undergo numerous modifications over time. Its principal entrance faced a large open area known as the Augustaion, which gave access to a large bath complex built or remodeled by Constantine and known as the Baths of Zeuxippos. The Augustaion also opened onto the area set aside for the major churches of the city, Hagia Eirene and Hagia Sophia (Holy Peace and Holy Wisdom).[44] Nothing of the original churches survives, and there is confusion in the sources as to whether Constantine built both or was responsible for only the former, in part because Hagia Sophia was dedicated only in 360. Both structures were, however, enclosed within a common precinct wall, suggesting that both were planned from the beginning, and it is difficult to imagine that Constantine would not have built for his new capital what he had built in the old one – a cathedral. Two other churches honoring local martyrs were built by Constantine in the city, echoing the interest in such shrines that he had exhibited in Rome. These were St. Acacius and St. Mocius, the latter located in the cemetery area outside of the land walls.[45] His greatest church in the city, that of the Holy Apostles, was built towards the end of his reign (more on this later).

Nor were Constantine's ecclesiastical benefactions limited to his new capital. Eusebius reports that he "honored" Nicomedia with "a very large and splendid church . . . to his Savior from his personal funds, a monument of victory over his enemies and the foes of God."[46] In doing so, Constantine was following a long-established Roman tradition of making a votive offering in the form of a place of worship. Nevertheless, to do so in Nicomedia, the starting point of the Great Persecution, emphasized how very different imperially sanctioned worship had become. Further east, in Antioch, he constructed what must have been one of his most interesting churches near the palace precincts on the island in the Orontes River, a building known as the "Great Church" or, more descriptively, the "Golden Octagon." Dedicated to Homonoia (Concordia or Harmony), this church was begun in 327 and set within a large enclosure. Its roof was domed and gilded, its interior decorated with marble revetment and gold mosaic. It must have been a remarkable building, but unfortunately it no longer survives.[47]

With his domain extended to include the Holy Land, it is only natural that Constantine would, perhaps at the urging of Helena, turn his attention to the sites made sacred by Christ's life.[48] As early as 326, construction projects were begun at the site of Christ's birth at Bethlehem; at Jerusalem, at the sites of his death and resurrection and of his ascension; and at Mamre, where the three angels had appeared to Abraham (Gen. 18:1–33).

The church at Bethlehem featured another variation on the basilica type: a porticoed atrium led to a wide and relatively short basilica, with nave and side aisles, whose proportions would become common in this region (Plan 5).[49] At the end of the nave, where one would expect to find an apse, was instead an entrance into an octagonal structure built directly above the sacred grotto of the nativity. A hole cut through the roof of the grotto allowed the faithful a view down onto the very spot of the Incarnation. Just outside of Jerusalem on the Mount of Olives, another somewhat humble basilica preceded by an atrium and known as the Eleona served a double function. The polygonal apse at the end of the nave was constructed over the grotto where Christ was believed to have taught the apostles and whence he was believed to have ascended into heaven.[50]

What would become the most venerated site in Christendom, the site of Christ's death, entombment, and resurrection, had been occupied by a pagan temple up to Constantine's reign.[51] Constantine took a personal interest in seeing that this sacred place would be properly embellished as its importance demanded. At his orders, the temple site, just outside the old city wall, was cleared and leveled, revealing both the top of the hill of Golgotha and the rock-cut tomb of the resurrection. In a letter written around 326 to Bishop Macarius of Jerusalem, the emperor instructed the bishop to begin work on the complex, stating that it was to be built at public expense and to be "superior to those in all other places;" he suggested the use of columns, marble revetment, and a coffered gilded ceiling.[52] The east end of the complex fronted one of the major streets of the city (Plan 4). Here a propylaeum (monumental gateway) was constructed that gave access to an atrium, an arrangement like that at Old St. Peter's. The atrium led to a basilica, referred to in sources as the "martyrium." It was wide, with double side-aisles and a gallery on each side. Its semicircular apse was contained within a straight exterior wall and was located next to the top of Golgotha. Behind the western wall of the basilica was an open courtyard with porticoes. On the opposite end of the courtyard was the entrance to the tomb site. The tomb was freed from the surrounding hill, and its rock exterior was cut to form what appeared to be an octagonal structure. Eventually, it was surrounded by a huge rotunda, known as the Anastasis (Resurrection) and modeled on the architecture of Roman imperial mausolea. There is some question as to whether the rotunda was an original part of the project or a later addition. Both the masonry of the lower walls, identical with that of other Constantinian structures on the site, and the concept of a monumental structure marking a holy site point to Constantine. It is furthermore difficult to believe that the rotunda – a structure already used by Constantine at SS. Marcellino e Pietro – was an afterthought.

The rotunda was aligned so that the tomb aedicula was located near its center. A circle of columns and piers enclosed this sacred space and rose to support a gallery, a drum, and a dome. An ambulatory encircled this central space and was marked with three apses placed on the cardinal points. Its closest relative among surviving structures is the rotunda of S. Costanza in Rome, the mausoleum of Constantine's daughter. Another close relative may have been the building destined to house Constantine's own mortal remains, the church of the Holy Apostles in Constantinople.

Begun in the last years of Constantine's life, the church was located on a hill just inside of the new city walls built as the city was expanded. According to Eusebius, Constantine at first kept the true purpose of the building unknown, but eventually it became clear that this was to be his mausoleum as well as a church. Destroyed by the Turks soon after their conquest of the city in 1453, it is known through Eusebius's description and from other scattered references in later sources.[53] The description is imprecise and mentions that the church stood in a courtyard surrounded by porticoes, it possessed a drum and/or dome, it reached to an "unimaginable height," and it was lavishly decorated with marbles, bronze, and gold. The description does not clearly indicate the architectural form of the building, though it is clear that at a later date the site possessed a cruciform church and a circular mausoleum (Plan 2). The lack of precision in the earliest sources has led some to believe that the church was built from the beginning as a cruciform structure and that the mausoleum was added later by Constantius II.[54] Another interpretation has it that the original building was the circular mausoleum and that Constantius added the cruciform structure.[55] The typology of late Roman imperial mausolea and the form of the Anastasis rotunda in Jerusalem would argue in favor of the latter interpretation.[56]

Eusebius is clear on what Constantine intended with this building: it was to be both a mausoleum for himself and a memorial to the Apostles. Accordingly, the emperor ordered twelve *thekai* (repositories or cenotaphs) erected near his sarcophagus, all placed near the altar, where he "might benefit from the worship which would be conducted there in honor of the Apostles."[57] In the year before his death (our sources record the date as June 22, 336), Constantine had "relics" of the Apostles Andrew and Luke brought to Constantinople and deposited in the church, and two decades later his son Constantius apparently added to these the relics of Paul's apostolic assistant Timothy.[58] This represents the first time a permanent transfer of relics occurred in Christianity.

This building nicely sums up Constantine's building program, the work of a Roman emperor who oversaw the construction of new cities, public buildings, and places of worship. Like other emperors before him, he provided a place for his eventual entombment and did so in grandiose – some would say megalomaniacal – fashion. As the first emperor to be involved with the construction of Christian buildings and the patron of the first large churches, he had demonstrated an open mind to a variety of building types: variations on the basilica but also octagons and circular buildings. He was also in large part responsible for the concept of memorial structures built to honor the tombs of saints or sites connected with the life of Christ, linking architecture with Christian history and the growing importance of the cult of the saints and their relics. In this, his last major construction, Constantine – who had begun his rule as a pagan and then embraced the Christian faith – wanted not only the grandeur of an imperial mausoleum and proximity in his burial place to important saints, he also wanted the grandeur of both state and church to coincide and meld into one. He made for himself an impressive tomb in a prominent location in the city that bore his name and in a church dedicated to the original champions of the Christian message. Whether the transfer of the Apostles' relics came during his lifetime or afterwards, by linking his tomb with a memorial to the Apostles, he had created an arrangement that would leave the impression that he was to be considered an Apostle, or even a Christ-like figure in his own right.[59]

FURTHER READING

Most of the literary source material on Constantine's building program can be found in Eusebius's *Life of Constantine* (esp. 3.25–53) and the anonymous *Liber pontificalis* (esp. 34–35). The best modern surveys of Constantinian architecture in English are S. Alexander's "Studies in Constantinian Architecture," *Rivista di archeologia cristiana* 67 (1971): 281–330, and R. Krautheimer's *Early Christian and Byzantine Architecture* (1986) and *Three Christian Capitals* (1983). F. A. Bauer's *Stadt, Platz, und Denkmal in der Spätantike* (1996) is also extremely valuable and has a more up to date bibliography. On Rome specifically, J. Curran's *Pagan City and Christian Capital: Rome in the Fourth Century* (2000) and R. R. Holloway's *Constantine and Rome* (2004) are now indispensable, and H. Brandenburg's *Roms frühchristliche Basiliken des 4. Jahrhundert* (1979) remains useful, especially for its illustrations. On Constantinople, C. Mango's *Studies on Constantinople* (1993) and *Le développement urbain de Constantinople (IVe–VIIe siècles)* (1990c) cover the sparse remains judiciously. For Jerusalem, see P. W. L. Walker's *Holy City, Holy Places? Christian Attitudes to Jerusalem and the Holy Land in the Fourth Century* (1990).

NOTES

1 Krautheimer 1993.
2 Reusch 1956. For Trier in general, see Wightman 1971; Heinen 1996.
3 *Pan. Lat* 6(7).22.5.
4 Krautheimer 1980, 3–31; Curran 2000, 70–115.
5 Minoprio 1932.
6 The literature on the arch is vast. Recent studies include Peirce 1989 and Elsner 2000a.
7 Messineo and Calci 1989; cf. Kuhoff 1991.
8 Steinby 1993–2000, 5:49.
9 Aur. Vict. *Caes.* 40.26–7.
10 Colli 1996; Barbera 2000.
11 Guidobaldi 1998; Cima 2000.
12 For the Christian buildings in Rome, see Krautheimer, Corbett, and Frazer 1937–77; Krautheimer 1983, 6–40; Brandenburg 1979a; Holloway 2004, 57–119.
13 Krautheimer, Corbett, and Frazer 1937–77, 5:90; Curran 2000, 94–5.
14 Krautheimer 1983, 28–9; cf. Curran 2000, 95–6, on the choice of site.
15 *Liber pont.* 34.9–12. On the church, see Krautheimer, Corbett, and Frazer 1937–77, 5:1–92; Holloway 2004, 57–61.
16 Kinney 2001a.
17 Blaauw 2001a; cf. Chapter 11 n. 50 in this volume.
18 Krautheimer 1967.
19 See below in this chapter around n. 52.
20 O. Brandt 1997–8, 2001; Holloway 2004, 73–6.
21 *Liber pont.* 34.13–14. The present arrangement of columns around the font and the drum and dome that they support are the product of a remodeling undertaken by Pope Sixtus III in the fifth century.

22 *Liber pont.* 34.22; Krautheimer, Corbett, and Frazer 1937–77, 1:165–95; Brandenburg 1979a, 160–9; Argentini and Ricciardi 1996–7; Blaauw 1997.

23 *Liber pont.* 35.3; Alexander 1971, 291–2; Cecchelli 1992.

24 For the growth of the cult of the saints, see Brown 1981.

25 Krautheimer, Corbett, and Frazer 1937–77, 5:165–279.

26 I follow Krautheimer 1989.

27 The inscription is reported at *Liber pont.* 34.17. On Helena's title Augusta, see Drijvers 1992, 39–54. Bowersock 2003, argues, unconvincingly, that the church is post-Constantinian.

28 Krautheimer 1969, 35–58; Brandenburg 1979a, 61–120; Tolotti 1982; Schumacher 1987; La Rocca 2000. Contrast Lehman 2003, who discounts the circus symbolism of the Constantinian cemetery churches.

29 Krautheimer, Corbett, and Frazer 1937–77, 4:99–147.

30 Jastrzebowska 1983.

31 Guyon 1987; Holloway 2004, 86–93.

32 Rasch et al. 1998.

33 *Liber pont.* 34.26–7.

34 Krautheimer 1983, 23.

35 Krautheimer, Corbett, and Frazer 1937–77, 2:1–144; Holloway 2004, 110–11.

36 *Liber pont.* 34.24–5.

37 *Liber pont.* 34.23; cf. Holloway 2004, 93–104.

38 *Liber pont.* 35.3; Fiocchi Nicolai 1995–6; Holloway 2004, 111–2.

39 Pagano and Rouget 1984.

40 *Liber pont.* 34.28–29; Bauer 1999; Bauer et al. 1999.

41 Krautheimer 1986, 48–50.

42 Mango 1993b, studies II–IV; Bauer 1996, 167–87.

43 Krautheimer 1983, 41–67; Mango 1990c; Barsanti 1992.

44 Bauer 1996, 143–67; Alexander 1971.

45 Alexander 1971, 329–30.

46 Eus. *VC* 3.50.1 (trans. Cameron and Hall).

47 Eus. *VC* 3.50.2; *LC* 9.15; Downey 1961, 342–9; Alexander 1971, 314–7.

48 Eus. *VC* 3.41–43 attributes the churches of the Nativity and the Ascension to Helena. See also Hunt 1997; J. W. Drijvers 1992, 55–72; Lenski 2004.

49 Eus. *LC* 9.17; *VC* 3.43.1–2; Soc. 1.17.1–13; Soz. 2.1.1–2.2; Krautheimer 1986, 59–60; Walker 1990, 171–98.

50 Eus. *VC* 3.43.3–4; Corbo 1959–60; Walker 1990, 199–234.

51 Corbo 1981–2; Krautheimer 1986, 60–5; Walker 1990, 235–81; Patrich 1993; Krüger 2000, 39–81.

52 Eus. *VC* 3.30–31 (trans. Cameron and Hall).

53 Eus. *VC* 4.58–60. Further sources are gathered and analyzed at Speck 2000.

54 Krautheimer 1969, 27–34; 1983, 56–60; 1986, 69–70.

55 Mango 1990a.

56 So Effenberger 2000, who suggests a building like the mausoleum of Constantina in Rome.

57 Eus. *VC* 4.60 (trans. Cameron and Hall); cf. *VC* 4.71.2.

58 The translation of these relics is disputed, with some arguing that they were first brought to Constantinople only in 357. See Burgess 2003.

59 On this theme, see Rebenich 2000.

13: Constantine in Legendary Literature

Samuel N. C. Lieu

"**C**onstantine sitting amongst the Christian bishops at the oecumenical council of Nicaea is in his own person the beginning of Europe's Middle Age." This oft-quoted sentence with which Norman Baynes concludes his chapter on Constantine in the first edition of the *Cambridge Ancient History* looks forward to the legacy of Constantine as founder of a Christian Byzantium and the Christian Roman empire of Pippin and Charlemagne in the medieval west.[1] However, it was not Constantine the founder of "Caesaropapism" whom the historians and hagiographers of the Middle Ages – both east and west – chose to commemorate.[2] His legacy in the Middle Ages, and in the west in particular, was partially obscured by those of two other figures of his reign who were the more popular as saints for veneration, pope Sylvester, who occupied the see of St. Peter for much of his reign, and Constantine's mother, Helena Augusta.

The Sylvester Legend and the Baptism of Constantine

According to the *Liberian Catalogue*, Sylvester (feast, December 31) succeeded Miltiades as bishop of Rome on January 31, 314. At the time of Sylvester's death, which occurred, according to the *Depositio episcoporum*, on December 31, 335, Constantine had transformed the relationship between the Roman state and Christian Church. He had personally heard the appeals from both sides of the Donatist dispute and had summoned the first ecumenical council to Nicaea in May 325 without the authority of Sylvester. The establishment of Constantinople as the new capital undermined further the importance of both the city of

Rome and its bishop. His baptism by the Arian bishop Eusebius of Nicomedia in 337, though necessitated by historical and geographical circumstances, was nevertheless seen as a further snub to the papacy. Later generations found it difficult to accept that the papacy could have played such a minor role in the reign of the first Christian emperor, and before the end of the fifth century a romantic account of Sylvester's life had emerged in which he was portrayed as a key figure in both the conversion of Constantine and the establishment of Christianity as the state religion of the Roman empire. The legend survives today as the *Actus beati Silvestri papae* (*CPL* 2235), which has its fullest manifestation in a fifteenth-century Latin manuscript utilized by the Italian humanist Bononius Mombritius in his edition published c. 1480.[3] Elements of the same legend are more popularly known through the *Golden Legend* (*Legenda Aurea*) of the Dominican preacher and scholar Jacobus de Voragine, published around 1260.[4]

The *Actus*, purportedly the work of Eusebius of Caesarea, begins with an account of Sylvester's early philanthropic career looking after the pilgrims who came to Rome and his ordination by Pope Miltiades.[5] The latter was alleged to have perished in the Great Persecution, and Sylvester, who was in hiding at a place called "Serapte," later identified with Soracte, was summoned by the new persecutor Constantine to cure him of a vile bodily illness – elephantaic leprosy, a medically impossible disease. His pagan priests, consisting of doctors and magicians, had advised bathing in the blood of infants – that is, a pagan caricature of Christian baptism with overtones of the *taurobolium*. But Constantine was overcome by the wailing of the children rounded up for slaughter and of their mothers and ordered their release.[6] That same night saints Peter and Paul appeared to him like a Christian version of the Dioscuri, promising as recompense for his humane gesture cure from his hideous illness provided he seek out Sylvester and follow his commands. When summoned to the emperor's presence, Sylvester showed him images of Peter and Paul, and these were duly recognised by Constantine as those who had appeared to him. He was then given Christian instruction, and after a solemn fast he was allegedly baptized in the Lateran Basilica – though it was not yet built at the time. A bright light was seen when he entered the water, and he was instantly healed. This was followed by a flood of legislation against paganism and in favour of Christianity. A week after his baptism, Constantine also began the construction of a church in the Lateran Palace.[7]

The baptism of Constantine by Sylvester absolved the medieval church, both east and west, of a major source of embarrassment, namely, his deathbed baptism by an Arian bishop. It was hard for the church to accept the fact that an emperor who could summon councils and claim to be the "bishop of those outside the church" was not baptised shortly after his victory over Maxentius. The romantic story of his healing, conversion, and baptism was also, however, a foil against pagan propaganda. Already in the 360s, Constantine's nephew Julian had charged him with turning to Christianity as an antidote to the sin of having murdered his son Crispus and his wife Fausta without trial. By the late fourth century, the historian Eunapius seems to have argued that Constantine's pagan advisor Sopater had denied that forgiveness for such a crime was possible among the pagan gods and that in response Constantine was forced to turn to Christian baptism. Though the fifth-century church historian Sozomen already countered this charge with the simple contention that Constantine's conversion predated the family murders, the Sylvester legend seems to have constituted a more elaborate response to the same charge.[8]

Though Roman in origin, the Sylvester story might thus have contained and responded to eastern elements, and it certainly found its way into Greek Byzantine *vitae* of Constantine. The story of Constantine's baptism as related in the *Actus* was certainly known in Byzantium by the sixth century, when it was depicted in a mosaic in the church of Hagios Polyeuktos built by Anicia Juliana between 512 and 527.[9] Later, one of the historically best informed of the Byzantine *vitae* (the Opitz-*Vita*, discussed later) shows clear literary connection with the *Actus* as well. Here the legend was clearly put to political use, for Anicia Juliana's mosaic seems to have been completed in anticipation of a visit to Constantinople by Pope John I in an effort to heal the rifts between the eastern and western churches that had arisen in the previous century. Similar issues were at play in the formation of the *Actus* in the west. It is not impossible that Eusebius of Nicomedia, Constantine's Arian baptiser, had already been replaced by Pope Eusebius of Rome in the legend of the discovery of the True Cross as attested in the Byzantine *Visio Constantini*.[10] Since Eusebius of Nicomedia later became bishop of Constantinople – the New Rome – it would have only been a short mental leap to replace him with his namesake from the old Rome. When it was then found that the pontificate of Eusebius (*sedit* April 18, 308, exiled September 309) did not coincide with Constantine's time in Rome,[11] he was replaced by Sylvester, the confessor-pope.[12] For the papacy, the image of Sylvester as a confessor became vital counterpropaganda to the allegation made by the Donatists that Pope Miltiades (*sedit* July 2, 311–January 10, 314), an African, was a *traditor*, an allegation that naturally cast suspicion on Miltiades' proteges Marcellus and Sylvester.[13]

This chronological shift is necessary given Sylvester's prominence as confessor in the Great Persecution, for which he would enjoy cultic veneration. The *Actus* takes great pains to stress the hospitality he accorded at great personal risk to Timothy, who was fleeing persecution from Antioch, and also the fact that his self-imposed exile at "Syrapte" was for devotion in preparation for martyrdom and not an attempt to escape the persecutions.[14] Once the starting date of his pontificate had been extended, no one would have known that this was in the time before his elevation to bishop of Rome; Sylvester thus became the confessor-pope. From this the natural conclusion must be drawn that Sylvester had led the Roman Church before Constantine's defeat of Maxentius. It is also interesting to note that, by the time the fullest version of Helena's *Vita* was compiled in the late medieval west, the story of Constantine as persecutor was replaced by the story of him as victor over the pagan Maxentius – the falsity of the Sylvester legend had at last been recognized.[15]

THE "DONATION" OF CONSTANTINE

Closely related to the Sylvester legend is a quasi-hagiographical and quasi-juridical Latin document known as the "Donation of Constantine," a text that was readily available to churchmen and scholars in the Middle Ages in any copy of Gratian's *Decretum* at Chapter 14 of the 96th Distinction.[16] It was compiled no later than the early fifties of the eighth century, and despite its legendary character, its authenticity was not challenged until the late Middle Ages.[17] While the events of the pontificate of Stephen II (752–7) seem most appropriate for the fabrication of the text, its place of origin is not certain; involvement by the papal chancery could not be ruled out. The compiler or forger reworked elements of Constantine's brief sojourn in Rome into an abridged version of the *Actus Sylvestri* combined with a quasi-constitutional document, the *Constitutum Constantini*. It claims that on the day after his baptism Constantine, as a solemn act of personal recognition of the authority of the pope, handed over to him all the imperial accoutrements, including his sceptre, lance, orb, standards, and various other *ornamenta*. He also offered to place his crown on the head of Sylvester as a sign of true imperial power, but the latter refused to wear it above his clerical tonsure (Fig. 38). For the medieval papacy, the most important aspect of the document was not its implication of the pope's right to crown Roman emperors but the eternal possession of the Lateran Palace, which tied *urbs Roma* to the papacy, and above all the emancipation of the papacy from the imperial framework through Constantine's "donation" of imperial dominion into the hands of the pope in order that he could grant it back to the emperor:

> To correspond to our own Empire and so that the supreme Pontifical authority may not be dishonoured, but may rather be adorned with glorious power greater than the dignity of any earthly empire, behold, we give to the often-mentioned most holy Pontiff, our father Sylvester, the Universal Pope, not only the above mentioned palace [i.e., the Lateran], but also the city of Rome and all the provinces, districts, and cities of Italy and the Western regions, relinquishing them to the authority of himself and his successors as Pontiffs by a definite Imperial grant. We have decided that this should be laid down by this our divine, holy, and lawfully framed decree and we grant it on a permanent legal basis to the holy Roman Church.[18]

A major contemporary factor that impacted on the the *Constitutum* was the role assumed by the Byzantine emperor in promulgating religious doctrine, especially after 482, when Emperor Zeno issued a decree of religious unity that deliberately avoided reference to the bishop of Rome. The absence of the Roman emperor from Rome was prophetically explained in the *Constitutum* in terms which seemed to justify the Papacy's detachment from any obligation to the eastern monarch:

> Therefore we have seen it to be fitting that our Empire and the power of the kingdom should be transferred and translated to the Eastern regions and that in the province of Byzantium in the most suitable place a city should be built in our name and our Empire established there; because it is not just that an earthly Emperor should exercise authority where the government of priests and the Head of the Christian religion have been installed by the heavenly Emperor.[19]

The forger thus acknowledged Constantinople as the capital of the Roman empire through the residence of the emperor, but the crown was there by papal acquiescence only, for the transfer was presented "as the effluence of papal volition."[20] The impact of the *Constitutum* was most strongly felt in the reign of Charlemagne. He was addressed by his court poet as Flavius Anicius Carolus ("Flavius" being the name borne by Christian Roman emperors from Constantine onwards), and time and again the Carolingian chancery referred to Constantine as a model for Charlemagne, the "new Constantine." Later a crown supposedly used for the coronation of Constantine – who of course was never *crowned* – was used for the coronation of Charlemagne's son Louis the Pious. The city of Rome, granted by Constantine to Sylvester, reflected the pope's imperial standing, while the fact that Rome was within Charlemagne's domains also strengthened his claim to the imperial crown.[21] Despite its obvious usefulness in the Carolingian period, the earliest certain appeal to the *Constitutum* was made by Pope Leo IX in a letter to Michael Cerularius, the patriarch of Constantinople, in 1054; from then on it was frequently employed in papal claims to territorial possessions and as a weapon of the spiritual powers against the temporal. Its description of how the temporal possessions of the Roman pontiff were "gifted" to him by the first Christian emperor and founder of Constantinople rendered the "Donation" entirely acceptable to Byzantine churchmen, and the *Constitutum* did not therefore take long to become part of the Byzantine hagiographical tradition regarding Constantine.

The *Constitutum Constantini*, like its partner text the *Actus Sylvestri*, could easily have been challenged by any scholar in the Latin Middle Ages. Most used Cassiodorus's *Historia Tripertita* – a source based on excellent authorities – for their church history, and Cassiodorus plainly contradicts the *Actus* and *Constitutum*, not just with his silence about the donation and indeed any contact between Constantine and Sylvester, but also with his clear statement that Constantine was baptised in 337 by the Arian Eusebius. But in the Middle Ages, this silence and even this contradiction were not considered grounds to disprove the authenticity of an account or document. More to the point, the premise of the forgery, aimed as it was at strengthening the position of the papacy vis-à-vis temporal powers, was not likely to be challenged by the Roman Church in the west, which had the most to gain from it and also possessed the main research facilities for its exposure.

THE CONVERSION OF HELENA AND THE *INVENTIO CRUCIS*

A major part of the *Actus Sylvestri* tradition concerns the conversion of Constantine's mother Helena. She was apparently greatly distressed by the news of her son's conversion and wrote to him from her abode in Drepanum, on the Sea of Marmara, urging him to adopt Judaism instead. In response, a public theological disputation between Pope Sylvester and twelve rabbis on the superiority of their respective monotheistic faiths was organized on August 13, 315. The highlight of the encounter occurred when the rabbis caused a bull to die by whispering the name Jehovah into its ear, but Sylvester was able to restore it to life by uttering the name of Jesus Christ. Helena was so astonished by this that she instantly accepted the Christian faith.[22]

Separate from the *Actus Sylvestri* and even earlier in the tradition is the attribution of the discovery of the True Cross to Helena Augusta as part of her sedulous efforts to reclaim the main Christian sites and remains from the Jews of Palestine. Although Constantine hardly features in these legends, except as a builder of churches, they deserve mention because of their great popularity in late antiquity and the Middle Ages (Fig. 13). In his *Life of Constantine*, Eusebius makes no overt mention of the discovery during his account of the empress's peregrinations in the east, but some version very probably featured in the lost history of Gelasius of Caesarea, written already in the fourth century,[23] and the story thus found its way into all main church histories after Eusebius.[24] Rufinus, who certainly used Gelasius, preserves an account that, though brief, carries many of the defining characteristics of the legend as retold in a multitude of versions in the Middle Ages. Helena was said to have searched for the Cross on arrival at Jerusalem, but the task was made difficult by the presence of a temple dedicated to Venus on the site of Golgotha, so that if any Christian wished to worship Christ there, he had to give the appearance of worshipping Venus. The empress immediately began to clear the site and found three crosses jumbled together, those of Christ and the two thieves with whom he was crucified, but the remains of the True Cross were distinguished from the other two through a healing miracle. The story was sufficiently well known for it to be included by Ambrose in his obituary sermon on the emperor Theodosius delivered in 395, and Paulinus of Nola was eager to recount his version of it in a letter to the historian Sulpicius Severus in 402/3.[25] In fact, the veneration and possibly the discovery of fragments of the True Cross may have taken place in Jerusalem already before 325 but did not make the headlines until Helena's pilgrimage to the Holy Land in 327.[26]

In the Greek and Syrian Orient, the legend of the discovery of the True Cross by Helena was later embroidered with two further legends. The first of these, known to scholars as the Kyriakos legend, was probably of Greek origin and was known to Sozomen c. 450, although the earliest manuscript version is in Syriac.[27] This has Helena summoning the Jews in Jerusalem and accusing them of deliberately concealing the relics of the True Cross. She orders them to produce men who truly knew the Law. A Jew by the name of Judas, who was distantly related to the protomartyr St. Stephen, duly presents himself and shows her where the crosses had been buried. This Judas was later baptized under the name of "Kyriakos" (he who belongs to the Lord) and became bishop of Jerusalem and even a martyr under Julian the Apostate. The legend gained widespread acceptance and was circulated in both Greek and Latin;[28] the most readily available medieval version is again found in the *Golden Legend*.[29] A second legend, almost certainly of Syrian origin, features Protonike, a fictional wife of the emperor Claudius, as the first discoverer of the True Cross. The circumstances of the discovery were almost identical to those of the Judas-Kyriakos legend, and the gradual acceptance of this additional legend led Helena to be regarded as the "rediscoverer" of the True Cross in some Syriac sources.[30]

Here, as earlier, we find history rewritten in order to bring Constantine and his family into greater prominence in the providential history of Christianity. In the absence of firmer testimony about the actual discovery of the True Cross – accepted as a historical given by the mid-fourth century[31] – Constantine's mother, who had indeed visited the Holy Land, was conveniently inserted into the tradition by the fertile late antique imagination. In the process she was transformed into a heroine of salvific history and an archetypal proselytizer for Christianity against pagans and Jews.

THE BYZANTINE *VITAE* OF CONSTANTINE

In the Byzantine Church, Constantine was venerated as a saint and an equal of the Apostles (*isapostolos*). His joint feast day with Helena was and still is celebrated on May 21. The cult of the saints in Byzantium demanded that the saints' ascetical achievements be celebrated in hagiography and summarized in menologia – collections of saints' or martyrs' lives arranged according to their feast date. One of the best and most available examples of a Byzantine menologion is the *Synaxarium* of Constantinople, which consists of about two thousand condensed biographies up to the tenth century.[32] The relatively brief entry devoted to Constantine begins with his descent from the emperor Claudius – a claim that goes back to Constantinian propaganda before the battle of

Milvian Bridge.[33] The rest of the entry, however, is fairly close to our knowledge of Constantine as transmitted in late antique sources: his early interest in Christianity, his refusal to persecute, the vision of the Cross, his victory over the infidel Maxentius, the discovery of the True Cross by Helena, his summoning of the Council of Nicaea to combat Arianism, and his death in Nicomedia. It thus omits the story of his conversion and baptism by Sylvester, which necessitates a reinterpretation of the events surrounding the battle of the Milvian Bridge, even though it was already known in Byzantium as early as the early sixth century.[34]

The main story of the *Actus* does feature, however, in many Byzantine *vitae* of Constantine. The number of extant Greek *vitae* from the Byzantine period is very large; the most easily available published ones – conveniently named after their principal editors – are as follows:[35]

(1) The "Winkelmann-*Vita*,"[36] an eighth- or ninth-century epitome of a pre-sixth-century proto-vita, contains many of the features found in later and longer *vitae*, such as the discovery of the True Cross by Helena and Constantine's consecration of his eponymous city with the bishops who attended the Council of Nicaea during the patriarchate of Metrophanes.

(2) The "Guidi-*Vita*,"[37] with more than forty extant manuscripts of its two versions (one earlier, viz. eleventh century, and one late, twelfth century), is by far the most popular of the Byzantine lives of Constantine and is the only one available in full English translation.[38] The work is of substantial length and contains a number of features that are commonly found in later Byzantine lives:

a. Constantius Chlorus's visit to Drepanum, his meeting with Helena at an inn, and the conception of Constantine under unusual auspices;

b. recognition of the young Constantine by courtiers and his physical resemblance to his father; his subsequent reunification with Constantius and his assignment to the court of Diocletian for grooming as a future emperor;

c. the baptism of Constantine by Pope Sylvester in Rome after the emperor's refusal to cure his leprosy through bathing in the blood of innocent children;

d. Constantine's Persian campaign, his capture and escape;

e. the foundation of Constantinople and the earlier history of Byzantium;

    f. the Arian controversy and miraculous happenings at the Council of Nicaea;

    g. the discovery of the True Cross by Helena and her building programme in Palestine;

    h. victories for Constantine in various battles through the symbol of the cross.

These became so standard in Constantinian hagiography that they soon passed from legend into history in Byzantium. Substantial parts of the Guidi-*Vita* are reproduced in the sections on the reign of Constantine in the massive *Ecclesiastical History* of Nicephorus Callistus (compiled c. 1320).[39] A distinctive feature of this *vita* is the detailed account of the foundation of churches on holy sites in Palestine by Helena. It also repeatedly stresses the important role played by the True Cross in Constantine's military victories. These features are not found in the "Vorvita" (i.e., *BHG* 365z etc.) and are likely to have developed during the Iconoclast Controversy (eighth century), when there was an increase in the veneration of the cross as a replacement for images.

    (3) The "Opitz-*Vita*,"[40] dated between the end of the ninth and the eleventh centuries, is sadly acephalous and begins with Constantine's activities in Rome after his victory over Maxentius.[41] This work is unusual for its extraordinary familiarity with earlier sources, including the pagan historian Zosimus. It also makes substantial use of material from the western (?) *Actus Sylvestri* tradition. A feature not found in earlier *vitae* is the role played by a legendary figure, the chamberlain Euphratas, in the conversion of Constantine.

    (4) The "Halkin (or Patmos)-*Vita*,"[42] the product of a twelfth- or thirteenth-century monk from Beroea in the neighbourhood of Thessalonica, contains a number of fascinating local details as well as some geographical errors. It nevertheless displays much material not found in other lives. The trials of the young Constantine at the court of Galerius, for instance, were graphically depicted as the labours of a new Hercules or Jason, with Constantine singlehandedly defeating a bear and lion as well as thirty men armed with rocks. The *vita* also contains a uniquely detailed account of Euphratas's role in the foundation of Constantinople.

    (5) The "Gedeon-*Vita*"[43] is a highly mechanical compilation of material from earlier sources and from the *Vita Constantini* of Eusebius. The purpose of the work is to produce an ideal Constantine totally shorn of controversy and complication. Its panegyrical section on Helena was equally wholesome and omits any mention of her low origin or her "affair" with Constantius Chlorus.

SOME BIOGRAPHICAL AND HISTORICAL *TOPOI* FROM THE BYZANTINE *VITAE*

The Byzantine *vitae* are genuine attempts at popular biographical writing, and they embody biographical and historical details not found in late antique sources like Eusebius's *Vita Constantini*. These details became so popular that they were generally regarded as genuine and came to be absorbed into the Byzantine historical tradition as attested in histories of Nicephorus Callistus, Cedrenus, and Zonaras.

The Helena-Recognition Theme

Common to the Guidi, Opitz, and Halkin *vitae* is the semimiraculous and certainly fictional story of Constantine's conception and his later "recognition" by his father. The story also fleshes out the link between Constantine and Drepanum, his mother's home town which he eventually rebuilt and renamed Helenopolis after her death. According to legend, Constantine was conceived when Constantius Chlorus, then serving as an imperial guardsman (*protector*), satisfied his sexual needs with Helena, the daughter of an innkeeper in Drepanum whom he met while he was sent on a diplomatic mission to the Parthians [*sic*]. The morning after their union, Constantius gave Helena a purple chiton and a golden necklace. He also instructed the innkeeper to look after their offspring because he guessed from a vision that he received from Apollo that Helena had conceived. Many years later, after Constantius had become emperor, another Roman embassy passing the same way to Persia stayed at the same inn, and when they heard that the handsome young man they met there spoke of himself as the son of the reigning emperor, they burst out laughing. The lad went crying to his mother, who reproached the officials and showed them the purple chiton. They duly reported to Constantius their discovery of a young man who was a "copy" of him. Constantine was promptly sent for and reunited with his father.

Interestingly the recognition theme, thoroughly grounded in the legendary tradition of Constantine in Byzantium, would later resurface in the medieval west and become the main plot of a romantic novella on the young Constantine.[44] Helena appears in this not as an innkeeper of dubious reputation from Drepanum but as a Christian pilgrim from Trier – a city with strong associations with the Tetrarchs – who came to Rome to visit the churches of Peter and Paul when Constantius was emperor. The latter fell madly in love with her after catching a glimpse of her on a bridge over the Tiber, forcibly entered her room in the hostel, and raped her. After learning that she was a Christian, the pagan Constantius left her with two valuable gifts, an imperial shoulder ornament and a ring. Helena did not return to Trier but settled in Rome and told everyone there that the father of the child she subsequently bore had died. Constantine grew into a handsome young man imbued with strong moral principles. Later hostilities broke out between the king of Rome (i.e., Constantius) and the unnamed "King of Constantinople, or rather of the Greeks." At that time there lived in Rome two merchants who enjoyed the exclusive right to trade between the two empires. They conceived a plan to kidnap the child, rear him, and pass him off as a Roman prince to the king of the Greeks, who had no son. The plan succeeded, but instead of bringing Constantine and his Greek bride back to Rome, the merchants dumped them on a desert island and made off with the riches sent by the Greek king as a dowry. The couple were forced to sustain themselves by eating wild fruit and drinking seawater – a strong indication that the story originated somewhere in the heart of Europe. They were subsequently rescued by sailors and reunited joyously with Helena, who had opened an inn as a *stabularia* – the profession with which Helena was traditionally associated.[45] Later Constantius chanced upon his son, who was distinguishing himself in tournaments, and was struck by his physical resemblance to himself. He could not believe that he was someone without wealth and connection and therefore summoned his mother, who duly produced the ring from the occasion of their union. Constantius was overjoyed, and hearing the story of the conspiracy of the merchants, he had them executed and their property given to Constantine. The latter was proclaimed heir apparent, and as the Greek king did not have a son, Constantine eventually became emperor by treaty of both halves of the empire and was baptized by Pope Sylvester. The story, which echoes elements of the adventures of Prinz Manfred in the Middle Ages, seems to have exercised a strong influence on the development of storytelling in Europe and might have even contributed to the formation of the Cinderella legend.

The "Christian" Eunuch Euphratas

An important figure in the Byzantine legends of Constantine that has no western parallel is the eunuch Euphratas. He appears in the Opitz-*Vita* as instrumental in explaining the meaning of the crucial vision that Constantine witnessed before the battle of Milvian Bridge and warned him of the consequences of not following its obvious implication. Constantine is said to have asked,

> "What means could there be in this predicament to assure me of such a great victory?" "Provided" replied Euphratas "that you reject the many gods and properly treat them with contempt, for they are not gods at all, and it is madness to consider them as such, and that, turning to the only true God, you take his son, Christ, as your ally in this situation and throughout your life. Consider the superiority of his power: although by undergoing the Cross he was plunged into the deepest and most undeserved humiliation, by the strength of his works he obliged the majority of the human race to worship him and to recognise him as God. His glory advances unceasingly for all time: in public and in private, in all cities and nations and peoples, almost the whole of humanity seeks his favour. As for those who raised their hands against him, the Jews in particular, you see how they have perished, they and their city with them; those who escaped live scattered over all the world, they live a hard and wandering life, forced most harshly to serve their worst enemies as slaves.
>
> "After them Nero, Domitian, Decius and many more in between and finally Maximinus in our day, have all come to a catastrophic end, receiving death as punishment for their acts of violence against the Church. Suppose I tell you from the beginning about the deserved misfortunes that were inflicted upon the impious ones. Diocletian became insane and abdicated his imperial status; he was forced to wear the garb of a private citizen; worn away by a long illness, he was cut off from the land of the living. Maximianus Herculius ended his life by hanging; Maximianus Galerius, struck down by an incurable ulcer, his body eroded by the putrefaction of his genitals and consumption by worms, sang a palinode and revoked persecution against the Christians by public decrees, but later, falling under the influence of Theotecnos, the magician of Antioch, he again worked terror against the Christians and was destroyed by the previous illness. Maximinus' fate was worse than all that, and the former Caesar Severus, who had been sent by Maximianus

Galerius to arrest Maxentius, was put to death himself, his soldiers having betrayed him.

"If you consider, emperor, all this, you will abandon your many gods and bring yourself to join Christ and pray to him. Truly through his help you will conquer your enemies, then, trusting in him, you will be able henceforth to attend to affairs of State. If you follow my advice I promise you that the enemy will not even give battle, and that if they do so they will immediately be routed and turn tail without a confrontation. Thus the supreme power over all affairs will be yours."[46]

Convinced by this plea, Constantine called upon Christ to preserve him in battle and protect the state and thus won his great victory. Euphratas interestingly does not appear again in the historically fairly reliable Opitz-*Vita*, but in the later Halkin-*Vita* he becomes a dominant figure who plays a vital role in the establishment of Constantinople as a second Rome during and after Constantine's Persian war(s) (discussed in the next section). One of the first tasks the eunuch accomplished before the emperor set off on his campaign was the construction of the sewers. First of all he created the inflow and outflow of the water channels according to the lie of the land, digging wells and laying underground cisterns from place to place. Because most of the work was carried out underground and thus out of sight, some men denounced him before the emperor as having squandered the large sums of money entrusted to him without even clearing the trees from the hillside. Constantine however stayed loyal to his eunuch, and when Euphratas came before him at Chalcedon, he said no hostile word towards him but instead inquired in a friendly manner as to how the construction work was going. When Euphratas replied that work was progressing in line with his instructions, the emperor asked why they were not able to see any sign of it. Euphratas then took Constantine across the Bosporus and led him through the underground series of vaults as far as the foundation of the great column on which the statue of the emperor rests (i.e., the famous "Burnt Column"; Fig. 2). There were to be found many and frequent subterranean vaults through which all the refuse from the meat markets and the sewers could be discharged. When Constantine expressed his amazement at this, he was told by Euphratas that the structures were designed to take the overflow during heavy rains and that, with them in place, building the walls would be a simple matter.

Amazed, Constantine then entrusted Euphratas with the building of a great church and with bringing "not only Romans but also people of all nations" to settle in the new capital. Euphratas consented to this but only on condition that the emperor take the signet rings from the leaders of the Roman Senate, mark each of them, and send them in a letter to him. This Constantine promised to do, and he carried out his promise at a convenient time. When Euphratas was then asked to create for Constantinople a senate as noble as the one in Rome, he used the rings in a ruse designed to lure the established senators and their families to move to the new city. According to pagan authors like Zosimus, Constantine constructed houses for those senators who followed him to the new capital,[47] and a later source, Hesychius of Miletus, claims that these were built at the emperor's own expense.[48] These legends underscore the difficulty that Constantine must have faced in attracting a senatorial class to Constantinople or creating one in the city. The solution attributed to Euphratas reflects the level of ingenuity demanded for such an undertaking:

> Now Euphratas . . . had received from the emperor the signet rings of the leading men. He summoned men with knowledge of the leaders' houses at Rome and appointed houses to be built following the design of each house, with exact similarities as to setting and position with regard to air and sea. Then he sent by letters, and with the security of boats, the leaders' actual signet rings to their wives as if from their own husbands. They did not realise the deception, but rather filled with joy that they were on their way to their own husbands, embarked on the boats with all their most valuable possessions and with their whole household they all reached Byzantium. There they entered the city built for the mother of God, and each of them went to the house that had been made the same as hers in Rome, filled with extraordinary amazement. . . . So each of them thanked their divinity as best they were able and awaited the arrival of their own husbands. Meanwhile the most pious emperor Constantine had returned to Chalcedon with his army after his destruction of Persia. The most loyal Euphratas was the first to meet him and made the following proposal: "When your majesty returns to the palace at dead of night with your boats, then give each leader by the hand to me to escort to his own home. What happens next you will learn later." So

the emperor returned to the palace as arranged and taking each of the leaders by the hand passed him on to Euphratas, saying: "Take him to his own house." He went off with torches and a large bodyguard. Each man stood at the gates of the house and inspected the entrance, inspected the outward impression of the house, and in particular its appearance, and the surprised shout of the servant girls and the uproar that passed among the servants, and the greeting of his children and the embrace of his wife. He was astonished and could not explain it, but heard his relatives saying: "We received your letter and boats, and came to find things here." And for more certain confirmation they displayed the letter itself and the signet ring.[49]

Astonished with their painless migration, reassured that it represented the will of the Virgin, and enticed with monetary emoluments, the Roman aristocrats were easily persuaded to stay in their new homes. Nor did Euphratas's achievements end here. At the time of Constantine's death, he had also surveyed the site and laid the foundation for Hagia Sophia so that the church had reached the level of the colonnade.[50] Euphratas then continued the work in the reign of Constantius II, and by the time of his own death the structure was beginning to be lavishly furnished; he also bequeathed an almshouse that later became a church and in which he was buried. The locals called the church, which was situated near the Leomacellium, "the Euphratas."[51]

How such an intricate legend arose in the first place is intriguing; one could imagine that posterity believed Constantine's numerous achievements were possible only if he had some kind of Christian vizier and that Euphratas, who would enter later Byzantine annals as a historical figure, was introduced to fill this gap. Novelistic elements are also clearly at play, for at this point Constantine had metamorphosed into a generic symbol of Byzantium and Byzantine rulership more generally.

The "Persian Wars" of Constantine

Historically, Constantine was victorious over the Franks, Sarmatians, and Goths and over his imperial rivals, but the one all-important victory that eluded him his entire lifetime was against the Persians. Despite plans to campaign against the Sassanians – plans that were nearly put into effect at the end of his life – "Persicus Maximus" was a title that he was never able to display legitimately in his titulature.[52] Beset first by Persians and later the Arabs and then the Turks, the Byzantines would dream of what Constantine could have achieved had he lived long enough to bring his "crusade" against the Persians to a triumphal conclusion. In their legends, however, they were able to ensure that their model emperor personally triumphed over Rome's traditional eastern enemy not once but twice. The first campaign, according to the Halkin-*Vita*, followed shortly after his sojourn in Rome. In an effort to fend off a Persian attack, Constantine set off into uncharted Persian territory, where his army was attacked and fled into the nearby woods:

> Others were taken prisoner, among them the emperor Constantine who was overpowered and condemned to serve as a sacrificial victim to their idol. But reflect on God's goodness, and how he provides a way when there seems no way out! The guards of the abominable rite of the Persians went out to gather wood that they would need for the sacrifice, and when they approached the place where a few men were hidden and began trying to cut the brushwood, the men leapt out and overwhelmed them. They were dragged into the thicket. Then they asked them to tell in all truth what had happened to the Roman emperor. They were panic stricken and clasped their feet, saying: "We are slaves of the Persians, as you can see, though we too are Romans. If our lives are saved, we will tell you everything in detail. If you like, you can trust us. We will also suggest a very useful plan." And after making an oath to them the guards continued: "The king of the Persians and his rulers have announced the celebration of his birthday in the temple of their god and that your emperor will be produced as a sacrifice. . . . Around the altar is a high wall, the enclosure that we call the temple. The middle parts of the temple are covered over, but the parts around it have no roof. All the people enter this temple with the king. Since it is the Persians' custom to approach any sacrifice without even the weapons they have on them, we can lead you into the temple in the evening, if you are in agreement. The next day, when the crowd comes in, we will place you behind the gates. At the moment when your emperor is about to be sacrificed, we will close the gates and join you in cutting down the Persians. And we shall liberate your emperor."

The Romans put their faith in their words, and at dead of night they followed them and were brought inside the temple where they enjoyed breakfast and a rest. At dawn the heralds shouted, and they stood behind the doors with their weapons concealed. The whole Persian assemblage entered. Emperor Constantine was led forward in chains and placed next to the altar. As the Persians were dancing, the guards in accordance with their promise secured the gates and bade the Romans cut down the Persians. They released the emperor Constantine from his bonds and produced weapons and joined equally in the slaughter. All the Persians in the temple along with their king were killed. "Great you are, God of the Christians," shouted the Romans, "and who apart from you works miracles without number?" Then they came out of the temple following the guards and overran all the sentry posts and freed any men in them that were Romans. But the Persians that they encountered they killed without mercy, while the men who were hidden in the mountains they called out through heralds. Then they returned to the stronghold where they had carried out the massacre, and after setting in order the arrangements for the journey they entered Byzantium, wreaking great destruction in the villages they found en route. So that is what occurred.[53]

The Persians could hardly leave such a shameful defeat unavenged. When they counterattacked, the Persians advanced as far as Chalcedon unopposed and laid waste to the city. Constantine raised an army in Macedon and marched through Bithynia up to the rear of the Persian lines, thus causing them to withdraw:

The pious emperor heard about their invasion, gathered together his army and crossed through Macedonia. While he was approaching Persian territory he first secured the roads that led to Bithynia. Then he changed the appearance of the soldiers so that they would not be recognised as being Romans. In this way he entered Persian lands. He found only women and children and separated the women and killed them. Any that were pregnant they pretended to roast their embryos and eat them. The children they tied up and beat them with threshing implements as if it were harvest time. They did many other strange acts so that they would not be recognised for who they were.

At this the Persian queen made use of places of refuge in the area and sent frequent letters every day to her own husband to make clear her situation. But the men of the pious emperor who had secured the roads as has been said passed all these letters into his hands. This continued to happen for a whole year. After this she managed to get a letter through to the Persian king. Emperor Constantine discovered this and straight away withdrew from Persian territory and set up a close guard on the roads. So that was what took place. When the Persians learned of the disconcerting turn of events from the letters that had got through, each of them with all speed and without a thought for their king, and lacking any military formation, hurried away to their own homes. . . . When the Persians in their small numbers encountered the Romans who were guarding the roads, they were killed by them without mercy. Their king heard of this and received the survivors and took to flight by trackless empty mountains and secured his own safety. At these successes won by the holy and adorable cross the pious emperor was glorified and the whole army gratified, and they returned to their own lands.[54]

This entire narrative is larded with echoes of Heraclius's successful campaigns behind the Persian lines to relieve the siege of Constantinople by the combined forces of the Avars and the triumphant Persian armies of Chosroes Parwez encamped at Chalcedon in 610. Indeed, the early seventh century was precisely the period when the legendary Constantine came into his own. As Michael Whitby has well noted,

For Constantine as an imperial model the breakthrough came in the seventh century with Heraclius: his eldest son was named Constantine, and the Heraclian author of Chronicon Paschale gave more attention to Constantine than had Malalas, and used him more in the dating calculations that adorn his work. For Heraclius the resonances of Constantine as the Christian who came out of the west to overthrow eastern persecutors, reunite the Roman empire, and promise to extend Christianity to Persia may all have been potent factors.[55]

With the Persian legends as well, then, Constantine was reshaped to fit an imperial ideal suited to the demands of contemporary politics and culture.

CONCLUSION

No other emperor in the Byzantine world enjoys a literary and hagio-graphical heritage as rich and as widespread as that of Constantine – and his mother Helena. As Rome's first Christian emperor, he offered the obvious exemplar of Christian rulership for generations of late Roman and especially Byzantine emperors. As an emperor who, by virtue of his lengthy reign, sweeping reforms, and lasting dynasty cast a long shadow over the subsequent history of the Roman empire, he also offered tremendous symbolic capital to those hoping to legitimize their own claims to power. As an imperial prototype, however, Constantine's career as a Christian Roman emperor as known from late antique sources was far from ideal. The judicial murder of his son, the execution without trial of his wife, his deathbed baptism by an Arian prelate, and his unfinished campaign against Rome's traditional enemy were all aspects of his vita that had to be sanitized and replaced with legend. These legends became so popular in the Middle Ages that they replaced the more contemporary sources from late antiquity in both Byzantium and the medieval west. The rediscovery of the historical Constantine had to await the arrival of critical scholarship in the Renaissance.

BIBLIOGRAPHICAL GUIDE

Sources: Despite the importance of the Constantine legend for both scholars of late antiquity and the Middle Ages, the main sources remain largely untranslated. The best edition of the *Actus Sylvestri* is P. De Leo, *Il Constitutum Constantini, compilazione agiografica del sec. VIII* (1974), 153–221. Most scholars however still use the edition of B. Mombritius, *Sanctuarium seu Vitae Sanctorum*, vol. 2 (1910), 508–31. There is no known English translation of this text, but the abridged version of it in the *Legenda Aurea* could be conveniently consulted in translation in W. G. Ryan, *Jacobus de Voragine, The Golden Legend* (1993), 62–71. The standard and most often consulted edition of the *Donatio Constantini* is found in C. Mirbt and K. Aland, *Quellen zur Geschichte des Papsttums und des römischen Katholizismus* (1967), 251–6, and complete translations of the document can be found in E. F. Henderson, *Select Historical Documents of the Middle Ages* (1925), 324–35, and M. Edwards, *Constantine and Christendom: The Oration to the Saints, The Greek and Latin Accounts of the Discovery of the Cross, The Edict of Constantine to Pope Silvester* (2003), 92–115. Of the five Byzantine (post-Eusebian) lives of Constantine, only one (the Guidi-*Vita*) is available in English translation; the translation, by F. Beetham, is found in S. N. C. Lieu and D. A. Montserrat, *From Constantine to Julian: Pagan and Byzantine Views* (1996): 106–46. English translations of the Opitz-*Vita*, the Winklemann-*Vita*, and the Halkin-*Vita* have been completed by a team of scholars and are awaiting publication in learned journals and collected studies.

Secondary works: The majority of modern studies are in German. Among English contributions to the subject, the most important ones are C. B. Coleman, *Constantine the Great and Christianity* (1914); A. Linder, "The Myth of Constantine the Great in the West: Sources and Hagiographic Commemoration," *Studi Medievali*, 3rd ser. 16.1 (1975): 43–95; A. Kazhdan, "'Constantin imaginaire': Byzantine Legends of the Ninth Century about Constantine the Great," *Byzantion* 57 (1987): 196–250; G. Fowden, "The Last Days of Constantine, Oppositional Versions and Their Influence," *Journal of Roman Studies* 84 (1994b): 146–70; and S. N. C. Lieu, "From History to Legend and Legend to History: The Medieval and Byzantine Transformation of Constantine's *Vita*," and T. Wilfong, "Constantine in Coptic: Egyptian Constructions of Constantine the Great," both in *Constantine, History, Historiography and Legend* (1998), 136–88. On Helena, see the standard biography by J. W. Drijvers, *Helena Augusta: The Mother of Constantine the Great and the Legend of Her Finding of the True Cross* (1992), which makes full use of hagiographical sources. So also does S. Borgehammar, *How the Holy Cross Was Found* (1991), which also includes editions of important medieval texts. The recent study of A. Harbus, *Helena of Britain in Medieval Legend* (2002), is essential for those interested in western medieval legends on Constantine, many of which are unrelated to those that can be traced back to late antiquity.

NOTES

This chapter is dedicated to the late Professor Walter Ullmann, FBA, formerly Professor of Medieval History at Cambridge University, who first instilled in the present author an interest in the Constantinian legacy during the Middle Ages.

1 Baynes 1939, 699. On medieval and Byzantine rulers claiming to be new Constantines, see Grünewald 1992 and the articles in Magdalino 1994.

2   On the legends of Constantine in Byzantium, see esp. Kazhdan 1987, and in the west, Linder 1975. On the legends in general and their relation to medieval historical sources on Constantine, see also Lieu 1998.

3   The manuscript in question is Bibliothèque Royale Albert Ier, Réserve Précueyse B 1414. The most easily available edition is Mombritius 1910, 508–31. The text is reprinted with extensive commentary in De Leo 1974. Cf. Pohlkamp 1988, 418 n. 21. There is no known English translation of the *Actus Sylvestri*.

4   The best critical edition now is Maggioni 1998, XII (De Sancto Silvestro) 1:108–19. For an English translation, see Ryan 1993, 62–71. On Constantine and Sylvester in the Legenda, see esp. Reames 1985, 109–11. On Jacobus de Voragine, see esp. Cushing 1935.

5   Mombritius 1910, 508–10; cf. De Leo 1974, 155–60.

6   For an excellent summary of the contents of the *Actus*, see Fowden 1994b. See also Pohlkamp 1988, 449–59.

7   On the laws, see the important study of Linder 1988.

8   Jul. *Caes*. 336a–b; cf. Jul. *Con. Gal.* fr. 59 and Soz. 1.5.1 with Fowden 1994b, 155–8.

9   Milner 1994; Fowden 1994a. See also Malalas 13.2 (p. 317) and R. Scott 1994, 62.

10 Cf. Nestle 1895. For Latin versions, see Borgehammar 1991, 255–71 (versio A), 282–8 (versio B).

11 In the Middle Ages, the belief circulated that it was not Constantine but his father with a similar sounding name (i.e., Constantius I) who was baptised by Eusebius. Cf. Jacobus de Voragine *Legenda Aurea* 68 (64). The same source also refuted the claim that Constantine was baptised by Eusebius of Nicomedia as stated by the *Historia Tripartita* of Cassiodorus, a work that is an amalgam of the main continuations of the *Ecclesiastical History* of Eusebius. The *Actus Sylvestri*, in a variant of Ruf. *HE* 10.8, ends with a claim to be a direct translation of Eusebius from the Greek. Cf. Levison 1924, 176.

12 A view first put forward by Dölger 1913, esp. 416–26. See further elaborations and additional support for the thesis, esp. from the Syriac Julian Romance, in Fowden 1994b, 158–60.

13 Aug. *De unico baptismo* 16.27 (*CSEL* 53:28): "Marcellinus et presbyteri eius Miltiades, Marcellus et Siluester traditionis codicum diuinorum et turificationis ab eo crimine arguuntur." Cf. Frend 1971, 22; Pohlkamp 1984, 368.

14 *Actus Sylvestri* (Mombritius 1910, 508.27–509.6, 511.33–37 = De Leo 1974, 1:25–28, 302–5 [pp. 156–7, 163]). Cf. Pohlkamp 1984, 369–71.

15 See *Vita de S. Helena* 23–24 (*AASS* August Vol. 3:587d–e [August 18]). On the main medieval legends on Helena in the west (including those in Old English), which state she was born in Britain, see now the excellent comprehensive study by Harbus 2002, esp. 152–82, which offers an edition of the *Vita Sancte Helene* of Jocelin of Furness.

16 The best and most convenient version of the text is that of Zeumer found in Mirbt and Aland 1967, 251–6. See also the useful remarks and edition of S. Williams 1964. For an English translation, see Edwards 2003, 92–115; cf. Ehler and Morrall 1954, 15–22 (superior but incomplete); also Henderson 1925, 324–35 (inferior but complete).

17 On this see esp. Ullmann 1955, 74–86; 1967. For a summary of the varied use and reputation of the text in the Middle Ages, both west and east, see Lieu 1998,

145–9. There is a vast literature on this subject, the most important works being Levison 1924 and Polhkamp 1988, 435–64.

18 *Constitutum Constantini* 17 (Mirbt and Aland 1967, 255 = Ehler and Morrall 1954, 21–2; cf. Edwards 2003, 112–13).

19 *Constitutum Constantini* 18 (Mirbt and Aland 1967, 255 = Ehler and Morral 1954, 22; cf. Edwards 2003, 113).

20 Ullmann 1955, 82.

21 On this, see the important observations of Krautheimer 1980, 117–21.

22 *Actus Sylvestri* (Mombritius 1910, 508.27–510.34 = De Leo 1974, 156–61).

23 On Gelasius in general, see my comments in Lieu and Montserrat 1996, 34–5; Borgehammar 1991, 31–55.

24 Ruf. *HE* 11.7; Soc. 1.17.1–13; Soz. 2.1.1–11; Theod. *HE* 2.18.1–9.

25 Ambrose *De obit. Theod.* 43–51; Paulinus Nolanus *Ep.* 31.3–6 (*CSEL* 39:2, 269–75).

26 On the date, see Borgehammar 1991, 130–9; cf. J. W. Drijvers 1992, 81–93.

27 Soz. 2.1.4. For the Syriac (BL Add. 14644 of the fifth or sixth century AD), see the edition and translation of H. J. W. Drijvers and J. W. Drijvers 1997, 36–73.

28 See Latin sources collected in Borgehammar 1991, 255–302; cf. Holder 1889. The best known version of the Judas-Kyriakos story in Greek is that published by Nestle 1895.

29 *Legenda Aurea* 64 (Maggioni 1998, 459–70 = Ryan 1993, 277–84).

30 The earlist known version of the Protonike legend is found in the Syraic *Doctrina Addai*; cf. Howard 1981, 20–35.

31 See, e.g., Cyril of Jerusalem's references to the cross from the 340s (Catechesis 4.10, 10.19 = *PG* 33:470, 685–7) or the mid-fourth-century inscription *CIL* 8:9255 attesting a relic of the cross in North Africa.

32 *Propylaeum ad Acta Sanctorum Novembris: Synaxarium ecclesiae Constantinopolitanae e codice Sirmondiano nunc Berolinensi adiectis synaxariis selectis*, ed. H. Delehaye (*AASS* November Vol. 1). On this important exemplum of a Byzantine menologion, see Kazhdan 1996, esp. 484–9.

33 See Lieu in Lieu and Montserrat 1996, 69–70; cf. Chapter 3 n. 40 in this volume.

34 Cf. above n. 9.

35 For a fuller discussion of these lives and their contents, see Lieu in Lieu and Montserrat 1996, 101–5; Lieu 1998, 153–4.

36 *BHG* 365z, 366, and 366a, edited at Winkelmann 1987. An English translation of the text by Mark Vermes awaits publication.

37 *BHG* 364, edited at Guidi 1907.

38 The translation by Beetham is revised and reprinted in Lieu and Montserrat 1996, 106–46.

39 *PG* 145:1241–1325. On this, see Gentz 1966, 73, 84.

40 *BHG* 365, edited at Opitz 1934b. See also the earlier edition of Franchi de' Cavalieri 1896–7. An English translation of this important text by Frank Beetham remains unpublished as a new edition of the text based on an examination of both the Vatican and the Sabba (see next note) manuscripts is urgently required.

41 Though additional sections from part of its lost beginning could be supplied by *Codex Sabbaiticus gr.* 366 (13 C.) foll. 9–22, cf. Bidez 1935; Halkin 1960a, 1960b.

42 *BHG* 365n, edited by Halkin 1959a, 73–105; 1959b. An English translation of the text by Mark Vermes awaits publication.

43 *BHG* 363, edited by Gedeon 1900. There is no known translation of this text into a modern European language.

44 *Libellus de Constantino Magno euisque matre Helena* in Giangrasso 1999.

45 This was acknowledged as early as the end of the fourth century, see above Chapter 3 n. 3. Ambrose *De obit. Theod.* 42 regarded this lowly occupation favourably because Jesus was born in the stables of an inn.

46 Halkin 1960a, 7–8, sec. 1–5 (trans. Beetham and Vermes in Lieu 1998, 161–3).

47 Zos. 2.31.3.

48 Hesychius 40–1.

49 Halkin 1959a, 89–90, sec. 12 (trans. Vermes, unpublished, here and below).

50 Halkin 1959a, 100–1, sec. 18.

51 Halkin 1959a, 102, sec. 20.

52 See Chapter 16 of this volume.

53 Halkin 1959a, 84–5, sec. 9. Constantine as a victor over the Persians is a frequently encountered theme in oriental *vitae* of Constantine. On this, see Wilfong 1998, 185–6.

54 Halkin 1959a, 88–9, sec. 11.

55 Whitby 1994, 92–4.

SECTION V

EMPIRE AND BEYOND

14: WARFARE AND THE MILITARY

Hugh Elton

৵

Aurelius Gaius, son of the same, I served in Legio I Italica of
the Moesians, was selected for Legio VIII Augusta in Germany
and the [Legio I] Iovia Scythica in the provinces of Scythia and
Pannonia. As a recruit I served as an apprentice cavalryman,
then as a *lanciarius, optio triarius, optio ordinatus, optio princeps,* and
optio of the imperial *comites* [drawn from?] Legio I Iovia Scythica.
I travelled around the empire, to Asia [?], Caria, [missing
region], Lydia, Lycaonia, Cilicia, [missing region], Phoenicia,
Syria, Arabia, Palestine, Egypt, Alexandria, India, [missing region],
Mesopotamia, Cappadocia, [missing region], Galatia, Bithynia,
Thrace, [missing region], Moesia, the Carpians' territory, [missing
region], Sarmatia four times, Viminacium, [missing region], the
Goths' territory twice, Germany, [missing region], Dardania,
Dalmatia, Pannonia, [missing region], Gaul, Spain, Mauretania,
and [missing region]. Then advancing and after much toil I came
to my native land Pessinus where I was brought up, [and am
now] dwelling in Cotyaeum . . . with [my daughter?] Macedonia.
In tribute to Julia [Are]scusa my dearest [wife] I have erected this
stele from the fruits of my own labours as a memorial till the
Resurrection. Farewell all.[1]

When Aurelius Gaius erected this now damaged memorial to
his wife at Cotyaeum in central Asia Minor, he could be
excused for thinking that he had been involved in every war
fought in the age of Constantine. He certainly participated in foreign
wars fought against Germans, Sarmatians, Persians, Moors, and Arabs to
defend the imperial frontiers; nor did he even mention the many civil
wars in which he may have fought for imperial power. The constant

military pressures implicit in his catalogue forced the army to continue developing between the late third century and mid-fourth century. In this broader span, three major periods can be distinguished: the Tetrarchy (284–305), the civil wars (305–24), and the House of Constantine (324–63). During the early years of the fourth century, the large numbers of emperors, the frequent civil wars, and the changes of allegiance by troops meant that the army was not a homogeneous body but an organisation with a complicated history and many local variations. During the three decades that Constantine was Roman emperor, the forces under his command grew from a quarter of the Roman army to its entirety; there was thus no single body that can be described as Constantine's army.

Beyond this organisational complexity, a substantial human element had to be contended with. Take, for example, Flavius Abinnaeus, who enlisted c. 304 in the regiment of the Parthosagittarii in Egypt and served with them for thirty-three years, that is, under Diocletian, Maximin, Licinius, and Constantine. He escorted a group of refugees to Constantinople in 336 and a group of Egyptian recruits to Syrian Hierapolis in 339–40. At the court in Syria, he was rewarded with the command of the Ala Quinta Praelectorum at Dionysias in Egypt, but when he arrived at Alexandria to have his appointment confirmed, he discovered that other officers had claimed the same post. Initially denied his promotion because one of his rivals had the support of Valacius, the *dux Aegypti*, Abinnaeus was forced to petition the emperor Constantius II before he could take up his position.[2]

ORGANISATION

When Constantine became emperor in 306, he inherited the army of his father, the Tetrarch Constantius I. Constantius's army was similar to that of the other Tetrarchs, Diocletian, Maximian, and Galerius. Most of their troops were deployed on the borders of the empire, but each emperor also had his own field army. In the third century, imperial expeditionary forces, though in theory only temporarily detached from border service, had in practice become standing field armies, known informally as the *comitatus*. With two Augusti reigning from 285, there were two field armies, and with the addition of the two Caesars in 293, this number was increased to four. This allowed the empire to deal simultaneously with problems on four fronts. So in 298 Constantius held the Rhine against the Franks while Maximian was in Africa, probably fighting the Laguatan. Meanwhile, in Syria Galerius invaded Persia while Diocletian was in Egypt suppressing the revolt of Aurelius Achilleus. Despite the number of emperors, they were still forced to move long distances; by 299 Maximian had moved on to Rome and Diocletian was in Syria.[3] Diocletian's *comitatus* was formed around the legion of the Ioviani and two elite cavalry regiments, the Lanciarii and the Comites, while Galerius's was based on three Moesian legions, Legio IV Flavia, VII Claudia and XI Claudia, and the elite cavalry regiment of the *promoti*.[4] The core was supplemented by other infantry and cavalry regiments and by various guard units.

During the third century, legions at full strength contained about five thousand men in ten cohorts. This continued to be the case under the Tetrarchy, when Diocletian and Maximian raised two new elite legions, the Ioviani and Herculiani, at a strength of six thousand. An inscription from Sitifis in Mauretania mentions cohorts VII and X of Legio II Herculia, probably brought there by Maximian in 298, and tile stamps from Galerius's palace at Gamzigrad mention five different cohorts from Legio V Macedonica.[5] Not all legions in the *comitatus* were full strength, and some were detachments, known as *vexillationes* and commanded by a tribune. Many of these were absent from their bases for long periods. Under Licinius, a combined detachment of the Phoenician-based legions III Gallica and I Illyricorum were in Egypt for at least six years, being attested at Coptos in 315/6 and at Syene in 321, in both cases under the command of the same Praepositus, Victorinus.[6] In a separate development during the late third century, eastern legions became more complex owing to the creation of subunits of *lanciarii* (elite infantry) and stronger cavalry elements, known as *promoti*.[7] Thus in Egypt in 299, Legio II Traiana consisted of a *vexillatio* at Apollinopolis Superior, some *lanciarii* at Ptolemais, and some *promoti* at Tentyra, all in the Thebaid, as well as a base unit at Parembole further north.[8] By the middle of the fourth century, many of these detachments had become entirely separate units, which, like most legions in the *comitatus*, were now under tribunes, about one thousand strong.

The same need for more flexibility was felt in western armies, though the response was different. Instead of creating subunits from legions, a new type of elite infantry unit, the *auxilia palatina*, was created. Some of these regiments were existing auxiliary cohorts like the Batavi or Mattiaci, transferred into the *comitatus* and possibly increased in size to about one thousand men. Others were new creations, many of which were raised by Constantius I and Constantine on the Rhine. At the point of recruitment, many of their number were of extra-imperial origin (the Romans would have said "barbarian"), but subsequent recruits would have diluted this character.[9] Stronger western cavalry forces were created through a new series of cavalry corps, generically referred to as the Illyriciani, composed of numerous regiments of Dalmatae, Mauri, Scutarii, and Stablesiani.[10] All the new cavalry regiments in both east and west were *vexillationes* – confusingly they used the same name as legionary detachments – and had an establishment of circa six hundred.[11]

Emperors usually travelled with the *comitatus* but were always protected by guard troops. Under the Tetrarchy, this meant some division of the ten cohorts of praetorians, each one thousand strong under an equestrian tribune, supported by the one thousand cavalry of the Equites Singulares.[12] Constantine disbanded Maxentius's praetorians after the battle of the Milvian Bridge in 312 and Licinius's after Chrysopolis in 324, but we have no evidence for what happened to his own praetorians.[13] The need for guards of course remained, and this was met by Constantine's creation of new units, the *Scholae Palatinae*, regiments of cavalry five hundred strong. By the end of Constantine's reign, there were five Scholae – the Primi, Secundi, and Tertii Scutarii; the Armaturae; and the Gentiles – though their numbers probably varied according to the number of emperors.[14] The emperor's personal security was the responsibility of forty *candidati* who were picked from the Scholae (Fig. 39).[15] Emperors were also surrounded by Protectores Augusti (known as Domestici from perhaps the 350s), imperial staff officers who were often later promoted to command regiments. Their commander was an important figure, and in this period several became emperors, including Diocletian in 284, Constantius I in 293, and Jovian in 363.[16] Many early Protectores maintained links with their units, like Traianus Mucianus, Protector in Legio XIII Gemina at the end of the third century.[17] When the office of *magister militum* was created by Constantine, Protectores were also attached to his staff, though many served away from the *magister's* headquarters.

This variety of guard troops formed an effective and visible cordon around emperors on almost all occasions. No emperor was assassinated during this period, while Julian's death in Mesopotamia in 363 occurred because he had not put on his breastplate and had left his *candidati* behind in his haste to enter the fighting. Constantine's appearance without a military escort was a surprising feature of his attendance at the Council of Nicaea in 325; even in the imperial palace "others led the way, not some of the usual guards and soldiers, but only of his faithful friends." Far more typical was what happened at the celebration of his twentieth anniversary as emperor, when "guards and soldiers ringed the entrance to the palace, guarding it with drawn swords."[18] These troops were not only for display or personal security. They fought often and hard, as in 355, when Arintheus led a counterattack at the head of the Schola Armaturarum at Lake Brigantia together with the Comites and Promoti, the elite cavalry regiments instituted under Diocletian and Galerius.[19]

The regular troops in the *comitatus* were often supplemented by foreign troops, usually described as *foederati* or *auxilia*, who were recruited for a specific campaign and dismissed at its end. Licinius, for example, had a large number of allied Goths under Alica in the 324 campaign against Constantine.[20] In the east at this period, the Romans were often allied with the various Arab tribes, though these alliances tended to produce scouts and intelligence rather than troops for major battles. A good example of these was the Lakhmid chief Imru' al-Qays, buried at the Roman fort at Namara in the province of Arabia in 328.[21] He served simultaneously as both chief of his own people and ally of the Roman army.

The *comitatus* was supported by warships and transports deployed in fleets throughout the Mediterranean and in northern Europe.[22] Ravenna was the most important western base, though other fleets were based at Misenum and around the English Channel and Rhine delta. In the east, Constantinople replaced Nicomedia as the major fleet base from the 330s, while other smaller fleets were based in Egypt at Alexandria and in the south Aegean. A typical use for such fleets is attested in the transport of four regiments of *auxilia palatina* from Gaul to Britain in 360 in response to raids on the northern frontier.[23] Fleets were of more use in civil wars, when the Mediterranean might be divided between rival emperors, forcing both sides to construct fleets rapidly in order to gain control of seaways. Thus in 324 both Constantine and Licinius hastily built fleets in the Aegean which met in a two-day battle near Gallipoli. Similarly, Constantius II built a fleet in Egypt to support his campaign in Italy against Magnentius in 351–2, then sent it against Carthage and in turn to Spain.[24]

COMMAND STRUCTURES

Before Diocletian, the troops in the border provinces were commanded by the provincial governor, who also handled civil matters. Heavy fighting power was provided by large and unwieldy legions concentrated on the Rhine and Danube, in Britain and Syria. These were drawn on for detachments for the *comitatus* but were also broken up for garrison purposes, as with Legio II Adiutrix in Valeria, which was divided into six parts. They were supported by cavalry *alae* (wings), infantry cohorts (mostly about five hundred strong), and river fleets.[25] From Diocletian's reign, however, military and civil responsibilities were reallocated, so that by the end of Constantine's reign, a province's military aspects were administered by a *dux* (commander, whence the title "duke"), and civil matters generally by a separate governor. Some of the new military frontier commands covered more than one civil province, producing officers such as the *dux Pannoniae Primae et Norici Ripensis* or the *dux Aegypti Thebaidos utrarumque Libyarum*.[26] Such arrangements were still developing in the early fourth century but were at least similar to those at the end of the century, when there were two ducates in Britain, twelve along the length of the Rhine and Danube, eight in the east, and seven in Africa.[27] The transition to the new structure was gradual, and *duces* could still sometimes carry out some civic duties, as evidenced by a rescript of Constantine to Ursinus, *dux* of Mesopotamia, asking him to enforce a ban on castration.[28] Usually their duties were more mundane. Thus when Valacius, the *dux Aegypti* who had tried to stymie Abinnaeus's promotion, ordered an inspection of all the forts under his command c. 340, he discovered the fort of Psobthis needed a new coat of limewash.[29] Similarly, some civil governors may have retained military functions into Constantine's reign, as suggested by a dedication from the tribune Successus to Arrius Maximus, *consularis* (consular governor) of Syria Coele.[30]

The separation of civil and military hierarchies had consequences beyond provincial administration. With no need to hold civic offices, soldiers could now be career officers rather than aristocrats with military responsibilities. This enabled the creation of an imperial aristocracy based on office-holding rather than land. Once these barriers to advancement were removed, emperors could pick candidates from the whole army, not just the senatorial and equestrian orders. Diocletian, born the son of a freedman, and Galerius, who had been a herdsman, benefitted from these changes. Less spectacular was the contemporary career of Valerius Thiumpus, who served in Legio XI Claudia, then as a *lanciarius* in the *comitatus* before becoming a Protector and going on to command Legio II Herculia.[31] These changes affected men from outside the Roman empire too. Thus the Frank Bonitus fought for Constantine against Licinius and had a Roman wife; and Crocus, an Alamannic king, played a role in Constantine's accession in 306 because he was in command of troops at York when Constantius I died.[32] This enabled the promotion of non-Romans into higher ranks, a process often described as "barbarisation." It was not a deliberate policy change but an unintended consequence of the changes in command structures.

After the final defeat of Licinius, his last imperial rival, in 324, Constantine was able to reunite all Roman armed forces under his own direct authority. Campaigning against foreign enemies continued, but there were now opportunities for reorganisation. Although the core of his army had been inherited from his father, it had successively incorporated the forces of Maxentius (including troops of Domitius Alexander and Maximian) and of Licinius (including troops of Diocletian, Severus, Galerius, and Maximin). Some traces of this history remain in the *Notitia Dignitatum*, which lists, among other offices, the units of the late fourth-century army. When the two halves of the *Notitia* were finalized in the late fourth and early fifth centuries, Legio III Diocletiana, I Maximiana, and the Gallic legion Prima Flavia Constantia – all named after members of the first Tetrarchy – were still in existence. We cannot identify any units named after Galerius, but these may only be undetectable because they would have used his official name Maximian. However, the lack of units named after Licinius, Severus, Maxentius, Maximin Daia, or Alexander is suggestive. Although they could have been destroyed or disbanded, trained manpower was valuable, and the units were probably renamed. This would explain a group of five legions in Africa: Prima Flavia Pacis, Secunda Flavia Victrix, Tertia Flavia Salutis, Flavia Victrix Constantina, and Secunda Flavia Constantiniana. These were probably named for Maxentius or Alexander and then renamed after Constantine took control of Africa in 312.[33]

Constantine's most significant reforms probably took place after his final defeat of Licinius. The members of the *comitatus* were now given a separate status as field army troops (*comitatenses*). They mainly differed from the troops left on the borders (now known variously as *limitanei, burgarii,* or *ripenses*) by having higher physical standards and a shorter length of service before receipt of full benefits on retirement. The efficiency and morale effects of these measures are harder to assess but may have led to a slight decline in the quality of the border troops.[34] The troops on the borders remained under the command of *duces*, but the *comitatus* came to be commanded by two new officers, the *magister peditum* (master of infantry) and *magister equitum* (master of cavalry).[35] These titles should not be taken literally; *magistri peditum* and *equitum* both commanded infantry and cavalry and were often loosely referred to as *magistri militum* (masters of soldiers).[36] *Magistri militum* had authority over *duces* from the time of their creation. However, the unity of the new field army was rapidly fractured as Constantine assigned military responsibilities to his family. Even from as early as 318 or 319, while Licinius was still in power, Crispus led his own army in Gaul, where he won several victories against Franks and Alamanni.[37] After Constantine's death in 337, his sons divided the empire and the *comitatus* so that there were field armies in Gaul (Constantine II), Illyricum (Constans) and the east (Constantius II). Constantine and Constans each had his own *magister equitum* and *magister peditum*, while Constantius II divided his forces between the Balkans and the east – where he commanded personally – with a *magister militum* in each region. This fragmentation did mean that the resources available to any individual emperor were reduced. By 353 Constantius ruled alone, leading a central imperial army with two *magistri militum* while leaving the three regional field armies in Gaul, Illyricum, and the east, each under its own *magister militum*.[38] The army's structure was thus complex but flexible. Transfers of men and units around the empire were common, and though Abinnaeus's experiences show the problems that might arise, they need to be set against an organisation that was efficient enough to tunnel under the walls of the Persian stronghold of Maiozamalcha in 363, record the names of the men first out of the tunnel, and then reward them for their achievements.[39]

NUMBERS AND RECRUITS

We cannot be certain of the size of the Roman army at the start of the fourth century, though a figure provided by the sixth-century writer John Lydus is attractive. He stated that Diocletian had an army of 389,704 and a navy of 45,562. This figure may be broadly accurate (even if its extreme precision seems dubious) since Lydus worked as an imperial secretary and could have had access to official records.[40] The largest field army known in the third or fourth century was Julian's expeditionary force of 83,000 in Persia in 363, drawn from the entire empire. This was the eastern field army, supplemented by local border troops, the imperial army of Constantius II, and troops brought by Julian from Gaul.[41] More typical than Julian's army of 363 was the 38,000-man force available for operations in Gaul in 357, composed of 13,000 from the Gallic army under Julian and 25,000 from part of the imperial army led by the *magister peditum* Barbatio.[42] Given the wide range of resources drawn upon for Julian's 363 expedition, it is unlikely that larger figures are plausible without extensive supporting evidence. Thus for the 312 war between Constantine and Maxentius, Zosimus's figures of 98,000 men under Constantine (from Spain, Gaul, and Britain) and 188,000 for Maxentius (from Italy and Africa) cannot represent field army strengths.[43]

The early fourth-century writer Lactantius claimed that each Tetrarch worked to increase the size of his own army. Many new units were certainly raised at this period; Diocletian, for example, raised a series of six legions, three named Iovia for himself and three named Herculia for Maximian.[44] Other "new" units, however, were assembled out of older units, by detachment or renaming. Furthermore, many of the units known from the early third century no longer existed.[45] Lastly, though it has been argued that unit sizes were reduced during this period, the evidence for this is not compelling.[46]

For the army, whatever its size, to function, it needed supplies of rations, animals, equipment and manpower. The supply process was the responsibility of the praetorian prefect. Before Constantine's reforms, praetorian prefects commanded the praetorian guards and had military functions until the creation of the *magistri militum*.[47] Collection and distribution within a province was handled by local officials, and then surpluses were sent on to other provinces. The ordered running of the system was complicated by troop movements, especially those involving the emperor. Providing for these movements required extensive planning in advance, as suggested by a letter of September 23, 298, ordering the construction of a bakery at Panopolis in Egypt in preparation for a visit of Diocletian and by the stockpiling of 3 million *medimnoi* (about 120,000 metric tons) of wheat in Brigantia and 3 million more in the Cottian Alps as part of Constantius II's preparations for his campaign against Julian.[48] A letter authorising the delivery of 8,280 *litrai* (= 3,764 kilograms) of oil and 8,280 Italic *sextarii* (= 5,645 kilograms) of salt to a detachment of Legio III Diocletiana at Syene in 299 was meant to cover only a period of four months.[49] Other ration items included meat, wheat, and wine as well as chaff and barley for horses. Specialised studfarms existed to provide some horses, though others were levied from the populace, and the army also needed large numbers of mules, donkeys, camels, and oxen. A sense of the need for horses can be gained from the fact that the sons of cavalrymen would only be enrolled as cavalry troopers if they provided their own horses.[50] Once delivered to their destination, these supplies were handed out by *actuarii* (requisitions officials), who according to Aurelius Victor, governor of Pannonia II in 361, "are a kind of man, especially at this time, who are venal, sly, factious, and greedy, as if made by nature for committing and concealing fraud."[51]

The most difficult item to supply, however, was always manpower. Most new troops came from levies provided by local communities.[52] In the third century, many successful soldiers, such as Galerius and Diocletian, came from the Danubian provinces. In the fourth century, Gaul and Illyricum were famous for producing good soldiers, and it was said of Gauls that "all ages are most suitable for military service."[53] Recent arrivals to the empire were treated no differently from those who had been resident for generations. A panegyrical description of one of Constantius I's settlements of Franks in northern Gaul noted that "if he is summoned to the levy, he comes running and is crushed by discipline; he submits to the lash and congratulates himself upon his servitude by calling it soldiering."[54] This is an idealised view, for another common reaction to a call to service was to cut off a finger or thumb.[55] Military service was also hereditary, a Tetrarchic formalisation of a frequent custom in the early empire. In the mid-fourth century, for example, Abinnaeus received a letter stating, "I write to you about my wife Naomi's brother. He is a soldier's son and gave his name so that he might serve." The writer hoped Abinnaeus could win for the man a release, or at least exemption from the *comitatus*.[56] The government continually tried to root out dodgers, showing the value placed on this source of troops.[57] These levies were supplemented by volunteers from inside and outside the empire. Many men entered the empire to volunteer for military service, perhaps encouraged by the prospect of regular pay and food. Military actions sometimes brought troops into the army, like the conscripts levied from the defeated Limigantes by Constantius II in 358.[58] Individual prisoners were also recruited, like the Alamannic king Vadomarius, who was kidnapped by Julian in Gaul in 361 and went on to become the *dux Phoenices* in the early 360s.[59] Defectors also joined the army, like Hormisdas, a disaffected Persian prince who served as a cavalry officer under Constantius and Julian.[60] Recruits from outside the empire came mostly from across the Rhine and Danube, though some Moors, Armenians, and Persians also served. Although the number of soldiers recruited from outside the empire is unknown, the majority of Roman regiments consisted of men born in the empire.[61]

This system of recruitment generally worked well, and there are no signs of a shortage of military manpower.[62] However, the standard process of recruiting had to be stepped up when wars were planned. In 312 Constantine "increased preparations for war, levying troops from the barbarians he had conquered and the Germans and the other Celtic peoples together with those collected from Britain."[63]

Regardless of when they joined the army, the state gave recruits a new identity, setting them off from civilians and their prior lives. They received the names borne by all imperial servants, Valerius under the Tetrarchy, Flavius under Constantine.[64] They swore an oath to the emperor and were given dog tags (*bullae*). They also received the standard equipment of tunic, belt, cloak, and boots. In many cases, they would have to have learned at least a basic vocabulary in the army language, Latin. Some left the army after a short period, but others had long careers. In the mid-fourth century, Flavius Memorius spent twenty-eight years in the Ioviani as well as fourteen years in other positions, for a total of forty-two years of service. Service in the Ioviani alone would have qualified him for the full discharge bonuses received after twenty years – changed by 325 to twenty years in the *comitatus* or twenty-four years of border service.[65]

CHRISTIANITY

Before 313, being a Christian was not generally felt by the state to be a bar to military service, though refusal to obey orders was a problem. When the soldier-martyr Marcellus refused to take the military oath at an imperial birthday parade in 298, he had already achieved the rank of centurion; the crisis was his, not the state's.[66] From a Christian perspective, there was no consensus that military service was wrong, and there were numerous Christian soldiers under the Tetrarchy who were prepared to accept the state's demands. When trying to persuade the reluctant Maximilianus in 295, Cassius Dio, the *proconsul Africae*, observed that "in the sacred *comitatus* of our lords Diocletian, Maximian, Constantius, and Galerius there are Christian soldiers and they serve."[67] One of these men was the empire-trotting Aurelius Gaius, whose inscription appears at the head of this chapter, though he may have left service in 303 when Diocletian's persecution began. But from 324, all emperors were Christian, with the brief exception of Julian (361–3).[68] With a Christian emperor, the commandment "Thou shalt not kill" could have taken on a greater importance. At one of Constantine's first church councils, at Arles in August 314, the assembled bishops agreed to excommunicate soldiers who put down their arms in peacetime, implying that Christianity offered no impediment to armed service.[69] Although there were many Christian soldiers after 313, most troops remained pagan, drawn from the countryside where the majority were non-Christian until at least the end of the fourth century. Changes were only introduced slowly, as shown by the greetings given by some veterans to Constantine in 320 (or 326): "Augustus Constantine, May the gods preserve [*servent*] you for us. Your security [*salus*] is our security."[70] Diocletian's elite legions of the Ioviani and Herculiani remained at the top of the army precedence list at the end of the fourth century despite being named after pagan deities. By contrast, a growing number of officers can be identified as Christians, like the *magister militum* in Gaul Silvanus. This unfortunate, accused of plotting against Constantius II, was cut down on his way to church in 355.[71]

Of course, Christianity did bring some changes. Constantine ordered his soldiers to paint the sign of the cross on their shields before the battle of the Milvian Bridge in 312. This practice did not become universal, and even though the Chi-Rho symbol was found subsequently on the shields of some soldiers, it was usually confined to those around the emperor, perhaps the *candidati*. A new imperial standard was also created, the labarum (Coin 31).[72] Sozomen claimed that regimental chaplains were part of every regiment from Constantine onwards, though there is little evidence until the fifth century. Regular services were held for Christians, balanced by regular prayers for others.[73]

Regardless of the religious inclination of its members, the army remained an instrument of the state. Under Diocletian, it was used to destroy churches and persecute Christians. At Nicomedia in 303,

> The prefect came to the church with *duces*, tribunes and *rationales*; they forced open the doors and searched for the image of God; they found the scriptures and burnt them; all were granted booty; the scene was one of plunder, panic, and confusion. The rulers themselves from their vantage-point (the church was built on high ground and so was visible from the palace) argued with each other for a long time whether the building ought to be set on fire. Diocletian won the argument by warning that a large fire might cause some part of the city to go up in flames; for the church was surrounded on all sides by a number of large houses. So the praetorians came in formation, bringing axes and other iron tools, and after being ordered in from every direction, they levelled the lofty edifice to the ground within a few hours.[74]

Two decades later, the same army was used by Constantine to destroy pagan temples, like that of Asclepius at Cilician Aegae, but also to enforce the suppression of Donatists in North Africa between 317 and 321. Thus the tribune Marcellinus was in charge of troops who massacred a congregation in the church of Avioccala.[75]

THE ARMY IN POLITICS

Despite the importance of religion, imperial power in the age of Constantine depended on military support alone. To seize power, one needed the support of a large number of officers and men, all of whom had sworn loyalty to the incumbent. Such support was difficult to obtain, and many plots were extinguished before they began or spread far. Typical of attempts to seize power was an uprising by Calocaerus, in charge of the emperor's camels, who declared himself emperor in Cyprus in 334. An expedition under Constantine's half-brother Dalmatius was rapidly landed on the island and defeated Calocaerus, who was then brought to Tarsus, where he was burnt alive.[76] Even so, uprisings were hardly impossible, and failure to pay attention to the army left emperors vulnerable. Because there was no way to replace an emperor except by force, opposition tended to be expressed by declaring a new emperor. Thus for Diocletian to become emperor in 284, he first had to be acclaimed by some troops. He then had to have Numerianus killed and in turn to defeat Carinus at the battle of Margus. After this, he, like any other emperor, could only remain in power as long as he could hold off other challengers. The existing emperor(s) usually suppressed challengers by force since failure to do so would only encourage other rivals.[77] But some men who seized power were accepted by the ruling emperor. Constantine's seizure of power in Britain in 306 was accepted, albeit grudgingly, by Galerius, though that of Maxentius was not. And Vetranio was removed through diplomacy, not by force. More often, though, seizing power led to armed conflict. Civil war battles were often bloody – there were allegedly fifty-four thousand casualties at Mursa in 351 – and required real leadership of the emperors involved.

Most imperial figures in the late third-century, successful or not, came from the Balkans and were often, like Diocletian and Maximian, from obscure backgrounds.[78] They were given this opportunity by the third-century senatorial aristocracy's attachment to Italy and disinclination to hold imperial offices. From Diocletian's reign, the separation of military and civil hierarchies, along with the consequent lack of need to go to Rome to hold office, accelerated this process. But once a man was established as emperor, power passed through his relatives, a process approved of by the army. The importance of the army to imperial power and the constant military pressures created strong links between emperors and the army. Emperors were expected to lead armies and, if necessary, to fight in person. Constantine was wounded at the battle of Adrianople in 324, and Julian was attacked in 363 while carrying out a reconnaissance of the fortress of Maiozamalcha in Persia.[79] Participating in such actions would have endeared the leaders to their troops. The frequency of campaigning was reflected in imperial titulature. In an inscription of 337, for example, Constantine was commemorated officially as Germanicus Maximus IIII, Sarmaticus Maximus II, Gothicus Maximus II, and Dacicus Maximus, meaning he had defeated the Germans four times, the Sarmatians twice, and so on.[80] Tetrarchic propaganda placed a greater emphasis on showing the emperor as a soldier. The emperor now publicly portrayed himself on coins and statues with a day's stubble and wearing an undress cap, much as his troops often saw him (Coins 5, 7, 8, and 26). Similarly, the arches erected by Constantine in Rome and Galerius in Thessalonica show the closeness of troops to the emperor (Fig. 40).[81] Licinius's actions in 313, suggest the number of miles the emperor could cover in the company of his troops. In early February 313, he left Carnuntum on the Danube for Milan, where he married Constantine's sister Constantia. By April 30, he was back in the Balkans, where he defeated Maximin Daia in battle at Adrianople. By the autumn of that year, he had defeated Maximin again near Tarsus in Cilicia and then moved to Syrian Antioch, either on campaign against the Persians or preparing for it.[82] Some 2,700 kilometres, two campaigns, two battles and a wedding in one year. Rank helped Licinius, but it would not keep away saddle-sores, flies, sweat and sunburn.

Outside the *comitatus*, few soldiers saw the emperor regularly and instead had to make do with imperial images. These were widely distributed, as statues and paintings in cities and camps, as gifts, but most widely on coins. The relationship between emperors and individual soldiers was reinforced by donatives, cash gifts from the emperor on his accession as Caesar or Augustus and at five-year intervals thereafter. Smaller gifts were also given for imperial birthdays and consulships. In the late third century, donatives were cash payments, as for example the 1,097,500 denarii received by the Praepositus Tinto in 299 to celebrate the anniversary of Diocletian's accession.[83] By the middle of the fourth century, the accession donative had become a fixed sum of five solidi and a pound of silver per man, while quinquennial donatives were of five solidi.[84] Though these sums were more easily distributed than the billions of denarii required earlier, the distribution still required special minting arrangements, and each donative in the mid-fourth century required about two million gold solidi. The coins usually showed emperors in military garb on the obverse, while the reverses showed defeated barbarians, military camps, and triumphant emperors, accompanied by a legend like GLORIA EXERCITUS (The glory of the army) or ALAMANNIA DEVICTA (Alamannia has been conquered) (Coins 24 and 32).

Imperial concern for the troops' welfare was also expressed in the programme of discharge benefits, as mentioned by Licinius in the Brigetio tablet of 311:

> Considering the labours of our same soldiers who support the stability and welfare of the state by their constant move-ments, we believe that it should be provided and arranged that at the time of their military service they may happily enjoy the pleasant fruits of their labours as a result of our foresight, and that after their military service they may obtain peaceful leisure and fitting security.[85]

Veterans received assistance in buying land and setting up farms as well as exemptions from tax for themselves and, depending on length of service, their families.[86] Their right to these privileges was certified by a discharge certificate.[87]

ROMAN IMPERIAL STRATEGY

Unlike the early Roman empire, Roman frontier strategy from the third century onwards was defensive, with no major attempts being made to conquer new territory. During the mid-third century, emper-ors were mostly reactive, but the gradual reestablishment of central imperial power under the Tetrarchy is often said to have brought in a new programme of fortification and deployment. According to the sixth-century writer Malalas,

> Diocletian also built fortresses on the *limites* from Egypt up to the Persian borders and stationed *limitanei* soldiers in them, and he appointed *duces* for each province to be stationed further back from the fortresses with a large force for their security.[88]

Despite this passage and a road that bears his name, the Strata Diocletiana, there is a danger of assigning too much credit to Diocletian. Tetrarchic constructions in the east are identified through inscriptions, so the evidence reflects both the Tetrarchic propaganda machine as well as frontier activity. Nor is it clear if all these sites were military. Mobene in the province of Arabia (modern Qasr Bshir in Jordan) (Fig. 41) was built "from the foundations" by the provincial governor at a point between 293 and 305, rebuilding an earlier Nabatean site. Although it looks like a fort, no military unit was named in the inscription, contrary to usual practice, nor is Mobene attested in the list of military sites in the *Notitia Dignitatum*. From this, it has been argued that the site was not military but a *praetorium*, a base for a governor while away from the provincial capital. Its classifications as such is not conclusive, however, since the function of the site may have changed after its construction; further, not all Roman military bases are known, and it could have been occupied by a detachment from a unit headquartered elsewhere.[89] All that we can say, therefore, is that there were many new constructions during the Tetrarchic era in the east, mostly known from inscriptions. Tetrarchic construction is rarely attested in Europe and Africa. However, there was continuing work on defences on all frontiers throughout the third and fourth centuries.[90]

A second view on frontier policy comes from the late fifth-century writer Zosimus:

> Constantine did something else which gave the barbarians unhindered access to the territory under the Romans. By the forethought of Diocletian, the frontiers of the Roman Empire everywhere were covered, as I have already said [in a lost section] with cities, fortresses, and towers. Since the whole army had its home in these, it was impossible for the barbarians to cross the frontier because they were confronted everywhere by forces capable of resisting their advances. Constantine destroyed this security, removing the majority of the soldiers from the frontiers and stationing them in cities which did not need help. This stripped help from those troubled by the barbarians and subjected the cities left by them to the outrages of the soldiers so that from this point most became deserted. Moreover, he made the troops soft by giving them shows and luxuries; to speak plainly, he was the origin and beginning of the present destruction of the state.[91]

Zosimus's hostility to Constantine is clear and leads to exaggeration. To say that barbarians could not cross the frontier when Diocletian was emperor is simply untrue, as is the assertion that Constantine removed "the majority" of the troops from the frontiers or that most of the cities had become deserted. Moreover, allowing the troops to go soft was a cliché of long standing. This passage also reads awkwardly when contrasted with the words of Constantine's contemporary panegyrist describing the emperor's treatment of the defeated troops of Maxentius:

> Now forgetful of the delights of the Circus Maximus, the theatre of Pompey and famous baths, they are stationed on the Rhine and Danube, they keep watch, suppress plundering, and lastly, after having been defeated in a civil war, they compete with the victors to be matched with the enemy.[92]

All of these passages place great stress on the personal role of the emperor in determining policy, but in many cases emperors could only react to events that began beyond the frontiers or that were outside imperial control. This was certainly the case with civil wars. Once a usurpation had begun, almost inevitably it would be resolved by force. Civil wars were sometimes given higher priority than foreign wars. When Constantius II had to choose between Persia and Magnentius's usurpation in 350, he marched west, but in 360 he decided to fight Persia first rather than attack Julian immediately.[93]

Emperors, as we have seen, led armies personally. But with more emperors spending more time on the frontiers, there was a greater need for palaces and military bases. These new "Tetrarchic capitals" were usually located either close to the frontier or on major communication routes. Thus Trier and Antioch were well placed for action on the Rhine and in the east respectively. In Italy, Milan was preferable to Rome as a base since it was closer to both the Rhine and Danube. In the central Balkans, Serdica and Sirmium were well situated for both action on the Danube and moving east and west. The importance of Serdica to Constantine was such that he even called it "my Rome."[94] Lastly, Nicaea, Nicomedia, and Constantinople were all well placed for reaching the lower Danube and the eastern frontier as well as being easily accessible by sea. There was thus an emphasis on the ability to despatch forces to one or more frontier regions easily.

Roman enemies fell into three main groups: the Persians, the barbarians on the Rhine and Danube, and a third group, peoples at the fringes of the empire, that is, North Africa and Egypt, Palestine and

Britain. Any military problems with the third group were usually dealt with by local forces, though there was an occasional need for the deployment of regional or imperial troops. Constantius I, for example, had deployed to Britain shortly before his death at York in 306, Maximian fought in North Africa in 297–8, Galerius in Egypt in 295, and Diocletian there as well in 297–8 and 301–2. The second area, the Rhine and Danube, posed a more serious threat. On the Rhine, the Romans called the tribes to the north "Franks," those to the south "Alamanni," while they called the western Danubian tribes "Sarmatians" and the easterners "Goths." Some of these tribes occasionally united under capable leaders and were then able to challenge the army directly in field battles, but generally the Romans had the upper hand. Although the Romans were on the strategic defensive, imperial policy usually dealt with frontier issues by entering barbarian territory and plundering. These campaigns took Aurelius Gaius into Carpian territory once, Gothic territory twice, and Sarmatian territory four times. Troops reached barbarian territory in various ways. There always were forts in barbarian territory, and new forts continued to be built across the Rhine or Danube, such as at Bononia (Vidin) and Aquincum (Budapest) in 294.[95] New bridges were also built which facilitated crossings. In 309–10, Constantine built a bridge over the Rhine at Colonia (Cologne) connecting the Roman bank with a new fort at Deutz, and he built a bridge across the Danube at Oescus (Gigen) in 328.[96] Another way of crossing was to ferry troops. In some areas this was made easier by using fortified landing places opposite Roman forts, like the one constructed by Constantine at Constantiana Daphne and proudly advertised on his coinage (Coin 20). These were small walled enclosures with corner towers and a gateway.[97] The army could also build pontoon bridges. In addition to this offensive strategy, the border itself was defended by a dense line of forts and watchtowers garrisoned by border troops. During the third century, the design of fortifications had developed, and a greater emphasis was placed on being able to fight from military bases, which now tended to have projecting towers.

The most serious threat was posed by the Sassanid Persians. With Persia perhaps more than with other enemies, Rome often regulated war and peace through mutual negotiation and imperial initiative.[98] Control of the eastern frontier was centered on the field army based at Antioch, and most activity took place in the valley of the Euphrates (see Map 2). Offensive campaigns against the Persians took place under Diocletian in 296 and Galerius in 296–7 and 298; these ended in an extension of

Roman control up to the Tigris and created a peace that lasted until the end of Constantine's reign. By then preparations were again being made for war. As part of these, Constantine's nephew Hannibalianus was made king of Armenia in 335, replacing a Sassanid ally. This action reflected the growing importance of Armenia as a second theatre of war north of Mesopotamia. From 337, there was constant warfare until 350, though the reduction in resources available to Constantius II meant a change in strategy. Under the Tetrarchs there had been an offensive policy (i.e., a policy of fighting field battles), but Constantius II was forced to rely on a screen of heavily fortified cities – Nisibis (Nisib), Amida (Diyarbakir), and Singara – backed up by the field army in Antioch. During this period there were one or two major battles at Singara (344 and/or 348) and three major sieges of Nisibis (337–8, 346, and 350). In the last of these, the Persians breached the walls but could not capture the city. After a period of uncertain peace, hostilities restarted in 359 with the Persian capture of Amida. Constantius's riposte, however, was interrupted by the need to deal with Julian's seizure of power. In 363, with all imperial resources under his control, Julian was able to return to an offensive posture and led a force of sixty-five thousand men down the Euphrates to Ctesiphon, last attacked by Roman troops in 298. The campaign was difficult, and when Julian was killed in battle, a peace was negotiated which surrendered Nisibis in order to extract the army from Persia. The border now moved to the Chabur River, where it remained for the rest of antiquity.

CONCLUSION

The age of Constantine witnessed constant threats to imperial security from both internal and external foes. These pressures caused ongoing change and development in the way in which armies were structured and the way in which emperors related to armies. The dominant characteristics of the organisation were flexibility and professionalism, yet these were combined with inefficiency, corruption, and other flaws of human nature. Perhaps more important than religion or structure, however, was obedience. Armies were generally loyal to the emperor, and his power, which depended on them, generally remained stable. This interdependence meant that armies were well rewarded, but it also gave emperors an instrument that allowed them to suppress dissent and to defend the lives and homes of Romans.

FURTHER READINGS

There is no comprehensive work on the army and warfare during this period, though a number of studies deal with particular aspects. Short modern introductions are provided for the period 337–425 by *The Cambridge Ancient History*, vol. 13 (1998), in the chapters by A. D. Lee on "The Army," and R. C. Blockley on "Warfare and Diplomacy." M. J. Nicasie, *The Twilight of Empire: The Roman Army from the Reign of Diocletian until the Battle of Adrianople* (1998), covers structures for this period. H. Elton, *Warfare in Roman Europe AD 350–425* (1996b), covers aspects of warfare during this period, but only in Europe after 350. The introductory study by P. Southern and S. Dixon, *The Late Roman Army* (1996) is heavily dependent on A. H. M. Jones, *The Later Roman Empire* (1964), chap. 17, itself still fundamental for understanding structures and administration. These recent works – and others – are discussed in a series of review articles by J.-M. Carrié and S. Janniard, "L'armée romaine dans quelques travaux récents," *Antiquité Tardive* 8–10 (2000–2). M. Whitby, *Rome at War AD 293–696* (2003), offers a brief introduction to the subject and excellent photographs.

Amongst primary sources, the history of Ammianus Marcellinus, who fought in Gaul and on the eastern frontier, is of outstanding value. This vivid account, often supplemented by eyewitness testimony, is well studied in J. F. Matthews, *The Roman Empire of Ammianus* (1989). Far more dry but equally important for administration and structures are Egyptian papyri, especially the Panopolis Papyri, a government archive of letters and receipts relating to the supply of troops in Egypt between 298 and 300; see T. C. Skeat, *Papyri from Panopolis in the Chester Beatty Library, Dublin* (1964). Another useful archive is that of Flavius Abinnaeus, commander of the Ala Quinta Praelectorum at Dionysias in the mid-fourth century; see H. I. Bell, *The Abinnaeus Archive: Papers of a Roman Officer in the Reign of Constantius II* (1962). Lastly, archaeological evidence about fortifications is usually collected in the triennial publications of the Roman Frontiers (Limes) conferences, most recently, P. Freeman, *Limes XVIII* (2002).

NOTES

1 *AE* 1981, 777 = *SEG* 31:1116; Drew-Bear 1981; cf. Zuckerman 1994b, 67–8.
2 *P. Abinn.* 1; T. D. Barnes 1985a.
3 *Pan. Lat.* 9(4).21.2; T. D. Barnes 1982, 49–64.
4 Van Berchem 1952; Seston 1955; Leadbetter 2000.
5 Vegetius 1.17; *ILS* 4195; Christodoulou 2002.

6   *ILS* 8882; *AE* 1900, 29.

7   Hoffmann 1969–70, 1:218–22; Brennan 1998.

8   *P. Panop. Beatty* 2.181, 198, 260; Parembole, *Not. Dign. or.* 28.19.

9   Hoffmann 1969–70, 1:131–73; Zuckerman 1993; Speidel 1996.

10   Speidel 1974.

11   Elton 1996b, 90 n. 3.

12   Thus we find the third praetorian cohort serving with Maximian in Africa c. 297; Zos. 2.9.1, 3; *CIL* 8:21,021.

13   Zos. 2.17.2.

14   Frank 1969; Jones 1970; Barlow and Brennan 2001.

15   Frank 1969, 127–42.

16   Lenski 2000.

17   *IGRR* 1:1496.

18   On Julian, see AM 25.3.3–6. On Constantine, see Eus. *VC* 3.10.2, 15.2.

19   AM 15.4.10–12.

20   *Origo* 27; Jord. *Get.* 110.

21   Isaac 1990, 239–40; cf. Chapter 16 n. 43 in this volume.

22   Reddé 1986; cf. Bounegru and Zahariade 1996.

23   AM 20.1.3.

24   On Constantine and Licinius, see Zos. 2.22–24; *Origo* 23–7; cf. Chapter 3 nn. 97–8 in this volume. On Constantius, see Jul. *Or.* 1.40c.

25   Elton 1996b, 99–101.

26   *Not. Dign. oc.* 34.13; *ILS* 701.

27   Mann 1977.

28   *CJ* 4.42.1.

29   *P. Oxy.* 55:3793; cf. Zuckerman 1994a.

30   *AE* 1940, 168.

31   *ILS* 2781.

32   AM 15.5.33; *Epit.* 41.3.

33   *Not. Dign. oc* 5.249–53 = 7.146–50.

34   See Van Berchem 1952, with *CTh* 7.20.4 (325).

35   Zos. 2.33.3.

36   Demandt 1970; Crump 1973.

37   Pohlsander 1984, 87–9; cf. Chapter 3 n. 88 in this volume.

38   Elton 1996b, 208–10.

39   AM 24.4.23.

40   Joh. Lyd. *De mens.* 1.27; cf. Treadgold 1995, 43–64.

41   Zos. 3.12.5–13. 1.

42   AM 16.11.2, 12.2.

43   Zos. 2.15.1–2.

44   Lact. *DMP* 7.2; Veget. 1.17; Aur. Vict. *Caes.* 39.18.

45   Roxan 1976.

46   Duncan Jones 1978, though see the objections of Coello 1996, 37–42.

47   Zos. 2.33.3–4. See Chapter 8 in this volume.

48   *P. Panop. Beatty* 1.374–80; Jul. *Ep. ad Ath.* 286b.

49   *P. Panop. Beatty* 2.244–9.

50   *CTh* 7.22.2 (326).

51   Aur. Vict. *Caes.* 33.13.

52 Zuckerman 1998b.
53 AM 15.12.3.
54 *Pan. Lat.* 8(5).9.4 (trans. Nixon and Rodgers).
55 AM 15.12.3.
56 *P. Abinn.* 19.
57 *CTh* 7.22.1 (313), 2 (326).
58 AM 17.13.3.
59 AM 21.3–4.
60 Zon. 13.5.30–4; AM 24.1.2.
61 Elton 1996b, 136–52.
62 Boak 1955 with Finley 1958.
63 Zos. 2.15.1.
64 Keenan 1973.
65 *ILS* 2788; *CJ* 10.55.3 (284/305); *CTh* 7.20.4 (325).
66 Lanata 1972.
67 *Acta Maximiliani* 2.9 (Musurillo 1972, 246).
68 Tomlin 1998.
69 Optat. *App.* 4 canon 3.
70 *CTh* 7.20.2, dated at Corcoran 2000, 257–9.
71 AM 15.5.31.
72 Lact. *DMP* 44.5–6; Eus. *VC* 1.28–31.
73 Jones 1953, 249–50, with Soz. 1.8.11–13. Cf. Eus. *VC* 4.18.3–20.2 and *LC* 9.10.
74 Lact. *DMP* 12.2–5 (trans. Creed, with modifications).
75 Eus. *VC* 3.56.2; *Sermon on the Passion of Saints Donatus and Advocatus* 2 (Tilley 1996, 53).
76 Theoph. a.m. 5825; Jer. *Chron.* s.a. 334; Aur. Vict. *Caes.* 41.11–12.
77 Wardman 1984.
78 T. D. Barnes 1982, 30–45.
79 *Origo* 24; AM 24.4.3–4.
80 T. D. Barnes 1982, 17–27.
81 R. R. R. Smith 1997.
82 T. D. Barnes 1982, 81.
83 *P. Panop. Beatty.* 2.259–65; cf. 197–203 and see Chapter 10 in this volume.
84 Jones 1964, 624.
85 *FIRA* 1:93.
86 *CTh* 7.20.3 (320), 4 (325).
87 *CTh* 7.20.1 (324); *FIRA* 1:93.
88 Malalas 12.40 (trans. Jeffreys, Jeffreys, and Scott).
89 Isaac 1990, 172–5; Gregory 1995–6; Kennedy 2000, 140–3.
90 Lewin 2002.
91 Zos. 2.34.1–2 (trans. Ridley, with modifications).
92 *Pan. Lat.* 12(9).21.3 (trans. Nixon and Rodgers, with modifications).
93 Blockley 1992.
94 *Anon. Cont. Dio* 15 (*FHG* 4:199).
95 Brennan 1980.
96 *Pan. Lat.* 6(7).13.1–5; *Chron. Pasch.* p. 527.
97 Lander 1984, 248–9.
98 Dodgeon and Lieu 1991.

15: CONSTANTINE AND THE NORTHERN BARBARIANS

Michael Kulikowski

Rome's northern frontiers, running the length of the Rhine and Danube rivers from the North Sea to the Black Sea, faced outwards towards a world filled with peoples not subject to Roman government. In the century that separated the reign of Gallienus from the reign of Julian, we hear of more than a dozen barbarian groups along the Rhine-Danube line: Iuthungi, Franci, Alamanni, Iazyges, Vandali, Carpi, Sarmatians, Goths, Tervingi, Taifali, and so on. Collectively we may refer to them as "barbarians," a term of art that, despite its pejorative connotation in Greek, Latin, and English, has the signal advantage of making no assumptions about ethnicity. This is important, because the nature of barbarian ethnicity is nowadays a matter of considerable controversy, and the relationship of different barbarian groups to one another is often unclear. The one thing that unites third- and fourth-century barbarians, both as an object of study and as a historical phenomenon, is their collective designation in the sources by the Graeco-Roman idea of the barbarian – the uncivilized "other" outside the borders of the civil world of the empire, the *externae gentes* (external peoples), who were to be subdued and turned from savagery to gentleness, or harried from imperial territory like wild beasts.[1]

The barbarians we meet in our texts provided the rhetorical alterity that was defined by a sense of Hellenic or Roman identity and against which that latter identity could be defined. We know nothing of the barbarians' identity or sense of self, nothing of their own sense of ethnicity. The barbarians are accessible to us only through the prism of an *interpretatio romana*, because the literary sources are exclusively

Graeco-Roman in their perspective, and no alternative sources can make up that deficit.[2] Our sources were concerned with the *externae gentes* only insofar as they impinged upon imperial horizons as threats or annoyances. The interest of Greek and Roman commentators in barbarians was always closely circumscribed, which in turn closely circumscribes the perspectives open to us.

BARBARIAN IDENTITY AND BARBARIAN ARCHAEOLOGY

That assessment may seem pessimistic given the current scholarly enthusiasm for studying barbarians in light of their ethnicity. Barbarian "ethnogenesis," a neologism for the coming into being of a barbarian ethnic group, dominates recent textbooks and reference works.[3] Proponents of ethnogenesis theory locate barbarian ethnicity not in communities of descent but rather in what they call *Traditionskerne* (nuclei of tradition), small groups of aristocratic warriors who carry ethnic traditions with them from place to place and transmit them from generation to generation; then larger ethnic groups go on to coalesce and dissolve around these nuclei of tradition in a process of continuous becoming or ethnic reinvention. Barbarian ethnic identities were not, therefore, expressions of genuine kinship but evanescent and freely available for adoption by those who wanted to participate in them.[4]

Little of this is actually new, and ethnogenesis theory in fact dresses up old, and often discredited, approaches to the barbarians in a new vocabulary drawn from anthropology and literary theory.[5] The biological heterogeneity of the barbarian groups named in our sources was already generally acknowledged even in the 1930s. The rest of ethnogenesis theory transfers old ideas of ethnic migration from broad-based free populations to small aristocratic groups. It relies, in nineteenth-century fashion, on speculative philological reconstructions to identify pure barbarian ideas about themselves and to trace barbarian ethnic ideas back to an ancient past, before contact with Rome.[6] In other words, ethnogenesis theory and its correlative approaches to the barbarians are a new formulation of a very old project: creating a Germanic past independent from Rome and tracing an ancient Germanic identity through the late Roman period into the Middle Ages and thence to modern Germany. Treasured topoi of nineteenth-century and early-twentieth-century *germanische Altertumskunde* are thus salvaged, among them a Scandinavian *Urheimat* (proto-homeland) of barbarian identity and heroic Germanic migrations, plotted on arrow-strewn maps. The project is the same, but the descriptive vocabulary has changed, marketing old ideas in a postmodern guise.[7] Yet all this fails at the most basic methodological level to respect what little evidence for the barbarians survives from antiquity, and it also ignores the most basic limitation of our sources – none of them tells us what the barbarians believed about themselves. They merely report to us what Roman observers saw or heard, and then thought worth recording, about the neighbours who confronted them.

The material remains of the frontier regions, for their part, are an invaluable source for social change beyond the Roman frontier, but they are as useless as the extant literary sources when it comes to questions of ethnicity. For the better part of the twentieth century, it was generally assumed that material artefacts themselves carry ethnicity: that one particular form of brooch is Gothic, another Vandalic, and that wherever we find such brooches we can locate Goths and Vandals; or that artefacts can distinguish the habits of one ethnic group from another, so that Gepids were farmers, Ostrogoths aristocratic horsemen.[8] Despite the ubiquity of this ethnic ascription, it has now been definitively shown that artefacts do not carry ethnicity in such a fashion and that we can almost never match archaeological cultures to ancient ethnic divisions.[9] Whether it is the cemeteries whence most of our artefacts come or the remains of barbarian settlements, material evidence tells us far more about vertical social relationships – those between different status levels within a society – than it does about horizontal relationships between ethnic or linguistic groups with separate identities. The difficulty is inherent in the way we define an archaeological culture: even if our selection of defining characteristics successfully isolates those that are not actually quite widely diffused (and that is not always the case), we are still making the assumption that the characteristics we select as definitive are those that contemporaries would have recognized as defining a sense of identity and, conversely, a sense of alterity.[10] That assumption is in fact never possible in purely archaeological terms – we need the human voice of the past to communicate a sense of identity. In the case of the barbarians, that voice does not exist apart from the *interpretatio romana*.

Nevertheless, there do exist cases in which we can legitimately draw connections between certain sets of artefacts and historically attested peoples. If a well-dated material assemblage is widely present in a region where our sources locate a named ethnic group over a substantial period of time, then we can say with some certainty that the named ethnic group participated in that material culture. But that fact has no follow-on consequences. We cannot say that the material culture in question was exclusive to the particular named ethnic group, nor that elements of the material culture that appear outside the region necessarily represent the presence of that ethnic group. The concrete example of the Goths is instructive. There can be no doubt that, in the later third century and the fourth century, groups of people collectively described as Goths in our literary sources dwelt in the large swathe of modern Ukraine, Moldova, and Romania within which was located the archaeological culture that we call Sîntana-de-Mureş or Černjachov (see Map 2). This relatively homogeneous material culture, defined by its artefacts and its burial practices, was clearly common to the entire population of the region. But the literary sources make it equally clear that the region's entire population was not Gothic. To call the Černjachov culture "Gothic," as many do, is to make a statement instantly falsified by the evidence.[11] The literary sources allow us to say that people known as Goths were politically dominant in the territory encompassed by the Černjachov culture during the fourth century; they do not allow us to state that the brooches, antler combs, or pots of that archaeological culture communicate the distinctive attributes of Goths. Thus a geographical expansion of the material culture might as easily reflect the migration of Gothic subjects as the extension of Gothic hegemony. Similarly, a Černjachov artefact found outside the culture's chief distribution zone – in Italy, for instance, or in Pannonia – need not represent the presence of a Goth.

Yet if the material evidence has a very limited role in the study of barbarian ethnicity, it is quite informative about barbarian society in broader terms, precisely because of its capacity to reveal vertical relationships within an archaeological assemblage and changes among those relationships over time. Here we can do little more than sketch general observations that seem to be borne out at many sites excavated in central and northern Europe. A relatively stable archaeological culture reaching back to the Neolithic era existed all across this region, but changes in settlement patterns and technology become evident in the second century AD. In general terms, barbarian society became increasingly stratified from that point onwards. The most famous illustration of the trend is probably the site of Feddersen Wierde on the Weser estuary, much rebuilt after AD 100; it contains a clearly visible chieftain's house inside its own enclosure, a house much larger than the fifty or more smaller houses that occupy the site.[12] Other examples of planned villages centered on a chieftain's house can be multiplied, particularly from the Rhine and Weser regions, but the evidence is sufficiently similar across barbarian Europe for us to postulate increasingly hierarchical societies both close to the frontiers and in the central European interior. That this trend towards a more stratified society probably corresponds to the concentration of wealth in the hands of a few disproportionately powerful leaders is suggested by the increasing prominence of isolated, lavish burials in various parts of barbarian Europe, not least in territory close to the Roman frontiers. These so-called princely graves (*Fürstengräber*) contain an abundance of both native material and rich Roman imports and demonstrate substantial contacts with the imperial Roman world even in parts of central Europe, like Moravia or the Elbe River valley, that are almost invisible in the Graeco-Roman literary tradition.

Although archaeology cannot confirm the existence of such typically "Germanic" institutions as the chieftain's retinue (*Gefolgschaft, comitatus*), there can be little doubt that the barbarian elites laid to rest in the *Fürstengräber* were responsible for much redistribution of wealth throughout barbarian society.[13] The rural and agricultural society over which they ruled was not only becoming wealthier, it was becoming more populous: throughout barbarian Europe, settlements grew in size between the second and fourth centuries, even as larger tracts of marginal land came to be exploited. In the Černjachov regions, a new and increasingly homogeneous archaeological culture came into being during the third century, oriented towards the harvesting, storage, and redistribution of agricultural products. Along the Rhine and Upper Danube, by contrast, there is no visible break in the archaeological culture of the third century, when such new ethnic names as those of the Franks and Alamanni begin to dominate our sources. On the other hand, the excavation of cemeteries and settlements in ever greater numbers seems to confirm the same picture of growing social differentiation, while fortifications within the abandoned Roman *limes* of Upper Germany and Raetia (e.g., the Glauberg and the Gelbe Burg) were definitely turned into barbarian strongholds during the third century.

The picture of barbarian Europe that develops without reference to the literary evidence is remarkably consistent: across the continent, almost certainly beginning in those regions closest to the *limes*, settlements were growing larger and more differentiated in terms of wealth and status. At the same time, more and more portable wealth circulated among the barbarian populations of the continent. These changes correspond roughly to the period in which Roman authority faced real challenges from beyond the northern frontiers. We are practically compelled to infer that profound social changes in barbarian Europe made it possible, for the first time, for barbarians to contemplate the Roman empire as an entity capable of being challenged. Any attempt to explain the precise nature of these changes in terms of kingship theories or ethnic change founders for lack of evidence, and we may be certain that there were impulses to change within the *barbaricum* that remain wholly invisible to us.

On the other hand, the one overwhelming fact of barbarian Europe in the later second century and third century is the Roman empire itself. The barbarians who raided or invaded the Roman provinces between the 170s and the 330s had dwelt beside a prosperous, stable, and powerful empire for three, or five, or seven generations. The wealth of that empire and the example of rulership it offered through the mere fact of its existence, not to mention the deliberate political interventionism in which emperors and their legates might dabble, spurred the great changes that overtook the barbarian world in the second and third centuries and that we can witness in the archaeological record without the Roman sources interposing themselves.[14] How we explain the conflicts between Rome and its barbarian neighbours in the reigns of Constantine's predecessors is in some ways immaterial – Romans had always fought their neighbours, whoever they happened to be. What had changed was the ability of the barbarians to pose a sustained challenge to Roman armies and to mount successful, if transitory, campaigns deep inside imperial territory. That they could do this was probably a result of the social changes that decades of contact with the empire had wrought on barbarian society. Unfortunately, we lack any record of the barbarian perspective on ensuing events, which we can reconstruct only on the basis of Roman sources.

ROMAN EMPERORS AND THE NORTHERN BARBARIANS IN THE THIRD CENTURY

From the perspective of observers within the empire, the Rhine and Danube frontiers were an increasingly important focus of attention from the reign of Marcus Aurelius onwards. However, the patterns of frontier conflict that still dominated the age of Constantine were only established in the middle of the third century. The reign of Gallienus (253–68) in particular was remembered as a time of devastation when "many enemies invaded the Roman empire."[15] In fact, all four decades after 240 brought with them barbarian raids on a scale unprecedented in imperial history. Although the increased potency of barbarian leaders no doubt played a part in this, the sheer number of military challenges that third-century emperors had simultaneously to confront was of far greater consequence. Much the most dangerous challenge was usurpation, and during the third and fourth centuries, conflict with barbarian neighbours is almost never separable from conflict among contenders for the imperial throne.[16] Save in the brief interlude of Constantine's sole reign, the intensity of barbarian aggression along the Rhine and Danube ebbed and flowed as Roman civil conflict provided greater or lesser opportunity. In the same way, the determination of emperors to campaign on the Rhine and Danube frontiers nearly always coincided with a lapse in civil conflict. It was precisely this vicious cycle of foreign invasion and consequent usurpation out of which the Tetrarchy emerged — and that it was designed, in large part, to redress.

Our miserable sources for the third century record nearly annual fighting, although they do not record line upon line of barbarian migrants toppling one another like dominoes into the Roman *limes*. A rhetoric of tidal invasions sustains many modern narratives, but it ignores the relative consistency of the warfare along the Rhine and Danube frontiers and their consequent stability.[17] Emperors themselves never made this mistake, as we can see from the consistent priority they gave to the eastern frontier. The prestige of the Persian front never lessened, no matter how severe a particular crisis on the Rhine or Danube frontier became.[18] The reason for this was the same under Gallienus as it was to be under Constantine — however violent or devastating a barbarian invasion might be, the barbarians were on their own quite incapable of seizing a Roman province and keeping it. They could do so only if the imperial government allowed them to. This happened in the third century when the Agri Decumates (see Map 1), the stretch of land between the sources of the Rhine and Danube, ceased to be garrisoned and was gradually occupied by Alamanni; it happened again when Aurelian removed the garrison of trans-Danubian Dacia.

At other times, barbarian invasion presented a secondary threat because it was believed, rightly, that the invaders could always be destroyed or driven out after more pressing concerns abated.[19] A concentrated Roman army could nearly always overmaster its barbarian enemies by weight of arms alone — as Ammianus puts it, Roman armies "thought that the most difficult portion of their work had been done once the enemy was discovered."[20] By the time of Constantine, the disparity between Roman and barbarian arms and tactics was less dramatic than it had once been, both because of the imitation of Roman techniques by barbarians and also because of the increasing employment of barbarians in imperial armies.[21] Even in the fourth century, however, the discipline and, particularly, the generalship of Roman armies were usually decisive. It is, for instance, not clear that any Tetrarchic or Constantinian army suffered a defeat at the hands of a barbarian army. The military superiority, regardless of whether it lay in armament or in command and control, was usually overwhelming. The difficulty was bringing it to bear, and on that point Constantine and his immediate predecessors learned the lessons of the third century.

The third- and fourth-century barbarians about whom we hear the most are the Alamanni and the Goths, while the Franks are increasingly prominent from the Tetrarchic period onwards.[22] The Franks and the Alamanni may represent new political groupings brought into being by centuries of contact with Romans and made up of older, smaller barbarian groups.[23] We are told as much explicitly of the Franks, though the evidence for the Alamanni is less clear-cut.[24] It is harder to fit the Goths into the same sort of evolutionary conception, but historical models that explain the Gothic Danubian polities by migration from either north or east must rely on highly doubtful ethnic-ascriptive archaeology.[25] Regardless of origins, these barbarians were formidable. It was a Gothic army, after all, that killed the emperor Decius (r. 249–51) and sacked Philippopolis in 251.[26] Raids by Goths and others penetrated into the Balkans in 252 and later into Asia Minor. Having defeated one such group of raiders in 253, the governor of Moesia, Aemilianus, was acclaimed emperor by his troops (r. 253), establishing the iron link between invasion and usurpation that plagued the remainder of the third century.[27]

The phenomenon is constant: the murder of Aemilian precipitated invasions in the reign of his successor, Valerian (r. 253–60) and the latter's son and coemperor Gallienus (r. 253–68).[28] Barbarian piracy into Asia Minor and Achaea from the Black Sea coast was a major feature of the reign, yet though such raids could be devastating, they were not coordinated military campaigns any more than were those of the Marcomanni and various Rhineland barbarians during the 250s.[29] Rather, opportunistic invasions went hand in hand with civil strife, as with the Iuthungian raid into Italy that inspired the usurpation of Postumus: his success against the Iuthungi in April 260, freeing many Italian captives, allowed him to inaugurate a separate imperial succession that lasted in Gaul for over a decade, from 260 to 274.[30] Postumus may briefly have held the Raetian *limes* intact, but his subsequent withdrawal to the line of the Rhine left the Agri Decumates ungarrisoned and open to a gradual occupation by the Alamanni. The rest of Gallienus's reign appears in the sources as a catalogue of disasters: Alamannic raids into Italy as far as

Rome; Roxolani, Iazyges, Sarmatians, and Quadi in Pannonia; *Germani* penetrating as far as Tarraco in northeastern Spain.[31] Gallienus's military reforms, particularly the creation of a mobile cavalry force, were probably inspired by his need to move swiftly between looming threats as quickly as they arose, but while he was fighting Goths in the Balkans, one of his generals revolted in Italy, and Gallienus was murdered in the course of the campaign to suppress him.

The revolt against Gallienus in Italy had inspired a massive invasion of the Balkans by "Scythians" (named variously as Heruli, Peuci, and Goths). His successor Claudius (r. 268–70) defeated them twice, winning the victory title *Gothicus* by which he is generally known before succumbing to the plague.[32] Claudius died at Sirmium in August 270, and his successor Aurelian's proclamation faced opposition in Italy, perpetuating the now familiar pattern: Vandals invaded Pannonia, Alamanni and Iuthungi Italy.[33] For that reason we find Aurelian (r. 270–5) entering his first consulship at Siscia on January 1, 271, in the midst of a rare winter campaign against the Vandals. When this proved successful, the emperor marched immediately to Italy, where the Iuthungi and Alamanni initially routed his exhausted army but were later turned back from their march on Rome at Fanum. Despite their defeat, the barbarians refused to make any act of submission, leaving the iron-willed Aurelian to harry their march out of Italy and eventually annihilate them in pitched battle outside Ticinum. Aurelian now took the title *Germanicus Maximus* and, with renewed confidence, marched his army beyond the Danube – the first time an emperor had done so in decades – on a massive punitive expedition in 271. Aurelian may possibly have killed a Gothic king named Cannobaudes, and he certainly took the title *Gothicus Maximus* for a campaign whose success was still remembered more than a hundred years later.[34] Success against the Goths kept the Danube quiescent during Aurelian's Palmyrene campaign, and his victorious march back to Rome included a detour against the Carpi.[35] In 274, Aurelian suppressed his Gallic rival Tetricus, and one may suspect that the campaigns of early 275, in Gaul, Raetia, and the Balkans, were made necessary by barbarian attempts to exploit the civil war.

That fact suggests that, despite Aurelian's prodigious battlefield successes, nothing fundamental had changed in the political dynamic of the frontier. In the aftermath of Aurelian's murder (275), his successors Tacitus (r. 275–6) and Probus (r. 276–82) faced raids from across the Rhine and Danube, some reaching as far as Cilicia in Asia Minor.[36] Probus launched a major offensive into German territory, and it is now that Franks are first securely attested in our sources, settled by Probus along the coastline of Gaul, where some of them rebelled, seized boats, and sailed into the Mediterranean as pirates.[37] A fourth-century author makes explicit the link between imperial disarray and barbarian invasion: "all the barbarians seized the opportunity to invade when they learned of the death of Probus [in 282]."[38] Probus's praetorian prefect Carus became his successor (r. 282–3), left his elder son Carinus (r. 283–5) in charge of the western provinces, and led an army against the Quadi and Sarmatians on the Danube before launching the invasion of Persia during which he met his end.[39] The accession of Diocletian at Nicomedia in 284 prompted the inevitable civil war against Carinus. The latter had restored the Rhine frontier in the year before his defeat and death at the Margus in 285, but his march eastwards to face Diocletian seems to have allowed for new barbarian raids on the Gallic coast. In that same year, Diocletian campaigned against the Sarmatians on the Danube and appointed a new coemperor, Maximian, to counter two invading barbarians armies, composed of Burgundians, Alamanni, Chaibones, and Heruli, who had crossed the Rhine into Gaul.[40] The decision to place Carausius, a general of barbarian origin, in charge of a fleet to fight the Franks and Saxons was militarily sound, but his successes led, predictably enough, to his usurpation (287–93).

Thus, although the accession of Diocletian marks a symbolic turning point for the modern historian, the first years of his reign reflect the long-standing pattern of usurpation and barbarian invasion. Nevertheless, both Diocletian and Maximian manifested the renewed imperial willingness to lead armies beyond the *limes*. Barbarian raids in January of 287 provoked Maximian to campaign beyond the Rhine later in the year.[41] In the next year, he concentrated on Carausius while both his praetorian prefect Constantius and the senior Augustus invaded Germany. Constantius's campaigns produced real success, for the Frankish king Gennobaudes sued for peace and was confirmed in his position and settled near Trier.[42] In the subsequent years, before his elevation to the rank of Caesar, Constantius continued to fight beyond the Rhine, penetrating into "Alamannia" and taking prisoner a barbarian king.[43] Diocletian, meanwhile, campaigned on the Danube against Tervingi and Taifali.[44]

After the appointment of Constantius and Galerius as Caesars in 293, the value of the Tetrarchic experiment became increasingly evident: an imperial college, made up of competent generals who would not go to war against each other, meant that Roman power could be projected beyond the frontiers with a regularity unknown since the Severan period and with little danger of usurpation supervening. Thus almost immediately after driving Carausius out of Gaul, Constantius marched against Franks, Chamavi, and Frisii, presumably the usurper's former allies, deporting many to Gaul and settling them there as farmers.[45] All the emperors took the title *Germanicus Maximus* for this victory, and while Constantius consolidated this success by launching his invasion of Britain, Maximian maintained the newly imposed peace on the Rhine.[46] In 293 or 294, Diocletian built a fortress across the Danube in the territory of the Sarmatians, and in the following year the Carpi, who dwelt some way to the east of the Sarmatians, submitted to Roman authority.[47] The Marcomanni were defeated in 299 or 300.[48] Meanwhile, Constantius persisted with his reign of terror in the Rhineland, campaigning against the Franks in 299 or so, and then defeating a major invasion of three barbarian groups between 302 and 304.[49]

ROMAN EMPERORS AND THE NORTHERN BARBARIANS, 305–337

There appears to be some slackening of frontier warfare in the years before the abdication of the Augusti in 305. Although this might be an illusion born of the sparse evidence, it is just as likely to reflect the Tetrarchy's success in reducing the third century's endemic frontier instability. Either way, it seems likely that co-opting more and more barbarian support into imperial circles did contribute to stability. It was, after all, the Alamannic king Crocus who supposedly engineered Constantine's acclamation at York in 306, perhaps as a client of the dead Augustus Constantius.[50] That acclamation, however, marked the breakdown of the succession arrived at in 305 and led promptly to what we have come to expect, an outburst of frontier warfare to accompany internal discord. Thus by late 306 or 307, Constantine was already campaigning on the lower Rhine, leading a number of Frankish kings in triumph at Trier in a spectacle that made a considerable impression on his panegyrists.[51] By early 307, Galerius had fought a Sarmatian campaign, and in the following summer he attacked the Carpi.[52] In that same year, Constantine laid waste the trans-Rhenan territory of the Bructeri.[53] In 310, he attacked the Franks, building a bridge across the Rhine to carry the campaign to them.[54] This provided the opportunity for diplomatic contacts, which in turn led to substantial recruitment of Franks into Constantine's army. The evidence for this recruitment exists in later army rolls listing units of Bracchiati and Cornuti that probably date back to this period and in the reliefs of the Arch of Constantine at Rome, which clearly distinguish the dress of Constantine's barbarian supporters.[55] While Constantine was occupied in the Rhineland, Licinius took over the Danube front from his patron Galerius and won a victory over the Sarmatians in 310.[56]

It is quite possible to read all these campaigns in terms of barbarian exploitation of Roman disunity, but other possibilities suggest themselves as well. It had always been part of the emperor's job to extend his protection to his subjects and to trample the foes of the Romans underfoot. Yet by the end of the third century, as one would expect in a period of military crisis, this aspect of imperial duties had come to embody the largest part of the imperial majesty. The emperor's very claim to hold the throne might rest on his military success. That attitude persists in the literary assessments of the fourth century: bad emperors were those, like Gallienus, who allowed barbarians to run amok in the provinces.[57] For Aurelius Victor, imperial decline set in when emperors worked harder to dominate their subjects than to defeat barbarians.[58] A pagan writer like Zosimus, virulently hostile to Constantine, could condemn that emperor's army reforms precisely for removing soldiers from the frontiers, thereby encouraging barbarians to invade.[59] The emperors certainly understood how important military victory was to their image, not least in the imagery of their coins (see Fig. 29 and Coins 2, 20, 24, 25, and 32).[60] We can see it made verbally explicit in the preface to Diocletian's Price Edict, the very first sentence of which proclaims that the emperors, having first suppressed the rapine of the barbarian nations, can now provide for the economic tranquility of the empire.[61] When those Christians who rejected Diocletian's order to sacrifice also mocked his claim to Gothic and Sarmatian victories, they were doing more than just defying his commands. They were also challenging the foundations of his claim to rule.[62]

Given this substantive element of the imperial image, many of the northern campaigns of 306–12 may represent the need of Constantine and his rivals to assert their military qualifications for rulership. Indeed, it has been suggested that, for much of the fourth century, the dangers posed by Rhine barbarians were less than fully real and instead were inflated because of the emperors' need for enemies on whom to exercise military might and thereby shore up their image.[63] This view, though exaggerated, is not without merit. In this light, although Constantine had many good reasons to repudiate the Herculian name that represented his connection to Maximian, his decision to substitute Claudius Gothicus as his supposed ancestor beginning in 310 is significant.[64] Claudius was one of the previous century's great military heroes, and his name was satisfyingly free of Tetrarchic associations. The site of his greatest victories may likewise be significant, for they were won in the Balkans, perhaps adumbrating Constantine's own territorial ambitions, ambitions on which he soon acted. It was, after all, the exigencies of frontier warfare that eventually brought Constantine and Licinius to blows. During the uneasy truce of 312–16, both Augusti campaigned against their respective barbarian neighbours: Constantine on the lower Rhine against Franks and Alamanni, Licinius against the Goths in the Balkans.[65] After the first war between the two emperors, Constantine sent his Caesar Crispus to Trier in 317 to guard the Rhine frontier and campaign against the Franks and Alamanni, while he himself took over Licinius's residence at Sirmium, dividing his time between there and nearby Serdica.[66]

Constantine's Danubian campaigns also precipitated the final conflict with Licinius. In 323, he attacked the Sarmatians on the frontiers of Pannonia, winning one battle, over a king called Rausimod, at Campona in the Pannonian province of Valeria, and a second considerably further downstream at the confluence of the Danube and Morava in Moesia Superior.[67] Coins issued at Trier, Arles, Lyons, and Sirmium celebrated the success with the legend SARMATIA DEVICTA (Sarmatia has been subdued; Coin 2), Constantine took the title *Sarmaticus*, and the gladiatorial *ludi Sarmatici*, known epigraphically, may also have celebrated this victory.[68] The winning of the second victory, however, had taken Constantine on a march through parts of Licinius's territory and provoked their final break. In the ensuing civil war, Goths fought on the side of Licinius, some of them under a leader called Alica, while Constantine's army made substantial use of Franks, at least one of whom, Bonitus, had reached a position of rank.[69]

Although emperors had always recruited northern barbarians into the Roman *auxilia*, and later into the regular units of the army, the years before 324 may represent a new phase in the habits and scale of that recruitment. Because the *externae gentes* represented a seemingly inexhaustible reservoir of manpower, it paid to preserve as much barbarian strength as one safely could. The recruits might be used to fight other barbarians – *Germanorum auxilia contra Germanos* (units of Germans against Germans).[70] Alternatively, they might be used in foreign adventures, as in the case of the Sarmatians and Goths employed by Galerius against Persia. But barbarian soldiers were even more useful in civil wars, and their recruitment for that end was already well entrenched by the middle of the third century, when Trebonianus Gallus first used "Scythians" against Decius and then concluded a pact with them in the expectation of their future utility.[71] On the other hand, it is generally assumed that the Constantinian period formed a decisive stage in the use of barbarian soldiers by Roman generals.[72] The years between 312 and 324 were the first period since the onset of military crisis in the third century during which rival emperors had really ample leisure in which to recruit troops for themselves. In his campaign against Maxentius in 312, Constantine had already made great use of Frankish auxiliaries, recruited both from beyond the Rhine and from barbarian prisoners of war settled by his father and Maximian in Gaul.[73] Julian's *Caesares* is scathing on Constantine's recruitment and subsidy of barbarians, Licinius seems to have relied systematically on Danubian recruits, and the recruitment of barbarians grew steadily in the course of the fourth century.[74] That being the case, it seems likely that the precedent set by Constantine and Licinius was validated by its very success: Constantine routed Licinius in 324.

That victory allowed Constantine a free hand in the Balkans, which he used partly for grandiose construction schemes. Some of these were eminently practical, but they were also symbolic, not least the bridge over the Danube from Oescus to Sucidava, which in 328 established an actual, as well as an ideological, bridgehead onto what one source now calls the *ripa Gothica*.[75] The campaigns that followed on these ventures, including an unsuccessful attack on an invading force of Taifali in 330,[76] ended in 332 with a Gothic peace that has become one of the most controverted events of Constantine's reign. The war against the Goths began in support of certain Sarmatians who had beseeched the emperor's aid and was won "in the lands of the Sarmatians," thus beyond the Pannonian section of the Danube frontier.[77] The Caesar Constantine II led the imperial armies, driving many Goths – the sources speak improbably of a hundred thousand – to die of hunger and cold and demanding hostages, amongst them the son of a Gothic king called Ariaric.[78] That, in full, is what the sources tell us of the 332 campaign.

That it was a major and lasting victory need not be doubted – it remained worthy of note two decades later when, in 355, Constantine's nephew Julian delivered his panegyric to the emperor Constantius.[79] Likewise, some Goths clearly developed a special loyalty to the Constantinian dynasty, as evidenced by their support of the usurper Procopius – who claimed connections to the Constantinian dynasty – against Valens in the 360s.[80] Perhaps because the war of 332 and the peace are so obscure, they have permitted highly speculative reconstruction, much of it ideologically inspired. It is actually very difficult to find evidence for continuity between the Goths of 332 and groups attested later, like the Tervingi, or to fit Ariaric into a continuous stream of Gothic royal history.[81] The early evidence says nothing more than that Ariaric held a royal title and ruled over many Goths, but by no means necessarily all the Danubian Goths.[82] Discussion of the terms of the peace is similarly complicated. It is clear that the emperor dictated the treaty's terms: "the Goths finally learned to serve the Romans," as Eusebius put it a few years after 332.[83] Goths likewise continued to serve in Roman armies after 332, just as they had done before that year, but we have no evidence that the treaty of 332 provided a new framework for their doing so.[84] There is little point in attempting to eke out our understanding of 332 by appeal to general models of Roman diplomacy, for instance, by postulating a formal *deditio* (full surrender) unattested by the sources or by deriving its terms from Romano-Gothic relations attested later in the fourth or even the fifth and sixth centuries.[85] Nor do we get very far following those who invent precise technical connotations for the generic Latin noun *foedus*, which simply means "formal treaty."[86] Many hypotheses based on such approaches have found their way, as fact, into the modern literature; some have even claimed that the whole late Roman concept of *foederati* stems from Constantine's treaty of 332.[87] None is implicit in the evidence for 332.[88] Viewed without preconceptions, the peace of 332 seems rather ordinary, important because it was militarily decisive, not because it represents a new phase in Gothic history and Gothic kingship or introduces new principles into imperial policies towards the barbarians.

After 332, Goths continued to be employed by the emperors as they had been before, as military recruits in times of specific need, while the Danube frontier remained generally peaceful until 367, when Valens launched his first Gothic war.[89] Thirty-five years of frontier stability was no small matter, but a still more lasting consequence was less demonstrably intentional, Christianisation. It is sometimes argued that Constantine deliberately imposed Christianity on those Goths with whom he made peace, but the evidence for that is not good.[90] It is, however, quite likely that Constantine's victory, his dictating of its terms, and his subsequent regular interventions in the trans-Danubian territories made it easier for Christianity to take hold there.[91] The years after Constantine's victory of 332 were far more significant in this respect, especially because they led to the consecration and mission of the Gothic bishop Ulfila. Our information on the life of Ulfila is limited.[92] He was descended from Cappadocians taken captive in the Gothic raids of

Gallienus's reign, but he himself bore a Gothic name. He came on an embassy to the emperor – perhaps Constantine, perhaps Constantius II – and was consecrated in either 336 or 341 by Eusebius of Nicomedia and other bishops in order to minister to Christians in Gothic lands.[93]

We do not know what percentage of the population of Gothic lands was already Christian in 332, but it was perhaps large enough to worry Gothic leaders. For reasons more or less obscure to us, they began a persecution against the Christians of Gothia in 347 or 348 during which Ulfila and his followers were driven out and granted lands in Moesia.[94] In this period, Ulfila created an alphabet with which to write Gothic and translated into that language the text of the Bible. Ulfila was theologically inclined towards the semi-Arian (homoian) views of his consecrator, Eusebius of Nicomedia, but it seems most likely that the main part of his theological activity dates from after his settlement inside the empire.[95] On the other hand, it is unclear whether or not the Christian Gothic community of Moesia maintained close connections with coreligionists beyond the Danube, though reliable sources make it clear that such coreligionists existed. For that matter, the possibility of Ulfila's continued involvement in diplomacy between emperors and Goths up to and including the fateful year 376, when a large group of Goths entered the empire never to be fully subdued, rests on very uncertain ground, though it is not altogether unlikely.[96]

In some ways a product of Constantine's Gothic peace, Ulfila's mission would only gain dramatic significance in retrospect with the entry of a substantial Gothic population into the empire and their use of his Gothic literary language as one important marker of their political identity. The short-term political consequences of Constantine's victory merely shifted the focus of confrontation to a new set of barbarian enemies, this time in a Sarmatian campaign of 334.[97] It appears that the Sarmatians' slaves rebelled against them and that many Sarmatians – thirty thousand, according to one source – fled into Roman service on Roman territory, being divided among the Balkan and Italian provinces.[98] Constantine again took the title *Sarmaticus Maximus*, and he appears to have campaigned extensively beyond the Danube thereafter, leading to his assumption of the title *Dacicus Maximus*, perhaps as part of an effort to claim a restoration of Trajan's province of Dacia. Though the old Dacia was certainly not reannexed and subjected to Roman administration, the claim may make reference to small conquests or bridgeheads established north of the Danube.[99] These proved ephemeral, but Constantine could clearly exercise control beyond the *limes*, as is illustrated by the large number of barbarian ambassadors present at the celebration of his *tricennalia* in 335.[100] The diplomatic front was stable enough that the emperor's death two years later brought few major changes to the relationship between the northern barbarians and the three sons who succeeded Constantine, although before 340 both Constantius and Constans had taken the title *Sarmaticus*, implying either a joint campaign or two consecutive ones.[101]

ROMAN EMPERORS AND THE NORTHERN BARBARIANS, 337–363

The strife that eventually broke out among the imperial siblings swiftly revived old patterns in which civil war triggered hostile opportunism on the frontiers. Thus in both 341 and 342 Constans launched campaigns against the Franks, the second a clear imperial victory, commemorated on a recently discovered silver dish from Kaiseraugst.[102] The history of the 340s is notoriously obscure, but the aftermath of Magnentius's usurpation (350–3), which is described in the earliest portion of Ammianus still extant, fits squarely into the pattern just described. Ammianus, in fact, makes the link between usurpation and barbarian invasion explicit in the speech that he puts in the mouth of Constantius II before his appointment of Julian as Caesar.[103] The murder of Constans and the accession of the usurper had precipitated major wars in the Rhineland, supposedly encouraged by Constantius: the barbarians "were like wild beasts who have acquired the habit of stealing their prey through the negligence of the shepherds."[104] As a result, once Magnentius was suppressed, the Rhine and the Upper Danube frontiers became a serious source of concern to Constantius. In 354, Constantius himself took up summer quarters at Valence, planning to campaign against the Alamannic royal brothers Gundomar and Vadomar.[105] Peace was made without fighting, but the following year brought further campaigns.[106] In 355, Silvanus was sent to the Rhineland to deal with the raids there but was accused of rebellion and was murdered.[107] In the immediate aftermath of this upheaval, Cologne was taken by Franks, supposedly the first news Julian received after his appointment as Caesar to cope with the barbarian threat.[108] Stabilizing the Rhine frontier would occupy Julian continuously until his acclamation as Augustus.

In spring 356, hearing of an attack on Autun, Julian determined to chastise the barbarians while they were scattered about the countryside plundering. After relieving Troyes and winning a series of skirmishes,

Julian cleared the countryside and recovered Cologne.[109] His mere presence in the Rhineland sufficed to extract better terms from the Franks along the lower reaches of the river, and in 356/7 he overwintered in Sens, defeating an Alamannic attempt to besiege him there. Julian then spent the whole of 357 on campaign. The culmination was the famous battle of Strasbourg (Argentoratum), described with great circumstantial detail by Ammianus.[110] There, Julian defeated a coalition of seven Alamannic kings with an army of thirty-five thousand men, testimony to the sheer scale of the manpower they could muster. Between six thousand and eight thousand of these were killed in the battle with Julian's army, and after his stunning victory, Julian threw a bridge across the Rhine and implemented a series of punitive attacks and security measures against the Alamanni.[111] The summer of 358 was spent in a new campaign against the Franks, who had used the Alamannic wars as an excuse to penetrate the Roman province of lower Germany, and another against the Alamanni, still smarting from the disaster of Strasbourg.[112] Later in 358, Julian carefully prepared another large campaign in Germany aimed at deliberately sowing terror in the hope of preventing further attacks.[113]

Meanwhile, Constantius's victorious sojourn in Rome was cut short in 357 by news of Suebic attacks on Raetia, Quadic attacks on Pannonia, and Sarmatian attacks on Pannonia and Moesia.[114] In 358, before the start of the summer campaigning season, when an invasion would not yet be expected, Constantius crossed the Danube against the Sarmatians and Quadi. He forced the Sarmatians to restore their Roman prisoners, sat in judgment over the petty kings of the whole region, and forced the Limigantes, who had previously been subject to the Sarmatians, to relocate beyond the Tisza (Parthiscus) River in order to prevent them from posing a further threat to the empire.[115] By the next year, however, the subdued Limigantes had abandoned the territory into which Constantius had hoped to confine them, instead seeking settlement inside the empire. As this was being contemplated, the Limigantes rose up and were subject to wholesale slaughter.[116]

When Julian became Augustus, he quite correctly feared his cousin's opposition. It therefore became more important than ever for him to look the part of emperor. In 360 he attacked the Frankish Attuarii down towards the mouth of the Rhine, where imperial armies rarely appeared, and destroyed large numbers of them before granting them peace and accepting them into the empire as settlers.[117] It was perhaps then that he took the title *Francicus maximus*.[118] Meanwhile, the

Alamannic king Vadomar, with whom Julian had been at peace for several years, decided that 361 was an opportune moment to exploit the brewing hostilities between Constantius and Julian. Rumour suggested that Vadomar was acting on orders of Constantius, who hoped to detain his rebellious Caesar with an Alamannic invasion. Julian, at any rate, intercepted correspondence from Vadomar to Constantius, on which grounds he exiled the king to Spain before marching against Constantius.[119] The northern frontiers seem to have remained quiet during Julian's brief sole reign. When that ended in the disaster of the Persian war, Valentinian and Valens were confronted with long years of renewed conflict.[120] That, however, lies beyond the scope this chapter, though one might usefully point out that, until the Goths' Danube crossing was botched in 376, the basic dynamic of imperial relations with the northern barbarians remains largely what it had been since the later days of Constantine.

TRENDS AND PATTERNS IN ROMAN-BARBARIAN RELATIONS

Two trends with roots in the Constantinian empire grow ever more visible as the fourth century progresses. The first is the impact of Christianity on the barbarians, at which we have already briefly looked. During the reign of Valentinian and Valens, Christianity became widespread enough among the Danubian Goths that Gothic leaders felt it necessary to launch a persecution of Gothic Christians, who may have been viewed as a sort of fifth column. The Gothic martyr Saba died in these persecutions, and the account of his martyrdom offers our best insight into Gothic social life beyond the *limes*.[121] Conversion to the imperial version of Christianity may have been encouraged by Valens early in the 370s, while others of the Tervingi may have been converted upon their mass admission to the empire in 376.[122] Either way, those Goths who converted did so to Valens's favoured brand of Arian Christianity, which would come to be an important badge of barbarian identity within the increasingly heterogeneous population of the fifth-century empire.

A phenomenon with much deeper roots in the Constantinian period is the presence of northern barbarians in the highest reaches of the Roman military. As we have seen, the use of barbarian recruits in imperial armies may have grown in scale under Constantine and Licinius. It certainly continued under Constantine's sons, as when

Constantius took Goths on his eastern campaigns of 356–8 and then requested Gothic recruits to fight Julian.[123] In 358 he employed Taifali to fight the Quadi and Sarmatians.[124] To the same period may date the many Alamannic units noted in the *Notitia Dignitatum* as stationed in the provinces of Egypt and Syria, although other Rhine barbarians objected to service beyond the Alps and made exemption from such service a condition of their enlistment.[125] And though Julian could express contempt for the power of the Goths, famously leaving them to the Galatian slave traders while he turned to the weightier problem of Persia, this did not stop him recruiting Goths for precisely that campaign.[126] All of these examples conform to practices of very long standing. On the other hand, the ascent of Rhine and Danubian barbarians to the highest ranks of the officer corps was a newer development, at least on the scale that emerges under Constantius and Julian. This impression is no doubt partly exaggerated by our sudden access to the detail of Ammianus after 353, but it does seem that many more barbarian officers reached the apex of a Roman military career from the middle of the fourth century on. Since many of their careers will have begun in the ranks well before we meet them, their recruitment and first promotions probably belong to the reign of Constantine. Of the *magistri militum* attested between the death of Constantine and the death of Theodosius, more than half were barbarians; if one adds the various barbarian *tribuni* of the palatine *scholae* and the *comites stabuli*, the barbarian dominance of military commands looks even more pronounced.[127]

Under Constantius, Alamanni are particularly prominent – for instance, that Agilo who rose from *tribunus stabuli*, to Tribune of the Gentiles and Scutarii, to *magister peditum* after the emperor had cashiered Ursicinus.[128] Another Alamannic officer, Scudilo, was entrusted with luring Gallus away from the safety of Antioch.[129] Franks, who dominate the reigns of Valentinian, Valens, and Theodosius, are under Constantius very nearly as prominent as Alamanni: Silvanus's father Bonitus had served under Constantine, and it was Silvanus himself who handed Constantius the victory against Magnentius. Silvanus belongs to an older type, the second-generation barbarian. The Tetrarchic general and usurper Carausius fitted this profile, as did the usurper Magnentius.[130] On the other hand, alongside Silvanus we meet a host of other Frankish officers, some of whom were certainly recruited from beyond the Rhine: Malarich, Mallobaudes, Laniogaisus, and many lesser men.[131] Half the high command appointed by Julian before his march to the east had barbarian names.[132] The Sarmatian Victor was made *magister equitum*, while another officer, Nevitta, became consul in 362, an appointment which Ammianus deplores in an emperor who had mocked Constantine for advancing barbarians to the consulship.[133]

The presence of so many barbarians in positions of command could lead to tension and to the open expression of suspicions. When, in 354, Constantius found the Alamanni at Augusta Raurica prepared to repel his attack, suspicion at once fell on some of his lower-ranking Alamannic officers, though in the long run their careers did not suffer as a result.[134] Such suspicions must have been galling, particularly because so many barbarian officers dissociated themselves entirely from their origins as they rose through the ranks. Thus when Silvanus found himself accused of plotting usurpation, he contemplated flight to the Franks, only to be forestalled by a fellow Frank's reminder that the Franks across the Rhine would either kill him or sell him back to the emperor.[135] Of ethnic fellow-feeling he says nothing, though it is worth noting that it was the Frankish officer corps in Italy that exposed the plot against Silvanus, and it was two Franks, Mallarich and Mallobaudes, who offered to stand surety for him.

From another vantage point, however, the suspicion that the Roman bureaucracy could manifest against the barbarian officer corps is unsurprising. It was difficult to have a visual or social assurance of loyalty because it was increasingly difficult to tell Roman from barbarian in the military context. A striking example of this comes from 356, when the Caesar Julian himself appeared before the gates of Troyes, only to find them barred by a population that believed his imperial army to be a band of marauding barbarians.[136] What was more, some men could pass easily between the Roman and the barbarian worlds, even if others, like Silvanus, could not. Mallobaudes, whom we have met as *tribunus Scholae Armaturarum* under Constantius, reappears as a *rex Francorum* (king of the Franks) in 378, when he is simultaneously *comes domesticorum*.[137] The Alamannic king Vadomar had been a frequent enemy of Julian and was sent into Spanish exile by him, but he entered Roman service as *dux Phoenices* under Julian and Jovian, and fought for Valens against Procopius.[138] The Alamannic noble Mederich, brother of king Chnodomar and perhaps a king himself, had been initiated into the mysteries of Serapis while living as a hostage in Gaul and changed his son's name from "Agenarich" to "Serapio" accordingly.[139] Yet this Serapio, whatever he might owe to the impact of provincial Roman society on his father, was also one of the seven kings who assaulted Julian at Strasbourg. Lower down the social hierarchy, it was an Alamannic deserter from the Scutarii who informed the seven kings of Julian's manpower shortage just before that battle.[140]

CONCLUSION

All these men passed back and forth between barbarian and Roman worlds. The ease with which they did so marks a major change from earlier periods and can be attributed to Constantine's relationship with the barbarian world, the outlines and precedents of which have occupied us in the foregoing pages. Constantine's reign began a process that had the profoundest consequences for the history of late antiquity. As the fourth century progressed, and more definitively throughout the fifth century, Roman provincials at all levels of society had to learn how to accommodate a growing number of non-Romans in their midst. Doing so posed a challenge to the old assumptions of ancient ethnography, which posited an almost ontological divide between Greek, Roman, and barbarian. Lived experience threatened, sometimes quite literally, the comfortable distinctions to which the classical world had long been accustomed. In the pages of Ammianus, himself a product of the Constantinian empire, we can see the first real attempt to record barbarian realities in a way not automatically dependent upon Roman stereotypes. Ammianus did not like barbarians, to be sure. But he recognized them as a fact of life in his world, susceptible of empirical description and with motives capable of analysis in a Roman fashion. It is perhaps not coincidental that Ammianus's pages offer us so many insights into the accommodation, if not the assimilation, of Roman and barbarian worlds: Alamanni beyond the *limes* living in Roman villas in a Roman fashion, imperial treaties made with barbarians in barbarian form, Julian raised up on his barbarian soldiers' shields by way of imperial acclamation.[141] None of these examples does more than hint at the changes that Roman society would feel in the decades following Adrianople. But they are part of the historical process that led to that imperial cataclysm.

Constantine's reign is pivotal here. He inherited the Tetrarchic system that had once and for all eliminated the cycle of frontier violence and usurpation that afflicted the third century. Constantine's accession to sole power did not much alter the basic patterns of frontier relations, but his conflicts with Maxentius and Licinius and the sheer scale of his success certainly encouraged the recruitment of men from beyond the frontiers into the imperial armies, men who over the next generation rose to positions of enormous power. That accommodation of barbarian ambitions within the empire can, ultimately, be read as the culmination of imperial responses to the brute fact of barbarian strength, a strength felt repeatedly, if unsystematically, since the later second century.

Constantine's reign, in its turn, offers us the first glimpse of new historical phenomena, phenomena that would, in time, create the postimperial
world.

FURTHER READING

Most of the best older work on the topic is in German, particularly L. Schmidt's *Geschichte der deutschen Stämme bis zum Ausgang der
Völkerwanderung* (1938) and K. F. Stroheker's *Germanentum und Spätantike*
(1965). In English, one may consult, on the Roman frontiers, C. R.
Whittaker's *Frontiers of the Roman Empire* (1994) and H. Elton's *Frontiers
of the Roman Empire* (1996a). In general, the political history of imperial
relations with the northern barbarians is better served by the standard
narrative histories than by the monographic literature on the barbarians themselves, with the signal exception of P. Heather's *Goths and
Romans, 337–489* (1991), an exemplary political history. The articles by
J. Drinkwater, cited in the notes, offer a stimulating alternative approach
to the political history of the fourth-century Rhineland.

The best general overview of the archaeological evidence and
barbarian social history is still M. Todd's *The Northern Barbarians* (2nd
ed., 1987); he covers the same ground with less technical detail but
better illustrations in *The Early Germans* (1992). Apart from these, different barbarian groups still tend to be treated individually: E. James's
The Franks (1988) is better for the Merovingian period than earlier
ones but is well illustrated; E. Zöllner's *Geschichte der Franken* (1970) is
much the best narrative; on the Goths, E. A. Thompson's *The Visigoths in the Time of Ulfila* (1966) should not be read without reference
to P. Rousseau, "Visigothic Migration and Settlement, 376–418: Some
Excluded Hypotheses," *Historia* 41 (1992): 34–61; there are no reliable
treatments of the Alamanni in English, but D. Geuenich's *Geschichte der
Alemannen* (1997) is an exceptionally fine short introduction.

The ethnogenesis theory of H. Wolfram's Vienna school is readily
available in his *History of the Goths* (1988), though his *Die Germanen* (2nd
ed., 1995) and W. Pohl's *Die Germanen* (2000) are the most lucid expo-
sitions of the theory and demonstrate how little it has advanced since
R. Wenskus published his much-cited and little-read *Stammesbildung und
Verfassung* (1961). P. Geary offers an Americanization of Viennese doctrine in *Before France and Germany* (1987), bedeviled with factual errors,
and in his "Barbarians and Ethnicity" in *Late Antiquity: A Guide to the
Post-Classical World*, ed. G. W. Bowersock, P. Brown, and O. Grabar

(1999), 107–29. Several volumes in the European Science Foundation's vast Transformation of the Roman World series include relevant contributions. See in particular W. Pohl and H. Reimitz, eds., *Strategies of Distinction: The Construction of Ethnic Communities, 300–800* (1998), and W. Pohl, ed., *Kingdoms of the Empire: The Integration of Barbarians in Late Antiquity* (1997). All of these works should be read in conjunction with the critical essays in A. Gillett, ed., *On Barbarian Identity: Critical Approaches to Ethnicity in the Early Middle Ages* (2002).

NOTES

1   Cf. the rhetoric of Eus. *VC* 1.25.1.
2   The only two literary texts that have any claim to a "barbarian" perspective come from mid-sixth-century Constantinople (Jordanes) and very late seventh-century Italy (Paul the Deacon); their date alone makes them useless as testimony for barbarian history before contact with the Graeco-Roman world and its literary conventions, within which both works exist. For Jordanes as a fundamentally Byzantine, rather than Gothic, author, see Croke 1987 and Gillett 2000. On the limitations of his narrative as a source, see Heather 1989, 1991, 34–67.
3   Ethnogenesis theory is closely associated with Herwig Wolfram and his disciples at the Österreichische Institut für Geschichtsforschung, but its current popularity owes much to American apostles like Patrick Geary.
4   That description summarizes the *Lehre* of Wenskus 1961 and Wolfram 1988. The leading recent proponent of the school, Walter Pohl, claims in polemical contexts (e.g., Pohl 1998, 2002b) to have added subtlety and nuance to the theories of Wenskus and Wolfram, shearing them of their dogmatism, which might be plausible if the author's various introductory studies (e.g., Pohl 2000, 2002a) did not follow their forebears in very doctrinaire fashion.
5   Demonstrated by Murray 2002.
6   For the philological argument, see Wenskus 1961, and for the extremes to which the approach can be taken, see Wolfram 1988, 25 n. 58.
7   Witness the sweeping synchronic deployment of late Roman, Tacitean, and hypothetical philological evidence in Wolfram 1997, 1–34, in the service of a timeless *Germanentum*. The postmodernism is supplied by, e.g., Pohl 1998, with its references to Barth and Bourdieu.
8   The ascription of ethnicity to artefacts is associated most of all with the early-twentieth-century archaeologist G. Kossina, whose *Siedlungsarchäologie* postulated that materially homogeneous archaeological cultures were coterminous with the ethnic groupings attested in our sources and with the language groups defined by philologists. The rigidity of Kossina's approach has long been repudiated, but its legacy remains pervasive (e.g. Pohl 2000, 34; 2002b).
9   See especially Brather 2000 with extensive references to earlier literature; cf. Brather 2002 for a case study.
10   The statistical approach to the incidence of artefacts used by Siegmund 2000 can at least ensure that we do not mistakenly take the atypical as normal, though it cannot overcome the subjectivity of our selection criteria.

11   See, e.g., Heather and Matthews 1991, 51–101, which treats the Sîntana-de-Mureş/Černjachov culture as self-evidently Gothic. Heather 1998a, 489–91, is both more cautious and more plausible in its attempt to understand the mixed ethnicity of the area.

12   Haarnagel 1979.

13   Steuer 1992. They will certainly have reaped the profits of such large-scale industry as existed beyond the *limes*, the most impressive evidence for which are the ironworks in the Lysa Gora hills of Poland, and, to a lesser degree in Silesia and Bohemia as well; see Todd 1992, 133–4.

14   For a case study in Roman interventionism, see Pitts 1989.

15   *Cons. Const.* s.a. 261: *hostes multi inruerunt in Romania* (sic).

16   As recognized by Shaw 1999.

17   The standard narrative, Demougeot 1969–79, is structured around precisely this notion of continuous barbarian pressure on the frontiers. Wolfram 1988 turns scattered references to Goths into a grand narrative of Gothic conflict with the empire by ignoring precisely their disconnectedness. The first chapter of Goffart 1980 remains the best antidote to the overly rhetorical treatment of Romano-barbarian relations.

18   Recognized by Pohl 2000, 29.

19   Elton 1996b, 199–233.

20   AM 18.2.14.

21   See Lebedynsky 2001 on armaments.

22   The Goths are first attested in the 240s, the Alamanni perhaps as early as the reign of Caracalla (Dio Cass. 77.13), although this may well be the work of the later epitomator; see Geuenich 1997, 18. On the earliest authentic attestation of the Franks – the Gallic panegyric of 289 – see T. D. Barnes 1996b.

23   Demandt 1993 summarizes the *status questionis* of the 1970s on the large barbarian groups of the third century.

24   Greg. Tur. *Hist.* 2.9, drawn from the fifth-century Sulpicius Alexander, speaks of Bructeri, Chamavi, Amsivarii, and Chatti making up the Franks, to which one may add the (Ch)attuarii, identified as Franks by AM 20.10. There are no evidentiary grounds for regarding Frankish identity as particularly vested in *Kriegergruppen, pace* Pohl 2000, 34. Geuenich 1997, 9–18, is much the best summary of Alamannic origins. Siegmund 2000, 8–14, outlines recent controversy with bibliography.

25   Rightly recognized by Todd 1998, 483. The putative archaeological evidence is laid out at Bierbrauer 1992, 1994; Kazanski 1993.

26   Zos. 1.23; Eutr. 9.4; Aur. Vict. *Caes.* 39; *Epit.* 29.3; Dexippus fr. 22 (*FGH* 2A100:465); Jord. *Get.* 103; AM 31.5.17. For the precise, disputed, date, see Potter 1990, 278–81. For a recent summary of third-century history, see Potter 2004, 217–98.

27   Zos. 1.27.1, 28.1. Zosimus mentions Scythians, Urogundi, and Borani. He uses the term "Scythians" indiscriminately for trans-Danubian barbarians, not exclusively for the Goths, as some modern scholars assume: see, e.g., 1.37.1, 42.1. The canonical letter of Gregory Thaumaturgos (*PG* 10:1020–48) preserves an eyewitness account of the raids into Asia Minor. It is translated at Heather and Matthews 1991, 1–11.

28   Zos. 1.29.1; *Epit.* 31.2; Aur. Vict. *Caes.* 31–2; Eutr. 9.5–7.

29 Contra, Wolfram 1988, 53–5. Zos. 1.31–2, 34–6, which draws largely on the eyewitness account of Dexippus, is the most complete testimony. On the Rhine campaign, see Zos. 1.29.2, 37, with Paschoud 1971, 150–1 on a date of 254. On the Rhine and Gallienus's victory title of 258, *Germanicus Max V*, see Zos. 1.37. On victory titles and their contribution to imperial history, see Kneissl 1969 and the important methodological strictures of T. D. Barnes 1982, 17–29.

30 In the same way, Gallienus's campaigns against Marcomanni and Roxolani, and their settlement within the imperial frontiers, were associated with the suppression of Ingenuus (r. 260); cf. Zos. 1.38–9. For Postumus's victory, see the recently discovered victory altar from Augsburg in Bakker 1993a, 1993b.

31 Eutr. 9.7–8; Jer. *Chron.* s.a. 221, followed by Oros. 7.22; cf. Aur. Vict. *Caes.* 33.3, who calls them Franks. See also Zos. 1.30.2 and T. D. Barnes 1996b on the supposed Franks.

32 Zos. 1.42–3, 45–6; Eutr. 9.11.

33 For Claudius's death, see Eutr. 9.11; Zos. 1.46. For invasions at the start of Aurelian's reign, see Aur. Vict. *Caes.* 34; *Epit.* 35; Zos. 1.48–9; Dexippus fr. 7 (*FGH* 2A100:460–1); cf. Watson 1999. The relationship of Iuthungi to the larger Alamannic group is disputed – AM 17.6.1 maintains that the Iuthungi were a subdivision of the Alamanni, but late fourth-century evidence need not hold true for the third century. Postumus's victory altar speaks of *barbaros Semnonum sive Iouthungorum*. For the problem, see Geuenich 1997, 37–40.

34 AM 31.5.17. The dead Gothic king is attested only in the almost worthless *Historia Augusta* (*Aur.* 22.2).

35 Some of them were settled in Roman territory; Aur. Vict. *Caes.* 39; *SHA Aur.* 30.4.

36 For Tacitus, see Zos. 1.63–4; Aur. Vict. *Caes.* 37; *SHA Prob.* 10. For Probus, see Zos. 1.68; Eutr. 9.17. *SHA Prob.* 12.3–4 is embellishment.

37 T. D. Barnes 1996b, 16; Zos. 1.71.2; *Pan. Lat.* 8(5).18.3.

38 Aur. Vict. *Caes.* 38.1. On the death of Probus and succession of Carus, see Eutr. 9.17; *Epit.* 37.1; *SHA Prob.* 21–2; Zos, 1.71; Joh. Ant. fr. 160 (*FHG* 4:600).

39 Eutr. 9.18; *SHA Car.* 8. But note that the *ludi Sarmatici* attested in *SHA Car.* 19.3, and probably the great Sarmatian victory at 9.4, are nowhere else on record and may well be invented.

40 *Pan. Lat.* 10(2).4.2; Aur. Vict. *Caes.* 39.19; Eutr. 9.20.3.

41 He celebrated a victory; *Pan. Lat.* 10(2).6.2.

42 *Pan. Lat.* 10(2).10.3, 11.4, 11(3).7.2, 8(5).21.1.

43 *Pan. Lat.* 8(5).2.1.

44 In 289 and 291, *Pan. Lat.* 11(3).17.

45 *Pan. Lat.* 8(5).5.8–9, 8.1, 9.3, 21.1, 6(7).5.3.

46 *Pan. Lat.* 8(5).13.3.

47 Aur. Vict. *Caes.* 39; *Cons. Const.* s.a. 294, 295; *Pan. Lat.* 8(5).5.1; AM 28.1.5.

48 *Cons. Const.* s.a. 299. Vague references to Carpi, Iuthungi, and Quadi at *Pan. Lat.* 8(5).18.5, and 10.4 presumably refer to these campaigns.

49 *Pan. Lat.* 6(7).6.2.

50 *Epit.* 41.3.

51 *Pan. Lat.* 6(7).10.12, 4(10).16.4, 7(6).4.2.

52 For the Sarmatian campaign, see T. D. Barnes 1981, 299 n. 15. For the Carpi, see T. D. Barnes 1981, 300 n. 20.

53   *Pan. Lat.* 7(6).4.2, 6(7).10.2; Lact. *DMP* 29.3; Eus. *VC* 1.25.

54   *Pan. Lat.* 6(7).10.1.

55   See Hoffmann 1969–70, 1:130–45, for the troops, and A. Alföldi 1959 for the iconography.

56   *ILS* 660 (June 27, 310).

57   E.g., *Pan Lat.* 9(5).18, 11(2).15.3, 8(5).10.1, 18.3.

58   Aur. Vict. *Caes.* 24. See also the attitude of Eusebius, n. 1 above.

59   Zos. 2.34.1–2, drawn from the presumably similar attacks of Eunapius. The passage is quoted above at Chapter 14 n. 91 in this volume.

60   Cf. Stroheker 1965, 15–17.

61   *Ed. de pretiis* praef. ll. 19–26.

62   Lact. *DMP* 12.12; Eus. *HE* 8.5.1.

63   See esp. Drinkwater 1996, 1997.

64   *Pan. Lat.* 6(7).2.1. See Chapter 3 at n. 39 in this volume.

65   On Constantine, see *Pan. Lat.* 12(9).21.5, for the years 313/14. On Licinius, see *ILS* 696, 8942, by 315.

66   *Pan. Lat.* 4(10).17.2; Optat. Porf. *Carm.* 10.24; *RIC* 7 Trier 237–41.

67   Optat. Porf. *Carm.* 6; Zos. 2.21. *Origo* 21 describes the victory as Gothic, but the numismatic and epigraphic evidence is decisive. Contrast Chapter 3 n. 93 in this volume.

68   *RIC* 7 Lyons 209–24; *AE* 1934, 158; *CIL* 1²: 2335. For the appropriate date, see Lippold 1992, 377.

69   *Origo* 27, accepting the emendation of Valesius, which may be supported by Jord. *Get.* 111. The Frank Bonitus was the father of Constantius's general Silvanus; cf. AM 15.5.33.

70   *SHA Marc.* 21.7.

71   Zos. 1.24–25.

72   In general for barbarian recruitment in this period, see Bang 1906; Schenk von Stauffenberg 1947, 16–34; Waas 1965, 5–9.

73   Zos. 2.15.1, with Hoffmann 1969–70, 1:140.

74   Jul. *Caes.* 329a. See Hoffmann 1969–70, 1:141–308, for fourth-century developments.

75   Aur. Vict. *Caes.* 41; *Epit.* 14.3; *Chron. Pasch.* p. 527; Zos. 2.34; commemorated on coins at *RIC* 7 Rome 298. For the *ripa Gothica*, see *Origo* 35. See Tudor 1965 for Sucidava. See also the bridgehead at Daphne, Procop. *Aed.* 4.7.7; *RIC* 7 Constantinople 36–8 (cf. Coin 20 in this volume).

76   Zos. 2.31.3, with Paschoud 1971b, 229, for the date of the battle with the Taifali.

77   *Cons. Const.* s.a. 332.

78   Eus. *VC* 4.5; *Origo* 31; Aur. Vict. *Caes.* 41; Eutr. 10.7. *Origo* 32 may attest a campaign against the Sarmatians undertaken immediately after the Gothic victory, but the reference might also allude to the well-known campaign of 334.

79   Jul. *Or.* 1.9.

80   Eun. *Hist.* fr. 37 (Blockley); Zos. 4.10; AM 26.10.3.

81   Our sources speak in resolutely generic terms of Goths and Scythians (or the antiquarian *Getae* of Jul. *Or.* 1.9). On the other hand, many scholars (e.g., Brockmeier 1987) regularly identify the Goths of 332 as Visigoths (a name not attested until the sixth century) or Tervingi by reference to a Gothic group prominent in Ammianus

Marcellinus's narrative of the 360s and 370s. The only evidentiary basis for connecting the Goths of 332 with those of 376–8 and after is the Byzantine history of Jordanes. His *Getica* 142 implies that the Tervingian *iudex* Athanaric was, in 381, the direct inheritor of the terms of the peace of 332, but Heather 1989 has expertly demonstrated the complex fictions behind Jordanes' royal genealogies, and there are no grounds for preferring his late testimony to that of our less precise, but almost certainly more accurate, fourth-century sources.

82 Correctly recognized in Lippold 1992, 382, much the best treatment of the peace, but see now the moderate reading of Lenski 2002b, 122–7. Heather 1991, 97–107, usefully clears away the hypothetical superstructures of E. A. Thompson 1966 and Wolfram 1988, but even he assumes too much Gothic unity unattested in the sources.

83 *VC* 4.5.2. Clear Roman superiority is recognized by Brockmeier 1987 and Lippold 1992.

84 The late report of Jordanes (*Get.* 112) states that 40,000 Gothic troops were sent to Constantine as the result of a treaty. But a contemporary observer who had reason to know, Eusebius (*VC* 4.5), is vague on Gothic military service, even though he could be very specific on such matters when there was reason to be (as at 4.6 on the Sarmatians).

85 Contra, Brockmeier 1987. Schmidt 1938, 224, already recognized the inherent limitations of the evidence and is followed by Lippold 1992, 382, with full references to the bewildering number of pseudo-technical treatments that have proliferated over the years. For a cautious assessment of fourth-century treaties, see Lenski 2002b, 341–3.

86 E.g., Barceló 1981, 154; Chrysos 1973, 55; Brockmeier 1987, *passim*. Heather 1991, 111–14, is a surer guide.

87 Chrysos 1973.

88 On the contrary, Eus. *VC* 4.5 shows the Goths not receiving a federate's salary but rather offering tribute.

89 Demonstrated by Lippold 1992, 384–5. The evidence is Lib. *Or.* 59.89 (348); AM 20.8.1 (360), 23.2.7 (363).

90 T. D. Barnes 1981, 258, argues that conversion was a part of the price of peace, and Chrysos 1973 that bishops were sent to the Goths after 332. However, Eus. *VC* 4.5, which states that Constantine subdued the barbarians under the sign of the cross, does not demonstrate religious stipulations in the treaty, while no specifics can be read into *VC* 4.14.1, where all nations are said to be steered by the single helmsman Constantine. The evidence of Eusebius on this point is surely to be preferred to the fifth-century Soc. 1.18.8 and Soz 1.8.8 and 2.6.1, where legendary accretions are to be suspected.

91 See Brockmeier 1987.

92 It comes from just two sources, Philost. 2.5 and a letter of Ulfila's disciple Auxentius, transmitted from the so-called Arian scholia to the Council of Aquileia in 381, for which see Gryson 1980. There is a translation into English in Heather and Matthews 1991, 134–53.

93 The arguments for the earlier date are laid out in T. D. Barnes 1990, for the later in Heather and Matthews 1991, 142–3. The latter is marginally more convincing, but the evidence does very much suggest consecration at a church council, hence 341 at Antioch rather than Heather and Matthews's 340.

94 The region of settlement is guaranteed by the letter of Auxentius. The more specific reference to Nicopolis (ad Istrum) at Jord. *Get.* 267 is likely.

95 Convincingly set forth by Heather and Matthews 1991, 139–41.

96 Soz. 6.37.

97 *Cons. Const.* s.a. 334; *Origo* 32.

98 Eus. *VC* 4.6; *Origo* 31. Interpretations of this event are particularly illustrative of the flaws of modern ethnogenesis theory, which, as per Wolfram 1988, 62, requires reading a conflict described exclusively in class or social terms as an ethnic conflict.

99 Jul. *Caes.* 329. For the Dacian question, see Brockmeier 1987, 91–3.

100 Eus. *VC* 4.7, which represents eyewitness testimony.

101 T. D. Barnes 1981, 262, with references.

102 *Cons. Const.* s.a. 341, 342. For the dish, see *AE* 1999, 1123.

103 AM 15.8.5–8.

104 AM 16.5.17. The tradition of Constantius encouraging the Alamannic invaders to attack Magnentius is found at Lib. *Or.* 18.33; Zos. 2.53; Soc. 3.1. It is accepted with reservations by Drinkwater 1997.

105 AM 14.10.1.

106 Against Lentienses and other Alamanni, cf. AM 15.5.

107 AM 15.6. Drinkwater 1994 argues very persuasively that Silvanus never actually usurped the imperial title.

108 AM 15.8. Drinkwater 1997 argues that the Frankish capture of Cologne was the result of its virtual abandonment by Roman troops because of the confused chain of command in Gaul after Silvanus's murder.

109 AM 16.2–3.

110 AM 16.11 for the campaigns of early 357.

111 AM 17.1.1–11.

112 AM 17.10.5–8.

113 AM 18.2.1–15.

114 AM 16.10.20.

115 AM 17.12–13; Aur. Vict. *Caes.* 42.

116 AM 19.11.1–16. Lenski 2002b, 350, contends plausibly if unprovably that such tension-filled episodes were quite normal in the process of barbarian settlements.

117 AM 20.10.1–2.

118 *ILS* 8945; cf. Arce 1984, 109, no. 98. The inscription dates from the emperor's third consulate, of 360, which provides the *terminus ante quem*.

119 AM 21.3–4.

120 Though the scale of the threat to the Rhine has been plausibly questioned by Drinkwater 1997.

121 The Greek *Life of Saba* is translated into English at Heather and Matthews 1991, 109–17.

122 Heather 1986; Lenski 1995.

123 AM 20.8.1.

124 AM 17.13.19.

125 For the units in the *Notitia*, see Stroheker 1965, 34. Obviously when the *Notitia* was redacted (on which, see Kulikowski 2000 and Brennan 1995), these units need no longer have had the slightest connection to the Rhineland. For barbarian objections to long-distance service, see AM 20.4.4.

126 AM 22.7.8, 23.2.7; Zos. 3.25.6.

127 Waas 1965 remains the best overview.

128 In general, see Stroheker 1965, 31–53. For Agilo, see Waas 1965, 81–2, with evidence.

129 AM 14.11.11. He is first attested in 351; Waas 1965, 122–3.

130 For Carausius, see Aur. Vict. *Caes.* 39.20, with Casey 1994, 46–9. References to Magnentius's parentage are collected at *PLRE* 1 Fl. Magnus Magnentius.

131 Malarich was tribune of the Gentiles (AM 15.5.6); Mallobaudes *tribunus Scholae Armaturarum* (AM 14.11.21); Laniogaisus a *tribunus* otherwise unspecified (AM 15.5.16). In general, see Stroheker 1965.

132 Viz., the *magister equitum Nevitta* and the chief of the Protectores, *Dagalaifus* (AM 21.8), plus the prefects, including Agilo, named at AM 22.3.

133 Full references for Victor at *PLRE* 1 Victor 4. For Nevitta, see AM 21.10, 21.12, with Waas 1965, 117–19.

134 Viz., Scudilo, Agilo, and Latinus. That Ammianus was himself personally hostile to Alamanni, as suggested by Stroheker 1965, 31, is not borne out by his text.

135 For Silvanus as a Roman, see Stroheker 1965, 19–21; Waas 1965, 34–5.

136 AM 16.2.7.

137 AM 30.3.7.

138 References at Waas 1965, 128–30.

139 AM 16.12.25.

140 AM 16.12.2.

141 AM 20.4.17.

16: CONSTANTINE AND THE PEOPLES OF THE EASTERN FRONTIER

Elizabeth Key Fowden

> With the power of this God as my ally, beginning from the shores of Ocean I have raised up the whole world step by step with sure hopes of salvation.
>
> Constantine's letter to Shapur II, King of Persia (Eus. *VC* 4.9.)

I

For the Emperor Constantine, the east was both a goal and a return. By the end of his reign, victory over the Persian empire was "what he had still to achieve,"[1] but his motivations for eastern conquest were complex. Strategic concerns about Rome's eastern provinces were joined with a vision of a universal Christian empire in an intimate marriage of interests that has perplexed commentators both ancient and modern. Constantine's propaganda repeats the image suggested in the epigraph above, not just in this letter to the Persian shah, Shapur II (309/10–379), but also in the emperor's letter to the eastern provincials. So too, in his *Life of Constantine*, Eusebius of Caesarea portrays Constantine's triumphal progress from Britain and the remotest western Ocean, eastward toward India and the sun:

> [Constantine] campaigned against the land of the Britons and the dwellers at the very Ocean where the sun sets. He annexed the whole Scythian population, which was in the

far north divided into numerous barbarian tribes; and once he had also extended his Empire in the extreme south as far as the Blemmyes and the Aethiopians, he did not treat the acquisition of what lay in the orient as beyond his scope, but illuminating with beams of light of true religion the ends of the whole inhabited earth, as far as the outermost inhabitants of India and those who live round the rim of the whole dial of earth, he held in subjection all the toparchs, ethnarchs, satraps and kings of barbarian nations of every kind.[2]

In the rhetoric of his day, Constantine's reign initiated a restoration, a return to the unity designed by God for all humankind, even in its teeming variety.[3] If we do not start with this universal theological ideal, we are doomed to a fragmentary understanding of Constantine's relations with the myriad peoples of the eastern frontier.

Constantine was not blind to similarities between himself and past giants: he minted coins bearing his own portrait closely resembling that of Alexander the Great (Coin 29); his building of bridges over the Danube openly imitated Trajan, another conqueror of Persia. Constantine also enjoyed a special relationship with the first Roman emperor, Augustus, during whose reign Christ had been born. Origen, whose work was well known to Eusebius, had already observed that "Jesus was born during the reign of Augustus, the one who reduced to uniformity, so to speak, the many kingdoms on earth so that he had a single empire";[4] roughly two generations earlier, Melito of Sardis had pointed out to Marcus Aurelius that "our philosophy first grew up among barbarians, but its full flower came among your nation in the great reign of your ancestor Augustus."[5] It was left to Constantine to conjoin the unifying power of Augustus's western empire with that of Christ's philosophy, which had grown up in the Orient.

As a young member of the imperial entourage, Constantine had traveled through and beyond Rome's eastern frontier regions. Later, as Rome's single ruler, he used the image of the fallen glory of Memphis and Babylon that had struck him as a youth to illustrate the dangers of straying from God's will.[6] Nor were early tours the extent of his experience of the east. He had lived and been educated for several years at Diocletian's court at Nicomedia, where scholars of both Greek and Latin culture resided, and Constantine himself became an adequate if somewhat reluctant speaker of Greek.[7] Little wonder then that he conceived a wish to visit the eastern provinces after his final victory over Licinius on September 18, 324. His plan had been to visit Alexandria, but ecclesiastical infighting there caused him to abort further eastward travels once he had reached Antioch. This decision, based on political realism, must have represented a great personal as well as symbolic disappointment for the new ruler of a united empire.[8]

In late 324 Constantine began a fresh campaign in the east, this time using the power of words and images to win over the peoples of the newly acquired provinces. Less than two months after becoming sole emperor, he began work on a new capital on the Bosporus. Around the same time, he inaugurated a form of self-presentation that, in addition to buildings, inscriptions, and coins, used open letters as universal circulars to explain his views of empire and religion.[9] Through these theological exhortations, Constantine asserts the universal sway of Rome under her first Christian emperor. This assertion is backed up by his belief in the cumulative, concrete realization of a politico-religious ideal already present in the mind of God and the hearts of all discerning believers. Formal declarations of credal unity, for example, or regarding the date of Easter are understood as indicators of movement toward this goal. Constantine's urgings that theologians ignore their differences in favor of their shared faith in the Supreme God may have been viewed even at the time as overly simplistic.[10] But his vision of the universal took for granted individual variance – by virtue of a healthy realism about the imperfect nature of human knowledge, he recognized that "we neither all agree among ourselves in wanting the same thing, nor does one single being and mind operate in us."[11]

This acknowledgement of diversity within the universal faith also informed Constantine's vision of universal empire. Diversity could include the rule of other kings, whose sovereignty was overarched by God's unique "teacher of true devotion. . . for all nations."[12] The business of day-to-day government required that Constantine think about empire in terms of political frontiers. Given his theological convictions, however, our attention cannot be limited to these. On one level the emperor's job was to defend territory and satisfy the needs of his subjects. But Constantine's horizon was not circumscribed by the lines drawn after battles and diplomatic haggling. This chapter will investigate how the environmental, political, cultural, and religious diversity of Rome's eastern frontier zone – broadly defined – was molded by the universalist ideas of Constantine and the Christian empire he founded.

II

Control of Rome's broad eastern frontier zone was vital for the integrity of the empire against Persian encroachment as well as for any aspirations to universal rule. The strategic importance of this middle ground had been grasped already by Augustus, who through diplomacy and the military expeditions of his legates had made the Roman presence felt in both Transcaucasia, including Armenia, at the northern end of this zone and in South Arabia and Ethiopia in the south.[13] The notion that the Caucasus in the north and Egypt or "India" in the south were counterparts in the *oikoumene* was adumbrated in myth long before its geopolitical significance was grasped by Augustus or Constantine.[14] For example, traditional Greek geography had pictured the Caucasian river Phasis and the Egyptian Nile as tributaries linked by the earth-girdling river Ocean.[15] Though this view was gradually challenged, Hellenistic geographers still conceived of a vast, continuous mountain range that joined the Taurus and the Caucasus proper and continued "southwards" as far as the Hindu Kush, identifying the whole range as the "Caucasus."[16]

The middle ground, where Rome and Persia encountered each other, stretched between the poles of Transcaucasia and Egypt/India and was embraced not just by one range to the east but by a great elliptical sequence of ranges, the "Mountain Arena."[17] In the north, the mountain circumference was composed of the Taurus, separating Syria from the Anatolian plateau, and the Transcaucasian bulwark of Armenia and Georgia. From there the mountain rim continues southeastward into Persia's Zagros range, which follows a northwest-southeast course that leads down to the Persian Gulf before continuing south and west as the mountains of South Arabia (Yemen), whence chains run along both sides of the Red Sea depression and join up once more in the sequence of coastal ridges running parallel to the Mediterranean before reconnecting with the Taurus (see Map 2).

Constantine, like Augustus, was alive to the strategic importance of the Mountain Arena, cultivating close relations with Armenia and Iberia as well as in South Arabia and Aksum (modern Ethiopia) before his final preparations for war against Persia. By dominating this vast region, a Roman ruler might place himself in a strong position to control the more exposed lowlands of Syria and Mesopotamia that shaded into Persian country. This arena was not just a geographical given but also the lively scene of cultural interaction, economic exchange, and religious cross-pollination – as well as military confrontation both large and small scale. It was traditionally home to speakers of Aramaic and Syriac, Greek, Middle Persian, and Arabic and to worshippers of Graeco-Roman and Semitic deities and adherents of Zoroastrianism, Judaism, Christianity, and Manichaeism. Such broad ecumenicity was deeply woven into the fabric of the eastern provinces. Syria, Osrhoene, Mesopotamia, Palestine, and Arabia were fonts of material and cultural wealth that percolated westward and eastward; they were hybrid places where Hellenic and Semitic cultures had long mingled. A century before Constantine appeared on the eastern stage, Mesopotamia had produced the Christian philosopher Bardaisan, for example, whose intellectual frame of reference spanned all the peoples from Britain to India, reaching even as far as China.[18] For many late antique writers – as well as for the countless individuals who lived below the radar of modern historians – the area within the Mountain Arena was the world's center, formed by the peripheries of two world empires.[19]

III

When on November 8, 324, foundation ceremonies were celebrated for New Rome at the meeting of Europe and Asia, Constantine was continuing a Tetrarchic trend of palace building that put the emperor in closer proximity to important regional centers as well as critical frontiers.[20] Constantinople provided easy access to the east without turning its back on the west. The foundation of Constantinople was just one sign of the prominence now granted the empire's eastern half. Eusebius, looking back, will describe Constantine acting in the west as "a universal bishop appointed by God, convoking councils of the ministers of God."[21] In May 325, less than a year after assuming control over the eastern provinces, Constantine convened the first ecumenical church council at Nicaea. In theory it embraced all Christian bishops, but the overwhelming majority came from the eastern empire and its fringes. Though only a handful of western bishops are known to have participated, the Armenian Aristakes and the Lazican (West Georgian) Stratophilus were in attendance, and Eusebius takes care to note that "even a Persian bishop was present at the council."[22]

In confronting the range of religious traditions and theological speculation that was to be found in the eastern Mediterranean and West Asia, Constantine presented himself through his letters to those living in the eastern provinces as a divinely led unifier. His guiding principle was at once theological and political, and we would be unwise to try to separate the two. We see this exemplified in the famous incident when, at dinner with some bishops, Constantine remarked, "You are bishops of those within the Church, but I am perhaps appointed by God over those without."[23] Constantine considered his flock to be those outside the church *regardless* of political boundaries.[24] The groundwork for this universalism was to be laid in the form of mission, alliance, and warfare. We should not be misled into thinking that for Constantine it was sufficient merely to discern the universality of Christianity. Discernment was a prelude to the unification of all peoples into one political empire. Although political restraints limited his lawgiving to "all those under Roman government,"[25] Constantine's ecumenical council and cultivation of holy sites were international in scope. The emperor made the site of Christ's resurrection, where the incarnate God fully revealed himself on earth, the epicenter of his own universal Christian empire.[26] As if to demonstrate this, on July 25, 336, the thirtieth anniversary of his reign, he assembled clergy and laity at Jerusalem for the dedication of the church over Christ's tomb. As with Nicaea, bishops came from all over the east, including "all Syria and Mesopotamia, Phoenicia, and Arabia with Palestine itself," and there was even a "sacred member of the Persian bishops."[27] Constantine's plans for a campaign against the Persians worked in concert with these dedications and celebrations.[28] But before we consider these preparations, we need to examine more closely the situation that was evolving in the wide frontier zone between the two great powers.

IV

The flayed hide of the emperor Valerian played a role in fourth-century Roman-Persian relations that should not be underestimated. Valerian's defeat on a Mesopotamian battlefield in 260 led to his prolonged servitude under Shapur I (239/40–270/2), who, when the emperor finally died, had his skin removed and dyed vermillion and then hung in a fire temple as a memorial.[29] This image remained an awful spectre that marked the way generations of Romans viewed their archfoe.[30] Emperor Galerius may have been born the same year as Valerian's capture, and Constantine's birth is dated just over a decade later.[31] The memory of Rome's greatest humiliation was still fresh for the Tetrarchs.

While Valerian's son and successor, Gallienus, struggled with pretenders in the west, Rome's eastern territory was purged of Persian invaders by the ruler of Syrian Palmyra, Odaenathus, who in 261 pursued Shapur's forces as far as Ctesiphon. What followed the Palmyrene victory is well known: Odaenathus was assassinated (possibly at the instigation of a wary Gallienus) in spring 267; Zenobia and their son Vaballathus sought to avenge his death and extend Palmyra's protection across Roman Egypt, Arabia, Palestine, and Syria and into Asia Minor; finally Aurelian – allegedly with the help of Zenobia's Arab opponents – turned their brilliant successes into humiliation when, having defeated Zenobia in battle, he celebrated a triumph in Rome with the queen as his prize trophy.[32]

Not surprisingly, Valerian's capture served as the impetus for a complex sequence of realignments as Rome, Persia, and the Arab populations between them struggled to reestablish an equilibrium in the frontier zone. Contemporary evidence from Egypt and Arabia suggests that support existed for Palmyrene control of the middle ground.[33] And the *Historia Augusta* (c. 400) preserves a tantalizing hint of the pivotal role played by the Mountain Arena's inhabitants. We see Zenobia at the center of the world: she calls herself Cleopatra and Augusta; drinks with Persians and Armenians; speaks Greek, halting Latin, and perfect Egyptian.[34] Accompanying her in Aurelian's triumph were said to be Blemmyes, Aksumites, Arabs from Arabia Felix, Indians, Bactrians, Iberians, Saracens, and Persians.[35] The *Historia Augusta* is notorious for its deep vein of creative history and cannot be taken at face value. Regardless of how great or small the germ of truth it contains, the text represents late fourth-century recognition of the potential unity of the peoples of the Mountain Arena. It was precisely this orchestration of the peoples of the eastern frontier that Constantine and his successors sought – with one significant addition, the critical unifying force of Christianity.[36]

In addition to necessitating an eastern defensive strategy that encouraged participation by the frontier populations in the Roman project of empire, Valerian's fate produced a mood of vengeful adamancy: never again would Rome be so humiliated. For Shapur, the victory confirmed his own claim to the status of "king of kings of Iran and non-Iran." In separate reliefs at Bishapur in the southern Zagros and at Naqsh-i-Rustam, he had himself represented on his steed, triumphing over the vanquished Valerian (for the latter, see Fig. 6). Also at Naqsh-i Rustam on the Ka ʿba-i Zardušt, the freestanding cubic structure built in front of a cliff face adorned with Achaemenid tombs, Shapur dedicated a monumental trilingual inscription in which he proclaimed publicly in Middle Persian, Parthian, and Greek the westward expansion of his rule, the divine support he enjoyed for his conquests, and his own displays of personal piety.[37] Following this example, Shapur's son Narseh (293–302) inscribed a proclamation of his own enthronement as king of kings of Iran and non-Iran on a cliffside at the Paikuli Pass, which opens out from the Zagros into central Mesopotamia.[38] This vaunting inscription documented Sassanian dominion over most of Armenia and Mesopotamia – territorial claims that were upset almost entirely in 297, when Diocletian's Caesar Galerius descended southward into Persian-held Armenia, defeated Narseh's army, and captured his harem before pushing on into Media. The Roman victory was devastating. Had Galerius managed to take Narseh too, Roman vengeance for Valerian's capture would have been complete.[39] The resulting treaty, struck in 298, long remained an open wound for the Persians: they lost extensive territory east of the Tigris and in northern Mesopotamia and dominion over Armenia and Iberia, all of which handed Rome the chance to develop friendly relationships in these areas. Perhaps most resented of all was Rome's acquisition of the powerful fortress city of Nisibis and its designation as the exclusive trading post between the two empires.[40] According to the late-fourth-century historian Aurelius Victor, Galerius had further territorial ambitions and longed to incorporate central Sassanian lands into a new Roman province. Diocletian was more farsighted and determined to focus his resources on establishing a dependable strategy for frontier defense.[41] In the long term, even Diocletian's stabilizing efforts in Mesopotamia were considered a *casus belli* from the Sassanian point of view.

In the years between Galerius's victory and Constantine's death there was no full-scale war between Rome and Persia.[42] Subsequently, Constantius II (337–61) engaged in armed conflict with his father's rival, but it was not until Julian (361–3) that Constantine's plan of outright invasion of Persia was implemented. Julian's haste and ill fortune, however, led to a harried retreat from Ctesiphon with no decisive victories and, then, his own death in combat. It was left to Julian's successor Jovian to make a settlement – but one that redressed the balance in Persia's favor. The period from 298 to 363 can be seen as one during which both Roman and Persian leaders maneuvered to establish and confirm their influence among the peoples along their shared frontier zone.

V

New alliances among the Arabs gradually filled the power vacuum caused by Palmyra's fall in 272. Certainly by Constantine's reign the process of consolidation had advanced sufficiently for one Arab leader, Imru' al-Qays, to call himself "king of all the Arabs." His much-discussed funerary inscription, dating to 328, was found at Namāra in the basalt steppe east of the Jabal Ḥawran, approximately 120 kilometers southeast of Damascus and roughly 800 kilometers northwest of Ḥira on the Euphrates.[43] If he had managed to survive into his sixties, Imru' al-Qays would have been a boy when Zenobia was defeated and Palmyrene control over the middle ground loosened forever. No doubt he would have heard the Arabic odes retelling the fortunes of al-Zabbā', as Zenobia was known in Arabic.[44] He flourished in a period when the inhabitants of the middle ground again found themselves in the delicate position of finding means to maintain a distinct identity while at the same time allying themselves with the great powers, in the interest of both survival and political advancement.

Their geographical position allowed the Arabs to learn from both sides and eventually adopt cultural traditions from Rome and Persia, developing their own distinctive fusion of late antique cultural forms.[45] The Namāra inscription is an important early witness to this distinctive process. The language is Arabic, while the letters are carved in Nabataean script within a Roman *tabula ansata*. The words themselves offer no straightforward answer to whether Imru' al-Qays was an independent ruler or one allied with Rome or Persia, or even both at different times. But the location just within Roman territory, where the rocky steppe blurs into desert, evokes better than words the liminal position occupied by the Arabs between Rome and Persia. From this and other evidence, the picture that emerges of the Arabs in the late third century and early fourth century is one of military mobility and the consolidation of authority.

Though Imru' al-Qays remains a shadowy figure, he stands on the cusp of a new era in Arab relations with the Roman empire, an era in which Christianity would play a powerful diplomatic role. Indeed, Eusebius already knew of Christian Arab communities,[46] and Pamphilus, bishop of the Arabs, attended the Council of Nicaea. We know that by 378 the Tanūkh queen Mavia had both a formal alliance with Rome and a bishop, supposedly of Arab background, for her tribe.[47] Our evidence suggests that the "king of all the Arabs" ruled over his subjects at a time when all around the eastern frontier the idea of sealing alliances through Christianity was just beginning to take hold. Whether Constantine was actively involved in forging such associations with Arab leaders is simply not known, but that it would have appealed to his understanding of the universal Christian empire is evinced by his relations with other peoples of the middle ground.

Other figures known to have been expanding territorial claims at this time included Shammar Yuhar'ish III, who ruled Ḥimyar (South Arabia) from approximately 275 to 310, and the African rulers across the Red Sea in Aksum.[48] The third-century religious visionary Mani had counted Aksum as one of the world's four great empires, alongside Rome, Persia, and China.[49] As the bulwarks of the Mountain Arena's southern end, both the Himyarite and Aksumite kingdoms held a critical position in trade relations between the Mediterranean and the Indian Ocean. For this reason both were also caught up in the broader efforts of Rome and Persia to control this area. Arabia was "confined on top of a rock between (the two lions) Persia and Rome."[50] Christianity existed in the Gulf and South Arabia already in the early fourth century, but it seems to have been still a foreign implant that showed few signs of taking root in the indigenous population at this stage. Pockets of Zoroastrians and possibly Manichaeans could be found amidst devotees of the traditional Arabian pantheon.[51] In 325/6, Shapur II projected a Sassanian military presence through Bahrayn deep into central Arabia to the vicinity of Yathrib, returning through the Syro-Arabian desert.[52] Constantine too may have cultivated Roman influence in South Arabia, and Imru' al-Qays is probably best considered, at least at the end of his life, as a Roman ally promoting Rome's presence in the region to counterbalance that of Persia.

Similarly, in early fourth-century Aksum it appears that king Ezana confronted many of the issues relating to Christianity and political power that Constantine was facing at roughly the same time. Ezana formally embraced Christianity, probably around 330, when most of his subjects were still faithful to the traditional gods of Ethiopia. His gold coinage is marked by the appearance of a cross and can be dated based on his efforts to follow monetary developments in the Roman empire: his first gold coins with crosses are based on the same weight standard as eastern Roman aurei from before Constantine's victories over Licinius in 324; only later are Aksumite gold issues brought into line with the weight standards of the solidus, introduced in the east after 324.[53] Inscriptions from Ezana's reign are preserved in Ge'ez and Greek, the latter containing overt references to the Trinity, while the inscription in the local tongue appeals to the "Lord in heaven."[54] The difference may reflect Ezana's awareness of internal resistance coupled with a desire to strengthen ties to Christian Rome – though we should not forget that Constantine too often appealed to "the Most High God" without further specificity.

VI

The classic example of the struggle to maintain a balance between Rome and Persia is Armenia. Armenian culture and society were deeply colored by a long-standing kinship with Persia, while the Armenian people had also enjoyed a history of political alliances with Rome.[55] Tacitus in the late first century had grasped the predicament inherent in Armenia's geographical position:

> They have been an ambiguous race from ancient times, both in the instincts of the people and in their country's situation, since, extending a broad frontier along our provinces, they stretch deep into the Medes: they are interposed between, and more often disaffected toward these greatest of empires, with hatred for the Romans and resentment of the Parthian.[56]

The Parthian Arsacid rulers of Persia were displaced by the Sassanians already in the 220s, but Persia maintained a hold on the ruling elite in Greater Armenia as late as 428. During the course of those two centuries, Armenian society was exposed to a variety of influences from the Fertile Crescent and further east, as Zoroastrians, Manichaeans, and Christians spread their customs and ideas across Armenia's rugged mountains and alluvial plains.[57] With the treaty of 298, Rome won control of Armenian marcher territories even beyond the upper Tigris, leaving the majority of Armenians under Roman suzerainty. From that time Armenia evolved from being a Persian satellite state to a Roman dependency, yet Armenia's cultural debt to Persia still ran deep. The "Armenian world," like the "Syriac world," was often blind to political frontiers drawn up by negotiators. Syriac Christianity, for instance, penetrated into Armenian lands at least two centuries before Armenia's official conversion in 314. Early accounts of the baptism of King Trdat (Tiridates III, c. 287–c. 330) preserve traces of Syriac initiation ritual that were gradually erased by other practices superimposed by later Greek missionaries.[58] This more authentically Greek variety of Christianity reached Armenia from Anatolia. Gregory the Illuminator, the bishop credited with baptizing Armenia's first Christian king, was of Parthian descent but educated in Cappadocian Caesarea. Gregory brought with him back to Armenia Greek clergymen and the Greek liturgy, though at first the use of Greek as the primary liturgical language was a stumbling block, as it was unknown to many of Trdat's subjects, who spoke Armenian and kept alive traditions that were still Persian in inspiration. In the fourth and early fifth centuries, the issue of language became highly politicized in Armenia, illustrating the Janus-like position Armenia struggled to maintain.

Trdat's career reflects Rome's characteristic attempts to mold Armenian affairs to its advantage against Persia. Given safe haven in the Roman empire when in 252/3 Shapur I seized Armenia, the soldierly Trdat served with Probus against the Goths before being installed on the Armenian throne by the Romans in c. 287. Both he and Constantine converted within roughly two years of each other, and in the aftermath of Constantine's takeover of the eastern provinces, Armenia cemented its military alliance with the Roman empire using its shared religious interests as a catalyst.[59] In 325, Armenian Christians were represented at Nicaea by Aristakes of Greater Armenia, and if we include in the Armenian world adjacent areas known to have been demographically and linguistically Armenian, then the number of Armenian representatives increases to as many as eight.[60]

It should not be forgotten that in the treaty of 298 two of the five main points involved Transcaucasia: Armenia came under Roman protection and the king of Iberia (eastern Georgia) was to be given his symbols of office by the emperor of Rome. But as in Armenia, Persian influence in Iberia was intricately woven into society and its kinship relations. In the case of Iberia, geographical and strategic factors also favored Persia over Rome. The privilege of bestowing the symbols of power granted the Roman emperor some modicum of influence over Iberia, but the treaty offered only a springboard for transforming formal influence into real Roman authority. The Christianization of Iberia provided the means by which the privilege of 298 became an alliance firm enough to resist (sometimes) Persian encroachment in Transcaucasia.[61]

Possibly as early as 324, or as late as 337, the Iberian king followed Trdat's example, adopted Christianity, and sent to Constantinople for spiritual leaders – and most likely a formal political alliance too.[62] Like Trdat again, the Iberian king was not a trendsetter. On the contrary, eastward-facing burials, some containing Christian symbols, suggest that Iberian Christians existed already in the late second century.[63] While Iberia's official conversion was closely linked with Rome's, Iberian, like Armenian, Christianity did acquire a momentum of its own.[64]

VII

As if competition in Iberia, in Armenia, and among the Arabs was not enough to bring Rome and Persia to another full-scale armed encounter, Constantine during the same years was asserting his position as protector of the Christians within Persian territory, whom he viewed as no less than subjects of his universal Christian rule.[65] According to Eusebius, Constantine composed a letter to Shapur that was in circulation in the bishop's own lifetime. It is undated but must have been written between 324 and 337. Eusebius relates that Constantine directed the letter to Shapur, perhaps in response to a Persian embassy sent to congratulate him as conqueror of the Roman east – or possibly in response to rumors of Constantine's aspirations to extend his reach even further eastward.[66] A date of 324/5 makes sense given the existence of similar claims to universal rule found in other writings by Constantine and by a contemporary writer, Publilius Optatianus Porfyrius, the "Ovid of the Constantinian age."[67] Porfyrius composed three poems in praise of the emperor that take a distinctly wide-angle view of his eastern relations: Indians, Arabians, Ethiopians, Medes, and Armenians are said to pay homage to the new sole ruler and conqueror of the east. Like Eusebius throughout his *Vita*, Porfyrius infuses his portrait of Constantine with light imagery: no obstacle shall stand in the way of his eternal effulgence. The future tense anticipates further conquests.[68]

The letter to Shapur II demonstrates Constantine's ability both to conceive an ideal Christian world and to attempt to realize that ideal on earth. Constantine asserts that by allying himself with the Christian God he has become the earthly regent of the whole world, and from that position he writes a benevolent letter to another earthly sovereign. At the same time, he was deeply versed in the historical realities of Roman-Persian relations. Thus when Constantine explains that the greatest wrong perpetrated by humankind was violence against divine will, he embeds this abstraction in historical reality by focusing on the pivotal figure of Valerian, a violent persecutor of Christians who, Constantine argues, was delivered by God into Persian hands. Echoes of the famous inscription of Shapur I resound in Constantine's letter and were no doubt placed there for the second Shapur's benefit. Both the inscription and the letter – at least the part we possess – start out by proclaiming the divine orientation of each ruler, then claim divine support for territorial conquests, after which the focus in both turns to Valerian's defeat, followed by further expansion on Shapur's Constantine's divine right to rule. At the end of his inscription, Shapur I prays that his successors will follow in his pious footsteps, while Constantine urges Shapur II to behave benevolently toward the Christians of Persia.

Constantine's compact letter is at once a historical record of Roman-Sassanian relations and a theoretical model for his new Christian empire, by nature a universal empire, governed by the supreme God, the "sovereign lord of the universe," whose ambassador on earth is Constantine.[69] By stressing that the Christian God is the Father of All,[70] Constantine implicitly airs the possibility that Christianity could flourish under Sassanian rule if Shapur too, like Rome's other neighbours, would convert and come under the overarching protection of Christian Rome. As an experienced ruler, Constantine himself cannot have held out much hope for a loyalist Christian Shapur in the mold of Trdat. Eusebius is more prone to wishful thinking. His comment on Constantine's letter is to imagine "all nations of the world being steered by a single pilot," namely, Constantine.[71] Still, the letter affords us a glimpse of the union of idealism and historically grounded pragmatism that characterizes Constantine's thought and action.[72]

Diplomacy aside, already by 325 signs were accumulating that Constantine was thinking in terms of conquest. The burden of having wrongs to right seems to have weighed heavily on his conscience.[73] In this same heady milieu of c. 325, a bronze medallion was minted depicting Constantine as Jupiter, holding in his right hand an orb surmounted by the Phoenix, much-beloved symbol of regeneration arising from the east (Coin 33).[74] Like so many Constantinian images, here too room is left for the viewer to assign meaning according to his own discernment.[75] One reading sees opposite the seated emperor his son Crispus, leaning forward to receive the orb and dressed as the New Dionysus, Conqueror of the East. A panther, Dionysus's exotic pet, crouches beside him facing Jupiter enthroned.[76] In the traditional symbolic language of empire, Constantine as the orb-holding king extends his sovereignty to the east. More interesting is the appearance of Dionysus, who had been so closely associated with Galerius, especially as a symbol of his own eastern triumph, his Persian victory in 297.[77] Constantine's adoption of Dionysus suggests a confidence in the strength of his own authority to overcome any lingering Galerian associations, even those once deliberately designed as anti-Christian. It would appear that the image was too potent for Constantine to resist as a symbol of his projected empire. Dionysus, the mythical conqueror of India, combined with the Phoenix looked forward not simply to the defense of Rome's eastern frontier but to expansion toward the world's eastern reaches.[78]

VIII

Ancient and modern attempts to determine "who started it" are doomed to failure in a region whose very geographical nature had taught its inhabitants to be perpetually shifting, however slightly, so as to keep the great powers adjusting their position as well. It is in this light that we must view the occasion when, in 336, a party of Armenian noblemen came to Constantinople, appealing to a treaty in order to gain Constantine's assistance against the violent incursions of Rome's foe.[79] The Armenian king Tiran had been blinded and supplanted by Shapur's brother Narseh. Constantine's response to the Armenians' distress was caught up in his much broader plan for Persian conquest, which had been slowly germinating and was now afforded the chance to spring to life. A crucial step in his preparations against Persia was to name his nephew Hannibalianus "King of Kings," giving him control over Armenia and Pontus, and to offer him his daughter's hand before dispatching him to Caesarea in Cappadocia, Rome's window onto Armenia.[80] In 335 he issued a silver coin at Constantinople inscribed FL (H)ANNIBALIANO REGI (for Flavius Hannibalianus King) with Euphrates personified, and the legend FELICITAS PVBLICA (public good fortune) on the reverse (Coin 34).[81] These were heavily loaded, practical decisions that shifted the momentum of conquest steadily eastward, preparing the way for Constantine's incremental assumption of universal rule.

Shapur's invasion of Armenia a decade after Porfyrius's intimations of conquest was, from the Sassanian point of view, an attempt to reclaim lost territory, but it provided Constantine a *casus belli*. Already in 335, the latter had sent his son and Caesar Constantius II to the eastern frontier to confront encroachment in Mesopotamia, though there seems to have been no serious fighting at this time other than the usual raids.[82] But the strained situation in Armenia was reaching a breaking point owing to a complicated intersection of political and religious developments. Even though many strategists had averred that ideally the best weapon against

Persia was surprise, news of Constantine's massive war preparations had clearly reached Shapur. Constantius's fortification project at the frontier town of Amida would have been enough to raise serious suspicions.[83] When in the winter of 336/7 Shapur's emissaries sought Constantine out in order to defuse the situation through diplomacy, there was no room for settlement, and they were sent away from the capital utterly disappointed.[84] Eusebius's portrait captures Constantine amidst quickening preparations: he summons bishops to accompany him, readies a cross-shaped tent to serve as a mobile church, makes plans for his baptism in the Jordan – whether en route to battle or on his triumphant return after his victory over Persia.[85] Constantine's realization of his vision is cut short when he falls ill and dies on May 22, 337, at the end of Pentecost, having advanced only as far as Nicomedia, just 80 kilometers from Constantinople. Constantius immediately returns from the eastern frontier to Nicomedia, whence he accompanies his father's body to the capital and its resting place beneath the dome of his mausoleum, surrounded by cenotaphs for the twelve Apostles.

IX

In the years following Constantine's death, any plans for dynamic expansion of the Roman empire eastward seem to have evaporated – except for Julian's grandiose but failed Persian invasion. At the same time, however, the new universal Christian commonwealth embracing Armenians, Iberians, Arabs, and Aksumites that Constantine had initiated continued to take shape. Amidst the tense atmosphere that had been building on both sides, Shapur took advantage of the unexpected turn of events and launched devastating attacks around Nisibis, personally besieging that fortress city in 337/8 and again in 346 and 350. Shapur justified his aggression with an ancestral claim reaching as far as the Macedonian river Strymon, though in his letter to Constantius he magnanimously offered to settle for just Mesopotamia and Armenia.[86] Desire for recompense for the settlement of 298 remained at the heart of Sassanian military and diplomatic relations with Rome.

Constantius was detained further west by military uprisings following his father's death and returned to Antioch only in August 337, where his response was largely to fall back on the fortifications of northern Mesopotamia. Throughout his twenty-four-year reign, Constantius found himself pulled in many directions, putting down usurpers as well as trouble on the empire's frontiers. Ultimately, ineffective seasonal raiding by Romans and Persians had a debilitating effect on both armies as well as the local populations. This state of affairs, which dragged on throughout most of Constantius's reign, at times led to disillusionment in Mesopotamia and Syria, where, as in many other circles, Constantius's defensive strategy in the face of Persian sieges and raids was little esteemed, if understood at all.[87] The Arian Constantius learned that Christianization alone did not guarantee allegiance to Rome but could in fact complicate loyalties, as in 360–1, when he had to resort to special inducements to counterbalance threats from the anti-Arian Armenians and Iberians to turn back to Persia.[88] It was amidst preparations for an expected full-scale military confrontation with Persia that, in 361, Constantius learnt of Julian's rebellion and progress eastward. With his troops already assembled opposite the Tigris, Shapur chose to withdraw, an unexpected move that allowed Constantius the reprieve he needed to confront his nephew. But that engagement too was foiled when Constantius died in Cilicia on November 3, 361, leaving Julian, who rivalled Constantine in his zeal to meet the Persian challenge, sole emperor.

Julian's admirers portrayed his revolt as a return to the traditions his uncle had trampled. Constantine's universal empire ran counter to Julianic politico-religious theory, grounded as it was on civic patriotism. What Julian did share with Constantine was the ambition to overpower Persia. But his own unexpected death in Mesopotamia on June 26, 363, clouded any understanding of Julian's plans for conquest.[89] Less than a month after Julian's death, his successor Jovian was forced into a devastating settlement with Shapur. Ammianus, who participated in the campaign, claimed that Shapur had demanded a return to the status quo before 298. In fact, Rome relinquished five Transtigritane regions with fifteen forts as well as the Mesopotamian cities of Nisibis and Singara, without their civilian populations. As for Armenia, the Romans agreed not to aid its king Arsak against the Persians.[90] The terms, though less comprehensive than Narseh's losses, represented such a mighty blow to Rome's grasp on the frontier zone that generations to come felt called, according to their own ideological preferences, to find a scapegoat for such a lasting defeat. As we have seen, the hostilities had been too long and complex for any such limited explanation to be satisfying. The treaty of 363 was agreed as a thirty-year peace, but in practice it marked the end of formal armed hostilities between Rome and Persia until 502. Nonetheless, Armenia and Iberia, as well as the Arabs in the south, remained open fields for competition between the two powers until the Arab conquests.

X

Constantine's ideal – that the creed propounded at Nicaea should serve as the canopy under which the world's peoples might flourish – though only ever partially realized on the ground, was not forgotten. As the church slowly fragmented under the strain of doctrinal disagreement, Constantine and Nicaea remained a widely acceptable point of theological, ecclesiological, and political reference in the nascent Christian commonwealth, especially once Arianism loosened its grip on the Germanic successor states. Constantine's cultivation of universal Christian holy places would also have lasting effect. Nearly four hundred years after the construction of the church of the Anastasis by Constantine, it was this domed monument to the incarnate God that the Umayyad caliph Abd al-Malik chose to rival with his own holy place on Mount Moriah.[91] The foundation inscription inside the Dome of the Rock is a direct response to Constantine's original memorial of Christ's divinity: "Believe therefore in God and His apostles, and say not 'Three'. . . God is only one God." That Nicaea and Jerusalem remained focal points for the Christian commonwealth that emerged as Constantine's legacy in the east would not probably have come as a surprise to the first Christian emperor of Rome. Abd al-Malik's monument might have perplexed him, though, by virtue of its familiarity. The One God–One Empire ideal that underpinned the Islamic empire had been Constantine's own vision. But in practice the Trinitarian doctrine had led to division rather than unity, as was often observed in the Qur'an. What Constantine could not have envisioned was that it would require the coming of another prophet before his ideal was realized on earth.[92]

FURTHER READING

The footnotes are designed to suggest further reading. In addition, see the *Barrington Atlas of the Greek and Roman World* (Princeton 2000), Maps 3 and 4, which together cover most of the Mountain Arena, and, for local detail, parts 5 and 6.

NOTES

1   Eus. *VC* 4.56.1 (trans. Cameron and Hall, here and below).
2   Eus. *VC* 1.8.2–4. For the reference in the letter to the eastern provincials, see *VC* 2.28.2, a passage whose authenticity is confirmed by a papyrus fragment of

Constantine's original letter, *P. Lond.* 3:878 with Jones and Skeat 1954. Cf. *VC* 2.67, 4.50 on the spiritual authority of the east.

3 This universalist thinking runs through the writing of Lactantius, who was more intimate with Constantine and more practiced in imperial politics than Eusebius; for instance, on Lactantius's incorporation of oriental wisdom into Christian universalism, see Nicholson 2001a.

4 Origen *Contra Celsum* 2.30 (trans. Chadwick).

5 Quoted by Eus. *HE* 4.26.7. (trans. Lake). Cameron and Hall 1999, 273, draw attention to Augustus's restoration of the temples (*Res Gestae* 20–21) as a parallel to Constantine's decontamination of Christian holy sites in Palestine; Eus. *VC* 3.25–53 and below.

6 On his role as an officer in Persian campaigns (293–6), see T. D. Barnes 1981, 25, and Chapter 3 n. 8 in this volume. For Memphis and Babylon, see *OC* 16.4.

7 On his education, see T. D. Barnes 1981, 73–6. On his ability to speak Greek, see Eus. *VC* 3.13.2; cf. *CTh* 8.15.1.

8 See T. D. Barnes 1982, 76.

9 Lane Fox 1986, 635.

10 Eus. *VC* 2.64–72.

11 Eus. *VC* 2.71.6. The heading at *VC* 2.64 asserts that this letter was addressed by Constantine to Alexander and Arius, but Hall 1998 has argued that the original addressees were not just these two but all the bishops assembled at the Council of Antioch in early 325.

12 Eus. *VC* 1.5.2; cf. 3.1.8–2.2.

13 The Augustan expedition to Ethiopia led by Cornelius Gallus reached as far south as the fourth cataract. On the area between Transcaucasia and Ethiopia as a political-geographical focus, see Fowden 1993, 101–4.

14 The geographical label "India" could in ancient authors mean anywhere from east Africa to the Indian subcontinent; Mayerson 1993, 169–74.

15 Herodotus 2.20–3, 103–5, 4.8, 36. Excellent discussion in Braund 1994, 17–19.

16 Eratosthenes in Arrian *Anabasis* 3.28.5, 5.5.2–5; cf. *Indica* 2–3.2; Strabo 15.1.8.

17 On the Mountain Arena, see Fowden 1993, 15–19.

18 Bardaisan moves easily between Hatrans, Kushanites, Romans, and those on the, "further side of the Euphrates, toward the East." Cf. *The Book of the Laws of Countries*, 591; generally 583–99 (trans. Drijvers 40–55). On the cultural and geopolitical centrality of Syria-Mesopotamia, the "middle ground," see Brown 2003, esp. 37–52, 267–94, an elegant synthesis of much recent thinking about West Asia and late antiquity's two superpowers.

19 *Expositio totius mundi et gentium* 22.

20 Kolb 2001, 42–4, 80–4. On the foundation of Constantinople at this time, see Chapter 3 n. 105 in this volume.

21 Eus. *VC* 1.44.1–2. "Universal" here translates κοινός.

22 Eus. *VC* 3.7.1.

23 Eus. *VC* 4.24.

24 For interpretations of this phrase, see the comments and bibliography in Cameron and Hall 1999, 320.

25 Eus. *VC* 4.18.2; cf. 4.23.

26 Eus. *VC* 3.30–2, Constantine's letter to Macarius, bishop of Jerusalem.

27 Eus. *VC* 4.43.3–4.

28 Eus. *VC* 4.56–7.

29 Lact. *DMP* 5. See also Chapter 2 at n. 1 for this incident.

30 The sources are conveniently assembled in Dodgeon and Lieu 1991, 57–65. See also Winter and Dignas 2001, 93–100, for commentary, a bibliography, and illustrations of the Bishapur relief and the Paris cameo, both showing Shapur's triumph over Valerian – though, for the latter, see Greatrex and Lieu 2002, 9, on the possibility that Shapur's opponent is Jovian.

31 T. D. Barnes 1982, 37 with n. 43; cf. Chapter 3 n. 1 in this volume.

32 *SHA Aurelian* 33.1–34.6. For context and bibliography, see Winter and Dignas 2001, 188–96.

33 The important article by Graf 1989 draws especially on Semitic epigraphy to emphasize the ecumenism of Zenobia's reign; cf. Bowersock 1983, 129–37.

34 *SHA Thirty Tyrants* 30.13–22. Other sources contribute to this image of Zenobia's Syro-Mesopotamian catholicity, as she is also said variously to have been a Zoroastrian, Jewess, or Christian, and is known to have hosted the learned polytheist Longinus at her court.

35 *SHA Aurelian* 33.4. Cf. 28.2, where Saracens and Armenians are mentioned as reinforcements defending Palmyra.

36 Another pregnant claim is that an offer to liberate the captive emperor was made by the Iberians, a people poised at the northern end of the Mountain Arena and so in a position to act as mediator between the two great powers; *SHA Valerian* 4.1.

37 *ŠKZ* 284–371.

38 Herzfeld 1924; Humbach and Skjærvø 1978–83.

39 Lact. *DMP* 9.6 uncharitably names Diocletian's fear of suffering Valerian's fate as the motive behind his choice to send Galerius against Narseh rather than go himself. Cf. Petr. Patr. fr. 13 (*FHG* 4:188), where Galerius reminds Narseh's envoy of Shapur's outrage against Valerian. On the chronology, see Chapter 2 n. 19 in this volume.

40 On the treaty of 298 see Petr. Patr. fr. 14 (*FHG* 4:189). For other sources relating to the campaign, see Dodgeon and Lieu 1991, 125–33. For commentary, bibliography, and a map, see Winter and Dignas 2001, 144–55, and also 209–13 on Nisibis and trade between Rome and Persia.

41 Aur. Vict. *Caes.* 39.6–37. See Lewin 1990.

42 In 312 Maximin Daia, Augustus in the east from 310 to 313, sent forces into Persian-controlled Armenia, though the reasons behind this brief engagement – possibly related to his Christian persecutions – are obscure; cf. Eus. *HE* 9.8.2–4; Malalas 12.46–8. For a concise summary of eastern military developments from Constantine until the treaty of 363, see Blockley 1992, 8–30, with Howard-Johnston 1994.

43 The present account focuses on Imru' al-Qays and the Arabs between Rome and Persia. For philological discussion of the inscription and full bibliography, see Retsö 2003, 467–85; Shahîd 1984, 31–64, with the review of Bowersock 1986b, 113–16; Calvet and Robin 2001, 265–9, with the response of Shahîd 2002 [2003], 73–102.

44 Al-Ṭabarī 1.757–71 (trans. Perlmann 139–50).

45 Again Palmyra is a foreshadowing. In Inscription Inv. 3.19 (*CIS* 2:3946 = Dodgeon and Lieu 1991, 88 no. 4.7.2), Odaenathus is called, in Palmyrene Aramaic translation, by both the Persian title "King of Kings," and the Roman "Restorer

of All the Orient." On the translation and connotations of the Palmyrene term *mtqnn'* (restorer or corrector) see Swain 1993, 157–64; Potter 1996, 271–85.

46 Eus. *Comm. in Is.* p. 273 (Ziegler).

47 Sources and interpretation at Bowersock 1994, 127*–40* with emendations; Lenski 2002b, 204–9.

48 On Ḥimyar, see Robin 1989. On Aksum, see Munro-Hay 1991.

49 *Kephalaia* 77.

50 Qatāda, late seventh or early eighth century, cited by Kister 1980, 143.

51 Crone 1987, 46–50.

52 Al-Ṭabarī 1.838–40. See the commentary and translation of Bosworth 1999, 54–8.

53 Munro-Hay 1991, 189–91, with Beeston 1992, 250–1.

54 For translations, see Munro-Hay 1991, 227–30.

55 For Armenia between Rome and Persia, see Garsoïan 1982; Garsoïan 1983; Redgate 1998, 94–139 with bibliography; Lenski 2002b, 153–67, including Iberia.

56 Tacitus *Annales* 2.56 (trans. Woodman).

57 Russell 1987, 121–36; Lieu 1992, 104–6.

58 For Syriac cultural and linguistic layers in Armenian Christianity, see Winkler 1982, 47–101; Thomson 1982, esp. 139–43.

59 For versions of the two rulers' relationship, see Thomson 1997.

60 Garsoïan 1988, 257–60.

61 Iberian willingness to go over to Persia would continue. The Roman-approved Sauromaces was ousted in favor of his cousin Aspacures, who received his regalia from Shapur II; cf. AM 27.12.4, 16; Braund 1994, 260.

62 Ruf. *HE* 10.11; Gel. Cyz. *HE* 3.10.1–21; Theod. *HE* 1.24. Soc. 1.20.11 and Soz. 2.7.12, mention a political alliance. More on the Christianization of Georgia in Peeters 1932 and at Thelamon 1981, 94–6. For an English translation of the Rufinus passage and discussion of his source, the Hellenized Armenian Bacurius, see Braund 1994, 246–61.

63 Braund 1994, 239. The bishop of Pityus in Lazica (western Georgia) was at Nicaea.

64 On the relationship between Armenia and Georgia, see Thomson 1996, esp. introduction; Braund 1994, 215–16.

65 For the positive response of the Persian Christian Aphrahat, see T. D. Barnes 1985b.

66 Eus. *VC* 4.8–14. T. D. Barnes 1981, 397 n. 144, claims the letter could be as early as 324; Lane Fox 1986, 636–9, discusses the letter in the context of Constantine's other public statements around 324/5.

67 Lane Fox 1986, 639; cf. T. D. Barnes 1981, 212.

68 Optat. Porf. *Carm.* 5, 14, 18. Eus. *VC* 4.7 also records foreign tribute.

69 Eus. *VC* 4.9.

70 Eus. *VC* 4.11.

71 Eus. *VC* 4.14.1.

72 Interpretations of Constantine's motives for launching the Persian campaign vary considerably. For a survey of sources, see Dodgeon and Lieu 1991, 143–63.

73 E.g., Eus. *VC* 2.53.

74 *RIC* 7 Rome 279.

75 Bryce 1989, 13–19.

76 Christodoulou 1998, 26 (Greek)/62–3 (English), medallion illustrated in color on jacket; cf. A. Alföldi 1947, 15.

77 Nicholson 1984, 253–61.

78 Closely related may be the Phoenix imagery at Lact. *De ave phoenice*, esp. ll. 31–89. Lane Fox 1986, 639–41, discusses the poem in connection with Constantine's intended tour of the eastern provinces, to conclude in Egypt.

79 *BP* 3.21; cf. Matthews 1989, 136 with n. 13.

80 On the title, see AM 14.1.2; *Origo* 35; *Epit.* 41.20; Zos. 2.39.2. On the marriage, see Philost. 3.22.

81 *RIC* 7 Constantinople 100. *RIC* 7 Constantinople 145–8 offers a related type that bears the reverse legend SECVRITAS PVBLICA. Seeck 1920–3, 4:25, sees the title as an indication that Hannibalianus was intended as a replacement for Shapur, an idea endorsed by T. D. Barnes 1981, 259; 1985b, 132.

82 Jul. *Or.* 1.13b. On "barbarian rumblings" on the frontier, see Eus. *VC* 4.56.1; Eutr. 10.8.2.

83 Joh. Lyd. *De mag.* 3.33–4. On the element of surprise, see Kaegi 1981. Lee 1993, 112–18, makes it clear, however, that major military expeditions were almost never kept secret. On Amida, see AM 18.9.1.

84 Eus. *VC* 4.57; Festus 26; Lib. *Or.* 59.71–2. Cf. T. D. Barnes 1981, 397.

85 Eus. *VC* 4.56. On Constantine's last days, see T. D. Barnes 1981, 258–60; Fowden 1994b; Burgess 1999a, 1999b, 221–32.

86 Shapur looks back to the Achaemenid empire in his letter; AM 17.5.3–8. Interpretations at Fowden 1993, 28–30; Winter and Dignas 2001, 83–4 with bibliography.

87 On Constantius's defensive strategy, see the lucid Warmington 1977.

88 AM 21.6.7–8.

89 Lib. *Ep.* 1402.3 claims that Julian planned to replace Shapur with Hormisdas, the Sassanian prince who had fled to the Roman court under Constantine and served also under Constantius; cf. AM 16.10.16; Zos. 2.27.1–4.

90 AM 25.7.9–14. Blockley 1992, 26–30; Greatrex and Lieu 2001, 1–19; Lenski 2002b, 161–7.

91 For the Dome of the Rock, see Grabar 1996, 21–116.

92 I have benefited from the learned comments of Oliver Nicholson, Noel Lenski, and Garth Fowden.

Appendix i: Stemmata

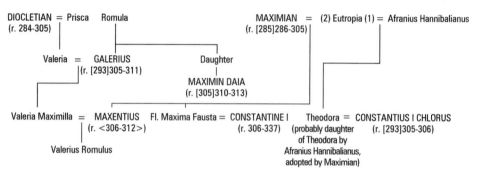

1. Family Connections of the Tetrarchs

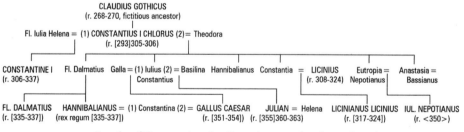

2. Family of Constantine the Great (parents, brothers, sisters)

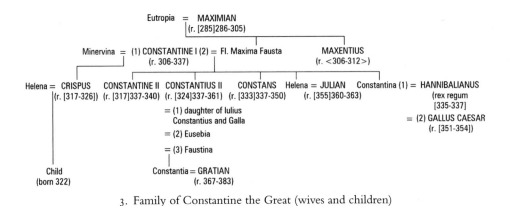

3. Family of Constantine the Great (wives and children)

APPENDIX 2: TIMELINE

250–1	Decius persecutes Christians
257–8	Valerian persecutes Christians
260	Valerian defeated and captured by Shapur I
268–70	Claudius Gothicus reigns
270–5	Aurelian reigns
272(?)	Constantine born
284	(Nov. 20) Diocletian accedes as emperor
285	Diocletian defeats Carinus; appoints Maximian as Caesar
286	Diocletian promotes Maximian to Augustus; Carausius revolts in Gaul and Britain
293	(Mar. 1) Diocletian appoints Galerius and Constantius I as Caesars; Carausius murdered by Allectus
296	Constantius defeats Allectus in Britain; Galerius defeated by Persians
297	Galerius defeats Persian king Narseh, captures Ctesiphon
298	Treaty with Persians regains upper Mesopotamia for Rome
301	(Sept. 1) Diocletian retariffs the coinage; (Nov./Dec.) issues Prices Edict
303	(Feb. 23) The Great Persecution begins; (Nov. 20) Diocletian and Maximian celebrate *vicennalia* in Rome
305	(May 1) Diocletian and Maximian abdicate, Galerius and Constantius become Augusti, and Maximin Daia and Severus Caesares; Constantine meets Constantius I in Boulogne
306	(July 25) Constantius I dies at York, and Constantine proclaimed emperor; (Oct. 28) Maxentius proclaimed emperor in Rome; Maximian resumes role of Augustus

307	(early) Severus captured in Ravenna after attacking Maxentius; (summer) Constantine fights Franks; (Aug./Sept.) Constantine marries Fausta; (autumn) Galerius fails to unseat Maxentius
308	(Spring) Maxentius and Maximian break off relations; (Summer) Constantine campaigns against Bructeri; L. Domitius Alexander revolts in Africa; (Nov. 11) at conference of Carnuntum Licinius proclaimed Augustus, Maximian forced to abdicate for the second time
309	Constantine introduces the solidus
310	Constantine completes bridge over the Rhine at Cologne, campaigns against Franks, and has vision of Apollo; Maximian revolts against Constantine and is captured in Marseilles; Constantine strikes an alliance with Licinius; Maxentius strikes an alliance with Maximin Daia
311	(Apr. 30) Galerius issues "Edict of Toleration" and dies shortly thereafter
312	(summer) Constantine crosses Alps and defeats Maxentius's forces at Susa, Turin, and Verona; (Oct. 28) Constantine defeats Maxentius at the battle of the Milvian Bridge
313	(early) Constantine and Licinius meet, consecrate Licinius's marriage with Constantia, and issue "Edict of Milan"; (Apr. 30) Licinius defeats Maximin Daia in Battle at Adrianople; (Aug.) Maximin Daia dies at Tarsus; (Oct.) council at Rome rejects Donatists
314	(Aug.) council at Arles again rejects Donatists
315	(July 25) Constantine celebrates *decennalia* in Rome
316	(autumn) Constantine defeats Licinius at Siscia, Cibalae, and Campus Ardiensis
317	Treaty arranged between Constantine and Licinius; (Mar. 1) Crispus, Constantine II, and Licinius II proclaimed Caesares; Constantine begins residing at Serdica
318	Crispus sent west to battle barbarians on Rhine
321	Constantine and Licinius break off relations
322(?)/323	Constantine campaigns against the Sarmatians (and Goths?)

324	Constantine constructs fleet at Thessalonica; (summer) Crispus defeats Licinius's fleet in the Propontis; (July 3) Constantine defeats Licinius at Adrianople then besieges him in Byzantium; (late summer) Licinius flees to Chalcedon and appoints Martinianus co-Augustus; (Sept. 18) Constantine defeats Licinius at Chrysopolis; (autumn) travels as far east as Antioch (?); (Nov. 8) Constantius II proclaimed Caesar, and Constantine initiates his refoundation of Byzantium as Constantinople
325	(May-June) Council of Nicaea; (July 25) Constantine celebrates his *vicennalia* in Nicomedia; Licinius I executed at Thessalonica
326	(July 25) Constantine celebrates his *vicennalia* again in Rome; refuses to sacrifice on the Capitoline; Licinius II executed at Thessalonica; (late) Crispus and Fausta executed
327	empress Helena visits the Holy Land
328	empress Helena dies in Rome (possibly 329); Constantine bridges the Danube at Oescus
330	(May 11) Constantine dedicates Constantinople; campaign against the Taifali
332	(early) Constantine II defeats Goths and forces them into a treaty
333	(Dec. 25) Constans proclaimed Caesar
334	Free Sarmatians are settled in Roman territory; Council at Antioch; Calocaerus revolts on Cyprus and is suppressed by Dalmatius the elder
335	Dalmatius the younger proclaimed Caesar and Hannibalianus proclaimed King of Kings; synod of Tyre, followed by Athanasius's meeting with Constantine in Constantinople
337	(May 22) Constantine dies near Nicomedia
337	(summer) Dalmatius, Hannibalianus, and other Constantinian dynasts executed; (Sept. 9) Constantine II, Constantius II, and Constans claim the title Augustus and divide empire
340	Constans defeats and kills Constantine II in battle near Aquileia
341	council of Antioch

343	council of Serdica
350	Magnentius revolts against Constans and kills him; Nepotian revolts in Rome and is killed by Magnentius's operatives; Vetranio revolts in Sirmium but is convinced to abdicate by Constantius II
351	Constantius II proclaims Gallus Caesar; Constantius defeats Magnentius at the battle of Mursa
353	Magnentius and Decentius executed
354	Gallus Caesar executed
355	Silvanus executed on suspicion of usurpation; (Nov. 6) Constantius II proclaims Julian Caesar
357	Julian defeats the Alamanni at Strasbourg
360	Julian proclaimed Augustus at Rheims
361	Julian marches east against Constantius II; (Nov. 3) Constantius II dies at Mopsucrene
363	(June 26) Julian killed during a skirmish inside Persia

MAPS

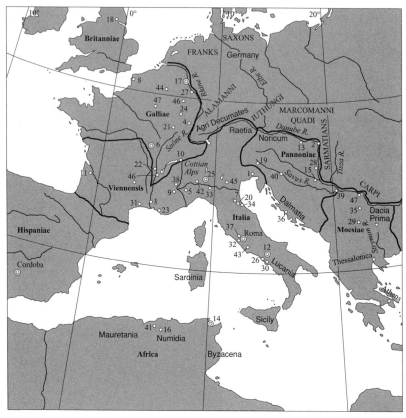

1. Aquileia
2. Aquincum (Budapest)
3. Arelate (Arles)
4. Argentoratum (Strasbourg)
5. Augusta Taurinorum (Turin)
6. Augustodunum (Autun)
7. Bononia (Bologna)
8. Bononia (Boulogne)
9. Brigantio (Briançon)
10. Brigantium (Bregenz)
11. Burdigalia (Bordeaux)
12. Capua
13. Carnuntum
14. Carthage
15. Cibalae
16. Cirta/Constantina
17. Colonia (Cologne)

18. Eburacum (York)
19. Emona
20. Fanum
21. Grand (Vosges)
22. Lugdunum (Lyon)
23. Massalia (Marseilles)
24. Mediomatrici (Metz)?
25. Milan (Mediolanum)
26. Misenum
27. Moguntiacum (Mainz)
28. Mursa
29. Naissus
30. Naples (Neapolis)
31. Nemausus (Nîmes)
32. Ostia
33. Placentia (Piacenza)

34. Ravenna
35. Romuliana (Gamzigrad)
36. Salona/Split
37. Saxa Rubra
38. Segusio (Susa)
39. Sirmium
40. Siscia
41. Sitifis
42. Ticinum
43. Tres Tabernae
    (south of Rome)
44. Trier (Augusta Treverorum)
45. Verona
46. Vienne
47. Viminacium

MAP I. The Western Empire

1. Adrianople (Edirne)	18. Damascus	35. Nicomedia
2 Aegae	19. Dionysias	36. Nisibis
3. Alexandria	20. Drepanum/Helenopolis	37. Oenoanda
4. Amida	21. Edessa	38. Oescus
5. Ancyra (Ankara)	22. Elaeus	39. Orcistus
6. Antioch	23. Gaza	40. Oxyrhynchus
7. Aphaca	24. Heliopolis	41. Palmyra
8. Aphrodisias	25. Hierapolis	42. Panopolis
9. Beroea (Stara Zagora)	26. Jerusalem	43. Pessinus
10. Bethlehem	27. Lampsacus	44. Philippopolis
11. Byzantium/Constantinople	28. Maiozamalcha	45. Ptolemais
12. Caesarea (Palestine)	29. Maiuma/Constantia	46. Scythopolis
13. Callipolis	30. Mamre	47. Singara
14. Chrysopolis	31. Memphis	48. Tarsus
15. Constantiana Daphne	32. Mobene (Qasr Bshir)	49. Transmarisca
16. Coptos	33. Namāra	50. Tropaium Traiani
17. Cotyaeum	34. Nicaea	51. Tyre

MAP 2. The Eastern Empire

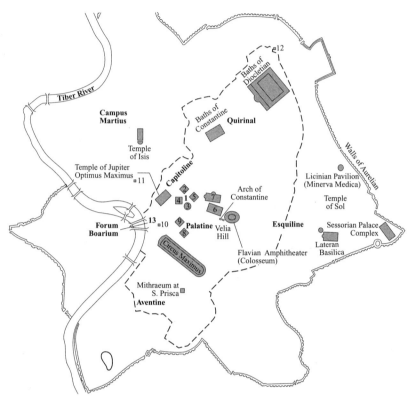

1. **Forum Romanum**
2. Curia
3. Temple of Vesta
4. Temple of Vespasian
5. Temple of Antoninus and Faustina
6. Temple of Venus and Roma
7. Basilica of Maxentius and Constantine
8. Temple of Apollo
9. Temple of Cybele
10. Janus Quadrifrons
11. S. Marco a Piazza Venezia
12. Temple of Fortuna at the Colline Gate
13. **Forum Boarium**

MAP 3.1. Rome Inside the Walls

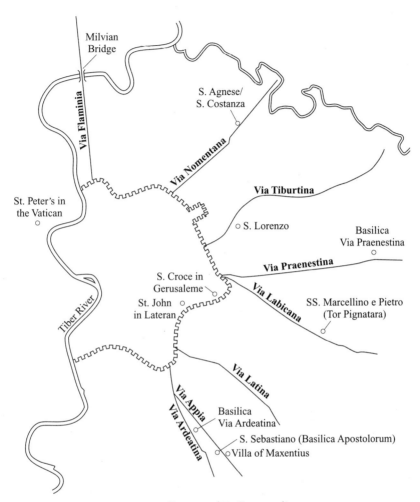

MAP 3.2. Rome and Its Surroundings

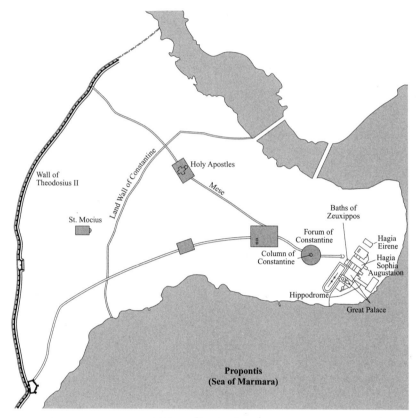

Wall of
Theodosius II

Land Wall of Constantine

Holy Apostles

Mese

St. Mocius

Baths of
Zeuxippos

Forum of
Constantine

Hagia
Eirene

Column of
Constantine

Hagia
Sophia

Augustaion

Hippodrome

Great Palace

Propontis
(Sea of Marmara)

MAP 4. Constantinople

Primary Sources and Translations

This bibliography excludes primary sources for the legend of Constantine, which are to be found in the notes for Chapter 13 and the secondary bibliography.

Acta Martyrum: *The Acts of the Christian Martyrs*, ed. H. Musurillo (Oxford 1972).

Al-Ṭabarī: *Ta'rīkh al rusul wa'l-mulūk*, ed. M. J. de Goeje et al. (Leiden, 1879–1901). Translation: *The History of Al-Ṭabarī (Ta'rīkh al-rusul wa'l-mulūk)*, vol. 4, *The Ancient Kingdoms*, trans. M. Perlmann (Albany, NY, 1987), and vol. 5, *The Sasanids, the Byzantines, the Lakhmids, and Yemen*, trans. C. E. Bosworth (Albany, 1999).

A(mmianus)**M**(arcellinus): *Rerum gestarum libri qui supersunt*, ed. C. U. Clark (Berlin [1910] 1963). Translation: *Ammianus Marcellinus*, trans. J. C. Rolfe. 3 vols. (Cambridge, MA, 1935–9), or *The Later Roman Empire (AD 354–378)*, trans. W. Hamilton (London and New York, 1986).

Ambrose *De Obit. Theod.*: *Sancti Ambrosii Oratio De Obitu Theodosii: Text, Translation, Introduction, and Commentary*, ed. and trans. M. D. Mannix (Washington, DC, 1925).

Ambrose *Ep.*: *Sancti Ambrosii Epistulae*. CSEL 82.1–2, ed. O. Faller and M. Zelzer (Vienna, 1968–90).

Anon. Cont. Dio: Anonymous Continuator of Dio at pp. 191–9 in *FHG* 4 (Paris, 1851).

Anonymous Arian historian: *Fragmente eines Arianischen Historiographen* at pp. 202–41 in *Philostorgius Kirchengeschichte mit dem Leben des Lucian von Antiochien und den Fragmenten eines arianischen Historiographen*, ed. J. Bidez and F. Winkelmann, 3d ed. (Berlin, 1981).

Arrian *Anabasis*: *Anabasis*, ed. A. G. Roos and G. Wirth, 2d ed. (Munich and Leipzig, 2002). Translation: *The Campaigns of Alexander*, trans. A. de Selincourt and J. R. Hamilton (London and Baltimore, 1971).

Artem.(ii) Pass.(io): Translation: *[John the Monk], Artemii Passio* at pp. 224–62 in *From Constantine to Julian: Pagan and Byzantine Views*, ed. S. N. C. Lieu and D. Montserrat (London, 1996).

Athan.(anasius) ***Apol. con. Arian.***: *Apologia contra Arianos (Apologia secunda)* at pp. 87–168 in *Athanasius Werke*, vol. 2.1, *De decretis Nicaenae synodi, De sententia Dionysii, Apologia de fuga sua, Apologia secunda, Epistula encyclica, De morte Arii, Historia Arianorum, De synodis, Apologia ad Constantium*, ed. H. G. Opitz (Berlin, 1936). Translation at pp. 100–47 in *NPNF* 2.4 (Peabody, MA [1891] 1995).

Athan. Con. gen.: *Contra gentes and De Incarnatione*, ed. and trans. R. W. Thomson (Oxford, 1971).

Athan. *De Incarn.*: in Athan. *Con. gen.*

Athan. *Hist. Arian*.: *Historia Arianorum* at pp. 183–230 in *Athanasius Werke*, vol. 2.1, *De decretis Nicaenae synodi, De sententia Dionysii, Apologia de fuga sua, Apologia secunda, Epistula encyclica, De morte Arii, Historia Arianorum, De synodis, Apologia ad Constantium*, ed. H. G. Opitz (Berlin, 1936). Translation at pp. 266–302 in *NPNF* 2.4 (Peabody, MA [1891] 1995).

Athan. *V. Anton*.: *Athanase d'Alexandrie Vie d'Antoine*. SCh 400, ed. and trans. G. J. M. Bartelink (Paris, 1994). Translation (of Evagrius's Latin version) at pp. 7–70 in *Early Christian Lives*, trans. C. White (London and New York, 1998).

Aug.(ustine) *Brev*.: *Breviculus collationis cum Donatistis* at pp. 261–306 in CCSL 149A, ed. S. Lancel (Turnhout, 1974).

Aug. *CD*: *Sancti Aurelii Augustini Episcopi De Civitate Dei Libri XXII*, 5th ed., ed. B. Dombart, A. Kalb, and J. Divjak, 2 vols. (Stuttgart and Leipzig, 1981). Translation: *The City of God against the Pagans*, trans. R. W. Dyson (Cambridge, 1998).

Aug. *Cresc*.: *Contra Cresconium grammaticum et Donatistam libri 4* at pp. 325–582 in *CSEL* 52, ed. M. Petschenig (Vienna, 1909).

Aug. *De doct. Christ*.: *Augustine De doctrina Christiana*, ed. and trans. R. P. H. Green (Oxford, 1995).

Aug. *Ep*.: *Epistulae 31–123*, CSEL 34.2, ed. A. Goldbacher (Vienna, 1898). Translation: *Augustine Letters*, Fathers of the Church 81, trans. W. Parsons, and R. Eno, 6 vols. (Washington, DC, 1964–89).

Aur.(elius) Vict.(or) *Caes*: *Sexti Aurelii Victoris Liber De Caesaribus*, ed. F. Pichlmayr (Leipzig, 1961). Translation: *Liber de Caesaribus of Sextus Aurelius Victor*, *TTH* 17, trans. H. W. Bird (Liverpool, 1994).

Bardaisan: *Philippus (Bardaisan): The Book of the Laws of Countries*, ed. and trans. H. J. W. Drijvers (Assen, 1965).

BP: *Buzandaran Patmut'iwink' (The Epic Histories): Also Known as Patmut'iwin Hayoc' (History of Armenia)*, ed. N. Garsoïan (Delmar, NY [1883] 1984). Translation: *Buzandaran Patmut'iwink': The Epic Histories Attributed to P'awstos Buzand (Buzandaran Patmut'iwink')*, trans. N. G. Garsoïan (Cambridge, MA, 1989).

Cedrenus: *Historiarum Compendium*, CSHB 34–5, ed. I. Bekker (Bonn, 1838).

Chron. *Pasch*.: *Chronicon Paschale*, CSHB 16–17, ed. L. Dindorf (Bonn, 1832). Translation: *Chronicon Paschale 284–628 AD. TTH* 7, trans. M. Whitby and M. Whitby (Liverpool, 1989).

CJ: *Corpus Iuris Civilis*, vol. 2, *Codex Justinianus*, ed. P. Krueger (Berlin, 1895).

Codinus: *Ps.-Codini Origines* at pp. 135–289 in *Scriptores Originum Constantinopolitanarum*, ed. T. Preger (Leipzig, 1901–7).

Coll. *Mos. et Rom. Leg*.: *Mosaicarum et romanarum legum collatio* at pp. 541–90 in *FIRA* 2 (Florence, 1940).

Cons. *Const*.: *The Chronicle of Hydatius and the Consularia Constantinopolitana: Two Contemporary Accounts of the Final Years of the Roman Empire*, ed. and trans. R. W. Burgess (Oxford, 1993).

Const. *Sirm*.: *Constitutiones Sirmondianae* at pp. 907–21 in *CTh*.

CTh: *Codex Theodosianus*, vol. 1.2, *Theodosiani libri XVI cum constitutionibus Sirmondianis*, ed. T. Mommsen and P. Krueger (Hildesheim [1905] 2000). Translation: *The Theodosian Code and Novels and the Sirmondian Constitutions*, trans. C. Pharr et al. (Princeton, 1952).

Cyprian *Ep*.: *Thascii Caecilii Cypriani Epistulae*, CCSL 3B, ed. G. F. Diercks (Turnhout, 1994).

Dig.: *Corpus Iuris Civilis*, vol. 1, *Institutiones Digesta*, ed. T. Mommsen and P. Krueger (Berlin, 1900). Translation: *Digest (Pandecta) of Justinian*, trans. A. Watson et al. (Philadelphia, 1985).

DRB: *De rebus bellicis*, ed. R. I. Ireland (Leipzig, 1984). Translation: *A Roman Reformer and Inventor, Being a Text of the Treatise De rebus bellicis*, trans. E. A. Thompson (Chicago [1952] 1996).

Ed. de pretiis: *Edictum Diocletiani et collegarum de pretiis rerum venalium*, ed. M. Giacchero (Genoa, 1974). Partial translation at pp. 422–26 in *Roman Civilization: Selected Readings*, vol. 2, *The Empire*, ed. N. Lewis and M. Reinhold, 3d ed. (New York, 1990).

Epiph.(anius) **Anc.**: *Ancoratus, GCS*, ed. K. Holl (Berlin, 1915).

Epiph. Pan.: *Panarion Haeresiarum, GCS*, ed. K. Holl and J. Dummer, 3 vols. (Berlin, 1915–85). Translation: *The Panarion of Epiphanius of Salamis*, trans. F. Williams. 2 vols. (Leiden, 1987–94).

Epit.: *Epitome de Caesaribus* at pp. 131–76 in *Sexti Aurleii Victoris Liber de Caesaribus*, ed. F. Pichlmayr (Leipzig, 1961).

Eun.(apius) **Hist.**: *Historiarum Fragmenta* at pp. 2–150 in *The Fragmentary Classicising Historians of the Later Roman Empire*, vol. 2, ed. and trans. R. C. Blockley (Liverpool, 1981).

Eun. VS: *Vitae Sophistarum*, ed. I. Giangrande (Rome, 1956). Translation: *Philostratus and Eunapius: The Lives of the Sophists*, trans. W. C. Wright (Cambridge, MA, 1921).

Eus.(ebius) **Comm. in Is.**: *Eusebius Werke*, vol. 9, *Der Jesajakommentar, GCS*, ed. T. Ziegler (Berlin, 1975).

Eus. DE: *Eusebius Werke*, vol. 6, *Demonstratio Evangelica, GCS*, ed. I. Heikel (Leipzig, 1913). Translation: *Eusebius: The Proof of the Gospel*, trans. W. J. Ferrar (London, 1920).

Eus. HE: *Eusebius Werke*, vol. 2.2–3, *Die Kirchengeschichte, GCS*, ed. E. Schwartz and T. Mommsen (Berlin, 1999). Translation: *Eusebius: The History of the Church from Christ to Constantine*, trans. G. A. Williamson and A. Louth (London and New York, 1989).

Eus. MP: *Eusèbe de Césarée Histoire Ecclésiastique Livres VIII–X et les martyrs en Palestine, SCh* 55, ed. and trans. G. Bardy (Paris, 1958).

Eus. PE: *Eusebius Werke*, vol. 8.1–2, *Die Praeparatio Evangelica*, ed. K. Mras, 2 vols. (Berlin, 1982–3). Translation: *Preparation for the Gospel: Eusebius*, trans. E. H. Gifford, 2 vols. (Grand Rapids, MI, 1981).

Eus. Tric.: *Tricennalia* at pp. 195–259 in *Eusebius Werke*, vol. 1, *Über das Leben Constantins, Constantins Rede an die Heilige Versammlung, Tricennatsrede an Constantin, GCS*, ed. I. A. Heikel (Leipzig, 1902). Translation: *In Praise of Constantine: A Historical Study and Translation of Eusebius' Tricennial Orations*, trans. H. A. Drake (Berkeley, 1975).

Eus. VC: *Eusebius Werke*, vol. 1.1, *Über das Leben des Kaisers Konstantin, GCS*, ed. F. Winkelmann (Berlin, 1975). Translation: *Eusebius: Life of Constantine*, trans. A. Cameron and S. G. Hall (Oxford, 1999).

Eutr.(opius): *Eutropii Breviarium ab urbe condita*, ed. C. Santini (Stuttgart, 1979). Translation: *The Breviarium Ab urbe condita of Eutropius, TTH* 14, trans. H. W. Bird (Liverpool, 1993).

Exp. tot. mundi: *Expositio totius mundi et gentium, SCh* 124, ed. and trans. J. Rougé (Paris, 1966).

Festal Index: *Histoire "acephale" et index syriaque des Lettres festales d'Athanase d'Alexandrie, SCh* 317, ed. and trans. A. Martin and M. Albert (Paris, 1985).

Festus: *The Breviarium of Festus: A Critical Edition with Historical Commentary*, ed. J. W. Eadie (London, 1967).

Firm.(icus) **Mat.**(ernus) **Err.**: M. *Minucii Felicis Octavius, Iulii Firmici Materni Liber de errore profanarum religionum, CSEL* 2, ed. C. Halm (Vienna, 1934). Translation: *Firmucus Maternus: The Error of the Pagan Religions*, Ancient Christian Writers 37, trans. C. A. Forbes (New York, 1970).

Firm. Mat. Math.: *Iulii Firmici Materni Matheseos libri VIII*, ed. W. Kroll and F. Skutsch (Stuttgart, 1968). Translation: *Ancient Astrology: Theory and Practice*, trans. J. R. Bram (Park Ridge, NJ, 1975).

Frag. Vat.: *Fragmenta Quae Dicuntur Vaticana* at pp. 461–540 in *FIRA* 2 (Florence, 1940).

Gel.(asius) **Cyz.**(icenus) **HE**: *Anonyme Kirchengeschichte (Gelasius Cyzicenus, CPG 6024)*, *GCS*, ed. G. C. Hansen (Berlin, 2002).

Greg.(orius) **Tur.**(onensis) **Hist.**: *Grégoire de Tours Histoire des Francs*, ed. and trans. R. Latouche, 2 vols. (Paris, 1975–9). Translation: *Gregory of Tours: The History of the Franks*, trans. L. Thorpe (London and New York, 1974).

Herodotus: *Herodoti historiae*, ed. C. Hude, 2 vols. (Oxford, 1908). Translation: *The History: Herodotus*, trans. D. Grene (Chicago, 1987).

Hesychius: *Hesychii Illustrii origines constantinopolitanae* at pp. 1–18 in *Scriptores Originum Constantinopolitanarum*, ed. T. Preger (Leipzig, 1901–7).

Irenaeus Adv. Haer.: *Irenée de Lyon Contre les heresies, SCh* 100, 153, ed. A. Rousseau, L. Doutreleau and C. Mercier, 2 vols. (Paris, 1951–65).

Jer.(ome) **Chron.**: *Eusebius Werke*, vol. 7, *Die Chronik des Hieronymus, GCS*, ed. R. Helm (Berlin, 1984).

Joh.(annes) **Ant.**(iochenus): *Historiarum Fragmenta* at pp. 535–622 in *FHG* 4 (Paris, 1851).

Joh.(annes) **Lyd.**(us) **De mag.**: *De magistratibus populi romani libri tres: On Powers or The Magistrates of the Roman State*, ed. and trans. A. C. Bandy (Philadelphia, 1982).

Joh. Lyd. De mens.: *Ioannis Lydi Liber de mensibus*, ed. R. Wuensch (Stuttgart [1898] 1967).

Jord.(anes) **Get.**: *Getica* at pp. 53–138 in *MGH.AA* 5. Translation: *Jordanes: The Origin and Deeds of the Goths*, trans. C. C. Mierow (Princeton, 1908).

Jul.(ian) **Caes.**: *Caesares* at vol. 2.2, pp. 32–71, in *Oeuvres Complètes*, ed. J. Bidez, C. Lacombrade, and G. Rochefort (Paris, 1932–64). Translation at vol. 2, pp. 341–414, in *The Works of the Emperor Julian*, trans. W. C. Wright (Cambridge, MA, 1913–23).

Jul. Con. Gal.: *Contra Galilaeos* at vol. 3, pp. 318–427, in *The Works of the Emperor Julian* (see Jul. *Caes.*).

Jul. Ep. ad Ath.: *Epistula ad Athenos* at vol. 1.1, pp. 213–35, in *Oeuvres Complètes* (see Jul. *Caes.*). Translation at vol. 2, pp. 239–91, in *The Works of the Emperor Julian* (see Jul. *Caes.*).

Jul. Or.: *Orationes I–III* at vol. 1.1, pp. 10–180, in *Oeuvres Complètes* (see Jul. *Caes.*). Translation at vol. 1, pp. 1–345, in *The Works of the Emperor Julian* (see Jul. *Caes.*).

Kephalaia: *The Kephalaia of the Teacher*, ed. and trans. I. Gardner (Leiden, 1995).

Lact.(antius) **De ave phoenice**: *Lactanti De ave phoenice*, ed. and trans. M. C. FitzPatrick (Philadelphia, 1933). Translation: *Lactantius Minor Works*, Fathers of the Church 54, trans. M. F. McDonald (Washington, DC, 1965), or at pp. 324–6 in *NPNF* 2.4 (Peabody, MA [1891] 1995).

Lact. DMP: *Lactantius De Mortuorum Persecutorum*, ed. and trans. J. L. Creed (Oxford, 1984).

Lact. **Div**. **Inst**.: *Divinae Institutiones et Epitome divinarum institutionum, CSEL* 19, ed. S. Brandt (Vienna 1890). Translation: *Lactantius: Divine Institutes, TTH* 40, trans. A. Bowen and P. Garnsey (Liverpool, 2003).

Lib.(anius) **Or**.: *Libanii Opera*, vols. 1–9, ed. R. Foerster (Leipzig, 1903–23). Translation: *Libanius, Selected Works*, trans. A. F. Norman, 2 vols. (Cambridge, MA, 1969–77), and *The Sons of Constantine: Libanius Or. LIX*, trans. M. H. Dodgeon at pp. 164–205 in *From Constantine to Julian: Pagan and Byzantine Views*, ed. S. N. C. Lieu and D. Montserrat (London, 1996).

Liber pont.: *Le Liber pontificalis*, ed. and trans. L. Duchesne, 2d ed. (Paris, 1955–7). Translation: *The Book of Pontiffs (Liber Pontificalis): The Ancient Biographies of the First Ninety Roman Bishops to AD 715, TTH* 6, trans. R. Davis (Liverpool, 1989).

Lucian **Peregrinus**: *De morte Peregrini* at pp. 188–205 in *Luciani opera*, vol. 3, *Libelli 44–68*, ed. M. D. Macleod (Oxford, 1980). Translation at vol. 5, pp. 2–51, in *Lucian*, trans. A. M. Harmon (Cambridge, MA, 1936).

Malalas: *Ioannis Malalae Chronographia*, Corpus Fontium Historiae Byzantinae 35, ed. J. Thurn (Berlin, 2000). Translation: *The Chronicle of John Malalas*, Byzantina Australiensia 4, trans. E. Jeffreys, M. Jeffreys, and R. Scott (Melbourne, 1986).

Marcian **Novels**: *Legum novellarum in oriente promulgatarum Marciani* at pp. 179–96 in *Codex Theodosianus*, vol. 2, *Leges novellae ad Theodosianum pertinentes*, ed. T. Mommsen and P. M. Meyer (Hildesheim [1905] 2000). Translation at pp. 562–7 in *The Theodosian Code and Novels and the Sirmondian Constitutions*, trans. C. Pharr et al. (Princeton, 1952).

Marc.(us) **Diac**.(onus) **V**. **Porph**.: *Marc le Diacre Vie de Porphyre eveque de Gaza*, ed. and trans. H. Grégoire and M.-A. Kugener (Paris, 1930). Translation: *The Life of Porphyry Bishop of Gaza by Mark the Deacon*, trans. G. F. Hill (Oxford, 1913).

Not. **Dign**.: *Notitia Dignitatum*, ed. O. Seeck (Berlin [1876] 1962).

OC: *Oratio Constantini* at pp. 149–92 in *Eusebius Werke*, vol. 1, *Über das Leben Constantins, Constantins Rede an die Heilige Versammlung, Tricennatsrede an Constantin, GCS*, ed. I. A. Heikel (Leipzig, 1902). Translation at pp. 1–62 in *Constantine and Christendom: The Oration to the Saints, The Greek and Latin Accounts of the Discovery of the Cross, The Edict of Silvester, TTH* 39, trans. M. Edwards (Liverpool, 2003).

Optat.(atus Milevitanus): *S. Optati Milevitani libri VII, CSEL* 26, ed. C. Ziwsa (Vienna, 1893), or *Optat de Milève Traité contre les Donatistes, SCh* 412, ed. and trans. M. Labrousse (Paris, 1995). Translation: *Optatus against the Donatists, TTH* 27, trans. M. Edwards (Liverpool, 1997).

Optat.(ianus) **Porf**.(yrius) **Carm**.: *Publilii Optatiani Porfyrii Carmina*, ed. J. Polara, 2 vols. (Torino, 1973).

Origen **Contra Celsum**: *Origenis contra Celsum libri VIII*, ed. M. Marcovich (Leiden, 2001). Translation: *Origen Contra Celsum*, trans. H. Chadwick (Cambridge, 1965).

Origo **(Constantini)**: *Excerpta Valesiana*, ed. J. Moreau (Leipzig, 1961). Translation: *The Origin of Constantine: The Anonymous Valesianus pars Prior (Origo Constantini)*, trans. S. N. C. Lieu at pp. 39–62 in *From Constantine to Julian: Pagan and Byzantine Views*, ed. S. N. C. Lieu and D. Montserrat (London, 1996).

Oros.: *Pauli Orosii Historiarum adversum paganos libri VII, CSEL* 5, ed. C. Zangemeister (Vienna, 1882). Translation: *The Seven Books of History against the Pagans*, Fathers of the Church 50, trans. R. J. Deferrari (Washington, DC, 1964).

P. **Abinn**.: *The Abbinaeus Archive: Papers of a Roman Officer in the Reign of Constantius II*, ed. H. I. Bell et al. (Oxford, 1962).

P. Cair. Isid.: *The Archive of Aurelius Isidorus in the Egyptian Museum, Cairo, and the University of Michigan (P. Cair. Isid.)*, ed. A. E. R. Boak and H. C. Youtie (Ann Arbor, 1960).

P. Panop. Beatty: *Papyri from Panopolis in the Chester Beatty Library Dublin*, Chester Beatty Monographs 10, ed. T. C. Skeat (Dublin, 1964).

P. Thead.: *Papryus de Théadelphie*, ed. P. Jouguet (Paris, 1911).

P. Turner: *Papyri Greek and Egyptian Edited by Various Hands in Honor of Eric Gardner Turner*, ed. P. J. Parsons et al. (London, 1981).

Pan. Lat.: *XII Panegyrici Latini*, ed. R. A. B. Mynors (Oxford, 1964). Translation *In Praise of Later Roman Emperors: The Panegyrici Latini*, trans. C. E. V. Nixon and B. S. Rodgers (Berkeley, 1994).

Pass. Mart. Abit.: *Acta martyrum Abintinianorum* at cols. 703–15 in *PL* 8 (Paris, 1865). Translation at pp. 27–49 in *Donatist Martyr Stories*, *TTH* 24, ed. M. Tilley (Liverpool, 1996).

Paulinus of Nola *Ep.*: *S. Pontii Meropii Paulini Nolani opera*, *CSEL* 29, ed. W. A. Hartel (Vienna, 1894). Translation: *Letters of St. Paulinus of Nola*, trans. P. G. Walsh, 3 vols. (New York, 1966–75).

Petr.(us) **Patr.**(icius): *Historiae* at pp. 184–91 in *FHG* 4 (Paris, 1851).

Philost.(orgius): *Philostorgius Kirchengeschichte mit dem Leben des Lucian von Antiochien und den Fragmenten eines arianischen Historiographen*, *GCS*, ed. J. Bidez and F. Winkelmann, 3d ed. (Berlin, 1981).

Pliny *Ep.*: *C. Plini Caecili Secundi epistularum libri decem*, ed. R. A. B. Mynors (Oxford, 1963). Translation: *The Letters of the Younger Pliny*, trans. B. Radice (London and New York, 1963).

Porph.(yrius) *V. Plot.*: *Plotinus*, vol. 1, *De vita Plotini et ordine librorum eius*, ed. A. H. Armstrong (London, 1966). Translation: *On the Life of Plotinus and the Arrangement of His Works* at pp. 1–54 in *Neoplatonic Saints: The Lives of Plotinus and Proclus by Their Students*, *TTH* 35, trans. M. Edwards (Liverpool, 2000).

Praxagoras of Athens: *Historiae* at pp. 948–9 in *FGH* 2B (Leiden, 1926). Translation at pp. 7–8 in *From Constantine to Julian: Pagan and Byzantine Views*, ed. S. N. C. Lieu and D. Montserrat (London, 1996).

Procop.(ius) *Aed.*: *Procopius Caesariensis opera omnia*, vol. 3.2, *De Aedificiis*, ed. J. Haury (Leipzig [1913] 2001). Translation: *Procopius*, vol. 7, *Buildings*, trans. H. B. Dewing and G. Downey (Cambridge, MA, 1940).

Procop. *BG*: *Procopius Caesariensis opera omnia*, vol. 2, *De bello Gothico*, ed. J. Haury (Leipzig [1913] 2001). Translation *Procopius*, vols. 3–5, *History of the Wars*, trans. H. B. Dewing (Cambridge, MA, 1919–28).

Ruf.(inus) *HE*: *Eusebii historia ecclesiastica translata et continuata* at pp. 957–1040 in *Eusebius Werke*, vol. 2.2, *Die Kirchengeschichte*, *GCS*, ed. E. Schwartz and T. Mommsen (Berlin, 1908). Translation: *The Church History of Rufinus of Aquileia*, trans. P. R. Amidon (New York, 1997).

SHA: *Scriptores Historiae Augustae*, 5th ed., ed. E. Hohl et al., 2 vols. (Leipzig, 1997). Translation: *The Scriptores Historiae Augustae*, trans. D. Magie, 3 vols. (Cambridge, MA, 1921–32).

ŠKZ: at pp. 284–371 in *Die sassanidischen Staatsinschriften*, ed. and trans. M. Back (Leiden, 1978). Translation at pp. 371–3 in *The History of Ancient Iran*, trans. R. Frye (Munich, 1984).

Soc.(rates): *Historia ecclesiastica*, *GCS*, ed. G. C. Hansen (Berlin, 1995). Translation: *Socrates Church History from AD 305–439*, *NPNF* 2.2, trans. A. C. Zenos (Peabody, MA [1890] 1995).

Soz.(omenus): *Historia ecclesiastica*, *GCS*, 2d ed., eds. J. Bidez and G. C. Hansen, (Berlin, 1995). Translation: *Sozomenus Church History from AD 323–425*, *NPNF* 2.2 (Peabody, MA [1890] 1995).

Suet.(onius): *Suetonius*, vol. 1, *De vita caesarum libri*, ed. M. Ihm (Stuttgart, 1993). Translation: *Suetonius the Twelve Caesars*, trans. R. Graves (London and New York, 1957).

Symm.(achus) *Rel*.: *Prefect and Emperor: The Relationes of Symmachus, A.D. 384*, ed. and trans. R. H. Barrow (Oxford, 1973).

Symm. *Ep*.: *Epistulae* at pp. 1–278 in *MGH.AA* 6.1, ed. O. Seeck (Berlin, 1883).

Tacitus *Annales*: *Cornelii Taciti annalium ab excessu Divi Augusti libri*, ed. C. D. Fisher (Oxford, 1906). Translation: *Tacitus the Annals*, trans. A. J. Woodman (Indianapolis, 2004).

Tertullian *Apol*.: *Apologeticum*, *CCSL* 1, ed. E. Dekkers (Turnhout, 1954). Translation: *The Apology* at pp. 17–55 in *The Ante-Nicene Fathers*, vol. 3, trans. S. Thelwall (Peabody, MA [1890] 1995).

Them. *Or*.: *Themistii Orationes*, ed. G. Downey, 3 vols. (Leipzig, 1965–74). Translation: *Politics, Philosophy, and Empire in the Fourth Century: Select Orations of Themistius, TTH* 36, trans. P. Heather and D. Moncur (Liverpool, 2001).

Theod.(oretus) *HE*: *Historia ecclesiastica*, *GCS*, 3d ed., ed. L. Parmentier and G. C. Hansen, (Berlin, 1998).

Theophan.(es): *Theophanis Chronographia*, ed. C. De Boor, 2 vols. (Hildesheim [1883] 1963). Translation: *The Chronicle of Theophanes Confessor: Byzantine and Near Eastern History AD 284–813*, trans. C. Mango and R. Scott (Oxford, 1997).

Veget.(ius): *Vegetius Epitoma rei militaris*, ed. M. D. Reeve (Oxford, 2004). Translation: *Vegetius: Epitome of Military Science, TTH* 16, ed. N. P. Milner (Liverpool, 1993).

Zon.(aras): *Ioannis Zonarae Epitome historiarum*, ed. C. Du Cange and L. A. Dindorf, 6 vols. (Leipzig, 1868–75). Translation: M. DiMaio, *Zonaras' Account of the Neo-Flavian Emperors: A Commentary* (Ph.D. diss., University of Missori, 1977).

Zos.(imus): *Zosime Historie Nouvelle*, ed. and trans. F. Paschoud, 3 vols. (Paris, 1971). Translation: *Zosimus: New History*, Byzantina Australiensia 1, trans. R. T. Ridley (Sydney, 1982).

SECONDARY BIBLIOGRAPHY

Ahlquist, A. 2001. "Cristo e l'imperatore romano. I valori simbolici del nimbo." Pp. 207–27 in *Imperial Art as Christian Art – Christian Art as Imperial Art*. Acta ad archaeologiam et artium historiam pertinenda 15, ed. J. R. Brandt and O. Steen. Rome.

Aiello, V. 1988. "Costantino, Lucio Domizio Alessandro e Cirta: Un caso di rielaborazione storiografica." Pp. 179–96 in *L'Africa Romana: Atti del VI convegno di studio Sassari, 16–18 dicembre 1988*, ed. A. Mastino. Sassari.

————. 1992a. "Costantino, la lebbra, e il battesimo di Silvestro." Pp. 17–58 in *Costantino il Grande dall'antichità all'umanesimo: Colloquio sul Cristianesimo nel mondo antico, Macerata 18–20 Dicembre 1990*, vol. 1, ed. G. Bonamente and F. Fusco. Macerata.

————. 1992b. "La fortuna della notizia geronimiana su Costantino eretico." *Messana* 13: 221–37.

————. 2000a. "Il controllo militare del Mediterraneo in età tetrarchica e costantiniana." Pp. 201–20 in *L'Africa Romana: Atti del XIV convegno di studio Sassari, 7–10 dicembre 2000*, ed. A. Mastino. Sassari.

————. 2000b. "Cronaca di una eclisse: osservazioni sulla vicenda di Silvestro I vescovo di Roma." Pp. 229–48 in *Il Tardoantico alle soglie del duemila: Diritto, Religione, Società*, ed. G. Lanata. Pisa.

Alexander, S. 1971. "Studies in Constantinian Architecture." *Rivista di archeologia cristiana* 67: 281–330.

Alföldi, A. 1947. "On the Foundation of Constantinople: A Few Notes." *Journal of Roman Studies* 37: 10–16.

————. 1948. *The Conversion of Constantine and Pagan Rome*, trans. H. Mattingly. Oxford.

————. 1959. "*Cornuti*: A Teutonic Contingent in the Service of Constantine the Great and Its Decisive Role in the Battle at the Milvian Bridge." *Dumbarton Oaks Papers* 13: 171–9.

Alföldi, M. 1963. *Die Constantinische Goldprägung*. Mainz.

————. 1964. "Die Sol Comes-Münze vom Jahre 325: Neues zur Bekehrung Constantins." Pp. 10–16 in *Mullus, Festschift Theodor Klauser*, Jahrbuch für Antike und Christentum Ergänzungsband 1. Münster. Reprint, pp. 52–9 in *Gloria Romanorum*, eds. H. Bellen and H.-M. von Kaenel. Stuttgart, 2001.

————. 1999. *Bild und Bildsprache der römischen Kaiser*. Mainz.

Alföldy, G. 1974. "The Crisis of the Third Century as Seen by Contemporaries." *Greek, Roman and Byzantine Studies* 15: 89–111.

Amarelli, F. 1978. *Vetustas Innovatio: Un'antitesi apparente nella legislazione di Costantino.* Naples.

Amelung, W. 1899. "Kybele-Orans." *Rheinisches Museum* 14: 8–12.

Amici, A. 2000. "Divus Constantinus: Le testimonianze epigrafiche." *Rivista Storica dell'Antichità* 30: 187–216.

Arce, J. 1984. *Estudios sobre el Emperador Fl. Cl. Juliano.* Madrid.

———. 1997. "Emperadores, Palacios y Villae (A propósito de la villa romana de Cercadilla, Córdoba)." *Antiquité Tardive* 5: 293–302.

Argentini, S., and M. Ricciardi. 1996–7. "Il complesso di S. Croce in Gerusalemme a Roma: Nuove acquisizioni ed ipotesi." *Atti della Pontificia accademia romana di archeologia, Rendiconti* 69: 253–88.

Arjava, A. 1996. *Women and Law in Late Antiquity.* Oxford.

Athanassiadi, P., and M. Frede, eds. 1999. *Pagan Monotheism in Late Antiquity.* Oxford.

Austin, N. J. E., and N. B. Rankov. 1995. *Exploratio: Military and Political Intelligence in the Roman World from the Second Punic War to the Battle of Adrianople.* London.

Bagnall, R. 1982. "Religious Conversion and Onomastic Change in Early Byzantine Egypt." *Bulletin of the American Society of Papyrologists* 19: 105–24.

———. 1985. *Currency and Inflation in Fourth Century Egypt.* Bulletin of the American Society of Papyrologists Supplement 5. Atlanta.

———. 1993a. *Egypt in Late Antiquity.* Princeton.

———. 1993b. "Slavery and Society in Late Roman Egypt." Pp. 220–40 in *Law, Politics and Society in the Ancient Mediterranean World*, ed. B. Halpern, and D. Hobson. Sheffield.

———. 2002. "The Effects of Plague: Model and Evidence." *Journal of Roman Archaeology* 15: 114–20.

Bagnall, R., A. Cameron, S. R. Schwartz, and K. A. Worp. 1987. *Consuls of the Later Roman Empire.* Atlanta.

Bakker, L. 1993a. "Die Siegesaltar zur Juthungenschlacht von 260 n. Chr.: Ein spektakulärer Neufund aus Augusta Vindelicium/Augsburg." *Archäologische Nachrichten* 24: 274–7.

———. 1993b. "Raetian unter Postumus: Das Siegesdenkmal einer Juthungenschlacht im Jahre 260 n. Chr. aus Augsburg." *Germania* 71: 370–86.

Banaji, J. 2001. *Agrarian Change in Late Antiquity: Gold, Labour, and Aristocratic Dominance.* Oxford.

Bang, M. 1906. *Die Germanen im römischen Dienst bis zum Regierungsantritt Constantins I.* Berlin.

Baratte, F. 1995. "Observations sur le portrait romain à l'époque tétrarchique." *Antiquité Tardive* 3: 65–76.

Barbera, M. 2000. "Dagli *horti Spei Veteris* al *Palatium Sessorianum*." Pp. 104–12 in *Aurea Roma: Dalla città pagana alla città cristiana*, ed. S. Ensoli and E. La Rocca. Rome.

Barceló, P. A. 1981. *Roms auswärtige Beziehungen unter der constantinischen Dynastie (306–363).* Regensburg.

Barlow, J., and P. Brennan. 2001. "*Tribuni Scholarum Palatinarum* c. A.D. 353–64: Ammianus Marcellinus and the *Notitia Dignitatum*." *Classical Quarterly* n.s. 51: 237–54.

Barnes, M. R. 1998. "The Fourth Century as Trinitarian Canon." Pp. 47–67 in *Christian Origins: Theology, Rhetoric and Community*, ed. L. Ayres and G. Jones. London.

Barnes, T. D. 1973. "Lactantius and Constantine." *Journal of Roman Studies* 63: 29–46.

———. 1975. "Publilius Optatianus Porfyrius." *American Journal of Philology* 96: 173–86.

————. 1976a. "Sosianus Hierocles and the Antecedents of the 'Great Persecution.'" *Harvard Studies in Classical Philology* 80: 239–52.

————. 1976b. "The Emperor Constantine's Good Friday Sermon." *Journal of Theological Studies*, n.s. 27: 414–23.

————. 1981. *Constantine and Eusebius*. Cambridge, MA, and London.

————. 1982. *The New Empire of Diocletian and Constantine*. Cambridge, MA, and London.

————. 1984. "Constantine's Prohibition of Pagan Sacrifice." *American Journal of Philology* 105: 69–72. Reprint, study IV in T. D. Barnes 1994.

————. 1985a. "The Career of Abinnaeus." *Phoenix* 39: 368–74. Reprint, study XV in T. D. Barnes 1994.

————. 1985b. "Constantine and the Christians of Persia." *Journal of Roman Studies* 75: 126–36. Reprint, study VI in T. D. Barnes 1994.

————. 1985c. "The Conversion of Constantine." *Echos du monde classique/Classical Views* 4: 371–91. Reprint, study III in T. D. Barnes 1994.

————. 1986. "The Constantinian Reformation." Pp. 39–57 in *The Crake Lectures, 1984*. Sackville, New Brunswick. Reprint, study V in T. D. Barnes 1994.

————. 1987. "Regional Prefectures." Pp. 13–23 in *Bonner Historia-Augusta-Colloquium, 1984/1985*, Antiquitas 4:19, ed. J. Straub. Bonn.

————. 1990. "The Consecration of Ulfila." *Journal of Theological Studies* n.s. 41: 541–5.

————. 1992. "Praetorian Prefects, 337–361." *Zeitschrift für Papyrologie und Epigraphik* 94: 249–60. Reprint, study XIII in T. D. Barnes 1994.

————. 1993. *Athanasius and Constantius: Theology and Politics in the Constantinian Empire*. Cambridge, MA.

————. 1994. *From Eusebius to Augustine: Selected Papers 1982–1993*. Aldershot.

————. 1996a. "Emperors, Panegyrics, Prefects, Provinces and Palaces (284–317)." *Journal of Roman Archaeology* 9: 532–52.

————. 1996b. "The Franci before Diocletian." Pp. 11–18 in *Historiae Augustae Colloquium Genevense* 2, ed. G. Bonamente and F. Paschoud. Macerata.

————. 1998. *Ammianus Marcellinus and the Representation of Historical Reality*. Ithaca and London.

————. 1999. "The Wife of Maximinus." *Classical Philology* 94: 459–60.

————. 2001. "Constantine's Speech to the Assembly of the Saints: Place and Date of Delivery." *Journal of Theological Studies* 52: 26–36.

Barsanti, C. 1992. "Costantinopoli: Testimonianze archeologiche di età costantiniana." Pp. 115–50 in *Costantino il Grande dall'antichità all'umanesimo: Colloquio sul Cristianesimo nel mondo antico, Macerata 18–20 Dicembre 1990*, vol. 1, ed. G. Bonamente and F. Fusco. Macerata.

Bartoli, A. 1963. *Curia Senatus: Lo scavo e il restauro*. Rome.

Barton, T. S. 1994. *Power and Knowledge: Astrology, Physiognomics, and Medicine under the Roman Empire*. Ann Arbor.

Bassett, S. 1991. "The Antiquities in the Hippodrome of Constantinople." *Dumbarton Oaks Papers* 45: 87–96.

————. 1996. "*Historiae Custos*: Sculpture and Tradition in the Baths of Zeuxippos." *American Journal of Archaeology* 100: 491–506.

————. 2004. *The Urban Image of Constantinople*. Cambridge.

Bastien, P. 1988. *Monnaie et "donativa" au Bas-Empire*. Numismatique Romaine 17. Wetteren.

Bauer, F. A. 1996. *Stadt, Platz und Denkmal in der Spätantike: Untersuchungen zur Ausstattung des öffentlichen Raums in den spätantiken Städten Rom, Konstantinopel und Ephesos.* Mainz.

———. 1999. "The Constantinian Bishop's Church at Ostia: Preliminary Report on the 1998 Season." *Journal of Roman Archaeology* 12: 342–53.

———. 2001. "Urban Space and Ritual: Constantinople in Late Antiquity." Pp. 27–62 in *Imperial Art as Christian Art – Christian Art as Imperial Art,* Acta ad archaeologiam et artium historiam pertinentia 15, ed. J. R. Brandt and O. Steen. Rome.

Bauer, F. A., M. Heinzelmann, A. Martin, and A. Schaub. 1999. "Untersuchungen im Bereich der konstantischen Bischofskirche Ostias: Vorbericht zur ersten Grabungskampagne 1998." *Mitteilungen des Deutschen Archäologischen Instituts, Römische Abteilung* 106: 289–341.

Bauer, W. 1971. *Orthodoxy and Heresy in Earliest Christianity.* Trans. and ed. R. A. Kraft and G. Krodel. Philadelphia.

Baynes, N. H. 1910. "Rome and Armenia in the Fourth Century." *English Historical Review* 25: 625–43.

———. 1929. *Constantine the Great and the Christian Church: The Raleigh Lecture on History, 29 October 1918.* Proceedings of the British Academy 15. London.

———. 1939. "Constantine." Pp. 678–99 in *The Cambridge Ancient History*, vol. 12, *The Imperial Crisis and Recovery A.D. 193–324*, ed. S. A. Cook et al. 1st ed. Cambridge.

Beard, M., J. North, and S. Price. 1998. *Religions of Rome.* 2 vols. Cambridge.

Beatrice, P. F. 2002. "The Word 'Homoousios' from Hellenism to Christianity." *Church History* 71: 243–72.

Beaucamp, J. 1990. *Le statut de la femme à Byzance (4e–7e siècle).* Vol. 1. Paris.

Becatti, G. 1969. *Scavi di Ostia.* Vol. 6. Rome.

Beeston, A. F. L. 1992. Review of *Aksum: An African Civilisation of Late Antiquity*, by S. C. Munro-Hay. *Journal of the Royal Asiatic Society* 2: 247–51.

Bell, H. I., et al., eds. 1962. *The Abinnaeus Archive: Papers of a Roman Officer in the Reign of Constantius II.* Oxford.

Berenson, B. 1954. *The Arch of Constantine or the Decline of Form.* London.

Bergmann, M. 1977. *Studien zum Römischen Porträt des 3. Jahrhunderts n. Chr.* Bonn.

———. 1998a. *Die Strahlen der Herrscher.* Mainz.

———. 1998b. "Der römische Sonnenkoloß, der Konstantinsbogen und die Ktistes-Statue von Konstantinopel." *Braunschweigische Wissenschaftliche Gesellschaft, Jahrbuch 1997* 14: 112–30.

———. 1999. *Chiragan, Aphrodisias, Konstantinopel.* Wiesbaden.

Betz, H. D., ed. 1986. *The Greek Magical Papyri in Translation.* Chicago.

———. 1991. "Magic and Mystery in the Greek Magical Papyri." Pp. 244–59 in *Magika Hiera: Ancient Greek Magic and Religion*, ed. C. A. Faraone and D. Obbink. New York.

Bianchi Bandinelli, R. 1971. *Rome: The Late Empire.* London.

Bidez, J. 1913. *Vie de Porphyre, le philosophe neo-platonicien.* Ghent.

———. 1935. "Fragments nouveaux de Philostorge sur la Vie de Constantin." *Byzantion* 10: 403–37.

Bidez, J., and F. Winkelmann, ed. 1981. *Philostorgius Kirchengeschichte mit dem Leben des Lucian von Antiochien und den Fragmenten eines arianischen Historiographen.* 3d ed. Berlin.

Bierbrauer, V. 1992. "Die Goten vom 1.–7. Jahrhundert n. Chr.: Siedelgebiete und Wanderbewegungen aufgrund archäologischer Quellen." Pp. 9–43 in *Peregrinatio Gothica III: Fredrikstad, Norway, 1991*, ed. E. Straume and E. Skar. Oslo.

————. 1994. "Archäologie und Geschichte der Goten vom 1.–7. Jahrhundert." *Frühmittelalterliche Studien* 28: 51–171.

Bird, H. W., trans. 1993. *The Breviarium Ab urbe condita of Eutropius.* TTH 14. Liverpool.

————, trans. 1994. *Liber de Caesaribus of Sextus Aurelius Victor.* TTH 17. Liverpool.

Blaauw, S. de. 1997. "Jerusalem in Rome and the Cult of the Cross." Pp. 55–73 in *Pratum Romanum: Richard Krautheimer zum 100. Geburtstag,* ed. R. Colella et al. Wiesbaden.

————. 2001a. "Imperial Connotations in Roman Church Interiors: The Significance and Effect of the Lateran *Fastigium.*" Pp. 137–46 in *Imperial Art as Christian Art – Christian Art as Imperial Art,* Acta ad archaeologiam et artium historiam pertinentia 15, ed. J. R. Brandt and O. Steen. Rome.

————. 2001b. "L'altare nelle chiese di Roma." Pp. 969–90 in *Roma nell'alto medioevo,* Settimane di studio del centro Italiano di studi sull'alto medioevo 48. Spoleto.

Black, E. W. 1987. *The Roman Villas of South-East England.* British Archaeological Reports British Series 171. Oxford.

Bleckmann, B. 1991. "Die Chronik des Johannes Zonaras und eine pagane Quelle zur Geschichte Konstantins." *Historia* 40: 341–65.

————. 1992. *Die Reichskrise des III. Jahrhunderts in der spätantiken und byzantinischen Geschichtsschreibung: Untersuchungen zu den nachdionischen Quellen der Chronik des Johannes Zonaras.* Munich.

————. 1996. *Konstantin der Große.* Reinbek bei Hamburg.

————. 1997. "Ein Kaiser als Prediger: Zur Datierung der konstantinischen Rede an die Versammlung der Heiligen." *Hermes* 125: 183–202.

————. 1999. "Zwischen Panegyrik und Geschichtsschreibung: Praxagoras und seine Vorgänger." Pp. 203–28 in *Geschichtsschreibung und politischer Wandel im 3. Jh. n. Chr.,* ed. M. Zimmermann. Stuttgart.

Bleicken, J. 1992. *Constantin der Große und die Christen: Überlegungen zur konstantinischen Wende.* Munich.

Blockley, R. C. 1992. *East Roman Foreign Policy: Formation and Conduct from Diocletian to Anastasius.* Leeds.

————. 1983. *The Fragmentary Classicising Historians of the Later Roman Empire.* Vol. 2. Liverpool.

————. 1998. "Warfare and Diplomacy." Pp. 411–436 in *The Cambridge Ancient History,* vol. 13, *The Late Empire* A.D. *337–425,* 2d ed., ed. A. Cameron and P. Garnsey. Cambridge.

Boak, A. E. R. 1924. "The Master of Offices in the Later Roman and Byzantine Empires." Pp. 1–160 in *Two Studies in Later Roman and Byzantine Administration,* University of Michigan Studies Humanistic Series 14, ed. A. E. R. Boak and J. E. Dunlap. New York.

————. 1955. *Manpower Shortage and the Fall of the Roman Empire.* London.

Bonamente, G., and F. Fusco, eds. 1993. *Costantino il Grande dall'antichità all'umanesimo: Colloquio sul Cristianesimo nel mondo antico, Macerata 18–20 Dicembre 1990.* 2 vols. Macerata.

Bonfils, G. de. 1981. *Il Comes et Quaestor nell'età della dinastia costantiniana.* Pubblicazioni della Facoltà giuridica dell'Università di Bari 62. Naples.

Borgehammar, S. 1991. *How the Holy Cross Was Found.* Bibliotheca Theologiae Practicae 47. Stockholm.

Boschung, D. 1993. *Die Bildnisse des Augustus.* Berlin.

Bosković, D., N. Duval, P. Gros, and V. Popović. 1973. "Recherches archéologiques à Sirmium, campagne Franco-Yougoslave 1973." *Mélanges d'Archéologie et d'Histoire de l'École Française de Rome, Antiquité* 86: 597–656.

Bosworth, C. E., trans. 1999. *The History of al-Tabarī (Ta'rīkh al rusul wa'l-mulūk).* Vol. 5, *The Sasanids, the Byzantines, the Lakhmids, and Yemen.* Albany.

Bounegru, O., and M. Zahariade. 1996. *Les forces navale du bas-Danube et de la Mer Noire aux Iᵉʳ–VIᵉ siècles.* Colloquia Pontica 2. Oxford.

Bousquet, B., and P.-Y. Péchoux. 1977. "La sismicité du bassin égéen pendant l'antiquité: Méthodologie et premiers résultats." *Bulletin de la Société géologique de France* 19.3: 683–4.

Bovini, G., and H. Brandenburg. 1967. *Repertorium der Christlich-Antiken Sarkophage.* Vol. 1, *Rom und Ostia.* Wiesbaden.

Bowersock, G. W. 1978. *Julian the Apostate.* Cambridge, MA.

———. 1983. *Roman Arabia.* Cambridge, MA.

———. 1986a. "From Emperor to Bishop: The Self-Conscious Transformation of Political Power in the Fourth Century AD." *Classical Philology* 81: 298–307.

———. 1986b. Review of *Byzantium and the Arabs in the Fourth Century,* by I. Shahîd. *Classical Quarterly* n.s. 36: 111–17.

———. 1990. *Hellenism in Late Antiquity.* Cambridge.

———. 1994. "Mavia, Queen of the Saracens." Pp. 477–95 in *Studien zur antiken Sozialgeschichte: Festschrift F. Vittinghoff.* Cologne, 1981. Reprint with corrections, pp. 127–40 in *Studies on the Eastern Roman Empire,* ed. G. W. Bowersock. Goldbach, 1994.

———. 2002. "Peter and Constantine." Pp. 209–17 in *Humana sapit: études d'Antiquité tardive offertes à Lellia Cracco Ruggini,* ed. J.-M. Carrié and R. Lizzi Testa. Turnhout.

Bowersock, G. W., P. Brown, and O. Grabar. eds. 1999. *Late Antiquity: A Guide to the Postclassical World.* Cambridge, MA.

Bowman, A. K., A. Cameron, and P. Garnsey, eds. 2005. *The Cambridge Ancient History.* Vol. 12, *The Crisis of Empire, A.D. 193–337.* 2d ed. Cambridge.

Bradbury, S. 1994. "Constantine and the Problem of Anti-Pagan Legislation in the Fourth Century." *Classical Philology* 89: 120–39.

———. 1995. "Julian's Pagan Revival and the Decline of Blood Sacrifice." *Phoenix* 49: 331–56.

Brakke, D. 1995. *Athanasius and the Politics of Asceticism.* Oxford.

Brandenburg, H. 1979a. *Roms frühchristliche Basiliken des 4. Jahrhunderts.* Munich.

———. 1979b. "Stilprobleme der frühchristlichen Sarkofagkunst Roms im 4. Jh." *Mitteilungen des Deutschen Archäologischen Instituts, Römische Abteilung* 86: 439–71.

———. 1985. "Zur Deutung der Deckenbilder aus der Trierer Domgrabung." *Boreas* 8: 143–89.

Brandt, H. 1998. *Geschichte der römischen Kaiserzeit von Diokletian und Konstantin bis zum Ende der konstantinischen Dynastie (284–363).* Berlin.

Brandt, O. 1997–8. "Il battistero lateranense da Costantino a Ilaro: Un riesame degli scavi." *Opuscula romana* 22–3: 7–65.

———. 2001. "Il battistero Lateranense dell'imperatore Costantino e l'archittettura contemporanea." Pp. 117–44 in *Late Antiquity: Art in Context,* Acta Hyperborea 8, eds. J. Fleischer, J. Lund, and M. Nielsen. Copenhagen.

Brather, S. 2000. "Ethnische Identitäten als Konstructe der frügeschichtlichen Archäologie." *Germania* 78: 139–77.

————. 2002. "Ethnic Identities as Constructions of Archaeology: The Case of the *Alamanni*." Pp. 149–76 in *On Barbarian Identity: Critical Approaches to Ethnicity in the Early Middle Ages*, ed. A. Gillett. Turnhout.

Braund, D. 1994. *Georgia in Antiquity: A History of Colchis and Transcaucasian Iberia, 550 BC–AD 562*. Oxford.

Bravo, G. 1979. "La funcion de los *agri deserti* en la economia imperial de Aureliano a Teodosio." *Memorias de historia antigua* 3: 157–69.

Brendel, O. 1979. *Prolegomena to the Study of Roman Art*. New Haven.

Brennan, P. 1980. "Combined Legionary Detachments as Artillery Units in Late Roman Danubian Bridgehead Dispositions." *Chiron* 10: 553–67.

————. 1996. "The *Notitia Dignitatum*." Pp. 147–78 in *Les littératures techniques dans l'antiquité romaine*, Entretiens Hardt 42, ed. C. Nicolet. Geneva.

————. 1998. "Divide and Fall: The Separation of Legionary Cavalry and the Fragmentation of the Roman Empire." Pp. 238–244 in *Ancient History in a Modern University: Proceedings of a Colloqium Held at Macquarie University, 8–13 July 1993*, vol. 2, ed. T. W. Hillard. Grand Rapids, MI.

Brilliant, R. 1984. *Visual Narratives*. Ithaca, NY.

Brockmeier, B. 1987. "Der Große Friede 332 n. Chr.: Zur Aussenpolitik Konstantins d. Großen." *Bonner Jahrbücher* 187: 79–100.

Brooks, C. E. P. 1950. *Climate through the Ages*. London.

Brown, P. 1971. "The Rise and Function of the Holy Man in Late Antiquity." *Journal of Roman Studies* 61: 80–101.

————. 1981. *The Cult of the Saints*. Chicago.

————. 1992. *Power and Persuasion: Towards a Christian Empire*. Madison, WI.

————. 1998. "Christianization and Religious Conflict." Pp. 632–64 in *The Cambridge Ancient History*, vol. 13, *The Late Empire A.D. 337–425*, 2d ed., ed. A. Cameron and P. Garnsey. Cambridge.

————. 2002. *Poverty and Leadership in the Later Roman Empire*. Hanover and London.

————. 2003. *The Rise of Western Christendom*. 2d ed. Oxford.

Bruns, G. 1948. *Staatskameen des 4. Jahrhunderts nach Christi Geburt*. Berlin.

Bruun, P. 1953. *The Constantinian Coinage of Arelate*. Helsinki.

————. 1958. "The Disappearance of Sol from the Coins of Constantine." *Arctos* 2: 15–37. Reprint, pp. 37–48 in Bruun 1991.

————. 1961. *Studies in Constantinian Chronology*. Numismatic Notes and Monographs 146. New York.

————. 1962. "The Christian Signs on the Coins of Constantine." *Arctos* 3: 5–35. Reprint, pp. 53–70 in Bruun 1991.

————. 1965. "Early Christian Symbolism on Coins and Inscriptions." Pp. 527–35 in *Atti del VI Congresso Internazionale di Archeologia Cristiana, Ravenna 1962*, Studi di Antichità Cristiana 26. Rome. Reprint, pp. 71–4 in Bruun 1991.

————. 1966. *The Roman Imperial Coinage*. Vol. 7, *Constantine and Licinius A.D. 313–337*. London.

————. ed. 1991. *Studies in Constantinian Numismatics: Papers from 1954 to 1988*. Rome.

Bryce, J. 1989. "Lactantius' *De Ave Phoenice* and the Religious Policy of Constantine the Great." *Studia Patristica* 19: 13–19.

Burckhardt, J. [1880] 1949. *The Age of Constantine the Great*. Trans. M. Hadas. New York.

Burgess, R. W. 1988. "Quinquennial Vota and the Imperial Consulship in the Fourth and Fifth Centuries, 337–511." *Numismatic Chronicle* 148: 77–96.

————. 1993. *The Chronicle of Hydatius and the Consularia Constantinopolitana.* Oxford.

————. 1999a. "AΧΥΡΟΝ or ΠΡΟΑΣΤΕΙΟΝ? The Location and Circumstances of Constantine's Death." *Journal of Theological Studies* n.s. 50: 153–61.

————. 1999b. *Studies in Eusebian and Post-Eusebian Chronography.* Stuttgart.

————. 2003. "The *Passio S. Artemii*, Philostorgius, and the Dates of the Invention and Translations of the Relics of Sts. Andrew and Luke." *Analecta Bollandiana* 121: 5–36.

Buttrey, T. V. 1983. "The Dates of the Arches of 'Diocletian' and Constantine." *Historia* 32: 375–83.

Calderone, S. 1993. "Costantinopoli: La 'seconda Roma.'" Pp. 723–49 in *Storia di Roma,* vol. 3.1: *L'età tardoantica, crisi e trasformazioni,* eds. A. Carandini, L. Cracco Ruggini, and A. Giardina. Turin.

————. 2001. *Costantino e il Cattolicesimo.* Florence.

Calvet, Y., and C. Robin. 2001. *Arabie heureuse, Arabie déserte: Les antiquités arabiques du Musée du Louvre.* Paris.

Calza, R. 1972. *Iconografia romana imperiale da Carausio a Giuliano (287–363 d. C.).* Rome.

Cameron, A. 1983. Review of *Constantine and Eusebius,* by T. D. Barnes. *Journal of Roman Studies* 73: 184–90.

Cameron, A., and P. Garnsey, eds. 1998. *The Cambridge Ancient History,* vol. 13, *The Late Empire* A.D., *337–425,* 2nd ed. Cambridge.

Cameron, A., and S. G. Hall, trans. and commentary. 1999. *Eusebius: Life of Constantine.* Oxford.

Carandini, A., A. Ricci, and M. de Vos. 1982. *Filosofiana: The Villa of Piazza Armerina.* Palermo.

Carrié, J.-M. 1993. "Observations sur al fiscalité du IVe siècle pour servir à l'histoire monétaire." Pp. 115–54 in *L'inflazione nel quarto secolo d.C.: Atti del convegno di studio, Roma 1988.* Rome.

————, ed. 1994. "La Tétrarchie (293–312): Histoire et archéologie." *Antiquité Tardive* 2. Turnhout.

————, ed. 1995. "*La Tétrarchie (293–312)*: Histoire et archéologie, 2e partie." Special issue. *Antiquité Tardive* 3. Turnhout.

Carrié, J.-M., N. Duval, and D. Feissel eds. 1998. "Les gouverneurs dans l'antiquité tardive." Special issue. *Antiquté Tardive* 6. Turnhout.

Carrié, J.-M., and S. Janniard. 2000–2. "L'armée romaine dans quelques travaux récents." *Antiquité Tardive* 8: 321–41; 9: 351–61; 10: 427–42.

Carrié, J.-M., and A. Rousselle. 1999. *L'empire romain en mutation des Sévères à Constantin 192–337.* Nouvelle Histoire de l'Antiquité 10. Paris.

Casey, P. J. 1994. *Carausius and Allectus: The British Usurpers.* London and New York.

Cataudella, M. R. 2001. "Costantino, Giuliano e l'*Oratio ad Sanctorum Coetum.*" *Klio* 83: 167–81.

Cecchelli, M. 1992. "S. Marco a Piazza Venezia: Una basilica romana del periodo costantiniano." Pp. 299–310 in *Costantino il Grande dall'antichità all'umanesimo: Colloquio sul Cristianesimo nel mondo antico, Macerata 18–20 dicembre 1990,* vol. 1, ed. G. Bonamente and F. Fusco. Macerata.

Cérati, A. 1975. *Caractère annonaire et assiette de l'impôt foncier au Bas-Empire.* Paris.

Chadwick, H. 1958. "Ossius of Cordova and the Presidency of the Council of Antioch, 325." *Journal of Theological Studies* n.s. 9: 292–304.

————. 1978. "Conversion in Constantine the Great." Pp. 1–13 in *Religious Motivation: Biographical and Sociological Problems for the Church Historian*, Studies in Church History 15, ed. D. Baker. Oxford.

————. 1980. *The Role of the Christian Bishop in Ancient Society*. Center for Hermeneutical Studies, Berkeley, Protocol of the Thirty-Fifth Colloquy, 25 February 1979, eds. E. C. Hobbs and W. Wuellner. Berkeley.

Charlesworth, M. P. 1937. "The Virtues of a Roman Emperor: Propaganda and the Creation of Belief." *Proceedings of the British Academy* 23: 105–33.

Chastagnol, A. 1962. *Les Fastes de la Préfecture de Rome au Bas-Empire*. Études Prosopographiques 2. Paris.

————. 1966a. "Un gouverneur Constantinien de Tripolitaine: Laenatius Romulus, *Praeses* en 324–326." *Latomus* 25: 539–52.

————. 1966b. "Zosime II, 38 et l'Historie Auguste." Pp. 43–78 in *Bonner Historia-Augusta-Colloquium, 1964/1965*, Antiquitas 4:3, ed. A. Alföldi. Bonn.

————. 1970. "Les modes de recrutement du Sénat au IVème siècle." Pp. 187–211 in *Recherches sur les structures sociales dans l'antiquité classique, Caen, 25–26 avril, 1969*, ed. C. Nicolet. Paris.

————. 1976a. "Constantin et le Sénat." Pp. 51–69 in *Accademia Romanistica Costantiniana: Atti 2° Convegno Internazionale, Spello, 18–20 settembre, 1975*. Perugia.

————. 1976b. "Remarques sur les sénateurs orientaux au IVème siècle." *Acta Antiqua Academiae Scientiarum Hungaricae* 24: 341–56.

————. 1986. "Les inscriptions africaines des préfets du prétoire de Constantin." Pp. 263–73 in *L'Africa romana: Atti del III convegno di studio Sassari, 13–15 dicembre 1985*, ed. A. Mastino. Reprint, pp. 81–92 in *Aspects de l'antiquité tardive*, Saggi di storia antica 6, Rome, 1994.

————. 1989. "Un nouveau préfect de Dioclétien: Aurelius Hermogenianus." *Zeitschrift für Papyrologie und Epigraphik* 78: 165–68. Reprint, pp. 171–76 in *Aspects de l'antiquité tardive*, Saggi di storia antica 6, Rome, 1994.

————. 1992. *Le sénat romain à l'époque impériale: Recherches sur la composition de l'assemblée et le statut de ses membres*. Paris.

————. 1994. *L'évolution politique, sociale et économique du monde romain de Dioclétien à Julien: La mise en place du régime du Bas-Empire (284–363)*, 3d ed. Paris.

Christodoulou, D. N. 1998. *The Figures of Ancient Gods on the Coinage of Constantine the Great (306–326 AD)*. Athens.

————. 2002. "Galerius, Gamzigrad and the Fifth Macedonian Legion." *Journal of Roman Archaeology* 15: 275–81.

Christol, M. 1986. *Essai sur l'évolution des carrières sénatoriales dans la 2ᵉ moitié du IIIᵉ s. ap. J.-C.* Études Prosopographiques 6. Paris.

————. 1997. *L'empire romain du IIIᵉ siècle: Histoire politique 192–325 après J.-C.* Paris.

Christol, M., and P. Sillières. 1980. "Constantin et la pénisule ibérique: À propos d'un nouveau milliare." *Revue des études anciennes* 82: 70–80.

Chrysos, E. 1973. "*Gothia romana*: Zur rechtslage des Föderatenlandes der Westgoten im 4. Jahrhundert." *Dacoromania* 1: 52–64.

Cima, M. 2000. "*Horti Liciniani*." Pp. 97–103 in *Aurea Roma: Dalla città pagana alla città cristiana*, ed. S. Ensoli and E. La Rocca. Rome.

Clark, G. 1993. *Women in Late Antiquity: Pagan and Christian Lifestyles*. Oxford.

————. 1999. "Translate into Greek: Porphyry of Tyre on the New Barbarians." Pp. 112–32 in *Constructing Identities in Late Antiquity*, ed. R. Miles. London and New York.

Clauss, M. 1973. *Untersuchungen zu den principales des römischen Heeres von Augustus bis Diokletian: Cornicularii, speculatores, frumentarii*. Bochum.

————. 1980. *Der Magister Officiorum in der Spätantike (4.–6. Jahrhundert): Das Amt und sein Einfluss aus der kaiserliche Politik*. Vestigia 32. Munich.

Coello, T. 1996. *Unit Sizes in the Late Roman Army*. British Archaeological Reports International Series 645. Oxford.

Coleman, C. B. 1914. *Constantine the Great and Christianity*. Columbia University Studies in History and Public Law 60.1. New York. Reprinted as monograph 1968.

Colli, D. 1996. "Il Palazzo Sessoriano nell'area archeologica di S. Croce in Gerusalemme: Ultima sede imperiale a Roma?" *Mélanges d'Archéologie et d'Histoire de l'École Française de Rome, Antiquité* 108: 771–815.

Corbo, V. C. 1959–60. "Scavi archeologici a ridosso della basilica dell'ascensione." *Liber annuus* 10: 205–69.

————. 1981–2. *Il Santo Sepolcro di Gerusalemme: Aspetti archeologici dalle origini al periodo crociato*. 3 Vols. Jerusalem.

Corcoran, S. 1993. "Hidden from History: The Legislation of Licinius." Pp. 97–119 in *The Theodosian Code*, ed. J. Harries and I. Wood. Ithaca, NY.

————. 2000. *The Empire of the Tetrarchs: Imperial Pronouncements and Government AD 284–324*. Revised edition. Oxford.

————. 2002. "A Tetrarchic Inscription from Corcyra and the *Edictum de Accusationibus*." *Zeitschrift für Papyrologie und Epigraphik* 141: 221–30.

Creed, J. L., ed. and trans. 1984. *Lactantius: De Mortibus Persecutorum*. Oxford Early Christian Texts. Oxford.

Croke, B. 1987. "Cassiodorus and the *Getica* of Jordanes." *Classical Philology* 82: 117–34.

Crone, P. 1987. *Meccan Trade and the Rise of Islam*. Oxford.

Crump, G. A. 1973. "Ammianus and the Late Roman Army." *Historia* 22: 91–103.

Cullhed, M. 1994. *Conservator Urbis Suae: Studies in the Politics and Propaganda of the Emperor Maxentius*. Stockholm.

Curcic, S. 1996. "From the Temple of the Sun to the Temple of the Lord: Monotheistic Contributions to Architectural Iconography in Late Antiquity." Pp. 55–61 in *Architectural Studies in Memory of Richard Krautheimer*, ed. C. Striker and J. S. Ackerman. Mainz.

Curran, J. 2000. *Pagan City and Christian Capital: Rome in the Fourth Century*. Oxford.

Cushing, E. C. 1935. *Materials for a Life of Jacopo da Varagine*. 2 vols. New York.

Dagron, G. 1974. *Naissance d'une capitale: Constantinople et ses institutions de 330 à 451*. Bibliothèque byzantine études 7. Paris.

Deckers, J. G., H. R. Seeliger, and G. Mietke. 1987. *Die Katakombe "Santi Marcellino e Pietro."* Vatican City.

De Decker, D. 1968. "La politique religieuse de Maxence." *Byzantion* 38: 472–562.

Deichmann, F. W. 1975. *Die Spolien in der spätantiken Architektur*. Munich.

Deichmann, F. W., and A. Tschira. 1957. "Das Mausoleum der Kaiserin Helena und die Basilika der heilige Marcellinus und Petrus an der Via Labicana vor Rom." *Jahrbuch des Deutschen Archäologischen Instituts* 72: 44–110.

Delbrueck, R. 1933. *Spätantike Kaiserporträts*. Berlin.

Delmaire, R. 1989. *Largesses sacrées et res privata: L'aerarium impérial et son administration du IVe au VIe siècle.* Collections de l'École française de Rome 121. Rome.

———. 1995. *Les institutions du Bas-Empire romain de Constantin à Justinien.* Vol. 1, *Les institutions palatines.* Initiations au christianisme ancien. Paris.

De Leo, P. 1974. *Il Constitutum Constantini, compilazione agiografica del sec. VIII: Note e documenti per una nuova lettura.* Ricerche sui falsi medioevali 1. Reggio Calabria.

Demandt, A. 1970. "*Magister militum.*" *Paulys Realencylopädie der classischen Altertumswissenschaft, Supplementband* 12: 553–788.

———. 1989. *Die Spätantike: Römische Geschichte von Diocletian bis Justinian, 284–565 n. Chr.* Berlin.

———. 1993. "Die westgermanischen Stammesbünde." *Klio* 75: 387–406.

Demarez, J.-D. 1987. *Les bâtiments à fonction économique dans les fundi de la provincia belgica.* Amphora 50. Brussels.

Demougeot, E. 1969–79. *La formation de l'Europe et les invasions barbares.* 2 vols. Paris.

Depeyrot, G. 1991. *Crises et inflation entre Antiquité et Moyen-Age.* Paris.

———. 1995a. *Histoire de la monnaie des origines au 18e siècle.* Vol. 1, *Introduction: de l'antiquité au treizième siècle.* Wetteren.

———. 1995b. *Les monnaies d'or de Dioclétien à Constantin I (284–337).* Wetteren.

———. 1996. *Les monnaies d'or de Constantin II à Zénon (337–491).* Wetteren.

———. 1999. *Zilil I: Colonia Iulia Constantia Zilil, Etude du numéraire.* Collection de l'Ecole française de Rome 250. Rome.

Derks, T. 1998. *Gods, Temples and Ritual Practices: The Transformation of Religious Ideas and Values in Roman Gaul.* Amsterdam.

Digeser, E. 1998. "Lactantius, Porphyry and the Debate over Religious Toleration." *Journal of Roman Studies* 88: 129–46.

———. 2000. *The Making of a Christian Empire: Lactantius and Rome.* Ithaca, NY.

Di Maio, M. 1977. "Zonaras' Acccount of the Neo-Flavian Emperors." Ph.D. diss., University of Missouri.

———. 1988. "Smoke in the Wind: Zonaras' use of Philostorgius, Zosimus, John of Antioch, and John of Rhodes in His Narrative on the Neo-Flavian Emperors." *Byzantion* 58: 230–52.

Di Maio, M., and W. H. Arnold. 1992. "*Per vim, per caedem, per bellum*: A Study of Murder and Ecclesiastical Politics in the Year 337." *Byzantion* 62: 158–211.

Dixon, S. 2001. *Reading Roman Women.* London.

Dodgeon, M. H., and S. N. C. Lieu. 1991. *The Roman Eastern Frontier and the Persian Wars AD 226–363: A Documentary History.* London and New York.

Dölger, F. J. 1913. "Die Taufe Konstantins und ihre Probleme." Pp. 377–477 in *Konstantin der Große und seine Zeit*, ed. F. Dölger. Freiburg im Breisgau.

Dörries, H. [1954] 1972. *Constantine the Great.* Trans. R. H. Bainton. New York.

Downey, G. 1961. *A History of Antioch in Syria, from Seleucus to the Arab Conquest.* Princeton.

Drake, H. A. 1976. *In Praise of Constantine: A Historical Study and New Translation of Eusebius' Tricennial Orations.* Berkeley.

———. 1983. Review of *Constantine and Eusebius*, by T. D. Barnes. *American Journal of Philology* 103: 462–6.

———. 1985. "Eusebius on the True Cross." *Journal of Ecclesiastical History* 36:1–22.

———. 1995. "Constantine and Consensus." *Church History* 64: 1–15.

————. 1996. "Lambs into Lions: Explaining Early Christian Intolerance." *Past and Present* 153: 3–36.

————. 2000. *Constantine and the Bishops: The Politics of Intolerance.* Baltimore.

Drew-Bear, T. 1981. "Les voyages d'Aurélius Gaius, soldat de Dioclètien." Pp. 93–141 in *La Géographie Administrative et Politique d'Alexandre à Mahomet, actes du Colloque de Strasbourg, 14–16 juin 1979.* Leiden.

Drijvers, H. J. W., and J. W. Drijvers, eds. and trans. 1997. *The Finding of the True Cross: The Judas Kyriakos Legend in Syriac, Introduction, Text and Translation.* Corpus Scriptorum Christianorum Orientalium 565 (Subsidia 95). Louvain.

Drijvers, J. W. 1992. *Helena Augusta: The Mother of Constantine the Great and the Legend of Her Finding of the True Cross.* Leiden.

Drinkwater, J. F. 1987. *The Gallic Empire: Separatism and Continuity in the North-Western Provinces of the Roman Empire A.D. 260–274.* Historia Einzelschriften 52. Stuttgart.

————. 1994. "Silvanus, Ursicinus and Ammianus: Fact or Fiction?" Pp. 568–76 in *Studies in Latin Literature and Roman History VII*, Collection Latomus 227, ed. C. Deroux. Brussels.

————. 1996. "The Germanic Threat on the Rhine Frontier: A Romano-Gallic Artefact?" Pp. 20–30 in *Shifting Frontiers in Late Antiquity*, ed. R. W. Mathisen and H. S. Sivan. Aldershot.

————. 1997. "Julian and the Franks, and Valentinian I and the Alamanni: Ammianus on Romano-German Relations." *Francia* 24.1: 1–15.

Duchesne, L. 1955. *Le Liber Pontificalis.* 3 vols. Paris.

Duncan Jones, R. P. 1978. "Pay and Numbers in Diocletian's Army." *Chiron* 8: 541–60. Reprint, pp. 105–17 in Duncan Jones, 1990.

————. 1990. *Structure and Scale in the Roman Economy.* Cambridge.

————. 1994. *Money and Government in the Roman Empire.* Cambridge.

Dupont, C. 1953. *Le droit criminel dans les constitutions de Constantin.* Vols. 1–2. Lille.

————. 1968. *Les constitutions de Constantin et le droit privé au début du IVe siècle: Les personnes.* Rome.

Edwards, M., ed. and trans. 1997. *Against the Donatists.* TTH 27. Liverpool.

————. 1999. "The Constantinian Circle and the *Oration to the Saints.*" Pp. 251–75 in *Apologetics in the Roman Empire: Pagans, Jews, and Christians*, ed. M. Edwards et al. Oxford.

————. 2000. *Neoplatonic Saints: The Lives of Plotinus and Proclus by their Students.* TTH 35. Liverpool.

————. 2003. *Constantine and Christendom: The Oration to the Saints, The Greek and Latin Accounts of the Discovery of the Cross, The Edict of Constantine to Pope Silvester.* TTH 39. Liverpool.

Effenberger, A. 2000. "Konstantinsmausoleum, Apostelkriche – und kein Ende?" Pp. 67–78 in *Lithostroton: Studien zur byzantinischen Kunst und Geschichte: Festschrift für Marcell Restle*, ed. B. Borkopp and T. Steppan. Stuttgart.

Effenberger, A., et al., eds. 1996. *Ägypten: Schätze aus dem Wüstensand.* Wiesbaden.

Ehler, S. Z., and J. B. Morrall. 1954. *Church and State through the Centuries: A Collection of Historic Documents with Commentaries.* London.

Elliott, T. G. 1978. "The Tax Exemptions Granted to Clerics by Constantine and Constantius II." *Phoenix* 32: 326–36.

————. 1987. "Constantine's Conversion: Who Needs It?" *Phoenix* 41: 420–38.

————. 1992–3. "Constantine's Preparations for the Council of Nicaea." *Journal of Religious History* 17: 127–37.

————. 1996. *The Christianity of Constantine the Great*. Bronx, NY.

Elsner, J. 1998a. *Imperial Rome and Christian Triumph*. Oxford.

————. 1998b. "Art and Architecture, 337–425." Pp. 736–61 in *The Cambridge Ancient History*, vol. 13, *The Late Empire A.D. 337–425*, 2d ed., ed. A. Cameron and P. Garnsey. Cambridge.

————. 2000a. "From the Culture of Spolia to the Cult of Relics: The Arch of Constantine and the Genesis of Late Antique Forms." *Papers of the British School at Rome* 68: 149–84.

————. 2000b. "Frontality in the Column of Marcus Aurelius." Pp. 251–64 in *Autour de la colonne Aurelienne*, ed. J. Scheid and V. Huet. Turnhout.

————. 2000c. "The *Itinerarium Burdigalense*: Politics and Salvation in the Geography of Constantine's Empire." *Journal of Roman Studies* 90: 181–95.

————. 2002. "The Birth of Late Antiquity: Riegl and Strzygowski in 1901." *Art History* 25: 358–79.

————. 2003. "Inventing Christian Rome: The Role of Early Christian Art." Pp. 71–99 in *Rome the Cosmopolis*, ed. C. Edwards and G. Woolf. Cambridge.

Elton, H. 1996a. *Frontiers of the Roman Empire*. Bloomington, IN.

————. 1996b. *Warfare in Roman Europe: AD 350–425*. Oxford.

Ensoli, S. 2000. "I colossi di bronzo a Roma in età tardoantica." Pp. 66–90 in *Aurea Roma: Dalla città pagana alla città Cristiana*, ed. S. Ensoli and E. La Rocca. Rome.

Ensoli, S., and E. La Rocca, eds. 2000. *Aurea Roma: Dalla città pagana alla città Cristiana*. Rome.

Ensslin, W. 1934. "Der konstantinische Patriziat und seine Bedeutung im 4. Jahrhundert." Pp. 361–76 in *Mélanges Bidez I*, Annuaire de l'Institut de philologie et d'histoire orientales 2. Brussels.

Errington, M. 1988. "Constantine and the Pagans." *Greek, Roman, and Byzantine Studies* 29: 309–18.

Evers, C. 1991. "Remarques sur l'iconographie de Constantin: À propos du remploi de portraits des 〈〈bons empereurs〉〉." *Mélanges d'Archéologie et d'Histoire de l'École Française de Rome, Antiquité* 103: 785–806.

Feissel, D. 1985. "Une dédicace en l'honneur de Constantin II César et les préfects du prétoire de 366." *Travaux et mémoires du Centre de recherches d'histoire et civilisation byzantine* 9: 421–34.

————. 1995. "Les constitutions des Tétrarques connues par l'épigraphie: Inventaire et notes critiques." *Antiquité Tardive* 3: 33–53.

————. 1999. "L'Adnotatio de Constantin sur le droit de cité d'Orcistus en Phrygie." *Antiquité Tardive* 7: 255–67.

Feissel, D., and J. Gascou. 1989. "Documents d'archives romains inédits du Moyen Euphrate (IIIᵉ siècle après J.-C.)." *Comptes rendus de l'Académie des Inscriptions et Belles-Lettres* 1989: 535–61.

————. 1995. "Documents d'archives romains inédits du Moyen Euphrate (IIIᵉ siècle après J.-C.)." *Journal des Savants* 1995: 65–119.

Février, P. A. 1964. "Notes sur le développement urbain en Afrique du Nord: Les exemples comparés de Djémila et de Sétif." *Cahiers archéologiques* 14: 1–47.

Finley, M. I. 1958. Review of *Manpower Shortage and the Fall of the Roman Empire*, by A. E. R. Boak. *Journal of Roman Studies* 48: 157–64.

————. 1985. *The Ancient Economy*. 2d ed. Cambridge.

Fiocchi Nicolai, V. 1995–6. "La nuova basilica circiforme della Via Ardeatina." *Atti della Pontificia Accademia Romana di archeologia, Rendiconti* 68: 69–233.

Fiocchi Nicolai, V., F. Bisconti, and D. Mazzoleni. 1999. *The Christian Catacombs of Rome*. Regensberg.

Fisher, E. 1982. "Greek Translations of Latin Literature in the Fourth Century A.D." *Yale Classical Studies* 27: 173–215.

Fittschen, K., and P. Zanker. 1985. *Katalog der römischen Porträts in der Capitolinischen Museen und den anderen kommunalen Sammlungen der Stadt Rom*. Vol. 1. Mainz.

Fleischer, J., J. Lund, and M. Nielsen, eds. 2001. *Late Antiquity: Art in Context*. Acta Hyperborea 8. Copenhagen.

Foss, C. 1996. *Survey of Medieval Castles of Anatolia II: Nicomedia*. British Institute of Archaeology at Ankara Monograph 21. London.

Fowden, G. 1978. "Bishops and Temples in the Eastern Roman Empire, AD 320–435." *Journal of Theological Studies* n.s. 29: 53–78.

————. 1987. "Nicagoras of Athens and the Lateran Obelisk." *Journal of Hellenic Studies* 107: 51–7.

————. 1991. "Constantine's Porphyry Column: The Earliest Literary Allusion." *Journal of Roman Studies* 81: 119–31.

————. 1993. *Empire to Commonwealth: Consequences of Monotheism in Late Antiquity*. Princeton.

————. 1994a. "Constantine, Silvester, and the Church of S. Polyeuctus in Constantinople." *Journal of Roman Archaeology* 7: 274–84.

————. 1994b. "The Last Days of Constantine: Oppositional Versions and Their Influence." *Journal of Roman Studies* 84: 146–70.

————. 1998. "Polytheist Religion and Philosophy." Pp. 538–60 in *The Cambridge Ancient History*, vol. 13, *The Late Empire A.D. 337–425*, 2d ed., ed. A. Cameron and P. Garnsey. Cambridge.

Frakes, R. M. 1995. "Cross-References to the Lost Books of Ammianus Marcellinus." *Phoenix* 49: 232–46.

————. 2001. *"Contra Potentium Iniurias"*: The *"Defensor Civitatis"* and Late Roman Justice. Münchener Beiträge zur Papyrusforschung und antiken Rechtsgeschichte 90. Munich.

Franchi de'Cavalieri, P. 1896–7. "Di un frammento di una Vita di Constantino." *Studi e Documenti di Storia e Diritto* 17–18: 89–131.

Frank, R. I. 1969. *Scholae Palatinae: The Palace Guards of the Later Roman Empire*. Papers and Monographs of the American Academy in Rome 23. Rome.

Frankfurter, D. 1998. *Religion in Roman Egypt: Assimilation and Resistance*. Princeton.

Frantz, A. 1988. *The Athenian Agora*, vol. 24, *Late Antiquity AD 267–700*. Princeton.

Frede, M. 1999. "Monotheism and Pagan Philosophy in Later Antiquity." Pp. 41–67 in *Pagan Monotheism in Late Antiquity*, ed. P. Athanassiadi and M. Frede. Oxford.

Freeman, P., et al., eds. 2002. *LIMES XVIII*. British Archaeological Reports, International Series 1084. Oxford.

Frend, W. H. C. 1971. *The Donatist Church: A Movement of Protest in Roman North Africa*. 2d ed. Oxford.

Fritts, H. C. 1976. *Tree-Rings and Climate*. New York.

Gager, J. G., ed. 1992. *Curse Tablets and Binding Spells from the Ancient World*. New York.

Gardner, J. 1997. "Legal Stumbling-Blocks for Lower-Class Families in Rome." Pp. 35–53 in *The Roman Family in Italy*, ed. B. Rawson and P. Weaver. Canberra and Oxford.

Garnsey, P. 1984. "Religious Toleration in Classical Antiquity." Pp. 1–27 in *Persecution and Toleration*, Studies in Church History 21, ed. W. J. Shiels. Oxford.

Garsoïan, N. 1982. "The Iranian Substratum of the 'Agathangelos' Cycle." Pp. 135–50 in *East of Byzantium: Syria and Armenia in the Formative Period*, ed. N. Garsoïan, T. F. Mathews, and R. W. Thomson. Washington, DC.

———. 1983. "Byantium and the Sasanians." Pp. 568–92 in *The Cambridge History of Iran*. Vol. 3, pt. 1, *The Seleucid, Parthian and Sasanian Periods*, ed. E. Yarshater. Cambridge.

———. 1988. "Some Preliminary Considerations on the Separation of the Armenian and Imperial Churches, 1: The Presence of 'Armenian' Bishops at the First Five Oecumenical Councils." Pp. 249–85 in *Kathegetria: Essays Presented to J. Hussey*. Camberley, Surrey. Reprint, study III in Garsoïan 1999.

———. 1999. *Church and Culture in Early Medieval Armenia*. Aldershot.

Gascou, J. 1967. "Le rescrit d'Hispellum." *Mélanges d'Archéologie et d'Histoire de l'École Française de Rome, Antiquité* 79: 609–59.

Gauthier, N., J.-C. Picard, and N. Duval. 1986–. *Topographie chrétienne des cités de la Gaule, des origines au milieu du VIIIe siècle*. 12 vols. Paris.

Geary, P. 1987. *Before France and Germany: The Creation and Transformation of the Merovingian World*. Oxford.

———. 1999. "Barbarians and Ethnicity." Pp. 107–29 in *Late Antiquity: A Guide to the Post-Classical World*, ed. G. W. Bowersock, P. Brown, and O. Grabar. Cambridge, MA.

Gedeon, M. I. 1900. "Δύο παλαιὰ κείμενα περὶ τοῦ μεγάλου Κωνσαντίνου." Εκκλεσιαστικὴ Ἀλήθεια 20: 253–4, 262–3, 279–80, 303–4.

Geffcken, J. [1920] 1978. *The Last Days of Greco-Roman Paganism*. Trans. S. MacCormack. Amsterdam.

Gentz, G. 1966. *Die Kirchengeschichte des Nicephorus Callistus Xanthopulus und ihre Quellen: Nachgelassene Untersuchungen von Günter Gentz*. Texte und Untersuchungen zur Geschichte der altchristlichen Literatur 98, ed. F. Winkelmann. Berlin.

Geuenich, D. 1997. *Geschichte der Alemannen*. Stuttgart.

Giacchero, M., ed. 1974. *Edictum Diocletiani et collegarum de pretiis rerum venalium in integrum fere restitutum e latinis graecisque fragmentis*. Genoa.

Giangrasso, G., ed. 1999. *Libellus de Constantino Magno eiusque matre Helena: La nascita di Constantino tra storia e leggenda*. Per Verba, Testi mediolatini con traduzione 13. Florence.

Giardina, A. 1977. *Aspetti della burocrazia nel Basso Impero*. Filologia e critica 22. Rome.

———. 2000. "The Family in the Late Roman World." Pp. 392–415 in *The Cambridge Ancient History*, vol. 14, *Late Antiquity: Empire and Successors A.D. 425–600*, ed. A. Cameron, B. Ward-Perkins, and M. Whitby. 2d ed. Cambridge.

Gibbon, E. [1776–81] 1994. *The History of the Decline and Fall of the Roman Empire*. Vols. 1 and 2 in a single volume, ed. D. Womersley. London and New York.

Gillett, A. 2000. "Jordanes and Ablabius." Pp. 479–500 in *Studies in Latin Literature and Roman History*, vol. 10, ed. C. Deroux. Brussels.

———, ed. 2002. *On Barbarian Identity: Critical Approaches to Ethnicity in the Early Middle Ages*. Turnhout

Giuliani, L. 2000. "Das Siegers Ansprache an das Volk: Zur politischen Brisanz der Frieserzählung am Constantinsbogen." Pp. 269–88 in *Rede und Redner: Bewertung und Darstellung in den antiken Kulturen*, ed. C. Neumeister and W. Raeck. Frankfurt.

Giuliano, A. 1956. *L'Arco di Costantino*. Milan.

———. 1991. "Augustus – Constantinus." *Bollettino d'Arte del Ministero per i Beni Culturali e Ambientali* 78.68–9: 3–10.

Goffart, W. 1980. *Barbarians and Romans, AD 418–584: The Techniques of Accommodation*. Princeton.

Goodburn, R., and P. Bartholomew, eds. 1976. *Aspects of the Notitia Dignitatum: Papers Presented to the Conference in Oxford, December 13 to 15, 1974*. British Archaeological Reports Supplementary Series 15. Oxford.

Gordon, R. L. 1996. *Image and Value in the Roman World: Studies in Mithraism and Religious Art*. Aldershot.

Grabar, O. 1996. *The Shape of the Holy: Early Islamic Jerusalem*. Princeton.

Gradara, C. 1918. "Restauri settecenteschi fatti all'Arco di Costantino." *Bullettino della Commissione Archeologica Communale di Roma* 46: 161–4.

Gradel, I. 2002. *Emperor Worship and Roman Religion*. Oxford.

Graf, D. F. 1989. "Zenobia and the Arabs." Pp. 143–67 in *The Eastern Frontier of the Roman Empire: Proceedings of a Colloquium held at Ankara in September 1988*, ed. D. H. French and C. S. Lightfoot. Oxford.

Greatrex, G., and S. N. C. Lieu, eds. 2002. *The Roman Eastern Frontier and the Persian Wars*. Part 2, *AD 363–630: A Narrative Sourcebook*. London.

Gregg, R., and D. Groh. 1981. *Early Arianism: A View of Salvation*. Philadelphia.

Grégoire, H. 1930–1. "La 'conversion' de Constantin." *Revue de l'Université de Bruxelles* 36: 231–72. Reprint in German at pp. 175–223 in *Konstantin der Grosse*, Wege der Forschung 131, ed. H. Kraft, Darmstadt.

———. 1938. "Eusèbe n'est pas l'auteur de la 'Vita Constantini' dans sa forme actuelle et Constantin ne s'est pas 'converti' en 312." *Byzantion* 13: 560–83.

———. 1939. "La vision de Constantin 'liquidée.'" *Byzantion* 14: 341–51.

Gregory, S. 1995–6. *Roman Military Architecture on the Eastern Frontier*. Amsterdam.

Grenier, A. 1931. *Manuel d'archéologie gallo-romaine*. Part 1, *Généralités, travaux militaires*. Paris.

———. 1960. *Manuel d'archéologie gallo-romaine*. Part 4, *Les monuments des eaux: Aqueducs, Thermes*. Paris.

Grenier, A., and J. Déchelette. 1931. *Manuel d'archéologie protohistorique, celtique et gallo-romaine*. Vol. 5, *Archéologie gallo-romaine*. Paris.

Grubbs, J. E. 1993. "'Marriage More Shameful than Adultery': Slave-Mistress Relations, 'Mixed Marriages' and Late Roman Law." *Phoenix* 47: 125–54.

———. 1995. *Law and Family in Late Antiquity: The Emperor Constantine's Marriage Legislation*. Oxford.

———. 2002. *Women and the Law in the Roman Empire: A Sourcebook on Marriage, Divorce and Widowhood*. London and New York.

Grünewald, T. 1990. *Constantinus Maximus Augustus: Herrschaftspropaganda in der zeitgenössischen Überlieferung*. Historia Einzelschriften 64. Stuttgart.

———. 1992. "*Constantinus novus*: Zum Constantin-Bild des Mittelalters." Pp. 461–86 in *Costantino il Grande dall'antichità all'umanesimo: Colloquio sul Cristianesimo nel mondo antico, Macerata 18–20 dicembre 1990*, vol. 1, ed. G. Bonamente and F. Fusco. Macerata.

Gryson, R. 1980. *Scolies ariennes sur le concile d'Aquilée*. SCh 267. Paris.

Guidi, I. 1907. "Un *BIOS* di Constantino." *Rendiconti della Reale accademia dei Lincei, Classe di Scienze Morali, Storiche e Filologiche,* 5th ser. 16: 306–40, 637–60.

Guidobaldi, F. 1998. "Il 'Tempio di Minerva Medica' e le strutture adiacenti: Settore privato del *Sessorium* costantiniano." *Rivista di archeologia cristiana* 74: 485–518.

Guthrie, P. 1966. "The Execution of Crispus." *Phoenix* 20: 325–31.

Guyon, J. 1987. *Le cimetière aux deux lauriers: Recherches sur les catacombes romaines.* Vatican City.

Haarnagel, W. 1979. *Die Grabung Feddersen Wierde.* Vol. 2, *Methode, Hausbau, Siedlungs- und Wirtschaftsformen, sowie Sozialstruktur.* Wiesbaden.

Habicht, C. 1958. "Zur Geschichte des Kaisers Konstantin." *Hermes* 56: 360–78.

Habicht, C., and P. Kussmaul. 1986. "Ein neues Fragment des Edictum de Accusationibus." *Museum Helveticum* 43: 135–44.

Hachlili, R. 1988. *Ancient Jewish Art and Archaeology in the Land of Israel.* Leiden.

———. 1998. *Ancient Jewish Art and Archaeology in the Diaspora.* Leiden.

Halkin, F. 1959a. "Une nouvelle vie de Constantin dans un légendier de Patmos." *Analecta Bollandiana* 77: 63–207.

———. 1959b. "Les deux derniers chapitres de la nouvelle vie de Constantin." *Analecta Bollandiana* 77: 371–72.

———. 1960a. "L'empereur Constantin converti par Euphratas." *Analecta Bollandiana* 78: 5–10.

———. 1960b. "Les autres passages inédits de la vie acéphale de Constantin." *Analecta Bollandiana* 78: 11–15.

Hall, S. G. 1998. "Some Constantinian Documents in the Vita Constantini." Pp. 86–103 in *Constantine: History, Historiography and Legend,* ed. S. N. C. Lieu and D. Monserrat. London.

Halsberghe, G. H. 1972. *The Cult of Sol Invictus.* Leiden.

Hamilton, W., trans. 1986. *Ammianus Marcellinus: The Later Roman Empire (A.D. 354–378).* London and New York.

Hanfmann, G. 1951. *The Seasons Sarcophagus from Dumbarton Oaks.* Cambridge, MA.

Hannestad, N. 1994. *Tradition in Late Antique Sculpture.* Aarhus.

———. 2001. "The Ruler Image of the Fourth Century: Innovation or Tradition." Pp. 93–107 in *Imperial Art as Christian Art – Christian Art as Imperial Art,* Acta ad archaeologiam et artium historiam pertinentia XV, ed. J. R. Brandt and O. Steen. Rome.

Hanson, R. P. C. 1988. *The Search for the Christian Doctrine of God: The Arian Controversy, 318–381.* Edinburgh.

Harbus, A. 2002. *Helena of Britain in Medieval Legend.* Woodbridge.

Harl, K. 1987. *Civic Coins and Civic Politics in the Roman East AD 180–275.* The Transformation of the Classical Heritage 12. Berkeley and Los Angeles.

Harries, J. 1988. "The Roman Imperial Quaestor from Constantine to Theodosius II." *Journal of Roman Studies* 78: 148–72.

———. 1999. *Law and Empire in Late Antiquity.* Cambridge.

Harrington, D. 1980. "The Reception of Walter Bauer's Orthodoxy and Heresy in Earliest Christianity during the Last Decade." *Harvard Theological Review* 73: 289–98.

Harrison, E. B. 1967. "The Constantinian Portrait." *Dumbarton Oaks Papers* 21: 81–96.

Hartranft, C. D., trans. 1890. *Sozomenus Church History from AD 323–425.* Nicene and Post Nicene Fathers of the Church 2.2. Peabody, MA.

Hatt, J. J. 1952. "La vision de Constantin au sanctuaire de Grand et l'origine celtique du Labarum." *Latomus* 9: 427–36.

Heather, P. J. 1986. "The Crossing of the Danube and the Gothic Conversion." *Greek Roman and Byzantine Studies* 27: 289–318.

———. 1989. "Cassiodorus and the Rise of the Amals." *Journal of Roman Studies* 79: 103–28.

———. 1991. *Goths and Romans 332–489 A.D.* Oxford.

———. 1994. "New Men for New Constantines? Creating an Imperial Elite in the Eastern Mediterranean." Pp. 11–33 in *New Constantines: The Rhythm of Imperial Renewal in Byzantium, 4th–13th Centuries*, Society for the Promotion of Byzantine Studies Publications 2, ed. P. Magdalino. Aldershot.

———. 1998a. "Goths and Huns, c. 320–425." Pp. 487–515 in *The Cambridge Ancient History*, vol. 13, *The Late Empire A.D. 337–425*, 2d ed., ed. A. Cameron and P. Garnsey. Cambridge.

———. 1998b. "Senators and Senates." Pp. 184–210 in *The Cambridge Ancient History*, vol. 13, *The Late Empire A.D. 337–425*, 2d ed., ed. A. Cameron and P. Garnsey. Cambridge.

Heather, P. J., and J. F. Matthews. 1991. *The Goths in the Fourth Century.* TTH 11. Liverpool.

Hefele, C. J. 1907–52. *Histoire des Conciles, d'après les documents originaux.* 11 vols. Trans. and corrected by H. Leclercq. Paris.

Heikel, I. A., ed. 1902. *Eusebius Werke.* Vol. 1, *Über das Leben Constantins, Constantins Rede an die Heilige Versammlung, Tricennatsrede an Constanin.* Leipzig.

Heinen, H. 1996. *Frühchristliches Trier: Von den Anfängen bis zur Völkerwanderung.* Trier.

Heintze, H. von. 1979. "Statuae quattuor marmoreae pedestres quarum basibus Constantini nomen inscriptum est." *Rheinisches Museum* 86: 399–437.

Henderson, E. F. 1925. *Select Historical Documents of the Middle Ages.* London.

Hendy, M. F. 1985. *Studies in the Byzantine Monetary Economy, c. 300–1450.* Cambridge.

Herzfeld, E. 1924. *Paikuli: Monument and Inscription of the Early History of the Sasanian Empire.* Berlin.

Hewsen, R. H. 1978–9. "The Successors of Tiridates the Great: A Contribution to the History of Armenia in the Fourth Century." *Revue des études arméniennes* n.s. 13: 99–126.

Hidalgo, R. 1996. *Espacio público y espacio privado en el conjunto palatino de Cercadilla (Córdoba): El aula central y las termas.* Sevilla.

Hoffmann, D. 1969–70. *Das spätrömische Bewegungsheer und die Notitia Dignitatum.* Epigraphische Studien 9. 2 vols. Düsseldorf.

Holder, A. 1889. *Inventio Crucis.* Leipzig.

Holloway, R. R. 2004. *Constantine and Rome.* New Haven.

Honoré, T. 1994. *Emperors and Lawyers.* 2d ed. Oxford.

Hopkins, K. 1978. *Conquerors and Slaves.* Cambridge.

———. 1998. "Christian Number and Its Implications." *Journal of Early Christian Studies* 6: 186–225.

———. 1999. *A World Full of Gods: Pagans, Jews and Christians in the Roman Empire.* London.

Horden, P., and N. Purcell. 2000. *The Corrupting Sea: A Study of Mediterranean History.* Oxford.

Howard, G., ed. and trans. 1981. *The Teaching of Addai*. Texts and Translations 16. Chico, CA.

Howard-Johnston, J. 1994. Review of *East Roman Foreign Policy: Formation and Conduct from Diocletian to Anastasius*, by R. C. Blockley. *Journal of Roman Studies* 84: 282–3.

Howgego, C. J. 1995. *Ancient History from Coins*. London and New York.

Humbach, H., and P. O. Skjærvø. 1978–83. *The Sassanian Inscription of Paikuli*. Wiesbaden.

Humphrey, J. H. 1986. *Roman Circuses: Arenas for Chariot Racing*. London and New York.

Hunt, E. D. 1997. "Constantine and Jerusalem." *Journal of Ecclesiastical History* 48: 405–24.

Huyse, P. 1999. *Die dreisprachige Inschrift Šabuhrs I. an der Kaʿba-i Zardušt (ŠKZ)*. Corpus Inscriptionum Iranicarum III.1.1. 2 vols. London.

Isaac, B. H. 1990. *The Limits of Empire*. Oxford.

Ison, D. 1985. The Constantinian Oration to the Saints: Authorship and Background. Ph.D. diss., University of London.

Jackson, B., trans. 1892. *The Ecclesiastical History, Dialogues and Letters of Theodoret*. Nicene and Post-Nicene Fathers of the Church 2.3. Peabody, MA.

Jacques, F. 1986. "L'ordine senatorio attraverso la crisi del III secolo." Pp. 81–225 in *Società Romana e Impero Tardoantico*, vol. 1, *Istituzioni Ceti Economie*, ed. A. Giardina. Rome.

James, E. 1988. *The Franks*. Oxford.

James, S. 1988. "The *fabricae*: State Arms Factories of the Later Roman Empire." Pp. 257–331 in *Military Equipment and the Identity of Soldiers: Proceedings of the Fourth Roman Military Equipment Conference*, British Archaeological Reports International Series 394, ed. J. C. N. Coulston. Oxford.

Janin, R. 1964. *Constantinople byzantine: Développement urbain et répertoire topographique*. Archives de l'Orient Chrétien 4A. 2d ed. Paris.

Jardé, A. 1925. *Les céréales dans l'antiquité grecque*. Vol. 1, *La production*. Paris.

Jastrzebowska, E. 1983. "La basilique des Apôtres à Rome: Fondation de Constantin ou de Maxence?" Pp. 223–39 in *Mosaïque: Recueil d'hommages à Henri Stern*. Paris.

Jones, A. H. M. 1949. *Constantine and the Conversion of Europe*. London.

———. 1953. "Military Chaplains in the Roman Army." *Harvard Theological Review* 46: 249–50.

———. 1954. "The Date and Value of the Verona List." *Journal of Roman Studies* 44: 21–9. Reprint, study 12 in *The Roman Economy: Studies in Ancient Economic and Administrative History*, ed. P. A. Brunt, Oxford, 1974.

———. 1959. "Over-Taxation and the Decline of the Roman Empire." *Antiquity* 33: 39–43.

———. 1964. *The Later Roman Empire 284–602: A Social, Economic and Administrative Survey*. 3 vols. Oxford.

———. 1970. Review of *Scholae Palatinae: The Palace Guards of the Later Roman Empire*, by R. I. Frank. *Journal of Roman Studies* 60: 227–9.

Jones, A. H. M., J. Martindale, and J. Morris. 1971. *The Prosopography of the Later Roman Empire*. Vol. 1, A.D. 260–395. Cambridge.

Jones, A. H. M., and T. C. Skeat. 1954. "Notes on the Genuineness of the Constantinian Documents in Eusebius's Life of Constantine." *Journal of Ecclesiastical History* 5: 196–200.

Jones Hall, L. 1998. "Cicero's *instinctu divino* and Constantine's *instinctu divinitatis*: The Evidence of the Arch of Constantine for the Senatorial View of the 'Vision' of Constantine." *Journal of Early Christian Studies* 6: 647–71.

Jonkers, E. J. 1954. *Acta et symbola conciliorum quae saeculo quarto habita sunt.* Textus minores in usum academicum 19. Leiden.

Kaegi, W. E. 1981. "Constantine's and Julian's Strategies of Strategic Surprise against the Persians." *Athenaeum* 69: 209–13.

Karayannopulos, J. 1958. *Das Finanzwesen des frühbyzantinischen Staates.* Südosteuropäische Arbeiten 52. Munich.

Kaster, R. A. 1988. *Guardians of Language: The Grammarian and Society in Late Antiquity.* The Transformation of the Classical Heritage 11. Berkeley.

Kazanski, M. 1993. *Les Goths.* Paris.

Kazhdan, A. 1987. "'Constantin imaginaire': Byzantine Legends of the Ninth Century about Constantine the Great." *Byzantion* 57: 196–250.

———. 1996. "Constantinopolitan Synaxarium as a Source of Social History of Byzantium." Pp. 484–515 in *The Christian East: Its Institutions and Its Thought: A Critical Reflection,* Orientalia Christiana Analecta 251, ed. R. F. Taft. Rome.

Keay, S. J. 1984. *Late Roman Amphorae in the Western Mediterranean, a Typology and Economic Study: The Catalan Evidence.* British Archaeological Reports International Series 196. Oxford.

Keenan, J. G. 1973. "The Names Flavius and Aurelius as Status Designations in Later Roman Egypt." *Zeitschrift für Papyrologie und Epigraphik* 11: 33–63.

Kelly, C. M. 1998. "Emperors, Government and Bureaucracy." Pp. 138–83 in *The Cambridge Ancient History,* vol. 13, *The Late Empire A.D. 337–425,* 2d ed., ed. A. Cameron and P. Garnsey. Cambridge.

———. 1999. "Empire-Building." Pp. 170–95 in *Late Antiquity: A Guide to the Postclassical World,* ed. G. W. Bowersock, P. Brown, and O. Grabar. Cambridge, MA.

———. 2004. *Ruling the Later Roman Empire.* Cambridge, MA.

Kelly, J. N. D. 1972. *Early Christian Creeds.* London.

Kennedy, D. L. 2000. *The Roman Army in Jordan.* London.

Kent, J. P. C. 1981. *The Roman Imperial Coinage.* Vol. 8, *The Family of Constantine I A.D. 337–364.* London.

Kent, J. P. C., and M. Hirmer. 1978. *Roman Coins.* London.

Kent, J. P. C., and K. Painter, eds. 1977. *Wealth of the Roman World: Gold and Silver AD 300–700.* London.

Kienast, D. 1996. *Römische Kaisertabelle: Grundzüge einer römischen Kaiserchronologie.* Darmstadt.

King, C. E. 1980. "The *Sacrae Largitiones*: Revenues, Expenditure and the Production of Coin." Pp. 141–73 in *Imperial Revenue, Expenditure and Monetary Policy in the Fourth Century A.D.: The Fifth Oxford Symposium on Coinage and Monetary History,* British Archaeological Reports International Series 76, ed. C. E. King. Oxford.

Kinney, D. 1995. "Rape or Restitution of the Past: Interpreting *Spolia*." Pp. 53–67 in *The Art of Interpreting,* Papers in Art History from the Pennsylvania State University 9, ed. S. C. Scott. University Park, PA.

———. 1997. "Spolia, *Damnatio* and *Renovatio Memoriae*." *Memoires of the American Academy at Rome* 42: 117–48.

———. 2001a. "The Church Basilica." *Acta ad archaeologiam et artium historiam pertinentia* 15 n.s. 1: 115–35.

————. 2001b. "Roman Architectural *Spolia*." *Proceedings of the American Philosophical Society* 145: 138–50.

Kister, M. J. 1980. *Studies in Jāhiliyya and Early Islam*. London.

Klauck, H.-J. 2000. *The Religious Context of Early Christianity: A Guide to Graeco-Roman Religions*. Edinburgh.

Klein, R. 1977. *Constantius II. und die christliche Kirche*. Darmstadt.

————. 1988. *Die Sklaverei in der Sicht der Bischöfe Ambrosius und Augustinus*. Forschungen zur Antiken Sklaverei 20. Stuttgart.

————. 1993. "Die Bestellung von Sklaven zu Priestern: Ein rechtliches und soziales Problem in Spätantike und Frühmittelalter." Pp. 473–93 in *Klassisches Altertum, Spätantike und frühes Christentum, Festschrift für A. Lippold*. Würzburg.

————. 2000. *Die Haltung der Kappadokischen Bischöfe Basilius von Caesarea, Gregor von Nazianz und Gregor von Nyssa zur Sklaverei*. Forschungen zur Antiken Sklaverei 32. Stuttgart.

Kleiner, D. E. E. 1992. *Roman Sculpture*. New Haven.

Kneissl, P. 1969. *Die Siegestitulatur der römischen Kaiser: Untersuchungen zu den Siegerbeinamen des 1. und 2. Jahrhunderts*. Hypomnemata 23. Göttingen.

Knudsen, S. 1989. "Spolia: The So-called Historical Frieze on the Arch of Constantine." *American Journal of Archaeology* 93: 267–8.

————. 1990. "Spolia: The Pedestal Reliefs on the Arch of Constantine." *American Journal of Archaeology* 94: 313–4.

Koch, G. 2000. *Frühchristliche Sarkophage*. Munich.

Koep, L. 1958. "Die Konsekrationsmünzen Kaiser Konstantins und ihre religionspolitische Bedeutung." *Jahrbuch für Antike und Christentum* 1: 94–105.

Koeppel, G. 1990. "Die historischen Reliefs der römischen Kaiserzeit VII: Der Bogen des Septimius Severus, die Decennalienbasis und der Konstantinsbogen." *Bonner Jarhbücher* 190: 1–64.

Kolb, A. 2000. *Transport und Nachrichtentransfer im römischen Reich*. Klio Beihefte n.F. 2. Stuttgart.

Kolb, F. 1987. *Diocletian und die erste Tetrarchie: Improvisation oder Experiment in der Organisation monarchischer Herrschaft?* Berlin and New York.

————. 2001. *Herrscherideologie in der Spätantike*. Berlin.

König, I. 1987. *Origo Constantini: Anonymus Valesianus Teil 1, Text und Kommentar*. Trierer Historische Forschungen. Trier.

Kotansky, R. 1994. *Greek Magical Amulets*. Opladen.

Kranz, P. 1984. *Jahreszeiten-Sarkophage*. Berlin.

Krautheimer, R. 1967. "The Constantinian Basilica." *Dumbarton Oaks Papers* 21: 115–40.

————. 1969. *Studies in Early Christian, Medieval and Renaissance Art*. New York.

————. 1980. *Rome: Profile of a City, 312–1308*. Princeton, NJ.

————. 1983. *Three Christian Capitals: Topography and Politics*. Berkeley and Los Angeles.

————. 1986. *Early Christian and Byzantine Architecture*. 4th ed. Harmondsworth.

————. 1989. "The Building Inscriptions and the Dates of Construction of Old St. Peter's: A Reconsideration." *Römisches Jahrbuch der Bibliotheca Herziana* 25: 1–24.

————. 1993. "The Ecclesiastical Building Policy of Constantine." Pp. 509–52 in *Costantino il Grande dall'antichità all'umanesimo: Colloquio sul Cristianesimo nel mondo antico, Macerata 18–20 dicembre 1990*, vol. 2, ed. G. Bonamente and F. Fusco. Macerata.

Krautheimer, R., S. Corbett, and A. Frazer. 1937–77. *Corpus Basilicarum Christianarum Romae: The Early Christian Basilicas of Rome (IV–IX Centuries)*. 5 vols. Vatican City.

Krüger, J., et al. 2000. *Die Grabeskirche zu Jerusalem. Geschichte, Gestalt, Bedeutung.* Regensburg.

Kuhoff, W. 1991. "Ein Mythos in der römishcen Geschichte: Der Sieg Konstantins des Großen über Maxentius." *Chiron* 21: 127–74.

———. 2001. *Diokletian und die Epoche der Tetrarchie: Das römische Reich zwischen Krisenbewältung und Neuaufbau (284–313 n. Chr.).* Frankfurt-am-Main.

Kulikowski, M. 2000. "The *Notitia Dignitatum* as a Historical Source." *Historia* 49: 358–77.

Kurfess, A. 1948. "Zur Echtheitsfrage und Datierung der Rede Konstantins an die Versammlung der Heiligen." *Zeitschrift für Religions- und Geistesgeschichte* 1: 355–8.

Lahusen, G., and E. Formiglioli. 2001. *Römische Bildnisse aus Bronze.* Munich.

Laiou, A. E. 2002. *The Economic History of Byzantian from the Seventh through the Fifteenth Century*, 3 vols. Washington, DC.

Lake, K., and J. E. L. Oulton, trans. 1926–32. *Eusebius: The Ecclesiastical History.* 2 vols. Cambridge, MA, and London.

Lallemand, J. 1964. *L'administration civile de l'Égypte de l'avènement de Dioclétien à la création du diocèse (284–382).* Paris.

Lamb, H. H. 1977. *Climate, Present, Past and Future.* Vol. 2. London.

Lanata, G. 1972. "Gli atti del Processo contro il Centurione Marcello." *Byzantion* 42: 509–22.

Lander, J. 1984. *Roman Stone Fortifications: Variation and Change from the First Century* AD *to the Fourth.* British Archaeological Reports International Series 206. Oxford.

Lane Fox, R. 1986. *Pagans and Christians in the Mediterranean World from the Second Century* AD *to the Conversion of Constantine.* London and New York.

La Rocca, E. 1993. "La fondazione di Costantinopoli." Pp. 553–84 in *Costantino il Grande dall'antichità all'umanesimo: Colloquio sul Cristianesimo nel mondo antico, Macerata 18–20 dicembre 1990*, vol. 1, ed. G. Bonamente and F. Fusco. Macerata.

———. 2000. "Le basiliche cristiane 'a deambulatorio' e la sopravvivenza del culto eroico." Pp. 204–20 in *Aurea Roma: Dalla città pagana alla città cristiana*, ed. S. Ensoli and E. La Rocca. Rome.

Lavan, L. 1999. "Late Antique Governors' Palaces: A Gazeteer." *Antiquité Tardive* 7: 135–64.

Leadbetter, B. 1998. "The Illegitimacy of Constantine and the Birth of the Tetrarchy." Pp. 74–85 in *Constantine: History, Historiography, and Legend*, ed. S. N. C. Lieu and D. Montserrat. London.

———. 2000. "Galerius and the Revolt of the Thebaid in 293/4." *Antichthon* 34: 82–94.

Lebedynsky, I. 2001. *Armes et guerriers barbares au temps des grandes invasions, IVe au VIe siècle après J.-C.* Paris.

Leclercq, H. 1907. *Les martyrs: Recueil de pièces authentiques sur les martyrs depuis les origines du christianisme jusqu'au xxᵉ siècle.* Vol. 4, *Juifs, sarrasins, iconoclastes.* Paris.

Lee, A. D. 1993. *Information and Frontiers: Roman Foreign Relations in Late Antiquity.* Cambridge.

———. 1998. "The Army." Pp. 211–37 in *The Cambridge Ancient History*, vol. 13, *The Late Empire* A.D. *337–425*, 2d ed., ed. A. Cameron and P. Garnsey. Cambridge.

———. 2000. *Pagans and Christians in Late Antiquity: A Sourcebook.* London.

Lehman, T. 2003. "Circus Basilicas, 'Coemeteria Subteglata,' and Church Buildings in the Suburbium of Rome." *Acta ad archaeologiam et artium historiam pertinentia* 17: 57–77.

Leeb, R. 1992. *Konstantin und Christus*. Berlin.

Lenski, N. 1995. "The Gothic Civil War and the Date of the Gothic Conversion." *Greek Roman and Byzantine Studies* 36: 51–87.

————. 1999. "Assimilation and Revolt in the Territory of Isauria." *Journal of the Economic and Social History of the Orient* 42: 413–65.

————. 2000. "The Election of Jovian and the Role of the Late Imperial Guards." *Klio* 82: 492–515.

————. 2002a. "Evidence for the *Audientia episcopalis* in the New Letters of Augustine." Pp. 93–97 in *Law, Society and Authority in Late Antiquity*, ed. R. Mathisen. Oxford.

————. 2002b. *Failure of Empire: Valens and the Roman State in the Fourth Century A.D.* The Transformation of the Classical Heritage 34. Berkeley and Los Angeles.

————. 2004. "Empresses in the Holy Land: The Creation of a Christian Utopia in Late Antique Palestine." Pp. 113–24 in *Travel, Communication and Geography in Late Antiquity*, ed. L. Ellis, and F. L. Kidner. Aldershot.

Lepelley, C. 1979. *Les cités de l'Afrique du nord au Bas-Empire*. Vol. 1, *La permanance d'une civilization romaine*. Paris.

Leppin, H. 1996. *Von Constantin dem Großen zu Theodosius II: Das christliche Kaisertum bei den Kirchenhistorikern Sokrates, Sozomenus und Theodoret*. Hypomnemata 110. Göttingen.

Levi, D. 1948. *Antioch Mosaic Pavements*. Oxford.

Levison, W. 1924. "Konstantinische Schenkung und Silvester-Legende." Pp. 159–247 in *Miscellanea Francesco Ehrle, Scritti di Storia e Palaeografia*, vol. 2, *Per la storia di Roma e dei papi*. Studi e Testi 38. Rome.

Levitan, W. 1985. "Dancing at the End of the Rope: Optatian Porfyry and the Field of Roman Verse." *Transactions of the American Philological Association* 115: 245–69.

Lewin, A. 1990. "Dall'Euphrate al Mar Rosso: Diocleziano, l'esercito e i confini tar-doantichi." *Athenaeum* 78: 141–65.

————. 2002. "Diocletian: Politics and *limites* in the Near East." Pp. 91–101 in *Limes XVIII: Proceedings of the XVIIIth International Congress of Roman Frontier Studies Held in Amman Jordan (September 2000)*, British Archaeological Reports International Series 1084, ed. P. Freeman et al. Oxford.

Lewis, N., and M. Reinhold, eds. 1990. *Roman Civilization: Selected Readings*. Vol. 2, *The Empire*. 3d ed. New York.

Liebeschuetz, J. H. W. G. 1979. *Continuity and Change in Roman Religion*. Oxford.

————. 1999a. "The Significance of the Speech of Praetextatus." Pp. 185–205 in *Pagan Monotheism in Late Antiquity*, ed. P. Athanassiadi and M. Frede. Oxford.

————. 2001. *The Decline and Fall of the Roman City*. Oxford

Lieu, S. N. C. 1992. *Manichaeism in the Later Roman Empire and Medieval China*. 2d ed. Tübingen.

————. 1998. "From History to Legend and Legend to History: The Medieval and Byzantine Transformation of Constantine's *Vita*." Pp. 136–76 in *Constantine: History, Historiography and Legend*, ed. S. N. C. Lieu and D. A. Montserrat. London and New York.

Lieu, S. N. C., and D. Montserrat, eds. 1996. *From Constantine to Julian: Pagan and Byzantine Views*. London.

————, eds. 1998. *Constantine: History, Historiography and Legend*. London and New York.

Lim, R. 1995. *Public Disputation, Power, and Social Order in Late Antiquity*. The Transformation of the Classica Heritage 23. Berkeley and Los Angeles.

Linder, A. 1975. "The Myth of Constantine the Great in the West: Sources and Hagiographic Commemoration." *Studi Medievali*, 3d ser. 16.1: 43–95.

————. 1988. "Constantine's 'Ten Laws' Series." Pp. 491–506 in *Fälschungen im Mittelalter: Internationaler Kongreß der Monumenta Germaniae Historica, München, 16.– 19. September 1986*, part 2, *Gefälschte Rechtstexte, der bestrafte Fälscher*. Monumenta Germaniae Historica Schriften 33. Hannover.

Lippold, A. 1992. "Konstantin und die Barbaren (Konfrontation? Integration? Koexistenz?)." *Studi Italiani di Filologia Classica* 85: 371–91.

L'Orange, H. P. 1933. *Studien zur Geschichte des spätantiken Porträts*. Oslo.

————. 1965. *Art Forms and Civic Life*. Princeton.

————. 1984. *Das spätantike Herrscherbild von Diokletian bis zu den Konstantin-Söhnen, 284–361 n. Chr.* Berlin.

L'Orange, H. P., and A. von Gerkan. 1939. *Der Spätantike Bildschmuck des Konstantinsbogens*. Berlin.

Lucien-Brun, X. 1973. "Constance II et le massacre des princes." *Bulletin de l'Association Guillaume Budé, Supplément Lettres d' Humanité*, 4th ser. 32: 585–602.

MacCormack, S. 1981. *Art and Ceremony in Late Antiquity*. The Transformation of the Classical World 1. Berkeley and Los Angeles.

Mackay, C. S. 1999. "Lactantius and the Succession to Diocletian." *Classical Philology* 94: 198–209.

MacMullen, R. 1968. "Constantine and the Miraculous." *Greek Roman and Byzantine Studies* 9: 81–96.

————. 1969. *Constantine*. Beckenham and New York.

————. 1971. "Social History in Astrology." *Ancient Society* 2: 105–16. Reprint, pp. 218–24 in *Changes in the Roman Empire: Essays in the Ordinary*, ed. R. MacMullen, Princeton, 1990.

————. 1981. *Paganism in the Roman Empire*. New Haven.

————. 1986. "Judicial Savagery in the Roman Empire." *Chiron* 16: 147–66. Reprint, pp. 204–217 in *Changes in the Roman Empire: Essays in the Ordinary*, ed. R. MacMullen, Princeton, 1990.

————. 1997. *Christianity and Paganism in the Fourth to Eighth Centuries*. New Haven.

Magdalino, P., ed. 1994. *New Constantines: The Rhythm of Imperial Renewal in Byzantium, 4th–13th Centuries*. Aldershot.

Maggioni, G. P., ed. 1998. *Legenda Aurea, Iacopo da Varazze*. Millennio medievale 6. Tavarnuzze-Firenze.

Magi, F. 1956–7. "Il coronamento dell' Arco di Costantino." *Atti della Pontificia Accademia Romana di Archeologia, Rendiconti* 29: 83–110.

Maier, J.-L., ed. 1987–9. *Le dossier du Donatisme*. 2 vols. Texte und Untersuchungen zur Geschichte der Altchristlichen Literatur 134–5. Berlin.

Mango, C. 1959. *The Brazen House: A Study of the Vestibule of the Imperial Palace of Constantinople*. Royal Danish Academy, Archaeologisk-kunsthistoriske Meddelelser 4.4. Copenhagen.

————. 1965. "Constantinopolitana." *Jahrbuch des Deutschen Archäologischen Instituts* 80: 305–36. Reprint, study II in Mango 1993b.

————. 1990a. "Constantine's Mausoleum and the Translation of Relics." *Byzantinische Zeitschrift* 83: 51–62. Reprint, study V in Mango 1993b.

————. 1990b. "Constantine's Mausoleum: An Addendum." *Byzantische Zeitschrift* 83: 434.

————. 1990c. *Le développement urbain de Constantinople (IVᵉ–VIIᵉ siècles).* Travaux et mémoires du Centre de recherche d'histoire et civilisation de Byzance, Monographies 2. 2d ed. Paris.

————. 1993a. "Constantine's Column." Study III in Mango 1993b.

————. 1993b. *Studies on Constantinople.* Aldershot.

————. 1994. "The Empress Helena, Helenopolis, Pylae." *Travaux et mémoires du Centre de recherches d'histoire et civilisation byzantine* 12: 143–58.

Mann, J. C. 1977. "*Duces* and *comites* in the Fourth Century." Pp. 11–15 in *The Saxon Shore*, ed. D. E. Johnston. London.

Mannix, M. D., ed. and trans. 1925. *Sancti Ambrosii Oratio De Obitu Theodosii: Text, Translation, Introduction and Commentary.* The Catholic University of America Patristic Studies 9. Washington, DC.

Marcone, A. 2000. *Costantino il Grande.* Rome.

————. 2003. "Il destino dell'impero e la fortuna di Costantino." Pp. 311–21 in *Consuetudinis Amor: Fragments d'histoire romaine (II–VI siècles) offerts à Jean-Pierre Callu*, ed. F. Chausson and É. Wolff. Rome.

Marlowe, L. 2004. "'That Customary Magnificance Which is Your Due': Constantine and the Symbolic Capital of Rome." Ph.D. diss., Columbia University.

Martin, D. B. 1996. "The Construction of the Ancient Family: Methodological Considerations." *Journal of Roman Studies* 86: 40–60.

Mathews, T., and N. Muller. 2005. "Isis and Mary in Early Icons," Pp. 3–12 in *Images of the Mother God: Perceptions of the Theotokos in Byzantium*, ed. M. Vassilaki. Aldershot.

Matthews, J. F. 1989. *The Roman Empire of Ammianus.* London and Baltimore.

————. 2000. *Laying Down the Law: A Study of the Theodosian Code.* New Haven.

Mattingly, H. 1933. "Fel. Temp. Reparatio." *Numismatic Chronicle* 94: 182–202.

Mayerson, P. 1993. "A Confusion of Indias: Asian India and African India in the Byzantine Sources." *Journal of the American Oriental Society* 113: 169–74.

Mazzarino, S. 1951. *Aspetti sociali del quarto secolo.* Rome.

McCormick, M. 2001. *Origins of the European Economy: Communication, and Commerce, A.D. 300–900.* Cambridge and New York.

McGinn, T. A. J. 1999. "The Social Policy of Emperor Constantine in *Codex Theodosianus* 4.6.3." *Tijdschrift voor Rechtsgeschiedenis* 67.1–2: 57–73.

McKechnie, P. 2002. "Roman Law and the Laws of the Medes and Persians: Decius' and Valerian's Persecutions of the Christians." Pp. 253–69 in *Thinking Like a Lawyer: Essays on Legal History and General History for John Crook on His Eightieth Birthday*, Mnemosyne Supp. 231, ed. P. McKechnie. Leiden, Boston, and Cologne.

Meier, H. R. 2001. "Christian Emperors and the Legacy of Imperial Art." Pp. 63–75 in *Imperial Art as Christian Art – Christian Art as Imperial Art*, Acta ad archaeologiam et artium historiam pertinentia 15, ed. J. R. Brandt and O. Steen. Rome.

Melucco Vaccaro, A., and A. M. Ferroni. 1993–4. "Qui costruì l'Arco di Costantino? Un interrogativo ancora attuale." *Atti della Pontificia Accademia Romana di Archeologia, Rendiconti* 66: 1–60.

Merkelbach, R., and J. Stauber. 1999. "Unsterbliche Kaiserpriester: Drei Dokumente der heidnischen Reaktion." *Epigraphica Anatolica* 31: 157–64.

Messineo, G., and C. Calci. 1989. *Malborghetto. Lavori e studi di archeologia.* Rome.

Michel, S. 2001. *Die magischen Gemmen im britischen Museum.* 2 vols. London.

Mickwitz, G., 1932, *Geld und Wirtschaft im römischen Reich des vierten jahrhunderts n. Chr.* Commentationes humanarum litterarum 4.2. Helsinki.

Migl, J. 1994. *Die Ordnung der Ämter: Prätorianerpräfektur und Vikariat in der Regionalverwaltung des Römischen Reiches von Konstantin bis zur Valentinianischen Dynastie.* Europäische Hochschulschriften 623. Frankfurt am Main.

Millar, F. 1969. "P. Herennius Dexippus: The Greek World and the Third-Century Invasions." *Journal of Roman Studies* 59: 12–29. Reprint, Chapter 13 in Millar 2004.

———. 1971. "Paul of Samosata, Zenobia and Aurelian: The Church, Local Culture and Political Allegiance in Third Century Syria." *Journal of Roman Studies* 61: 1–17.

———. 1983. "Empire and City, Augustus to Julian: Obligations, Excuses and Status." *Journal of Roman Studies* 73: 76–96. Reprint, Chapter 16 in Millar 2004.

———. 1992. *The Emperor in the Roman World (31 B.C.–A.D. 337).* 2d ed. London.

———. 1993. *The Roman Near East, 31 BC–AD 337.* Cambridge, MA, and London.

———. 2004. *Rome, the Greek World, and the East,* Vol. 2, *Government Society and Culture in the Roman Empire,* ed. H. M. Cotton and G. M. Rogers. Chapel Hill, NC.

Milner, C. 1994. "The Image of the Rightful Ruler: Anicia Juliana's Constantine Mosaic in the Church of Hagios Polyeuktos." Pp. 73–81 in *New Constantines: The Rhythm of Imperial Renewal in Byzantium, 4th–13th Centuries,* ed. P. Magdalino. Aldershot.

Minoprio, A. 1932. "A Restoration of the Basilica of Constantine." *Papers of the British School at Rome* 12: 1–25.

Mirbt, C., and K. Aland, eds. 1967. *Quellen zur Geschichte des Papsttums und des römischen Katholizismus.* Tübingen.

Mitchell, S. 1988. "Maximinus and the Christians in AD 312: A New Latin Inscription." *Journal of Roman Studies* 78: 105–24.

———. 1993. *Anatolia: Land, Men and Gods in Asia Minor.* 2 vols. Oxford.

———. 1995. *Cremna in Pisidia: An Ancient City in Peace and War.* London.

———. 1999. "The Cult of Theos Hypsistos between Pagans, Jews and Christians." Pp. 81–148 in *Pagan Monotheism,* ed. P. Athanassiadi and M. Frede. Oxford.

Mitrev, G. 2003. "*Civitas Heracleotarum*: Heracleia Sintica or the Ancient City at the Village of Rupite (Bulgaria)." *Zeitschrift für Papyrologie und Epigraphik* 145: 263–72.

Mócsy, A. 1974. *Pannonia and Upper Moesia.* London.

Mombritius, B. 1910. *Sanctuarium seu Vitae Sanctorum.* Vol. 2, ed. H. Quentin and A. Brunet. Paris.

Moreau, J. 1954. *Lactance de la mort des persécuteurs.* 2 vols. Paris.

Munro-Hay, S. 1991. *Aksum: An African Civilisation of Late Antiquity.* Edinburgh.

Murray, A. C. 2002. "Reinhard Wenskus on 'Ethnogenesis,' Ethnicity, and the Origin of the Franks." Pp. 39–68 in *On Barbarian Identity: Critical Approaches to Ethnicity in the Early Middle Ages,* ed. A. Gillett. Turnhout.

Musurillo, H. 1972. *The Acts of the Christian Martyrs.* Oxford.

Nakamura, B. J. 2003. "When did Diocletian Die? New Evidence for an old Problem." *Classical Philology* 98: 283–9.

Nathan, G. S. 2000. *The Family in Late Antiquity: The Rise of Christianity and the Endurance of Tradition.* London and New York.

Neri, V. 1992. *Medius Princeps: Storia e immagine di Costantino nella storiografia latina pagana.* Bologna.

Nestle, E. 1895. "Die Kreuzauffindungslegende: Nach einer Handscrift von Sinai." *Byzantinische Zeitschrift* 4: 325–31.

Nicasie, M. J. 1998. *Twilight of Empire: The Roman Army from the Reign of Diocletian until the Battle of Adrianople.* Dutch Monographs on Ancient History and Archaeology 19. Amsterdam.

Nicholson, O. 1984. "The Wild Man of the Tetrarchy: A Divine Companion for the Emperor Galerius." *Byzantion* 54: 253–75.

————. 1994. "The 'Pagan Churches' of Maximinus Daia and Julian the Apostate." *Journal of Ecclesiastical History* 45: 1–10.

————. 2001a. "Broadening the Roman Mind: Foreign Prophets in the Apologetic of Lactantius." *Studia Patristica* 36: 364–74.

————. 2001b. "*Caelum potius intuemini*: Lactantius and a Statue of Constantine." *Studia Patristica* 34: 177–96.

Nixon, C. E. V. 1981. "The Panegyric of 307 and Maximian's Visits to Rome." *Phoenix* 35: 70–6.

————. 1993. "Constantinus Oriens Imperator: Propaganda and Panegyric: On Reading Panegyric 7 (307)." *Historia* 42: 229–46.

Nixon, C. E. V., and Rodgers, B. S. 1994. *In Praise of Later Roman Emperors: The "Panegyrici Latini."* The Transformation of the Classical World 21. Berkeley and Los Angeles.

Nock, A. D. 1930. "*A Diis Electa*: A Chapter in the Religious History of the Third Century." *Harvard Theological Review* 23: 251–74.

————. 1947. "The Emperor's Divine *Comes*." *Journal of Roman Studies* 37: 102–16.

Noel, R. 1972. *Les dépôts de pollens fossiles.* Turnhout.

Noreña, C. 2001. "The Communication of the Emperor's Virtues." *Journal of Roman Studies* 91: 146–68.

North, J. 1992. "The Development of Religious Pluralism." Pp. 174–93 in *The Jews among Pagans and Christians in the Roman Empire*, ed. J. Lieu, J. North, and T. Rajak. London.

————. 2000. *Roman Religion.* Greece and Rome New Surveys in the Classics 30. Oxford.

Noy, D. 2000. *Foreigners at Rome: Citizens and Strangers.* London.

Odahl, C. M. 2004. *Constantine and the Christian Empire.* London and New York.

O'Donnell, J. J. 1977. "'Paganus': Evolution and Use." *Classical Folia* 31: 163–9.

Opitz, H.-G. 1934a. *Athanasius Werke.* Vol. 3.1, *Urkunden zur Geschichte des Arianischen Streites, 318–328.* Berlin.

————. 1934b. "Die *Vita Constantini* des Codex Angelicus 22." *Byzantion* 9: 535–93.

Orr, D. G. 1978. "Roman Domestic Religion: The Evidence of the Household Shrines." *Aufstieg und Niedergang der römischen Welt* 2.16.2: 1557–90.

Packer, J. 1997. *The Forum of Trajan in Rome.* Berkeley and Los Angeles.

Pagano, M., and J. Rouget. 1984. "Il battistero della basilica costantiniana di Capua (cosidetto *catabulum*)." *Mélanges d'Archéologie et d'Histoire de l'École Française de Rome, Antiquité* 96: 987–1016.

Panella, C. 1981. "Le anfore tardoantiche: Centro di produzione e mercati preferenziali." Pp. 251–84 in *Società romana e impero tardoantico.* Vol. 3, *Le merci, gli insediamenti*, ed. A. Giardina. Rome.

Paschoud, F. 1971a. "Zosime 2,29 et la version païenne de la conversion de Constantin." *Historia* 20: 334–53. Reprint, pp. 24–62 in *Cinq Études sur Zosime*, ed. F. Paschoud, Paris, 1975.

———. 1971b. *Zosime: Histoire Nouvelle*, Tome I, *Livres I–II*. Paris.

———. 2000. *Zosime: Histoire Nouvelle*, Tome I, *Livres I–II*, new ed. Paris.

Patrich, J. 1993. "The Early Church of the Holy Sepulchre in the Light of Excavations and Restoration." Pp. 100–17 in *Ancient Churches Revealed*, ed. Y. Tsafrir. Jerusalem.

Peeters, P. 1932. "Les debuts du christianisme en Géorgie d'après les sources hagiographiques." *Analecta Bollandiana* 50: 5–58.

Peirce, P. 1989. "The Arch of Constantine: Propaganda and Ideology in Late Roman Art." *Art History* 12: 387–418.

Pensabene, P. 1993. "Il reimpiego nell'età Costantiniana a Roma." Pp. 749–68 in *Costantino il Grande dall'antichità all'umanesimo: Colloquio sul Cristianesimo nel mondo antico, Macerata 18–20 dicembre 1990*, vol. 2, ed. G. Bonamente and F. Fusco. Macerata.

———. 1995. "Reimpiego e nuove mode architettoniche nelle basiliche Cristiane di Roma tra IV e VI secolo." *Jahrbuch für Antike und Christentum, Ergänzungsband* 20.2: 1076–96.

———. 1999. "Progetto unitario e reimpiego nell'Arco di Costantino." Pp. 13–42 in *Arco di Costantino: Tra archeologia e archeometria*, ed. P. Pensabene and R. Panella. Rome.

Pensabene, P., and C. Panella. 1993–4. "Reimpiego e progettazione architettonica nei monumenti tardo-antichi di Roma." *Atti della Pontificia Accademia Romana di Archeologia, Rendiconti* 66: 111–283.

———., eds. 1999. *Arco di Costantino: Tra archeologia e archeometria*. Rome.

Pfättisch, J.-M. 1913. "Die Rede Konstantins an die Versammlung der Heiligen." Pp. 96–121 in *Konstantin der Große und seine Zeit, gesammelte Studien: Festgabe A. de Waal*, Römische Quartalschrift für christliche Altertumskunde und für Kirchengeschichte, Supplementheft 19. Freiburg.

Pharr, C. T. 1952. *The Theodosian Code and Novels and the Sirmondian Constitutions*. Princeton.

Piganiol, A. 1932. *L'empereur Constantin*. Paris.

———. 1972. *L'Empire chrétien (325–395)*, ed. A. Chastagnol. Paris.

Pitts, L. F. 1989. "Rome and the German 'Kings' on the Middle Danube." *Journal of Roman Studies* 79: 45–58.

Plassard, J. 1968. "Crises séismique au Liban du quatrième au sixième siècle." *Mélanges de l'Université Saint-Joseph de Beyrouth* 44: 9–20.

Platner, S. B., and T. Ashby. 1929. *A Topographical Dictionary of Ancient Rome*. London.

Plesnicar-Gec, L. 1970–1. "Emona pozni antiki (Emona dans l'antiquité classique)." *Arheoloski vestnik* 21–2: 117–22.

———. 1972. "La citta di Emona nel tardo antico e i suoi ruderi paleochristiani." *Arheoloski vestnik* 23: 367–73.

Poeschke, J., ed. 1996. *Antike Spolien in der Architektur des Mittelalters und der Renaissance*. Munich.

Pohl, W., ed. 1997. *Kingdoms of the Empire: The Integration of Barbarians in Late Antiquity*. Leiden.

————. 1998. "Telling the Difference: Signs of Ethnic Identity." Pp. 17–69 in *Strategies of Distinction: The Construction of Ethnic Communities, 300–800*, ed. W. Pohl, and H. Reimitz. Leiden.

————. 2000. *Die Germanen*. Oldenbourg Enzyklopädie Deutscher Geschichte. Munich

————. 2002a. *Die Völkerwanderung: Eroberung und Integration*. Munich.

————. 2002b. "Ethnicity, Theory, and Tradition: A Response." Pp. 221–240 in *On Barbarian Identity: Critical Approaches to Ethnicity in the Early Middle Ages*, ed. A. Gillett. Turnhout.

Pohl, W., and H. Reimitz, eds. 1998. *Strategies of Distinction: The Construction of Ethnic Communities, 300–800*. Leiden.

Pohlkamp, W. 1984. "Kaiser Konstantin, der heidnische und der christliche Kult in den Actus Silvestri." *Frühe Mittelalterliche Studien* 18: 357–400.

————. 1988. "Privilegium ecclesiae Romanae pontifici contulit: Zur Vorgeschichte der Konstantinischen Schenkung." Pp. 413–90 in *Fälschungen im Mittelalter: Internationaler Kongreß der Monumenta Germaniae Historica, München, 16.–19. September 1986*, Pt. 2, *Gefälschte Rechtstexte, der bestrafte Fälscher*, Monumenta Germaniae Historica Schriften 33. Hannover.

Pohlsander, H. 1984. "Crispus: Brilliant Career and Tragic End." *Historia* 33: 79–106.

————. 1993. "Constantia." *Ancient Society* 24: 151–67.

————. 1995. "The Date of the *Bellum Cibalense*: A Re-examination." *Ancient World* 26: 89–101.

————. 1996. *The Emperor Constantine*. London.

Polara, J., ed. 1973. *Publilii Optatiani Porfyrii Carmina*. Torino.

Popović, V. 1971. "A Survey of the Topography and Urban Organisation of Sirmium in the Late Empire." Pp. 119–34 in *Sirmium: Archaeological Investigations in Syrmian Pannonia*, vol. 1, ed. V. Popović. Belgrade.

Porena, P. 2003. *Le origini della prefettura del pretorio tardoantica*. Saggi di storia antica 20. Rome.

Portmann, W. 1999. "Die politische Krise zwischen den Kaisern Constantius II. und Constans." *Historia* 48: 301–29.

Potter, D. S. 1990. *Prophecy and History in the Crisis of the Roman Empire: A Historical Commentary on the Thirteenth Sybilline Oracle*. Oxford.

————. 1994. *Prophets and Emperors: Human and Divine Authority from Augustus to Theodosius*. Cambridge, MA.

————. 1996. "Palmyra and Rome: Odaenathus' Titulature and the Use of the *imperium maius*." *Zeitschrift für Papyrologie und Epigraphik* 113: 271–85.

————. 2004. *The Roman Empire at Bay AD 180–395*. London and New York.

Poulter, A. 1992. "The Use and Abuse of Urbanism in the Later Roman Empire." Pp. 99–135 in *The City in Late Antiquity*, ed. J. Rich. London.

————. 1995. *Nicopolis ad Istrum: A Roman, Late Roman, and Early Byzantine City: Excavations 1985–1992*. London.

Preger, T. 1901. "Konstantinos-Helios." *Hermes* 36: 457–69.

Price, S. R. F. 1984. *Rituals and Power: The Roman Imperial Cult in Asia Minor*. Cambridge.

Purcell, N. 1983. "The *Apparitores*: A Study in Social Mobility." *Papers of the British School in Rome* 51: 125–73.

Rabb, T. K., and R. I. Rotberg, eds. 1980. "History and Climate: Interdisciplinary Explorations." Special issue. *Journal of Interdisciplinary History* 10. 4.

Raimondi, M. 2003. "Bemarchio di Cesarea, panegirista di Costantino e Costantinopoli: Per una reinterpretazione di Libanio, *Or.* I 39; 41." *Rivista Storica dell'Antichità* 33: 171–99.

Rapp, C. 2005. *Holy Bishops in Late Antiquity: The Nature of Christian Leadership in an Age of Transition.* Berkeley and Los Angeles.

Rasch, J., et al. 1998. *Das Mausoleum der Kaiserin Helena in Rom und der 'Tempio delle Tosse' in Tivoli.* Mainz.

Rathbone, D. 1991. *Economic Rationalism and Rural Society in Third Century A.D. Egypt: The Heroninos Archive and the Appianus Estate.* Cambridge.

Rea, J. 1984. "A Cavalryman's Career, AD 384(?)–401." *Zeitschrift für Papyrologie und Epigraphik* 56: 79–88.

Reames, S. L. 1985. *The Legenda Aurea: A Reexamination of Its Paradoxical History.* Madison, WI.

Rebenich, S. 2000. "Vom dreizehnten Gott zum dreizehnten Apostel? Der tote Kaiser in der Spätantike." *Zeitschrift für antikes Christentum* 4: 300–24.

Reddé, M. 1986. *Mare Nostrum.* Rome.

Redgate, A. E. 1998. *The Armenians.* Oxford.

Rees, R. 1993. "Images and Image: A Re-examination of Tetrarchic Iconography." *Greece and Rome* 40: 181–200.

———. 2002. *Layers of Loyalty in Latin Panegyric AD 289–307.* Oxford.

———. 2004. *Diocletian and the Tetrarchy.* Edinburgh.

Retsö, J. 2003. *The Arabs in Antiquity.* London.

Reusch, W. 1956. *Die Basilika in Trier: Festschrift zur Wiederherstellung 9. Dezember 1956.* Trier.

Richard, H. 1988. "Palynologie et climat." *Histoire et Mesure* 3: 359–85.

Richardson, L. 1975. "The Date and Program of the Arch of Constantine." *Archeologia Classica* 27: 72–8.

———. 1992. *A New Topographical Dictionary of Rome.* Baltimore.

Ridley, R. T., trans. 1982. *Zosimus New History: A Translation with Commentary.* Byzantina Australiensia 1. Sydney.

Riegl, A. 1901. *Spätrömische Kunstindustrie.* Vienna.

Rieß, W. 2001. "Konstantin und seine Söhne in Aquileia." *Zeitschrift für Papyrologie und Epigraphik* 135: 267–83.

Rist, J. M. 1967. *Plotinus: The Road to Reality.* Cambridge.

Rives, J. B. 1999. "The Decree of Decius and the Religion of Empire." *Journal of Roman Studies* 89: 135–54.

Rivière, Y. 2002. "Constantin, le crime et le christianisme: Contribution à l'étude des lois et des moeurs de l'antiquité tardive." *Antiquité Tardive* 10: 327–61.

Robert, L. 1973. "De Cilicie à Messine et à Plymouth." *Journal des savants* 1973: 162–211. Reprint, pp. 225–75 in *Opera Minora Selecta: Épigraphie et antiquités grecques*, vol. 7, ed. L. Robert, Amsterdam, 1990.

Robin, C. 1989. "Aux origines de l'état Himjarite: Himyar et Dhû Raydân." Pp. 104–12 in *Arabian Studies in Honour of Mahmoud Ghul: Symposium at Yarmouk University, December 8–11, 1984*, ed. M. M. Ibrahim. Wiesbaden.

Rodgers, B. S. 1980. "Constantine's Pagan Vision." *Byzantion* 50: 259–78.

Rolfe, J. C., trans. 1935–9. *Ammianus Marcellinus.* 3 vols. Cambridge, MA.

Rosafio, P. 2002. *Studi sul Colonato*. Puglia.

Rossignol, J.-P. 1845. *Virgile et Constantin le Grand*. Paris.

Roueché, C. M. 1989. *Aphrodisias in Late Antiquity*. London.

Rougé, J. 1958. "La Pseudo-Bigamie de Valentinien Ier." *Cahiers d'Histoire* 3: 5–15.

Rousseau, P. 1992. "Visigothic Migration and Settlement, 376–418: Some Excluded Hypotheses." *Historia* 41: 34–61.

Roxan, M. M. 1976. "Pre-Severan Auxilia Named in the Notitia Dignitatum." Pp. 59–80 in *Aspects of the Notitia Dignitatum*, British Archaeological Reports International Series 15, ed. R. Goodburn and P. Bartholomew. Oxford.

Rubin, Z. 1982. "The Church of the Holy Sepulchre and the Conflict between the Sees of Caesarea and Jerusalem." *Jerusalem Cathedra* 2: 79–105.

Russell, J. R. 1987. *Zoroastrianism in Armenia*. Cambridge, MA.

Rutgers, L. 2000. *Subterranean Rome*. Leuven.

Ryan, W. G. 1993. *Jacobus de Voragine, The Golden Legend*. Princeton.

Saller, R. 2000. "Family and Household." Pp. 855–74 in *The Cambridge Ancient History*, vol. 11, *The High Empire* A.D. *70–192*, 2d ed., ed. A. K. Bowman, P. Garnsey, and D. Rathbone. Cambridge.

Salway, R. W. B. 1994. "What's in a Name? A Survey of Roman Onomastic Practice from c. 700 B.C. to A.D. 700." *Journal of Roman Studies* 84: 124–45.

Sande, S. 2001. "The Iconography and Style of the Rothschild Cameo." Pp. 145–58 in *Late Antiquity: Art in Context*, Acta Hyperborea 8, ed. J. Fleischer, J. Lund, and M. Nielsen. Copenhagen.

Scagliarini, D. 1970. "L'insediamento residenziale e produttivo nel suburbio di Bologna romana." *Atti e memorie della Reale Deputazione di storia patria per le provincie di Romagna* 20: 137–92.

Schenk von Stauffenberg, A. 1947. *Das Imperium und die Völkerwanderung*. Munich.

Schiavone, A., ed. 1993. *Storia di Roma*. Vol. 3, *L'età tardoantica I: Crisi e trasformazioni*. Turin.

Schlumberger, J. A. 1989. "*Potentes* and *Potentia* in the Social Thought of Late Antiquity." Pp. 89–104 in *Tradition and Innovation in Late Antiquity*, ed. F. M. Clover and R. S. Humpheys. Madison, WI.

Schlunk, H. 1988. *Die Mosaikkuppel von Centcelles*. Mainz.

Schmidt, L. 1938. *Geschichte der deutschen Stämme bis zum Ausgang der Völkerwanderung*. Vol. 1, *Die Ostgermanen*. 2d ed. Munich.

Schumacher, W. 1987. "Die konstantinischen Exedra-Basiliken." Pp. 132–76 in *La catacomba dei Santi Marcellino e Pietro: Repertorio delle pitture*, ed. J. Deckers et al. Vatican City.

Scott, R. 1994. "The Image of Constantine in Malalas and Theophanes." Pp. 57–71 in *New Constantines: The Rhythm of Imperial Renewal in Byzantium, 4th–13th Centuries*, ed. P. Magdalino. Aldershot.

Scott, W. B. 1936. *Hermetica: The Ancient Greek and Latin Writings Which Contain Religious or Philosophic Teachings Ascribed to Hermes Trismegistus*. Vol. 4. Oxford.

Seeck, O. 1900. "Comites." *Paulys Realencylopädie der classischen Altertumswissenschaft* 4.1: 622–79.

————. 1919. *Regesten der Kaiser und Päpste für die Jahre 311 bis 476 n. Chr.* Stuttgart.

————. 1920–3. *Geschichte des Untergangs der antiken Welt*. 4th ed. Stuttgart.

Segrè, A. 1942–3. "Essays on Byzantine Economic History: The *annona civica* and the *annona militaris*." *Byzantion* 16: 393–444.

Seston, W. 1936. "La vision païenne de 310 et les origines du chrisme constantinien." *Annuaire de l'Institut de Philologie et d'Histoire Orientale*, Mélanges F. Cumont 4: 373–95.

———. 1955. "Du comitatus du Dioclétien aux comitatenses de Constantin." *Historia* 5: 284–96.

Setton, K. 1941. *Christian Attitudes towards the Emperor in the Fourth Century*. New York.

Shahîd, I. 1984. *Byzantium and the Arabs in the Fourth Century*. Washington, DC.

———. 2000 [2003]. "Byzantium and the Arabs during the Reign of Constantine: The Namāra Inscription, an Arabic Monumentum Ancyranum, AD 328." *Byzantinische Forschungen* 26: 73–124.

Shaw, B. 1999. "War and Violence." Pp. 130–69 in *Late Antiquity: A Guide to the Post-Classical World*, ed. G. W. Bowersock, P. Brown, and O. Grabar. Cambridge.

Siegmund, F. 2000. *Alemannen und Franken*. Ergänzungsbände zum Reallexikon der Germanischen Altertumskunde 23. Berlin.

Silli, P. 1987. *Testi Costantiniani nelle fonti letterarie*. Materiali per una palingenesi delle costituzioni tardo-imperiali 3. Milan.

Simon, E. 1986. *Die Konstantinischen Deckengemälde in Trier*. Mainz.

Sinnigen, W. G. 1959. "Two Branches of the Late Roman Secret Service." *American Journal of Philology* 80: 238–54.

———. 1962. "Three Administrative Changes Ascribed to Constantius II." *American Journal of Philology* 83: 369–82.

Skeat, T. C. 1964. *Papyri from Panopolis in the Chester Beatty Library, Dublin*. Dublin.

Smith, M. D. 1997. "The Religion of Constantius I." *Greek Roman and Byzantine Studies* 38: 187–208.

Smith, R. R. R. 1997. "The Public Image of Licinius I: Portrait Sculpture and Imperial Ideology in the Early Fourth Century." *Journal of Roman Studies* 87: 170–202.

Somme, J. 1977. *Les plaines du nord de la France et leur bordure: Étude géomorphologique*. Lille.

Southern, P., and K. R. Dixon. 1996. *The Late Roman Army*. London.

Speck, P. 2000. "Konstantins Mausoleum: Zur Geschichte der Apostelkirche in Konstantinopel." Pp. 113–66 in *Varia VII*, Poikila Byzantina 18, ed. P. Speck. Bonn.

Speidel, M. P. 1974. "*Stablesiani*: The Raising of New Cavalry Units during the Crisis of the Roman Empire." *Chiron* 4: 541–6.

———. 1996. "Raising New Units for the Late Roman Army: *Auxilia Palatina*." *Dumbarton Oaks Papers* 50: 163–70.

Spier, J. 1993. "Late Antique Cameos." Pp. 43–56 in *Cameos in Context*, ed. M. Henig and M. Vickers. Oxford.

Srejović, D. 1993. *Roman Imperial Towns and Palaces in Serbia*. Belgrade.

Srejović, D., and Č. Vasić. 1994. *Imperial Mausolea and Consecration Memorials in Felix Romuliana, Gamzigrad, Eastern Serbia*. Belgrade.

Stark, R. 1993. "Epidemics, Networks, and the Rise of Christianity." Pp. 159–75 in *Social Networks in the Early Christian Environment: Issues and Methods for Social History*, Semeia 56, ed. M. White. Alpharetta, GA.

———. 1996. *The Rise of Christianity*. Princeton.

Stein, E. 1928. *Geschichte des spätrömischen Reiches*. Vol. 1, *Vom römischen zum byzantinischen Staate (284–476 n. Chr.)*. Vienna.

Steinby, E. M., ed. 1993–2000. *Lexicon Topographicum Urbis Romae*. 6 vols. Rome.

Stemberger, G. 2000. *Jews and Christians in the Holy Land: Palestine in the Fourth Century.* Edinburgh.

Stern, H. 1958. "Les mosaiques de l'église de Ste-Costance à Rome." *Dumbarton Oaks Papers* 12: 157–218.

Steuer, H. 1992. "Interpretationsmöglichkeiten archäologischer Quellen zum Gefolgschaftsproblem." Pp. 203–57 in *Beiträge zum Verständnis der Germania des Tacitus,* ed. G. Neumann and H. Seemann. Göttingen.

Stewart, P. 1999. "The Destruction of Statues in Late Antiquity." Pp. 159–89 in *Constructing Identities in Late Antiquity,* ed. R. Miles. London.

Stirling, L. 2005. *The Learned Collector: Mythological Statuettes in Late Antique Gaul.* Ann Arbor.

Stoneman, R. 1992. *Palmyra and Its Empire.* Ann Arbor.

Straub, J. 1955. "Konstantins Verzicht auf den Gang zum Kapitol." *Historia* 4: 297–313. Reprint, pp. 100–18 in *Regeneratio Imperii* ed. J. Straub. Darmstadt, 1972.

Stroheker, K. F. 1965. *Germanentum und Spätantike.* Zurich and Stuttgart.

Strzygowski, J. 1901. *Orient oder Rom: Beiträge zur Geschichte der spätantiken und frühchristlichen Kunst.* Leipzig.

Sydow, W. von. 1969. *Zur Kunstgeschichte des spätantiken Porträts im 4 Jahrhundert n. Chr.* Bonn.

Syme, R. 1974. "The Ancestry of Constantine." Pp. 63–79 in *Bonner Historia-Augusta-Colloquium, 1971*, Antiquitas 4.11, ed. J. Straub. Bonn. Reprint, pp. 63–79 in *Historia Augusta Papers*, Oxford, 1983.

Sutherland, C. H. V., ed. 1967. *The Roman Imperial Coinage.* Vol. 6, *Diocletian to Constantine.* London.

Swain, S. 1993. "Greek into Palmyrene: Odaenathus as '*corrector totius orientis.*'" *Zeitschrift für Papyrologie und Epigraphik* 99: 157–64.

Tantillo, I. 2003. "Attributi solari della figura imperiale in Eusebio di Cesarea." *Mediterraneo antico* 6: 41–59.

Tavano, S. 1970. "Architettura Aquilenese tra IV e V secolo." *Memorie storiche Forogiuliesi* 50: 154–74.

Teasdale Smith, M. 1970. "The Lateran *Fastigium*: A Gift of Constantine the Great." *Rivista di Archeologia Cristiana* 46: 149–75.

Teitler, H. C. 1985. *Notarii and Exceptores: An Inquiry into the Role and Significance of Shorthand Writers in the Imperial and Ecclesiastical Bureaucracy of the Roman Empire (from the Early Principate to c. 450 A.D.).* Dutch Monographs on Ancient History and Archaeology 1. Amsterdam.

Temporini, H., ed. 1975. *Aufstieg und Niedergang der römischen Welt.* Vol. 2.2. Berlin.

Thelamon, F. 1981. *Païens et chrétiens au IVe siècle: L'apport de l'Histoire ecclésiastique de Rufin d'Aquilée.* Paris.

Thompson, E. A. 1966. *The Visigoths in the Time of Ulfila.* Oxford.

Thomson, R. W. 1982. "The Armenian Literary Tradition." Pp. 135–50 in *East of Byzantium: Syria and Armenia in the Formative Period*, ed. N. Garsoïan, T. F. Mathews, and R. W. Thomson. Washington, DC.

———. 1996. *Rewriting Caucasian History: The Medieval Armenian Adaptation of the Georgian Chronicles.* Oxford.

———. 1997. "Constantine and Trdt in Armenian Tradition." *Acta Orientalia Academiae Scientiarum Hungaricae* 50: 277–89.

Thomson, R. W., and J. Howard-Johnston, trans. and commentary, 1999. *The Armenian History Attributed to Sebeos. TTH* 31. 2 vols. Liverpool.

Tilley, M. 1996. *Donatist Martyr Stories. TTH* 24. Liverpool.

Todd, M. 1987. *The Northern Barbarians.* 2d ed. Oxford and New York.

———. 1992. *The Early Germans.* Oxford.

———. 1998. "The Germanic Peoples." Pp. 461–86 in *The Cambridge Ancient History*, vol. 13, *The Late Empire A.D. 337–425*, 2d ed., ed. A. Cameron and P. Garnsey. Cambridge.

Tolotti, R. 1982. "Le basiliche cimiteriali con deambulatorio del suburbio romano: Questione ancora aperta." *Mitteilungen des Deutschen Archäologischen Instituts, Römische Abteilung* 89: 153–211.

Tomlin, R. S. O. 1998. "Christianity and the Late Roman Army." Pp. 21–51 in *Constantine: History, Historiography and Legend*, ed. S. N. C. Lieu and D. A. Montserrat. London.

Toynbee, J. M. C. 1947. "Roma and Constantinopolis in Late Antique Art." *Journal of Roman Studies* 37: 135–44.

Tran Tam Tinh, V. 1973. *Isis Lactans.* Leiden.

Treadgold, W. 1995. *Byzantium and Its Army, 284–1081.* Stanford.

Tronzo, W. 1986. *The Via Latina Catacomb: Imitation and Discontinuity in Fourth-Century Painting.* University Park, PA.

Tudor, D. 1965. *Sucidava: Un cité daco-romaine byzantine en Dacie.* Brussels.

Ullmann, W. 1955. *The Growth of Papal Government in the Middle Ages.* London.

———. 1967. "Donation of Constantine." *New Catholic Encyclopaedia* 4: 1000–1.

Urbainczyk, T. 1997. *Socrates of Constantinople: Historian of Church and State.* Ann Arbor.

———. 2002. *Theodoret of Cyrrhus: The Bishop and the Holy Man.* Ann Arbor.

Van Berchem, D. 1952. *L'Armée de Dioclétien et la réforme Constantinienne.* Paris.

Van Dam, R. 2003. "The Many Conversions of the Emperor Constantine." Pp. 127–51 in *Conversion in Late Antiquity and the Early Middle Ages: Seeing and Believing*, ed. K. Mills and A. Grafton. Rochester.

Vanderspoel, J., and M. L. Mann. 2002. "The Empress Fausta as Romano-Celtic Dea Nutrix." *Numismatic Chronicle* 162: 350–5.

Varner, E., ed. 2000. *Tyranny and Transformation: From Caligula to Constantine in Roman Portraiture.* Atlanta.

Vermaseren, M. J., ed. 1956–60. *Corpus Inscriptionum et Monumentorum Religionis Mithrae.* 2 vols. The Hague.

———. 1977–89. *Corpus Cultus Cybelae Attidisque.* 6 vols. Leiden.

Vermaseren, M. J., and C. C. Van Essen. 1965. *The Excavations of the Mithraeum of the Church of Santa Prisca in Rome.* Leiden.

Vittinghoff, F. 1936. *Der Staatfeind in der römischen Kaiserzeit: Untersuchungen zur "damnatio memoriae."* Berlin.

Vogler, C. 1979. *Constance II et l'administration impériale.* Groupe de recherche d'histoire romaine de l'Université des sciences humaines de Strasbourg, Études et travaux 3. Strasbourg.

Waas, M. 1965. *Germanen im römischen Dienst im 4. Jahrhundert nach Christus.* Bonn.

Waelkens, M. 1985. "From a Phrygian Quarry: The Provenance of the Statues of the Dacian Prisoners in Trajan's Forum at Rome." *American Journal of Archaeology* 89: 641–53.

Walford, E., trans. 1854. *Theodoret Bishop of Cyrus: A History of the Church from A.D. 322 to the Death of Theodore of Mopsuestia, A.D. 427.* London.

Walker, P. W. L. 1990. *Holy City, Holy Places? Christian Attitudes to Jerusalem and the Holy Land in the Fourth Century.* Oxford.

Walker, S., and M. L. Bierbrier. 1997. *Ancient Faces: Mummy Portraits from Roman Egypt.* London.

Wallraff, M. 1997. *Der Kirchenhistoriker Sokrates: Untersuchungen zu Geschichtsdarstellung, Methode und Person.* Göttingen.

———. 2001. "Constantine's Devotion to the Sun after 324." *Studia Patristica* 34: 256–69.

Wardman, A. E. 1984. "Usurpations and Internal Conflicts in the Fourth Century AD." *Historia* 33: 220–37.

Ward-Perkins, B. 1984. *From Classical Antiquity to the Middle Ages: Urban Public Building in Northern and Central Italy, AD 300–850.* Oxford.

———. 1999. "Reusing the Architectural Legacy of the Past, *Entre Idéologie et Pragmatisme.*" Pp. 225–44 in *The Idea and Ideal of the Town between Late Antiquity and the Early Middle Ages,* ed. G. P. Brogiolo and B. Ward-Perkins. Leiden.

Warmington, B. 1977. "Objectives and Strategy in the Persian War of Constantius II." Pp. 509–20 in *Limes: Akten des XI. Internationalen Limeskongresses, Székesfehérvar, 1976,* ed. J. Fitz. Budapest.

———. 1981. "Ammianus Marcellinus and the Lies of Metrodorus." *Classical Quarterly* n.s. 31: 464–8.

———. 1999. "Some Constantinian References in Ammianus." Pp. 166–77 in *The Late Roman World and Its Historian: Interpreting Ammianus Marcellinus,* ed. J. W. Drijvers and E. D. Hunt. London and New York.

Watson, A. 1999. *Aurelian and the Third Century.* London and New York.

Weber, M. 1963. *The Sociology of Religion.* Trans. E. Fischoff. London and Boston.

Weber, W. 1984. *Constantinische Deckengemälde an dem römischen Palast unter dem Trierer Dom.* Trier.

Weiss, P. 1975. *Consistorium und Comites Consistoriani: Untersuchungen zur Hofbeamtenschaft des 4. Jahrhunderts n. Chr. auf prosopographischer Grundlage.* Würzburg.

———. 1993. "Die Vision Constantins." Pp. 143–69 in *Colloquium aus Anlass des 80. Geburtstages von Alfred Heuss,* Frankfurter Althistorische Studien 13, ed. J. Bleicken. Kalmünz.

———. 2003. "The Vision of Constantine." *Journal of Roman Archaeology* 16: 237–59.

Wenskus, R. 1961. *Stammesbildung und Verfassung: Das Werden der frühmittelalterlichen Gentes.* Cologne.

Whitby, M. 1994. "Images for Emperors in Late Antiquity: A Search for New Constantine." Pp. 83–94 in *New Constantines: Rhythm of Imperial Renewal in Byzantium, 4th–13th Centuries,* ed. P. Magdalino. Aldershot.

———. 2003. *Rome at War AD 293–696.* London and New York.

Whittaker, C. R. 1976. "*Agri deserti.*" Pp. 137–65 in *Studies in Roman Property,* ed. M. I. Finley. Cambridge.

———. 1996. *Frontiers of the Roman Empire: A Social and Economic Study.* Baltimore.

Wiemer, H.-U. 1994a. "Libanius on Constantine." *Classical Quarterly* n.s. 44: 511–24.

———. 1994b. "Libanios und Zosimus über den Rom-Besuch Konstantins I. im Jahre 326." *Historia* 43: 469–94.

Wightman, E. 1971. *Roman Trier and the Treviri*. New York.

Wiles, M. F. 1962. "In Defense of Arius." *Journal of Theological Studies*, n. s. 13: 339–47.

Wilfong, T. 1998. "Constantine in Coptic." Pp. 177–88 in *Constantine: History, Historiography and Legend*, ed. S. N. C. Lieu and D. A. Montserrat. London.

Wilkes, J. J. 1993. *Diocletian's Palace, Split: Residence of a Retired Roman Emperor*. Occasional publications, Ian Sanders Memorial Fund 1. Rev. ed. Sheffield.

Williams, R. 1987. *Arius*. London.

Williams, S. 1964. "The Oldest Text of the '*Constitutum Constantini*.'" *Traditio* 20: 448–61.

————. 1985. *Diocletian and the Roman Recovery*. London and New York.

Williamson, G. A., and A. Louth, trans. 1989. *Eusebius: The History of the Church*. 2d ed. London and New York.

Wilson, R. J. A. 1983. *Piazza Armerina*. Austin.

Winkelmann, F. 1987. "Die älteste erhaltene griechische hagiographische Vita Konstantins und Helenas (BHG N. 365z, 366, 366a)." Pp. 623–38 in *Texte und Textkritik: Eine Aufsatzsammlung*, Texte und Untersuchungen 133, ed. J. Dummer. Berlin.

Winkler, G. 1982. *Das armenische Initiationsrituale, Entwicklungsgeschichte und Liturgievergleichende: Untersuchung der Quellen des 3. bis 10. Jahrhunderts*. Rome.

Winter, E., and B. Dignas. 2001. *Rom und das Perserreich: Zwei Weltmächte zwischen Konfrontation und Koexistenz*. Berlin.

Wirth, G. 1990. "Hannibalian: Anmerkungen zur Geschichte eines überflüssigen Königs." *Bonner Jahrbücher* 190: 201–32.

Witschel, C. 1999. *Krise-Rezession-Stagnation? Der Westen des römischen Reiches im 3. Jahrhundert n. Chr.* Frankfurt-am-Main.

Wohl, B. 2001. "Constantine's Use of Spolia." Pp. 85–115 in *Late Antiquity: Art in Context*, Acta Hyperborea 8, ed. J. Fleischer, J. Lund, and M. Nielsen. Copenhagen.

Wolfram, H. 1988. *History of the Goths*. Trans. T. J. Dunlap. Berkeley and Los Angeles.

————. 1995. *Die Germanen*. Munich.

————. 1997. *The Roman Empire and its Germanic Peoples*. Trans. T. J. Dunlap. Berkeley and Los Angeles.

Woods, D. 1991. "The Date of the Translation of the Relics of SS Andrew and Luke to Constantinople." *Vigiliae Christianae* 45: 286–92.

————. 1998. "On the Death of the Empress Fausta." *Greece and Rome* 45: 70–86.

Wright, D. 1987. "The True Face of Constantine the Great." *Dumbarton Oaks Papers* 41: 493–507.

Zadoks-Josephus Jitta, A. 1966. "Imperial Messages in Agate II." *Bulletin van de Vereeniging tot Bevordering der Kennis van de Antieke Beschaving* 41: 91–104.

Zahariade, M. 1997. "The Halmyris Tetrarchic Inscription." *Zeitschrift für Papyrologie und Epigraphik* 119: 228–36.

Zanker, P. 1988. *The Power of Images in the Age of Augustus*. Ann Arbor.

Zazoff, P. 1983. *Die Antiken Gemmen*. Munich.

Zenos, A. C., trans. 1890. *Socrates Church History from AD 305–439*. Nicene and Post-Nicene Fathers of the Church 2.2. Peabody, MA.

Zöllner, E. 1970. *Geschichte der Franken bis zur Mitte des sechsten Jahrhunderts*. Munich.

Zuckerman, C. 1993. "Les 'barbares' romains: Au sujet de l'origine des *auxilia* tétrarchiques." Pp. 17–29 in *L'armée romaine et les barbares du IIIe au VIIe siècle*, ed. M. Kazanski and F. Vallet. Paris.

————. 1994a. "Le camp Psobthis/Sosteos et les catafractarii." *Zeitschrift für Papyrologie und Epigraphik* 100: 199–202.

————. 1994b. "Les campagnes des tétrarques, 296–298: Notes de chronologie." *Antiquité Tardive* 2: 65–70.

————. 1998a. "Comtes et ducs en Égypte autour de l'an 400 et la date de la *Notitia Dignitatum Orientis*." *Antiquité Tardive* 6: 137–47.

————. 1998b. "Two Reforms of the 370s: Recruiting Soldiers and Senators in the Divided Empire." *Révue des Études Byzantines* 56: 79–140.

INDEX